PREFACE

The Housing Act 1980 affects a very wide area of both landlord and tenant and housing law. Moreover, in some of its parts it evinces a shift of legislative policy, such as the provisions relating to the compulsory sale of local authority and other public sector housing (see Chapter I of Part I) and the introduction of the new, private sector, shorthold tenancy (see Part II). Much of the 1980 Act is amending, however, and the Housing Act 1974 and Rent Act 1977 have particularly been altered; the amendments to the latter having often as their prime object the easement of the landlord's position.

No work of this nature could be other than introductory, being produced under great pressure of time. The book takes the form of an introduction to the Act in sixteen chapters, followed by an anotated text of the Act itself, the aim of the annotations being chiefly that of analysis of the context, scope and possible difficulties of the enactment. The introduction to the Housing Act 1980 performs the function, it is hoped, of affording some guidance to the provisions, with particular emphasis on new or difficult ones.

I wish to express my thanks to my colleague Mr David Lloyd Evans, who has often kindly given me the benefit of his thoughts on the Act and topical news connected therewith; and also to the Law Librarian, University of Reading Library, Mr Ian Sainsbury, for his frequent and tireless assistance in unearthing sources. To the staff at Butterworths is owed perhaps the greatest debt; not only in relation to essential co-ordination, but also because of their efficient and willing assistance throughout the preparation of this work.

It is hoped that any errors or omissions, for which the author accepts sole responsibility, will not render the book unhelpful in the function it sets out to perform in relation to a rather long and at times somewhat difficult enactment. There is one point which must unavoidably be made, because it arose unfortunately after the manuscript went to the printer. It has become clear (see the Housing Act (Commencement No. 5) Order 1980 (S.I. 1980 No. 1706)) that the provisions in the Housing Act 1980 dealing with amending the procedure on applications for registration of rent will never be brought into force. In their place, reference should be made to the Regulated Tenancies (Procedure) Regulations 1980 (S.I.) 1980 No. 1696), which came into effect on 28th November 1980.

31st December 1980   P. F. SMITH

CONTENTS

v

TABLE OF CASES

vii

Table of Cases

ix

W

Y

CHAPTER 1

INTRODUCTION

Introduction—Housing policy—Parliamentary debates—Commencement and regulations

The Housing Act 1980 is a *pot-pourri* of legislative miscellany affecting a wide sweep of landlord and tenant and housing law. The Act is divided into nine separate Parts. **[1]**

Part I of the Act is subdivided into two chapters. Chapter I deals with the sale of public sector housing to tenants: in particular, council house tenants are enabled to buy their homes. Until the Act was passed, the sale of council houses was a matter for the discretion of the local authority concerned: see the Housing Act 1957, s. 104, and the Ministry of Housing and Local Government Circular No. 54/70. After the commencement of Part I of this Act (8 weeks from the date of Royal Assent) not only may a qualifying tenant insist on a right to buy and to a mortgage, but the central government has wide powers to force the hand of a recalcitrant local authority. **[2]**

Chapter II of Part I confers security of tenure on tenants of many public sector landlords, notably again local authorities. This is by close analogy with the Rent Acts, and there are favourable modifications of the common law in relation to tenants' improvements, though there is no regulation of rents. To prevent evasion of security by conferral of licences, there is a wide provision nullifying licences to occupy which are still permissible in the private sector. **[3]**

Part II of the Act deals with the private rented sector. It introduces a new form of shorthold tenancy which has the advantage from the landlord's point of view that he may in principle obtain vacant possession on expiry of the term under a mandatory case added to the Rent Act 1977. A new form of high-class tenancy is introduced—assured tenancies—in favour of such institutional landlords as insurance companies and the Rent Acts will not apply to these. On expiry of the contractual term, the Landlord and Tenant Act 1954, as modified by this Act, will apply. Part II also contains a number of amendments to the Rent Act 1977: in particular, security of tenure for tenants under restricted contracts is removed; controlled tenancies are abolished; the rules as to rent regulation are amended and the scope of the resident landlord provisions altered. **[4]**

Part III of the Act amends the law in relation to tenants repairs and improvements and Part IV deals with jurisdiction and procedure: of particular importance here are the sections restrictive of the court's discretion in actions for possession of land. **[5]**

Part V of the Act deals with the powers of sale of local authority housing: in particular, s. 104 of the Housing Act 1957 is replaced by a wider provision.

Part VI alters the rules applicable to housing subsidies and Part VII deals with finance: in particular, there are new powers given to local authorities and the Housing Corporation to guarantee mortgage advances and also provisions as to local authority mortgage interest rates. Part VIII of the Act deals with housing associations and the Housing Corporation: of particular importance are the new rules as to audits and accounts of registered housing associations. Part IX contains a number of miscellaneous provisions. **[6]**

HOUSING POLICY

In connection with general policy, the following documents may be referred to: in 1977 the then (Labour) government produced a Consultative Document entitled "Housing Policy" (Cmnd 6851) and the Department of the Environment published in that year a set of three Technical Volumes to accompany it. The fall of that government prevented its proposals, then in the form of a Bill, from ever reaching the statute-book. The incoming (Conservative) government, by the Department of the Environment, then produced a large number of consultation papers, and among them:

1. Housing Bill: Improvement and Repair.
2. Housing Bill: The Right to Buy.
3. Legislation of Housing: the tenants' charter provisions.
4. Local Authority Subsidy System.

It might be perhaps of some interest if one were to compare very briefly one or two points as to the contrast or otherwise between the stated policy of the government then in office in 1977 and that enacted by the new government in 1980. The subsequent bitter controversy has, it is thought, obscured the areas of substantial agreement between the parties. **[7]**

One matter which is thought to be very controversial is the sale of council housing. In Chapter 6 of the Consultative Document, for instance, the stated policy of the Labour government was that while it was not opposed to sales of council houses, it "... cannot accept indiscriminate and unregulated programmes for sales in areas where pressure for homes remains high and where the authority is not taking compensating action to keep up the supply of adequate housing." (Chapter 6, para 6.25; and see also Chapter 11, para 11.39.) As will become evident to anyone who reads Chapter I of Part I of this Act, the tenants of council houses *et alia* have a compulsory right to buy their homes, at a discount, with a very few exceptions. The suggestions of the 1977 Consultative Document to deal with the fact that by 1977 only 15% of total housing stock was in the private rented sector (cf. 1914: 90%) were not radical: there was a suggestion for speeding up the procedures for a resident landlord to re-gain possession (see Chapter 8, para 8.20) and also for a form of tenancy which would give (in effect) an assured rate of return in rented terms (see *ibid.*, para 8.23). This Act goes much further. In the first place, *all* procedures for obtaining possession (with some exceptions) have been speeded up (see Part IV of this Act) and security of tenure for tenants under restricted contracts has gone (see Part II). Also, there is not only an Assured Tenancy, for institutional landlords, as to some extent envisaged rather cautiously in the 1977 Consultative Document (see Part II of this Act) but there is a new form of private sector tenancy (Protected Shorthold Tenancies) under which there is an automatic right to possession at the end of the term. On the other hand, both the main political parties agree on the need for a Tenants' Charter (i.e. security of tenure in the public sector) and this is to be found in Chapter II of Part I of this Act, which in many of its parts adopts the defunct Labour Housing Bill. **[8]**

PARLIAMENTARY DEBATES
These were extremely copious but not always very enlightening from a legal standpoint.   They will be found as follows:

House of Commons
1st Reading: Hansard, vol. 976, 19th December 1979, col. 644.
2nd Reading: Hansard, vol. 976, 15th January 1980, cols 1443–1570.
Standing Committee F: This sat from 29th January 1980 to 30th April 1980 for 46 sittings: cols 1–2642.
Report and 3rd Reading: Hansard, vol. 984, 19th May 1980, cols 53–217; 20th May 1980, cols 264–461; 21st May 1980, cols 723–795.

House of Lords
1st Reading: Hansard, vol. 409, 2nd June 1980, col. 1109.
2nd Reading: Hansard, vol. 410, 9th June 1980, cols 17–26; 32–136.
Committee: Hansard, vol. 410, 26th June 1980, cols 1728–1805; 1809–1861; vol. 411, 30th June 1980, cols 9–110, 115–210; vol. 411, 2nd July 1980, cols 350–464; vol. 411, 3rd July 1980, cols 520–600, 610–650, 651–732; vol. 411, 4th July 1980, cols 763–841.
Report: Hansard, vol. 412, 21st July 1980, cols 10–32, 41–96, 106–184; vol. 412, 22nd July 1980, cols 207–290, 296–376.
3rd Reading: Hansard, vol. 412, 30th July 1980, cols 878–892, 898–950, 961–1031.

House of Commons (Lords' Amendments)
Hansard, vol. 990, 6th August 1980, cols 561–691. [**9**]

COMMENCEMENT AND REGULATIONS
At the date of going to press the position as to the commencement of provisions (see s. 153) was as follows:

Provisions in force on 8th August 1980 (date of Royal Assent)
Part V: the whole.
Part VI: the whole.
Sections 108, 112–113, 120, 122–127, 130, 131, 133–135, 137–140, 150, 151, 152 (2), 153–155.

Provision in force on 1st October 1980
Section 121 (Housing Act 1980 (Commencement No. 1) Order 1980, S.I. 1980 No. 1406).

Provisions in force on 3rd October 1980
Part I, both Chapter I and Chapter II (see s. 153 (1), (2)).

Parts III and IV, ss. 110, 111, 114, 116 (1) (so far as it relates to Sch. 14, Para. 6 (1), (2) and to s. 116 (2)), 128, 129, 132, 136, 141 (except in relation to Sch. 21, para. 7), 143–146, 148, 152 (1) (so far as it relates to Sch. 25, paras, 4, 6, 8–16, 18–20, 24–29, 31, 34, 36 and 61), 152 (3) (repeals) (for certain purposes only) (S.I. 1980 No. 1406, *supra*).

Provisions in force on 6th October 1980
Sections 56–58 (Housing Act 1980 (Commencement No. 2) Order 1980, S.I. 1980 No. 1466).

Provisions in force on 20th October 1980
Sections 78, 79, 118 (Housing Act 1980 (Commencement No. 3) Order 1980,
S.I. 1980 No. 1557).

Provisions in force on 27th October 1980
Sections 107 (except in relation to Sch. 12, paras. 4, 12 and 28–32), 147,
152 (1) (so far as it relates to Sch. 25, paras. 21 and 30), 152 (3) (so far as
it relates to the repeals of Housing Acts 1961, s. 16; 1969, s. 62; 1974, ss.
56 (1) (*d*), 57 (6), 62 (3), 64 (7), 67 (2) (*b*), (4), 84 (para. (*b*) of definition) (Housing
Act 1980 (Commencement No. 3) Order 1980 No. 1557).

Provision in force on 11th November 1980
Section 115 (Housing Act 1980 (Commencement No. 4) Order 1980, S.I.
1980 No. 1693).

Provisions in force on 28th November 1980
Part II (so far as not already in operation) except s. 59 (3), ss. 149, 152
(1) (in relation to Sch. 25, paras. 1–3, 17, 32, 33, 35 and 37–60), 152 (3) (in
relation to specified repeals) (Housing Act 1980 (Commencement No. 5) Order
1980, S.I. 1980 No. 1706).

Provisions in force on 15th December 1980
Sections 106, 107 (in relation to those paras. of Sch. 12 not already in
operation), 109, 152 (1) (in relation to those paras. of Sch. 25, Part I not
already in operation), 152 (3) (in relation to specified repeals) (Housing Act
1980 (Commencement No. 6) Order 1980, S.I. 1980 No. 1781).

Remaining provisions
The remaining provisions of the Act come into force on a day or days
to be appointed.

Regulations
As to regulations, see generally s. 151, *post.* **[10]**

CHAPTER 2

SALE OF HOUSES AND FLATS BY LOCAL AUTHORITIES AND OTHER PUBLIC SECTOR LANDLORDS

Introduction—Premises covered by right to buy—Persons to whom right to buy extends—Main landlords against whom right to buy may be exercised—Main landlords against whom right to buy cannot arise—Other cases where right to buy does not arise—The price payable—Landlord's notice of price and discount—Right of landlord to clawback in event of early disposal—Right to a mortgage—Amount of mortgage and terms—Conveyancing: children succeeding parents—Conveyancing: completion of sale or grant of lease—Landlord's notice to complete and deposit provision—Registration of title—Right of determination by district valuer—Power of secretary of state to intervene and to execute vesting orders—Miscellaneous.

INTRODUCTION

Secure tenants (as defined in s. 28 (3), viz. in principle individuals occupying dwelling-houses as their only or principal home) or persons who would have been secure tenants had Chapter I of this Act been in force (s. 27 (3)) of certain public sector landlords are given by Chapter I of this Act the right to buy the houses in which they live. This is at a generous discount; there is a right to a mortgage advance from the landlord (if a local authority) or the Housing Corporation. To make sure that the right is not blocked by recalcitrant local authorities, there is a sweeping intervention power in the Secretary of State for the Environment (s. 23). **[11]**

There will be discussed in what follows: the premises covered by the right to buy; the persons entitled to exercise it and the landlords against whom it is exercisable; conveyancing matters; the right to a mortgage; completion; registration of title and then the administrative provisions of Chapter I, notably the right of appeal to the district valuer and the ministerial intervention power. Technical and other points are dealt with in the annotations to each section. **[12]**

PREMISES COVERED BY THE RIGHT TO BUY

The right to buy is, under s. 1 (1), a right either to acquire the freehold,

5

if the dwelling-house is a house (para. (*a*)) or a long lease (125 years: s. 16 (1) (*b*)) if the dwelling-house is a flat (para. (*b*)). In the case of a lease, all references in Chapter I to "purchase price" are to include references to the consideration for the grant of a long lease: s. 1 (8). By s. 1 (1) (*c*), as part of the right to buy there is a right to a mortgage advance of the amount laid down in s. 9. **[13]**

The right to buy covers only dwelling-houses. In the case of a house, it is provided in s. 3 (2) that, leaving out of account land included with it under s. 50 (2), a dwelling-house is only a house if it is a structure reasonably so called. This connotes permanence: see the note to s. 3. As a result of s. 3 (2) (*a*), where a building is divided horizontally, the units into which it is divided are not houses and may only be flats; as a dwelling-house which is not a house is a flat (s. 3 (3)) a long lease may be obtained in such a case. By s. 3 (2) (*b*), where a building is divided vertically, the units may be treated as houses, and so the freehold may be bought. This is different from the result of the Leasehold Reform Act 1967, A.L.S. Vol 162, s. 2 (2), where the words therein "structurally detached" were held in *Parsons* v. *Viscount Gage* [1974] 1 All E.R. 1162, H.L., to exclude two houses in part of a terrace from enfranchisement. By s. 3 (2) (*c*), where a building is not structurally detached, it is not a house (it may be a flat) if a material part of it lies above or below the remainder of the structure. It is thought that the object of this is to restrict the right to buy to a lease in such cases. No doubt behind this is the impossibility of enforcing positive covenants on the freehold: see *Haywood* v. *Brunswick Permanent Building Society* (1881) 8 Q.B.D. 403, C.A. Land may be included in the dwelling-house if used for the purposes of the same, which the landlord and the tenant agree to include, s. 3 (4); by s. 50 (2), which is applicable (s. 27 (1)), the land is treated as part of the dwelling-house unless it is agricultural land exceeding 2 acres. See further the notes. **[14]**

In the case of a joint tenancy, the right to buy may be, by agreement, in favour of one of them only, or more of them, provided that the person or persons occupy the dwelling-house as his or their only or principal home (s. 4 (1)). Up to three family members of the secure tenant occupying the dwelling-house with him may be required by him to be included in the right to buy with him, subject to the conditions mentioned in s. 4 (2). In such a case the tenant and his family are treated as joint tenants, s. 4 (3), with the consequent beneficial effect on discounts (s. 7 (7)). **[15]**

PERSONS TO WHOM THE RIGHT TO BUY EXTENDS

The main persons entitled to exercise the right to buy are those treated as secure tenants when Chapter I comes into force (see s. 27 (3)) and those who become secure tenants in the future. There is a general residence requirement for 3 years; this is relaxed (see below) in some cases. The right to buy covers joint tenants and certain other persons, notably resident family members. The right to buy is initiated by a tenant's notice (s. 5) in the prescribed form (s. 22). See the Housing (Right to Buy) (Prescribed Forms) (No. 1) Regulations 1980, S.I. 1980 No. 1391. **[16]**

TABLE I

SUMMARY OF MAIN PERSONS ENTITLED TO EXERCISE
THE RIGHT TO BUY

1. The secure tenant.
2. A successor to a deceased secure tenant who is:

  (a) his spouse; or
  (b) a member of the deceased's family; or
  (c) a child qualified to succeed by permission of landlord.
 3. Joint tenants:
  (a) If the secure tenancy is a joint tenancy, all the joint tenants jointly;
  or
  (b) such one or more of the joint tenants as may validly be agreed
  between them. **[17]**

Position of secure tenant
   One is a secure tenant if within s. 28 (3), i.e. an individual occupying a
dwelling-house as one's only or principal home (a term discussed in the note
to s. 28). The right to buy arises only after the secure tenant has been secure
tenant for a period of not less than three years or for periods amounting
together to not less than three years (s. 1 (3)). Periods of residence in different
dwellings under different landlords may in principle be added together in computing the total residence requirement, because, by s. 1 (3) (*a*), neither the
landlord nor the dwelling-house need have been the same during the whole
of the period of residence. However, a period during which a secure tenant
was a tenant of a landlord against whom the right to buy does not arise (see
s. 2 as to this) is to be left out of account: s. 1 (3) (*b*). The restrictions in
the case of previous purchasers in s. 1 (6) and (7) should be noted. **[18]**
Extensions
   For the purpose of the residence condition in s. 1 (3), a person who, as
joint tenant under a secure tenancy, occupied a dwelling-house as his only
or principal home is to be treated as the secure tenant under the tenancy;
where the secure tenancy is a joint tenancy that condition need be satisfied
with respect to only one of the joint tenants (s. 1 (4)). By s. 1 (5), where
a secure tenant became secure tenant (by succession) on the death of his
spouse, the deceased spouse's residence is (subject to s. 1 (3) (*b*)) to count
in calculating the required residence period, provided that at the time of the
death the spouses occupied the same dwelling-house as their only or principal
home. **[19]**
   Section 15 (1) enables the landlord, if it thinks fit, to count the whole or
part of any period qualifying under s. 15 for the purposes of s. 1 (3), in cases
where a child within s. 15 (1) of the last secure tenant becomes the new secure
tenant. As to a period qualifying, see s. 15 (2). See also para. **[42]**, *post*. **[20]**

MAIN LANDLORDS AGAINST WHOM THE RIGHT TO BUY MAY BE EXERCISED
   The landlord must own the freehold: s. 2 (3). Table 2 summarises the
main landlords against whom the right to buy is exercisable. **[21]**

TABLE 2

LANDLORDS AGAINST WHOM THE RIGHT TO BUY
MAY BE EXERCISED

 1. A local authority.
 2. The Commission for the New Towns.
 3. The Development Board for Rural Wales.
 4. A development corporation.
 5. The Housing Corporation.
 6. Housing Associations within the Rent Act 1977, s. 15 (3).

7

7. Housing Co-operatives where the dwelling-house is comprised in a housing co-operative agreement (Sch. 20 to this Act).
8. Those county councils granting secure tenancies under their reserve powers in the Local Government Act 1972, s. 194.

Notes
In the case of nos 2 to 4 above, exceptions to the general rule are provided in Sch. 1 para. 2. **[22]**

MAIN LANDLORDS AGAINST WHOM THE RIGHT TO BUY CANNOT ARISE
As to these, see generally s. 2 and Sch. 1. Table 3 summarises the position. **[23]**

TABLE 3
LANDLORDS AGAINST WHOM THE RIGHT TO BUY
CANNOT ARISE

1. Charitable housing trusts.
2. Charitable housing associations.
3. Those housing associations within the Rent Act 1977, s. 15 (3) (*d*) or within s. 2 (2) (*c*) of this Act.
4. Cases where houses are held by a local authority otherwise than for the purposes of Part V of the Housing Act 1957.
5. Landlords within Sch. 1, paras. 2 to 4.

Notes
In the case of No. 4, however, there is a power to modify the exclusion in regulations, s. 2 (5). **[24]**

OTHER CASES WHERE THE RIGHT TO BUY DOES NOT ARISE
It is suspended in the case of tenant's rent arrears: see s. 16 (9). The right to buy cannot be exercised by the tenant where he is within Sch. 1 Part II, s. 2 (4), nor in the case of special dwellings for the elderly where Sch. 1, para. 5, applies. **[25]**

THE PRICE PAYABLE
The price depends, by s. 6 (1) on two elements: the value of the house at the date of service of the tenant's right to buy notice under s. 5 and the size of the discount, computed under s. 7. **[26]**
Value of the dwelling-house
The basic rule is that this is the price which the house or flat would realise if sold on the open market by a willing vendor, but certain artificial assumptions have to be made, which differ for the grant of the freehold and that of a long lease. As to these, see s. 6 (3) and (4). Under s. 6 (2), there must also in all cases be disregarded: (i) improvements made by the secure tenant and the persons specified in s. 6 (5); (ii) any failure by any of those persons to keep the dwelling-house in good internal repair. See the notes to this section as to these matters. The value goes to price and is determined by the landlord subject to the right of appeal to the district valuer in s. 11. **[27]**
Discount
Section 7 entitles a secure tenant exercising the right to buy to a generous discount from the price payable. But s. 7 (2) protects dwellings first let after

31st March 1974: here, the discount is not to reduce the price below the amount which, in accordance with any determination by the Secretary of State, represents costs incurred in respect of the dwelling-house, treated as incurred after 31st March 1974 and as relevant costs; if the pre-discount price is below this amount, then there is no discount (and see further s. 7 (3)). In any case, the discount is not to reduce the price by more than the prescribed sum in regulations (s. 7 (4)), which is £25,000 (S.I. 1980 No. 1342).

Apart from the above, the amount of the discount is, by s. 7 (1):

(a) 33 per cent. if the period of residence (see s. 7 (5)) is less than four years;

(b) 33 per cent. plus one per cent for each complete year by which the residence period exceeds three years, where the period of residence is over four years, but subject to a limit overall of 50 per cent. **[28]**

Period of residence

This is governed by s. 7 (5) and (6). The special rules for the Armed Forces are not detailed here. The basic rule is that the period of residence for discount is: (a) the aggregate of periods during which, before service of a right to buy notice, the secure tenant or his spouse or deceased spouse was either a secure tenant or the spouse of a secure tenant (s. 7 (5) (a)); further (b) a period is taken into account whether or not (i) the dwelling-house or (ii) the landlord was the same at the time of the service of the right to buy notice (s. 7 (6)) except that a period of residence under an exempt landlord (s. 2 (2)) is to be left out of account. By s. 7 (6), further, (a) periods of occupation by a spouse are only to be taken into account if the tenant and the spouse occupied the same dwelling-house as their only or principal home at the time of service of the right to buy notice; (b) no period during which the tenant's deceased spouse was a secure tenant or the spouse of a secure tenant is to be taken into account unless the tenant became secure tenant on the death of his spouse and at the time of the death both occupied the dwelling-house as their only or principal home; and (c) a period during which either the tenant or his spouse or deceased spouse was the spouse of a secure tenant is to be taken into account only if during that period both spouses occupied the same dwelling-house as their only or principal home. **[29]**

Joint tenants

In relation to joint tenants, s. 7 (7) relaxes the rules so that: (i) only one joint tenant need satisfy the residence requirements above; (ii) but if more than one joint tenant claims the right to buy (and members of a family claiming with the tenant are in this very position) then the period of residence of the joint tenant which will produce the largest amount of discount is to be taken into account. **[30]**

Section 7 (8) contains a restriction on periods of residence to count towards discount by a previous purchaser (this, by s. 7 (10) is to have the same meaning as in s. 1 (6)) to periods of residence by such persons after the completion of the purchase. Section 7 (9) enables periods of residence in Scotland and Northern Ireland as a secure tenant, etc., to count towards discount in the case where the tenant then moved to an English or Welsh dwelling-house, save in the case of Scottish housing associations. **[31]**

Some further points

1. What is occupation as one's residence is surely a question of fact; temporary residence will not do.

2. Obviously to the tenant's advantage is the possibility of joining up residence periods in different dwellings.

9

Example—T resided in house No. 1 for 18 months; then in No. 2 under a different landlord for 6 months and has again moved into No. 3 where he has lived for a further 18 months. 18 plus 6 plus 18=42 months' worth of discount, though it will relate to No. 3 where T has resided for 18 months only.

3. It is thought that there is nothing in s. 7 to prevent advantage being taken in the following case to maximise the discount. T was secure tenant from 1977 to 1981 and was then married to W, who lived with him in the same dwelling-house throughout. T died in 1981 and W (his successor) continues in residence and re-marries to X. In 1983 the two jointly claim the right to buy and are pleased to be entitled to 6 years' worth of discount: in X's case he has a triple premium on his 2 years of residence.

4. In general, the amount of discount will not vary from area to area (and the regulatory powers affect price not method). [**32**]

LANDLORD'S NOTICE OF PRICE AND DISCOUNT

Under s. 10 (1), where a secure tenant has claimed to exercise the right to buy and it has been established the landlord must, as soon as practicable (see the note: it does not mean "at once") serve on the tenant a notice which describes the dwelling-house and states: (a) the price at which, in the landlord's opinion, the tenant is entitled to have the freehold or a long lease conveyed or granted to him; and (b) the provisions which, in the landlord's opinion, should be contained in the conveyance or grant. By s. 10 (2), the notice must also state: (a) the value at the time of service of the tenant's right to buy notice; (b) the discount to which the tenant is entitled, stating (i) the period of residence to be taken into account under s. 7 (5), and (ii) (if applicable) the amount mentioned in s. 7 (2); and (c) the improvements disregarded under s. 6. By s. 10 (3), the notice must inform the tenant (a) of his right to have the value determined, etc., under s. 11 by the district valuer; (b) of the right to a mortgage; (c) of the effect of s. 12 and s. 16 (4) (the latter being the tenant's right to defer completion). The notice must also be accompanied by a form for the tenant's use in exercising the right to a mortgage. For forms, see S.I. 1980 Nos. 1391, 1465. [**33**]

RIGHT OF LANDLORD TO CLAWBACK OF DISCOUNT IN THE EVENT OF EARLY DISPOSAL

The landlord's right to a clawback of discount in the event of early disposal of the dwelling-house is in s. 8 (1): a conveyance or grant must both contain a covenant (where there is a discount) binding on the secure tenant or his successors in title (see the note for the uncertainties this creates) to pay the landlord on demand a given amount of the discount, in the event of the first or only disposal within a period of 5 years from the grant or conveyance. By s. 8 (2), the amount of the repayment is the amount of the discount, less 20 per cent. for each complete year from the conveyance or grant. The disposals caught by s. 8 are, by s. 8 (3): (a) a further conveyance of the freehold or an assignment of the lease; or (b) the grant of a lease or sub-lease for a term or more than 21 years otherwise than at a rack rent. In this, mortgage terms are excluded: s. 8 (6). There are two special exceptions in s. 8 (3). Section 8 (7) is anti-avoidance. [**34**]

The liability that may arise to repay discount is a charge on the dwelling-house: (a) taking effect as if created in a legal mortgage charge (s. 8 (4) (*a*)); and (b) having priority after any legal charge to secure amounts left outstanding by the tenant as part of his right to a mortgage (s. 8 (4) (*b*)). The Land

Registration Act 1925, s. 59 (2), applies to its protection and realisation and s. 59 (5) of that Act is displaced: s. 8 (6). **[35]**

THE RIGHT TO A MORTGAGE

As to the right itself, see s. 1 (1) (c) of this Act. To exercise it, by s. 12 (1), the tenant must serve a relevant (see s. 12 (3)) notice on the landlord, this not later than 3 months after service on him of a landlord's s. 10 or s. 11 notice, and then, as soon as practicable, the landlord must serve a counter-notice in writing under s. 12 (4) stating: (a) the amount of the mortgage, (b) how that amount has been arrived at; and (c) the provisions which, in the opinion of the landlord or Housing Corporation, should be contained in the mortgage deed. By s. 12 (5), the notice must inform the tenant of the effect of s. 16 (8) and be accompanied by a form for the tenant's use in claiming, under s. 16 (4) (c), deferral of completion. As to changes of secure tenant or landlord after service of a right to buy or right to mortgage notice, see ss. 13 and 14. **[36]**

AMOUNT OF MORTGAGE AND TERMS THEREOF
Amount of mortgage

This is governed by s. 9. By s. 9 (1), the amount which a secure tenant is entitled to leave outstanding or to have advanced to him is as follows (but by s. 12 (2), subject to its not exceeding the amount prescribed in regulations (s. 12 (4)) as the tenant's available annual income multiplied by the appropriate factor), see S.I. 1980 No. 1423:—

    (a) the purchase price;
    (b) the costs of the landlord or the Housing Corporation chargeable to the tenant under s. 21;
    (c) tenant's costs defrayed on his behalf by the above bodies. **[37]**

There are two relaxations to the appropriate factor: the first is apt to deal with cases where the right to a mortgage belongs to more than one person (see s. 4 (3): they are then treated as joint tenants); the limit is the aggregate of the amounts to be taken into account in accordance with regulations as the annual available income of each of them, after multiplying by the appropriate factor: s. 12 (3). Secondly, where the amount left outstanding is reduced by the limit imposed by s. 12, the landlord has a discretion under s. 12 (5), with the agreement of the tenant, to leave an amount over the limit up to the aggregate mentioned in s. 12 (1), such amount to be determined by the landlord. **[38]**

Terms of the mortgage

This is governed by s. 18. Unless these are otherwise agreed between the parties, and subject also to a power in the Secretary of State to prescribe additional terms or to vary (a) or (b) below in relation to deeds executed after the relevant order comes into force, the mortgage must contain the following provisions:

    (a) Repayment in equal instalments of principal and interest combined;
    (b) The period for repayment is to be 25 years, or, at the option of the mortgagor, a shorter period; it is capable of extension by the mortgagee.

By para. (c) of s. 18, the mortgage may contain such other terms as may be agreed between the parties or as may be determined by the county court to be reasonably required by either: see the note to s. 18. **[39]**

Before going further, it might be helpful if a table were given to summarise the operation of the various notices mentioned so far in the text. **[40]**

TABLE 4

SUMMARY OF MAIN NOTICES IN CONNECTION
WITH THE RIGHT TO BUY AND TO A MORTGAGE

1. The tenant (T) serves at any time (assuming residence requirement is satisfied) a s. 5 (1) right to buy notice on the landlord (L).
2. L must serve on T, within 4/8 weeks (if s. 5 (2) applies) a notice:

    (a) admitting right to buy; or
    (b) denying it with reasons.

3. If L admits T's right to buy or if T establishes it nevertheless (e.g. in proceedings), L must serve on T "as soon as practicable" a s. 10 notice of price and stating T's right to a mortgage, etc.
4. T may contest the value determined by L under No. 3 above by a s. 11 (2) notice served on L, not later than 3 months after the service on T of a s. 10 notice. As soon as practicable after a determination/redetermination under s. 11 by district valuer, L must serve on T a s. 11 (5) notice.
5. T, upon receipt of a s. 11 (5) notice, may serve within 3 months of service (this may be extended) a claim to mortgage notice under s. 12.
6. If however no part of Nos. 4 to 5 above applies, then T may serve on L a s. 12 notice within 3 months (this may be extended) of service on T of L's s. 10 notice.
7. In either eventuality, L must, as soon as practicable, serve on T a s. 12 (5) notice as to the amount of mortgage.

Notes. (1) As to changes of the secure tenant or landlord, see ss. 13 and 14. **[41]**
    (2) For form of notices, see notes to s. 5, *post.*

CONVEYANCING: CHILDREN SUCCEEDING PARENTS

Section 15 (1) enables the child of the secure tenant, where the secure tenant has died, which child occupies the dwelling-house as his only or principal home and becomes a new secure tenant, to claim that residence periods of his be taken into account as provided in s. 15 (2) provided the landlord thinks fit to do this. The periods, if accepted, may count: (a) in computing the residence qualification in s. 1 (3); or (b) for the purposes of the discount in s. 7 (5). Section 15 (2) states the circumstances in which a child's residence may be counted: in all cases since the child attained the age of 16 only. The rest of the section is consequential. **[42]**

CONVEYANCING: COMPLETION OF SALE OR GRANT OF LEASE

Once the right to buy has been established by a secure tenant, as soon as all matters relating to the grant and mortgage have been agreed or determined, the landlord must make to the tenant either:

    (a) in the the case of a house, the grant of an estate in fee simple absolute; or
    (b) in the case of a flat, the grant of a lease for a term of not less than 125 years. (See generally s. 16 (1).)

The reason why the 125 years were chosen was that the government thought that there was a move in the commercial world to 125 years: H.C. Committee, Col. 333. The grant of the freehold must comply with Sch. 2, Parts I and II, and that of a lease with Parts I and III of that Schedule: s. 17. (See generally the annotations.) On the conveyance or grant, the secure tenancy comes to an end, and, if there is a sub-tenancy, the Law of Property Act 1925, s. 139, is to apply: s. 16 (11). (See the annotations.) Part IV of Sch. 2 applies to certain charges: s. 17. **[43]**

The duty of the landlord in s. 16 (1) to make the relevant conveyance or grant is enforceable by injunction: s. 16 (10). It is not clear why this was thought necessary: presumably, specific performance would be available as with every contract for sale or lease. It is thought that s. 16 (10) envisages a mandatory injunction, in a proper case, it is supposed, against the landlord himself or by his servants or agents: *Marengo* v. *Daily Sketch and Sunday Graphic* [1948] 1 All E.R. 406. **[44]**

But by s. 16 (9), a landlord is not bound to complete and if a s. 16 (2) notice to complete is served on the tenant, he is deemed not to comply with it, if the tenant has failed to pay rent or any payment due from him as a tenant for 4 weeks after it has lawfully been demanded. This will last while the whole or any part of such sums remains outstanding. **[45]**

LANDLORD'S NOTICE TO COMPLETE AND DEPOSIT PROVISION

If the tenant fails to take all steps necessary to complete a transaction where all matters in relation thereto have been agreed or determined, then, under s. 16 (2), the landlord may serve a notice to complete within s. 16 (2), requiring the tenant to complete within the period stated in the notice, which must be not less than 28 days. A failure by the tenant to comply with this notice deems his right to buy notice to be withdrawn at the end of the time stated in the notice: no further right to buy notice served on the landlord within 12 months of the end of that period is to have effect: s. 16 (6). Section 16 (3) prevents the service of a s. 16 (2) notice to complete earlier than whichever of the three events therein stated is applicable:

(a) if the tenant has not claimed the right to mortgage, 3 months after the end of the period within which a mortgage notice could have been served by him; or

(b) if he has claimed the right to a mortgage, but is not entitled to defer completion, 3 months after service of a s. 12 (4) notice; or

(c) if he is entitled to defer completion (see s. 16 (4)) 2 years after service of a s. 5 (right to buy notice) or, if later, 3 months after service of a s. 12 (4) notice. By s. 16 (4), a tenant is entitled to defer completion if: (i) he has claimed the right to a mortgage; (ii) the amount to be left outstanding or advanced is less than the aggregate mentioned in s. 9 (1) (i.e. the price plus costs); and (iii) the tenant has, within 3 months from service on him of a s. 12 (4) notice (or as extended under s. 12 (5)) or within the period as extended under s. 16 (5) served a notice on the landlord which claims to defer completion, and has, within that period, deposited the sum of £100 with the landlord. Under s. 16 (5), not only may the landlord extend the period of service of a s. 16 (4) (c) notice, but the county court has power to do this if the landlord fails to extend: reasonable grounds for doing so must in either case be shown: s. 16 (5). As to further mortgage notices by a tenant entitled to defer completion, see s. 16 (8). **[46]**

Effect of deposit

Provided the above is complied with, then by s. 16 (7), should the tenant then deposit the sum of £100 with the landlord, then: (a) if he completes, the £100 goes to the purchase price; and (b) if he does not do this but withdraws or is deemed to withdraw (see s. 16 (9)) his right to buy notice, then the £100 is to be returned to the tenant. **[47]**

Some comments

The price payable on eventual completion after a tenant's £100 deposit, where applicable, will of course be based on figures arrived at or determined at a time not long after the right to buy notice was served. The extra residence of the tenant from then until eventual completion will not go to discount; but all the same, the £100 deposit will benefit the tenant where he has no funds at the time it is made but comes into them by the time he completes. He will complete on out-of-date prices. Thus, if in 1981 T paid a £100 deposit and the house then had a value of £10,000 (less discount) and then in 1983 T completes the deal (paying £1,000 less £100 to the 10 per cent. deposit) he will find that inflation between 1981 and 1983 might, if it kept up recent rates, give him a real extra discount of 60%: H.C. Committee, Cols 351–352. **[48]**

REGISTRATION OF TITLE

This will be obligatory in all cases, because, by s. 20 (1), the Land Registration Act 1925 will apply whether or not the dwelling-house is in an area of compulsory registration of title: s. 123 of the 1925 Act, applied by s. 20 (1). Registration must accordingly be applied for by the grantee: if he does not then the legal estate reverts to the grantor who holds it as a bare trustee for the grantee. In view of the state "guarantee" of title conferred by the 1925 Act, the certificate provisions in s. 20 (2) and (3) of this Act were required in the case of unregistered land. Should the applicant for registration be registered with an absolute title (see ss. 5 and 8 of the 1925 Act) no freedom is thereby conferred from overriding interest (see s. 70 (1) of that Act) and so there is always the danger of rectification to give effect thereto under s. 82 (3) thereof. Should the applicant claim title to land in fact vested in a squatter, for instance, the latter would obtain automatic rectification against the applicant: *Re 139 Deptford High Street* [1951] 1 All E.R. 950. **[49]**

As to indemnity, it is true that s. 20 (4) of this Act enables the Chief Land Registrar to accept a s. 20 (2) certificate relating to unregistered land as sufficient evidence of the matters stated therein, and confers a right of recovery by him in the event of a successful indemnity claim against him, from the landlord; but it seems that landlords or rather ex-landlords need have few fears on this matter. This is because no indemnity is obtainable under the Land Registration Act 1925 s. 83 unless a "loss" has been suffered, and none is where rectification is ordered to give effect to an overriding interest: *Re Chowood's Registered Land* [1933] Ch. 574. **[50]**

RIGHT OF DETERMINATION BY DISTRICT VALUER

By s. 11 (1), the district valuer (defined in s. 27 (2)) has a power to determine any question under Chapter I of this Act as to the value of the dwelling-house at the "relevant time" (see s. 3). **[51]**

Tenant requires value to be determined, etc.

The tenant may require the value to be determined or redetermined by notice in writing served on the landlord not later than 3 months after service of a landlord's s. 10 notice: s. 11 (2).

In cases where proceedings are pending or have been begun between the parties, then the time for service is modified: s. 11 (2) (*a*) and (*b*). The landlord has, where s. 11 (2) (*b*) applies, a right to require the district valuer to re-determine the value of the dwelling-house as provided in s. 11 (3). **[52]**
Further requirements

The district valuer, in making a determination or redetermination (as to what this means, see the note to this section) is bound to consider any representation made by either party within 4 weeks of the service of the appropriate notice: s. 11 (4). As soon as practicable after the decision of the district valuer, the landlord must then serve on the tenant a notice complying with s. 11 (5) and (6). **[53]**

POWER OF THE SECRETARY OF STATE TO INTERVENE AND TO EXECUTE VESTING ORDERS

Section 23 contains a sweeping, highly subjective and almost unreviewable (as to this see the annotations) power of intervention in the Secretary of State for the Environment. By s. 23 (1), where it appears to him that tenants generally, or a tenant or tenants of a particular landlord, or tenants of a description of landlords have or may have difficulty in exercising the right to buy effectively and expeditiously, he may use his s. 23 powers, on giving the landlord or landlords written notice of his intention to do so. It is not stated in s. 23 (1) whether a notice without a fixed duration would be bad; all that s. 23 (1) does say as to time is that a notice is deeded to be given 72 hours after it has been sent—received, known about or not, therefore. This is better than the 24 hour limit in the first copy of the Housing Bill; and the reason for it at all was stated by the government to be to create certainty as to the moment in time of exercise of the intervention power: H.C. Committee, Col. 493. **[54]**

Except in so far as the notice otherwise provides, once given, a s. 23 notice annuls (in effect) any steps taken by the landlord or landlords to whom it is given; by s. 23 (2), no step taken by the landlord(s) is to have any effect, while the notice is in force or before it was given, in relation to the tenant's exercise of the right to buy or to a mortgage. **[55]**

Having thus annulled the landlords' acts, s. 23, by s. 23 (3), seems to give the Secretary of State total dictation: he may, while a notice continues in force, do all such things as appear to him (note the subjectivity and see the annotations) necessary or expedient to enable the secure tenants in question to exercise the right to buy and to a mortgage. Obscurely, s. 23 (3) states that the Secretary of State is not to be bound to take the steps which a landlord would have been bound to take, but what, apart from the notice and conveyancing procedure, this refers to is not at once self-evident.
[56]

Section 23 (4) deals with the case where a secure tenant having exercised the right to buy, a landlord on whom a s. 23 notice then in force has been served becomes his mortgagee. Essentially, the Secretary of State is put in the latter's place while the s. 23 notice continues in force. Section 23 (5) gives the Secretary of State a subjectively worded power, where it appears to him necessary or expedient for the exercise of his powers under s. 23, by service of yet another notice on the landlord (or mortgagee, etc.) to require them, within the time stated in the notice, or such longer time as the Secretary of State may allow, to produce any document or supply any information. Also, in this, any officer of the landlord (see the notes) designated in the notice for this purpose or having custody and control of the document or in a position to give the information must take all reasonable steps to ensure that the notice is complied with. **[57]**

A s. 23 notice may be withdrawn by a further notice as provided in s. 23 (6) and the withdrawal notice may contain directions to a landlord as to the completion of any transaction begun before the s. 23 (6) notice was given: see also s. 23 (7). These provisions also cover mortgagees. **[58]**

The rest of s. 23 deals with sums due to a landlord and costs. **[59]**

When a s. 23 notice is in force, then s. 24 applies. This, by s. 24 (1), enables the Secretary of State to make a vesting order in favour of the secure tenant(s); but the landlord is liable for the stamp duty thereon. In principle, a vesting order has the like effect as a conveyance (freehold) or grant (lease) under this chapter. In particular, therefore, by s. 24 (2), the landlord and tenant and their successors in title are bound to the same extent as if covenants contained in the order had been entered into by them. Section 24 deals also with registration and the Land Registry and some particular matters relating to this are discussed in the annotation to s. 24. **[60]**

Some comments

It is evident that ss. 23 and 24 are penal provisions. There is no requirement of prior consultation in s. 23, and an amendment to effectuate this was voted down in committee: H.C. Committee, Col. 505. Judicial review of the various powers in s. 23 is considered in the annotations: it is not in theory totally impossible, but in practice this will be the usual result. The section was criticised by an Opposition spokesman as being "little short of dictatorial": H.C. Committee, Col. 472. The reason for ss. 23 and 24 is that the government is determined, for good or bad reasons, to override any landlord averse to the sale of public sector housing. **[61]**

MISCELLANEOUS

Section 22 deals with the service of notices under this chapter (s. 22 (2)) and also gives a general regulatory power in connection therewith to the Secretary of State (s. 22 (1)). There is a special rule for service of notices on housing associations (s. 22 (3)). Section 26 contains a subjective power in the Secretary of State to repeal local enactments or parts thereof inconsistent with any provision of this chapter of the Act (s. 26 (1)); consultation is required (s. 26 (2)): this must be genuine: see the annotations. The annulment procedure applies to s. 26: s. 151. In committee this power was spoken of as an erasure power of non-operable statutes (it is not so confined) and the Huddersfield Act 1949 was cited as an example of a candidate for the erasure treatment: H.C. Committee, Col. 577. Section 18 provides for special protection by covenant in the case of a dwelling-house situate in National Parks, etc. Section 21 avoids certain agreements as to landlords' costs, but tenant's mortgage costs up to £50 are chargeable to him: s. 21 (2); S.I. 1980 No. 1375. As to the acceptance of statutory declarations, see s. 25. Finally, s. 27 is a definition section. As to commencement of Chapter I, see s. 153 (1): i.e. on 3rd October 1980. **[62]**

CHAPTER 3

SECURITY OF TENURE FOR PUBLIC SECTOR TENANTS

Introduction—Definition of secure tenancy—Succession rules—Re-grant to successor—Security of tenure—Grounds for possession—Omissions from security of tenure—Terms of secure tenancy—Assignments and sub-letting of whole premises—Improvements—Miscellaneous provisions.

INTRODUCTION

Chapter II of Part I of this Act introduces security of tenure for existing and future public sector tenants, with certain exceptions. Security of tenure is conferred even where there is a licence, the terms of which are overridden. There are provisions similar to those in the Rent Act 1977 as to the recovery of possession where there is a secure tenancy, and succession provisions, but, unlike the Rent Act, one succession only is permitted. The common-law rules as to assignments and sub-letting are modified in relation to secure tenants and so are the rules as to improvements. It will be noted, however, that the fixing of the level of rents remains for the landlord to decide and there is no rent regulation in the public sector similar to that in the Rent Act 1977. **[63]**

DEFINITION OF A SECURE TENANCY

By s. 28 (1), for there to be a secure tenancy, both the landlord and the tenant condition must be satisfied, and there must be a letting of a dwelling-house (see s. 50 (2)) as a separate dwelling. In fact, as will be seen, licences are in principle treated by s. 48 (1) as though they were tenancy agreements.
[64]

Tenant condition

By s. 28 (3), the condition is that the tenant is an individual who occupies the dwelling-house as his only or principal home. In the case of joint tenancies, each of the joint tenants must be individuals, but only at least one of them must satisfy the residence requirement. **[65]**

Landlord condition

If there is to be security, then the landlord must be one of those landlords listed in s. 28 (2) or (4). Table 1 summarises the position. **[66]**

TABLE 1

LANDLORDS UNDER WHICH SECURITY OF TENURE MAY ARISE
1. A local authority.
2. The Commission for the New Towns.

3. A development corporation.
4. The Housing Corporation.
5. A housing trust which is a charity within the Charities Act 1960.
6. The Development Board for Rural Wales.
7. Housing associations within the Rent Act 1977, s. 15 (3) (but see s. 49).
8. Housing co-operatives where the dwelling-house is comprised in a housing co-operative agreement.
9. Where the landlord's interest is held by a county council granting the tenancy under reserve powers in the Local Government Act 1972, s. 194.

Notes—As to housing co-operative agreements, see Sch. 20 to this Act. **[67]**
Further exclusions
　　These will be found in Sch. 3 to this Act. The position is summarised in Table 2: the numbers correspond to the paragraph numbers in Sch. 3. **[68]**

TABLE 2
EXCLUSIONS FROM SECURITY OF TENURE

1. Long tenancies.
2-3. Tenancies held by employees of certain landlords.
4. Dwelling-house is situated on land acquired for development.
5. Accommodation provided for homeless persons under the Housing (Homeless Persons) Act 1977.
6. Temporary accommodation for persons seeking employment.
7. Leases of short-life accommodation to the landlord.
8. Dwelling-house available for occupation during works to tenant's other home.
9. Agricultural holdings.
10. Licensed premises.
11. Student lettings.
12. Business premises.
13. Almshouses.

Notes—Despite the deeming provision for licences in s. 48 (1) (and see further the annotations) there is also no security where there is a licence granted as a temporary expedient to a person who entered the dwelling-house or any other land as a trespasser (whether or not before the grant another licence to occupy that or another dwelling-house had been granted to him): s. 48 (2). **[69]**
Licences deemed to be secure tenancies
　　By s. 48 (1), it is provided that, where a person who is not the tenant of a dwelling-house has a licence (whether or not granted for a consideration) and the circumstances are such that, if the licence were a tenancy, it would be a secure tenancy, then, with the exception of temporary licences (see s. 48 (2)) there is to be (in effect) security of tenure and Chapter II is to apply as much to the "licence" as it would had there been a tenancy: in other words, the terms of the licence are overriden. The scope and intendment of this provision is considered in the annotations. It suffices to remark here that it was difficult at common law to prove that a licence did not mean what it said: this could only be done in the case of a sham or where the agreement did not truly represent the real intentions of the parties. **[70]**

It is next proposed to deal with devolution on death and then with security. After that, the terms of a secure tenancy will be considered plus miscellaneous matters. **[71]**

SUCCESSION RULES

The rules, which are difficult and superimposed on the existing law, may be divided into those which apply to cases of death of a secure tenant entitled to a fixed-term tenancy and those where he dies entitled to a periodic tenancy, whether it originated as such or followed on a fixed-term tenancy. **[72]**

Death of tenant entitled to a fixed-term tenancy

On the death of the tenant, the fixed-term tenancy will pass as real estate to his personal representatives, under the Administration of Estates Act 1925, s. 1 (1), with the notable exception of a secure joint tenancy: see s. 3 (4). Eventually, by s. 36 (2) and (4) of the 1925 Act, the secure tenancy will be vested by an assent in the person named, if there is such a person. In the case of a joint tenancy, there is a survivorship. Section 28 (5) of this Act appears to act as a bridge from the death until the assent or other events: the tenancy is to remain, after the death, a secure tenancy during administration (while the personal representative have full property) until either:

(a) the tenancy is vested (by assent) or otherwise disposed of in the course of the administration of the tenant's estate; or
(b) it is known that when the tenancy is so vested or disposed of it will not be a secure tenancy. **[73]**

Paragraph (*a*) of s. 28 (5) deals with a case where, for instance, P assents to the vesting of the residue of a 10-year term in R, where R is not a person qualified to succeed the deceased. Paragraph (*b*) looks to a time before vesting, but when the personal representatives become aware that the beneficiary who will ultimately obtain an assent is not qualified to succeed. But for para. (*b*), the bridge of security might have to last until the actual vesting, at any rate where the beneficiary was a residuary legatee and so, during administration, without title to the term: see, *e.g.*, *Commissioner for Stamp Duties (Queensland)* v. *Livingston* [1965] A.C. 694; [1964] 3 All E.R. 692. **[74]**

What s. 28 (5) does not say is what is to happen after the artificial extension of security through the administration comes to an end. It is thought that the answer to this will be found in the succession provisions. One thus asks if there is a person qualified to succeed the tenant within sub-ss. (2) and (3). (This is dealt with below.) If there is such a person, then the tenancy remains secure. If not, then security is lost owing to s. 28 (5). **[75]**

Example 1—T, a secure tenant, entitled to a 15-year term, with 10 years to run at the date of his death, dies, disposing of the residue of the term to his wife W. Section 28 (5) gives W bridging security of tenure until assent and thereafter she obtains full security.

Example 2—T as above dies intestate leaving W as above. There is bridging security of tenure until vesting in W under s. 47 of the Administration of Estates Act 1925, with results as above.

Example 3—T as above dies intestate but the only possible claimant, all his other relatives being dead, is R, who has only resided with T for 11 months during his last illness. Once this is discovered, then s. 28 (5) (*b*) comes into play and interim security ends. **[76]**

"Artificial" succession on assignments permitted by s. 37 (1) (b)

In general, assignment of a secure tenancy causes it to cease to be a secure tenancy: s. 37 (1).   Section 37 (1) (*b*), not on its face an easy provision, appears to allow for an assignment of a fixed-term secure tenancy—and also a periodic tenancy—*inter vivos* by the present secure tenant to a person who would be qualified to succeed on the death of the present secure tenant.   In the case of a periodic secure tenancy, this results from these words in s. 37 (1) (*b*) ". . . the assignment is to a person in whom the tenancy would or might have vested by virtue of section 30 . . . had the tenant died immediately before the assignment."   In the case of a fixed-term secure tenancy, it is conceived (with difficulty) that this ought to be the end result of the last words of s. 37 (1) (*b*) ". . . or in whom it would or might have vested had the tenancy been a periodic tenancy."   (The last words of s. 37 itself appear to save assignments by vesting or other disposals by the personal representatives of a deceased secure tenant.) **[77]**

Example—T could decide to pre-empt matters as follows.   Assuming that at a given date, X, his favourite niece (part of his "family" under s. 50 (3)) has been residing with him for 24 months to date and he wishes to provide for her rather than some other relative whom he dislikes.   T assigns to X his secure tenancy: it is saved from loss of secure status by s. 37 (1) (*b*), be it fixed-term or periodic.   Now, as X became a secure tenant on assignment, s. 31 (1) (*d*), in the case of a periodic tenancy, treats her as a successor: on her death, there can be no further succession. **[78]**

Periodic tenancies

On the death of a secure periodic tenant, the periodic tenancy will form part of his estate under the Administration of Estates Act 1925, ss. 1 (1) and 3 (1); but, were it not for s. 30 (1) of this Act, the landlord could serve a notice to quit on the deceased's personal representatives and thus possibly put an end to security of tenure thereby.   This is avoided by s. 30 (1), except where the tenant was a successor.   Apart from this—it is the one-succession rule—on the death of the secure tenant, where there is a person qualified to succeed him (see s. 30 (2) and (3)) the periodic tenancy vests by virtue of s. 30 (1) in that person.   A person is qualified to succeed if, by s. 30 (2), which applies also to fixed-term tenancies, the person occupied the dwelling-house as his only or principal home at the time of the tenant's death and is either:

(a)   the tenant's spouse; or
(b)   another member of the tenant's family (see s. 50 (3)) and has resided with the tenant throughout the period of twelve months ending with the tenant's death. **[79]**

Section 30 (3) deals with the resolution of competing claims where there is more than one person qualified to succeed the tenant. **[80]**

Meaning of successor

The meaning of successor—and there can only be one succession to a secure tenancy—is dealt with in s. 31 (1).   The following are deemed to be the successors to a periodic tenancy:

(a)   a person in whom the tenancy is vested by s. 30 (1); or
(b)   an individual who was a joint tenant (with the deceased) but who has become the sole tenant (under the right of survivorship); or
(c)   the tenant is a person to whom a fixed-term tenancy was granted jointly with another person or where the fixed-term tenancy was granted to another person than the tenant; in either case, where the fixed-term tenancy ended and a periodic tenancy arose under s. 29; or

(d) the tenant became tenant by virtue of an *inter vivos* assignment under s. 37 (1) (*b*) (discussed above); or on the tenancy being vested in him on the death of the previous tenant.

In the case of a tenant to whom the tenancy was assigned under an order under the Matrimonial Causes Act 1973, s. 24, the tenant is only a successor if the other party to the marriage was himself a successor. This means that the order will not result of itself in there being a succession. **[81]**

Paragraph (*c*) of s. 31 (1) is not easy and two examples may be given.

Example 1—Joint tenants. In 1980 T and X were jointly granted a 5-year secure tenancy. In 1985 this expired and T died in 1986. In 1985 s. 29 "bit" and T and X obtained continued security under the periodic tenancy which then arose. But from 1986 X is a successor. As a result, should X die, his wife (for instance) cannot claim to succeed as a person qualified to do so as X is a successor.

Example 2—Grant to another person. In the case of a fixed-term tenancy, the successor provision does not apply: it only applies to periodic tenancies. Suppose that T, a secure tenant, died during a fixed-term tenancy leaving W (his spouse) as a person qualified to succeed. The tenancy expired in 1986 and then a periodic tenancy arose. On that event, W becomes a successor because, under para. (*c*) of s. 31 (1), the first tenancy was granted to another person (T). **[82]**

In view of the complexity of the provisions, it is hoped that a brief résumé is in order. **[83]**

TABLE 3

SUMMARY OF MAIN SUCCESSION RULES (SECURE TENANCIES)

A—*Fixed-term tenancies*
T dies entitled to a fixed-term tenancy.
   1. Is there a person qualified to succeed?
     (i) Spouse, or
     (ii) Resident member of family.
   2. If so, then s. 28 (5) applies and personal representative vests fixed-term tenancy in that person.
   3. If not, then no security as soon as it is known that this is so: s. 28 (5).

B—*Periodic tenancies*
T dies entitled to a periodic tenancy.
   1. It vests by virtue of s. 30 (1) in the person qualified to succeed, if such a person, as above.
   2. The person qualified to succeed is a successor: s. 31 (1) (*a*).
   3. If successor dies, then no vesting by virtue of s. 30 (1) and no further security, as one succession only.

Notes—(a) In the case of *inter vivos* assignments of any secure tenancy, assignee becomes successor whether the tenancy be periodic or fixed term (deemed to be so in this case): s. 37 (b). If there is a survivorship to a joint tenancy, then the survivor is the successor and there can be no person qualified to succeed him, *e.g.* his spouse. **[84]**

RE-GRANT TO A SUCCESSOR

To enable a new tenancy to be granted to a successor tenant which, though itself a secure tenancy, will not confer on the successor a right to transmit a further succession, there is s. 31 (2). It applies only where a secure periodic tenancy ends and the tenant was a successor thereto, and a new periodic tenancy is then granted to him within six months of the termination of the former tenancy. Provided, in this, that either the landlord or the dwelling-house (or both) are the same as under the former tenancy, then the tenant is treated as a successor in relation to the new tenancy (unless the contract of tenancy otherwise provides). None of this applies if there is a re-grant after six months from the termination of the former periodic tenancy; nor of course to the grant of a fixed-term lease, for however short a period, within the six-month period. **[85]**

Section 31 (2) might work as follows. R, a local authority, granted T a two-year term in January 1979 of "Bellavista", a house. From January 1981, T held over as a secure periodic tenant and died in January 1982. X, his nephew, succeeds as a family member under s. 30, having taken up residence to look after T. In January 1983 the periodic tenancy is terminated by a tenant's notice to quit to R from X and he moves to "Seaview" another house owned by R, which may, between January 1983 and July 1983, re-grant X a periodic tenancy of "Seaview" without fearing that there will be a further succession in any event (say X should die in October 1983, leaving a resident son). On X's death, the security ends. **[86]**

SECURITY OF TENURE

The concept of security of tenure will not be unfamiliar to those conversant with the Rent Acts; but in this Act, the rules applicable differ at the outset as to termination, between periodic and fixed-term tenancies. It may be said that the basic idea is to bring about, if it is not there already, a periodic tenancy, which is then terminable only, as a secure tenancy, in accordance with the grounds set out in Sch. 4 and subject to s. 34. In what follows, the rules for termination of periodic and fixed-term tenancies are dealt with; mention is then made of the last stage—the grounds for possession—but these are analysed in detail in the annotations and call for outline treatment here only. **[87]**

Security of tenure: periodic tenancies

Assuming that the secure tenancy is a periodic tenancy, then a notice to quit served by the landlord will not suffice to obtain possession. The landlord will have to obtain an order of court for possession, on proof of grounds for possession; if obtained, the tenancy ends on the date specified in the order for possession: s. 32 (1). As to grounds for possession, see s. 34 and Sch. 4. **[88]**

Before proceedings for possession may be entertained, a statutory notice in the prescribed form must be served in accordance with s. 33 on the tenant; proceedings must be begun after the date specified in the notice, which must still be in force at the time proceedings are begun: s. 33 (1). A date must be specified for the commencement of proceedings and the notice itself ceases to be in force twelve months after this date: s. 33 (3). The date after which proceedings may be begun for possession cannot be earlier than the date of termination by notice to quit at common law: s. 33 (3)—see further the annotations. **[89]**

Security of tenure: fixed-term tenancies

If the fixed-term tenancy ends by effluxion of time, then the periodic tenancy which arises automatically is, broadly, terminable under the periodic tenancy rules. If it is terminated by forfeiture, then the forfeiture does not of itself confer a right to possession: the procedure as for termination of the periodic tenancy which will arise on forfeiture must be followed. [**90**]

Termination by effluxion of time

Where this takes place, then the landlord has no right to possession; s. 29 applies and automatically, under it, a periodic tenancy of the same dwelling-house arises. The only thing which will prevent this is the grant of a new fixed-term lease or periodic tenancy, to begin on the coming to an end of the first tenancy: s. 29 (1). [**91**]

Broadly, the periods of the tenancy arising under s. 29 are the same as those for which rent was last payable under the fixed-term tenancy (s. 29 (2) (a)): this affects the date to be specified in the necessary statutory notice to terminate the periodic tenancy under s. 33. The parties and terms are to be the same as at the end of the first tenancy (s. 29 (2) (b)) but they must be compatible with a periodic tenancy (s. 29 (2))—see further the annotations. They will not include a right of re-entry or forfeiture. This statute-implied periodic tenancy may then only be terminated in accordance with the procedure outlined above. [**92**]

Termination by forfeiture

A forfeiture action will not of itself obtain possession for the landlord: s. 32 (1). If the landlord is not prepared to await the expiry of the fixed term and the availability of the procedure for obtaining possession where the statute-implied periodic tenancy arises, then he must first forfeit the tenancy and then terminate the periodic tenancy which arises under s. 29 on proof of one of the grounds for possession in Sch. 4 and satisfying s. 34 and, in this, a notice under s. 33 must be served as well as any notice under the Law of Property Act 1925, s. 146 (1), in the forfeiture action. [**93**]

In the forfeiture action, the first stage, it is provided that the Law of Property Act 1925, s. 146 (except s. 146 (4), the power to vest the tenancy in underlessees or mortgagees) applies, and any enactment or rule of law likewise: s. 32 (3): this is dealt with in the annotations. If the court forfeits the lease, it cannot order possession under the forfeiture; it makes an order under s. 32 (2) which terminates the secure tenancy on the date specified in the order. [**94**]

The result of a s. 32 (2) order will then be to attract s. 29 and the statute-implied periodic tenancy will come to an end on the date specified in the order for the giving up of possession. The s. 33 notice which the landlord is required to serve on the secure tenant as a pre-condition of obtaining possession not only applies to the fixed-term tenancy but also, by s. 33 (4), to any periodic term which arises under s. 29 and s. 33 is consequently relaxed in this instance. [**95**]

GROUNDS FOR POSSESSION

As is the case with a protected tenant under the Rent Acts, a landlord can only remove a secure tenant by obtaining an order for possession from the county court (see s. 87) and this only on proof of the matters required by s. 34 and the grounds set out in Sch. 4. Thus, as with the Rent Acts, an extra obstacle is placed in the path of the landlord's common law right to possession on termination at common law: *cf. Kennealy* v. *Dunne* [1977] 2 All E.R. 16, CA. The burden of proof of the requirements of s. 34 and of grounds in Sch. 4 is on the landlord. [**96**]

In the case of grounds 1 to 6 and 10 to 13, no order may be made for possession in any case unless the court considers it reasonable to do so: s.

34 (2) and (3). In the case of grounds 7 to 13, there is an overriding requirement that no order may be made unless the court is satisfied that suitable
alternative accommodation will be available to the tenant when the order
takes effect: *ibid.* These matters are considered in detail in the annotations. **[97]**

To obtain possession under a ground, it must be specified in the statutory
notice under s. 33 which must be served: s. 33 (1), but the grounds specified
may be altered or added to with the leave of the court: s. 34 (1). **[98]**

By s. 87 (1), in the case of proceedings under Grounds 1 to 6 or 10 to
13 of Sch. 4, the court has a general discretion to adjourn the proceedings
for such a period or periods as it thinks fit. There are in s 87 (2) wide powers
of staying, suspension and postponement of the order for possession. If these
powers are exercised and execution postponed, etc., then by s. 87 (3) conditions must be imposed as to the payment by the tenant of rent arrears or
mesne profits, save only where to do so would cause exceptional hardship
on the tenant. The court may also impose such other conditions as it thinks
fit and if complied with, it may discharge or rescind the order: s. 87 (4). Section 87 is extended by s. 87 (5) and (6) to spouses with rights of occupation
under the Matrimonial Homes Act 1967. The suspensory powers and s. 87
(3) are discussed further in the annotations. **[99]**

OMISSIONS FROM SECURITY OF TENURE

It was stated earlier that there are a number of specific exclusions from
security of tenure, stated in Sch. 3. One or two omissions in particular deserve
mention here, as of particular interest. **[100]**

The omission (by Sch. 3, para. 2) of job-related accommodation from being
a secure tenancy is to be noted; it was stated that 200,000 persons are affected
by this omission: H.C. Committee, Col. 708. The government excluded them
because it feared queue-jumping of housing waiting lists otherwise: H.C. Committee, Col. 713. A public sector short-let tenant holding under a sub-lease
from a local authority landlord, itself a lessee of a private landlord on a lease
terminable on notice has no security of tenure (Sch. 3 para. 7). (As to these
sub-leases, see an article in (1977) 128 New Law Journal, p.677.) The government omitted these sub-tenants to avoid causing a useful supply of shortlet housing to dry up: H.C. Committee, Col. 704. **[101]**

TERMS OF A SECURE TENANCY

In general, of course, the terms of a secure tenancy will be governed by
the contract of tenancy, subject, in the case of a periodic tenancy arising by
virtue of s. 29 to the compatibility requirement; but Parliament has imposed
special rules in relation to assignments, sub-lettings and lodgers, and there
are modifications of the consent rules.

By s. 35 (1), it is declared to be a term of every secure tenancy that the
tenant may allow any persons to reside as lodgers in the dwelling-house. This
right is not dependent on the landlord's consent. By s. 35 (2), it is a term
of every secure tenancy that the tenant will not, without the written consent
of the landlord, sub-let or part with possession of part of the dwelling-house.
The landlord's consent cannot be unreasonably withheld: if it is, then it is
treated as given (s. 35 (3)) and this means that the tenant may sub-let without
fear of committing a breach of covenant. By s. 35 (4), s. 113 (5) of the Housing
Act 1957 is repealed. **[102]**

Section 36 (1) casts the burden of proving reasonableness on the landlord,
and this reverses the common law (see the annotations). If the landlord

proves (a) that his consent would lead to overcrowding within the Housing Act 1957, s. 77; or (b) that he proposes to carry out certain works (see the annotations), then he may discharge the burden of proof of reasonable with-holding of consent: s. 36 (1). It is thought that—as with the Landlord and Tenant Act 1954, Part II, s. 30—the proposal to carry out works should be firm and relate to action which the landlord is able to carry out, not just a mere hope or expectation: *Cunliffe* v. *Goodman* [1950] 1 All E.R. 720, C.A. (and see the annotation to Sch. 4, para. 8). A consent is stated by s. 36 (2) to be valid though it follows an action requiring it; but no conditions may be imposed in the consent: if they are, they will be ignored: s. 36 (3). An example might be a condition as to the payment of landlords' costs. The common law is still further altered in relation to secure tenancies by s. 36 (4), wherein it is provided that where a tenant has applied in writing for a consent, then:

    (a) If the landlord refuses his consent, reasons must be given in writing. It is not clear at law how far one has to give reasons; but see *Lovelock* v. *Margo* [1963] 2 All E.R. 13, C.A.
    (b) If the landlord does not give or refuse to give his consent within a reasonable time (this is considered in the annotations) then consent is deemed withheld. [**103**]

ASSIGNMENT AND SUB-LETTING OF THE WHOLE PREMISES
    By s. 37 (1), if a secure tenancy is assigned, it ceases to be a secure tenancy. There are two exceptions to this rule:

    (a) where the assignment is made in pursuance of an order under s. 24 of the Matrimonial Causes Act 1973; and
    (b) (See the discussion above of the succession rules as to this). [**104**]

The secure tenancy similarly ceases to be a secure tenancy where, on the death of the tenant, it is vested or otherwise disposed of in the course of the administration of his estate: s. 37 (1). In such a case, where the secure tenancy is a periodic tenancy, the person in whom it is assigned or vested after the death is a successor under s. 31 (1) (*d*). [**105**]

    By s. 37 (2), if the secure tenant parts with possession of the dwelling-house or sub-lets the whole of it (or sub-lets first part of it and then the remainder) the tenancy ceases to be a secure tenancy. [**106**]

    By s. 37 (3), where (a) a tenancy ceases to be a secure tenancy by virtue of s. 37, or (b) at a time when a tenancy is not a secure tenancy, it is assigned or the tenant parts with possession of the dwelling-house or sub-lets the whole of it (or sub-lets first part then the remainder) then the tenancy cannot become a secure tenancy. This prevents a non-secure tenant from conferring by assignment, etc., security on some other person. [**107**]

IMPROVEMENTS
    Some element of compensation for improvements (see a statutory defini-tion in s. 81 (5) and also the annotation to s. 6) and also a provision as to the effect on rent of an improvement are to be found in ss. 38–39. In broad terms, "improvement" means the addition to property of something new which was not there before: *Morcom* v. *Campbell-Johnson* [1955] 3 All E.R. 264, C.A. Examples would be installing a new floor or central heating. [**108**]

    Where s. 38 applies (see s. 38 (1)) then, where the landlord or his prede-cessor in title has consented in writing to the improvement (for consent provisions see Part III of this Act) then s. 38 applies, on two further conditions. These are:

(a) that work on the improvement was begun not earlier than the commencement of Part I of this Act (s. 38 (1) (*b*)) and

(b) that the improvement must have added materially to the price which the dwelling-house may be expected to fetch on sale on the open market or the rent which the landlord may be expected to charge on letting the dwelling-house (s. 38 (1) (*c*)).

(It is to be noted that at common law there may be an improvement within the meaning of the Landlord and Tenant Act 1927, s. 19 (2), though it not only does not add to the value of the property but reduces it: see the note to s. 6.) **[109]**

Where s. 38 applies then the landlord has a discretion under s. 38 (2) at or after the end of the tenancy to make to the tenant or his personal representatives such a payment in respect of the improvement as he considers appropriate. By s. 38 (3), in no case may the amount of the payment exceed the cost or likely cost of the improvement; and from the payment there must be deducted any grant-aid for the improvement paid under the Housing Act 1974, Part VII. In other words, this provision applies only if and so far as the cost is borne by the secure tenant out of his own pocket. Also, in that the payment is to be based on cost, subsequent inflation in the value of the improvement will benefit the landlord in due course. There is no compulsory re-imbursement by the landlord: this is because the government thought that to have it would cause an undesirable administrative burden and a proliferation of refusals of consents: H.C. Committee, Col. 798. But the discretion to make the payment exists where the landlord is treated by the Act as having given his consent: see as to this Part III. **[110]**

Section 39 alters the common law as to the effect of an improvement on rent. Where an improvement was carried out by a business tenant at his own expense, it was held that the improved value must be reflected in a rent review: *Ponsford* v. *HMS Aerosols Ltd.* [1978] 2 All E.R. 837, H.L. To some extent the principle that the uplift in the value of property resulting from an improvement must always be reflected in the rent is modified by s. 39 in relation to secure tenancies. This provides that where a secure tenant has lawfully made an improvement (*i.e.* with the landlord's consent or where the landlord's consent is treated as given) and has borne the whole or part of its cost, or would, but for a grant under the Housing Act 1974, Part VII, have borne the whole or part of its cost, then in determining whether or to what extent to increase the rent, against two classes of secure tenant, the landlord cannot increase the rent in so far as the increase is attributable to the cost of an improvement paid for by the tenant, personally or grant-aided. The persons are: (a) the secure tenant who made the improvement, and (b) where he is dead but the tenancy vested in his spouse under s. 30, while the improver or his spouse are secure tenants of the dwelling-house improved. This means that so soon as they are not, the effect of the improvement may be taken fully into account in increasing the rent.

The section does not apply to any increase attributable to rates. **[111]**

MISCELLANEOUS PROVISIONS

It has already been remarked that there is no rent regulation in the case of secure tenancies. Accordingly, the rent will remain charged under the Housing Act 1957 s. 111 (1), though the system is to some extent adjusted by Part VII of this Act. There is no provision in any part of Chapter II corresponding to the Rent Act 1977, s. 147. This disallows distress for rent in the case of protected or statutory tenancies without the leave of the county court. An amendment to incorporate some similar provision into Chapter II was not accepted in the House of Lords by the government: the main reason given was that rent arrears stood, at the time, at £70 million; rent arrears were a rising trend and local authorities resisted the restriction: H.L. Committee, 30 June 1980, Cols 207–208. **[112]**

Brief mention is next made of a statutory procedure for variation of the terms of a secure tenancy; as to the publication of information and other matters. **[113]**

Variation

As to this, by agreement or notice, see s. 40. Space forbids detailed coverage, but the advantage of a rent increase by notice of variation is that it will be no longer necessary to raise the rent by first serving a notice to quit on the tenant. **[114]**

Before a notice of variation is served, except for rent, rates or services, there is a procedure for service of a preliminary notice (s. 40 (6) and (7)). The comments of the tenant (but note the absence of a requirement to consider comments by a tenants' association) must then be considered before the notice of variation is served: s. 40 (6) (*b*). **[115]**

Publication of information

Section 41 lays down a duty on public sector landlords to publish the information listed therein plus explanations of the effect of relevant parts of this Act and ss. 32 and 33 of the Housing Act 1961 (landlord's implied covenant to repair). The form of the information must be such as the landlord considers best suited to explain the relevant legislation and only so far as the landlord considers appropriate. This discretion is not thought by the government to avoid a need to explain, say, the right to buy provisions; but it does avoid one's having to explain every nook and cranny of the Acts: H.C. Committee, Col. 842. As to supply of copies of the information to tenants, see s. 41 (3). There must also be a statement of the terms of the tenancy special to the tenant in question: s. 41 (3) (*b*). As to the date of the required supply of information, see s. 41 (4). **[116]**

Housing management

Certain public sector landlords are bound to provide information to and to consult with their tenants as to matters of housing management (s. 42 (1) and (2)) but not in relation to rent or service charges. The latter have special rules in Sch. 19. Section 43 sets out the consultation requirements. The Development Board for Rural Wales or a development corporation, though caught by the above, may apply to the Secretary of State for an exemption certificate—see s. 45 as to this. **[117]**

Housing allocation

Landlords within s. 42 are under a duty to publish a summary of their housing allocation rules and also their rules dealing with certain other matters set out in s. 44. The Secretary of State has a power to make grants or loans to assist moves by secure tenants: s. 46. **[118]**

Scope of Part II; definitions

Both existing tenancies and those granted after the commencement of the Act are secure tenancies: s. 47. As was mentioned above, s. 48 (1) confers security even on certain licensees. Section 49 excludes Chapter II in the case of certain housing associations. Section 50 is a definition section. **[119]**

CHAPTER 4

PROTECTED SHORTHOLD TENANCIES

Introduction—Framework of protected shorthold tenancies—Two preliminary points—Formal characteristics of a protected shorthold tenancy—Termination by tenant of protected shorthold tenancy—Subletting—Assignments—Terms following protected shorthold tenancy—Landlord's mandatory right to possession: Case 19—Conclusion: Case 19 as mandatory case.

INTRODUCTION

Sections 51 to 55 of this Act introduce a new form of protected tenancy in the private residential sector—a protected shorthold tenancy (hereinafter "PST" for short). The most important feature of it is that a PST is a lease of a fixed term of not less than one nor more than five years in duration; during this term, the full protection of the Rent Acts will in principle apply; but, on its expiry, subject to any agreement between the parties before or after expiry, the landlord may obtain possession as of right under a new mandatory Case for possession, on the simple basis that the fixed term has expired. The provisions are of some complexity and are outlined in what follows. **[120]**

As a matter of policy, the government takes the view that a landlord's inability at the time of writing, to obtain vacant possession as of right at the expiry of a protected tenancy acts as a disincentive to letting empty residential property. It is therefore believed by them that, where a landlord has empty property, shortlets will offer him a third alternative of letting, knowing that re-possession on expiry of the lease will be automatic, as opposed to selling with vacant possession or going into personal occupation of the property (H.C. Committee, Cols 1101 and 1107). It remains to be seen whether this hope is realised as a result of the new provisions: after all, a landlord may always take advantage of the resident landlord provisions where appropriate (see the Rent Act 1977, s. 12 and Sch. 2, as amended by Part II of this Act, *q.v.*). Also, restricted contracts have become still more attractive because of the removal of security of tenure in Part II of this Act (*q.v*).
[121]

It is thought only fair to landlords and their advisers to allude to this: the Labour party's attitude in Parliament during the passage of the provisions was hostile to them; it stated more than once its intention to repeal the provisions relating to PSTs in the event of taking office at some future date and then to confer on existing shortlet tenants and successors full Rent Act security of tenure. (See, *e.g.*, H.C. Committee, Col. 1180; H.C. Report and Third Reading, Cols 378–379.) **[122]**

FRAMEWORK OF PROTECTED SHORTHOLD TENANCIES

The following is an outline of the framework of PSTs, and there follows after it an analysis of each relevant provision.

1. During the term itself, the tenancy is a protected tenancy under the Rent Act 1977; a rent must in principle be registered at the time the tenancy is granted; a succession to the PST is always possible. (See s. 52).

2. The PST must, to be such, be a term certain of not less than one nor more than five years (s. 52 (1)).

3. It may not be terminated by the landlord before its expiry save in the case of forfeiture or re-entry (s. 52 (1) (*a*)).

4. Moreover, before the grant of a PST, the landlord must serve on the tenant a notice in the prescribed form stating that the tenancy is to be a protected shorthold tenancy (s. 52 (1) (*b*)). Unless this is done, the tenancy will not be a PST at all and would attract full protection in some cases, depending on the circumstances, though the court may treat the tenancy as a PST nevertheless (s. 55 (2)).

5. The tenant may not (in principle) assign his interest under a PST (s. 54 (3)); but he has a right (which cannot be excluded or restricted) to terminate the PST by a suitable tenant's notice complying with the time limits laid down in s. 53.

6. Upon expiry of the PST, one of at least two things may happen:

   (i) The landlord, having made up his mind to obtain possession on expiry of the PST, will have served an "appropriate notice" under s. 55 on the tenant; if he does this, he may rely on Case 19 to the Rent Act 1977, Sch. 15, Part II (s. 55)) to obtain possession in 14 days of the order (s. 89 (1)).

   (ii) The parties may have agreed on one of two types of extension to the original term certain (the PST)—see s. 52 (5)—but, even where this is so, the landlord may, on expiry of the extended term, which is a protected tenancy, obtain possession under Case 19. If the extended term is periodic then a notice to quit will be required to end the contractual term and also an "appropriate notice" as above. [**123**]

TWO PRELIMINARY POINTS

Before passing to the details of the PST provisions, two preliminary points should be made. First, no protected shorthold tenancy may be granted save after the commencement of the PST provisions. Secondly, and vitally, by virtue of s. 52 (2), a tenant under an existing protected tenancy of a dwelling-house cannot be granted a PST of the same dwelling-house. But nothing would prevent the parties from agreeing that such a tenant were to be granted a shortlet of *another* dwelling-house, whether or not in the same building. Also, in that s. 52 (2) only applies to existing protected tenants, nothing would prevent a landlord, if it were to his advantage, from granting a PST of the same dwelling-house to for instance a tenant holding under him as resident landlord (Rent Act 1977, s. 12). [**124**]

FORMAL CHARACTERISTICS OF A PROTECTED SHORTHOLD TENANCY

The tenancy is, for the term certain, a "protected tenancy" (s. 52 (1)) and so the Rent Act 1977 will apply to it. Accordingly, by s. 1 of that Act, there must be a "tenancy under which a dwelling-house . . . is let as a separate dwelling." (For comments as to this, see the note to s. 28 of this Act.) No PST may therefore be granted by landlords outside the Rent Act (see, *e.g.*, s. 14 of the 1977 Act): the PST is for the private residential sector. [**125**]

By s. 52 (1), further, a PST is a protected tenancy "granted" after the commencement of s. 52. This, it is thought, requires an express and not an implied grant: see the note. Accordingly, in principle the formal requirements of the Law of Property Act 1925, ss. 52 and 54, must be complied with by the landlord. To pass the legal estate, therefore, a deed will be required if the fixed term is to exceed three years: s. 52 (1) and 54 (2) of the 1925 Act; if the fixed term is for less than this, no formality may be required to pass the legal estate provided the term takes effect in possession and satisfies s. 54 (2) of the 1925 Act. While it is difficult to see how "granted" could include implied grant at law, it might enable the landlord to pass an estate in equity (say for a fixed written term of 4 years) which could be a PST provided the term were specifically enforceable within the doctrine of *Walsh* v. *Lonsdale* (1882) 21 Ch.D. 9, C.A. [**126**]

Section 52 (1) continues "for a term certain of not less than one year nor more than five years ..." Thus, a fixed term at law for 11 months cannot be a PST, nor a term for 5 years 1 month. Since a PST must be a term certain, a landlord cannot grant a periodic tenancy expressly or by implication of law and fall within s. 52 (1). So even a yearly periodic tenancy granted expressly would be fully protected under the Rent Act 1977 if that Act applied to it; no part of the PST provisions could apply to it, though if the original grant of the PST (*e.g.* for 4 years certain) included, at the end of the term certain, a yearly tenancy following it, while the yearly tenancy would not be a PST, the landlord could still obtain possession on its expiry under Case 19 (see s. 52 (5) and 55 (2)). [**127**]

Section 52 contains three crucial conditions which the term certain must satisfy to qualify as a protected shorthold tenancy. They are as follows. [**128**]

First condition: no termination by landlord during term certain

By s. 52 (1) (*a*), the term certain, if it is to be a PST, must be such that it "cannot be brought to an end before the expiry of the term" subject to an exception (*q.v.*). This is however subject to the tenant's right to terminate a PST by the notice procedure laid down in s. 53. As regards the landlord, he is unable to insert, for instance, an option to determine a term certain, granted for, say, 4 years, at the end of the first 2 by notice. This provision would disqualify the whole term certain from being a PST and it might then attract full Rent Act protection without the benefit of Case 19—the mandatory ground for re-possession on expiry of a PST. The only exception for a landlord is that stated in s. 52 (1) (*a*) "except in pursuance of a provision for re-entry or forfeiture or for non-payment of rent or breach of any other obligation of the tenancy." The landlord may thus insert such a provision for his own self-protection without fear of losing the benefit of the term being a PST. [**129**]

Second condition: Prescribed form of notice served on tenant by landlord

A second condition precedent to there being a PST is that mentioned in s. 52 (1) (*b*), that "before the grant the landlord has given the tenant a valid notice stating that the tenancy is to be a protected shorthold tenancy." "Before the grant" is apt to prevent a landlord from granting a term to take effect in possession at a later date and then serving the notice only at the later date. The significance of "valid notice" is that, by s. 52 (3), the notice must comply with regulations made by the Secretary of State. See the Protected Shorthold Tenancies (Notice to Quit) Regulations 1980, S.I. 1980 No. 1707 (operative as of 28th November 1980). Non-compliance with the notice requirements will not necessarily be fatal to a landlord's action for possession under Case 19 because s. 55 (2) enables the court, in such a case, where satisfied that it is just and equitable to make the order for possession, to treat the tenancy as a PST. Whether this discretion would be exercised in favour of a landlord who had completely failed at any time to serve a notice remains to be seen; service slightly later than the grant without sharp practice would appear to qualify for the discretion however. **[130]**

Third condition: Requirement of registration of rent

In that, for the duration of the term certain, Rent Act protection applies for the term certain, a PST is a regulated tenancy, and so s. 52 (1) (c) provides a third condition which the term certain must satisfy to be a PST: either a rent for the dwelling-house must be registered at the time the tenancy is granted or (i) a certificate of fair rent has, before the grant, been issued under the Rent Act 1977, s. 69, and the rent payable under the tenancy, for any pre-regulation period, does not exceed the rent specified in the certificate; and (ii) an application for the registration of such a rent (see the Rent Act 1977, Sch. 11) is made not later than 28 days after the beginning of the term and is not withdrawn. However, first, the Secretary of State has, under s. 52 (4), a power to direct by order that the requirements of s. 52 (1) (c) are to be omitted either generally or in relation to any regulation area specified in the order. Secondly, even if this is not applicable, the court's dispensation power in a case where the requirements of s. 52 (1) (c) are not complied with applies to allow a landlord to obtain possession, despite the lack of a registered rent (which means that the term is not a PST) in a case where it is just and equitable to make an order for possession. In this case (see s. 55 (2)) the tenancy is treated as a PST. An example was thought to be where a landlord applied for registration of a rent in 29 rather than 28 days: H.C. Committee, Col. 1169. **[131]**

TERMINATION BY THE TENANT OF A PROTECTED SHORTHOLD TENANCY

Section 53 (1) enables the tenant under a PST to bring the tenancy to an end before the expiry of the term certain by means of a notice in writing to the landlord. The right to serve such a notice is given "notwithstanding anything in the terms of the tenancy" (s. 53 (1)) and s. 53 (2) renders void any agreement relating to a PST, whether in the tenancy agreement or collateral to it, in so far as it purports to impose any penalty or disability on the tenant in the event of his giving a s. 53 (1) notice. By s. 53 (1), the notice must be of the "appropriate length" which is:

(a) One month if the term certain is two years or less; and
(b) Three months if it is more than two years. **[132]**

SUBLETTING

There is nothing in s. 54, which deals with sub-letting and assignments, to preclude a shorthold tenant from subletting the dwelling-house or part of it to a sub-lessee. If the tenant has sub-let, then s. 54 (1) provides that where there is a sub-letting of the whole or part of a dwelling-house let under a protected shorthold tenancy during the continuous period specified in s. 54 (3) and, during that period, the landlord becomes entitled, as against the tenant, to possession of the dwelling-house, he is also to be entitled to possession against the sub-tenant. In this, the Rent Act 1977, s. 137, is excluded. (This, by s. 137 (1), provides that an order for possession against a protected or statutory tenant or the equivalent under the Rent (Agriculture) Act 1976 is not in principle to give a right to possession against the sub-tenant.) However, it would not appear to matter at all whether the sub-tenancy is or is not itself a PST. So, where the head lease is a PST, the common law principle that the destruction of the head-lease automatically terminates the sub-lease applies to PSTs as much as to tenancies unaffected by the Rent Act 1977 or other enactments: see generally *Moore Properties (Ilford) Ltd.* v. *McKeon* [1977] 1 All E.R. 262. [**133**]

The exclusion of s. 137 of the Rent Act 1977 and the general entitlement of the landlord to possession against a sub-tenant holding under a PST applies only during the "continuous period" mentioned in s. 54 (3): s. 54 (1). The discussion following of this applies also to assignments of a PST during the "continuous period" (s. 54 (2)) which are prohibited during it. The continuous period provides a span of time to cover the duration of the PST and also any term derived out of it; and is framed to apply to a case where there was a succession, during this time, to a PST following on the death of the original tenant. [**134**]

Under s. 54 (3), the continuous period during which the Rent Act 1977, s. 137, is not to apply and during which (in principle) the PST and terms derived out of it may not be assigned, is a period *beginning* with the grant of the PST. Therefore, if the grant precedes the commencement of the term certain, the continuous period will antecede the commencement date thereof. Under s. 54 (3), further, the period is to continue until either:

(a) no person is in possession of the dwelling-house as a protected or statutory tenant; or

(b) a protected tenancy of the dwelling-house is granted to a person who is not, immediately before the grant, in possession of the dwelling-house as a protected or statutory tenant. [**135**]

Section 54 (3) (*a*) would seem to deal with the case of, for instance, a short-hold tenant or a successor thereto who sub-lets the whole of part of the dwelling-house and then quits. In such a case, the landlord, before granting any new lease of the whole dwelling-house to another person on a shortlet (or in any other case) would be well advised to evict the sub-tenant who, at this time, would not be able to reply on s. 137 of the 1977 Act. [**136**]

As to s. 54 (3) (*b*), this indicates a point in time at which the span beginning with the grant of the PST comes to an end; it will have lasted through terms derived out of the PST under s. 52 (5). (What happens after that depends on whether there is or is not a re-grant by the landlord of a new PST so as to begin a new continuous period.) A tentative example may be helpful here to illustrate the possible operation of s. 53 (1) (*b*) and assumes that the landlord will be in principle entitled to rely on Case 19 to obtain vacant possession in due course. In January 1981 the landlord (L) lets the whole of a dwelling-house to a tenant (T) on a 3 year shortlet. In July 1982 T sub-lets the top floor to a sub-tenant (X) on a monthly tenancy. In August 1983 T dies, leaving his widow Q as his successor to the shortlet (Rent Act 1977, Sch. 1, para. 2, as amended by s. 76 of this Act.) L refrains (perhaps ill-advisedly) from serving on Q a Case 19 notice between October and December 1983 and must now wait until October 1984 to do this (s. 55 (1) (iii) (*b*)). He re-grants a yearly tenancy to Q from January 1984 but the span is thought to continue in that Q seems to be outside s. 53 (3) (*b*) at this stage. If L serves his Case

19 notice in time in 1984, it seems that he may recover possession from January 1985 both from Q and X. If, in this, Q had obligingly quit the premises in July 1984, L would certainly wish to serve a notice to quit on X and then rely on Case 19 to obtain possession at the earliest possible moment; if L were to re-grant a new tenancy to any person, this will end the continuous period in s. 54 (3) (*b*). [**137**]

ASSIGNMENTS

By s. 54 (2), a protected shorthold tenancy of a dwelling-house and any protected tenancy of the same dwelling-house granted during the continuous period specified in s. 54 (3) are not capable of being assigned except under a court order under the Matrimonial Causes Act 1973 s. 24. As to the continuous period, see the discussion under sub-letting in the previous paragraphs. The protected tenancy referred to in the prohibition is a tenancy derived out of the original PST or one granted by the landlord to the shortlet tenant or his successor imediately following a PST of the same dwelling-house. [**138**]

TERMS FOLLOWING THE PROTECTED SHORTHOLD TENANCY

Since the advantage of a PST from a landlord's point of view is the absolute right under Case 19 (s. 55) to possession on expiry of the term certain, the legislation confers no right whatever on the tenant to continued possession against the landlord's wishes, whether this be by way of first refusal of a new tenancy or in any other way. Now, if a landlord wishes to take advantage of Case 19 on the expiry of a PST, assuming he is in a position to do this, he should take care to serve his "appropriate notice" within s. 55 (1) during the last 3 months of the PST, because, failure to do this will force him to wait for at least a year from the beginning of the last 3 months of the PST before he may again serve an appropriate notice (s. 55 (1) (iii) (*b*)). Also, the landlord should obviously avoid an implied grant of a new (protected) tenancy after the expiry of the shortlet to a person not in possession immediately before the grant as protected or statutory tenant (*i.e.* the sitting tenant) where no term is, under the terms of the grant of the original PST, expressly to follow the shortlet. If the landlord were to make such a grant impliedly to a person not the sitting tenant on expiry of the PST, he might find that this person was fully protected under the Rent Act 1977. However, to the landlord's fortunate advantage, the law is reluctant to imply a re-grant in cases such as this: see for instance *Marcroft Wagons Ltd.* v. *Smith* [1951] 2 All E.R. 271, C.A. [**139**]

If however the landlord and the tenant agree at the time of granting the term certain on a further term to follow the initial protected shorthold tenancy, then s. 52 (5), a difficult provision, applies. By this, if a protected tenancy is granted (after the commencement of s. 52) and either:

"(*a*) for such a term certain as is mentioned in subsection (1) above, to be followed, at the option of the tenant, by a further term; or
(*b*) for such a term certain and thereafter from year to year or some other period;
    and satisfies the conditions stated in that subsection, the tenancy is a protected shorthold tenancy until the end of the term certain." [**140**]

This means that the renewed term (para. (*a*)) or the periodic tenancy following the PST (para. (*b*)) will be fully protected tenancies. On expiry of the former or termination of the latter by notice to quit, however, the landlord will still able in general to obtain possession under Case 19. This is because under para (*a*) of that case (s. 55 (1)), while there has been a grant of a further tenancy, it was (where to the sitting tenant) to a person who immediately before the grant, was in possession as a protected or statutory tenant (under the preceding shortlet). [**141**]

But if the landlord and the tenant do not agree, before the grant of the PST, with what, if anything, is to happen upon its expiry, then no part of s. 52 (5) appears to apply and so the safest thing to say here is, it is thought, that the landlord must seek to obtain possession from the tenant under the s. 55 procedure at the earliest possible moment, as was mentioned in the first part of this discussion. There is otherwise the danger of implied re-grant of a fully protected tenancy outside s. 52 (5) and therefore outside Case 19. [**142**]

LANDLORD'S MANDATORY RIGHT TO POSSESSION: CASE 19

In general terms, where a dwelling-house has been let under a PST which has expired, or where a term derived thereout has likewise expired, then the landlord has a mandatory right to possession under a new Case 19 against the original tenant and any successor of his. The new Case is added to the Rent Act 1977, Sch. 15, Part II, by s. 55 (1). [**143**]

Preliminary matters to be proved by the landlord

Though the new Case 19 is mandatory, there is presumably a burden of proof on the landlord (*cf.* in this *Kennealy* v. *Dunne* [1977] 2 All E.R. 16, C.A., dealing with the owner-occupier provision in Case 11) that, within s. 55 (1), the dwelling-house was let under a PST and therefore that the three conditions set out in s. 52 (1) are satisfied. If either or both of the prior notice requirement (s. 52 (1) (*b*)) or the registration of rent provision (s. 52 (1) (*c*)) are not complied with, the landlord will have to persuade the court to ignore these matters on the ground that it is just and equitable for the court to do so—as with a trivial slip as to the time of registration—and to make the order for possession nevertheless. If he succeeds then the court will, under s. 55 (2), treat the tenancy as a PST and as falling within Case 19. [**144**]

Scope of Case 19: s. 55 (1) (a)

The first circumstance in which Case 19 will be available to a landlord will be where a PST expires and no further tenancy of the dwelling-house is granted to the tenant (s. 55 (1) (*a*)). In such a case, to obtain possession, the landlord must comply in any event with the requirements of service of an "appropriate notice" and also satisfy s. 55 (1) (*b*). The second instance in which Case 19 is available to a landlord is where a PST expired but a further tenancy was granted to a person who immediately before the grant was in possession of the dwelling-house as a protected or statutory tenant. Here too, the two requirements just mentioned must be complied with by the landlord. In either case, failure to comply with the requirements will lead to failure to obtain possession. The second instance would be available where, for example, s. 52 (5) applied: L grants T a PST for 2 years in 1981 with an option to renew once only in 1983 for a further 2 years. Suppose that in 1983, after exercising the option to renew, T died leaving W (his widow) as successor. In 1985, L may still rely on Case 19 provided he takes good care as to the service of his appropriate notice. It is the same if it were W who obtained the renewal from L, because she is a person who, within Case 19, was, immediately before the grant, in possession as a statutory tenant. [**145**]

Requirement of service of "appropriate notice"

In order to bring proceedings for possession based on Case 19, the landlord must have served on the tenant, whether protected or statutory, an "appropriate notice": s. 55 (1) (*b*). If this is done, the landlord must then bring proceedings for possession not later than 3 months after the expiry of the notice (*ibid*.). **[146]**

In Case 19 (s. 55 (1)) there is set out four requirements which all have to be complied with (except for the last, which is dependent on special circumstances) before a notice is appropriate: non-compliance is thus disastrous. These are (the nos. correspond to the four paras. of Case 19):

1. The notice must be in writing; it must state that proceedings for possession under Case 19 may be brought after its expiry; and

2. It must expire not earlier than 3 months after it is served nor, if, when it is served, the tenancy is a periodic tenancy, before that periodic tenancy could be brought to an end by a notice to quit served by the landlord on the same day. So the longer the period of the periodic tenancy following a PST, the longer the appropriate notice may have to be if served with a notice to quit.

3. It is served:
  (a) in the period of 3 months immediately preceding the date on which the protected shorthold tenancy comes to an end; *or*
  (b) if that date has passed, in the period of 3 months immediately preceding any anniversary of that date; and

4. In a case where a previous notice has been served by the landlord on the tenant and that notice was an appropriate notice, it is served not earlier than 3 months after the expiry of the previous notice. **[147]**

As has been mentioned above, if the landlord, during the last 3 months of a PST (outside s. 52 (5)) fails to serve an appropriate notice on the tenant, the condition 3 will oblige him to wait for at least 9 months from the expiry of the PST before he is able to serve a Case 19 notice. So, in this case, if the landlord wishes to obtain vacant possession he must serve his Case 19 notice without hesitation during the last 3 months of the PST. In fact, even if the landlord is in doubt whether he wishes to have vacant possession promptly or whether he wishes for instance, to negotiate a new tenancy with the tenant, it is thought as well to serve a Case 19 notice on the tenant within the last 3 months of the PST as a sort of insurance policy and begin, if need be, proceedings for possession not later than 3 months after expiry of the notice. **[148]**

CONCLUSION: CASE 19 AS A MANDATORY CASE

To the initial remarks made on Case 19, the following additional points come to mind in conclusion, based on the fact that it is a mandatory case within the Rent Act 1977, Sch. 15, Part II. **[149]**

First, there is no overriding discretion in the (county) court to refuse to make the order for possession once the landlord has satisfied the basic requirements of Case 19, on the ground of its being reasonable to do this. **[150]**

Secondly, the landlord will not be denied his right to possession under Case 19 because of an absence of provision of suitable alternative accommodation to be provided by him for the tenant. **[151]**

These two obstacles only apply to Part I of Sch. 15 to the Rent Act 1977. In fact, a court which implied a discretion to refuse to make the order for possession on some ground of reasonableness (at any rate expressly) would, as was the case with owner occupiers (*Kennealy* v. *Dunne* [1977] 2 All E.R. 16, C.A.), be overruled on appeal.   And so the main obstacle to the landlord's common-law right to re-possession on expiry of a shortlet is chiefly that of compliance with the elaborate formal requirements mentioned in this chapter. [**152**]

CHAPTER 5

ASSURED TENANCIES

*Introduction—Nature of assured tenancies—Conditions precedent—
Loss of approved body status—Application and modification of Landlord and Tenant Act 1954, Parts II and IV to assured tenancies.*

INTRODUCTION

The government believes there to be room in the private sector for the
private institutional investor, such as pension funds, insurance companies and
building societies (these it has in mind as "approved bodies", *q.v.*: H.C. Committee, Col. 1213). So it has produced assured tenancies. These are denied
Rent Act security of tenure; accordingly, during the contractual term, the
full market rent may be charged. On termination of the term, the Landlord
and Tenant Act 1954, Part II, will apply to assured tenancies; it is modified
to suit their requirements by Sch. 5. Existing buildings are not covered by
assured tenancies, which will be available in relation only to buildings constructed after 6th October 1980. **[153]**

NATURE OF ASSURED TENANCIES

To be an assured tenancy, the landlord's interest must belong to an
"approved body", in a case where the tenancy would otherwise have been
a protected tenancy under the Rent Act 1977 or a housing association
tenancy (the latter having a "rent limit" under Part VI of the Rent Act 1977
but no security of tenure). **[154]**

If a dwelling-house is let as a separate dwelling (see the notes) but the
interest of the landlord belongs to an approved body within s. 56 (4) (*i.e.* a
body or description of bodies specified in regulations; see the notes) and certain other conditions are satisfied, then, by s. 56 (1), the tenancy is an assured
tenancy. The Rent Act 1977 is excluded: s. 16A, inserted by s. 56 (5) of
this Act; as are the provisions in that Act relating to housing association
tenancies.

But s. 56 does not apply, by s. 56 (6), if, before the grant of the tenancy,
the landlord has given the tenant a valid notice (see sub-s. (7)) stating that
the tenancy is to be a protected or housing association tenancy, as the case
may be. A landlord with approved body status may thus let under, for instance, an arrangement with a local authority, part of a building under regulated tenancies and the rest under assured tenancies. **[156]**

CONDITIONS PRECEDENT

By s. 56 (2), to be an assured tenancy:

    (a) The interest of the landlord must, since the creation of the tenancy,
        belong to an approved body (see s. 56 (4));

(b) The dwelling-house must be, or form part of, a building (see the note to s. 56) which was erected and on which construction work first began after the passing of this Act;
(c) Before the tenant first occupied the dwelling-house, no part of it had been occupied by any person as his residence except under an assured tenancy. **[157]**

LOSS OF APPROVED BODY STATUS

If this is lost, then, subject to what follows, the tenancy is no longer assured. If however, the reason for the loss of the landlord's approved body status is a variation in the bodies or descriptions of bodies specified in regulations, then the landlord continues to be treated as though an approved body in relation to the existing tenancy and also any re-grant of a tenancy to a person who, immediately before the grant, was an assured tenant in possession as such of the dwelling-house: s. 57 (I). But, if a tenancy were granted to one not in possession e.g. a new applicant for a tenancy, then the tenancy could not be an assured tenancy. **[158]**

If the reason for loss of status by the landlord is not as above and the result of the loss is that the tenancy would become a housing association tenancy or a protected tenancy, there is a 3-month interim suspension period during which the interest of the landlord may be held by a non-approved body see—s. 57 (2). If, at the expiry of this period, the interest of the landlord then comes to be held by an approved body, continuity is preserved and the tenancy remains assured; but if not, then not. This provision would apply where an approved body lost its status by engaging in an activity which it had been a condition of obtaining its status; the body then has 3 months to transfer the reversion to another approved body: *quaere*, in this, whether the suspension ends with the conclusion of a binding contract for an assignment or only on completion? **[159]**

APPLICATION AND MODIFICATION OF LANDLORD AND TENANT ACT 1954, PARTS
II AND IV TO ASSURED TENANCIES

This is achieved by s. 58. The detailed consequences of this are dealt with in the annotations to Sch. 5, which is applied by s. 58. **[160]**

Broadly, however, four important results of this will be:

(a) On termination of the contractual term of the assured tenancy, s. 24 of the 1954 Act will continue the term;
(b) The tenant may then agree with the landlord, if appropriate, as to a new tenancy; or apply to the court for a new tenancy under s. 26 of the 1954 Act;
(c) The landlord may obtain possession on proof by him of one of the grounds for possession set out in s. 30 of the 1954 Act;
(d) There will be no regulation of rent during any part of the contractual term and, on its termination, only the rent provisions of the 1954 Act Part II will apply. **[161]**

CHAPTER 6

AMENDMENTS TO THE RENT ACT 1977

Introduction—Rents under regulated tenancies: amendments by this Act—Abolition of controlled tenancies—Restricted contracts— Amendments to resident landlord provisions—Extensions of Rent Act 1977, Sch. 15, Cases 11 and 12—Miscellaneous.

INTRODUCTION

Part II of this Act amends some parts of the Rent Act 1977 and also corresponding parts of the Rent (Agriculture) Act 1976. Sections 59 to 63 amend the rules relating to regulated fair rents and controlled tenancies are abolished by s. 64. By ss. 70 to 72 the rules as to reasonable rents for restricted contracts are altered as a result of the changes made in the case of fair rents; security of tenure is removed for restricted contracts and is replaced by a limited discretion in the county court in actions for possession; the Protection from Eviction Act 1977 is extended to cover certain licences. There are also amendments to the resident landlord exception (s. 65) and also to two of the mandatory Cases for possession (cases 11 and 12: and see s. 66). There are many consequential amendments; some of these are noted in the annotations to Sch. 25. **[162]**

RENTS UNDER REGULATED TENANCIES: AMENDMENTS BY THIS ACT

First, the scope of rent officer schemes (see the Rent Act 1977, s. 63) is extended by s. 59 (1) of this Act. Secondly, by s. 59 (2), there is substituted in the 1977 Act, s. 67 (2), a new sub-s. (2), as a result of which, an application for a registration of rent must be in the prescribed form and also:

   (a) it must specify the rent which it is sought to register;

   (b) where the rent contains a payment by the tenant for services in a landlord's application, the sum must be specified and accompanied by details of the expenditure incurred by the landlord in providing the services; and

   (c) contain such other particulars as may be prescribed.

Paragraph (b) (which is quite new) could assist a tenant where he contested the services. The procedure for applications for registration of rent is altered by the Regulated Tenancies, etc., Regulations 1980, S.I. 1980 No. 1696, from 28th November 1980. **[163]**

Reduction of time-bar

There is a time-bar in the Rent Act 1977, s. 67 (3) and (4) on new applications for registration of a fair rent: the length of the bar is cut by s. 60 (1) of this Act to 2 years from the "relevant date". This term is re-defined by virtue of s. 61 (5), by substitution of a new s. 67 (5) in the 1977 Act: the general rule is that the relevant date is the date from which registration takes effect. As to this, see the (new) s. 72 of the 1977 Act: this is substituted by s. 61 (1) of this Act. The new 2-year time-bar is not retrospective: s. 60 (2). The cut of one-third in the time-bar was because of inflation: in Committee it was stated that between 1970 and 1979, unfurnished rents rose by 111% but earnings by 261%: H.C. Committee Col. 1254. **[164]**

Phasing—alterations

1. As a result of s. 61 (6), in the Rent Act 1977, Sch. 8 para. 1, and the corresponding provision in the Rent (Agriculture) Act 1976, the definition of "period of delay" is altered so as to read, in general, a period of one year beginning with the date of registration of a rent. **[165]**

2. In consequence of this single-year phasing, the mathematical formula in each relevant schedule (para. 3 in each) is replaced by s. 60 (3)'s new para. 3 formula. As before, by the new para. 3 (2) the maximum permitted increase is an increase to the registered rent. **[166]**

But by the new para. 3 (1), the permitted increase for a period within the period of delay is an increase to an amount calculated by applying a formula: the service element is left out of phasing (as before) and is payable in full from registration. The raise allowed in rent by the new formula is one-half of the difference between (in effect) the old rent and the new registered rent. This results from applying the formula:

$$\tfrac{1}{2}(P+S+R)$$

where *P* is the previous rent limit, *S* the service element and *R* the registered rent. **[167]**

3. The special phasing provisions in relation to (a) phasing of rent increases following certain grant-aided improvements (see Rent Act 1977, s. 56); (b) phasing of rent increases after conversion of controlled tenancies (*ibid.*, s. 114); and (c) the consequential Sch. 9 to the 1977 Act are all repealed by s. 60 (4). **[168]**

4. Section 60 (5) to (7) contain wide regulatory and consequential powers and provisions so that the Secretary of State for the Environment may, in particular, by s. 60 (5), by order make provision:

(a) for reducing or increasing the period of delay in the Rent Act 1977 s. 67 (3) and (4); or

(b) as above in relation to the appropriate phasing Schedules; or

(c) repealing the phasing provisions in the 1977 and 1976 Acts altogether. **[169]**

Effect of registration of rent

Section 61 (1) substitutes a new s. 72 in the Rent Act 1977, and the main result of this is that registration of a fair rent only becomes effective from the date of registration or that of the decision of the rent assessment committee; this contrasts with the previous position, which was effectiveness from the date of application for registration. Section 61 also amends the relevant provisions of the Rent (Agriculture) Act 1976. **[170]**

Rents: miscellaneous

Section 73 of the Rent Act 1977 (this deals with applications for cancellation of registration of rent) is extended by s. 62 of this Act, so as to be able to deal with a case where, in effect, there is no regulated tenancy at the date of the application. At present, s. 73 of the 1977 Act applies only to the case of rent agreements providing for increases of rent (tied up to fair rents in any case: s. 73 (4) of the 1977 Act). New Regulations as to procedure for cancellation of registered rent are in the Rent Regulations, etc., Regulations 1980, S.I. 1980 No. 1698, in force from 28th November 1980. **[171]**

Other amendments to the regulated rent system will be found in ss. 61 (4)–(8) and 63. In addition, Sch. 25 to the Act makes a number of consequential amendments: see esp. paras. 37 and 41, noted in the annotations. **[172]**

Rent agreements

The first alteration made by this Act is that by s. 68 (1), s. 51 (4) of the Rent Act 1977 is amended. Section 51 deals with cases where there is no registered rent and sets out formalities which must, on pain of irrecoverability, be observed. The requirements are set out in s. 51 (4), and it is s. 51 (4) (*b*), setting out the required contents of the statement (in characters not less conspicuous than those used in any other part of the agreement) which the agreement must contain, that is amended by a new para (ia) so that it must be stated that if the agreement were not made but instead a rent registered under Part IV of the 1977 Act, then part only of the increase over the rent previously recoverable would be payable by the tenant during the first year. **[173]**

The second alteration is by s. 68 (2) which substitutes a new s. 52 into the 1977 Act. The new s. 52 deals with cases where a controlled tenancy is converted (as defined in s. 52 (4) so as to include de-control by this Act) into a regulated tenancy. The new s. 52 applies to rent agreements entered into from 28th November 1980 if the tenancy became or has become a regulated tenancy by conversion (s. 52 (1)). Any agreement purporting to increase the rent is void if entered into when no rent is registered for the dwelling-house under Part IV of the 1977 Act (s. 52 (2)). If the agreement grants a regulated tenancy, rent in excess of the rent limit applicable to the previous tenancy is irrecoverable, but not if a rent is subsequently registered (s. 52 (3)). No part of the new s. 52 applies to any agreement where the tenant is neither, at conversion, the tenant nor a statutory tenant by succession (s. 52 (5)); and s. 52 (6) excludes rent agreements submitted to the rent officer in connection with cancellation of a fair rent from the new s. 52. **[174]**

Section 57 of the 1977 Act, which deals with recovery of sums paid in excess of recoverable rent from the landlord and other matters, is amended by s. 68 (3) which inserts a new s. 57 (3), so that, in place of a general 2 year limitation period, it is provided that no amount which a tenant is entitled to recover from the landlord or his personal representative is recoverable at any time after the expiry of—

(a) one year, in the case of an amount irrecoverable under s. 54; or

(b) two years in any other case. **[175]**

ABOLITION OF CONTROLLED TENANCIES

Section 64 (1) provides that, from its commencement date (see para. 10) every controlled tenancy is to cease to be controlled and will become regulated. This means that, by Sch. 25, para. 35, the Rent Act 1977, ss. 18 (4) and 115 (these deal with conversion and the applicability of the consequential Sch. 17 to the 1977 Act) are repealed and replaced by a new s. 18A, which applies the (amended: para. 59) Sch. 17 to the 1977 Act in all cases set out in the repealed provisions, plus s. 64 of this Act. **[176]**

There is no regulated tenancy on decontrol where s. 64 (2) applies. By this, if the only reason why the Landlord and Tenant Act 1954, Part II, does not apply to the controlled tenancy is s. 24 (2) of the 1977 Act, or the 1954

Act would apply in any case, then the tenancy, on decontrol, is treated as if it were a term of years which expired and was continued by s. 24 of that Act. **[177]**

Consequential provisions will be found in Sch. 25 to this Act. Apart from para. 35, considered above, para. 52 modifies the rent limit in the Rent Act 1977, s. 145, on subsidised private houses. In consequence of para. 55, Sch. 22 to the 1977 Act is repealed. There are notes to the other relevant paragraphs (47, 48, 57 and 58) in the annotations to Sch. 25. **[178]**

It appears that decontrol affects 200,000 tenants: H.C. Committee, Col. 1283. But it is not a pre-requisite of de-control that the dwelling-house be fit for human habitation within the Housing Act 1957, s. 4. **[179]**

RESTRICTED CONTRACTS
Reasonable rents

The Rent Act 1977 contains a system of registration of reasonable rents in the case of restricted contracts: ss. 79 to 82. By s. 70 (1) of this Act, the time-bar on reconsideration of a new rent, in s. 80 of the 1977 Act, is cut to 2 years, from 28th November 1980: s. 70 (2), and, as with regulated tenancies, an extension is made to s. 81 of the 1977 Act by s. 71 (1) of this Act. **[180]**

Rent tribunals are abolished by s. 72 (1) and so s. 76 of the 1977 Act is repealed. By s. 72 (2), their functions are transferred to rent assessment committees, which, by s. 73 (3), when carrying out the functions previously assigned to rent tribunals, will be known as rent tribunals. Consequential provisions will be found in s. (2) and also Sch. 25 paras 40, 42, 44 and 45. **[181]**

Abolition of limited security of tenure

By virtue of s. 69 (3), in relation to any restricted contract entered into after 28th November 1980, the limited security of tenure conferred by the Rent Act 1977, ss. 103 to 106, will not apply: new s. 102A of the 1977 Act. If, after the commencement of s. 69 of this Act, the tenant under a restricted contract entered into after the commencement thereof refers a rent to the rent tribunal, it seems that the landlord may respond to this by a notice to quit followed by proceedings—the notice to quit will be fully effective. **[182]**

Moreover, from the commencement date of s. 69, there is only a limited discretion in the county court where proceedings are brought for possession by the landlord in the case of a restricted contract. Section 69 (2) inserts into the Rent Act 1977 a new s. 106A. The result of this is that, provided there is an action in court for possession and the required minimum period of 4 weeks' notice to quit in the prescribed form is served by the landlord on the tenant (see the Protection from Eviction Act 1977, ss. 3 and 5) then possession will normally be granted to the landlord. While the court has, in relation to the order for possession, a power to stay or suspend its execution or to postpone the date for delivery of possession for such period as it thinks fit (s. 106A (2)) where an order for possession is made, the giving up of possession cannot be postponed to a date later than three months from the making of the order (s. 106A (3)). Conditions as to the payment of rent arrears and mesne profits, must be imposed except in the case of exceptional hardship to the lessee or where it would otherwise be unreasonable, in all cases where the power to stay, suspend or postpone is exercised: s. 106A (4). Also, the court may impose such other conditions as it thinks fit: s. 106A (4), but, in this instance, its discretion is absolute. The burden of proof of exceptional hardship or unreasonableness will presumably fall on the tenant: *cf. Sims* v. *Wilson* [1946] 2 All E.R. 261, C.A. **[183]**

There is an extension of the right to obtain a stay, etc., of possession orders to a lessee's spouse or ex-spouse with rights of occupation under the Matrimonial Homes Act 1967: s. 106A (5) to (6), which is dependent on the applicant remaining in occupation. For a discussion of this and some other points, see the note to s. 87 below.

Extension of Protection from Eviction Act 1977, s. 3

Section 3 of this Act requires the owner to obtain possession in court proceedings only, of premises let under a restricted contract where, *inter alia*, the agreement is terminated and the occupier continues in residence. By s. 69 (1) of this Act, which inserts a new s. 3 (2A) into the 1977 Act: the result is that the Protection from Eviction Act will apply in future to a restricted contract which creates a licence. **[185]**

AMENDMENTS TO THE RESIDENT LANDLORD PROVISIONS

First, by s. 65 (1), s. 12 (1) of the Rent Act 1977 is substituted so that a landlord who shares a flat with a tenant is to be within the benefit of the resident landlord exception, as much as a landlord who shares the same house with the tenant. Consequential amendments are made to Sch. 2 of the 1977 Act by s. 65 (2) (3) (*b*) and (4). It may be noted that the term "building" in s. 12 continues in use and is not affected by these amendments: the problems which this term will continue therefore to create are mentioned in the annotations. The extension to flat-sharing is non-retrospective: s. 65 (6). **[186]**

Secondly, by s. 69 (4), from 28th November 1980, s. 12 (2) and (3) of the Rent Act 1977 are replaced by a new s. 12 (2), and the result of this is that the exception for resident landlords will continue not to be available for grant to any sitting protected or statutory tenant in the building. However, because the old s. 12 (2) (*b*) has disappeared, it seems that, from the commencement of s. 69, a fixed-term tenancy may be granted to a sitting tenant whose previous tenancy was within the exception which will not itself be outside the exception either. **[187]**

Thirdly, Schedule 2 to the Rent Act 1977 is amended as follows by s. 65 (3) and (5):

1. The period for an intending owner-occupier to take possession without notice following his acquisition of the reversion is retrospectively extended from 14 to 28 days—s. 65 (3) (*a*). amending Sch. 2, para. 1.

2. The period of suspension during which s. 12 continues to apply following the death of the landlord and the consequent vesting of his interest in his personal representatives etc., is retrospectively extended from 12 months from the date of vesting to 2 years: s. 65 (3) (*c*), amending Sch. 2, para. 1.

3. Section 65 (5) provides new rules as to the vesting in personal representatives of the landlord by insertion of a new para. 2A in the 1977 Act, Sch. 2. The old rule is non-retrospectively repealed: s. 65 (2) (*c*). The effect, in relation to personal representatives, is to reverse the decision in *Landau* v. *Sloane* [1980] 2 All E.R. 539. **[188]**

As to what the amendments to Sch. 2 do *not* do, see the annotations: in particular, they do not affect the question of what is to occur when the suspension period comes to an end. **[189]**

EXTENSIONS OF RENT ACT 1977, SCH. 15, CASES 11 AND 12

In Part II of Sch. 15 to the Rent Act 1977, there are cases under which orders for possession may be obtained mandatorily by the landlord: they are not subject to the requirement of suitable alternative accommodation, nor to the discretion to refuse to make the order for possession on the ground that it would be unreasonable to do so. Section 66 of this Act extends the scope of Cases 11 and 12. The former enables the recovery of possession by certain owner-occupiers and Case 12 deals with the case of a person who buys a house in anticipation of retirement but who then lets it beforehand. The extension to these cases is achieved by replacing in the relevant cases the existing para. (c) with a new para. (c), which then refers to a new Part V of Sch. 15, which is added by Sch. 7 to this Act (s. 66 (1) (2) and (3)). Section 98 of the 1977 Act is amended accordingly: s. 66 (3). **[190]**

By s. 66 (4), Case 12 is amended so that it will apply in any case where the landlord (the "owner") intends to occupy the dwelling-house as his residence at such time as he might retire from regular employment and has let it on a regulated tenancy before he retired. The relaxation in this is that a landlord need not have to show, to come within Case 12, that he *acquired*, etc., the dwelling-house with a view to residential occupation on his retirement, only that he intended retiring into it, so to speak, when letting it. What amounts in Case 12 to "regular employment" remains at best uncertain. **[191]**

Essentially, what both Cases 11 and 12 are extended to cover is instances of recovery of possession following the death of the owner by resident family members at the date of the owner's death, also to enable recovery of possession by the owner's successors in title or mortgagees, death or no death. If possession by a resident family member is sought after a death, then the dwelling-house must be required by him as a residence; if sought by a successor in title (defined in Sch. 7, para. 1 and note thereto) then as a residence or for sale; if by a mortgagee, for disposal. Case 11 is also extended to instances of requiring possession for sale of the house where it has become unsuitable from the owner's point of view, having regard to his place of work, and he intends to purchase, with the sale-proceeds, a new dwelling-house. See generally Sch. 7 para. 2 (b) to (f). It may be noted that sub-paras (c) and (d) of Sch. 7, para. 2, are not available for Case 11 where the tenancy was granted and the owner died before the commencement of s. 66: s. 66 (6); and subpara. (d), *ibid.*, is not available in such a case to Case 12: s. 66 (6). **[192]**

The offer by a landlord, in proceedings for possession of a dwelling-house let on a protected or statutory tenancy, of alternative accommodation to be held under circumstances where a mandatory case for possession would be available to the landlord is not deemed to be suitable alternative accommodation for the purposes of the Rent Act 1977, Sch. 15, Part IV: Sch. 25, para. 58. **[193]**

MISCELLANEOUS

In what follows, the amendment to the Rent Act 1977, s. 100, and the corresponding provision in the Rent (Agriculture) Act 1976, the new definitions of "successor" to a statutory tenancy, the new rules as to tenants' realisations of long tenancies and the altered definition of "premium" in the Rent Act 1977, s. 128, all fall for outline consideration. The Act also contains elaborate new definitions of housing association and housing trust tenancies (s. 74 and Sch. 9.) and Sch. 10 amends Part VI of the Rent Act 1977 (s. 77). Schedule 25, paras 34 to 60, contains minor and consequential amendments to the Rent Act 1977. Section 73 and Sch. 8 apply the 1977 Act and other enactments to the Crown in certain cases. **[194]**

Amendment to the Rent Act 1977, s. 100

Section 100 of the 1977 Act at present gives a discretion to the court to adjourn for such period or periods as it thinks fit proceedings for possession of a dwelling-house let on a protected tenancy or subject to a statutory tenancy. Section 75 (2) of this Act, in keeping with the general policy of this Act, replaces s. 100 (3) with a new sub-s. (3). In place of a discretion to impose conditions, the new sub-s. (3) imposes a special new rule for rent, arrears of rent and mesne profits viz., that unless the court considers that to impose conditions as to payment of these sums, would cause exceptional hardship to the tenant or would otherwise be unreasonable, then conditions as to payment of these sums must be imposed. The general discretion there-fore applies only to other conditions. **[195]**

By the insertion of a new s. 100 (4A) and 100 (4B), s. 75 (3), extends the court's powers under s. 100 of the 1977 Act to the case of spouses or ex-spouses with rights of occupation under the Matrimonial Homes Act 1967. See the note to s. 87. **[196]**

The rest of s. 75 amends in a similar manner, the corresponding section (s. 7) in the Rent (Agriculture) Act 1976. **[197]**

New definitions of successor to a statutory tenancy

Section 76 (1) replaces the Rent Act 1977, Sch. 1, para. 2, with a new para. 2, the changes being that the first successor to a statutory tenancy is defined as the "surviving spouse" (*cf.* the previous word "man") of the original tenant "if residing in the dwelling-house immediately before the death of the original tenant" (rather than "with him"). The second succession rule is updated in similar modern manner by s. 76 (2), and s. 76 (3) makes a minor amendment to the rules in the Rent (Agriculture) Act 1976, s. 3. None of these amendments is retrospective: s. 76 (4). **[198]**

Long tenancies which are protected tenancies

Despite the fact that the Rent Act 1977 contains prohibitions on premiums, it is possible to realise certain long tenancies as mentioned in s. 127 of that Act. This deals essentially with tenancies at less than a market rent but which are outside s. 5 of the 1977 Act. Section 78 amends 1977 Act, s. 127, so as to allow for the lawful realisation of a premium on a long tenancy at a low rent where the rent has subsequently risen to $\frac{2}{3}$ or above of the rateable value of the premises on the "appropriate day". The condi-tions vary depending on whether the tenancy was granted before 16 July 1980 or after 15 July 1980. Also, s. 127 (2) of the 1977 Act is amended so that, if the long tenancy contains an "Adler" clause, no part of s. 127 will apply and no lawful realisation by a premium will be allowable. **[199]**

New definition of "premium"

The previous definition of "premium" in the Rent Act 1977, s. 128 (1), is replaced by a new definition in s. 79. The new words are in para. (*c*), which prohibits any sum paid by way of a deposit; but not a sum which does not exceed one-sixth of the annual rent and which is reasonable in relation to the potential liability in respect of which it was paid. Note the overlap of this, in relation to protected tenancies, with s. 126 of the 1977 Act. The scope of the new definition is discussed in the note to s. 79. **[200]**

Dwellings forming part of Crown Estates

Section 73 (1) substitutes a new s. 13 in the Rent Act 1977. The new s. 13 (1) is the same as the old s. 13 (1) and (2). But the new s. 13 (2) provides that an interest belonging to Her Majesty in right of the Crown is not to prevent a tenancy from being a protected tenancy or a person from being a statutory tenant if the interest is under the management of the Crown Estate

Commissioners. Consequentially, s. 73 (2) amends s. 19 (5) (*b*) of the 1977
Act so as to bring lettings within the new s. 13 (2) of that Act within the
jurisdiction of a rent tribunal where there is a restricted contract. The rest
of s. 73 makes consequential amendments to the Rent (Agriculture) Act 1976,
s. 5, and the Landlord and Tenant Act 1954, s. 56 and 21 (6). Section 73
(5) applies Sch. 8 to this Act, which is consequential. It was estimated that
about 3,100 tenants, mostly in London, would benefit from these changes:
H.L. Committee, 3 July 1980, Col. 750. **[201]**

CHAPTER 7

TENANT'S REPAIRS AND IMPROVEMENTS

Part III of the Act, which generally applies to tenancies granted before the commencement of the Act as well as to those granted after such commencement (s. 85 (2)) modifies the law relating to repairs and improvements in relation to tenants generally, and mostly in a favourable manner from their point of view. The special alterations to the Housing Act 1974 grant system are considered in a later chapter. **[202]**

Section 80 contains a new list of exclusions from the obligation to repair the structure and exterior, etc., on a short lease imposed by the Housing Act 1961, s. 32. The new exclusions apply to any lease (not just to secure tenancies for instance) granted after 3rd October 1980, by the bodies mentioned in s. 80 (1): specified educational institutions or bodies, certain housing associations, local authorities and the Crown, except for certain Crown Estate tenancies. **[203]**

Sections 81 and 82 modify the law relating to improvements in the case of secure, protected and statutory tenancies. Section 81 replaces the Landlord and Tenant Act 1927, s. 19 (2), in relation to these tenancies, by a new rule. By s. 81 (2), it is to be a term of every secure, protected and statutory tenancy that the tenant will not make any improvement without the written consent of the landlord. The landlord's consent cannot be unreasonably withheld; if it is, then it is treated as given (s. 81 (3)). The law is further altered in the tenant's favour by s. 82 (3), under which, where a tenant has applied in writing for a consent:

(a) if the landlord refuses his consent, it must give the tenant a written statement of the reasons why the consent was refused;
(b) if the landlord neither gives nor refuses consent within a reasonable time, the consent is taken to have been withheld.

Further, in this, if the consent is given but subject to an unreasonable condition, it is taken to have been unreasonably withheld. The burden of proving reasonableness of a condition is cast by s. 82 (4) on the landlord. **[204]**

Contrary to the common law (which is discussed in the annotation to this section) the burden of proof that a withholding of consent is not unreasonable is cast on the landlord by s. 82 (1), and, in this, the court is bound to have regard to the extent to which the improvement would be likely to fall within any of the three matters (all of which would obviously seriously damage the landlord's reversion) set out in s. 82 (1). **[205]**

A provision beneficial to the landlord is s. 82 (2), by which a consent may be given notwithstanding that it follows, instead of preceding, the action requiring it, and, it may, subject of course to s. 82 (3) and (4), mentioned

49

above, be subject to a condition.   In the case of a reasonable condition, failure
by a tenant to comply with it is to be treated, thanks to s. 83, under (in effect)
Sch. 4 to this Act or Sch. 15, Part I, to the Rent Act 1977 as the case may
be, as a breach of an obligation in the tenancy or previous protected tenancy
as the case may be. **[206]**

Neither s. 81 nor s. 82 apply in the cases mentioned in s. 81 (4).   There
is a special statutory definition of "improvement" in s. 81 (5) which appears
to extend the usual meaning of the term.   Part III of this Act is also excluded
in the case of certain registered housing associations (s. 84). **[207]**

CHAPTER 8

JURISDICTION AND PROCEDURE

Extended discretion of the court—Restriction of discretion of the court in possession actions.

Part IV of the Act gives the county court a general jurisdiction to determine matters arising under Parts I to III of this Act (s. 86) and contains two provisions, one of which, s. 87, is similar to the Rent Act 1977, s. 100, and extends the discretion of the court in relation to actions for possession of certain secure tenancies. Section 89 restricts the discretion of the court in other actions for possession of land, save in four exceptional cases. **[208]**

EXTENDED DISCRETION OF THE COURT

This is governed by s. 87, which applies to actions for possession of a dwelling-house let under a secure tenancy, based on grounds 1 to 6 and 10 to 13 of Sch. 4 to this Act.

By s. 87 (1), the court is enabled to adjourn the proceedings for possession for such period or periods as the court thinks fit. By s. 87 (2), on making the order for possession, or at any time before execution of the order, the court may:

(a) stay or suspend the execution of the order, or
(b) postpone the date of possession,

in either case for such period or periods as the court thinks fit. **[209]**

In the case both of adjournments or where s. 87 (2) applies, however, s. 87 (3) requires the court to impose conditions on the tenant with regard to the payment by him of any rent arrears and rent or mesne profits; it also has a discretion to impose such other conditions as it thinks fit. The only cases where conditions as to rent or mesne profits may not be imposed is if the court is satisfied (presumably by the tenant) that to impose such conditions would cause him exceptional hardship or would otherwise be unreasonable: s. 87 (3) Compliance with conditions enables the court, in its discretion, to discharge or rescind the order (s. 87 (4)). **[210]**

The discretionary powers mentioned in s. 87 (1) to (2) are extended by s. 87 (5) to a case where, in effect, a secure tenancy is terminated in proceedings, but the tenant's spouse or former spouse is then in occupation of the dwelling-house by virtue of rights of occupation conferred on her by the Matrimonial Homes Act 1967. Where this is so, then by s. 87 (6), the spouse or former spouse may apply in her own behalf to the court and invoke for her own benefit the powers in s. 87 (1) and (2) notwithstanding the termination of the tenancy. **[211]**

Section 87 is similar in its policy to the corresponding provisions in the Rent Act 1977 (s. 100) in favour of protected or statutory tenants, and thus imposes a further obstacle in the path of landlords; but the requirements of s. 87 (3), weakening this obstacle, are new, as is the protection of spouses and former spouses in s. 87 (5) to (6). **[212]**

Section 88 (1) provides for an extended discretion in the court in the case of possession proceedings against persons in possession under rental purchase agreements (as defined in s. 88 (4)). Such persons, until this section was enacted, were protected neither by the Rent Act 1977, s. 100 (because not protected tenants), nor by the Administration of Justice Act 1970, s. 36 (not mortgagors). By s. 88 (5), the new protection is generally retrospective: it is similar to that in the Administration of Justice Act 1970, s. 36. Moreover, to assist rental purchasers further, by Sch. 25, para. 61, the Protection from Eviction Act 1977 is extended so as to cover them. [213]

RESTRICTION OF THE DISCRETION OF THE COURT IN POSSESSION ACTIONS

The general discretion of the court in making orders for the possession of land is restricted by s. 89 (1), with exceptions in s. 89 (2). By s. 89 (1), where a court makes an order for possession, the giving up of possession cannot be postponed to a date later than 14 days after the order is made, unless it appears to the court that exceptional hardship would be caused by requiring possession to be given up by that date; and in any event possession cannot be postponed to a date later than six weeks after the making of the order. **[214]**

The exceptions to this are stated in s. 89 (2) and are:

(a) Orders for possession in a mortgagee's action for possession. In such cases, the court has, where the land consists of or includes a dwelling-house, powers of suspension, etc., given by the Administration of Justice Acts 1970 (s. 36) and 1973 (s. 8).

(b) Orders in an action for forfeiture of a lease.

(c) Cases where the court has power to make the order for possession only if it considers it reasonable to do so. This is so in the case of protected or statutory tenancies within the non-mandatory cases for possession in the Rent Act 1977 (s. 98 and Sch. 15, Part I) or the corresponding provisions in the Rent (Agriculture) Act 1976 (s. 7 and Sch. 4, Part I; also in the case of secure tenancies.

(d) The order relates to a dwelling-house which is the subject of a restricted contract within the Rent Act 1977, s. 19.

(e) The order is made in proceedings under s. 88. **[215]**

CHAPTER 9

AMENDMENTS TO THE HOUSING ACT 1957, PART V

Section 90 and following make alterations to Part V of the Housing Act 1957, relating chiefly to the powers of disposal of land held by local authorities. The following simply calls attention briefly to the effect of these alterations. **[216]**

Section 90 amends the Housing Act 1957, s. 91, in such a way that a local authority is no longer bound, as often as occasion arises, to prepare and submit to the Minister its proposals for new houses. The power of the Minister to serve a notice on a local authority requiring it to submit proposals within 3 months is also removed by s. 90 of this Act. **[217]**

At present, a local authority has, under the Housing Act 1957, powers in connection with the provision of housing accommodation (s. 92) and ancillary powers of acquisition (ss. 96–97) and development. Section 91 (1) of this Act alters the power of disposal of land held by a local authority for the purposes of Part V of the 1957 Act. The existing power in s. 104 of the 1957 Act is replaced by a new s. 104. As a result, a disposal requires ministerial consent (s. 104 (2)) except for a letting on secure tenancies within s. 28 of this Act or a letting falling within Sch. 3, paras 2–13, of this Act (s. 104 (3)). The price premium payable may be secured by mortgage (s. 104 (4)). **[218]**

What is quite new about the new s. 104 is that, instead of giving on sale, etc., a power in the local authority to impose conditions (which, under the old s. 104 (3), it could have been required to impose), s. 104 (5) allows the local authority on a "disposal" (widely defined in s. 104 (9): it includes the grant of an option to purchase) of "land" to impose any covenants and conditions as it thinks fit. So the power of the Minister to compel the imposition of conditions has gone. The conditions mentioned in the new s. 104 (6) may only be imposed with the consent of the Minister. **[219]**

As a ministerial consents generally see now s. 92, which inserts a new s. 104A after the new s. 104 of the 1957 Act. **[220]**

Section 91 (2) repeals certain parts of s. 105 and the whole of s. 106 of the 1957 Act. The repeal of parts of s. 105 means that the sole power of disposal of a local authority of land held for the purposes of Part V of the 1957 Act is contained in the new s. 104. Section 106 enabled the Minister to impose conditions when giving his consent to sales, etc., of land held in the Housing Revenue Account. Section 91 (3) repeals s. 39 of the Town and Country Planning Act 1968, and therefore there are now no exceptions to the Town and Country Planning Act 1959, s. 26. **[221]**

Section 92 inserts new s. 104B and 104C into the Housing Act 1957. As to these provisions, *cf.* ss. 8 and 18 above. **[222]**

Section 93 (*a*) makes it clear that the power to acquire land in s. 96 of the 1957 Act includes powers to acquire land for the purpose of disposing (as defined in s. 104) of houses erected or to be erected, on the land, or of disposing of the land to a person who intends to provide housing accommodation on it. At present, s. 96 seems to have been designed only for land to be acquired for the provision of council accommodation.   Section 93 (*b*) modifies, in accordance with the above extension of s. 96 of the 1957 Act, s. 92 of that Act. Section 94 is a saving provision for options to purchase to the tenant of a house granted (where there was no ministerial consent as is now required by s. 104 (6)) at any time before the commencement of s. 91 of this Act. [**223**]

Section 95 prevents a local authority which has acquired or appropriated any land for the purposes of Part V of the Housing Act 1957 from appropriating, without ministerial consent, for any other purposes any part of that land on which there is a house: this is, by the new s. 110A (1) in the Housing Act 1957.   The rest of the new s. 110A is consequential. [**224**]

CHAPTER 10

HOUSING SUBSIDIES

Housing subsidies: to whom payable from 1981/82—Calculation—Miscellaneous.

This chapter briefly draws attention to the main features of the new housing subsidy system, to come into effect from 1st April 1981 (see s. 105). There are certain withdrawals of central government funds (s. 96 and Sch. 11); the rules as to the calculation of the subsidy are to be found in ss. 97–100; there is a recoupment provision in favour of the central government (s. 102) and certain miscellaneous provisions (ss. 101, 103–104). **[225]**

HOUSING SUBSIDIES: TO WHOM PAYABLE FROM 1981/82
The rules as to the provision of housing finance are modified as follows by s. 96 (1): by s. 96 (1) (*a*) a housing subsidy is to be payable (for the year 1981/82 and subsequent years) to local authorities, new town corporations and the Development Board for Rural Wales (the first two bodies being defined in s. 105). But no payment is to be made from the year 1981/82 under the following enactments (see Sch. 11, Part I—s. 96 (1) (*b*)):

    (a) the Housing Rents and Subsidies Act 1975 ss. 2 & 4. (This means that the housing subsidy is, from 1981/82, no longer to be calculated in accordance with the four elements listed in s. 2 of the 1975 Act; the expanding towns subsidy is withdrawn from 1981/82 because of the repeal of s. 4 of the 1975 Act.)
    (b) The Development Board of Rural Wales Act 1976, s. 18. **[226]**

No payment is to be made for the year 1981/82 as mentioned in s. 96 (1) (*c*) under the following enactments (listed in Sch. 11, Part II):

    The Housing Act 1969 ss. 17 to 19;
    The Housing Act 1971, ss. 1 and 2;
    The Housing Act 1974, s. 79. **[227]**

Sections 17 to 19 of the 1969 Act relate to payments in respect of conversion or improvement of an authority's stock of houses; ss. 1 and 2 of the 1971 Act relate to "additional financial assistance" in development and intermediate areas and s. 79 of the 1974 Act (repealed) related to payments out of central government funds of certain improvement contributions. Section 96 (2) states that from 31st March 1981, no grant for building experiments under the Housing (Financial Provisions) Act 1958 s. 14, may be made. It seems that this provision (repealed by Sch. 26) was little used: H.C. Committee, Col. 1801. **[228]**

In the above, whenever the word "year" is used, it means the period of 12 months beginning on a 1st April (s. 105). **[229]**

CALCULATION

In the case of local authorities, the amount of the housing subsidy payable for any year is to be calculated in accordance with the formulae set out in ss. 98–100. There are modifications to these rules in the case of the Development Board for Rural Wales and new town corporations (s. 101). There is a wide and subjectively worded power of recoupment of subsidy in s. 102. **[230]**

MISCELLANEOUS

Section 103 relates to the administration of payment of the housing subsidy; s. 104 is transitional and s. 105 is a definition section. **[231]**

CHAPTER 11

REPAIRS AND IMPROVEMENTS

Grants for tenants—Grants towards losses on sale—Modification of grant system.

Sections 106 to 108 and Sch. 12 modify the statutory provisions applicable to repairs and improvements. The objectives of the changes are: first, to remove unnecessary statutory or administrative restrictions both on the availability of grant aid and on local authority improvement policies, and secondly, to introduce more flexibility within the grant system. Thirdly, to adapt the existing grant system so that more recognition can be given to the needs of individual householders (see Department of the Environment Consultation Paper "Housing Bill—Improvement and Repair"). **[232]**

GRANTS FOR TENANTS
It will be remembered that four kinds of grant are available from a local authority under Part VII of the Housing Act 1974, s. 56: improvement grants, intermediate grants, special grants and repairs grants. The first three types of grant relate to the provision of standard amenities (though improvement grants are not confined to these), as defined in s. 58 of the 1974 Act. This Act extends the availability of these grants to the public and private sector tenants listed in s. 106 (1), notably, *inter alia*, to protected or statutory tenants, secure tenants and tenancies within the Rent (Agriculture) Act 1976. However, no application may be entertained by a local authority for an improvement grant in respect of works required for the provision of a dwelling: s. 106 (1). **[233]**
The local authority has a discretion to refuse to entertain an application by a tenant within s. 106 (1) unless the application is accompanied by a certificate satisfying the requirements of s. 106 (2), and provided by a "qualifying person" (see s. 106 (3)). If the application is accompanied by a certificate, then the authority may impose the grant conditions as to letting, etc., mentioned in s. 74 (2) of the Housing Act 1974; if it is not so accompanied, then no conditions may be imposed. **[234]**

GRANTS TOWARDS LOSSES ON SALE
Section 108 (1) empowers the Secretary of State, with the consent of the Treasury, to make regulations for paying contributions to the net cost to local authorities of acquiring and disposing of dwellings of the kind listed in s. 108 (2), where the authority has made the disposal after carrying out works of repair, improvement or conversion. There is a £5,000 limit of total cost for any one dwelling (s. 108 (3)) which may be raised by regulations (*ibid.*). By

s. 108 (5), s. 79 of the Housing Act 1974 is repealed: the system above outlined supersedes it. **[235]**

The requirements of the schemes will not be rigid: what the government has in mind is chiefly old and vacant properties; any significant works of repair, improvement or conversion would be grant-eligible: H.C. Committee, Col. 1924. The level of grant would be 75% on the first £4,000 of the net cost and 25% of the next £1,000, with a maximum contribution of £3,250 for any one dwelling: H.C. Committee, Col. 1925. **[236]**

Because of the repeal of s. 79 of the Housing Act 1974 (s. 108 (5)) housing revenue account dwellings acquired for improvement or resale will benefit from s. 108. In relation to dwellings not on housing revenue accounts—*e.g.* county council dwellings occupied by their employees—improvement expenditure will apparently count as relevant expenditure for the purposes of the rate support grant: H.C. Committee, Cols 1920–1921. **[237]**

In what follows, it is hoped briefly to pinpoint the main alterations made to the grant system by Sch. 12 to this Act (s. 107)—which came into operation on 27th November 1980, apart from paras 4, 12, 28–32, operative on 15th December 1980, see S.I. 1980 Nos. 1557, 1781. **[238]**

MODIFICATION OF GRANT SYSTEM
In tabular form the main modifications made in Sch. 12 are as follows:

1. A new formula as to the "appropriate percentage" of the cost of works (para. 4).
2. New provision as to certificates of owner-occupation (para. 5).
3. Altered rules as to the availability of improvement grants (paras 7 and 8).
4. New rules as to the approval of intermediate grants (paras 9 to 11).
5. Widening of the availability of repairs grants (paras 12 to 14).
6. Extension of the availability of special grants (paras 15 to 19).
7. Alteration of the standard of repair required to be attained for improvement and repairs grants (para. 20).
8. Amendment of the general conditions applicable to all types of grant (paras 21 to 24). **[239]**

Each of these falls to be considered; the alterations are made by insertions into the relevant parts of the Housing Act 1974. **[240]**

Calculation of appropriate percentage
In relation to the standard amenities (see the Housing Act 1974, Sch. 6) the amount of any grant is limited to the "appropriate percentage" of the cost of the works. Under the old rules this was usually 50%; but para. 4 of Sch. 12 to this Act substitutes a new s. 59 into the 1974 Act, and the new rule therein is flexible. The appropriate percentage will, from the commencement of the new rule, be that contained in regulations. **[241]**

Certificates of future occupation
The main changes which result from Sch. 12, para. 5, which substitutes a new s. 60 (3) and (4) into the Housing Act 1974, are these: **[242]**

1. In a case where the applicant for a certificate applies himself, the applicant must state the intention that the dwelling will be the only or main residence of and occupied exclusively by, either, as at present, the applicant himself and members of his household, or, and this is new, by a person who is a member of the applicant's family, or a grandparent or grandchild of the applicant or his spouse and members of that person's household (if any). The

period of required intended residence is unchanged. (See generally new s. 60 (3) to the 1974 Act.) **[243]**

2. By the new s. 60 (4), there is a similar extension to family, etc., where an applicant is the personal representative of a deceased person or by trustees. **[244]**

3. By para. 6, s. 60 (5) of the 1974 Act is amended so that there is to be left out of account, in dealing with the 5-year period required for a certificate of availability for letting, any part of the period when neither s. 60 (5) (*a*) nor (*b*) applies but the dwelling is occupied by a protected occupier under the Rent (Agriculture) Act 1976. **[245]**

Improvement grants

Schedule 12, para. 7 excludes the operation of the Housing Act 1974, s. 62 (1) and (2) (which impose rateable value limits above which no grant is payable) where the dwelling is in a housing action area. By para. 7, inserting a new s. 62 (6) into the 1974 Act, the restrictions in s. 62 (1) and (2) are eased in the case of a disabled applicant. **[246]**

Because, by para. 8, s. 64 (7) of the 1974 Act is omitted, there need be no adjustment of an improvement grant where other grants have been made in respect of the dwelling. **[247]**

Intermediate grants

These are to pay for standard amenities. The rather elaborate rules governing conditions precedent for approval by a local authority of an application for an intermediate grant in the 1974 Act, s. 66, with the differentiation between a "full standard" (including all standard amenities, good repair and compliance with thermal insulation) and the "reduced standard" (a 15-year life, as a rule), have been repealed. By Sch. 12, para. 9, there is a new s. 66 in the 1974 Act and, by this, no application for an intermediate grant may be approved unless:

    (a) the local authority is satisfied that on completion of the works the dwelling or dwellings will be fit for human habitation, within the Housing Act 1957, s. 4; or

    (b) it seems reasonable to approve the application though the above standard will not be reached on completion of the works. **[248]**

It may be that this is a lowering of standards (at any rate in semantic terms) when one compares it with the "full standard", because it seems that a dwelling may be fit for human habitation without being, at any rate in all respects, in good repair: see *Jones* v. *Geen* [1925] 1 K.B. 659. **[249]**

In consequence of the above, as was said, the distinction formerly made between full standard and reduced standard in s. 67 (2) to (3) of the 1974 Act is removed by para. 10 (1) and (2). By para. 10 (2), there is a new s. 67 (3) in the 1974 Act. If the works are thought by the local authority to include works of repair or replacement (see the note to para. 9 as to this) to put the dwelling into what is called "reasonable repair" having regard to the age, character and locality of the dwelling and its likely life (in effect) as a dwelling, then they may vary the application, with the applicant's consent, so that the works:

    (a) are confined to works other than of repair or replacement; or

    (b) include only such works of repair or replacement (taken with the rest of the works) as will, in the opinion of the local authority, put the dwelling into reasonable repair.

They may then approve the application as so varied. **[250]**

The local authority must, as is known, determine, where they approve
an application for an intermediate grant, the amount of the proper expenses
eligible for grant; and the amount of the expenses which are proper to incur
in relation solely to the provision of standard amenities (s. 68 (1) of the 1974
Act). The amount of the eligible expenses, in this, determined under s. 68
(3) of the 1974 Act, is altered by Sch. 12. By para. 11 (1), in place of "£800
or such other amount as may be prescribed" there is inserted "the relevant
limit" which is governed by para. 11 (2), inserting a new s. 68 (3A), (3B)
into the 1974 Act. **[251]**

Repairs grants

The main alterations are these. First, para. 12 (1) replaces s. 71 (2) of
the 1974 Act (this requires the question of undue hardship to the applicant
to be considered) with a new s. 71 (2) which limits the power of a local authority to make a repairs grant to cases where either (a) they are satisfied that
the relevant works are of a substantial and structural character, or (b) the
relevant works satisfy requirements prescribed in regulations. Secondly, the
former restriction of repairs grant availability to housing action areas or
general improvement areas is removed (para. 12 (2)) and a new restriction is
imposed thereby, which is by addition of a new s. 71 (3A): no application
for a repairs grant may be approved except in the case of an old dwelling
(to be defined in regulations); if the dwelling is outwith a housing action area
but accompanied by a certificate of owner-occupation, then the dwelling
must be within the rateable value limits to be laid down in regulations. **[252]**

The discretion of a local authority to turn down an application for a repairs
grant is removed by para. 13 by insertion of a new s. 71A into the 1974 Act
in cases where the application relates to a notice to execute works under the
Housing Act 1957, s. 9 (*i.e.* works to put the dwelling in a state fit for human
habitation) and in such a case (a) no certificate of owner-occupation is then
required; and (b) the application must be duly made and the authority
satisfied that the works are necessary for compliance with the notice. Where
the new s. 71A applies, the amount of the grant is to be governed by para.
14 (2) (new s. 72 (4)). **[253]**

Special grants

A special grant is payable in respect of improvements to a house in multiple occupation, under s. 56 (2) of the Housing Act 1974, which, as now
amended by Sch. 12, para. 15, to this Act, will cover the provision not only,
as at present, of "standard amenities" (see as to this s. 58 and Sch. 6 of the
1974 Act) but also, and this is new, the provision of means of escape from
fire. **[254]**

Further, if an application for a special grant relates to the provision of
standard amenities, it cannot be refused by the local authority, if the application is duly made and the authority satisfied that the works are necessary
for compliance with such parts of a notice under the Housing Act 1961, s.
15, as relates to standard amenities: s. 69A (1) of the 1974 Act, added by
Sch. 12, para. 17. There is a similar mandatory special grant in the case of
means of escape from fire in relation to works in that regard following in a
notice under the Housing Act 1961, s. 16 (s. 69A (2) to the 1974 Act, added
by para. 17). **[255]**

The general conditions as to the payment of special grants are altered by
para. 16 (1), which substitutes a new s. 69 (2) into the Housing Act 1974.
This means that an application for a special grant must not only state the
standard amenities the house is already provided with, but also its means
of escape from fire. The new s. 69 (2A) to (2C), added by the same paragraph,

adopt the same policy as is contained in paras 10 and 11. Section 84 of the 1974 Act is amended accordingly by para. 16 (2). In accordance with the policy of the Act, the amount of a special grant is to be determined by a new s. 70 of the 1974 Act, inserted by para. 18 (1). Section 70 (2), as replaced, is similar to the previous provision; but the basis of calculation has changed and is found in s. 70 (3) and 70A (added by para. 19). Under the old rules, the amount of grant was the cost of the works for providing the standard amenities as limited in Sch. 6 to the Housing Act 1974, and then was the "appropriate percentage" of this cost. Now, in the case of a non-mandatory special grant (*i.e.* one outside para. 17) the amount of the grant is such as is fixed by the local authority, but never above the appropriate percentage of the eligible expense as determined for a mandatory special grant: new s. 70 (3) (*b*) of the 1974 Act (para. 18 (1)). At present, of course, the appropriate percentage is at fixed levels. In the case of a mantatory special grant, its amount is the appropriate percentage of the eligible expense—never less— new s. 70 (3) (*a*) (para. 18 (1)). The amount of the eligible expense is now to be calculated in accordance with the new s. 70A (inserted into the 1974 Act by para. 19). One has to find the "contributory elements" and then aggregate them (new s. 70A (1)). In the case of standard amenities, the method is as before: new s. 70A (2). In the case of means of escape from fire, there is an overall upper limit of £6,750 or such sum as may be prescribed (new s. 70A (3)). In the case of works of replacement or repair, the overall limit is £2,000 or such sum as may be prescribed: new s. 70A (4). [**256**]

Improvement grants

The standard of repair required to be attained is, as with the rest of Sch. 12, lowered from "good" to "reasonable" repair: para. 20 (1), amending s. 61 (3) (*b*)) of the 1974 Act. There is also a discretionary power in the local authority to dispense with the conditions in s. 61 (3) (*a*) to (*c*) on the ground of undue hardship in the applicant: para. 20 (2). [**257**]

Repairs grants: Standard of repair

Paragraph 20 (3) lowers this to "reasonable repair" by the appropriate amendment to s. 71 (5) of the 1974 Act. [**258**]

General grant conditions for improvement, intermediate or repairs grants

Section 73 of the Housing Act 1974 deals with the conditions which must apply during the first 5 years of occupation after the completion of the works. The house must be occupied exclusively by a "qualifying person" or available for letting. The definition of qualifying person is extended by para. 21 (*a*), by insertion into the 1974 Act of a new s. 73 (3) (*a*) to any person deriving title through or under the applicant where the application was accompanied by a certificate of owner-occupation, and also (in the case where the application was accompanied by a certificate of availability for letting) to any person deriving title through or under the applicant otherwise than by a conveyance for value. [**259**]

Paragraph 21 (*b*) and (*c*) extend the persons who are qualifying persons by means of insertion into s. 70 (3) of the 1974 Act new paragraphs (*aa*) and (*bb*). Paragraph 22 amends s. 73 (4) so as to leave out of account as a qualifying letting the case of a protected occupier under the Rent (Agriculture) Act 1976. This is because, in such a case, no further condition may be imposed on the grant: s. 74 (3) (*d*) of the 1974 Act, as inserted by para. 24 (1). The exception from the power to impose further conditions in the case of owner-occupiers (s. 74 (3) (*b*) of the 1974 Act) is extended to certain "family" lettings: new s. 74 (3A), added by para. 24 (2). There is, by para. 23 a new dispensation power given by the new s. 74 (2A) in the local authority to dispense with conditions required by s. 74 (1) if it appears to them in the special circumstances of the case that it would be reasonable to do this. **[260]**

Miscellaneous

Paragraph 25 alters the rules as to payment of grant by instalments. Because of para. 29, a certificate of future occupation will not have to be provided in the case of a tenant's application under s. 106 of this Act: see the new s. 60 (1A). Accordingly, para. 28 amends s. 57 (3) of the 1974 Act. In such a case, s. 106 (2) applies; so para. 30 makes the necessary amendment to s. 73 (4) of the 1974 Act. The annulment procedure which generally applies to orders made under the Housing Act 1974 does not apply to expenditure out of monies: hence its exclusion in relation to the financial regulatory machinery in the new s. 58, 68, 70A and 72 of the 1974 Act, inserted by Sch. 12: para. 27 amends s. 128 (4) of the 1974 Act accordingly. Finally, para. 26 makes consequential amendments to s. 57 (3) and (5) of the 1974 Act. **[261]**

CHAPTER 12

GENERAL IMPROVEMENT AREAS AND HOUSING ACTION AREAS

Introduction—Housing Action Areas—Priority Neighbourhoods.

INTRODUCTION

The notion of a general improvement area was introduced in its present form in the Housing Act 1969, Part II. The aim was to enable block improvements in an area of substandard housing, with the emphasis on standard amenities. This Act removes some of the modifications to the scheme made in the Housing Act 1974, s. 50, and also alters the basis of the contributions payable to a local authority in a general improvement area from central government funds (see esp. Sch. 13, paras 1 to 6). Schedule 13 to this Act deals also with housing action areas, *viz.*, those where the need for improvements is greater than in a general improvement area. As to housing action areas in general, see Part IV of the Housing Act 1974, which is modified by Sch. 13 to this Act. **[262]**

GENERAL IMPROVEMENT AREAS

By Sch. 13 (s. 109 (1)) paras 1 to 4, provision is made for the removal of various ministerial controls: **[263]**

    (a) The elaborate provisions in the Housing Act 1974, Sch. 5, Part I, as to criteria to be adopted, etc., in the creation of a general improvement area are repealed and replaced by the old rules they had superseded (Housing Act 1969, s. 28): para. 1. **[264]**

    (b) This means that the supervisory role of the Secretary of State in such areas is removed: *ibid.* **[265]**

    (c) The power of the Secretary of State to terminate the status of a general improvement area is abolished: para. 2; owing to para. 3, the only body which may exclude land from a general improvement area or remove the status totally from land is a local authority. **[266]**

    (d) The general restriction on consents to disposals, etc., of general improvement land without ministerial consent is removed by para. 4. **[267]**

Paragraph 5 of Sch. 13 alters the basis of central government contributions towards general improvement areas; the substituted s. 37 (1) of the

Housing Act 1969, for instance, renders the power to make contributions quite general; s. 37 (3) raises the "multiplier" to £400 and para. 6 is consequential.
[268]

HOUSING ACTION AREAS
    Schedule 13 (s. 109 (1)) amends the law as to these. **[269]**
Removal of ministerial controls
    No approval by the Secretary of State of a resolution by a local authority incorporating a general improvement area into a housing action area will be required: para. 7; para. 8 is consequential on this. **[270]**
Environmental works
    These are eligible for financial assistance under the Housing Act 1974, s. 45, which is amended by para. 9 (2), one result of which is that in future the authority itself may carry out the works—but not interior works—or give assistance under s. 45 of the 1974 Act towards such works by others.   Paragraph 9 (3) excludes any assistance under s. 45 where any application for a grant under Part VII of the 1974 Act has been approved. **[271]**
Basis of central government contribution
    This is altered by para. 10, which substitutes a new s. 46 in the Housing Act 1974.   In effect, the basis is as for general improvement area (see para. 5) and not, as at present, 50 per cent of the expenditure incurred by the authority. **[272]**

PRIORITY NEIGHBOURHOODS
    This category was supposed to protect an area adjoining a housing action area or a general improvement area from deterioration; but the whole of the legislation on the matter is redundant from the commencement of s. 109 (2), which repeals the whole of Part VI of the Housing Act 1974, save in relation to areas declared priority neighbourhoods before 15th December 1980.   In consequence of this, s. 29B of the Housing Act 1969 (consequential) is repealed: s. 109 (3).   The reason for these repeals is that local authorities were stated to think, after consultation, that there was no place for priority neighbourhoods: H.C. Committee, Col. 1929. **[273]**

CHAPTER 13

MORTGAGES AND HOME OWNERSHIP

Interest Rates—Indemnity—Vesting power—Housing subsidies (mortgages)—Option notices—Other amendments relating to subsidised home loans.

Part VII of the Act contains a number of amendments and alterations to local authority mortgage financing. Section 110 deals with local authority mortgage interest rates and s. 111 gives local authorities and the Housing Corporation the power to indemnify building societies. The option mortgage scheme rules are amended by ss. 114–116 and Sch. 14 and there is a limited vesting power in local authorities which sell under their old powers (prior to the commencement of this Act): see ss. 112–113. **[274]**

INTEREST RATES

In the instances set out in s. 110 (2) and where a mortgage advance etc., is made by a local authority (s. 110 (3)) within s. 110 (1), then the rate of interest must comply with s. 110 (3) and be the higher of (a) the standard national rate (defined in s. 110 (4)) and (b) the applicable local average rate (see as to this s. 110 (5)). Also, local authorities will be bound under s. 110 (6) to review at regular intervals their rates of interest, and where the rate is varied, then the procedure for notices of variation applies (s. 110 (8) to (9)). There is a directory power in the Secretary of State in s. 110 (10) in relation to rates, presumably to be invoked where a local authority charges the lower of the two rates mentioned above. There is a saving of certain interest-free loans (s. 110 (13)) and certain loans to housing associations (s. 110 (14)), and also for waiver/reduction of interest in the cases mentioned in s. 110 (11) and (12).

Section 110 (11) and (12) relax the strict requirements of the rest of s. 110 in a case of property bought in a state of disrepair or needing improvement, but only for a 5-year period. **[275]**

INDEMNITY

Section 111 enables local authorities and the Housing Corporation to enter into an indemnity agreement with certain building societies as therein provided. **[276]**

VESTING POWER

The right of pre-emption of a local authority, obtainable under its powers of disposal in the (repealed) s. 104 of the Housing Act 1957, was held in *Williams* v. *Wellingborough BC* [1975] 3 All E.R. 462, C.A., not to enable a local authority to transfer the property to itself in circumstances where it was entitled to exercise its statutory power of sale as mortgagee. Section 112, which applies only to cases where a local authority has sold property under the (repealed) s. 104 of the 1957 Act, enables the vesting to take place in cases where s. 112 is satisfied, in particular where the local authority has become entitled to exercise its statutory power of sale: s. 112 (2). This and s. 113 (consequential rules as to compensation and accounting) being limited in scope, no further mention of them need be made; but some technical points are dealt with in the notes. **[277]**

HOUSING SUBSIDIES (MORTGAGES)
    Sections 114–116 and Sch. 14 modify the present rules as to "option mortgages": these are a form of assistance to persons desirous of acquiring or improving their dwellings. **[278]**

OPTION NOTICES
    In general, it may be recalled, a notice of intention to give an option notice (this is an election for a susbsidised loan under Part II of the Housing Subsidies Act 1967) must be given to the lender at the time when the loan was applied for or by such later time as the lender allows; also the option notice must be signed not later than when a repayment contract was first entered into. Now, as a result of s. 114 (1) of this Act, if an option notice is given but the above things are not done, with the lender's agreement and in such cases as are specified in regulations, then the option notice is nevertheless effective. The option notice will also be effective, irrespective of the above, despite non-compliance with the things mentioned, provided it is given not earlier than 12 months after the date of the repayment contract (s. 114 (1) (*b*)). Section 114 (2) governs the date when such an option notice takes effect. Cancellation of an option notice is allowed for by s. 114 (3) and (7) but except as provided in s. 114 (4) (*a*); cancellation is final and no further option notice is thereafter possible in relation to that repayment contract: s. 114 (4) (*b*). There is a general regulatory power as to the giving and the cancellation of notices in s. 114 (5) to (6); consultation is required beforehand: s. 114 (8). **[279]**

OTHER AMENDMENTS RELATING TO SUBSIDISED HOME LOANS
    These are contained in Sch. 14 (s. 116 (1)). Paragraph 1 of this amends s. 24 of the 1967 Act so as to enable the Secretary of State to prescribe regulations governing entitlement to subsidy. Paragraph 3 removes the power to subsitute a trustee for the lender; the general disposition power from the conditions mentioned in s. 24 (3) (*a*) and (*b*) of the 1967 Act is repealed; but see now s. 114 of this Act. By para. 4, there is added a new s. 24A to the 1967 Act and s. 24B thereof disappears so that the £25,000 limit on loans, for instance, goes. Paragraph 6 extends the power of the Secretary of State to confer a "qualifying lender" status, and para. 6 (2) expressly adds 3 bodies as qualifying lenders. **[280]**
    Finally, s. 115 applies Part II of the 1967 Act to loans under annuity schemes in the case of persons over 65. **[281]**

CHAPTER 14

LOCAL AUTHORITY FINANCE

Part VII of the Act alters some aspects of the rules relating to rent rebates and the like. There is a scheme in the Housing Finance Act 1972 for a subsidy on rent allowances; this is, by s. 117 (1), to be 90 per cent. of the standard amount of rent allowances, as to which see s. 20 (8) of the 1972 Act. Essentially, this means the allowances granted under a model scheme, or which would be granted if such a scheme were operational. **[282]**

The rate of the modified rent rebate subsidy paid under the Housing Rents and Subsidies Act 1975, s. 3, is to be 90 per cent. (s. 117 (2) (*a*)). There is a like provision for the subsidy to the Development Board for Rural Wales (s. 111 (4)). The rate fund contribution falls to 10 per cent. (s. 117 (2) (*b*)). In view of s. 117 (3), since the rate fund contribution of the local authorities is not to count as "relevant expenditure" within the Local Government Act 1974, s. 1, it is left out of account in determining their expenditure out of the rate fund for the purposes of the rate support grant. **[283]**

A restriction is placed on rent rebates by s. 119: by s. 119 (1), no rebate or allowance is payable (in general) under Part II of the Housing Finance Act 1972 to any person if, to the knowledge of the authority, he is receiving supplementary benefit; or equally so, if his income or resources fall to be aggregated under the 1972 Act or the Supplementary Benefits Act 1976 with those of another person receiving the benefit. This might be so, for instance, under Sch. 1, Part I, para. 3 of the 1976 Act, where a husband and wife are members of the same household so that their requirements and resources are aggregated and treated as those of the husband; this also happens in the case of cohabitation. The rest of s. 119 is mostly consequential on this; note the power of the Secretary of State to obtain information from authorities. **[284]**

The rules relating to rent rebates and allowances are amended by Sch. 15 (s. 118). **[285]**

CHAPTER 15

HOUSING ASSOCIATIONS AND THE HOUSING CORPORATION

The Housing Corporation—Registered housing associations: Disposal of land—Accounts and audit—Registration of housing associations— Miscellaneous.

Part VIII of the Act contains a number of amendments to the rules relating to the Housing Corporation and housing associations. New rules as to the disposal of land by registered housing associations are provided for and there are new auditing and accounting rules. The following is only a brief résumé of the main provisions in Part VIII. **[286]**

THE HOUSING CORPORATION

Section 120 (1) raises the borrowing limits imposed on the Housing Corporation to £2,000 million; this may be further increased in regulations to £3,000 million. Section 121 deals with the provision of grants by the Secretary of State to the Housing Corporation. **[287]**

REGISTERED HOUSING ASSOCIATIONS: DISPOSAL OF LAND

Subject to the control of the Housing Corporation contained in the Housing Act 1974 s. 2, all registered housing associations are given in s. 122 of this Act a wide power to dispose of any land held by them in such manner as they think fit, subject to s. 122 (2) to (5) (s. 122 (1)). Section 2 of the 1974 Act is also amended: s. 123 of this Act. **[288]**

ACCOUNTS AND AUDIT

Section 124 enables the Secretary of State to make regulations requiring the preparation of accounts, etc., by registered housing associations (s. 124 (1)) and contains detailed requirements as to the accounts, applying Sch. 16, Part I, to the Act in this connection. Section 125 is an enforcement section; but no criminal proceedings may be commenced without the consent of the Director of Public Prosecutions or the Housing Corporation (s. 125 (4)). Certain payments to committee members of registered housing associations are prohibited by Sch. 16, Part II (which also provides for the clawback of such payments) (s. 126). The scope of these prohibitions is dealt with in the annotations: it is thought that they are very wide indeed, perhaps unnecessarily so. **[289]**

REGISTRATION OF HOUSING ASSOCIATIONS

By s. 127 (1), where a housing association is registered under the Industrial and Provident Societies Act 1965, it may remain registered by the Housing Corporation under the Housing Act 1974 s. 13 despite the fact that its objects include those set out in s. 127 (1). But for s. 127, continued registration under such circumstances would have been impossible. Thus, if a housing association which is registered keeps land for letting within s. 127 (2), it may remain registered; but notice that a premium on granting the lease should be taken; if it is not, then the benefit of s. 127 (1) is not conferred (s. 127 (2) (*a*)) unless s. 127 (2) (*b*) is satisfied. **[290]**

Section 128 enables the Housing Corporation to remove certain non-grant-aided registered housing associations, at their request, from the register. **[291]**

MISCELLANEOUS

Section 29 of the Housing Act 1974 (which enables the Secretary of State to pay a grant to registered housing associations in certain cases) is extended by s. 130 to the cases therein mentioned, subject to a clawback in s. 131. **[292]**

The powers of the Housing Corporation to inquire into the affairs of registered housing associations are tightened up by Sch. 17 (s. 129) which amends the existing powers (in the Housing Act 1974, ss. 19 and 20) accordingly. Section 132 amends s. 24 of the 1974 Act (this deals with restrictions on the powers of registered housing associations) and s. 133 is a definition section. **[293]**

CHAPTER 16

PART IX OF THE HOUSING ACT 1980

*Introduction—New rules as to accounts—Housing Co-operatives—
Exclusion of shared ownership tenancies from Leasehold Reform Act
1967 and Housing Act 1974—Amendments of Leasehold Reform Act
1967 and Housing Act 1974—Transfer of Jurisdiction to rent
assessment committees—Miscellaneous—Service charges.*

INTRODUCTION

Part IX of this Act contains an assortment of alterations in housing and landlord and tenant law. Of particular importance appear to be the new rules on service charges (s. 136 and Sch. 19); further amendments to the Leasehold Reform Act 1967 and consequential provisions (s. 141 and Sch. 21); the new rules as to overcrowding (s. 145) and the new penalties attached thereto (Sch. 23) and concerning fire escape (s. 147 & Sched. 24); and the extension of the Housing Act 1957, s. 9, by s. 149. Supplemental provisions will be found in ss. 150–155 and Sch. 25 brings minor and consequential amendments (especially of the Rent Act 1977) into play: many of these are mentioned in Chapter 6. **[294]**

In what follows, the important provisions are outlined with a view principally to signposting their effect and significance. Technical points are dealt with in the annotations. **[295]**

NEW RULES AS TO ACCOUNTS

Two changes are made here. First, by s. 134 it is no longer necessary for an authority keeping a Housing Revenue Account, governed by the Housing Finance Act 1972, Sch. 1, Part I, to avoid keeping a surplus beyond a "working balance": s. 134 removes the previous restriction to a working balance, which was imposed by the Housing Rents and Subsidies Act 1975, s. 1 (3). Secondly, s. 135 enables any local authority (as defined in s. 135 (10)) to keep for the year 1981/82 and subsequent years, a Housing Repairs Account, as governed by that section. **[296]**

HOUSING CO-OPERATIVES

By Sch. 20 (s. 139) the rules dealing with agreements between housing co-operatives and local authorities in relation to the exercise by housing co-operatives of the powers of a local authority under Part V of the Housing Act 1957 (provision of council housing) are modified in consequence of the provision in s. 102 enabling the recovery of subsidy from a local authority where the purpose of the subsidy was not fulfilled. **[297]**

EXCLUSION OF SHARED OWNERSHIP TENANCIES FROM THE LEASEHOLD REFORM
ACT 1967

Where a tenancy of a house is created by the grant of a lease at a premium
by a registered housing association or one of the bodies listed in s. 140 (2),
then the tenancy is excluded from the operation of the Leasehold Reform
Act 1967 as long as the interest of the landlord belongs to a registered housing
association or one of the above bodies (s. 141 (1)). In the case of these latter, the
tenancy, to be excluded, must comply with the requirements of s. 140 (3)
and in the case of a tenancy granted by a registered housing association
with those of s. 140 (4). "Registered housing association" means, by s. 140
(6), an association registered under the Housing Act 1974, s. 13. **[298]**

AMENDMENTS OF THE LEASEHOLD REFORM ACT 1967 AND THE HOUSING ACT
1974

A number of amendments to these are set out in Sch. 21 (s. 141). The
main points are as follows (s. 141 and Sch. 21 commenced, apart from para.
7, on 3rd October 1980: S.I. 1980 No. 1406): **[299]**

1. The period of residential occupation required by s. 1 (1) (*b*) of the 1967
Act is cut from 5 years or 5 years of the last 10 years to 3 years or 3 years
of the last 10: para. 1 (1). Consequential amendments are therefore made
to s. 9 (3) (*b*) and 23 (2) (*b*) of the 1967 Act by para. 1 (2): these reduce the
timebars therein to 3 years. **[300]**

2. In the 1967 Act there is inserted a new s. 1 (4A) by para. 2. This applies
the Housing Act 1974, Sch. 8, to a case where the tenant wishes to have the
rateable value of the house or premises reduced under s. 1 of the 1967 Act
in consequence of tenant's improvements. **[301]**

3. At present, the proviso to s. 3 (1) of the 1967 Act excepts from the
definition of a long tenancy, a tenancy granted so as to become terminable
after a death or marriage. Now, if the notice to terminate the tenancy is
capable of being given at any time after the death of the tenant, the length
of the notice should be no more than 3 months and also the terms of the
tenancy itself should preclude both its assignment and the subletting of
the whole of the premises comprised in it (para. 3 (*b*)). If this is so, then
advantage may still be taken of the proviso to s. 3 (1) and the tenancy will then
be outside the 1967 Act. But if not, then para. 3 (*a*) will apply, where the
tenancy was not granted before 18th April 1980. The reason for this is to deny
the benefit of s. 3 (1) of the 1967 Act to a tenancy which contains an option to
determine it at any time after the death of the last survivor of any issue of King
George VI living at the date when the lease was granted. **[302]**

4. By para. 4, there is inserted a new s. 16 (1A) to the 1967 Act so that,
where an extended tenancy is granted, and at the time after the commencement of para. 4, a rent is registered for the dwelling-house, then the tenant
cannot be obliged to pay more than the registered rent until the next rental
period after the landlord has served notice on the tenant, in writing, that
the registered rent no longer applies. **[303]**

5. Paragraph 5 extends the scope of s. 29 of the 1967 Act, which will now
enable reservations for future development in a s. 8 conveyance under the
1967 Act to be made by a university body in favour of development by a
related university body (i.e. a university and the colleges of that university:
see s. 29 (6) (*b*) of the 1967 Act). **[304]**

6. Paragraph 6 means that, from the commencement of the schedule, s.
9 and Sch. 1, para. 7, to the 1967 Act, governing the calculation of the price
payable for a superior tenancy, will apply only to tenancies which are

not minor superior tenancies within para. 6. Where para. 6 applies, then a new formula must be resorted to: see new para. 7A to Sch. 1 of the 1967 Act. **[305]**

7. By para. 7, the required particulars in a tenant's notice of desire to enfranchise, etc., are extended; and para. 8 amends Sch. 8 to the Housing Act 1974 (this deals with reduction in rateable values). In particular, owing to para. 8 (*b*), a right of appeal from the county court is conferred; para. 8 (*d*) eases the landlord's position as regards costs of investigation. **[306]**

TRANSFER OF JURISDICTION TO RENT ASSESSMENT COMMITTEES

In relation to all matters set out in s. 21 (1) to (3) of the Leasehold Reform Act 1967 (e.g. the price payable on enfranchisement (s. 9) or the determination of what are the premises (s. 10)) the jurisdiction to determine them is transferred by s. 142 (1) to rent assessment committees constituted under 1977 Act, Sch. 10 from the Lands Tribunal; the rent assessment committee is to be known as a leasehold valuation tribunal: s. 142 (2). Leasehold Valuation Tribunals are governed by Sch. 22, Part I (s. 142 (3)), and the rest of this schedule contains consequential amendments of the 1967 Act. **[307]**

MISCELLANEOUS

The most important of the provisions are discussed below. **[308]**

Extension of Land Compensation Act 1973, s. 42

This is extended by s. 138: s. 43 requires a re-housing authority to be indemnified by a displacing authority against any loss of the former. Now, s. 42 will apply to cases where the displacing authority, though it has functions under Part V of the Housing Act 1957 (this normally excludes s. 42 of the 1973 Act) acquired or re-acquired the land otherwise than in discharge of those functions. **[309]**

Apportionment of rents

Apportionment of rent may be made by order by the Secretary of State under the Landlord and Tenant Act 1927, s. 20 (1): this on application by any person interested in the rent or payment or on the land in respect of which it is payable. If, in this, the person is entitled to the rent or payment applies, the Secretary of State may require that any apportioned part of the rent which does not exceed £5 per annum (in the place of £2: 1980 Act, s. 143 (1)) must be redeemed forthwith in accordance with the Law of Property Act 1925, s. 191. The amount of £5 is, by s. 143 (2), to be variable by regulations; and s. 143 (3) enables the Secretary of State to order that the amount apportioned to any part of the land in respect of which the rent or payment is payable to be nil. **[310]**

Penalties for failure by landlord to comply with Housing Act 1974, ss. 121 and 122.

By s. 121 of the Housing Act 1974, tenants (not business tenants within the Landlord and Tenant Act 1954, Part II) are given the right to obtain the landlord's name and address; s. 122 of the 1974 Act puts a new landlord under a duty to inform the tenant by notice of his name and address within 2 months of the assignment. The penalties for non-compliance with these duties are raised by s. 144 of this Act to £500 from 3rd October 1980.

[311]

Overcrowding

Schedule 23 (s. 145) alters the penalties for overcrowding in the cases set out in Sch. 23 from 3rd October 1980. **[312]**

Overcrowding in lodging-houses

The existing rules, contained in the Housing Act 1957, s. 90, are repealed and replaced with a new s. 90 by s. 146 (1) of this Act, but the new rules do not apply to any notice served under the old s. 90 before 3rd October 1980: s. 146 (2). **[313]**

By the new s. 90 (1), a local authority may serve an overcrowding notice on the occupier of the premises or on any person having control or management thereof, if it appears to them that in the case of a house in their district occupied by persons not forming *a single household* (the italicised words are not new), an excessive number of persons is being or is *likely to be* (these words are new) accommodated on the premises having regard to the rooms available. The overcrowding notice must comply with s. 90 (2) and (3) and include either the requirement in s. 90 (4) or s. 90 (5). **[314]**

The requirement in s. 90 (2) is similar to the old s. 90 (1) (*a*) but the notice must refer to every room in the premises; the requirement in s. 90 (3) resembles the old s. 90 (2). Section 90 (4) and (5) deal with the requirements of the two types of overcrowding notice which may now be served. Section 90 (4) resembles the old s. 90 (4) except that the new form of notice is (in accordance with the policy of s. 90 (2)) to deal with every room in the premises. Section 90 (5) is quite new, however, and provides for a notice in the case of overcrowding of new residents in the premises, as defined in s. 90 (6). A s. 90 (5) notice may be withdrawn at any time and a s. 90 (4) notice served in its place (s. 90 (7)). Section 90 (8), which is new, compels a local authority, not less than 7 days before serving an overcrowding notice, to inform the persons mentioned in s. 90 (8) of the authority's intention to serve an overcrowding notice; it must afford any such person the opportunity of making representations. Section 90 (9) enables a local authority to obtain information from the occupier of premises in respect of which an overcrowding notice is in force: again this is novel. The right of appeal in s. 90 (10) in any person aggrieved is the same as that it replaces (old s. 90 (3)). By s. 90 (11) (new) a local authority may at any time, on the application of any person having an estate or interest in the house, revoke an overcrowding notice or vary it so as to allow more people to be accommodated in the house; s. 90 (12) confers a right of appeal by such a person in the event of refusal within the time mentioned therein by the local authority to revoke or vary. The penalties in s. 90 (13) and (14) replace those contained in the Housing Act 1961, s. 20, which is, accordingly, repealed: Sch. 26. The penalty on any person who contravenes an overcrowding notice is raised, on summary conviction, to a fine not exceeding £500 (s. 90 (13)). It was previously £100; but imprisonment ceases to be available. Section 90 (14) punishes deliberate failure to comply with a s. 90 (9) information notice with a fine on summary conviction not exceeding £50. **[315]**

Extension of Housing Act 1957, s. 9

This is by s. 149 of this Act, which inserts a new s. 9 (1B) and 9 (1C) into the 1957 Act. By the new s. 9 (1B), where a local authority is satisfied, on a representation made by an occupying tenant, that a house is in such a state of disrepair that, although it is not unfit for human habitation, the condition of the house is such as to interfere materially with the personal comfort of the occupying tenant, they may serve on the person having control of the house (as to this, see the Housing Act 1957, s. 39 (2)) a s. 9 (1A) notice. By s. 9 (1C) "occupying tenant" has the same meaning, in relation to a dwelling which consists, or forms part of, the house concerned, as in the Housing Act 1974, s. 104. The reason for the passing of s. 149 of this Act may be that the relevant provisions in the Public Health Act 1936 to deal with such problems had been narrowed down by the courts: see further the annotation to this section. **[316]**

Provisions for pensions for certain officers of rent assessment panels

As to this, see s. 148 amending the Rent Act 1977, Sch. 10. **[317]**

Avoidance of unauthorised disposals

In the case of disposals to which the Housing Act 1957, s. 104 (as substituted by s. 91 (1) of this Act) or to which the Housing Act 1974, s. 2, apply, which are after 18th July 1980 by a local authority or housing association, and the disposal is of a house, then it is void (1980 Act, (s. 137)) unless to an individual or to two or more individuals. **[318]**

Houses in multiple occupation: means of escape from fire

By s. 147 (1), the rules in Sch. 24 replace those in the Housing Act 1961, s. 16, and the Housing Act 1969, s. 60, except in relation to notices served, undertakings accepted or orders made before 3rd October 1980. The rest of s. 147 amends the penalties in s. 60 of the 1969 Act in relation to pre-commencement breaches of undertakings (s. 147 (2)) and s. 147 (3) is a saving provision. Some particular aspects of Sch. 24 are noted in the annotations.

[319]

SERVICE CHARGES

New rules are provided in s. 136 and Sch. 19 to this Act which replace the previous rules (Housing Finance Act 1972, ss. 90 and 91A, repealed in Sch. 26). In relation to works begun earlier than 6 months after 3rd October 1980 the new rules in paras 2–6 of Sch. 19 do not apply and the previous ones remain in force: s. 136 (2). **[320]**

The new rules are regrettably no less elaborate than those they replace and are discussed also in the notes. Some points are made here to highlight the main changes in the rules. **[321]**

1. *Definitions.* "Service charge" is defined in para. 1 (1) and is similar to the previous definition in the 1972 Act save that, notably, there may be recovered in principle the landlord's costs of management. "Relevant costs" are defined in para. 1 (1) so as to include costs or estimated costs (including overheads) incurred *or to be incurred*, etc. The italicised words are new; but in relation to them, it will be noted that para. 2 limits this head of charge so that there may only be recovered costs to be incurred if to a reasonable amount and though service charges in advance of expenditure are recoverable, this is subject to re-adjustment after the expenditure is incurred (para. 2(b)). As to the other definitions, see paras 16 to 21. **[322]**

2. *Double general limit on relevant costs.* By para. 3 there is a double limit on costs: (a) they are only recoverable to the extent that "reasonably incurred", and (b) in the case of costs incurred in the provision of services or the carrying out of works, only if these are of a reasonable standard. **[323]**

3. *Costs within para. 4.* This applies where the amount of the costs of works on a building exceed the amount mentioned in para. 4 or (if applicable) prescribed in regulations, and where this is so, then, subject to the dispensation power of the court in para. 6, para. 5 requiring estimates, etc., will apply. The amounts are £25 times the number of flats in the building or £500, whichever is the greater, subject to the regulatory power to substitute a different amount. **[324]**

4. *Information.* Paragraphs 7 to 10 enable the tenant or a recognised tenants' association (para. 20) to obtain information as to service charges from the landlord and require a landlord to obtain it, where a tenants' request has

been made under para. 7, from a superior landlord (para. 8). There are penalties for non-compliance in para. 13. **[325]**

5. *Court proceedings.* The jurisdiction of the county court to grant purely declaratory relief in relation to service charges is contained in para. 12 and see further para. 11 on the exclusion of certain agreements by the tenant. **[326]**

6. *Exclusions.* The most important is that in para. 15 of tenants of flats where the rent is registered as a fair rent unless it is registered as a variable amount. **[327]**

THE HOUSING ACT 1980

(1980 c. 51)

PART II

PRIVATE SECTOR TENANTS

Protected shorthold tenancies

PART IX

GENERAL

Housing Revenue Account and Housing Repairs Account

81

An Act to give security of tenure, and the right to buy their homes, to tenants of local authorities and other bodies; to make other provision with respect to those and other tenants; to amend the law about housing finance in the public sector; to make other provision with respect to housing; to restrict the discretion of the court in making orders for possession of land; and for connected purposes.   [8th August 1980]

POWERS OF LOCAL AUTHORITIES
Nothing in the Local Government Act 1972, ss. 111–130, A.L.S. Vol. 209, or in Part VIII of that Act, affects or empowers a local authority to act otherwise than in accordance with, any provision contained in, or in any instrument made under, this Act and relating to any dealing in land by a local authority or the application of capital money arising from any such dealing, see s. 131 (1) and (2) of that Act, as amended, in case of s. 131 (2), by s. 152 (1) and Sch. 25, para. 23, *post.*

NORTHERN IRELAND
Only ss. 152 (1), 153 and 155 and Sch. 25, paras. 11, 12, 18 and 19, *post*, extend to Northern Ireland, see s. 155 (3), *post.*

PART I

PUBLIC SECTOR TENANTS

CHAPTER I

THE RIGHT TO BUY

1. Right to acquire freehold or long lease

(1) A secure tenant has the right—

    (*a*) if the dwelling-house is a house, to acquire the freehold of the dwelling-house;

    (*b*) if the dwelling-house is a flat, to be granted a long lease of the dwelling-house; and

    (*c*) in either case, to leave the whole or part of the aggregate amount mentioned in section 9 (1) outstanding on the security of a first mortgage of the dwelling-house or, if the landlord is a housing association, to have the whole or part of that amount advanced to him on that security by the Housing Corporation;

in the circumstances and subject to the conditions and exceptions stated in the following provisions of this Chapter.

(2) In this Chapter the right mentioned in subsection (1) (*a*) and (*b*) above is referred to as the right to buy and that mentioned in subsection (1) (*c*) above as the right to a mortgage.

(3) The right to buy only arises after the secure tenant has been a secure tenant for a period of not less than three years of for periods amounting together to not less than three years; but—

    (*a*) neither the landlord nor the dwelling-house need have been the same during the whole of that period; and

    (*b*) any period during which the secure tenant was a tenant of a body specified in subsection (1) or (2) of section 2 shall be left out of account; and

    (*c*) this subsection is subject to subsections (4) to (7) below.

(4) In determining whether the condition in subsection (3) above is satisfied a person who, as a joint tenant under a secure tenancy, occupied a dwelling-house as his only or principal home shall be treated as the secure tenant under that tenancy; and where the secure tenancy is a joint tenancy that condition need be satisfied with respect to one only of the joint tenants.

(5) Where the secure tenant became a secure tenant on the death of his spouse, and at the time of the death they occupied the same dwelling-house as their only or principal home, any period during which the deceased spouse was a secure tenant is to be counted for the purposes of subsection (3) above unless excluded by paragraph (b) of that subsection.

(6) In determining whether the condition in subsection (3) above is satisfied in the case of a person who is, or of persons one of whom is, a previous purchaser, a period counts as a period during which the previous purchaser or his spouse was a secure tenant only if it fell after the completion of the previous purchase or, if more than one, the last of them.

(7) In subsection (6) above "previous purchaser" means a person who has exercised the right to buy or the right to purchase conferred by Part I of the Tenants' Rights, Etc. (Scotland) Act 1980 on a previous occasion (whether he has exercised it alone or jointly with another person) and "previous purchase" has a corresponding meaning.

(8) References in this Chapter to the purchase price include references to the consideration for the grant of a long lease. **[330]**

COMMENCEMENT
This Chapter (ss. 1–27 and Schs. 1 and 2, *post*) came into operation on 3rd October 1980; see s. 153 (1), *post*, and the note thereto.

SUB-S. (1): HOUSING ASSOCIATION
This expression is not defined for the purposes of this Act, but by virtue of ss. 28 (1), (2) (b), 49 (2) and 150, *post*, in this Part of this Act it generally means a housing association falling within the Rent Act 1977, s. 15 (3), A.L.S. Vol. 255, other than an association which is both registered with the Housing Corporation under the Housing Act 1974, s. 13, A.L.S. Vol. 223, and is registered under the Industrial and Provident Societies Act 1965, and otherwise falls within s. 15 (3) (d) of the Act of 1977. Moreover the right to buy does not arise if the landlord is a housing association falling within the descriptions set out in s. 2 (2), *post*.

HOUSING CORPORATION
As to this body, see the Housing Act 1964, s. 1, Sch. 1, A.L.S. Vol. 149, and the Housing Act 1974, s. 1, Sch. 1, A.L.S. Vol. 223.

THIS CHAPTER
I.e., Chapter I (ss. 1–27) of Part I of this Act.

RIGHT TO BUY
In an answer to a Parliamentary Question the Prime Minister invented a new kind of right in this connection, a "compulsory right". However this may be, the right to buy is backed up, in particular, by the right of the tenant (in effect) to challenge the landlord's valuation before the district valuer (s. 11); the tenant's right to a mortgage (s. 12); and, very strikingly, the subjectively worded, sweeping and draconian power in the Secretary of State for the Environment to intervene (s. 23) and conduct forced sales over the landlord's head (s. 24). This means that the fact that a local authority has a policy of not embarking on indiscriminate or unplanned sales may only cause a particular tenant or class of tenants some delay if the Secretary of State is apprised of the policy.
One only has the right to buy subject to the various exclusions mentioned in s. 2 and Sch. 1 to this Act, and only where one is a secure tenant, so that not only is there no right to buy in any case where Sch. 3 applies, *e.g.* short-term arrangements (para. 7), but there will be none where the residence requirement, *i.e.* occupation of the dwelling-house as one's only or principal home (s. 28 (3)) is not satisfied. As to this, see further the note to that

provision; obviously, this is a question of fact; what is intended is a domestic quality of residence: cf. *Reidy* v. *Walker* [1933] 2 K.B. 266. A two-home tenant, a figure which crops up in relation to statutory tenancies mostly in theory (but see *Langford Property Co. Ltd.* v. *Tureman* [1949] 1 K.B. 29; 1948 2 All E.R. 722, C.A., and *Hallwood Estates Ltd* v. *Flack* [1950] W.N. 268, C.A.) could not have two rights to buy at one and the same time and would be put on his election in a marginal case, one may presume. It will be seen that different periods of residence may be accumulated in different dwelling-houses over a period of time: see sub-s. (3); and one has to reside as a secure tenant for 3 years or for a total of 3 years.

JOINT TENANT (SUB-S. (4))

The right to buy provisions in general are favourable to one out of several joint tenants: it is also of interest to note that the common law rules have been relaxed in relation to succession to statutory tenancies: see *Lloyd* v. *Sadler* [1978] Q.B. 774; [1978] 2 All E.R. 529, C.A. The joint tenant landlord is not so favoured: thus in relation to Case 10 of the Rent Act 1977, Sch. 15, Part I, one joint tenant's reasonable requirements are not enough: *Tilling* v. *Whitman* [1978] 3 All E.R. 1103, C.A.; also *McIntyre* v. *Hardcastle* [1948] 1 All E.R. 696, C.A.

The following is a brief list of those sections of this Act relating to the right to buy: s. 2 and Sch. 1, *post* (exceptions); s. 4, *post* (joint tenants and members of the family to be included in the right to buy); s. 5, *post* (notice claiming exercise of the right to buy); s. 6, *post* (purchase price); s. 7, *post* (discount); s. 8, *post* (repayment of discount on early disposal of freehold or lease); s. 10, *post* (landlord's notice of purchase price and right to a mortgage); s. 11, *post* (right of tenant to have values determined by district valuer); s. 13, *post* (change of secure tenant after notice claiming right to buy); s. 14, *post* (change of landlord after notice claiming right to buy); s. 16, *post* (completion); s. 17 and Sch. 2, *post* (conveyance of freehold and grant of lease); s. 19, *post* (dwelling houses in National Parks and areas of outstanding natural beauty, etc.); s. 20, *post* (registration of title); s. 21, *post* (costs); ss. 23 and 24, *post* (Secretary of State's power to intervene); s. 41, *post* (landlord's obligation to provide information about the right to buy, etc.); and s. 48, *post* application of this Part (ss. 1–50) to licences).

RIGHT TO A MORTGAGE

See, further, in connection with the right to a mortgage, s. 4, *post* (joint tenants and members of the family included in right to mortgage); s. 9, *post* (amount to be secured); s. 10, *post* (notice of purchase price and right to mortgage); s. 12, *post* (claim to a mortgage); s. 14, *post* (change of landlord after notice claiming right to a mortgage); s. 18, *post* (terms of mortgage deed); s. 21 (2), *post* (costs); s. 23, *post* (Secretary of State's power to intervene); s. 41, *post* (landlord's obligation to provide information about the right to mortgage, etc.); s. 48, *post* (application of this Part (ss. 1–50) to licences) and s. 110, *post* (local authority mortgage interest rates).

SUB-S. (3): HAS BEEN A SECURE TENANT FOR ... NOT LESS THAN THREE YEARS, ETC.

As to children succeeding parents, see however, s. 15, *post*; and as to the inclusion of periods before the commencement of Chapter II of Part I on 3rd October 1980, see s. 27 (3), *post*.

JURISDICTION OF COUNTY COURT

By s. 86 (1), *post*, a county court has, subject to s. 11, *post*, jurisdiction to determine any question arising under this Part (ss. 1–50) of this Act and to entertain any proceedings brought thereunder and any claim (for whatever amount) in connection with a secure tenancy; and by s. 86 (2), *post*, the jurisdiction as conferred includes jurisdiction to entertain proceedings on any question arising under this Chapter (ss. 1–27) notwithstanding that no other relief is sought than a declaration. See also s. 86 (3), *post*, as to non-recovery of costs of proceedings in the High Court, and s. 86 (4)–(6), *post*, as to procedure, etc., in the county court.

DEFINITIONS

For "flat" and "house", see s. 3 (1)–(3), *post*; for "dwelling house", see s. 3 (1), (4), *post* and s. 50 (2) as applied by s. 27 (1), *post*; for "landlord", see s. 27 (2), *post*; for "secure tenant" and "secure tenancy", see ss. 27 (3), 28, 49 (2) and 150, *post*. Note as to "the right to buy" and "the right to a mortgage", sub-s. (2) above, and as to "previous purchaser" and "previous purchase", sub-s. (7) above.

TENANTS' RIGHTS ETC. (SCOTLAND) ACT 1980

1980 c. 52.

2. Exceptions to right to buy

(1) The right to buy does not arise if the landlord is a housing trust which is a charity within the meaning of the Charities Act 1960.

(2) The right to buy does not arise if the landlord is a housing association which either—

(*a*) is a charity (within the meaning of the Charities Act 1960); or

(*b*) falls within paragraph (*d*) of section 15 (3) of the 1977 Act (certain societies registered under the Industrial and Provident Societies Act 1965); or

(*c*) has at no time received a grant under section 119 (3) of the 1957 Act, section 29, 31, 32 or 33 of the 1974 Act or under any enactment mentioned in paragraph 2 of Schedule 2 to that Act.

(3) The right to buy does not arise unless the landlord owns the freehold.

(4) Subject to subsection (5) below, the right to buy—

(*a*) does not arise in any of the circumstances mentioned in Part I of Schedule 1 to this Act, and

(*b*) cannot be exercised in any of the circumstances mentioned in Part II of that Schedule.

(5) The Secretary of State may by order enable the right to buy to be exercised in relation to dwelling-houses held by local authorities otherwise than under Part V of the 1957 Act or such descriptions of such dwelling-houses as may be specified in the order; and any such order may contain such supplementary provisions, including provisions modifying the following provisions of this Chapter, as appear to the Secretary of State necessary or expedient. **[331]**

COMMENCEMENT
See the note to s. 1, *ante*.

SUB-S. (1): RIGHT TO BUY
See s. 1, *ante*, and the notes thereto.

SUB-S. (2): HOUSING ASSOCIATION
Cf. the note to s. 1, *ante*.

SUB-S. (5): SECRETARY OF STATE
I.e., one of Her Majesty's Principal Secretaries of State; see the Interpretation Act 1978, s. 5, Sch. 1, A.L.S. Vol. 258. The Secretary of State here concerned is the Secretary of State for the Environment or, as respects Wales, the Secretary of State for Wales.

THIS CHAPTER
I.e., Chapter I (ss. 1–27) of Part I of this Act.

APPEAR
For a discussion as to the effect of the use of this and similar expressions such as "in the opinion" and "satisfied", on the power of the courts to review administrative action, see 1 Halsbury's Laws (4th Edn.), para. 22.

JURISDICTION OF COUNTY COURT
See the note to s. 1, *ante*.

DEFINITIONS
For "the right to buy", see s. 1 (2), *ante*; for "dwelling-house", see s. 3 (1), (4), *post*, and s. 50 (2) as applied by s. 27 (1), *post*; for "landlord", see s. 27 (2), *post*: for "local authority", see s. 50 (1) as applied by s. 27 (1), *post*; by virtue of ss. 27 (1) and 50 (1), *post*, for "housing trust", see the Rent Act 1977, s. 15 (5), as substituted by s. 74 (2), *post*.

CHARITIES ACT 1960
For the meaning of "charity", see s. 45 (1), (2) of that Act, A.L.S. Vol. 132.

RENT ACT 1977, S. 15 (3) (*d*) (SUB-S. (2))

By the Rent Act 1977, A.L.S. Vol. 255, s. 15 (1), a tenancy whereof the interest of the landlord is held by a housing association is not a protected tenancy, but by *ibid.*, s. 15 (3) (*d*), there is, as a result of s. 2 (2) of this Act, no right to buy if the housing association is a registered society within the meaning of the Industrial and Provident Societies Act 1965, s. 74, and its rules restrict membership to persons who are tenants or prospective tenants of the association and preclude the granting or assigning of tenancies to persons other than members.

1977 ACT

I.e., the Rent Act 1977; see s. 150, *post*

INDUSTRIAL AND PROVIDENT SOCIETIES ACT 1965

See Vol. 17, p. 333.

1957 ACT

I.e., the Housing Act 1957; see s. 150, *post*. For Part V and s. 119 (3) of that Act, see A.L.S. Vol. 109. Part V (ss. 91–134) is amended by ss. 35 (4), 90–95 and 152 (1) and Sch. 25, paras. 5–7, *post*, and is partly repealed by s. 153 (3) and Sch. 26, *post*; and s. 119 (3) is partly repealed by s. 152 (2) and (3) and Sch. 25, para. 6, and Sch. 26, *post*.

1974 ACT

I.e., the Housing Act 1974; see s. 150, *post*. For ss. 29, 31, 32 and 33 of, and Sch. 2, para. 2, to that Act, see Vol. 44, pp. 433, 436–438, 524. Section 29 is amended by s. 130 (4) and Sch. 18, paras. 1, 2, *post*; s. 31 is repealed, except in relation to grants payable in pursuance of applications made before 8th August 1980, by ss. 130 (4), 152 (3), Sch. 18, para. 8, and Sch. 26, *post*; and ss. 32 and 33 are amended and partly repealed by ss. 130 (4), 152 (3), Sch. 18, paras. 9, 10, and Sch. 26, *post*.

ORDERS UNDER THIS SECTION

At the time of going to press no orders had been made under sub-s. (5) above.

For general provisions as to orders, see s. 151, *post*.

3. Meaning of "house", "flat", "dwelling-house" and "relevant time"

(1) The following provisions apply to the interpretation of "house", "flat", "dwelling-house" and "relevant time" when used in this Chapter.

(2) A dwelling-house is a house if, and only if, it (or so much of it as does not consist of land included by virtue of section 50 (2) of this Act) is a structure reasonably so called; so that—

(*a*) where a building is divided horizontally, the flats or other units into which it is divided are not houses; and

(*b*) where a building is divided vertically, the units into which it is divided may be houses; and

(*c*) where a building is not structurally detached it is not a house if a material part of it lies above or below the remainder of the structure.

(3) Any dwelling-house which is not a house is a flat.

(4) There shall be treated as included in the dwelling-house any land used for the purposes of the dwelling-house which the landlord and the tenant agree to include.

(5) The relevant time is the date on which the tenant's notice claiming to exercise the right to buy is served; except that, if that notice is served within six months of the commencement of this Chapter, the relevant time is the date on which this Act is passed. **[332]**

COMMENCEMENT

See the note to s. 1, *ante*.

SUB-S. (1): THIS CHAPTER

I.e., Chapter 1 (ss. 1–27) of Part I of this Act.

SUB-S. (2): DWELLING-HOUSE
This will not be an easy provision to apply. There is a distinction between houses, which must be a structure reasonably so called, and a flat, which is not subject to this condition. Accordingly, a detached or semi-detached house would be a house and one could buy the freehold of either if eligible to do so. Owing to sub-s. (2) (b), a single terraced house in a longer terrace would also be a house within s. 3.

As to what is a "structure reasonably so called", the meaning of this is not clear. It appears to connote permanence: *South Wales Aluminium Co Ltd.* v. *Neath Assessment Committee* [1943] 2 All E.R. 587; *Jewish Blind Society Trustees* v. *Henning* [1961] 1 All E.R. 47, C.A. So, a temporary structure, such as a caravan or house-boat, would not be a house within s. 3 (2); cf. *Kingston Plastics* v. *Esher U.D.C.* 68 L.G.R. 401.

Section 3 (2) refers to "units"—*i.e.* living units. So, no right to buy is possible except where the premises, house or flat, are used as a dwelling: all the major activities of life should normally be carried on, such as sleeping, cooking and feeding: *Wright* v. *Howell* 204 L.T. Jo. 299, C.A.; *Curl* v. *Angelo* [1948] 2 All E.R. 189, C.A.

The physical extent of the "dwelling-house" will be a question of fact and degree: cf. *Bardrick* v. *Haycock* (1976) 31 P. & C.R. 420, C.A. (considering the Rent Act 1977, s. 12). By s. 3 (4) of this Act, land used for the purposes of the dwelling-house is treated as part of the dwelling-house. It is thought that, accordingly, as with the Rent Act 1977, s. 6, one may have, in the case of agreement between the landlord and tenant only (s. 3 (4)), a composite entity of dwelling-house and land: see *Langford Property Co Ltd.* v. *Batten* [1950] 2 All E.R. 1079, H.L. Examples would be a garage, outbuilding or garden; for it is conceived that, as with the Rent Acts, "land" in s. 3 (4) may comprise buildings.

It is possible also that, as with the Rent Acts, two living units physically separated but held under the same secure tenancy might be taken as a single entity for the purposes of the right to buy: *Langford Property Co Ltd.* v. *Goldrich* [1949] 1 All E.R. 402, C.A., envisaged this.

It seems that "dwelling-house" should not be construed so as to connote only that part of a building in which the occupant dwells and that it therefore includes such parts as a cellar (*Grigsby* v. *Melville*, [1973] 3 All E.R. 455, C.A., at p. 462, *per* Stamp, L.J.).

A caravan jacked up and resting on bricks and connected to the electricity and water supplies has been held to be a dwelling-house (*Makins* v. *Elson (Inspector of Taxes)*, [1977] 1 All E.R. 572).

See further on the meaning of "dwelling-house", 2 Words and Phrases (2nd Edn.) 127–131; and note sub-s. (4) above and s. 50 (2) as applied by s. 27 (1), *post*.

LAND
For meaning, see the Interpretation Act 1978, s. 5, Sch. 1, A.L.S. Vol. 258.

STRUCTURE
In *Hobday* v. *Nicol*, [1944] 1 All E.R. 302, Humphreys, J. (with whom the other members of the Court agreed), said: "Structure, as I understand it, is anything which is constructed; and it involves the notion of something which is put together, consisting of a number of different things which are so put together or built, constructed as to make one whole which is then called a structure". See also the cases cited in 5 Words and Phrases (2nd Edn.) 131 *et seq.*

BUILDING
As usual in statutes where this term is used, there is no definition of "building" in s. 3. "... To attempt a definition," it was rightly remarked in *Bell* v. *Edinburgh Workmen's Dwelling-Houses Improvement Co.* (1957) S.L.T. 10, p. 12, (Sh. Ct.) "which would cover all the various diversity of structures affected by this Act would tax the ingenuity of the most hardened Parliamentary draftsman."

This may excuse brevity here. It seems that the courts tend to content themselves with holding that there is no general rule (*Humphery* v. *Young* [1903] 1 K.B. 44); that a popular usage may be relevant to the decision (*Moir* v. *Williams* [1892] 1 Q.B. 264, C.A.: held that 14 chambers in a single structure but with separate entrances, one single "building" for the purposes of the Metropolitan Building Act 1855, Sch. 2, Part I).

The courts may also apply the mischief test, as was done in relation to resident landlords (s. 12 of the Rent Act 1977) in *Bardrick* v. *Haycock* (1976) 31 P. & C.R. 420, C.A.). See also the cases cited in 1 Words and Phrases (2nd Edn.) 191 *et seq.*

SUB-S. (5): NOTICE CLAIMING TO EXERCISE THE RIGHT TO BUY
See s. 5, *post*.

WITHIN SIX MONTHS OF, ETC.
The general rule in cases where an act is to be done within a specified time from a certain date is that the day of that date is to be exluded; see *Goldsmiths' Co.* v. *West Metropolitan Rail. Co.*, [1904] 1 K.B. 1; [1900–3] All E.R. Rep. 667, C.A.; *Stewart* v. *Chapman*, [1951] 2 K.B. 792; [1952] 2 All E.R. 613; and the cases cited in 37 Halsbury's Laws (3rd Edn.), p. 95, para. 168. "Months" means calendar months; see the Interpretation Act 1978, s. 5, Sch. 1.

COMMENCEMENT OF THIS CHAPTER
I.e., 3rd October 1980; see s. 153 (1), *post*, and the note thereto.

DATE ON WHICH THIS ACT IS PASSED
I.e., 8th August 1980, the date of the Royal Assent.

JURISDICTION OF COUNTY COURT
See the note to s. 1, *ante*.

DEFINITIONS
For "the right to buy", see 1 (2), *ante*; for "landlord", see s. 27 (2), *post*.

4. Joint tenants and members of family occupying dwelling-house otherwise than as joint tenants

(1) Where a secure tenancy is a joint tenancy then, whether or not each of the joint tenants occupies the dwelling-house as his only or principal home, the right to buy and the right to a mortgage belong jointly to all of them or to such one or more of them as may be validly agreed between them; and the agreement is not valid unless the person or at least one of the persons to whom the right to buy is to belong occupies the dwelling-house as his only or principal home.

(2) A secure tenant may, in his notice under section 5 claiming to exercise the right to buy, require that not more than three members of his family who are not joint tenants but occupy the dwelling-house as their only or principal home should share the right to buy with him; but he may validly do so in the case of any such member only if—

　　(*a*) that member is his spouse or has been residing with him throughout the period of twelve months ending with the giving of the notice; or
　　(*b*) the landlord consents.

(3) Where by such a notice any members of the tenant's family are validly required to share the right to buy with the tenant, both the right to buy and the right to a mortgage belong to the tenant and those members jointly and he and they shall be treated for the purposes of this Chapter as joint tenants. **[333]**

COMMENCEMENT
See the note to s. 1, *ante*.

RIGHT TO BUY; RIGHT TO A MORTGAGE
See s. 1, *ante*, and the notes thereto.

REQUIRE THAT NOT MORE THAN THREE MEMBERS OF HIS FAMILY ... SHARE THE RIGHT TO BUY
Section 13 (1)–(3), *post* (change of secure tenant after notice claiming right to buy), do not confer any right on a person required in pursuance of sub-s. (2) above to share the right to buy unless he could have been validly so required had the notice claiming to exercise the right to buy been given by the new tenant; see s. 13 (4), *post*.
　　As to which persons are members of another's family, see s. 50 (3), as applied by s. 27 (1), *post*.

RESIDING WITH HIM
Cf. the note to the Rent Act 1977, Sch. 1, Part I, A.L.S. Vol. 255.

MONTHS
 I.e., calendar months; see the Interpretation Act 1978, s. 5, Sch. 1, A.L.S. Vol. 258.

THIS CHAPTER
 I.e., Chapter I (ss. 1–27) of Part I of this Act.

JURISDICTION OF COUNTY COURT
 See the note to s. 1, *ante*.

DEFINITIONS
 For "the right to buy" and "the right to a mortgage", see s. 1 (2), *ante*; for "dwelling-house", see s. 3 (1), (4), *ante*, and s. 50 (2) as applied by s. 27 (1), *post*; for "landlord", see s. 27 (2), *ante*; for "secure tenancy", see ss. 27 (3), 28 and 49 (2), *post*; for "member of his family", see s. 50 (3) as applied by s. 27 (1), *post*.

5. Notice claiming exercise of right to buy

(1) Where a secure tenant serves on the landlord a written notice claiming to exercise the right to buy, the landlord shall (unless the notice is withdrawn) serve on the tenant, within four weeks, or in a case falling within subsection (2) below, eight weeks, either—

 (*a*) a written notice admitting the tenant's right; or

 (*b*) a written notice denying the tenant's right and stating the reasons why, in the opinion of the landlord, the tenant does not have the right to buy.

(2) A case falls within this subsection if the periods counting towards the three years required by section 1 (3) above include a period during which the landlord was not the landlord on which the tenant's notice under subsection (1) above is served.

(3) A tenant's notice under subsection (1) above may be withdrawn at any time by notice in writing served on the landlord. [334]

COMMENCEMENT
 See the note to s. 1, *ante*.

SERVE
 As to the regulatory power as to the form of notices, see s. 21 (1).
 By s. 21 (2), any notice under this Chapter may be served by sending it by post. Under the Interpretation Act 1978, A.L.S. Vol. 258, s. 7, service of a notice by post is deemed to be effected by properly addressing, prepaying and posting a letter containing the document and, unless the contrary is proved, service is deemed to have been effected at the time at which the letter would be delivered in the ordinary course of the post.
 There is thus created a presumption of due service, which is in general irrebuttable: *Moody* v. *Godstone R.D.C.* [1966] 2 All E.R. 696. However, where the time of service is crucial, the presumption is rebuttable and evidence is admissible to prove that there was in fact no service, or that it was out of time: *Hewitt* v. *Leicester County Council* [1969] 2 All E.R. 802, C.A.; *Maltglade* v. *St Albans R.D.C.* [1972] 3 All E.R. 129. In the case therefore of a right to buy notice (s. 5) due service will be irrebuttably presumed; but in the case for instance of notices under ss. 11 (1) and 12 (right to have value determined by district valuer and right to a mortgage respectively) the presumption is not irrebuttable, time being crucial there.
 Where a landlord's notice under ss. 10 (1), 11 (4) or 12 (3) is served as above in relation to joint tenants, it is possible that service on one joint tenant will be sufficient, irrespective of whether the other or others receive the notice: cf. *Re 88 Berkeley Road, London, N.W. 9, Rickwood* v. *Turnsek* [1971] 1 All E.R. 254.

WRITTEN; WRITING
 Expressions referring to writing are, unless the contrary intention appears, to be construed as including references to other modes of representing or reproducing words in a viable form; see the Interpretation Act 1978, s. 5, Sch. 1, A.L.S. Vol. 258.

NOTICE

As to claiming in the notice that members of a secure tenant's family shall share the right to buy, see s. 4 (2), (3), *ante*; and as to notice generally, see s. 22, *post*. A separate notice claiming to exercise the right to a mortgage is required; see s. 12, *post*.

By the Housing (Rights to Buy) (Prescribed Forms) (No. 1) Regulations 1980, S.I. 1980 No. 1391 (made under s. 22 (1), post), the following forms are prescribed for use under sub-s. (1) above:—

Form No. 1: Secure tenant's notice claiming to exercise the right to buy.

Form No. 2: Notice in reply to secure tenant's notice claiming to exercise the right to buy—for use where the landlord is not a development corporation, the Commission for the New Towns or the Development Board for Rural Wales.

Form No. 3: Notice in reply to secure tenant's notice claiming to exercise the right to buy—for use where the landlord is a development corporation, the Commission for the New Towns or the Development Board for Rural Wales.

RIGHT TO BUY

See s. 1, *ante*, and the notes thereto.

WITHIN FOUR (EIGHT) WEEKS

See the note "Within six months of, etc." to s. 3, *ante*

JURISDICTION OF COUNTY COURT

See the note to s. 1, *ante*.

DEFINITIONS

For "the right to buy", see s. 1 (2), *ante*; for "landlord", see s. 27 (2), *post*; for "secure tenant", see ss. 27 (3), 28, 49 (2) and 150, *post*.

6. Purchase price

(1) The price payable for a dwelling-house on a conveyance or grant in pursuance of this Chapter is—

    (a) the amount which, under this section, is to be taken as its value at the relevant time; less

    (b) the discount to which the purchaser is entitled under this Chapter.

(2) The value of a dwelling-house at the relevant time shall be taken to be the price which, at that time, it would realise if sold on the open market by a willing vendor on the assumptions stated, for a conveyance, in subsection (3) below and, for a grant, in subsection (4) below, and disregarding any improvements made by any of the persons specified in subsection (5) below and any failure by any of those persons to keep the dwelling-house in good internal repair.

(3) For a conveyance the assumptions are that—

    (a) the vendor was selling for an estate in fee simple with vacant possession;

    (b) neither the tenant nor a member of his family residing with him wanted to buy; and

    (c) the dwelling-house was to be conveyed with the same rights and subject to the same burdens as it would be in pursuance of this Chapter.

(4) For the grant of a lease the assumptions are that—

    (a) the vendor was granting a lease for 125 years with vacant possession (subject to pargraph 11 (2) of Schedule 2 to this Act);

    (b) neither the tenant nor a member of his family residing with him wanted to take the lease;

    (c) the ground rent would not exceed £10 per annum; and

    (d) the grant was to be made with the same rights and subject to the same burdens as it would be in pursuance of this Chapter.

(5) The persons mentioned in subsection (2) above are—

    (*a*) the secure tenant;

    (*b*) any person who under the same tenancy was a secure tenant before him; and

    (*c*) any member of his family who, immediately before the secure tenancy was granted, was a secure tenant of the same dwelling-house under another tenancy. **[335]**

COMMENCEMENT
    See the note to s. 1, *ante*.

SUB-S. (1): CONVEYANCE OR GRANT IN PURSUANCE OF THIS CHAPTER
    I.e., under s. 16 or 24, *post*.

VALUE AT THE RELEVANT TIME
    For the right of the tenant to have the value of a dwelling-house at the relevant time determined by a district valuer, see s. 11, *post*.
    The value at the relevant time and the improvements disregarded in pursuance of this section are two items that must be stated in the landlord's notice under s. 10, *post*; see s. 10 (2) (*a*) and (*c*), *post*.

DISCOUNT TO WHICH THE PURCHASER IS ENTITLED
    See s. 7, *post*.

SUB-S. (2): SOLD ON THE OPEN MARKET
    I.e., without restrictions as to the price payable. The legislature did not use terms such as the best price reasonably obtainable (as in the Building Societies Act 1962, s. 36) but little turns on this: it is the proper price at the time in question of the actual (not a hypothetical) market that will presumably govern: cf. *Priestman Collieries Ltd.* v. *Northern District Valuation Board* [1950] 2 K.B. 398; [1950] 2 All E.R. 129. For cases on sale in the open market, see *Inland Revenue Comrs.* v. *Clay*, [1914] 3 K.B. 466; [1914–15] All E.R. Rep. 882, C.A.; *Earl of Ellesmere* v. *Inland Revenue Comrs.*, [1918] 2 K.B. 735; *Inland Revenue Comrs.* v. *Crossman*, [1937] A.C. 26; [1936] 1 All E.R. 762, H.L.; *Raja Vyricheria Narayana Gajapatiraju* v. *Revenue Divisional Officer, Vizaqapatam*, [1939] A.C. 302; [1939] 2 All E.R. 317, P.C.; *Priestman Collieries, Ltd.* v. *Northern District Valuation Board*, [1950] 2 K.B. 398; [1950] 2 All E.R. 129; *Rolex Watch Co., Ltd.* v. *Customs and Excise Comrs.*, [1956] 2 All E.R. 589, C.A.; *J. and C. Moores, Ltd.* v. *Customs and Excise Comrs.*, [1964] 2 All E.R. 983, H.L.; *Salomon* v. *Customs and Excise Comrs.*, [1967] 2 Q.B. 116; [1966] 3 All E.R. 871, C.A.; *Morisis Products, Ltd.* v. *Customs and Excise Comrs.*, [1969] 3 All E.R. 1096, C.A.; *Lynall* v. *Inland Revenue Comrs.*, [1972] A.C. 680; [1971] 3 All E.R. 914. H.L.; *Crabtree* v. *Hinchcliffe (Inspector of Taxes)*, [1972] A.C. at p. 725; [1971] 3 All E.R. 967, H.L. and *Byrne* v. *Low* [1972] 3 All E.R. 526.

IMPROVEMENT (SUB-S. (2))
    Because of this sub-s. and the effect of sub-s. (5) below, the effect of *Ponsford* v. *HMS Aerosols Ltd.* [1978] 2 All E.R. 837, H.L., and *Cuff* v. *J. & F. Stone Property* [1978] 2 All E.R. 833, has been swept away. As to the removal of the rule that improvements carried out on business premises by a predecessor in title to the tenant would not be disregarded, despite the Landlord and Tenant Act 1954, s. 34 (so held in *Re "Wonderland", Cleethorpes* [1965] A.C. 58, H.L.) see the Law of Property Act 1969, A.L.S. Vol. 187, s. 1 (1). Parliament has thus maintained in this subsection its hostility to the common-law rules.

Meaning of "improvement"
    For a statutory definition which applies to this Part of the Act, see s. 81 (5) and the note thereto.
    An improvement need not, to be such, actually raise the value of the landlord's reversionary interest: *F. W. Woolworth & Co. Ltd.* v. *Lambert* [1937] Ch. 37; [1936] 2 All E.R. 523, C.A.; *Lambert* v. *F. W. Woolworth & Co. Ltd* [1938] Ch. 883; [1938] 2 All E.R. 664, C.A.
    It is not always easy to distinguish an improvement from extensive subordinate renewals with better materials than those used originally, carried out under a covenant to repair: see *Lurcott* v. *Wakely and Wheeler* [1911] 1 K.B. 905, C.A.; *Ravenseft Properties Ltd.* v. *Davstone (Holdings) Ltd.* [1979] 1 All E.R. 929. It has however been held that in general, an improvement is work which is the provision of something new for the benefit of the

occupier: *Morcom* v. *Campbell-Johnson* [1956] 1 Q.B. 106; [1955] 2 All E.R. 264; *Mackie* v. *Gallagher* 1967 S.C. 59. Accordingly, the following have been held, in various contexts, to amount to improvements: the installation of a new roof (*Re Gaskell's SE* [1894] 1 Ch 485); new sanitary facilities (*Strood Estates* v. *Gregory* [1936] 2 K.B. 605; [1936] 2 All R.R. 355, C.A.); a better replacement floor (*Wales* v. *Rowland* [1952] 1 All E.R. 470, C.A.) and the provision of new central heating (*Pearlman* v. *Harrow School Governors* [1979] Q.B. 56; [1979] 1 All E.R. 365, C.A.).

But merely to replace old worn-out fittings (see *Hulme* v. *Brigham* [1943] 1 All E.R. 204, at p. 207) is not to carry out an improvement: *Morcom* v. *Campbell-Johnson, supra.*

GOOD INTERNAL REPAIR (SUB-S. (2))

Internal repair

Cf. the references to "internal decorative repairs" in the Law of Property Act 1925, s. 147 (1) and the Housing Repairs and Rents Act 1954, s. 30 (3), but there is no definition of the term in either statute, nor in this Act. It is conceived that, obviously, improvements are outside the ambit of the term, and, on the other hand, that it is meant to cover decoration and minor repairs of the type that a tenant would be obliged to carry out under a covenant to paint and decorate every seventh year. It might also cover those little jobs about the place which a reasonable tenant even in the absence of covenant, must do: see *Warren* v. *Keen* [1954] 1 Q.B. 15; [1953] 2 All E.R. 1118, C.A., pp. 20 and 1121.

Good internal repair

Cf. the term "good tenantable repair" as the general standard of repair laid down for all but long terms in *Proudfoot* v. *Hart* (1890), 25 Q.B.D. 42, C.A. It means such repair as, having regard to the age, character and locality of the house, would make it reasonably fit for the occupation of a reasonably-minded tenant of the class likely to take it (*ibid.*, at p. 52). The prefix "good" in sub-s. (2) is not thought to add anything significant to the standard of repair itself: *Calthorpe* v. *McOscar* [1924] 1 K.B. 716, C.A., at p. 722.

DISREGARDING ANY IMPROVEMENTS

See also the second paragraph of the note "Value at the relevant time" above.

SUB-S. (3): FEE SIMPLE

As to this estate generally, see the Law of Property Act 1925, s. 1, Vol. 27, p. 346, and the notes thereto.

RESIDING WITH HIM

Cf. the note to the Rent Act 1977, Sch. 1, Part I, vol. 47, p. 558.

SAME RIGHTS AND ... SAME BURDENS AS IT WOULD BE IN PURSUANCE OF THIS CHAPTER

See generally, as to the provisions of conveyances and grants made in pursuance of this Chapter, s. 17 and Sch. 2, *post.*

DEFINITIONS

For "dwelling-house", see s. 3 (1), (4), *ante*, and s. 50 (2) as applied by s. 27 (1), *post*; for "relevant time", see s. 3 (1), (5), *ante*; for "secure tenant", and "secure tenancy", see ss. 27 (3), 28, 49 (2) and 150, *post*; for "member of his family", see s. 50 (3) as applied by s. 27 (1), *post*; for "improvement", see s. 81 (5), *post.*

7. Discount

(1) A person exercising the right to buy is entitled to a discount equal, subject to the following provisions of this section, to the following percentage of the price before discount, that is to say—

　(*a*) if the period to be taken into account under subsection (5) below is less than four years, 33 per cent.; and

　(*b*) if that period is four years or more, 33 per cent. plus one per cent. for each complete year by which that period exceeds three years, but not together exceeding 50 per cent.

(2) The discount shall not reduce the price below the amount which, in accordance with any determination made by the Secretary of State, is to be taken as

representing so much of the costs incurred in respect of the dwelling-house as, in accordance with the determination, is to be treated as incurred after 31st March 1974 and as relevant for the purposes of this subsection; and if the price before discount is below that amount, there shall be no discount.

(3) A determination under subsection (2) above may make different provision for different cases or descriptions of case, including different provision for different areas, and may provide for exceptions from the requirements of that subsection.

(4) The discount shall not in any case reduce the price by more than such sum as the Secretary of State may by order prescribe.

(5) The period to be taken into account for the purposes of the discount is, subject to the following provisions of this section, the aggregate of the periods during which, before the service of the notice claiming to exercise the right to buy,—

  (a) the secure tenant or his spouse or deceased spouse was either a secure tenant or the spouse of a secure tenant; or

  (b) the secure tenant occupied accommodation provided for him as a member of the regular armed forces of the Crown or the secure tenant's spouse occupied accommodation so provided for the secure tenant's spouse.

(6) A period shall be taken into account under subsection (5) (a) above whether or not the dwelling-house or the landlord was the same as at the time of the service of the notice claiming to exercise the right to buy, unless the landlord was then a body specified in subsection (1) or (2) of section 2 of this Act; but—

  (a) no period during which the tenant's spouse was a secure tenant or the spouse of a secure tenant shall be so taken into account unless both the secure tenant and his spouse occupied the dwelling-house as their only or principal home at the time of the service of the notice; and

  (b) no period during which the tenant's deceased spouse was a secure tenant or the spouse of a secure tenant shall be so taken into account unless the tenant became the secure tenant on the death of his spouse and at the time of the death both occupied the dwelling-house as their only or principal home; and

  (c) a period during which either the tenant or his spouse or deceased spouse was the spouse of a secure tenant shall be taken into account only if during that period the spouses occupied the same dwelling-house as their only or principal home; and

  (d) subsection (5) (b) above applies only if the secure tenant or, as the case may be, his spouse was a member of the regular armed forces of the Crown on or after 21st December 1979.

(7) For the purposes of subsections (5) and (6) above a person who, as a joint tenant under a secure tenancy, occupied a dwelling-house as his only or principal home shall be treated as the secure tenant under that tenancy; and where the right to buy is exercised by joint tenants those subsections shall be construed as if for the secure tenant there was substituted that one of the joint tenants whose substitution will produce the largest discount.

(8) Where the person or one of the persons exercising the right to buy, or the spouse or deceased spouse of that person or of any of those persons, is or was a previous purchaser, a period shall be taken into account as a period during which the previous purchaser was, or was the spouse of, a secure tenant or during which he or his spouse occupied accommodation provided for him or his spouse as a member of the regular armed forces of the Crown, only if it falls after the completion of the previous purchase or, if more than one, the last of them.

93

(9) Subsections (5) to (8) above shall have effect as if—

    (*a*) the references to a secure tenancy included a tenancy which either was a secure tenancy within the meaning of the Tenants' Rights, Etc. (Scotland) Act 1980 or would have been such a tenancy if Part II of that Act had been in force and the bodies mentioned in section 10 (2) of that Act had included the predecessor of any such body; and

    (*b*) the references to a secure tenant included the tenant under such a tenancy as is mentioned in paragraph (*a*) above, except when the landlord was a body specified in paragraph (*e*) or (*g*) of section 10 (2) of the Act of 1980, and also included a tenant of the Northern Ireland Housing Executive or of a predecessor of that Executive.

(10) In subsection (8) above "previous purchaser" and "previous purchase" have the same meaning as in section 1 (6) above.

(11) In this section "regular armed forces of the Crown" has the same meaning as in section 1 of the House of Commons Disqualification Act 1975. **[336]**

COMMENCEMENT
    See the note to s. 1, *ante*.

SUB-S. (1): RIGHT TO BUY
    See s. 1, *ante*, and the notes thereto.

DISCOUNT
    As to repayment of the discount on early disposal of the freehold or lease, see s. 8, *post*.
    The discount to which the tenant is entitled, stating the period to be taken into account under sub-s. (5) above, and, where applicable, the amount mentioned in sub-s. (2) or (4) above, is one of the items that must be stated in the landlord's notice under s. 10, *post*; see s. 10(2) (*b*), *post*.

PRICE BEFORE DISCOUNT
    As to the price payable under this Chapter, see s. 6, *ante*.

DETERMINATION MADE BY THE SECRETARY OF STATE
    Such determinations are not published in the S.I. series but information about them may be obtained from the Housing Directorate, Department of the Environment, 2 Marsham Street, London, SW1P 3EB. As to the Secretary of State, see the note to s. 2, *ante*.

31ST MARCH 1974
    I.e., the day before the reorganisation of local government in England and Wales under the Local Government Act 1972, A.L.S. Vol. 209, took effect; see s. 273 (1) of that Act.

SUB-S. (5): PERIOD TO BE TAKEN INTO ACCOUNT, ETC.
    As to the position where a child succeeds his parent as the secure tenant, see s. 15, *post*.

NOTICE CLAIMING TO EXERCISE THE RIGHT TO BUY
    This notice is to be served under s. 5 (1), *ante*.

SUB-S. (7): RIGHT TO BUY IS EXERCISED BY JOINT TENANTS
    As to the exercise of the right to buy by joint tenants, see, in particular, s. 4 (1), *ante*.

JURISDICTION OF COUNTY COURT
    See the note to s. 1, *ante*.

DEFINITIONS
    For "the right to buy", see s. 1 (2), *ante*; for "dwelling-house", see s. 3 (1), (4), *ante* and s. 50 (2) as applied by s. 27 (1), *post*; for "landlord", see s. 27 (2), *post*; for "secure tenant", see ss. 27 (3), 28, 49 (2) and 150, *post*. Note as to "previous purchaser" and "previous purchase", sub-s. (10) above, and as to "regular armed forces of the Crown", sub-s. (11) above.

TENANTS' RIGHTS, ETC. (SCOTLAND) ACT 1980
    1980 c. 52.

ORDER UNDER THIS SECTION

The Housing (Right to Buy) (Maximum Discount) Order 1980, S.I. 1980 No. 1342 (made under sub-s. (4) above; prescribing the sum of £25,000 as the maximum sum by which the price payable for a dwelling-house may be reduced by discount under this section).

As to orders generally, see s. 151, *post*.

8. Repayment of discount on early disposal of freehold or lease

(1) A conveyance of the freehold or grant of a lease in pursuance of this Chapter shall (unless there is no discount) contain a covenant binding on the secure tenant and his successors in title to pay to the landlord on demand the amount specified in subsection (2) below if, within a period of five years, there is a disposal falling within subsection (3) below; but if there is more than one such disposal, then only on the first of them.

(2) The amount payable under the covenant is an amount equal to the discount to which the secure tenant was entitled, but reduced by 20 per cent. of that discount for each complete year which elapses after the conveyance or grant and before the disposal.

(3) A disposal falls within this subsection if it is—

    (*a*) a further conveyance of the freehold or an assignment of the lease; or

    (*b*) the grant of a lease or sub-lease for a term of more than twenty-one years otherwise than at a rack rent;

whether the disposal is of the whole or part of the dwelling-house; but a disposal in pursuance of an order under section 24 of the Matrimonial Causes Act 1973 or under section 2 of the Inheritance (Provision for Family and Dependants) Act 1975 or a vesting in a person taking under a will or on an intestacy is not a disposal falling within this subsection.

(4) The liability that may arise under the covenant required by subsection (1) above shall be a charge on the dwelling-house—

    (*a*) taking effect as if it had been created by deed expressed to be by way of legal mortgage; and

    (*b*) having priority immediately after any legal charge securing any amount left outstanding by the tenant in exercising the right to buy or advanced to him by a body specified in subsection (5) below for the purpose of enabling him to exercise it or further advanced to him by that body.

(5) The bodies referred to in subsection (4) (*b*) above are—

    (*a*) the Housing Corporation;

    (*b*) any building society; and

    (*c*) any of the bodies specified in paragraph 6, 7 or 8 of the Schedule to the Home Purchase Assistance and Housing Corporation Guarantee Act 1978.

(6) A charge taking effect by virtue of subsection (4) above shall, notwithstanding subsection (5) of section 59 of the Land Registration Act 1925, be a land charge for the purposes of that section, and subsection (2) of that section shall apply accordingly with respect to its protection and realisation.

(7) The reference in subsection (3) above to a lease or sublease does not include a mortgage term.

(8) In this section "building society" means a building society within the meaning of the Building Societies Act 1962 or the Building Societies Act (Northern Ireland) 1967; and for the purposes of this section the grant of an option enabling a person to call for a disposal falling within subsection (3) above shall be treated as such a disposal. **[337]**

COMMENCEMENT
See the note to s. 1, *ante*.

SUB-S. (1): CONVEYANCE ... OR GRANT ... IN PURSUANCE OF THIS CHAPTER
I.e., under s. 16, *post*; and cf. s. 24, *post*.

COVENANT
As a positive covenant, the covenant to repay discount runs presumably, only by virtue of s. 8 of this Act—a positive covenant does not run with the freehold at law: *Austerberry* v. *Oldham Corporation* (1885) 29 Ch.D. 750 (unless the Law of Property Act 1925, s. 79, reverse this: *sed quaere*).

In relation at any rate to the freehold, with respect to which the following remarks are confined, a question arises as to the extent of the term "successors in title" in s. 8 (1). This is because a wide meaning was given to it where used in the Law of Property Act 1925, s. 78 (1), so as to comprehend not just the freeholder but even a tenant for years: *Smith and Snipes Hall Farm* v. *River Douglas Catchment Board* [1949] 2 K.B. 500; [1949] 2 All E.R. 179, C.A., cf. *Federated Homes Ltd* v. *Mill Lodge Properties Ltd.* [1980] 1 All E.R. 371, C.A. If this is to be applied to s. 8 (1) (and the present section is new, rather than merely a re-enactment of previous legislation) then it would certainly mean that one would not need to have to show that the defendant had the same legal estate as the original covenantor as a condition precedent to liability to repay discount. So, on this admittedly wide view, suppose that X, on a conveyance of the freehold of a house in 1981, leased the whole of it to T for 30 years in 1982 at an annual rent of £50 (presumably this attracts s. 8 (1): s. 8 (3) (*b*)) not only is X liable as the original covenantor, but so too is T as a successor in title; this would be useful to the plaintiff supposing one of the two of them to be insolvent at the date of the action. It must be said that the question is open.

SUB-S. (2): DISCOUNT TO WHICH THE SECURE TENANT WAS ENTITLED
See s. 7, *ante*.

SUB-S. (3): RACK RENT
The expression is not defined for the purposes of this Act, but cf., for example, the Housing Act 1957, s. 39 (2), A.L.S. Vol. 109, where the expression is defined to mean a rent which is not less than two-thirds of the full net annual value.

SUB-S. (4): CHARGE ... TAKING EFFECT AS IF IT HAD BEEN CREATED BY ... LEGAL MORTGAGE
As to the effect of the creation of such a charge, see the Law of Property Act 1925, s. 87. The effect of this provision is that the chargee is enabled to exercise the powers mentioned in s. 101, of that Act. For a case in point, see *Payne* v. *Cardiff Rural District Council*, [1932] 1 K.B. 241; [1931] All E.R. Rep. 479.

CHARGEE'S RIGHTS
As to these, see the Law of Property Act 1925, s. 87 (1). The only person to whom the chargee is postponed is the prior legal mortgagee in respect of sums advanced to the secure tenant (sub-s. (4) (*b*)). Subsection (5) of this section overrides s. 59 (5) of the Land Registration Act 1925, which excludes a puisne legal mortgage from its operation. So the charge is sub-s. (4) is a registrable land charge within s. 59, *ibid.*, and may accordingly be registered either as a caution or a notice.

REGISTRATION AS A CAUTIONER
If the landlord is unable to procure the Land Certificate, then he will seek registration of the charge as a cautioner: see the Land Registration Act 1925, s. 54 (1), and for the prescribed forms and particulars, see the Land Registration Rules 1925, rr. 215–228, and esp. also Form No. 63. By the Land Registration Act 1925, s. 55 (1), the cautioner is entitled to object to a dealing with the land affected by it upon being warned off by the Land Registry as provided in the Land Registration Rules, 1925, rr. 218–220. He has 14 days to object: *ibid.*, r. 218 (2).

A cautioner does *not* lose his rights just because of the ignorance, say, of a transferee of the property from the secure tenant, even where such ignorance results from a mistake at the Land Registry: *Parkash* v. *Irani Finance Ltd.* [1970] Ch. 101; [1969] 1 All E.R. 930.

After the lapse of 5 years from the date of the conveyance to the secure tenant, the liability to repay ceases, and presumably the registered proprietor for the time being could then apply if need be for the removal of the caution under s. 82 (1) (*b*) of the 1925 Act.

REGISTRATION OF A NOTICE
Despite what has been said about the registration of the charge as a caution where no Land Certificate can be produced, since the notice is the more effective protection, it is to be hoped that despite the Land Registration Act 1925, s. 64 (1) (*c*), such production will not be a condition precedent to registration of the charge under sub-s. (4) as a notice. After all, it is unnecessary to do this where a lessee applies for registration of a lease (*Strand Securities Ltd.* v. *Caswell* [1965] Ch. 958; [1965] 1 All E.R. 820, C.A.).

If available, then the chargee's protection by a notice is such that by the Land Registration Act 1925, s. 52 (1), any subsequent dealing with the land takes effect subject to the notice and the proprietor is deemed to be affected with the notice: *ibid.*, s. 48 (1), as are his successors in title.

The application for registration of a notice must, by the Land Registration Rules 1925, r. 190 (1), be in Form 59.

SIGNIFICANCE OF BEING A CHARGEE
By the Law of Property Act 1925, s. 87 (1), the chargee under sub-s. (4) is entitled, as such, to the "same protection, powers and remedies" as if he had a mortgage by demise or sub-demise. If the prior mortgagee is a building society, the chargee will be protected by the fact that it is under a duty to obtain the best price reasonably obtainable on sale (see the Building Societies Act 1962, s. 36). If the first mortgagee is not a building society, then the chargee is protected by the negligence duty on sale: *Tomlin* v. *Luce* (1889) 43 Ch. D. 191, CA; also *Cuckmere Brick Co. Ltd.* v. *Mutual Finance Ltd.* [1971] Ch. 949; [1971] 2 All E.R. 633, C.A. If the first mortgagee were to bring a foreclosure action, the chargee could apply under the Law of Property Act 1925, s. 91 (2) for an order for sale in lieu. Neither of these possibilities would affect his personal action on the covenant in s. 8 (1) of this Act to repay the discount: cf. *Rudge* v. *Ritchens* (1873) L.R. 8 C.P. 358; 42 L.J.C.P. 127.

OPTION (SUB-S. (7))
This prevents the avoidance of a liability to repay discount by the tenant granting, within the 5 year period, an option to purchase the dwelling-house to one who intends to purchase. The latter might then be allowed to take possession; but in any case, were it not for sub-s. (7), it is thought that the granting of the option would not have been a "disposal" and would not have been caught by s. 8.

AMOUNT LEFT OUTSTANDING BY THE TENANT
As to the tenant's right to do this, see s. 1 (1) (*c*), *ante*.

SUB-S (5): HOUSING CORPORATION
See the note to s. 1, *ante*.

DWELLING-HOUSES IN NATIONAL PARKS, ETC.
This section is excluded by s. 19 (7), *post*, in relation to houses in National Parks, etc.

JURISDICTION OF COUNTY COURT
See the note to s. 1, *ante*.

DEFINITIONS
For "the right to buy", see s. 1 (2), *ante*; for "dwelling-house", see s. 3 (1), (4), *ante*, and s. 50 (2) as applied by s. 27 (1), *post*, for "landlord", see s. 27 (2), *post*; for "secure tenant", see ss. 27 (3), 28, 49 (2) and 150, *post*. Note as to "lease" and "sub-lease", sub-s, (7) above; as to "building society", sub-s. (8) above; and as to "disposal falling within subsection (3)", sub-ss. (3) and (8) above.

MATRIMONIAL CAUSES ACT 1973, S. 24
See A.L.S. Vol. 217.

INHERITANCE (PROVISION FOR FAMILY AND DEPENDANTS) ACT 1975, S. 2
See A.L.S. Vol. 236.

HOME PURCHASE ASSISTANCE AND HOUSING CORPORATION GUARANTEE ACT 1978, SCHEDULE, PARAS. 6–8
See A.L.S. Vol. 258.

BUILDING SOCIETIES ACT 1962
For the meaning of "building society", see s. 1 of that Act.

BUILDING SOCIETIES ACT (NORTHERN IRELAND) 1967
   1967 C. 31 (N.I.).

9. Right to a mortgage–amount to be secured

(1) The amount which a secure tenant exercising the right to a mortgage is entitled to leave outstanding, or have advanced to him, on the security of the dwelling-house is, subject to the limit imposed by this section, the aggregate of—

   (a) the purchase price;
   (b) so much of the costs incurred by the landlord or the Housing Corporation as is chargeable to the tenant under section 21; and
   (c) any costs incurred by the tenant and defrayed on his behalf by the landlord or the Housing Corporation.

(2) The amount mentioned in subsection (1) above is subject to the limit that it does not exceed the amount to be taken into account, in accordance with regulations under this section, as the tenant's available annual income multiplied by such factor as, under the regulations, is appropriate to it.

(3) Where the right to a mortgage belongs to more than one person the limit is the aggregate of the amounts to be taken into account in accordance with the regulations as the available annual income of each of them, after multiplying each of those amounts by the factor appropriate to it under the regulations.

(4) The Secretary of State may by regulations make provision for calculating the amount which is to be taken into account under this section as a person's available annual income and for specifying a factor appropriate to it; and the regulations—

   (a) may provide for arriving at a person's available annual income by deducting from the sums taken into account as his annual income sums related to his needs and commitments, and may exclude sums from those to be taken into account as a person's annual income; and
   (b) may (without prejudice to the generality of section 151 (3) of this Act) specify different amounts and different factors for different circumstances.

(5) Where the amount which a secure tenant is entitled to leave outstanding on the security of the dwelling-house is reduced by the limit imposed by this section, the landlord may, if it thinks fit and the tenant agrees, treat him as entitled to leave outstanding on that security such amount exceeding the limit but not exceeding the aggregate mentioned in subsection (1) above as the landlord may determine. **[338]**

COMMENCEMENT
   See the note to s. 1, *ante*.

SUB-S. (1): RIGHT TO A MORTGAGE
   See s. 1, *ante*, and the notice thereto.

PURCHASE PRICE
   See ss. 6 and 7, *ante*.

HOUSING CORPORATION
   See the note to s. 1, *ante*.

SUB-S. (3): RIGHT TO A MORTGAGE BELONGS TO MORE THAN ONE PERSON
   I.e., by virtue of s. 4, *ante*.

SUB-S, (4): SECRETARY OF STATE
   See the note to s. 2, *ante*.

JURISDICTION OF COUNTY COURT
   See the note to s. 1, *ante*.

For "the right to a mortgage", see s. 1 (2), *ante*; as to "purchase price", see s. 1 (8), *ante*; for "dwelling-house", see s. 3 (1), (4), *ante*, and s. 50 (2) as applied by s. 27 (1), *post*; for "landlord", see s. 27 (2), *post*; for "secure tenant", see ss. 27 (3), 28, 49 (2) and 150, *post*.

REGULATIONS UNDER THIS SECTION
The Housing (Right to Buy) (Mortgage Limit) Regulations 1980, S.I. 1980 No 1423 (made under sub-s. (4) above).
As to regulations generally, see s. 151, *post*.

10. Notice of purchase price and right to a mortgage

(1) Where a secure tenant has claimed to exercise the right to buy and that right has been established (whether by the landlord's admission or otherwise) the landlord shall, as soon as practicable, serve on the tenant a notice describing the dwelling-house and stating—

(a) the price at which, in the opinion of the landlord, the tenant is entitled to have the freehold conveyed or, as the case may be, the long lease granted to him; and

(b) the provisions which, in the opinion of the landlord, should be contained in the conveyance or grant.

(2) The notice shall, for the purpose of showing how the price has been arrived at, state—

(a) the value at the relevant time;

(b) the discount to which the tenant is entitled, stating—

(i) the period to be taken into account under section 7 (5); and, where applicable,

(ii) the amount mentioned in section 7 (2) or (4); and

(c) the improvements disregarded in pursuance of section 6.

(3) The notice shall also inform the tenant—

(a) of his right under section 11 to have the value at the relevant time determined or re-determined by the district valuer;

(b) of the right to a mortgage; and

(c) of the effect of section 12 and section 16 (4) below;

and shall be accompanied by a form for use by the tenant in exercising the right to a mortgage. **[339]**

See the note to s. 1, *ante*.

CLAIMED TO EXERCISE THE RIGHT TO BUY
I.e., pursuant to a notice under s. 5, *ante*.

RIGHT HAS BEEN ESTABLISHED (WHETHER BY THE LANDLORD'S ADMISSION OR OTHERWISE)
As to such admission, see s. 5, *ante*, and as to proceedings in the county court to establish the right to buy, see the note "Jurisdiction of county court" to s. 1, *ante*.

PRACTICABLE
The meaning of this word and the difference between "practicable" and the less strict standard of "reasonably practicable" have been most frequently considered by the courts in connection with the occurrence of these terms in safety legislation; see, in particular, the note "So far as practicable" to the Factories Act 1961, s. 4, Vol. 13, p. 408, and 20 Halsbury's Laws (4th Edn.), para. 553, and the cases there cited. See also *Hammond* v. *Haigh Castle & Co., Ltd.* [1973] 2 All E.R. 289; *Owen* v. *Crown House Engineering, Ltd.* [1973] 3 All E.R. 618; and *Dedman* v. *British Building and Engineering Appliances, Ltd.* [1974] 1 All E.R. 520, C.A.

In relation to the term "as soon as reasonably practicable" in the Road Safety Act 1967, A.L.S. Vol. 165, s. 2 (1), it has been held that it is a question of fact for the recorder: *Arnold* v. *Kingston-upon-Hull Constable* [1969] 3 All E.R. 646; *Reg.* v. *Pearson (Donald)* [1974] R.T.R. 92, C.A.; and it depends on the context: *Rickwood* v. *Cochrane* [1978] R.T.R. 218.

While it is thought that, as with the term "as soon as possible", action is required as soon as convenient: *Re Rooke* [1953] Ch. 716; 1953 2 All E.R. 110, it does not necessarily mean "at once": cf. *Albinson* v. *Newroyd Mill Ltd.* [1926] 134 L.T. 171, C.A.

NOTICE

As to notices generally, see s. 32, *post*.

PRICE AT WHICH . . . THE TENANT IS ENTITLED TO HAVE THE FREEHOLD CONVEYED, ETC.

As to the computation of this price, see ss. 6 and 7, *ante*.

PROVISIONS WHICH . . . SHOULD BE CONTAINED IN THE CONVEYANCE OR GRANT

I.e., in accordance with s. 17 and Sch. 2, *post*.

VALUE AT THE RELEVANT TIME

As to the calculation of this value, see s. 6 (2)–(5), *ante*.

DISCOUNT TO WHICH THE TENANT IS ENTITLED

See s. 7, *ante*.

RIGHT TO A MORTGAGE

See s. 1, *ante*, and the notes thereto.

JURISDICTION OF COUNTY COURT

See the note to s. 1, *ante*.

DEFINITIONS

For "the right to buy" and "the right to a mortgage", see s. 1 (2), *ante*; for "dwelling-house", see s. 3 (1), (4), *ante* and s. 50 (2) as applied by s. 27 (1), *post*; for "district valuer" and "landlord", see s. 27 (2), *post*; for "relevant time", see s. 3 (1), (5), *ante*; for "secure tenant", see ss. 27 (3), 28, 49 (2) and 150, *post*; for "improvement", see s. 81 (5), *post*.

11. Right of tenant to have value determined by district valuer

(1) Any question arising under this Chapter as to the value of a dwelling-house at the relevant time shall be determined by the district valuer in accordance with this section.

(2) A tenant may require that value to be determined or, as the case may be, re-determined by a notice in writing served on the landlord not later than three months after the service on him of the notice under section 10; except that—

(a) if proceedings are then pending between the landlord and the tenant for the determination of any other question arising under this Chapter, the notice may be served at any time within three months of the final determination of the proceedings, and

(b) if such proceedings are begun after a previous determination under this section the notice may be served within four weeks of the final determination of the proceedings and, whether or not such a notice is served, the landlord may at any time within those four weeks require the district valuer to re-determine the value of the dwelling-house at the relevant time.

(3) Where the landlord requires a re-determination to be made in pursuance of subsection (2) (b) above it shall serve on the tenant a notice stating that the requirement is being or has been made.

(4) Before making a determination or re-determination in pursuance of this section the district valuer shall consider any representation made to him by the landlord or the tenant within 4 weeks from the service of the tenant's notice under this section, or, as the case may be, from the service of the landlord's notice under subsection (3) above.

(5) As soon as practicable after a determination or re-determination has been made in pursuance of this section the landlord shall serve on the tenant a notice stating the effect of the determination or re-determination and the matters mentioned in subsections (1) and (2) of section 10.

(6) A notice under subsection (5) above shall inform the tenant of the right to a mortgage and of the effect of section 12 below and shall be accompanied by a form to be used by the tenant in exercising the right to a mortgage. **[340]**

COMMENCEMENT
See the note to s. 1, *ante*.

SUB-S. (1): VALUE ... AT THE RELEVANT TIME
As to the calculation of this value, see s. 6 (2)–(5), *ante*.

SUB-S. (2): TENANT MAY REQUIRE THAT VALUE TO BE DETERMINED, ETC.
A landlord's notice under s. 10, *ante*, must inform the tenant of his right under this section to have the value determined by a district valuer; see s. 10 (3) (*a*), *ante*.

NOTICE
As to notice generally, see s. 22, *post*.

WRITING
See the note "Written; writing" to s. 5, *ante*.

NOT LATER THAN THREE MONTHS AFTER, ETC.
The general rule in the computation of periods of time is that, unless there is a sufficient indication to the contrary, the day on which the initial event occurs is to be excluded and the last day is to be included and that fractions of a day are to be ignored; see generally 37 Halsbury's Laws (3rd Edn.), pp. 92, 100. "Months" means calendar months"; see the Interpretation Act 1978, s. 5, Sch. 1, A.L.S. Vol. 258.

PROCEEDINGS ... FOR THE DETERMINATION OF ANY OTHER QUESTION ARISING UNDER THIS CHAPTER

These proceedings would normally take place in a county court; see the note "Jurisdiction of county court" to s. 1, *ante*.

WITHIN THREE MONTHS (FOUR WEEKS) OF, ETC.
See the note "within six months of, etc." to s. 3, *ante*.

SUB-S. (4): DETERMINATION OR RE-DETERMINATION
Procedure
Judicial review is governed by the procedure under R.S.C. Ord. 53. By r. 2 the application for *certiorari* is subject to a 6 month time limit, which may be extended at discretion: r. 3.
    Assuming that the determination of a district valuer is reviewable for excess of jurisdiction or for error of law on the face of the record, four remedies seem relevant: *certiorari*, prohibition, *mandamus* and a declaration.

Excess of jurisdiction
Judicial review is thought to be available against the district valuer, because his decision under s. 11 as to the value of a dwelling-house will affect the rights of subjects whether or not he is acting judicially: *R.* v. *Electricity Commissioners* [1924] 1 K.B. 171, C.A.; *Ridge* v. *Baldwin* [1964] A.C. 40; [1963] 2 All E.R. 77, H.L. Accordingly, *certiorari* has been held to lie against planning authorities: *R.* v. *London Borough of Hillingdon, ex parte Royco Homes Ltd.* [1974] Q.B. 720; [1974] 2 All E.R. 643; also against valuation officers: *R.* v. *Paddington Valuation Officer, ex parte Peachey Property Corporation Ltd.* [1966] 1 Q.B. 380; [1965] 2 All E.R. 836, C.A.

It thus appears that the court may review any initial decision of the district valuer as to whether or not he had jurisdiction within Chapter I. He might well have to decide whether or not the premises are a "dwelling-house" within s. 3. If he wrongly assumes a jurisdiction there is no determination or re-determination at all within this section and the decision (so-called) is liable to be quashed: *R.* v. *Tottenham and District Rent Tribunal, ex parte Northfield (Highgate) Ltd.* [1957] 1 Q.B. 103; 1956 2 All E.R. 863; *Anisminic Ltd.* v. *Foreign Compensation Commission* [1969] 2 A.C. 147; [1969] 1 All E.R. 208, H.L.

If, in the application for judicial review, prohibition is sought, it is available so soon as the district valuer indicates an intention to exceed his jurisdiction: *R.* v. *Tottenham etc. Rent Tribunal, supra.*

Error of law on the face of the record
A few select points from this tricky area may be made here. In the first place, the fact that the district valuer comes to a "wrong" decision does not suffice of itself to establish excess of jurisdiction: *R.* v. *Central Criminal Court J J* (1886) 17 Ch.D. 602; *R.* v. *Rent Tribunal for Paddington and St Marylebone* [1947] 1 All E.R. 448.

If there is an error of law on the face of the record which goes to jurisdiction (and possibly failure to comply with the statutory duty in sub-s. (4) to consider the representations of either or both landlord or tenant might, if it were a total refusal) then the court may quash the determination: *R.* v. *Northumberland Compensation Appeal Tribunal, ex parte Shaw* [1952] 1 K.B. 338; [1952] 1 All E.R. 122, C.A.; *R.* v. *Paddington North & St Marylebone Rent Tribunal, ex parte Perry* [1956] 1 Q.B. 229; [1955] 3 All E.R. 391. On this principle, it has been held that a valuation list, as a whole, which was shown to have been prepared on an erroneous basis, could be set aside: *R.* v. *Paddington Valuation Officer, ex parte Peachey Property Corporation Ltd.* [1966] 1 Q.B. 380; [1965] 2 All E.R. 836, C.A. In the case of the Commissioners of Inland Revenue, the court has power to interfere with a determination if, and only if, the facts found are such that no person acting judicially and properly instructed as the relevant law could have come to the determination in fact reached: the court has no alternative but to assume that an error of law was responsible for the (mis) determination: *Edwards* v. *Bairstow* [1956] A.C. 1; [1955] 3 All E.R. 48, H.L.; *Tyrer* v. *Smart* [1979] 1 All E.R. 321, H.L.

If a determination should be quashed, or for that matter in any case where the district valuer wrongfully refuses to comply with a tenant's requirement in sub-s. (2), then it is thought that *mandamus* would lie to compel the district valuer to determine the value of the dwelling-house: *R.* v. *Northumberland Compensation Appeal Tribunal, ex parte Shaw, supra; R.* v. *Pugh (Judge)* [1951] 2 K.B. 623; [1951] 2 All E.R. 307. Thus, a local authority under a duty to re-house a displaced tenant is subject to *mandamus* (if the applicant is not guilty of unreasonable delay): *R.* v. *Bristol Corporation, ex parte Hendy* [1974] 1 All E.R. 1047, C.A.

(I am grateful to Professor P. Jackson for commenting most helpfully on an earlier draft of this note; responsibility for the whole of it falls on the author.)

SHALL CONSIDER
Independently of this mandatory requirement, it may be that a failure by the district valuer to act in accordance with the principles of natural justice might afford grounds for *certiorari* by the person aggrieved: cf. *R.* v. *London Rent Assessment Committee, ex parte Hanson* [1977] 3 All E.R. 404, C.A., dealing with what is now Rent Act 1977 Sch. 11. As there, a matter of public interest, viz., a determination of price, is involved.

There is no express provision in any part of s. 11 as to withdrawal of a landlord's or tenant's notice to the district valuer, and it is conceived that, as with the Rent Acts, no right not to withdraw will be implied into s. 11: cf. *R.* v. *Hampstead & St Pancras Rent Tribunal, ex parte Goodman* [1951] 1 All E.R. 170.

WITHIN 4 WEEKS FROM, ETC.
See the note "Within six months of, etc." to s. 3, *ante.*

SUB-S. (5): PRACTICABLE
See the note to s. 10, *ante.*

SUB-S. (6): RIGHT TO A MORTGAGE
See s. 1, *ante,* and the notes thereto.

DEFINITIONS
For "the right to a mortgage", see s. 1 (2), *ante;* for "dwelling-house", see s. 3 (1), (4), *ante,* and s. 50 (2) as applied by s. 27 (1), *post;* for "relevant time", see s. 3 (1), (5), *ante;* for "district valuer" and "landlord", see s. 27 (2), *post.*

12. Claim to a mortgage

(1) A secure tenant cannot exercise his right to a mortgage unless he claims to exercise it by notice in writing served on the landlord or, if the landlord is a housing association, on the Housing Corporation, within the period of three months beginning with the service on the tenant of the relevant notice, or within that period as extended under subsection (2) below.

(2) Where there are reasonable grounds for doing so, the landlord or, as the case may be, the Housing Corporation, shall by notice in writing served on the tenant extend (or further extend) the period within which the tenant's notice claiming to exercise his right to a mortgage must be served; and if it fails to do so the county court may by order extend or further extend that period until such date as may be specified in the order.

(3) The relevant notice is—

    (a) if the tenant exercises his right under section 11, the notice served under subsection (5) of that section; and

    (b) if he does not exercise that right, the notice served under section 10 above.

(4) As soon as practicable after the service on it of a notice under subsection (1) above the landlord or Housing Corporation shall serve on the tenant a notice in writing stating—

    (a) the amount which, in the opinion of the landlord or Housing Corporation, the tenant is entitled to leave outstanding or have advanced on the security of the dwelling-house; and

    (b) how that amount has been arrived at; and

    (c) the provisions which, in the opinion of the landlord or Housing Corporation, should be contained in the deed by which the mortgage is to be effected.

(5) The notice shall also inform the tenant of the effect of section 16 (8) below and shall be accompanied by a form for use by the tenant in claiming, in accordance with section 16 (4) (c) below, to be entitled to defer completion.

(6) The Housing Corporation shall send to the landlord a copy of any notice served by it on the tenant under subsection (4) above. **[341]**

COMMENCEMENT
    See the note to s. 1, *ante*.

GENERAL NOTE (SUB-SS. (1) AND (2))
    But for sub-s. (2), which enables extensions to be made by the landlord or on application, the court, to the three-month time limit on the service of a tenant's mortgage notice, it is probable that time would have been held to be of the essence, because the right to a mortgage depends only on the initiative of the tenant to trigger it. In relation to the Landlord and Tenant Act 1954, A.L.S. Vol. 87, s. 29 (3), time has been held to be of the essence: *Beardmore Motors Ltd.* v. *Birch Bros (Properties) Ltd.* [1959] Ch. 298. It is true that in relation to rent review clauses with a trigger mechanism, the House of Lords has recently held time not to be of the essence, by (false) analogy with vendor-purchaser cases: *United Scientific Holdings Ltd.* v. *Burnley B.C.* [1977] 2 All E.R. 62, H.L.
    Quite apart from the extension enabling provision in sub-s. (2), a landlord could presumably accept service of a mortgage notice out of time (irrespective, therefore, of the existence of reasonable grounds for doing so): cf. *Kammins Ballrooms Co. Ltd.* v. *Zenith Investments (Torquay) Ltd.* [1971] A.C. 850; 1970 2 All E.R. 871, H.L.
    As to what will be reasonable grounds under sub-s. (2), this must be essentially a question of fact: *e.g.* T by error serves his notice 2 days out of time; or T, being abroad at the time for due service, returns after 2 further weeks and then serves it out of time.

SUB-S. (1): RIGHT TO A MORTGAGE
    See s. 1, *ante*, and the notes thereto.

NOTICE

As to notices generally, see s. 22, *post.*

A tenant who is entitled to defer completion may, at any time before the service on him of a notice under s. 16 (2), *post,* serve a further notice under sub-s. (1) above and, if he does so, sub-s. (4) above and (where applicable) sub-s. (6) above apply accordingly; see s. 16 (8), *post.*

A notice claiming to exercise the right to buy is to be served under s. 5, *ante.*

WRITING

See the note "Written; writing" to s. 5, *ante.*

HOUSING ASSOCIATION; HOUSING CORPORATION

See the notes to s. 1, *ante.*

THREE MONTHS BEGINNING WITH, ETC.

The use of the phrase "beginning with" makes it clear that in computing this period the day from which it runs is to be included; see *Hare* v. *Gocher,* [1962] 2 Q.B. 641; [1962] 2 All E.R. 763; and *Trow* v. *Ind. Coope (West Midlands), Ltd.* [1967] 2 Q.B. at p. 909; [1967] 2 All E.R. 900, C.A. "Months" means calendar months; see the Interpretation Act 1978, s. 5, Sch. 1, Vol. 48, pp. 1299, 1319.

SUB-S. (2): COUNTY COURT

I.e., a court held for a district under the County Courts Act 1959; see the Interpretation Act 1978, s. 5, Sch. 1, A.L.S. Vol. 258. As to the county court districts, see ss. 1 and 2 of the Act of 1959, and the orders noted to the said s. 2. As to the jurisdiction of the county court, see also the note thereon to s. 1, *ante.*

SUB-S. (3): NOTICE SERVED UNDER SUB-S. (5) OF THAT SECTION

That notice must inform the tenant of the effect of this section; see s. 11 (6), *ante.*

NOTICE SERVED UNDER S. 10

That notice must inform the tenant of the effect of this section; see s. 10 (3) (c), *ante.*

SUB-S. (4): PRACTICABLE

See the note to s. 10, *ante.*

AMOUNT WHICH ... THE TENANT IS TO LEAVE OUTSTANDING, ETC.

As to the computation of this amount, see s. 9, *ante.*

DEFINITIONS

For "the right to a mortgage", see s. 1 (2), *ante;* for "dwelling-house", see s. 3 (1), (4), *ante,* and s. 50 (2) as applied by s. 27 (1), *post;* for the "landlord", see s. 27 (2), *post;* for "secure tenant", see ss. 27 (3), 28, 49 (2) and 150, *post.* Note as to the "relevant notice", sub-s. (3) above.

13. Change of secure tenant after notice claiming right to buy

(1) Where, after a secure tenant (in this section referred to as "the former tenant") has given a notice claiming the right to buy, another person (in this section referred to as "the new tenant") becomes the secure tenant—

    (*a*) under the same secure tenancy; or

    (*b*) under a periodic tenancy arising by virtue of section 29 of this Act on the coming to an end of the secure tenancy;

the new tenant shall be in the same position as if the notice has been given by him and he had been the secure tenant at the time it was given.

(2) If a notice under section 10 of this Act has been served on the former tenant, the landlord shall serve on the new tenant a further form for his use in exercising the right to a mortgage and the new tenant may then serve a notice under section 12 (1) within the period of three months beginning with the service on him of that form or within that period as extended under subsection (3) below.

(3) Where there are reasonable grounds for doing so the landlord or, as the case

may be, the Housing Corporation shall by notice in writing served on the new tenant extend (or further extend) the period within which his notice claiming to exercise the right to a mortgage may be served; and if it fails to do so the county court may by order extend or further extend that period until such date as may be specified in the order.

(4) The preceding provisions of this section do not confer any right on a person required in pursuance of section 4 (2) to share the right to buy unless he could have been validly so required had the notice claiming to exercise the right to buy been given by the new tenant.

(5) The preceding provisions of this section apply with the necessary modifications if there is a further change in the person who is the secure tenant. **[342]**

COMMENCEMENT
　　See the note to s. 1, *ante*.

SUB-S. (1): NOTICE CLAIMING THE RIGHT TO BUY
　　See s. 5, *ante*.

ANOTHER PERSON ... BECOMES THE SECURE TENANT
　　For provisions which apply where there is a change of landlord after service of a notice claiming the right to buy, see ss. 14, *post*.

SUB-S. (2): THREE MONTHS BEGINNING WITH, ETC.
　　See the note to s. 12, *ante*.

SUB-S. (3): HOUSING CORPORATION
　　See the note to s. 1, *ante*.

NOTICE
　　As to notices generally, see s. 22, *post*.

WRITING
　　See the note "Written; writing" to s. 5, *ante*.

NOTICE CLAIMING ... THE RIGHT TO A MORTGAGE
　　See s. 12, *ante*.

COUNTY COURT
　　See the note to s. 12, *ante*.

SUB-S. (4): RIGHT TO BUY
　　See s. 1, *ante*, and the notes thereto.

DEFINITIONS
　　For "the right to buy" and "the right to a mortgage", see s. 1 (2), *ante*; for "landlord", see s. 27 (2), *post*; for "secure tenant" and for "secure tenancy", see ss. 27 (3), 28, 49 (2) and 150, *post*. Note as to "the former tenant" and "the new tenant", sub-s. (1) above.

14. Change of landlord after notice claiming right to buy or right to a mortgage

Where, after a secure tenant has given a notice claiming to exercise the right to buy or the right to a mortgage, the freehold of the dwelling-house passes from the landlord to another body, all parties shall be in the same position as if the other body had become the landlord before the notice was given and had been given that notice and any further notice given by the tenant to the landlord and had taken all steps which the landlord had taken. **[343]**

COMMENCEMENT
　　See the note to s. 1, *ante*.

NOTICE CLAIMING ... THE RIGHT TO BUY OR THE RIGHT TO A MORTGAGE
　　See ss. 5 and 12, *ante*.

FREEHOLD ... PASSES ... TO ANOTHER BODY
For provisions which apply where there is a change of secure tenant after service of a notice claiming the right to buy, see s. 13, *ante.*

DEFINITIONS
For "dwelling-house", see s. 3 (1), (4), *ante*, and s. 50 (2) as applied by s. 27 (1), *post*; for "landlord", see s. 27 (2), *post*; for "secure tenant", see ss. 27 (3), 28, 49 (2) and 150, *post.*

15. Children succeeding parents

(1) Where the secure tenant of a dwelling-house (in this section referred to as "the former tenant") dies or otherwise ceases to be a secure tenant of the dwelling-house, and thereupon a child of his who occupies the dwelling-house as his only or principal home (in this section referred to as "the new tenant") becomes the secure tenant of the dwelling-house (whether under the same or under another secure tenancy), the landlord may, if it thinks fit, count the whole or part of any period qualifying under this section—

    (a) for the purposes of section 1 (3) above; or

    (b) towards the period to be taken into account under section 7 (5) above for the purposes of discount;

or both (and may count different periods under paragraph (a) and (b) above).

(2) A period qualifies under this section if it is a period during which the new tenant, since reaching the age of sixteen, occupied as his only or principal home a dwelling-house of which a parent of his was the secure tenant or one of joint tenants under a secure tenancy, and either—

    (a) it was the period at the end of which he became the secure tenant; or

    (b) it was a period ending not earlier than two years before another period qualifying under this section.

(3) For the purposes of this section two persons shall be treated as parent and child if they would be so treated under paragraphs (a) and (b) of section 50 (3) of this Act.

(4) This section has effect, whether or not the former tenant and the new tenant are also the former tenant and the new tenant within the meaning of section 13 above. **[344]**

COMMENCEMENT
See the note to s. 1, *ante.*

REACHING THE AGE OF SIXTEEN
A person attains a particular age expressed in years at the commencement of the relevant anniversary of the date of his birth; see the Family Law Reform Act 1969, s. 9, A.L.S. Vol. 189.

DEFINITIONS
For "dwelling-house", see s. 3 (1), (4), *ante*, and s. 50 (2) as applied by s. 27 (1), *post*; as to "joint tenant", see s. 4 (3), *ante*; for "landlord", see s. 27 (2), *post*; for "secure tenant" and "secure tenancy", see ss. 27 (3), 28, 49 (2) and 150, *post*. Note as to "the former tenant" and "the new tenant", sub-s. (1) above, and as to "parent" and "child", sub-s. (3) above.

16. Completion

(1) Where a secure tenant has claimed to exercise the right to buy and that right has been established, the landlord shall be bound, subject to the following provisions of this section, to make to the tenant—

    (a) if the dwelling-house is a house, a grant of the dwelling-house for an estate in fee simple absolute; and (*b*) if the dwelling-house is a flat, a grant of a lease of the dwelling-house for a term of not less than 125 years (subject to paragraph 11 (2) of Schedule 2 to this Act);

as soon as all matters relating to the grant and to the amount to be left outstanding or advanced on the security of the dwelling-house have been agreed or determined.

    (2) If, after all those matters have been agreed or determined, the tenant does not take all steps necessary to complete the transaction, the landlord may serve on him a notice requiring him to complete the transaction within a period stated in the notice, but the period stated in the notice shall not be less than 28 days.

    (3) A notice under subsection (2) above shall not be served earlier than whichever of the following is applicable, that is to say—

    (*a*) if the tenant has not claimed to exercise the right to a mortgage, three months after the end of the period within which a notice claiming it could have been served by him;

    (*b*) if he has claimed the right to a mortgage, but is not entitled to defer completion, three months after the service of the notice under section 12 (4); and

    (*c*) if he is entitled to defer completion, two years after the service of his notice under section 5 claiming the exercise of the right to buy or, if later, three months after the service of the notice under section 12 (4) above.

    (4) A tenant is entitled to defer completion if—

    (*a*) he has claimed the right to a mortgage; and

    (*b*) the amount which he is entitled, or is treated as being entitled, to leave outstanding or have advnced on the security of the dwelling-house is less than the aggregate mentioned in section 9(1) above; and

    (*c*) he has, within the period of three months beginning with the service on him of the notice under section 12(4) above or within that period as extended under sub-section (5) below, served a notice on the landlord claiming to be entitled to defer completion and has, within the same period, deposited the sum of £100 with the landlord.

    (5) Where there are reasonable grounds for doing so the landlord shall extend (or further extend) the period within which a notice under subsection (4)(*c*) above must be served and the sum of £100 deposited; and if it fails to do so the county court may by order extend or further extend that period until such date as may be specified in the order.

    (6) If the tenant does not comply with the notice under sub-section (2) above, the notice claiming to exercise the right to buy shall be deemed to have been withdrawn at the end of the period stated in the notice under that subsection and no further notice claiming to exercise the right to buy shall have effect if served by the tenant on the landlord within twelve months of the end of that period.

    (7) If, in pursuance of a notice under subsection (4)*c*) above, the tenant deposited the sum of £100 with the landlord, then—

    (*a*) if he completes the transaction, that sum shall be treated as having been paid towards the purchase price; and

    (*b*) if he does not complete the transaction but withdraws his notice claiming to exercise the right to buy or is, by virtue of subsection (6) above, deemed to have withdrawn it, the sum deposited shall be returned to him.

    (8) A tenant who is entitled to defer completion may, at any time before the service on him of a notice under subsection (2) above, serve a further notice under

subsection (1) of section 12 and, if he does so, subsection (4) and (where applicable) subsection (6) of that section shall then apply accordingly.

(9) If the tenant has failed to pay the rent or any other payment due from him as a tenant for a period of four weeks after it has been lawfully demanded from him, then, while the whole or part of it remains outstanding—
    (*a*) the landlord shall not be bound to complete; and
    (*b*) if a notice under subsection (2) above has been served on the tenant, the tenant shall be deemed not to comply with the notice.

(10) The duty imposed on the landlord by subsection (1) above shall be enforceable by injunction.

(11) On the grant to a secure tenant of an estate in fee simple or of a lease in pursuance of this Chapter the secure tenancy of the dwelling-house shall come to an end and, if there is then a subtenancy, section 139 of the Law of Property Act 1925 shall apply as on a merger or surrender. **[345]**

COMMENCEMENT
    See the note to s. 1, *ante*.

SUB-S. (1): CLAIMED TO EXERCISE THE RIGHT TO BUY
    I.e., by notice under s. 5, *ante*. As to the right to buy, see s. 1, *ante*, and the notes thereto.

RIGHT HAS BEEN ESTABLISHED
    As to admission by the landlord of the tenant's right to buy, see s. 5, *ante*, and as to proceedings in the county court to establish that right, see the note "Jurisdiction of county court" to s. 1, *ante*.

LANDLORD SHALL BE BOUND, ETC.
    That duty is enforceable by injunction; see sub-s. (10) above.

GRANT
    A conveyance of the freehold under this section and a grant of a lease under this section must conform with Sch. 2, *post*; see s. 17, *post*. As to the registration of title, see s. 20, *post*.

FEE SIMPLE ABSOLUTE
    As to this estate generally, see the Law of Property Act 1925, s. 1, and the notes thereto, Vol. 27, p. 346.

AMOUNT TO BE LEFT OUTSTANDING, ETC.
    See s. 9, *ante*.

SUB-S. (2): NOTICE
    As to notices generally, see s. 21, *post*.

WITHIN A PERIOD STATED, ETC.
    See the note "Within six months of, etc." to s. 3, *ante*.

SUB-S. (3): CLAIMED TO EXERCISE THE RIGHT TO A MORTGAGE
    I.e., by notice under s. 12, *ante*. As to the right to a mortgage, see s. 1, *ante*, and the notes thereto.

THREE MONTHS (TWO YEARS) AFTER, ETC.
    See the note "Not later than three months after, etc." to s. 11, *ante*.

PERIOD WITHIN WHICH A NOTICE CLAIMING IT COULD HAVE BEEN SERVED
    As to this period see s. 12 (1)–(3), *ante*.

SUB-S. (4). TENANT IS ENTITLED TO DEFER COMPLETION, ETC.
    The effect of sub-s. (4) above must be set out in the landlord's notice of the purchase price, etc., served under s. 10, *ante* (see s. 10 (3) (*c*), *ante*), and the notice of the landlord or Housing Corporation concerning the amount to be left outstanding, etc., served under s. 12 (4), *ante* is to set out the effect of sub-s. (8) above and is to be accompanied by a form for claiming in accordance with sub-s. (4) (*c*) above it be entitled to defer completion (see s. 12 (5), *ante*).

THREE MONTHS BEGINNING WITH, ETC.
See the note to s. 12, *ante*.

SUB-S. (5): COUNTY COURT
See the note to s, 12, *ante*.

SUB-S. (6): NOTICE CLAIMING TO EXERCISE THE RIGHT TO BUY
See s. 5, *ante*.

SUB-S. (8): TENANT ... MAY ... SERVE A FURTHER NOTICE
See the first note to sub-s. (4) above.

SUB-S. (9): GRANT ... OF AN ESTATE IN FEE SIMPLE OR OF A LEASE, ETC.
I.e., under this section or s. 24, *post*.

SUB-S. (10): INJUNCTION
Just as the landlord is not bound to complete in the case of rent arrears under sub-s. (7), other non-trivial breaches of the tenancy agreement by the tenant might debar him from obtaining an injunction: *Western* v. *McDermott* (1866) 2 Ch. App. 72; *Chitty* v. *Bray* (1883) 48 L.T. 860. Inequitable conduct by the tenant would bar relief: *Litvinoff* v. *Kent* (1918) 34 T.L.R. 298 cf. *Coatsworth* v. *Johnson* (1886–90) All E.R. Rep. 597; 54 L.T. 520, C.A., as would unreasonable delay or acquiescence: *Shaw* v. *Applegate* [1978] 1 All E.R. 123, C.A.

If the court grants an injunction under sub-s. (8) then it has a jurisdiction to suspend its operation where, for instance, immediate compliance therewith is impossible (*Pride of Derby and Derbyshire Angling Association Ltd.* v. *British Celanese* [1953] Ch. 149; [1953] 1 All E.R. 179, C.A.) or for some other reason as a matter of discretion: *Wollerton & Wilson Ltd.* v. *Richard Costain Ltd.* [1970] 1 All E.R. 483.

SHALL BE ENFORCEABLE BY INJUNCTION
As to the jurisdiction of the county court, see the note thereto to s. 1, *ante*.

SUB-S. (11): SECTION 139 OF THE LAW OF PROPERTY ACT 1925 (SUB-S. (9))
This section, in the case of merger or surrender, deems the next vested interest in the land to be the reversion for the purposes of *inter alia*, enforcing covenants in the sub-lease. But for its extension by sub-s. (9), these would cease to be enforceable on the secure tenancy coming to an end. Now, if T, a secure tenant, held under L and sub-let part of the dwelling-house (with L's consent) to X, and then T buys the reversion, T is still able to sue X (and *vice versa*) for breaches of covenant, *e.g.* rent arrears: *Plummer and John* v. *David* [1920] 1 K.B. 326.

DEFINITION
For "the right to buy" and "the right to a mortgage", see s. 1 (2), *ante*; for "flat" and "house", see s. 3 (1)–(3), *ante*; for "dwelling-house", see s. 3 (1), (4), *ante*, and s. 50 (2) as applied by s. 27 (1), *post*; for "landlord", see s. 27 (2), *post*; for "secure tenant", and "secure tenancy", see ss. 27 (3), 28, 49 (2) and 150, *post*.

17. Conveyance of freehold and grant of lease

A conveyance of the freehold executed in pursuance of this Chapter shall conform with Parts I and of II Schedule 2 to this Act and a grant of a lease so executed with Parts I and III of that Schedule; and Part IV of that Schedule applies in relation to certain charges.

CONVEYANCE OF THE FREEHOLD EXECUTED IN PURSUANCE OF THIS CHAPTER; GRANT OF A LEASE SO EXECUTED
I.e., under s. 16, *ante*. It is thought that this section and Sch. 2, *post*, do not apply to vesting orders executed under s. 24, *post* (cf. sub-s. (1) of that section). As to the inclusion in the conveyance or grant of a covenant for the repayment of any discount on the purchase price where there is an early disposal of the freehold or lease, see s. 8, *ante*; and as to a covenant which may be included in a conveyance or grant of a dwelling-house in a National Park, etc., see s. 19, *post*.

18. Right to a mortgage—terms of mortgage deed

The deed by which a mortgage is effected in pursuance of this Chapter shall, unless otherwise agreed between the parties, conform with the following provisions—

    (a) it shall provide for repayments of the amount secured in equal instalments of principal and interest combined;

    (b) the period over which repayment is to be made shall be 25 years or, at the option of the mortgagor, a shorter period, but shall be capable of being extended by the mortgagee; and

    (c) it may contain such other terms as may be agreed between the mortgagor and the mortgagee or as may be determined by the county court to by reasonably required by the mortgagor or the mortgagee;

but the Secretary of State may by order prescribe additional terms to be contained in any such deed or vary the provisions of paragraphs (a) and (b) above, but only in relation to deeds executed after the order comes into force. **[347]**

COMMENCEMENT

    See the note to s. 1, *ante*.

MORTGAGE

    As to the right to a mortgage, see s. 1 (1) (c), *ante*, and the note "Right to a mortgage" to that section.

THIS CHAPTER

    I.e., Chapter 1 (ss. 1–27) of Part I of this Act.

TERMS AGREED

    The following are examples of terms which might be validly agreed between the parties:

      (i) A default clause in the mortgage, as to which see *Halifax Building Society* v. *Clark* [1973] Ch. 307; [1973] 2 All E.R. 33. It should be noted that the court may, in a possession action, ignore the default clause under the Administration of Justice Act 1973, A.L.S. Vol. 216, s. 8 (2), for the purpose of the exercise of its powers under the Administration of Justice Act 1970, A.L.S. Vol. 194, s. 36. This was done in *Centrax Trustees Ltd.* v. *Ross* [1979] 2 All E.R. 952.

      (ii) A covenant by the mortgagor to pay insurance premiums against, *e.g.* fire: and for the statutory power of the mortgagee to insure, see the Law of Property Act 1925, s. 101 (1) (ii) and further, *ibid.*, s. 108. In the event of the mortgagor covenanting to effect insurance, it is best to stipulate in the covenant that the monies will be held on trust for the mortgagee, owing to *Halifax Building Society* v. *Keighley* [1931] 2 K.B. 248.

      (iii) A term that the mortgagor will pay the mortgagee's costs on presumably a solicitor and client basis (if not, then see *Re Adelphi Hotel (Brighton) Ltd.* [1953] 2 All E.R. 498) but the regulatory power of the Secretary of State in relation to costs should be noted: see s. 21 (2) of this Act.

    It is obvious that a term which enabled the mortgagee to obtain an option to purchase the mortgaged property would be void in equity whether contained in the mortgage or not: *Samuel* v. *Jarrah Timber and Wood Paving Corporation Ltd.* [1904] A.C. 323, H.L.; *Lewis* v. *Frank Love* [1961] 1 All E.R. 446. *Quaere* whether the mortgagee could take a right of pre-emption in the event of a sale by the mortgagor: after all, it does not create an interest in land: *Pritchard* v. *Briggs* [1980] 1 All E.R. 294, C.A.

REASONABLY REQUIRED

    Should the mortgagor refuse to accept the terms mentioned above as reasonable to include in a mortgage by agreement, then presumably the court could impose them. But it would refuse to impose any term which it considered not reasonably required, and this is wider by far than the question of what is unconscionable or oppressive as understood in equity (see *Knightsbridge Estates Ltd.* v. *Byrne* [1939] Ch. 941; [1938] 4 All E.R. 618, C.A.; also *Multiservice Bookbinding Ltd.* v. *Marden* [1978] 2 All E.R. 489). An example of what would not be reasonably required would perhaps be excessive interest: cf. *Cityland and Property (Holdings) Ltd.* v. *Dabrah* [1968] Ch. 166; [1967] 2 All E.R. 639. *Quaere* how far, in deciding what was reasonably required between the parties, a court would be able to take into account the relative bargaining positions of the parties, as was done in *Lloyds Bank Ltd.* v. *Bundy* [1974] 3 All E.R. 757, C.A.

19. Dwelling-houses in National Parks and areas of outstanding natural beauty, etc.

(1) Where a conveyance or grant executed in pursuance of this Chapter is of a dwelling-house situated in a National Park, or an area designated under section 87 of the National Parks and Access to the Countryside Act 1949 as an area of outstanding natural beauty, or an area designated by order of the Secretary of State as a rural area, and it is executed by a local authority (as defined in section 50 of this Act), a county council, the Development Board for Rural Wales or a housing association ("the landlord") the conveyance or grant may contain a covenant limiting the freedom of the tenant and his successors in title to dispose of the dwelling-house in the manner specified below.

(2) The limitation is, subject to subsection (4), that, until such time (if any) as may be notified in writing by the landlord to the tenant or his successors in title there will be no disposal falling within subsection (8) below without the written consent of the landlord; but that consent shall not be withheld if the disposal is to a person satisfying the condition stated in subsection (3) below.

(3) The condition is that the person to whom the disposal is made (or, if it is made to more than one person, at least one of them) has, throughout the period of three years immediately preceding the application for consent, either—

   (a) had his place of work in a designated region which or part of which is comprised in the National Park or area; or
   (b) had his only or principal home in such a region;

or has had the one in part or parts of that period and the other in the remainder; but the region need not have been the same throughout the whole of the period.

(4) If the Secretary of State or, where the landlord is a housing association, the Housing Corporation, consents, the limitation specified in subsection (2) above may be replaced by the following limitation, that is to say, that until the end of the period of ten years beginning with the conveyance or grant there will be no disposal falling within subsection (8) below unless—

   (a) the tenant (or his successor in title) has offered to reconvey the dwelling-house or, as the case may be, surrender the lease, to the landlord for a consideration equal (subject to subsection (7) below) to the amount agreed between the parties or determined by the district valuer as being the amount which under subsection (6) below is to be taken as the value of the dwelling-house at the time the offer is made; and
   (b) the landlord has refused the offer or has failed to accept it within one month after it was made.

(5) The consent of the Secretary of State or of the Housing Corporation under subsection (4) may be given subject to such conditions as he or, as the case may be, the Housing Corporation thinks fit.

(6) The value of the dwelling-house at the time the offer is made shall be taken to be the price which, at that time, it would realise if sold on the open market by a

willing vendor on assumptions corresponding to those in subsection (3) or, as the case may require, subsection (4) of section 6 of this Act (but without the disregards required by subsection (2) of that section).

(7) If the landlord accepts the offer mentioned in subsection (4) above, and the offer was made within five years of the conveyance or grant to the tenant, the consideration shall be reduced by such amount as would fall to be paid on demand on a disposal made at the time the offer was made and falling within subsection (3) of section 8 of this Act; and no payment shall be required in pursuance of that section.

(8) A disposal falls within this subsection if it is—

(a) a further conveyance of the freehold or an assignment of the lease; or
(b) the grant of a lease or sub-lease for a term of more than twenty-one years otherwise than at a rack rent;

whether the disposal is of the whole or part of the dwelling-house; but a disposal in pursuance of an order under section 24 of the Matrimonial Causes Act 1973 or under section 2 of the Inheritance (Provision for Family and Dependants) Act 1975 or a vesting in a person taking under a will or on an intestacy is not a disposal falling within this subsection.

(9) Any disposal in breach of such a covenant as is mentioned in subsection (1) above shall be void.

(10) Where such a covenant imposes the limitation specified in subsection (2) above, the limitation shall be a local land charge and the Chief Land Registrar shall enter the appropriate restriction on the register of title as if application therefor had been made under section 58 of the Land Registration Act 1925.

(11) The reference in subsection (8) above to a lease or sublease does not include a mortgage term.

(12) In this section "designated region" means an area designated for the purposes of this section by order of the Secretary of State; and for the purposes of this section the grant of an option enabling a person to call for a disposal falling within subsection (8) above shall be treated as such a disposal made to him and a consent to such a grant as a consent to a disposal made in pursuance of the option. **[348]**

COMMENCEMENT
    See the note to s. 1, *ante*.

SUB-S. (1): CONVEYANCE OR GRANT EXECUTED IN PURSUANCE OF THIS CHAPTER
    I.e., under s. 16, *ante*; and cf. s. 24, *post*.

NATIONAL PARK
    As to National Parks, see the National Parks and Access to the Countryside Act 1949, Part II, A.L.S. Vol. 65 and the Countryside Act 1968, ss. 12 *et seq.*, A.L.S. Vol. 175.

SECRETARY OF STATE
    See the note to s. 2, *ante*.

COUNTY COUNCIL
    As to the counties in England and Wales and their councils, see the Local Government Act 1972, ss. 1 (1), (2), 2 (1), (3), 20 (1), (2), 21 (1), (3) Sch. 1, Parts I, II, Sch. 4, Part I, A.L.S. Vol. 209.

DEVELOPMENT BOARD FOR RURAL WALES
    This body is established under the Development of Rural Wales Act 1976, s. 1.

HOUSING ASSOCIATION
    See the note to s. 1, *ante*.

SUB-S. (2): NOTIFIED
As to notices generally, see s. 21, *post.*

WRITING: WRITTEN
See the note "Written: writng" to s. 5, *ante.*

HOUSING CORPORATION
See the note to s. 1, *ante.*

TEN YEARS BEGINNING WITH, ETC.
See the note "Three months beginning with, etc." to s. 12, *ante.*

SUB-S. (4): WITHIN ONE MONTH AFTER, ETC.
See the note "Within six months of, etc." to s. 3, *ante.*

SUB-S. (5): THINKS FIT
See the note "Appear" to s. 2, *ante.*

SUB-S. (6): SOLD ON THE OPEN MARKET
See the note to s. 6, *ante.*

SUB-S. (7): WITHIN FIVE YEARS OF, ETC.
See the note "Within six months of, etc." to s. 3, *ante.*

SUB-S. (8): RACK RENT
See the note to s. 8, *ante.*

SUB-S. (10): LIMITATION SHALL BE A LOCAL LAND CHARGE
As to the regulation of local land charges, see the Local Land Charges Act 1975, s. 1, Vol. 45. p. 1705.

CHIEF LAND REGISTRAR
I.e., a registrar appointed by the Lord Chancellor who conducts the business of Her Majesty's Land Registry; see the Land Registration Act 1925, s. 126 (1).

REGISTER OF TITLE
I.e., the register kept under the Land Registration Act 1925, s. 1.

JURISDICTION OF COUNTY COURT
See the note to s. 1, *ante.*

DEFINITIONS
For "dwelling-house", see s. 3 (1), (4), *ante,* and s. 50 (2) as applied by s. 27 (1), *post;* for "district valuer", see s. 27 (2), *post.* Note as to "the landlord", sub-s. (1) above; as to "lease" and "sub-lease", sub-s. (11) above; as to "designated region", sub-s. (12) above; and as to "disposal falling within subsection (8)", sub-ss. (8) and (12) above.

NATIONAL PARKS AND ACCESS TO THE COUNTRYSIDE ACT 1949, S. 87
See A.L.S. Vol. 65.

MATRIMONIAL CAUSES ACT 1973, S. 24
See A.L.S. Vol. 217.

INHERITANCE (PROVISION FOR FAMILY AND DEPENDANTS) ACT 1975, S. 2
See A.L.S. Vol. 236.

LAND REGISTRATION ACT 1925, S. 58
27, Halsbury's Statutes (3rd edn.) p. 832.

ORDERS UNDER THIS SECTION
The Housing (Right to Buy) (Designated Regions) Order 1980, S.I. 1980 No 1345 (made under sub-s. (12) above); the Housing (Right to Buy) (Designated Rural Areas and Designated Regions) (Wales) Order 1980, S.I. 1980, No. 1375 (made under sub-ss. (1) and (12) above).
As to orders generally, see s. 151, *post.*

20. Registration of title

(1) Section 123 of the Land Registration Act 1925 (compulsory registration of title) shall apply in relation to the conveyance of a freehold or grant of a lease in pursuance of this Chapter whether or not the dwelling-house is in an area in which an Order in Council under section 120 of that Act is for the time being in force.

(2) If the dwelling-house is not registered land, the landlord shall give the tenant a certificate stating that the landlord is entitled to convey the freehold or make the grant subject only to such incumbrances, rights and interests as are stated in the conveyance or grant or summarised in the certificate.

(3) A certificate under subsection (2) above—

    (*a*) shall be in a form approved by the Chief Land Registrar; and

    (*b*) shall be signed by such officer of the landlord or such other person as may be approved by the Chief Land Registrar.

(4) The Chief Land Registrar shall, for the purpose of the registration of title, accept such a certificate as sufficient evidence of the facts stated in it; but if, as a result, he has to meet a claim against him under the Land Registration Acts 1925 to 1971, the landlord shall be liable to indemnify him. **[349]**

COMMENCEMENT
    See the note to s. 1, *ante.*

GENERAL NOTE
    See, for some further particulars, the discussion in the main text, paras [49]–[50].
        Accordingly, the Land Registration Act is to apply whether or not the area is one of compulsory registration of title, as to which see the Registration of Title Order 1977, S.I. 1977 No. 828. As to the district land registry rules, see the Land Registration (District Registries) Order 1979, S.I. 1979 No. 1019.

CONVEYANCE OF A FREEHOLD OR GRANT OF A LEASE IN PURSUANCE OF THIS CHAPTER
    I.e., under s. 16, *ante.*

REGISTERED LAND
    That expression is not defined for the purposes of this Act, but by the Land Registration Act 1925, s. 3 (xxiv), "registered land" means land or any estate or interest in land the title to which is registered under that Act or any enactment replaced by that Act, and includes any easement, right, privilege, or benefit which is appurtenant or appendant thereto, and any mines and minerals within or under the same and held therewith.

CHIEF LAND REGISTRAR
    See the notes to s. 19, *ante.*

SUFFICIENT EVIDENCE
    See the note to s. 25, *post.*

DEFINITIONS
    For "dwelling-house", see s. 3 (1), (4), *ante,* and s. 50 (2) as applied by s. 27 (1), *post,* for "landlord", see s. 27 (2), *post.*

LAND REGISTRATION ACT 1925, SS. 120, 123
    See 27, Halsbury's Statutes Ord edn.), pp. 884, 885.

LAND REGISTRATION ACTS 1925 TO 1971
    For the Acts which may be cited by this collective title, see the Introductory Note to the Land Registration Act 1925.

21. Costs

(1) Any agreement between a tenant exercising the right to buy and the landlord shall be void in so far as it purports to oblige the tenant to bear any part of the costs

incurred by the landlord in connection with the tenant's exercise of that right, other than costs chargeable to the tenant under subsection (2) below.

(2) Where the tenant exercising the right to buy also exercises the right to a mortgage, the landlord or, as the case may be, the Housing Corporation, may charge to him the costs incurred by it in connection with the tenant's exercise of the right to a mortgage, but only to the extent that they do not exceed such amount as the Secretary of State may by order specify. **[350]**

COMMENCEMENT
See the note to s. 1, *ante.*

AGREEMENT
An agreement by the tenant to pay the mortgagee's costs on, say, a solicitor and client basis is thus avoided in principle, but regulations may provide for certain costs: sub-s. (2).

RIGHT TO BUY; RIGHT TO A MORTGAGE
See s. 1, *ante*, and the notes thereto.

HOUSING CORPORATION
See the note to s. 1, *ante.*

LANDLORD OR ... HOUSING CORPORATION; MAY CHARGE TO HIM THE COSTS, ETC.
The costs chargeable to the tenant under this section are one of the items which are to be included in calculating the amount which may be secured by mortgage; see s. 9 (1) (*b*), *ante.*

SECRETARY OF STATE
See the note to s. 2, *ante.*

JURISDICTION OF COUNTY COURT
See the note to s. 1, *ante.*

DEFINITIONS
For "the right to buy" and "the right to a mortgage", see s. 1 (2), *ante*; for "landlord", see s. 27 (2), *post.*

ORDER UNDER THIS SECTION
The Housing (Right to Buy) (Mortgage Costs) Order 1980, S.I. 1980 No. 1390 (made under sub-s. (2) above; specifying the amount of £50 as the maximum amount which may be charged in respect of the costs incurred in connnection with a tenant's right to a mortgage).
As to orders generally, see s. 151, *post.*

22. Notices

(1) The Secretary of State may by regulations prescribe the form of any notice under this Chapter and the particulars to be contained in any such notice.

(2) Any notice under this Chapter may be served by sending it by post.

(3) Where the landlord is a housing association, any notice to be served by the tenant on the landlord under this Chapter may be served by leaving it at or sending it to the principal office of the association or the office of the association with which the tenant usually deals. **[351]**

COMMENCEMENT
See the note to s. 1, *ante.*

GENERAL NOTE
The regulations made under this section are not subject to the annulment procedure, but, by the Statutory Instruments Act 1946, A.L.S. Vol. 36, s. 2 (1), immediately after it is made, a statutory instrument must be sent to the Queen's Printer and as soon as possible printed and sold. There is a Statutory Instrument Issue List: see Statutory Instruments Regulations 1947, S.I. 1948 No. 1, reg. 9.

SECRETARY OF STATE
See the note to s. 2, *ante.*

THIS CHAPTER
I.e., Chapter 1 (ss. 1, 27) of Part 1 of this Act.

MAY BE SERVED BY . . . POST
This provision brings into operation the provisions of the Interpretation Act 1978, s. 7, A.L.S. Vol. 258, to the effect that service is deemed to be effected by properly addressing, prepaying and posting a letter containing the document and, unless the contrary is proved, to have been effected at the time at which the letter would be delivered in the ordinary course of post. See, further, the notes to that section, A.L.S. Vol. 258.

Service by post may be effected by ordinary or registered letter; see *T.O. Supplies (London) Ltd.* v. *Jerry Creighton, Ltd.* [1952] 1 K.B. 42; [1951] 2 All E.R. 992. It follows that it is also permissible to use the recorded delivery service.

As this provision is permissive only, it is clear that, where a notice is served in a different manner and is received, this constitutes good service; see *Sharpley* v. *Manby,* [1942] 1 K.B. 217; sub nom. *Re Sharpley's and Manby's Arbitration,* [1942] 1 All E.R. 66, C.A.; and *Re Stylo Shoes Ltd.* v. *Princes Taylors, Ltd.* [1960] Ch. 396; [1959] 3 All E.R. 901.

LANDLORD
As to meaning, see s. 27 (2), *post.*

HOUSING ASSOCIATION
See the note to s. 1, *ante.*

PRINCIPAL OFFICE
This is the place where the business of the association is mangaged and controlled as a whole; cf. *Garton* v. *Great Western Rail Co.* (1858), E.B. & E, 837; *Palmer* v. *Caledonian Rail Co.* [1892] 1 Q.B. 823; and *Clokey* v. *London and North Western Rail Co.* [1905] 2 I.R. 251.

REGULATIONS UNDER THIS SECTION
The Housing (Right to Buy) (Prescribed Forms) (No. 1) Regulations 1980, S.I. 1980 No. 1391 (made under sub-s. (1) above; prescribing forms to be used for the purposes of s. 5, *ante*); The Housing (Right to Buy) (Prescribed Forms) (No. 2) Regulations 1980, S.I. 1980 No. 1465 (prescribing form of notice to be used by secure tenant claiming the right to a mortgage under s. 12, *ante*); The Housing (Right to Buy) (Prescribed Forms) (No. 1) (Welsh Forms) Regulations 1980, S.I. 1980 No. 1620.

As to regulations generally, see s. 151, *post.*

23. Secretary of State's power to intervene

(1) Where it appears to the Secretary of State that tenants generally, or a tenant or tenants of a particular landlord, or tenants of a description of landlords have or may have difficulty in exercising the right to buy effectively and expeditiously, he may, after giving the landlord or landlords notice in writing of his intention to do so and while the notice is in force, use his powers under the following provisions of this section; and any such notice shall be deemed to be given 72 hours after it has been sent.

(2) Where a notice under subsection (1) above has been given to a landlord or landlords no step taken by the landlord or any of the landlords while the notice is in force or before it was given shall have any effect in relation to the exercise by a secure tenant of the right to buy or the right to a mortgage, except in so far as the notice otherwise provides.

(3) While a notice under subsection (1) above is in force the Secretary of State may do all such things as appear to him necessary or expedient to enable secure tenants of the landlord or landlords to which the notice was given to exercise the right to buy and the right to a mortgage, and he shall not be bound to take the steps which the landlord would have been bound to take under this Chapter.

(4) Where, in consequence of the exercise by a secure tenant of the right to a mortgage a landlord becomes a mortgagee of a dwelling-house whilst a notice under subsection (1) above is in force in relation to the landlord and to the dwelling-house, then, while the notice remains in force—

    (*a*) the Secretary of State may, on behalf of the mortgagee, receive any sums due to it and exercise all powers and do all things which the mortgagee could have exercised or done; and

    (*b*) the mortgagee shall not receive any such sum, exercise any such power or do any such thing except with the consent of the Secretary of State, which may be given subject to such conditions as the Secretary of State thinks fit.

(5) Where it appears to the Secretary of State necessary or expedient for the exercise of his powers under this section, he may by notice in writing to a landlord require it within such period as may be specified in the notice or such longer period as he may allow, to produce any document or supply any information; and any officer of the landlord designated in the notice for that purpose or having custody or control of the document or in a position to give the information shall, without instructions from the landlord, take all reasonable steps to ensure that the notice is complied with.

(6) A notice under subsection (1) above may be withdrawn by a further notice in writing, either completely or in relation to a particular landlord or a particular case or description of case; and the further notice may give such directions as the Secretary of State may think fit for the completion of any transaction begun before the further notice was given.

(7) Directions contained in a notice under subsection (6) above shall be binding on the landlord and may require the taking of steps different from those which the landlord would have been required to take if the Secretary of State's powers under this section had not been used.

(8) Where, in consequence of the exercise of his powers under this section, the Secretary of State receives any sums due to a landlord he may retain them while a notice under subsection (1) above is in force in relation to the landlord, and he shall not be bound to account to the landlord for any interest accruing on any such sums.

(9) Where the Secretary of State exercises his powers under this section with respect to any secure tenants of a landlord he may calculate, in such manner and on such assumptions as he may determine, the costs incurred by him in doing so and certify a sum as representing those costs; and any sum so certified shall be a debt from the landlord to the Secretary of State payable on demand, together with interest at a rate determined by the Secretary of State from the date the sum was certified.

(10) Any sum payable under subsection (9) above may, without prejudice to any other method of recovery, be recovered from the landlord by the withholding of any sum due from the Secretary of State, including any sum payable to the landlord and received by the Secretary of State in consequence of his exercise of his powers under this section.

(11) The references in subsections (5) to (10) above to a landlord and to the powers of the Secretary of State with respect to the secure tenants of a landlord include respectively references to a body which has become a mortgagee in consequence of the exercise by a secure tenant of the right to a mortgage and to the powers of the Secretary of State to act on behalf of such a mortgagee. **[352]**

COMMENCEMENT
    See the note to s. 1, *ante.*

SUB-S. (1): WHERE IT APPEARS
SUB-S (3): AS APPEAR TO HIM
These two formulae are highly subjective, but they are not apt totally to exclude all possibility of judicial review. If no facts exist to give rise to the required state of affairs, then the Secretary of State cannot avoid review merely by the assertion that he is satisfied that the facts or state of affairs exist.

The evaluation of the facts is for the Secretary of State alone and he is, under these formulae, the sole arbiter on a matter of judgment; it is open to a court of law, on review, to ask whether the facts exist at all. Also, whether the judgment is based on a proper self-evaluation of the facts; whether those facts only were taken into account as are relevant, and whether irrelevant facts were left out of account. If these requirements are not satisfied, then the exercise of powers may be challenged in the courts. In this, the *bona fides* or *mala fides* of the Secretary of State is irrelevant. See as to these principles: *Secretary of State for Employment* v. *Associated Society of Locomotive Engineers and Firemen (No. 2)* [1972] 2 All E.R. 949, C.A.; *Secretary of State for Education and Science* v. *Metropolitan Borough of Tameside* [1976] 3 All E.R. 665, H.L.; *A.–G. of St. Christopher, Nevis and Anguilla* v. *Reynolds* [1979] 3 All E.R. 129, J.C.P.C.

SECRETARY OF STATE
See the note to s. 2, *ante*.

RIGHT TO BUY
See s. 1, *ante*, and the notes thereto.

NOTICE
As to notices generally, see s. 21, *ante*.

WRITING
See the note "Written: writing" to s. 5, *ante*.

SUB-S. (2): RIGHT TO A MORTGAGE
See s. 1, *ante*, and the notes thereto.

SUB-S. (3): SECRETARY OF STATE MAY DO ALL SUCH THINGS ... TO ENABLE SECURE TENANTS ... TO EXERCISE THE RIGHT TO BUY, ETC.
See also s. 24, *post*, as to the execution of vesting orders.

STEPS WHICH THE LANDLORD WOULD HAVE BEEN BOUND TO TAKE
See, in particular, ss. 5 (1), 10, 11 (5), 12 (2), (4), 13 (3), 16 and 20 (2), *ante*.

SUB-S. (4): THINKS FIT
See the note "Appear" to s. 2, *ante*.

SUB-S. (5): OFFICER
In this context, the safest thing to say is that an employee of the landlord would be an "officer": cf. *Walker* v. *Simpson* [1903] A.C. 208, J.C.P.C. (employee taken to mean salaried officer). So, a person employed by the landlord under a contract for services rather than under a contract of service might not be regarded as its officer: *Renfrewshire and Port Glasgow Joint Committee* v. *Minister of National Insurance* 1946 S.C. 83 (*held*, that "officer" denoted a person employed under contract of service with a special status to issue orders to other servants). It is tentatively suggested that, despite the width of subs. (5), a solicitor for, say, a housing association or local authority landlord would not be its officer within subs. (5): cf. *Brown* v. *Thames and Mersey Marine Insurance Co.* (1874) 43 L.J.C.P. 112.

CUSTODY OR CONTROL
It appears that possession of the documents would suffice to give the officer custody or control, if he had power to deal with them, but irrespective of whether he had property in them: *London and Yorkshire Bank* v. *Cooper* (1885) 15 Q.B.D. 7. "Control" requires there to be less than property, possession or a right to possession in the documents: *Roake, West and Smith* v. *Butler (Priory Filling Station)* [1963] C.L.Y. 3066.

SUB-S. (9)
Note the application of sub-s. (9) above by s. 24 (6), *post*.

JURISDICTION OF COUNTY COURT
See the note to s. 1, *ante*.

DEFINITIONS
    For "the right to buy" and "the right to a mortgage", see s. 1 (2), *ante*; for "dwelling-house", see s. 3 (1), (4), *ante*, and s. 50 (2) as applied by s. 27 (1), *post*; for "landlord", see s. 27 (2), *post*, for "secure tenant", see ss. 27 (3), 28, 49 (2) and 150, *post*. Note also as to "landlord" and to the powers of the Secretary of State with respect to the secure tenants of a landlord, sub-s. (11) above.

24. Vesting orders

(1) For the purpose of conveying a freehold or granting a lease in the exercise of his powers under section 23 the Secretary of State may execute a document, to be known as a vesting order, containing such provisions as he may determine; and for the purposes of stamp duty the vesting order shall be treated as a document executed by the landlord.

(2) A vesting order shall have the like effect, except so far as it otherwise provides, as a conveyance or grant duly executed in pursuance of this Chapter, and, in particular, shall bind the landlord and the tenant and their successors in title to the same extent as if the covenants contained in it and expressed to be made on their behalf respectively had been entered into by them.

(3) If the dwelling-house in respect of which a vesting order is made is not registered land the vesting order shall contain a certificate stating that the freehold conveyed or grant made by it is subject only to such incumbrances, rights and interests as are stated elsewhere in the vesting order or summarised in the certificate.

(4) The Chief Land Registrar shall, on a vesting order being presented to him, register the tenant as proprietor of the title concerned; and if the title has not been previously registered he shall so register him with an absolute title, and for the purpose of the registration the Chief Land Registrar shall accept any such certificate as is mentioned in subsection (3) above as sufficient evidence of the facts stated in it.

(5) Where the dwelling-house with respect to which the right to buy is exercised is registered land the Chief Land Registrar shall, if so requested by the Secretary of State, supply him (on payment of the appropriate fee) with an office copy of any document required by the Secretary of State for the purpose of executing a vesting order with respect to the dwelling-house and shall (notwithstanding section 112 of the Land Registration Act 1925) allow any person authorised by the Secretary of State to inspect and make copies of and extracts from any register or document which is in the custody of the Chief Land Registrar and relates to the dwelling-house.

(6) If any person suffers loss in consequence of a registration under this section in circumstances in which he would have been entitled to be indemnified under section 83 of the Land Registration Act 1925 by the Chief Land Registrar had the registration of the tenant as proprietor of the title been effected otherwise than under this section, he shall instead be entitled to be indemnified by the Secretary of State and section 23 (9) shall apply accordingly. **[353]**

COMMENCEMENT
    See the note to s. 1, *ante*.

SUB-S. (1): SECRETARY OF STATE
    See note to s. 2, *ante*.

STAMP DUTY
    Plainly, a conveyance of the fee simple or a lease for a term of years absolute for at least 125 years, by deed in either case, would be instruments within the Stamp Act 1891, s. 54 and Sch. 1. The landlord will accordingly, under this subsection, be liable *ad valorem*.

CONTAINING SUCH PROVISIONS AS HE MAY DETERMINE
These words would seem to imply that a vesting order executed under this section need not conform with s. 17, *ante*, and Sch. 2, *post*.

SUB-S. (2): CONVEYANCE OR GRANT . . . EXECUTED IN PURSUANCE OF THIS CHAPTER
See s. 16, *ante*.

SUCCESSORS IN TITLE
As to this, see s. 8 and note thereto.

SUB-S. (3): REGISTERED LAND
See the note to s. 20, *ante*.

SUB-S. (4): CHIEF LAND REGISTRAR
See the note to s. 19, *ante*.

ABSOLUTE TITLE
As to this, see the Land Registration Act 1925, s. 5 (freeholds) and s. 9 (leaseholds). The term "absolute title" is, as has been pointed out, misleading in view of the liability of the registered proprietor in possession to rectification against him under *ibid.*, s. 82, as amended by the Administration of Justice Act 1977 A.L.S. Vol. 254, s. 24, from 29th, August 1977.

REGISTER HIM WITH AN ABSOLUTE TITLE
For the effect of first registration with an absolute title; see the Land Registration Act 1925, ss. 5, 9, Vol. 27, pp. 789, 792.

SUFFICIENT EVIDENCE
See the note to s. 25, *post*.

SUB-S. (5): APPROPRIATE FEE
I.e., the fee prescribed by order under the Land Registration Act 1925, s. 145, Vol. 27, p. 908.

SECTION 112 OF THE LAND REGISTRATION ACT 1925
This provision, which does not apply to any person authorised by the Secretary of State, generally prohibits any person apart from the registered proprietor from inspecting the register.

SUB-S. (6): GENERALLY
As an example of the operation of sub-s. (6): T is registered as the proprietor of Blackacre with an absolute title pursuant to a vesting order. There turns out to be a defect in his so-called absolute title because the file plan is wrong and so the register is rectified under the Land Registration Act 1925, s. 82. *Prima facie* in this case T may obtain an indemnity from the Secretary of State (*Re Boyle's Claim* [1961] 1 All E.R. 620) who will then recover it as a debt from the landlord.

SUFFERS LOSS
It is thought that this word will be interpreted as narrowly as it has been under the Land Registration Act 1925 and will impose a brake on indemnity claims. There is no "loss" if the register is rectified so as to give effect to a state of affairs which existed before the transfer, as where it is to give effect to an overriding interest under the Land Registration Act 1925 s. 70 (1): *Re Chowood's Registered Land* [1933] Ch. 574; *Re Boyle's Claim, supra*.

Thus, for instance, T, who has been secure tenant for 15 years, eventually obtained a vesting order under s. 24 because his council refused to allow him the right to buy, claiming, as no doubt will be claimed, that T lives in an area of housing shortage. S is a successful squatter and obtains rectification against T, who may not have known of the squat: cf. *Re 139 Deptford High Street, ex parte British Transport Commission* [1951] Ch. 884; [1951] 1 All E.R. 950, and no indemnity will be payable, presumably because T suffered no loss.

PERSON
This includes a body of persons corporate or unincorporate; see the Interpretation Act 1978, s. 5, Sch. 1. Vol. 48, pp. 1299, 1320.

DEFINITIONS
For "the right to buy", see s. 1 (2), *ante*; for "dwelling-house", see s. 3 (1), (4), *ante*, and s. 50 (2) as applied by s. 27 (1), *post*; for "landlord", see s. 27 (2), *post*.

LAND REGISTRATION ACT 1925, SS. 83, 112
See 27, Halsbury's Statutes (3rd edn.), pp. 858, 882.

25. Statutory declarations

A landlord, the Housing Corporation or the Secretary of State may, if the landlord, Corporation or Secretary of State thinks fit, accept any statutory declaration made for the purposes of this Chapter as sufficient evidence of the matters declared in it.
[354]

COMMENCEMENT
See the note to s. 1, *ante.*

LANDLORD
As to meaning, see s. 27 (2), *post.*

HOUSING CORPORATION
See the note to s. 1, *ante.*

SECRETARY OF STATE
See the note to s. 2, *ante.*

STATUTORY DECLARATION
I.e., a declaration made by virtue of the Statutory Declarations Act 1835; see the Interpretation Act 1978, s. 5, Sch. 1, A.L.S. Vol. 258.

THIS CHAPTER
I.e., Chapter 1 (ss. 1, 27) of Part I of this Act.

SUFFICIENT EVIDENCE
This is not the same as conclusive evidence: see *Re Duce and Boots Cash Chemists (Southern) Ltd.'s Contract,* (1937) Ch. 642, *per* Bennett, J., at pp. 649, 650. It usually means no more than *prima facie* evidence (*Barraclough* v. *Greenhough* (1867), L.R. 3 Q.B. 612, at pp. 610, 620), but the matter is always one of interpretation of the particular statute.

26. Power to repeal or amend local Acts

(1) The Secretary of State may by order repeal or amend any provision of a local Act passed before this Act where it appears to him that the provision is inconsistent with any provision of this Chapter.

(2) Before making an order under this section the Secretary of State shall consult any local authority appearing to him to be concerned.

(3) An order made under this section may contain such transitional, incidental or supplementary provisions as the Secretary of State considers appropriate. **[355]**

COMMENCEMENT
See the note to s. 1, *ante.*

SECRETARY OF STATE
See the note to s. 2, *ante.*

PASSED BEFORE THIS ACT
I.e., passed before 8th August 1980, the date when this Act was passed (*i.e.,* received the Royal Assent).

APPEARS: CONSIDERS APPROPRIATE
See the note "Appears" to ss. 2, 21 (1), *ante.*

THIS CHAPTER
I.e., Chapter I (ss, 1, 27) of Part I of this Act.

SHALL CONSULT (SUB-S. (2))
Consultation must have the genuine objective of allowing views to be heard before a decision
is arrived at: *Sinfield* v. *London Transport Executive* [1970] Ch. 555; [1970] 2 All E.R. 264,
C.A. Mere formal so-called consultation by means of sending out a non-received letter
is insufficient: *Agricultural etc. Industry Training Board* v. *Aylesbury Mushrooms Ltd.*
[1972] 1 All E.R. 280. The proposals must be put to the local authority which must be
given a reasonably ample opportunity to state its own views: *Port Louis Corporation* v.
A.-G. of Mauritius [1965] A.C. 1111, P.C.; *Rollo and Another* v. *Minister of Town and Country
Planning* [1948] 1 All E.R. 13, C.A.; *Re Union of Whippingham and East Cowes' Benefices*
[1954] A.C. 245; [1954] 2 All E.R. 22, P.C.
    If no consultation takes place with a body which the Secretary of State is required to
consult, then it seems that a purported order made under this section would be void, a
possibility envisaged in *May* v. *Beattie* [1927] 2 K.B. 353; *R.* v. *Minister of Transport, ex
parte Skylark Motor Coach Co.* [1931] 47 T.L.R. 325; also *Hamilton City* v. *Electricity Distri-
bution Commission* [1972] N.Z.L.R. 605.

LOCAL AUTHORITY
For meaning, see s. 50 (1) as applied by s. 27 (1), *post.*

ORDERS UNDER THIS SECTION
At the time of going to press no order has been made under this section.
    As to orders generally, see s. 151, *post.*

27. Interpretation of Chapter I

(1) In this Chapter expressions used in Chapter II have, subject to subsections (2) and
(3) below, the same meanings as in that Chapter.

(2) In this Chapter—

"district valuer", in relation to any dwelling-house, means an officer of the
    Commissioners of Inland Revenue who is for the time being appointed by
    the Commissioners to be, in relation to the valuation list for the area in
    which the dwelling-house is situated, the valuation officer or deputy
    valuation officer, or one of the valuation officers or deputy valuation
    officers;

"flat", "house" and "relevant time" have the meanings given by section 3, and
    "dwelling-house" the extended meaning given by subsection (4) of that
    section;

"landlord", except in subsections (1) and (2) of section 2, does not include any
    body specified in those subsections; and

"the right to buy" and "the right to a mortgage" have the meanings given by
    section 1 (2).

(3) References in this Chapter to a secure tenancy or a secure tenant are, in
relation to any time before the commencement of Chapter II, references to a tenancy
which would have been a secure tenancy if Chapter II had then been in force or to a
person who would then have been a secure tenant; and for the purpose of determining
whether a person would have been a secure tenant and his tenancy a secure
tenancy—

(a) an authority not within the definition of "local authority" in section 50 (1)
    shall be deemed to have been a local authority within that definition if it
    was the predecessor of such an authority; and

(b) a housing association shall be deemed to have been registered under Part
    II of the 1974 Act if it was so registered at the commencement of Chapter
    II. **[356]**

COMMENCEMENT
See the note to s. 1, *ante.*

Chapter II

Security of Tenure and Rights of Secure Tenants

Secure tenancies

28. Secure tenancies

(1) A tenancy under which a dwelling-house is let as a separate dwelling is a secure tenancy at any time when the conditions described below as the landlord condition and the tenant condition are satisfied, but subject to the exceptions in Schedule 3 to this Act and to subsection (5) below and sections 37 and 49 of this Act.

(2) The landlord condition is that—

   (a) the interest of the landlord belongs to one of the bodies mentioned in subsection (4) below; or
   (b) the interest of the landlord belongs to a housing association falling within subsection (3) of section 15 of the 1977 Act; or
   (c) the interest of the landlord belongs to a housing co-operative and the dwelling-house is comprised in a housing co-operative agreement; or
   (d) the interest of the landlord belongs to a county council and the tenancy was granted by it in the exercise of the reserve powers conferred on county councils by section 194 of the Local Government Act 1972.

(3) The tenant condition is that the tenant is an individual and occupies the dwelling-house as his only or principal home; or, where the tenancy is a joint tenancy, that each of the joint tenants is an individual and at least one of them occupies the dwelling-house as his only or principal home.

(4) The bodies referred to in subsection (2) (a) above are—

   (a) a local authority;
   (b) the Commission for the New Towns;
   (c) a development corporation;
   (d) the Housing Corporation;

(e) a housing trust which is a charity within the meaning of the Charities Act 1960; and

(f) the Development Board for Rural Wales.

(5) Where a secure tenancy is a tenancy for a term certain and the tenant dies, the tenancy remains a secure tenancy until either—

(a) the tenancy is vested or otherwise disposed of in the course of the administration of the tenant's estate; or

(b) it is known that when the tenancy has been so vested or disposed of it will not be a secure tenancy. **[357]**

COMMENCEMENT
By s. 153 (2), *post*, thus Chapter (ss. 28, 50 and Schs. 3 and 4, *post*) was to come into operation on such day as the Secretary of State might by order appoint or, if no such order had been made on the expiry of the period of eight weeks beginning with the passing of the Act. As no such order was appointed this Chapter came into operation on 3rd October 1980. Note that by s. 47, *post*, this Chapter applies to tenancies granted before as well as tenancies granted after its commencement.

SUB-S. (I): TENANCY
Despite the use of this, if the occupier has only a licence but, apart from this, he would have a secure tenancy, then he is to be treated as a secure tenant because of s. 48 (1). As to tenancies generally, see Hill and Redman's Landlord and Tenant (16th Edn.), pp. 3 *et seq.*, and 23 Halsbury's Laws (3rd Edn.), pp. 407 *et seq.*

LET AS A SEPARATE DWELLING
Dwelling-house
What is or is not a dwelling-house must be a question of fact and degree. If the terms of the lease state the purpose of the lease, then this is decisive: *Wolfe* v. *Hogan* [1949] 2 K.B. 194; 1949 1 All E.R. 570, C.A. If none is stated, then one must look at the object of the lease, including whether the premises are suitable for use as a dwelling: *Wright* v. *Howell* (1947) 204 L.T. Jo. 299, C.A.; *Levermore* v. *Jobey* [1956] 2 All E.R. 362, C.A.; *Ponder* v. *Hillman* [1969] 3 All E.R. 694, C.A.; *St Catherine's College* v. *Dorling* [1979] 3 All E.R. 250, C.A.; *Regalian Securities Ltd.* v. *Ramsden* [1980] 2 All E.R. 497, C.A.

Land let with a dwelling-house
By virtue of s. 50 (2) (a), this is treated as part of the dwelling-house unless the land is agricultural land exceeding two acres. Cf. the Rent Act 1977, A.L.S. Vol. 255, ss. 6 and 26. For a definition of "agricultural land" see the General Rate Act 1967, s. 26; "use" therein is a question of fact: *Bradshaw* v. *Smith* (1980) 255 E.G. 699, C.A.

This means that the land is treated as part of the dwelling-house where it is let as an adjunct thereto and not the other way around: cf. *Langford Property Co., Ltd.* v. *Batten* [1951] A.C. 223, [1950] 2 All E.R. 1079, H.L. If land which, at the time in question is in fact enjoyed with the dwelling-house, be let on a different lease from the dwelling-house itself, then it is a question of intention whether the land was intended for use "with" the dwelling-house: cf. *Wimbush* v. *Cibulia* [1949] 1 K.B. 564; [1949] 2 All E.R. 432, C.A.; *Jelley* v. *Buckman* [1973] 3 All E.R. 853, C.A.

"A"
By analogy with the Rent Acts, it is thought that the letting of a house comprising several dwellings is outside this section: *Horford Investments Ltd.* v. *Lambert* [1976] Ch. 59; [1974] 1 All E.R. 131, C.A.; *St Catherine's College* v. *Dorling* [1979] 3 All E.R. 250, C.A.

Separate dwelling
Even if there is a tenancy or deemed tenancy under s. 48 (1) (q.v.) there must under s. 28 (1) always be a separate dwelling. Similar considerations to the Rent Acts would apply, so that the letting may be a composite entity comprising several elements: *Whitty* v. *Scott-Russell* [1950] 2 K.B. 32; 1950 1 All E.R. 884, C.A. There must at least be a separate unit of habitation; there is no secure tenancy, therefore, where the rooms do not form a separate unit: cf. *Neale* v. *Del Soto* [1945] 1 All E.R. 191, C.A. If there were a substantial sharing of accommodation with the landlord, this would negative the existence of a separate dwelling: *Goodrich* v. *Paisner* [1957] A.C. [1956] 2 All E.R. 176, H.L. But the mere reservation in favour of the landlord of a right of access would probably not avoid security of itself. If the agreement between the parties provided for sharing of the accommodation as a whole between the tenants (but described as licensees) then s. 48 (1) may require the

agreement to be treated as though a lease and a joint tenancy, overturning *Somma* v. *Hazlehurst* [1978] 2 All E.R. 1011, C.A., and the other cases mentioned in the note to s. 48 (1), in relation to secure tenancies.

Inclusion of licences
In relation to the Rent Acts, there have been a number of agreements recently in particular to avoid the protection of them by conferring what is in form a licence but may not differ much in substance from a lease: see the note to s. 48 (1). Some anti-avoidance provision was therefore needed for the public sector and it is contained in s. 48, which is noted in detail below. Suffice it to say here that, unlike the position under the Rent Act 1977, s. 1, the term "let" in s. 28 (1) of this Act includes licences deemed by s. 48 (1) to be tenancies.

SECURE TENANCY
For the main provisions relating to secure tenancies, see ss. 1, 2, *ante* (right to buy); s. 29, *post* (periodic tenancy following fixed term); s. 30, *post* (succession on death of tenant); s. 32, *post* (security of tenure); ss. 33, 34 and Sch. 4, *post* (proceedings for possession or termination); ss. 35 and 36, *post* (subletting and lodgers); s. 37, *post* (effect of assignment or subletting, etc.); ss. 38 and 39, *post* (effects of tenant's improvements); s. 40, *post* (variation of terms of secure tenancy); s. 41, *post* (landlord's obligation to provide information about tenancies); s. 43, *post* (consultation with secure tenants about matters of housing management); s. 44, *post* (duty of landlord authorities to provide information about housing allocation); s. 46, *post* (contributions towards the cost of transfers and exchanges); s. 47, *post* (application of this chapter (ss. 28–50) to existing tenancies); s. 48, *post* (application of this Part (ss. 1–50) to licences; ss. 81–83, *post* (tenant's improvements); and s. 106, *post* (grants to tenants for repairs and improvements).
Where one spouse (hereafter called the "first spouse") is entitled, either in his or her own right or jointly with the other spouse, to occupy a dwelling-house by virtue of a secure tenancy within the meaning of this section, and the marriage is terminated by the grant of a decree of divorce or nullity of marriage, the court by which the decree is granted may make an order transferring to and vesting in his or her former spouse, *inter alia*, the estate or interest which the first spouse had in the dwelling-house, and where the first spouse is a successor within the meaning of s. 31, *post*, his or her former spouse is deemed also to be a successor within the meaning of that section; see the Matrimonial Homes Act 1967, s. 7 (1), (2), A.L.S. Vol. 164, as amended by s. 152 (1) and Sch. 25, paras. 15, 16, *post*.
The provisions which allow a local authority to increase rents without a notice to quit do not apply to secure tenancies within the meaning of this section; see the Prices and Incomes Act 1968, s. 12, A.L.S. Vol. 175, as amended by s. 152 (1) and Sch. 25, para. 20, *post*.

SUB-S. (2): BELONGS TO A HOUSING ASSOCIATION, ETC.
By s. 49 (2), *post*, a tenancy is not a secure tenancy when the interest of the landlord belongs to a housing association which is both a registered association and a registered society (as defined in each case by s. 49 (1), *post*.

COUNTY COUNCIL
See the note to s. 19, *ante*.

SUB-S. (3): INDIVIDUAL
This word is used instead of the word "person" in order, presumably, to exclude bodies of persons corporate or unincorporate; cf. the Interptetation Act 1978, s. 5, Sch. 1, A.L.S. Vol. 258, and *Whitney* v. *Inland Revenue Comrs.*, [1926] A.C. 37, at p. 43, *per* Viscount Cave, L.C.

ONLY OR PRINCIPAL HOME
See s. 1 and the note thereto.

JOINT TENANT
See s. 1 and the note thereto.

SUB-S. (4): COMMISSION FOR THE NEW TOWNS
That body is established under the New Towns Act 1965, s. 35, Vol. 36, p. 402.

HOUSING CORPORATION
See the note to s. 1, *ante*.

DEVELOPMENT BOARD FOR RURAL WALES
See the note to s. 19, *ante*.

SUB-S. (5): TERM CERTAIN

Presumably vested in a person entitled to claim a succession to a secure tenancy: see s. 30. As to the vesting of property in the tenant's personal representatives, see the Administration of Estates Act 1925, ss. 1 and 3. (If one of two joint tenants dies, there is of course merely a survivorship to the other joint tenant and so s. 3 (4) of the 1925 Act excludes the tenancy from vesting in such a case.) The personal representatives will then assent by s. 36 (1) of the 1925 Act, to the vesting of the property in some other person: in that event, sub-s. (5) "bites". By s. 36 (2) of the 1925 Act, until the assent, if the person entitled is a residuary legatee, he has no interest in the property, but only an inchoate right therein. Until assent, therefore, sub-s. (5) (b) cannot "bite": see further: *Corbett* v. *I.R.C.* [1938] 1 K.B. 567; [1937] 4 All E.R. 700, C.A.; *Re Cunliffe-Owen* [1953] Ch. 545; [1953] 2 All E.R. 196, C.A.; *Commissioner of Stamp Duties (Queensland)* v. *Livingston* [1965] A.C. 694; [1964] 3 All E.R. 692, J.C.; *Re Leigh's W.T.* [1970] Ch. 277; [1969] 3 All E.R. 432. *Aliter* in the case of a specific legacy in which case it ought to be possible, to ascertain at once whether sub-s. (5) (b) is satisfied: see *I.R.C.* v. *Hawley* [1928] 1 K.B. 578.

JURISDICTION OF COUNTY COURT

See the note to s. 1, *ante.*

DEFINITIONS

For "development corporation", "housing co-operative agreement" and "local authority", see s. 50 (1), *post*; for "dwelling-house", see s. 59 (2), *post*; by virtue of s. 50 (1), *post*, for "housing co-operative", see Sch. 20, para. 1, *post*, and for "housing trust", see the Rent Act 1977, s. 15 (5), as substituted by s. 74 (2), *post*. Note as to "the landlord condition", sub-s. (2) above, and as to "the tenant condition", sub-s. (3) above.

1977 ACT

I.e., the Rent Act 1977; see s. 150, *post*. For s. 15 (3) of that Act, see A.L.S. Vol. 255.

LOCAL GOVERNMENT ACT 1972, S. 194

See A.L.S. Vol. 209.

CHARITIES ACT 1960

For the meaning of "charity", see s. 45 (1) and (2) of that Act, A.L.S. Vol. 132.

29. Periodic tenancy following fixed term

(1) Where a secure tenancy (in this section referred to as "the first tenancy") is a tenancy for a term certain and comes to an end by effluxion of time or by an order under section 32 (2) below, a periodic tenancy of the same dwelling-house arises by virtue of this section, unless the tenant is granted another secure tenancy of the same dwelling-house (whether a tenancy for a term certain or a periodic tenancy) to begin on the coming to an end of the first tenancy.

(2) Where a periodic tenancy arises by virtue of this section—

    (a) the periods of that tenancy are the same as those for which rent was last payable under the first tenancy; and

    (b) the parties and the terms of the tenancy are the same as those of the first tenancy at the end of it;

except that the terms are confined to those which are compatible with a periodic tenancy and do not include any provisions for re-entry or forfeiture. **[358]**

COMMENCEMENT

See the note to s. 28, *ante.*

SECURE TENANCY

Cf. the note to s. 28, *ante.*

SECURE TENANCY ... IN A TENANCY FOR A TERM CERTAIN AND COMES TO AN END BY EFFLUXION OF TIME

By virtue of s. 74 (3) and Sch. 9, paras. 1, 2, *post*, certain statutory tenancies which become housing trust tenancies are to be treated for the purposes of this Chapter as if they were secure tenancies for a term certain coming to an end by effluxion of time.

ORDER UNDER S. 32 (2)
This will be made where in a forfeiture action, the court would have ordered, but for s. 32 (1), a forfeiture. Instead, it orders termination of the secure tenancy on a date specified in the order.

TENANCY FOR A TERM CERTAIN; PERIODIC TENANCY; TERMS ARE CONFINED TO THOSE WHICH ARE COMPATIBLE WITH A PERIODIC TENANCY
As to these two kinds of tenancies and the differences between them, see 23 Halsbury's Laws (3rd Edn.), pp. 529 *et seq.*, 531 *et seq.*

PERIODIC TENANCY ... ARISES BY VIRTUE OF THIS SECTION
This means a tenancy for a period of one week, one month or one year for instance, depending on the periods for which rent is payable. For a discussion of the nature of a periodic tenancy see *Re Midland Railway Co's Agreement* [1971] Ch. 725; [1971] 1 All E.R. 1007, C.A., and *Centaploy Ltd.* v. *Matlodge Ltd.* [1974] Ch. 1; [1973] 2 All E.R. 720. A periodic tenancy has an inherent expansion potential, and, further, though at common law a landlord cannot totally deprive himself of his power to serve a notice to quit, by s. 32 (1) of this Act it is impossible to end the statutory periodic tenancy except by means of an order of court. The following provisions also apply to periodic tenancies arising by virtue of this section:—
        (1) Where a secure tenancy is a periodic tenancy the tenant is a successor within the meaning of s. 31, *post*, if the tenancy arose by virtue of this section and the first tenancy within the meaning of sub-s. (1) above was granted to another person or jointly to him and another person; see s. 31 (1) (*c*), *post*.
        (2) Where a notice under s. 33, *post*, notifying the tenant, *inter alia*, of the commencement of proceedings for possession or termination, is served with respect to a secure tenancy for a term certain it has effect also with respect to any periodic tenancy arising by virtue of this section on the termination of that tenancy, and s. 33 (1) (*a*) and (*b*) and (3), *post*, do not apply to the notice; see s. 33 (4), *post*.
        (3) S. 40, *post* (variation of terms of secure tenancy) applies in relation to the terms of a periodic tenancy arising by virtue of this section as it would have applied to the terms of the first tenancy within the meaning of sub-s. (1) above had the first tenancy been a periodic tenancy. See s. 40 (10), *post*.
        (4) Where, after a secure tenant has given a notice claiming the right to buy, a new tenant becomes the secure tenant under a periodic tenancy arising by virtue of this section on the coming to an end of the secure tenancy, the new tenant is in the same position as if the notice was given by him and he was the secure tenant at the time it was given; see s. 13 (1) (*b*), *ante*.
As instances of terms compatible with a periodic tenancy:
        (1) The implied covenant for quiet enjoyment: *Lavender* v. *Betts* [1942] 2 All E.R. 72.
        (2) Possibly a covenant by a landlord to provide services: *Engvall* v. *Ideal Flats Ltd.* [1945] K.B. 205; [1945] 1 All E.R. 230, C.A., but in any event certainly the implied covenants under the Housing Act 1957, A.L.S. Vol. 109, ss. 4 and 6 and the Housing Act 1961, A.L.S. Vol. 131, s. 32.
        (3) Presumably a right to store coal in a shed (*Wright* v. *Macadam* [1949] 2 K.B. 744; [1949] 2 All E.R. 565, C.A.) and other rights capable of passing under the Law of Property Act 1925, s. 62: *Goldberg* v. *Edwards* [1950] Ch. 247, C.A.
        (4) A covenant to pay a sum of money in lieu of dilapidations on quitting: *Boyer* v. *Warbey* [1953] 1 Q.B. 234; [1953] 1 All E.R. 269, C.A.
But purely personal covenants would not be "compatible" within sub-s. (2): *Boyer* v. *Warbey, supra. Quaere*, would a bonus provision for punctual payment of rent be "compatible" or not: *cf. Regional Properties Ltd.* v. *Oxley* [1945] A.C. 347; [1945] 2 All E.R. 418, H.L.

PROVISION FOR RE-ENTRY OR FORFEITURE
As to such provisions generally, see 23 Halsbury's Laws (3rd Edn.), pp. 665 *et seq.*

JURISDICTION OF COUNTY COURT
See the note to s. 1, *ante*.

DEFINITIONS
For "secure tenancy", see s. 28, *ante*, and s. 49 (2), *post*; for "dwelling-house", see s. 50 (2), *post*. Note as to "the first tenancy", sub-s. (1) above.

30. Succession on death of tenant

(1) Where a secure tenancy is a periodic tenancy and, on the death of the tenant, there is a person qualified to succeed him, the tenancy vests by virtue of this section in that person or, if there is more than one such person, in the one who is to be preferred in accordance with subsection (3) below, unless the tenant was a successor.

(2) A person is qualified to succeed the tenant under a secure tenancy if he occupied the dwelling-house as his only or principal home at the time of the tenant's death and either—

   (a) he is the tenant's spouse; or
   (b) he is another member of the tenant's family and has resided with the tenant throughout the period of twelve months ending with the tenant's death.

(3) Where there is more than one person qualified to succeed the tenant—

   (a) the tenant's spouse is to be preferred to another member of the tenant's family; and
   (b) of two or more other members of the tenant's family such of them is to be preferred as may be agreed between them or as may, where there is no such agreement, be selected by the landlord. **[359]**

COMMENCEMENT
   See the note to s. 28, *ante*.

GENERAL NOTE
   Succession to a secure tenancy depends on residential occupation of the dwelling-house as one's home. As with statutory tenants, therefore, the concept of secure tenancies generally is thought to rest on substantial use of the premises in a residential manner: cf. *Remon* v. *City of London Real Property Co. Ltd.* [1921] 1 K.B. 49, C.A.; *Hutchinson* v. *Jauncey* [1950] 1 K.B. 574; [1950] 1 All E.R. 165, C.A. A secure tenant cannot sub-let the whole of the premises: if he does so then there can be no succession because the tenancy ceases to be a secure tenancy: s. 37 (2). This follows the Rent Acts: see e.g. *Haskins* v. *Lewis* [1931] 2 K.B. 1. Business user of the whole premises would presumably have the same result, as one no longer uses the premises as one's home: cf. *Murgatroyd* v. *Tresarden* [1947] K.B. 316; [1946] 2 All E.R. 723.

SECURE TENANCY
   Cf. the note to s. 28, *ante*.

WHERE A SECURE TENANCY IS A PERIODIC TENANCY ETC.
   For provisions which apply where the secure tenancy is a tenancy for a term certain and the tenant dies, see s. 28 (5), *ante*.
   As to periodic tenancies, see 23 Halsbury's Laws (3rd Edn.), pp. 529 *et seq*.

TENANCY VESTS BY VIRTUE OF THIS SECTION IN THAT PERSON
   That person is a successor within the meaning of s. 31, *post*; see s. 31 (a), *post*.
   If a secure tenancy is assigned it ceases to be a secure tenancy, unless, *inter alia*, the assignment is to a person in whom the tenancy would or might have vested by virtue of this section had the tenant died immediately before the assignment, or in whom it would or might have so vested had the tenancy been a periodic tenancy, and similarly where, on the death of the tenant, a secure tenancy is vested or otherwise disposed of in the course of the administration of his estate; see s. 37 (1), *post*.

FAMILY
   For the wide statutory definition, see s. 50 (3). The position as regards succession of a "common law wife" is not quite settled either by this Act or by the courts. Thus, in *Gammans* v. *Elkins* [1950] 2 K.B. 328 [1950] 2 All E.R. 140, C.A.; in relation to the Rent Acts, it was held categorically that a mistress was not a member of the statutory tenant's "family", also *Ross* v. *Collins* [1964] 1 All E.R. 861, C.A. This was distinguished with some difficulty in *Dyson Holdings Ltd.* v. *Fox* [1976] Q.B. 503; [1975] 3 All E.R. 1030, C.A., on the ground that "family" must be construed in its popular sense and since the liason was permanent and stable, the mistress succeeded. See now *Watson* v. *Lucas* [1980] 3 All E.R. 647, C.A. *Quaere*, what is the amount of stability and permanence required

under s. 50 (3); *Helby* v. *Rafferty* [1978] 3 All E.R. 1016, C.A., it was stressed that a long duration might be required, and 5 years did not on the facts suffice.

It is also thought that, as with the Rent Acts, a relationship that did not result from a blood tie or artificially extended blood ties by s. 50 (3) of this Act, would not suffice to make the claimant to succession a "family" member, as where a man was "adopted" by an older woman: cf. *Carega Properties S.A.* v. *Sharratt* [1979] 2 All E.R. 1084, H.L.

RESIDED WITH THE TENANT
Cf. the note "Residing with him" to the Rent Act 1977, Sch. 1, Part I, Vol. 47, p. 558.

MONTH
See the note to s. 4, *ante*.

JURISDICTION OF COUNTY COURT
See the note to s. 1, *ante*.

DEFINITIONS
For "secure tenancy", see s. 28, *ante*, and s. 49 (2), *post*; for "successor", see s. 31, *post* (and see also s. 74 (3), and Sch. 9, paras. 1, 4, *post*); as to "member of the tenant's family", see s. 50 (3), *post*.

31. Meaning of successor

(1) Where a secure tenancy is a periodic tenancy the tenant is a successor if—

    (*a*) the tenancy vested in him by virtue of section 30 above; or

    (*b*) he was a joint tenant and has become the sole tenant; or

    (*c*) the tenancy arose by virtue of section 29 above and the first tenancy there mentioned was granted to another person or jointly to him and another person; or

    (*d*) he became the tenant on the tenancy being assigned to him or on its being vested in him on the death of the previous tenant;

but a tenant to whom the tenancy was assigned in pursuance of an order under section 24 of the Matrimonial Causes Act 1973 is a successor only if the other party to the marriage was himself a successor.

(2) Where within six months of the coming to an end of a secure tenancy which is a periodic tenancy (in this subsection referred to as the former tenancy) the tenant becomes a tenant under another secure tenancy which is a periodic tenancy; and—

    (*a*) the tenant was a successor in relation to the former tenancy; and

    (*b*) under the other tenancy either the dwelling-house or the landlord is or both are the same as under the former tenancy;

the tenant is a successor also in relation to the other tenancy, unless the agreement creating the other tenancy otherwise provides. **[360]**

COMMENCEMENT
See the note to s. 28, *ante*.

SECURE TENANCY
Cf. the note to s. 28, *ante*.

PERIODIC TENANCY
As to periodic tenancies, see 23 Halsbury's Laws (3rd Edn.), pp. 529 *et seq.*

SUCCESSOR
As to a tenant who is not to be treated as a successor for the purposes of this Chapter, see s. 74 (3) and Sch. 9, paras. 1, 4, *post*.
See also the second paragraph of the note "secure tenancy" to s. 28, *ante*.

WITHIN SIX MONTHS OF, ETC.
See the note to s. 3, *ante*.

JURISDICTION OF COUNTY COURT
See the note to s. 1, *ante*.

DEFINITIONS
For "secure tenancy", see s. 28, *ante*, and s. 49 (2), *post*; for "dwelling-house", see s. 50 (2), *post*.

MATRIMONIAL CAUSES ACT 1973, S. 24
See A.L.S. Vol. 217.

32. Security of tenure

(1) A secure tenancy which is either—

    (*a*) a weekly or other periodic tenancy; or

    (*b*) a tenancy for a term certain but subject to termination by the landlord;

cannot be brought to an end by the landlord except by obtaining an order of the court for the possession of the dwelling-house or an order under subsection (2) below; and where the landlord obtains an order for the possession of the dwelling-house the tenancy ends on the date on which the tenant is to give up possession in pursuance of the order.

(2) Where a secure tenancy is a tenancy for a term certain but with a provision for re-entry or forfeiture, the court shall not order possession of the dwelling-house in pursuance of that provision; but in any case where, but for this section, the court would have made such an order it shall instead make an order terminating the secure tenancy on a date specified in the order.

(3) Section 146 of the Law of Property Act 1925 (restriction on and relief against forfeiture), except subsection (4) (vesting in under-lessee), and any other enactment or rule of law relating to forfeiture shall apply in relation to proceedings for an order under subsection (2) above as if they were proceedings to enforce a right of re-entry or forfeiture. **[361]**

COMMENCEMENT
See the note to s. 28, *ante*.

GENERAL NOTE
Supposing that the landlord elects for forfeiture of the fixed term lease, he must not only comply with the requirements of the Law of Property Act 1925, s. 146: to be able to obtain possession he must comply with the notice requirements of s. 33 and also be able to obtain possession under s. 34 and one of the grounds set out in Schedule 4. If the landlord succeeds in the forfeiture action, then the court will make an order under s. 32 (2) which terminates the secure tenancy: this causes s. 29 (1) to bite and a periodic tenancy will arise thereunder. A notice served in the forfeiture proceedings as required by s. 33 will cover the possession proceedings also under s. 34: see s. 33 (4). As to the service of notices under the Law of Property Act 1925, s. 146, see *ibid.*, s. 196.

SECURE TENANCY
Cf. the note to s. 28, *ante*.

PERIODIC TENANCY; TENANCY FOR A TERM CERTAIN
As to these two types of tenancies, see 23 Halsbury's Laws (3rd Edn.), pp. 529 *et seq.*, 531 *et seq.*

ORDER ... FOR THE POSSESSION OF THE DWELLING-HOUSE; ORDER TERMINATING THE SECURE TENANCY
For a notice which must be served by the landlord on the tenant before proceedings for either kind of order are begun, see s. 33, *post*; for the grounds for possession, see s. 34 and Sch. 4, *post*; and as to the discretion of the court in certain proceedings for possession, see ss. 87 and 89, *post*.

    As to when a periodic tenancy arises where a secure tenancy for a term certain comes to an end by an order under sub-s. (2) above, see s. 29 (1), *ante*.

THE COURT

The county court has jurisdiction to hear and determine any action for the recovery of land where the net annual value for rating of the land does not exceed £1,000; see the County Courts Act 1959, s. 48 (1), as amended by the Administration of Justice Act 1973, s. 6, Sch. 2, Part I, A.L.S. Vol. 216; and by s. 86 (1), *post*, a county court has jurisdiction to determine any question arising under this Part of this Act and to entertain any proceedings brought thereunder and any claim (for whatever amount) in connection with a secure tenancy (see also s. 86 (3), *post*, concerning non-recovery of costs of proceedings in the High Court which could have been taken in the county court). See also, on the desirability of commencing proceedings for recovery of possession in the county court, rather than the High Court, in cases within the limits of the county court jurisdiction, *Russoff* v. *Lipovitch*, [1925] 1 K.B. 628, at pp. 639, 640; [1925] All E.R. Rep. 100, at pp. 108, 109; *Smith* v. *Poulter*, [1947] K.B. 339; [1947] 1 All E.R. 216; and *Peachey Property Corporation, Ltd.* v. *Robinson*, [1967] 2 Q.B. 543; [1966] 2 All E.R. 981, C.A.

As to procedure where the proceedings are brought in the High Court, see *Smith* v. *Poulter, supra*; *Peachey Property Corporation Ltd.* v. *Morley*, [1967] 3 All E.R. 30; *Lircata Properties, Ltd.* v. *Jones*, [1967] 3 All E.R. 386n; and as to procedure in the county court, see s. 86 (4)–(6), *post*.

SECTION 146 OF THE LAW OF PROPERTY ACT 1925 (SUB-S. (3))
Exclusion of s. 146 (4)
As a result of this, the court will have no jurisdiction to vest the residue of the term in any under-lessee or, presumably, any mortgagee: as to the latter in the normal case see *Grand Junction Co Ltd.* v. *Bates* [1954] 2 All E.R. 385.

Application of s. 146 (1) of the 1925 Act
Accordingly, the notice must specify the breach, require a remedy and compensation for the breach. If the breach is incapable of remedy then a remedy need not be asked for and compensation may not be required: *Rugby School Governors* v. *Tannahill* [1935] 1 K.B. 87, C.A. It is not always true that an immoral user covenant is incapable of remedy: *Glass* v. *Kencakes Ltd., West Layton Ltd.* v. *Dean* [1966] 1 Q.B. 611; [1964] 3 All E.R. 807.

Assignment or Sub-Letting of the whole premises
In the first place, in this case, s. 37 (1) and (3) provide that the tenancy ceases to be a secure tenancy, and so no part of ss. 33 and 34 will apply. The sole action would be for forfeiture in such a case: but if a lease is assigned even in breach of covenant, it is on the assignee alone that the s. 146 notice is to be served: *Kanda* v. *Church Comnrs for England* [1958] 1 Q.B. 332; [1957] 2 All E.R. 815, C.A.; *Church Comnrs for England* v. *Vi-Ri-Best Manufacturing Co. Ltd.* [1957] 1 Q.B. 238; [1956] 3 All E.R. 777; *Cusack-Smith* v. *Gold* [1958] 2 All E.R. 361; [1958] 1 W.L.R. 611; *Old Grovebury Manor Farm Ltd.* v. *W. Seymour Plant Sales & Hire Ltd.* (*No. 2*) [1979] 3 All E.R. 504, C.A. See also a note in 130 N.L.J. 130.

Bankruptcy
In the event of a right of re-entry on the bankruptcy of a surety, a s. 146 notice must be served on any surety: *Halliard Property Co. Ltd.* v. *Jack Segal Ltd.* [1978] 1 All E.R. 1219; [1978] 1 W.L.R. 377.

Mesne profits
As to this, see R.S.C. Ord 29, r. 18 (jurisdiction to award mesne profits in forfeiture action where lessee remains in possession, reversing *Moore* v. *Assignment Courier Ltd.* [1977] 2 All E.R. 842, C.A.) but this is not exercisable where the defendant has a *bone fide* counterclaim which exceeds the claim for mesne profits: *Old Grovebury Manor Farm Ltd.* v. *W. Seymour Plant Sales & Hire Ltd.* [1979] 1 All E.R. 573.

Elapse of reasonable time
A reasonable time must elapse between service of a s. 146 (1) notice and the action, and this is a question of fact: *Horsey Estate Ltd.* v. *Steiger* [1899] 2 Q.B. 79; *Civil Service Co-operative Society* v. *McGrigor's Trustee* [1923] 2 Ch. 347. If the breach is incapable of remedy, only a short time, e.g. 14 days, need elapse: *Scala House and District Property Co. Ltd.* v. *Forbes* [1974] Q.B. 575; [1973] 3 All E.R. 308, C.A.

Contents of notice
Precise information of the breach ought to be given in such detail as will enable the lessee to understand with reasonable certainty what he is required to do. If the premises are not specified the notice is bad (*Fletcher* v. *Nokes* [1897] 1 Ch. 271) or also where the breaches are not described (*Re Searle, Gregory* v. *Searle* [1898] 1 Ch. 652) but a notice which contains a claim not proved is not wholly invalidated thereby: *Pannell* v. *City of London Brewery Co.* [1900] 1 Ch. 496. See generally *Fox* v. *Jolly* [1916] A.C. 1, H.L.

Breach of covenant to repair
Where the tenancy was granted for a term certain of not less than seven years and at the
date of service of the s. 146 notice three years or more of the term remain unexpired, the
lessee may claim the benefit of the Leasehold Property (Repairs) Act 1938, A.L.S. Vol. 87
(ss. 7 (1) and 1). This stays all proceedings where a tenant's counter notice is served and then
leave to proceed must be obtained by the landlord on proof of the matters set out in s.
1 (5) of the 1938 Act (the grounds being alternatives—*Phillips* v. *Price* [1959] Ch. 181;
[1958] 3 All E.R. 386). The discretion to grant leave is interlocutory: *Re Metropolitan
Film Studio's Ltd.'s Application* [1962] 3 All E.R. 508; [1962] 1 W.L.R. 1315. A *prima
facie* case must be established by the landlord: *Sidnell* v. *Wilson* [1966] 2 Q.B. 67; [1966]
1 All E.R. 681, C.A.; *Charles A. Pilgrim* v. *Jackson* (1975) 29 P. & C.R. 328.

Relief against forfeiture
For the jurisdiction to grant relief against forfeiture, see the Law of Property Act 1925,
s. 146 (2). The landlord is "proceeding" within s. 146 (2) once he has served a s. 146 (1)
notice: *Pakwood Transport* v. *15 Beauchamp Place* (1978) 36 P. & C.R. 112, C.A.
     There are no rigid rules as to the granting or refusal of relief, as this is a matter of
discretion: *Hyman* v. *Rose* [1912] A.C. 623, H.L. Much depends on conduct: where there
was a deliberate breach of covenant relief was refused: *Duke of Westminster* v. *Swinton*
[1948] 1 K.B. 524; [1948] 1 All E.R. 248: also refused because of deliberate breach in *Egerton*
v. *Esplanade Hotels, London Ltd.* [1947] 2 All E.R. 88 and *Borthwick-Norton* v. *Romney
Warwick Estates Ltd.* [1950] 1 All E.R. 798. It is not inevitable that no relief will ever
be granted in the case of breach of the covenant against immoral user, but it is unusual:
Central Estates (Belgravia) Ltd. v. *Woolgar (No. 2)* [1972] 3 All E.R. 610, C.A.
     If relief be granted on terms as to time within which to rectify a matter, the court
may extend the time limits even where liberty to apply for an extension was not reserved
in the order: *Chandless-Chandless* v. *Nicholson* [1942] 2 K.B. 321; [1942] 2 All E.R. 315,
C.A.
     Where relief is granted, then there is deemed to have been no forfeiture of the lease
(and so the secure tenancy will continue): *Dendy* v. *Evans* [1910] 1 K.B. 263, C.A.
     Quaere whether, since only one of a number of joint tenants need satisfy the tenant condi-
tion mentioned in s. 28 (3), the court would have jurisdiction to grant relief on the application of one alone. The general rule for s. 146 (2) is that it has not: *T. M. Fairclough and
Sons Ltd.* v. *Berliner* [1931] 1 Ch. 60, but it is thought that it would be inconsistent with
the policy of Parliament in this Act to apply that case to this context.

Recovery of lessor's costs
By the Law of Property Act 1925, s. 146 (3), a lessor is entitled to recover certain costs
in two cases from the lessee: where, at the request of the lessee, he waives his right of re-
entry or forfeiture or where relief is granted by the court under s. 146 (2). It is therefore
usual to obtain a term in the lease as to the recovery of costs, which will be enforced as
a simple contract debt, since in a case where, say, the 1938 Act applied, no costs would
otherwise be recoverable: see as to this *Bader Properties Ltd* v. *Linley Property Investments*
(1968) 19 P. & C.R. 620; *Middlegate Properties Ltd.* v. *Gidlow-Jackson* (1977) 34 P. & C.R.
4, C.A., where there was such a covenant; and cf. *Skinner's Co.* v. *Knight* [1891] 2 Q.B.
542, C.A., where there was not.

Exclusions of s. 146 (1) of the 1925 Act
As to these see generally, s. 146 (9), considered in *Earl of Bathurst* v. *Fine* [1974] 2 All
E.R. 1160, C.A.

Decorative repairs
As to these, see the Law of Property Act 1925, s. 147, which is discussed under Sched.
2 para. 14.

ANY OTHER ENACTMENT
     The following appear to be the main enactments:
          (1) Common Law Procedure Act 1852, ss. 210 and 212. A tenant is thereby enabled
     to stay proceedings for forfeiture for non-payment of rent by paying into court the
     rent arrears and landlord's costs: there is a 6 month period from the execution of a
     forfeiture order for a tenant to apply for relief. As to the principles on which relief
     is granted, see *Howard* v. *Fanshawe* [1895] 2 Ch. 581; *Belgravia Insurance Co. Ltd.*
     v. *Meah* [1963] 3 All E.R. 828; [1964] 1 Q.B. 436, C.A.: it is usual to grant relief if
     the lessee repays the arrears of rent, costs and it is just and equitable to grant relief.
     In view of the exclusion of the Law of Property Act 1925, s. 146 (4) (relief to under-

lessees) by sub-s. (3) of this section, it is assumed that the like power in the 1852 Act (s. 210) is also inapplicable.

(2) Law of Property Act 1925, s. 147 (relief in relation to decorative repairs).

(3) *Ibid.*, s. 196. By s. 196 (1), a notice served under s. 146 (1) must be in writing; as to personal delivery, see s. 196 (2) and as to delivery by registered letter or recorded delivery, see s. 196 (4) and the Recorded Delivery Act 1962, s. 1 and Sched. Service on one joint tenant by the other is service whether or not the joint tenant actually sees the notice: *Re 88 Berkeley Road, London N.W. 9, Rickwood* v. *Turnsek* [1971] 1 All E.R. 254.

(4) Landlord and Tenant Act 1927, s. 18 (2): a right of re-entry or forfeiture for breach of a covenant to repair cannot be enforced unless the landlord proves that the fact of service of a s. 146 notice under the 1925 Act was known to the lessee or to certain other persons. If a notice is sent by registered post or recorded delivery to a person at his last-known place of abode in the U.K., the person has deemed knowledge of the fact of service from the time when the letter would in the ordinary course of the post have been delivered. As to this, see s. 5 and notes thereto.

(5) Leasehold Property (Repairs) Act 1938: see above.

OR RULE OF LAW

In addition to the principles discussed when dealing with a s. 146 notice under the 1925 Act, it may be mentioned that an attempt at disguised forfeiture will fail, whether this takes the form of an undated deed of surrender (*Plymouth Corporation* v. *Harvey* [1971] 1 All E.R. 623) or a provision for termination of the lease for non-payment of rent on three months' notice (*Richard Clarke & Co. Ltd.* v. *Widnall* [1976] 3 All E.R. 301, C.A.). The former cannot exclude the necessity for service of a s. 146 (1) notice, and the latter the equitable jurisdiction of the court to grant relief.

The rules as to waiver of forfeiture will apply. For a discussion of this, see Sch. 4, Part I, Ground I, note.

DEFINITIONS

For "secure tenancy", see s. 28, *ante*, and s. 49 (2), *post*; for "dwelling-house", see s. 50 (2), *post*.

33. Proceedings for possession or termination

(1) The court shall not entertain proceedings for the possession of a dwelling-house let under a secure tenancy or for the termination of a secure tenancy, unless the landlord has served on the tenant a notice complying with the provisions of this section and, if the tenancy is a periodic tenancy—

    (*a*) the proceedings are begun after the date specified in the notice; and

    (*b*) the notice is still in force at the time the proceedings are begun.

(2) A notice under this section must be in a form prescribed by regulations made by the Secretary of State and must specify the ground on which the court will be asked to make an order for the possession of the dwelling-house or for the termination of the tenancy and give particulars of that ground.

(3) If the secure tenancy is a periodic tenancy the notice—

    (*a*) must also specify a date after which proceedings for the possession of the dwelling-house may be begun; and

    (*b*) ceases to be in force twelve months after the date specified in it;

and the date specified in it must not be earlier than the date on which the tenancy could, apart from this Act, be brought to an end by notice to quit given by the landlord if the notice to quit were given on the same date as the notice under this section.

(4) Where a notice under this section is served with respect to a secure tenancy for a term certain it has effect also with respect to any periodic tenancy arising by virtue of section 29 above on the termination of that tenancy, and paragraphs (*a*) and (*b*) of subsection (1) and subsection (3) above do not apply to the notice. **[362]**

COMMENCEMENT
See the note to s. 28, *ante*.

THE COURT
See the note to s. 32, *ante*.

REGULATIONS (SUB-S. (2))
Owing to s. 151 (1), regulations made under this subsection are *not* subject to the annulment procedure. By the Statutory Instruments Act 1946, A.L.S. Vol. 36, s. 2 (1), immediately after it is made, a statutory instrument must be sent to the Queen's Printer and as soon as possible printed and sold. There is a Statutory Instrument Issue List: Statutory Instruments Regulations 1947, S.I. 1948 No. 1, reg. 9.

GROUND (SUB-S. (2))
If a landlord serves a statutory notice and wishes to rely on more than one ground, he should claim both in the notice. This may be done, it is thought, by mentioning the grounds in the front of the notice leaving the tenant to refer to standard-form notes on the back of the notice: cf. *Boltons (House Furnishers) Ltd.* v. *Oppenheim* [1959] 3 All E.R. 90, C.A.

NOT EARLIER THAN (SUB-S. (3))
This does not mean that the date of termination specified in the statutory notice must necessarily coincide with the correct date of termination for the periodic tenancy at common law.

A notice to quit which states the date of termination and correctly, will expire at midnight on that day: *Sidebotham* v. *Holland* [1895] 1 Q.B. 378; *Re Crowhurst Park, Sims-Hilditch* v. *Simmons* [1974] 1 All E.R. 991.

Dealing with the statutory notice, if the date of termination were, by some error on the landlord's part, incorrect (e.g. too early) then it is thought that, though the matter is not free from doubt, the court has no power to correct the slip and substitute the correct date: *Hankey* v. *Clavering* [1942] 2 K.B. 326; [1942] 2 All E.R. 311, C.A. A trivial mistake unrelated to the date of termination may be ignored and will not of itself invalidate the notice: *Frankland* v. *Capstick* [1959] 1 All E.R. 209, C.A. (incorrect name stated); *Germax Securities Ltd.* v. *Spiegal* (1979) 37 P. & C.R. 204, C.A. The doubt arises because it was held that, if the mistake is so absurd that a reasonable tenant would know it to be so, then the notice might be good: *Carradine Properties Ltd.* v. *Aslam* [1976] 1 All E.R. 573, criticised in 40 M.L.R. 490 (P. F. Smith). Even there, it is thought that if the notice leaves too much for the tenant to think out for himself then it is bad: cf. *Phipps & Co.* v. *Rogers* [1925] 1 K.B. 14, C.A.

PROCEEDINGS FOR THE POSSESSION OF A DWELLING-HOUSE ... OR FOR THE TERMINATION OF A SECURE TENANCY
Court orders for the possession of a dwelling-house let under a secure tenancy or terminating a secure tenancy are required by s. 32, *ante*. For the grounds for possession, see s. 34 and Sch. 4, *post*; and as to the discretion of the court in certain proceedings for possession, see ss. 87 and 89, *post*.

SECURE TENANCY
Cf. the note to s. 28, *ante*.

PERIODIC TENANCY; TENANCY FOR A TERMINATION
See the note to s. 32, *ante*.

SECRETARY OF STATE
See the note to s. 2, *ante*.

TWELVE MONTHS AFTER, ETC.
See the note "Not later than three months after, etc." to s. 11, *ante*.

DATE ON WHICH THE TENANCY COULD ... BE BROUGHT TO AN END BY NOTICE TO QUIT, ETC.
As to this date, see the note "Before that periodic tenancy could be brought to an end by a notice to quit, etc." to s. 55, *post*.

TENANCIES BECOMING HOUSING TRUST TENANCIES
The section is excluded in relation to certain protected or statutory tenancies which become

housing trust tenancies where proceedings for possession were begun before the tenancy ceased to be a protected or statutory tenancy; see s. 74 (3) and Sch. 9, paras. 1, 5, *post*.

DEFINITIONS
For "secure tenancy", see s. 28, *ante*, and s. 49 (2), *post*; for "dwelling-house", see s. 50 (2), *post*.

REGULATIONS UNDER THIS SECTION
The Secure Tenancies (Notices) Regulations 1980, S.I. 1980 No. 1339 (made under sub-s. (2) above, prescribing a notice of seeking possession and a notice of seeking termination of a tenancy and recovery of possession).
As to regulations generally, see s. 151, *post*.

TRANSITIONAL PROVISION
See s. 152 (2) and Sch. 25, para. 62, *post*.

34. Grounds and orders for possession

(1) The court shall not make an order for the possession of a dwelling-house let under a secure tenancy except on one or more of the grounds set out in Part I of Schedule 4 to this Act and shall not make such an order on any of those grounds unless the ground is specified in the notice in pursuance of which proceedings for possession are begun; but the grounds so specified may be altered or added to with the leave of the court.

(2) The court shall not make the order—

   (a) on any of grounds 1 to 6, unless the condition in sub-section (3) (a) below is satisfied;

   (b) on any of grounds 7 to 9, unless the condition in sub-section (3) (b) below is satisfied; and

   (c) on any of grounds 10 to 13, unless both those conditions are satisfied.

(3) The conditions are—

   (a) that the court considers it reasonable to make the order; and

   (b) that the court is satisfied that suitable accommodation will be available for the tenant when the order takes effect.

(4) Part II of Schedule 4 has effect for determining whether suitable accommodation will be available for a tenant. **[363]**

COMMENCEMENT
See the note to s. 28, *ante*.

GENERAL NOTE
This section and the provisions of Schedule 4 impose an additional obstacle on a landlord desirous of obtaining possession of property let on a secure tenancy. Before attempting to obtain possession under this section and Sch. 4, the landlord must of course be otherwise entitled to possession, as by effluxion of time or forfeiture if a fixed-term lease, or as the result of a properly served notice to quit. Also, a landlord cannot, it is thought, obtain possession under this section and Sch. 4 if he is deprived of it under the Limitation Act 1939, by the adverse possession of the tenant: *Parker* v. *Rosenberg* [1947] K.B. 371; [1947] 1 All E.R. 87, C.A.; *Moses* v. *Lovegrove* [1953] 2 Q.B. 533; [1952] 1 All E.R. 1279, C.A. The court will not lean in favour of landlords just because the Act cuts down their common-law rights—as with the Rent Acts: see *Kennealy* v. *Dunne* [1977] 2 All E.R. 16, C.A. The burden of proof of the requirements of each ground (the details of which and notes to which appear under Schedule 4) is on the landlord and it is also thought that, as with the Rent Acts, the court must be satisfied that the conditions of the Act are satisfied, whether or not they are impleaded by, say, the tenant: *Smith* v. *Poulter* [1947] K.B. 339; [1947] 1 All E.R. 216. It is also thought that, as with the Rent Acts, it will not be possible for a court merely to make a default order: cf. *Peachey Property Corporation Ltd.* v. *Robinson* [1966] 2 All E.R. 981, C.A. Should the tenant be persuaded to surrender his lease and then stay on rent-free as a licensee, even so, s. 48 treats him as a secure tenant, so that

Foster v. *Robinson* [1951] 1 K.B. 149; [1950] 2 All E.R. 342, C.A. does not apply in the case of secure tenants.

THE COURT SHALL NOT MAKE AN ORDER, ETC.
As to "the court", see the note to s. 32, *ante*. This section should be read in conjunction with s. 87, *post*, which relates to the powers of the court where proceedings are brought for possession on any of the grounds 1–6 or 10–13 in Sch. 4, Part I, *post*, and with s. 89, *post*, which restricts the discretion of the court in relation to the postponement of giving up possession except where under sub-ss. (2) (*a*), (*c*) and (3) (*a*) above the court had power to make the order only if it considered it reasonable.

SECURE TENANCY
Cf. the note to s. 28, *ante*.

NOTICE IN PURSUANCE OF WHICH PROCEEDINGS FOR POSSESSION ARE BEGUN
I.e., the notice given under s. 33, *ante*.

COURT CONSIDERS IT REASONABLE
Again by analogy with the Rent Acts (see now the Rent Act 1977, A.L.S. Vol. 255, s. 98 and Sch. 15) the burden of proof of reasonableness, where it is required to be shown, is on the landlord: *Barton* v. *Fincham* [1921] 2 K.B. 291; *Nevile* v. *Hardy* [1921] 1 Ch. 404. The question of reasonableness is one of fact and must be considered by the court in every case; *Peachey Property Corporation Ltd.* v. *Robinson, supra*. But what is reasonable is primarily a matter for the county court judge, taking in account all the circumstances which are relevant at the date of the hearing: *Cumming* v. *Danson* [1942] 2 All E.R. 653, C.A.; *Rhodes* v. *Cornford* [1947] 2 All E.R. 601; *Cresswell* v. *Hodgson* [1951] 2 K.B. 92; [1951] 1 All E.R. 710, C.A. Reasonableness must be considered even though the tenant is in breach of covenant: *Bell London and Provincial Properties Ltd.* v. *Reuben* [1947] K.B. 157; [1946] 2 All E.R. 547, C.A.; also *Smith* v. *Poulter, supra*; *Lircata Properties Ltd* v. *Jones* [1967] 3 All E.R. 386. The court will take into account both the conduct and the evidence of the parties: *Upjohn* v. *Macfarlane* [1922] 2 Ch. 256; *Yelland* v. *Taylor* [1957] 1 All E.R. 627; *Regional Properties* v. *Frankenschwerth and Chapman* [1951] 1 K.B. 631; [1951] 1 All E.R. 178, and indeed any other relevant factors at the date of the hearing. This includes the availability of suitable alternative accommodation: *Cumming* v. *Danson, supra*; *Bridden* v. *George* [1946] 1 All E.R. 609, C.A.; also the public interest: *Cresswell* v. *Hodgson, supra*.
Unless the county court judge can be shown to have misdirected himself, as by taking into account irrelevant factors or omitting to take into account a relevant factor (see *Darnell* v. *Millwood* [1951] 1 All E.R. 88, C.A.) then it is thought that, as with the Rent Acts, the Court of Appeal will assume that the decision was proper and will not interfere: *Tender* v. *Sproule* [1947] 1 All E.R. 193, C.A., *R. F. Fuggle Ltd.* v. *Gadsden* [1948] 2 K.B. 236; [1948] 2 All E.R. 160, C.A.

SUITABLE ACCOMMOCATION
Certain of the decisions on what amounts to suitable alternative accommodation which are cited in the relevant note to the Rent Act 1977, s. 98, A.L.S. Vol. 255, may be relevamt also for the purposes of determining undder sub-ss. (2) (*b*), (*c*) and (3) (*b*) above whether accommodation is suitable, but the provisions of Sch. 4, Part II, *post*, must be observed.

DEFINITIONS
For "secure tenancy", see s. 28, *ante*, and s. 49 (2), *post*; for "dwelling-house", see s. 50 (2), *post*.

Terms of a secure tenancy

35. Subletting and lodgers

(1) It is by virtue of this section a term of every secure tenancy that the tenant may allow any person to reside as lodgers in the dwelling-house.

(2) It is by virtue of this section a term of every secure tenancy that the tenant will not, without the written consent of the landlord, sublet or part with the possession of part of the dwelling-house.

(3) The consent required by virtue of this section is not to be unreasonably withheld and, if unreasonably withheld, shall be treated as given.

(4) Section 113 (5) of the 1957 Act shall cease to have effect. **[364]**

COMMENCEMENT
See the note to s. 28, *ante*.

LODGER
If a householder permits other persons to reside with him then these latter persons are his lodgers, provided that the householder is also resident on the premises: see *Honig* v. *Redfern* [1949] 2 All E.R. 15; a lodger has no control over the room he occupies for the purpose of rating: *Helman* v. *Horsham and Worthing Assessment Committee* [1949] 2 K.B. 335, [1949] 1 All E.R. 776, C.A.
    The right to include lodgers cannot be cut down, no matter what problems this causes or may cause to neighbours. Also, if the secure tenant dies, then no doubt any family lodgers may claim a succession under s. 30.
    As to "reside" in the case of lodgers, presumably this is a question of fact. Occupation as a temporary expedient would not, it is thought, suffice: cf. *Foreman* v. *Beagley* [1969] 3 All E.R. 838, C.A. (statutory tenancies). What is required is that one makes one's home with the secure tenant: *Morgan* v. *Murch* [1970] 2 All E.R. 100, C.A.; cf. *Collier* v. *Stoneman* [1957] 3 All E.R. 20.

IT IS ... A TERM, ETC.
Note that the terms of a secure tenancy implied by virtue of this section may not be varied; see s. 40 (2), *post*.

SECURE TENANCY
Cf. the note to s. 28, *ante*.

WRITTEN
See the note "Written; writing" to s. 5, *ante*.

CONSENT
For provisions as to consents required by this section, see s. 36, *post*.

SUBLET ... PART OF THE DWELLING-HOUSE
The effect of this is to attract in the landlord's favour ground 1 of Schedule 4, but this is subject to the overriding requirement of reasonableness.
    Parting with possession means losing the right to claim possession, as with a contract for a sub-lease or assignment: *Marks* v. *Warren*, [1979] 1 All E.R. 29. But to grant a licence will not involve parting with possession because no right to exclusive possession is conferred by most licences: *Marchant* v. *Charters* [1977] 3 All E.R. 918, C.A.; *Somma* v. *Hazlehurst* [1978] 2 All E.R. 1011. C.A.

IS NOT TO BE UNREASONABLY WITHHELD
As to this, see s. 36 and the note thereto. Because an unreasonably withheld consent is treated as given by sub-s. (3), the tenant, it is thought, could sub-let or part with possession of part of the dwelling-house without having to go to court and he would not risk disposses-sion. At common law, a covenant against assignment or sub-letting the whole or part of the demised premises is not required to be observed unless the landlord is or turns out to be reasonable in withholding consent: *Sear* v. *House Property and Investment Society* [1880] 16 Ch.D. 387; *Treloar* v. *Bigge* (1874) L.R. 9 Exch. 151.

EXCLUSION IN RELATION TO CERTAIN HOUSING ASSOCIATIONS
This section and ss. 36–46, *post*, do not apply to a tenancy at any time when the interest of the landlord belongs to a housing association which is a registered society as defined by s. 49 (1), post; see s. 49 (3), *post*.

DEFINITIONS
For "secure tenancy", see ss. 28, *ante*, and s. 49 (2), *post*; for "dwelling-house", see s. 50 (2), *post*.

1957 ACT
I.e., the Housing Act 1957; see s. 150, *post*. For s. 113 (5) of that Act see A.L.S. Vol. 109. That section is also repealed by s. 152 (3) and Sch. 26, *post*.

36. Provisions as to consents required by section 35

(1) If any question arises whether the withholding of a consent was unreasonable it is for the landlord to show that it was not; and in determining that question the following matters, if shown by the landlord, are among those to be taken into account, namely—

    (*a*) that the consent would lead to overcrowding of the dwelling-house (as determined for the purposes of the 1957 Act); and

    (*b*) that the landlord proposes to carry out works on the dwelling-house or on the building of which it forms part and that the proposed works will affect the accommodation likely to be used by the sub-tenant who would reside in the dwelling-house as a result of the consent.

(2) A consent may be validly given notwithstanding that it follows, instead of preceding, the action requiring it.

(3) A consent cannot be given subject to a condition, and if purporting to be given subject to a condition shall be treated as given unconditionally.

(4) Where the tenant has applied in writing for a consent then—

    (*a*) if the landlord refuses to give the consent it shall give to the tenant a written statement of the reasons why the consent was refused; and

    (*b*) if the landlord neither gives nor refuses to give the consent within a reasonable time the consent shall be taken to have been withheld.

(5) In this section a "consent" means a consent which is required by virtue of section 35 above. **[365]**

COMMENCEMENT
    See the note to s. 28, *ante*.

IF ANY QUESTION ARISES, ETC.
    As to the jurisdiction of the county court, see the second paragraph of the note "Is not to be reasonably withheld" to s. 35, *ante*.

IF SHOWN BY THE LANDLORD
    Accordingly, the burden of proof under this section is on the landlord. In relation to the Landlord and Tenant Act 1927, A.L.S. Vol. 87, s. 19 (1), it has been held, contrary to this, that the burden of proof of unreasonableness is on the tenant: *Shanley* v. *Ward* (1913) 29 T.L.R. 714, C.A.

MATTERS ... TO BE TAKEN INTO ACCOUNT (SUB-S. (1))
    In general
    No exact guidelines may now be given to landlords, following *West Layton Ltd.* v. *Ford* [1979] 2 All E.R. 657, C.A. Thus, it was said in *Bickel* v. *Duke of Westminster* [1977] Q.B. 517; [1976] 3 All E.R. 801, C.A., at pp. 524 and 804: "I do not think that the court can, or should, determine by strict rules the grounds on which a landlord may, or may not, reasonably refuse his consent." It is nevertheless thought that, in the context of this section, a refusal of consent which had nothing to do with the subject-matter of the lease or the personality of the proposed assignee or sub-lessee could not be justified: *Re Gibbs and Houlder Bros' Underlease* [1925] Ch. 575, C.A. A landlord may reasonably justify his refusal of consent if he can establish that the security of the rent is endangered: *Re Town Investments Ltd's Underlease McLaughlin* v. *Town Investments Ltd* [1954] Ch. 301; [1954] 1 All E.R. 585, but this must be a real possibility: *Balfour* v. *Kensington Gardens Mansions* (1932) 49 T.L.R. 29. It may be that, until proper information is forthcoming to the landlord, he may be able to withhold his consent, and this might be relevant in adjudging what under sub-s. (4), was a reasonable time: cf. *Fuller's Theatre and Vaudeville Co.* v. *Rofe* [1923] A.C. 435, H.L. If the landlord thought that, as a result of the assignment or underletting, he would have difficulty in re-letting some other property of his, this could not be justified as reasonable: *Re Gibbs and Houlder Bros' Underlease, supra*. Nor where there is no reasonable ground to fear a breach of covenant: *Parker* v. *Boggon* [1947 K.B. 346; [1947] 1 All E.R. 46

Para (a): Overcrowding
As to this, see the discussion in Sch. 4, para, 7.

Para (b): The landlord "proposes"
As to this, see the discussion in Sch. 4, para. 8: it is thought that the same interpretation would be given to "proposes" as to "intends" within that paragraph.

WRITING; WRITTEN
See the corresponding note to s. 5, *ante*.

REASONABLE TIME (SUB-S. (4))
It is thought that this is a question of fact. Even a protracted delay in dealing with an application for consent might not be a breach of the obligation to give or refuse consent within a reasonable time, provided that the delay was attributable to causes beyond the landlord's control, and he did not act negligently or unreasonably: *Carlton SS Co.* v. *Castle Meat Packets Co.* [1898] A.C. 486, H.L. There is no "reasonable time" in the abstract: *ibid.* No doubt, in dealing with any matter under sub-s. (4) (b), the court will take into account all relevant circumstances at the time of the hearing: *Cumming* v. *Danson* [1942] 2 All E.R. 655, C.A.; *Rhodes* v. *Cornford* [1947] 2 All E.R. 601, C.A.

EXCLUSION IN RELATION TO CERTAIN HOUSING ASSOCIATIONS
See the note to s. 35, *ante*.

DEFINITIONS
For "dwelling-house", see s. 50 (2), *post*. Note as to "consent", sub-s. (5) above.

1957 ACT
I.e., the Housing Act 1957; see s. 150, *post*. As to the meaning of "overcrowding", see s. 77 of that Act, Vol. 16, p. 176.

37. Effect of assignment or subletting, etc.

(1) If a secure tenancy is assigned it ceases to be a secure tenancy, unless—

   (a) the assignment is made in pursuance of an order under section 24 of the Matrimonial Causes Act 1973; or
   (b) the assignment is to a person in whom the tenancy would or might have vested by virtue of section 30 above had the tenant died immediately before the assignment, or in whom it would or might have so vested had the tenancy been a periodic tenancy;

and similarly where, on the death of the tenant, a secure tenancy is vested or otherwise disposed of in the course of the administration of his estate.

(2) If the tenant under a secure tenancy parts with the possession of the dwelling-house or sublets the whole of it (or sublets first part of it and then the remainder) the tenancy ceases to be a secure tenancy.

(3) Where—

   (a) a tenancy ceases to be a secure tenancy by virtue of this section; or
   (b) at a time when a tenancy is not a secure tenancy the tenancy is assigned or the tenant parts with the possession of the dwelling-house or sublets the whole of it (or sublets first part of it and then the remainder);

the tenancy cannot become a secure tenancy. **[366]**

COMMENCEMENT
See the note to s. 28, *ante*.

SECURE TENANCY
Cf. the note to s. 28, *ante*.

SIMILARLY WHERE, ON THE DEATH OF THE TENANT, A SECURE TENANCY IS VESTED, ETC.
The last limb of sub-s. (1) above should be read in conjunction with s. 28 (5), *ante*; see also the note to s. 28 (5).

IF THE TENANT . . . PARTS WITH THE POSSESSION OF THE DWELLING-HOUSE, ETC.
As to subletting or parting with the possession of part of the dwelling-house, see ss. 35 (2), (3) and 36, *ante*.

EXCLUSION IN RELATION TO CERTAIN HOUSING ASSOCIATIONS
See the note to s. 35, *ante*.

JURISDICTION OF COUNTY COURT
See the note to s. 1, *ante*.

DEFINITIONS
For "secure tenancy", see s. 28, *ante*, and s. 49 (2), *post*; for "dwelling-house", see s. 50 (2), *post*.

MATRIMONIAL CAUSES ACT 1973, S. 24
See A.L.S. Vol. 217.

38. Reimbursement of cost of tenant's improvements

(1) This section applies where a secure tenant has made an improvement and—

> (a) the landlord, or a predecessor in title of the landlord, has given its written consent to the improvement or is treated as having given its consent; and
>
> (b) work on the improvement was begun not earlier than the commencement of this Chapter; and
>
> (c) the improvement has materially added to the price which the dwelling-house may be expected to fetch if sold on the open market or the rent which the landlord may be expected to be able to charge on letting the dwelling-house.

(2) Where this section applies, the landlord shall (in addition to any other power to make such payments) have power to make, at or after the end of the tenancy, such payment to the tenant (or his personal representatives) in respect of the improvement as the landlord considers to be appropriate.

(3) The amount which a landlord may pay under subsection (2) above in respect of an improvement must not exceed the cost, or likely cost, of the improvement after deducting the amount of any grant in respect of that improvement under Part VII of the 1974 Act. **[367]**

COMMENCEMENT
See the note to s. 28, *ante*.

IMPROVEMENT
As to this, see further s. 81 and the note thereto. As to para. (c) of this subsection, a small improved value resulting from a repair which used better replacement materials than those used originally, will be left out of account.
In relation to the Housing Act 1974, A.L.S. Vol. 223, Sch. 8, para. 1 (2), "improvement" has been held to include the installation of a central heating system: *Pearlman* v. *Harrow School Governors* [1979] Q.B. 56; [1979] 1 All E.R. 365, C.A. In this, it is thought that what para. (c) may be intended to do is to prevent the tenant from claiming the benefit of s. 37 where, though what was done was an improvement from his point of view, it had no beneficial consequences for the landlord's reversion—as was the case in *F. W. Woolworth & Co. Ltd.* v. *Lambert* [1937] Ch. 37; [1936] 2 All E.R. 1523, C.A., and *Lambert* v. *F. W. Woolworth & Co. Ltd. (No. 2)* [1938] Ch. 883; [1938] 2 All E.R. 664, C.A. An example might be the fixing of a nameplate: *Frederick Berry Ltd.* v. *Royal Bank of Scotland* [1949] 1 All E.R. 706.

IMPROVEMENT GRANT (SUB-S. (3))
As to the conditions for the payment of an improvement grant, see the Housing Act 1974, A.L.S. Vol. 223, ss. 61–64.

WRITTEN
See the note "Written; writing" to s. 5, *ante*.

IS TREATED AS HAVING GIVEN ITS CONSENT
As to when this happens, see ss. 81 (3) and 82, *post*.

COMMENCEMENT OF THIS CHAPTER
See the note "Commencement" to s. 28, *ante*.

SOLD ON THE OPEN MARKET
See the note to s. 6, *ante*.

EXCLUSION IN RELATION TO CERTAIN HOUSING ASSOCIATIONS
See the note to s. 35, *ante*.

JURISDICTION OF COUNTY COURT
See the note to s. 1, *ante*.

DEFINITIONS
For "secure tenant", see s. 28, *ante*, and ss. 49 (2) and 150, *post*; for "dwelling-house", see s. 50 (2), *post*; for "improvement", see s. 81 (5), *post*.

1974 ACT.
I.e., the Housing Act 1974; see s. 150, *post*. For Part VII of that Act, see A.L.S. Vol. 223. That Part is amended by s. 107 and Sch. 12, *post*, and partly repealed by s. 152 (3) and Sch. 26, *post*.

39. Rent not to be increased on account of tenant's improvements

Where a person who is or was the secure tenant of a dwelling-house has lawfully made an improvement and has borne or would, but for a grant under Part VII of the 1974 Act, have borne, the whole or part of its cost, then in determining—

    (*a*) at any time whilst he is a secure tenant of that dwelling-house; or

    (*b*) if he has died and on his death the tenancy vested in his spouse under section 30, at any time whilst his spouse is a secure tenant of that dwelling-house;

whether or to what extent to increase the rent, the landlord shall treat the improvement as justifying only such part of any increase which would otherwise be attributable to the improvement as corresponds to the part of the cost which neither has nor would have been so borne (and accordingly as not justifying any increase if the whole of the cost has or would have been so borne).

This section does not apply to any increase attributable to rates. **[368]**

COMMENCEMENT
See the note to s. 28, *ante*.

GENERAL NOTE
This section follows the same legislative policy of disregarding improvements paid for by the tenant as is applied to the fixing of a reasonable rent for a new lease of business premises granted pursuant to the Landlord and Tenant Act 1954, Part II, s. 34, as amended by the Law of Property Act 1969, A.L.S. Vol. 187, s. 1. This overturned *Re "Wonderland" Cleethorpes* [1965] A.C. 58; [1963] 2 All E.R. 775, H.L. There is a similar provision to the present in the Rent Act 1977, A.L.S. Vol. 255, s. 70 (3) (*b*).

But unlike either of these provisions, there is no relief in favour of the tenant where the improvement was carried out by a predecesor in title to the secure tenant. Accordingly, in relation to an improvement carried out by a predecessor to the secure tenant, the rent may be raised if the value of the premises reflects the improvement: cf. *Ponsford* v. *H.M.S.*

Aerosols Ltd. [1979] A.C. 63; [1978] 2 All E.R. 837, H.L., and *Cuff* v. *J. & F. Stone Property Co. Ltd.* [1979] A.C. 87, n; [1978] 2 All E.R. 833. So there has been some compromise with the common law rules: see [1979] Conv. 215 (P. F. Smith).

SECURE TENANT ... HAS LAWFULLY MADE AN IMPROVEMENT
I.e., the tenant has made the improvement with the written consent of the landlord or its equivalent; see ss. 81 (2), (3) and 82, *post* (but see s. 81 (4), *post*).

SECURE TENANT ... HAS BORNE ... ITS COST
As to reimbursement by the landlord at or after the end of the tenancy, see s. 38, *ante.*

EXCLUSION IN RELATION TO CERTAIN HOUSING ASSOCIATIONS
See the note to s. 35, *ante.*

JURISDICTION OF COUNTY COURT
See the note to s. 1, *ante.*

DEFINITIONS
For "secure tenant", see s. 28, *ante* and ss. 49 (2) and 150, *post*; for "dwelling-house", see s. 50 (2), *post*; for "improvement", see s. 81 (5), *post.*

1974 ACT
See the note to s. 37, *ante.*

40. Variation of terms of secure tenancy

(1) The terms of a secure tenancy may be varied in accordance with the provisions of this section but not otherwise.

(2) This section does not apply to any term of a tenancy which is implied by an enactment (including this Act) or to such a term of a housing association tenancy as may be varied under section 93 of the 1977 Act (increase of rent without notice to quit).

(3) The variation may be effected—

    (*a*) by agreement between the landlord and the tenant; or

    (*b*) to the extent only that it relates to rent or to payments in respect of rates or services, by the landord or the tenant in accordance with any provision in the lease or agreement creating the tenancy or in any agreement varying it.

(4) If the tenancy is a periodic tenancy the variation may also be effected by the landlord by a notice of variation served on the tenant.

(5) A notice of variation must specify the variation effected by it and the date on which it takes effect; and the period between the date on which it is served and the date on which it takes effect must not be shorter than the rental period of the tenancy nor shorter than 4 weeks.

(6) Before serving a notice of variation on the tenant the landlord shall—

    (*a*) serve on him a preliminary notice informing him of the landlord's intention to serve a notice of variation, specifying the variation proposed to be effected and its effect and inviting him to comment on the proposed variation within such time, to be specified in the notice, as the landlord considers reasonable; and

    (*b*) consider any comment made by the tenant within the time specified in the preliminary notice;

and when the notice of variation is served it must be accompanied by such information as the landlord considers necessary to inform the tenant of the nature and effect of the variation.

(7) Subsection (6) above does not apply to a variation—

(a) of the rent or of payments in respect of services or facilities provided by the landlord; or

(b) of payments in respect of rates.

(8) Where a notice of variation is served on the tenant and the tenant, before the date specified in it, gives a valid notice to quit, the notice of variation does not take effect unless the tenant, with the written agreement of the landlord, withdraws his notice to quit before that date.

(9) References in this section to variation include addition and deletion; and for the purposes of this section the conversion of a monthly tenancy into a weekly, or a weekly into a monthly, tenancy is a variation of a term of the tenancy, but a variation of the premises let under a tenancy is not.

(10) This section applies in relation to the terms of a periodic tenancy arising by virtue of section 29 of this Act as it would have applied to the terms of the first tenancy mentioned in that section had that tenancy been a periodic tenancy. **[369]**

COMMENCEMENT
See the note to s. 28, *ante.*

SUB-S. (1): SECURE TENANCY
Cf. the note to s. 27, *ante*

SUB-S. (2): TERM ... WHICH IS IMPLIED BY ANY ENACTMENT
See *e.g.*, s. 35, *ante*, and s. 81 (1), (2), *post.*

HOUSING ASSOCIATION TENANCY
I.e., a housing association tenancy as defined by the Rent Act 1977, s. 86, A.L.S. Vol. 255.

SUB-S. (3): SERVICES
Cf. the use of this term in the Rent Act 1977, A.L.S. Vol. 255, s. 19 (8).
   The term is not defined for the purposes of this Chapter, but presumably, as with the Rent Acts, it would include attendance. In *Palser* v. *Grinling, Property Holding Co. Ltd.* v. *Mischeff* [1948] A.C. 291; [1948] 1 All E.R. 1, H.L., it was held that "attendance" meant a service personal to the tenant provided by the landlord under covenant for the benefit or convenience of the tenant, such as carrying coal or refuse to and from the tenant's premises, but not services common to all tenants, such as provision of a janitor. Coal delivery arrangements with a merchant are not attendance: *Feigenbaum* v. *Sutcliffe* (1942) 86 Sol. Jo. 27, C.A.

SUB-S. (4): PERIODIC TENANCY
As to periodic tenancies, see 23 Halsbury's Laws (3rd Edn.), pp. 529 *et seq.*

SERVED
As to this, see further s. 5 and the note thereto. It might be advisable for landlords to incorporate in the lease the provisions of the Law of Property Act 1925, s. 196.

SUB-S. (5): SHORTER THAN 4 WEEKS
Cf. the same requirement for notices to quit in the Protection from Eviction Act 1977, A.L.S. Vol. 255, s. 5. Presumably, following *Schnabel* v. *Allard* [1967] 1 Q.B. 627; [1966] 3 All E.R. 816, C.A. a notice which includes the day of service or of expiry would be valid for the purposes of this section.

SUB-S. (6): CONSIDER
If the analogy of public-law decisions is adopted, then because the requirement of consideration is mandatory ("shall") genuine consideration must be given to the matter: *Sinfield* v. *London Transport Executive* [1970] Ch. 550; [1970] 2 All E.R. 264, C.A.
   Also, it may be that a failure to consider any comment in a genuine manner would render any subsequent notice of variation bad: cf. *May* v. *Beattie* [1927] 2 K.B. 353; *R.* v. *Minister of Transport, ex p. Skylark Motor Coach Co.* (1931) 47 T.L.R. 325.

SUB-S. (9): VARIATION
It has been held, in relation to the Limitation Act 1939, s. 4 (3), that the issue of a new rent book for a weekly tenancy was merely a variation thereof: *Smirk* v. *Lyndale Developments Ltd.* [1975] Ch. 317; [1975] 1 All E.R. 690, C.A.

VARIATION OF PREMISES
Presumably the reason for excluding this from s. 40 is that, if a tenant occupies other land of the landlord's not demised to him, the additional land becomes an accretion to the tenancy: *J. F. Perrott & Co. Ltd.* v. *Cohen* [1951] 1 K.B. 705; [1950] 2 All E.R. 939, C.A. The landlord will re-acquire the land on the termination of the tenancy: *Tabor* v. *Godfrey* (1895) 64 L.J.Q.B. 245.

EXCLUSION IN RELATION TO CERTAIN HOUSING ASSOCIATIONS
See the note to s. 35, *ante.* Note also sub-s. (2) above.

JURISDICTION OF COUNTY COURT
See the note to s. 1, *ante.*

DEFINITIONS
For "secure tenancy", see s. 28, *ante*, and 49 (2), *post*; for "rental period" and "term", see s. 50 (1), *post.* Note as to "variation", sub-s. (9) above.

1977 ACT
I.e., the Rent Act 1977; see s. 150, *post.* That section is amended by s. 77 and Sch. 10, para. 5, *post*, and partly repealed by s. 152 (3) and Sch. 26, *post.*

41. Provision of information about tenancies

(1) Every body which lets dwelling-houses under secure tenancies shall, within two years of the commencement of this Chapter and thereafter from time to time, publish information about its secure tenancies in such form as it considers best suited to explain in simple terms and so far as it considers appropriate, the effect of—

    (a) the express terms of its secure tenancies;
    (b) the provisions of this Part, and Part III of this Act;
    (c) the provisions of sections 32 and 33 of the Housing Act 1961.

(2) Every such body shall ensure that, so far as is reasonably practicable, the information published under subsection (1) above is kept up to date.

(3) The landlord under a secure tenancy shall supply the tenant—

    (a) with a copy of the information for secure tenants published by it under subsection (1) above; and
    (b) with a written statement of the terms of the tenancy, so far as they are neither expressed in the lease or written tenancy agreement, if any, nor implied by law.

(4) The statement required by subsection (3) (b) above shall be supplied—

    (a) if the tenancy is granted after the commencement of this Chapter, on the grant of the tenancy or as soon as practicable afterwards; and
    (b) if the tenancy was granted before the commencement of this Chapter, within two years of that commencement. **[370]**

COMMENCEMENT
See the note to s. 28, *ante.*

EVERY BODY WHICH LETS DWELLING-HOUSES UNDER SECURE TENANCIES
For these bodies, see s. 28 (2) and (4), *ante.*

WITHIN TWO YEARS OF, ETC.
See the note "Within six months of, etc." to s. 3, *ante.*

COMMENCEMENT OF THIS CHAPTER
See the note "Commencement" to s. 28, *ante.*

PUBLISH
To publish means to make known to some person other than the originator; see *Dew* v. *Director of Public Prosecutions* (1926), 89 L.J.K.B. 1166; [1920] All E.R. Rep. 530; *Ranson* v. *Burgess*, [1927] All E.R. Rep. 667, and *A.-G.* v. *Walkergate Press, Ltd.* (1930), 142 L.T. 408. See, further, 4 Words and Phrases (2nd Edn) 229, 231.

SECURE TENANCIES
Cf. the note "secure tenancy" to s. 28, *ante.*

THIS PART
I.e., Part I (ss. 1–50) of this Act.

PART III OF THIS ACT
I.e., ss. 80, 85, *post.*

WRITTEN
See the note "Written; writing" to s. 5, *ante.*

STATEMENT OF THE TERMS OF THE TENANCY
A county court has jurisdiction to entertain proceedings on any question whether a statement supplied in pursuance of sub-s. (3) (*b*) above is accurate, notwithstanding that no other relief is sought than a declaration. See s. 86 (2), *post.* See, further, the note "Jurisdiction of county court" to s. 1, *ante.*

PRACTICABLE
See the note to s. 19, *ante.*

EXCLUSION IN RELATION TO CERTAIN HOUSING ASSOCIATIONS
See the note to s. 35, *ante.*

DEFINITIONS
For "secure tenancy:' and "secure tenant" see s. 28, *ante*, and ss. 49 (2) and 150, *post*; for "term", see s. 50 (1), *post*; for "dwelling-house", see s. 50 (2), *post.*

HOUSING ACT 1961, SS. 32, 33
See A.L.S. Vol. 131. S. 32 is restricted by s. 80 (1), (2), *post*, and s. 33 is amended by s. 80 (3), *post.*

Housing management

42. Meaning of "landlord authority" and "housing management"

(1) In this Chapter "landlord authority" means—

    (*a*) a local authority;

    (*b*) subject to section 49 of this Act, a housing association which falls within section 15 (3) of the 1977 Act;

    (*c*) a housing trust which is a charity within the meaning of the Charities Act 1960;

    (*d*) a development corporation; or

    (*e*) the Development Board for Rural Wales;

but neither the Development Board for Rural Wales nor a development corporation is a landlord authority for the purposes of this Chapter if an exemption certificate has been issued to it by the Secretary of State under section 45 of this Act.

(2) A matter is one of housing management for the purposes of this Chapter if, in the opinion of the landlord authority concerned, it—

(a) relates to the management, maintenance, improvement or demolition of dwelling-houses let by the authority under secure tenancies, or to the provision of services or amenities in connection with such dwelling-houses; and

(b) represents a new programme of maintenance, improvement or demolition or a change in the practice or policy of the authority; and

(c) is likely substantially to affect its secure tenants as a whole or a group of them.

(3) A matter is not one of housing management for the purposes of this Chapter in so far as it relates to the rent payable under any secure tenancy or to any charge for services or facilities provided by the landlord authority concerned.

(4) In this section "group" means a group of secure tenants who—

(a) form a distinct social group; or

(b) occupy dwelling-houses which constitute a distinct class (whether by reference to the kind of dwelling-house concerned or the housing estate or other larger area in which they are situated).

(5) In the case of a landlord authority which is a local authority, the reference in subsection (2) (a) above to the provision of services or amenities is to be taken by the authority acting in its capacity as landlord of the dwelling-houses concerned.

[371]

COMMENCEMENT
See the note to s. 28, *ante.*

SUB-S. (1): THIS CHAPTER
I.e., Chapter II (ss. 28, 50) of Part I of this Act.

HOUSING ASSOCIATION
See the note to s. 1, *ante.*

DEVELOPMENT BOARD FOR RURAL WALES
See the note to s. 19, *ante.*

SECRETARY OF STATE
See the note to s. 2, *ante.*

SUB-S. (2): AMENITIES
In the words of Scrutton, L.J. in *Re Ellis and Ruislip-Northwood Urban District Council,* [1926] 1 K.B. 343, C.A., at p. 370, this means "pleasant circumstances or features, advantages". Modern planning usage, however, has stretched the word to denote personal convenience, so that the convenient arrangement of different *but* inter-dependent uses of land (*e.g.,* shopping and housing) or the provision of a service such as a public lavatory is called an amenity. The word may be taken to express that element in the appearance and lay-out of town and country which makes for a comfortable and pleasant life rather than a mere existence; see *Ex parte Tooth & Co. Ltd., Re Parramatta City Council* (1955), 55 S.R. (N.S.W.), 282, at pp. 306, 308.

EXCLUSION IN RELATION TO CERTAIN HOUSING ASSOCIATIONS
See the note to s. 35, *ante.*

DEFINITIONS
For "secure tenancy" and "secure tenant", see s. 28, *ante,* and ss. 49 (2) and 150, *post;* for "development corporation" and "local authority", see s. 50 (1), *post;* for "dwelling-house", see s. 50 (2), *post;* for "improvement", see s. 81 (5), *post;* by virtue of s. 50 (1), *post,* for "housing trust", see the Rent Act 1977, s. 15 (5), as substituted by s. 74 (2), *post.* Note as to "landlord authority", sub-s. (1) above, as to "group", sub-s. (4) above, and as to "provision of services or amenities", sub-s. (5) above.

146

1977 ACT
I.e., the Rent Act 1977; see s. 150, *post*. For s. 15 (3) of that Act, A.L.S. Vol. 255.

CHARITIES ACT 1960
For the meaning of "charity", see s. 45 (1) and (2) of that Act, A.L.S. Vol. 132.

43. Consultation with secure tenants

(1) Every landlord authority shall, within 12 months of the commencement of this Chapter, make and thereafter maintain such arrangements as it considers appropriate to enable those of its secure tenants who are likely to be substantially affected by a matter of housing management—

    (*a*) to be informed of the authority's proposals in respect of that matter; and
    (*b*) to make their views known to the authority within a specified period.

(2) It shall be the duty of landlord authority, before making any decision on a matter of housing management, to consider any representation made to it in accordance with arrangements made by the authority under this section.

(3) Every landlord authority shall publish details of the arrangements which it makes under this section and a copy of any document published under this subsection shall—

    (*a*) be made available at the authority's principal office for inspection at all reasonable hours, without charge, by members of the public; and
    (*b*) be furnished, on payment of a reasonable fee, to any member of the public who asks for one.

(4) A landlord authority which is a housing association falling within section 15 (3) (*a*) of the 1977 Act (registered with Housing Corporation) shall, instead of complying with paragraph (*a*) of subsection (3) above, send a copy of any document published under that subsection—

    (*a*) to the Housing Corporation; and
    (*b*) to the council of any district or London borough in which there are dwelling-houses let by the association under secure tenancies.

(5) Where a copy of any document is sent to the council of a district or London borough under subsection (4) above, the council shall make it available at its principal office for inspection at all reasonable hours, without charge, by members of the public. **[372]**

COMMENCEMENT
See the note to s. 28, *ante*.

GENERAL NOTE
The Housing Act 1957, s. 111, puts responsibility for the general management, regulation and control of houses provided by a local authority on local authorities: in particular the fixing of the rent, and this is unaffected by anything in Chapter II of this Act. This section leaves the fixing of rents outside the ambit of the housing management duties. Also, the serving of notices to quit is unaffected by this section. At common law, the matter is one of discretion, though even where a notice to quit is served, the secure tenant may only be dispossessed as provided in Chapter II. For this reason, a secure tenant will have less interest in challenging a notice to quit than was the case when there was no security: and the authority is under no duty to consult the tenant beforehand nor to give him an opportunity to make representations: *Sevenoaks D.C.* v. *Emmott* (1980) 39 P. & C.R. 404, C.A. To impugn successfully the decision to serve a notice to quit, one had to show abuse of the local authority's power of management or that its decision to serve was such that no reasonable local authority could have reached: *Cannock Chase D.C.* v. *Kelly* [1978] 1 All E.R. 152, C.A.; *Bristol D.C.* v. *Clark* [1975] 3 All E.R. 976, C.A. It may be that some of the above reasoning depended on the fact that until the passing of this Act, council house tenants had no security of tenure, so that it was apparently thought fundamental by the

courts that, the Rent Acts not applying, "... the local authority should be able to pick and choose their tenants at will" (*Shelley* v. *London County Council* [1949] A.C. 56; [1948] 2 All E.R. 898, H.L., pp. 66 and 900).

SUB-S. (I): WITHIN 12 MONTHS OF, ETC.
See the note "Within six months of, etc." to s. 3, *ante*.

COMMENCEMENT OF THIS CHAPTER
See the note "Commencement" to s. 28, *ante*.

SECURE TENANTS
See the note "Secure tenancy" to s. 28, *ante*.

LIKELY
"Likely" has been construed so as to mean a "reasonable prospect" of something happening; see *Dunning* v. *Board of Governors of the United Liverpool Hospitals*, [1973] 2 All E.R. 454, C.A.

SUB-S. (2): IT SHALL BE THE DUTY
As to the remedies for failure to perform a statutory duty, see generally 36 Halsbury's Laws (3rd Edn.), pp. 440 *et seq.* and 1 Halsbury's Laws (4th Edn.), paras. 99, 195, 205.

SUB-S. (3): PUBLISH
See the note to s. 41, *ante*.

PRINCIPAL OFFICE
Cf. the note to s. 22, *ante*.

AT ALL REASONABLE HOURS
Cf. the note "At all reasonable times" to s. 44, *post*.

SUB-S. (4): HOUSING CORPORATION
See the note to s. 1, *ante*.

COUNCIL OF ANY DISTRICT
As to the districts in England and Wales and their councils, see the Local Government Act 1972, ss. 1 (1), (3), (4), 2 (2), (3), 20 (1), (3), 21 (2), (3), Sch. 1, Part I, Sch. 4, Part II, A.L.S. Vol. 209.

LONDON BOROUGH
For definition, see the Interpretation Act 1978, s. 5, Sch. 1, A.L.S. Vol. 258; and as to the London boroughs and their councils, see the London Government Act 1963, s. 1, Sch. 1, A.L.S. Vol. 138A, and the Local Government Act 1972, s. 8, Sch. 2.

EXCLUSION IN RELATION TO CERTAIN HOUSING ASSOCIATIONS
See the note to s. 35, *ante*.

DEFINITIONS
For "secure tenancy", and "secure tenant", see p. 28, *ante*, and ss. 49 (2) and 150, *post*; for "landlord authority", see s. 42 (1), *ante*; as to "matter of housing management", see ss. 42 (2), (5), *ante*; for "dwelling-house", see s. 50 (2), *post*.

1977 ACT
I.e., the Rent Act 1977; see s. 150, *post*. For s. 15 (3) (*a*) of that Act, see A.L.S. Vol. 255.

44. Provision of information about housing allocation

(1) Every landlord authority shall publish a summary of its rules—

    (*a*) for determining priority as between applicants in the allocation of its housing accommodation; and

    (*b*) governing cases where secure tenants wish to move (whether or not by way of an exchange of dwelling-houses) to other dwelling-houses let under secure tenancies by that landlord authority or by any other body.

(2) Every landlord authority shall—

    (*a*) maintain a set of those rules and of the rules which it has laid down governing the procedure to be followed in allocating its housing accommodation; and

    (*b*) subject to subsection (3) below, make them available at its principal office for inspection at all reasonable hours without charge by members of the public.

(3) A landlord authority which is a housing association falling within section 15 (3) (*a*) of the 1977 Act (registered with Housing Corporation) shall, instead of complying with subsection (2) (*b*) above, send a set of the rules mentioned in subsection (2) (*a*) above—

    (*a*) to the Housing Corporation; and

    (*b*) to the council of any district or London borough in which there are dwelling-houses let or to be let by the association under secure tenancies.

(4) Where a copy of any set of rules maintained under subsection (2) above is sent to the council of a district or London borough under subsection (3) above, the council shall make it available at its principal office for inspection at all reasonable hours, without charge, by members of the public.

(5) A copy of any summary published under subsection (1) above shall be furnished without charge, and a copy of any set of rules maintained under subsection (2) above shall be furnished on payment of a reasonable fee, to any member of the public who asks for one.

(6) At the request of any person who has applied to it for housing accommodation, a landlord authority shall make available to him, at all reasonable times and without charge, details of the particulars which he has given to the authority about himself and his family and which the authority has recorded as being relevant to his application for accommodation. **[373]**

COMMENCEMENT
    See the note to s. 28, *ante*.

SUB-S. (1): PUBLISH
    See the note to s. 41, *ante*.

SECURE TENANTS
    See the note "Secure tenancy" to s. 28, *ante*.

SUB-S. (2): PRINCIPAL OFFICE
    Cf. the note to s. 22, *ante*.

SUB-S. (3): HOUSING CORPORATION
    See the note to s. 1, *ante*.

COUNCIL OF ANY DISTRICT; LONDON BOROUGH
    See the notes to s. 43, *ante*.

SUB-S. (4): AT ALL REASONABLE HOURS
    Cf. the note "At all reasonable times" below.

SUB-S. (6): AT ALL REASONABLE TIMES
    What is a reasonable time is a question of fact. The time during which the premises in question are open for business purposes will ordinarily be deemed reasonable (cf. *Davies* v. *Winstanley* (1930), 144 L.T. 433) and presumably an inspector would not be justified, except in special circumstances, in demanding that premises should be opened at an unusual time such as Sunday afternoon (*Small* v. *Bickley*, (1875), 32 L.T. 726).

EXCLUSION IN RELATION TO CERTAIN HOUSING ASSOCIATIONS
See the note to s. 35, *ante*.

DEFINITIONS
For "secure tenancy" and "secure tenant", see s. 28, *ante*, and ss. 49 (2) and 150, *post*;
for "landlord authority", see s. 42 (1), *ante*; for "dwelling-house", see s. 50 (2), *post*.

1977 ACT
I.e., the Rent Act 1977; see s. 150, *post*. For s. 15 (3) (*a*) of that Act, see A.L.S. Vol. 255.

45. Exemption certificates

(1) On an application duly made by the Development Board for Rural Wales or by a development corporation, the Secretary of State may issue an exemption certificate to the applicant if—

> (*a*) he is satisfied that it has transferred, or otherwise disposed of, at least three-quarters of the dwellings which have at any time before the making of the application been vested in it; or
>
> (*b*) he has, before the commencement of this Chapter, given directions to it under section 3 (1) of the New Towns (Amendment) Act 1976 for the transfer of dwellings vested in it and is satisfied that when the transfer of those dwellings is completed it will have transferred, or otherwise disposed of, at least three-quarters of the dwellings which have at any time before that date been vested in it.

(2) An application under this section shall be in such form and shall be accompanied by such information as the Secretary of State may, either generally or in relation to a particular case, direct. **[374]**

COMMENCEMENT
See the note to s. 28, *ante*.

DEVELOPMENT BOARD FOR RURAL WALES
See the note to s. 19, *ante*.

DEVELOPMENT CORPORATION
For meaning, see s. 50 (1), *post*.

SECRETARY OF STATE
See the note to s. 2, *ante*.

EXEMPTION CERTIFICATE
If the Secretary of State issues an exemption certificate under this section, the applicant to which it was issued is not a landlord authority for the purposes of this chapter (*i.e.*, the applicant is not subject to the provisions of ss. 43 and 44, *ante*); see s. 42 (1), *ante*.

SATISFIED
See the note "Appear" to s. 2, *ante*.

COMMENCEMENT OF THIS CHAPTER
See the note "Commencement" to s. 28, *ante*.

EXCLUSION IN RELATION TO CERTAIN HOUSING ASSOCIATIONS
See the note to s. 35, *ante*.

46. Contributions towards the cost of transfers and exchanges

(1) The Secretary of State may with the consent of the Treasury make out of moneys provided by Parliament grants or loans towards the cost of arrangements for facilitating moves to and from homes by which—

(*a*) a secure tenant becomes, at his request, the secure tenant of a different landlord; or

(*b*) each of two or more tenants of dwelling-houses, one at least of which is let under a secure tenancy, becomes the tenant of the other or of one of the others.

(2) The grants or loans may be made subject to such conditions as the Secretary of State may determine, and may be made so as to be repayable or, as the case may be, repayable earlier, if there is a breach of such a condition. **[375]**

COMMENCEMENT
See the note to s. 28, *ante*.

SECRETARY OF STATE
See the note to s. 2, *ante*.

TREASURY
I.e., the Commissioners of Her Majesty's Treasury; see the Interpretation Act 1978, s. 5, Sch. 1, A.L.S. Vol. 258.

SECURE TENANCY
See the note to s. 28, *ante*.

EXCLUSION IN RELATION TO CERTAIN HOUSING ASSOCIATIONS
See the note to s. 34, *ante*.

DEFINITIONS
For "secure tenancy" and "secure tenant", see s. 28, *ante*, and ss. 49 (2) and 150, *post*; for "dwelling-house", see s. 50 (2), *post*.

Application to existing tenancies

47. Application to existing tenancies

This Chapter applies to tenancies granted before as well as tenancies granted after the commencement of this Chapter. **[376]**

COMMENCEMENT; COMMENCEMENT OF THIS CHAPTER
See the note "Commencement" to s. 28, *ante*.

THIS CHAPTER
I.e. Chapter II (ss. 28, 50) of Part I of this Act.

Application to licences

48. Application to licences

(1) Where a person who is not the tenant of a dwelling-house has a licence (whether or not granted for a consideration) to occupy the dwelling-house and the circumstances are such that, if the licence were a tenancy, it would be a secure tenancy, then, subject to subsection (2) below, this Part of this Act applies to the licence as it applies to a secure tenancy and, as so applying, has effect as if expressions appropriate to a licence were substituted for "landlord", "tenant", "tenancy" and "secure tenancy".

(2) Subsection (1) above does not apply to a licence which was granted as a temporary expedient to a person who entered the dwelling-house or any other land as a trespasser (whether or not before the grant another licence to occupy that or another dwelling-house had been granted to him). **[377]**

COMMENCEMENT
See the note to s. 28, *ante*.

GENERAL NOTE

It is thought that what sub-s. (1) is intended to do—the matter was not discussed in the H.C. Committee—is to nullify oral or written licences which have as their object the avoidance of Chapter II of this Act, by preventing a person who would, but for the licence, have a secure tenancy, from having security. As a result of sub-s. (1), it is thought that the first question to be asked, when faced with a licence of this kind is whether, leaving it out of account for the moment, there would be a secure tenancy. This is answerable by reference to the landlord and the tenant condition stated in s. 28: in particular, the tenant must be an individual occupying the dwelling-house as his only or principal home. So one is to ask oneself if "the circumstances are such that if the licence were a tenancy, it would be a secure tenancy" and if the Act bites as a result, that is the end of the matter. This is the exact opposite of the approach of the courts in relation to licences designed with the express object of avoiding the Rent Act 1977. Thus in *Aldrington Garages Ltd.* v. *Fielder* (1979) 37 P. & C.R. 461, C.A., for example Geoffrey Lane, L.J., at p. 471, stated that, when considering the effect of a licence designed to avoid the Rent Acts, one had to find out the true nature of the transaction and then see how the Act operated.

Section 48 (1) was essential to prevent avoidance of security of tenure by means of licences, and, subject to one matter to be mentioned at the end, it is to be hoped that it will be a difficult section to avoid, not only because of the special exclusion of licences to trespassers in some cases (sub-s. (2)) but also because there are a series of exemptions of certain short-let and other temporary arrangements in Sch. 3.

The necessity for a general provision such as sub-s. (1) to override the terms of a licence is obvious, because in relation to the private sector, the courts have tended to accept written licences stated to be licences and often also denying an intention to confer exclusive possession, at their face value. Thus, it was stated in *Buchmann* v. *May* [1978] 2 All E.R. 993, p. 998, C.A. that where a document (this was a "holiday let") stated a purpose, the expression of purpose was at least *prima facie* evidence of the true purpose; this could only be displaced on the narrow ground of proof by the licensee that the agreement was a sham and did not represent or reproduce the real transaction. See further *Somma* v. *Hazlehurst* [1978] 2 All E.R. 1011, C.A.; *O'Malley* v. *Seymour* (1979) 250 E.G. 1083, C.A. Only in the case of a "badly suspect" agreement in the private sector will the court be put on inquiry: *Demuren & Adefope* v. *Seal Estates* (1979) 250 E.G. 440, C.A.

One thing is clear about the private sector and explains further the need for s. 48 (1). The mere fact that the licence was obviously a device to avoid the Rent Acts while still enabling the "licensor" to draw money payments and even have the benefit of limited covenants not to damage the premises, did not and does not ruffle the courts, who have upheld them on the basis that "persons are entitled to arrange their affairs to their best advantage so long as the law allows it" (*Aldrington Garages Ltd.* v. *Fielder, supra*, p. 473). See also *Somma* v. *Hazlehurst, supra*, p. 1020.

Two examples may be taken as to the width of sub-s. (1). It seems evident that the mere fact that the document, if such it be, states that it is a licence, will not deny security of itself where s. 28 is satisfied. The mere reservation of a right of access or re-entry will certainly not suffice to deny security in the face of the combined operation of ss. 28 and 48 (1). Even at common law, the effect of such a term in an ambiguous document was doubtfully sufficient to exclude the Rent Acts: see *R.* v. *Battersea, Wandsworth, Mitcham and Wimbledon Rent Tribunal, ex parte Parikh* [1957] 1 All E.R. 352; *Walsh* v. *Griffiths-Jones* [1978] 2 All E.R. 1002, the latter having been reserved for future reconsideration in *Aldrington Garages Ltd.* v. *Fielder, supra*.

If there is a written licence which formally denies an intention to confer exclusive possession on the individual, this must surely be overriden where sub-s. (1) applies. If, however, the premises, otherwise capable of being the only or principal home of the *prepositi*, are jointly occupied and the agreement states that neither is to have exclusive possession against the other (perhaps also not against the "licensor"—this was done in *Somma* v. *Hazlehurst, supra*, for instance) then one could apply a mischief test and hold that there was a joint tenancy especially in view of the fact that s. 28 (3) may apply to joint tenants as much as to a single tenant. Such a test might have also to be applied where the form of the agreement was separate licences to each of the two co-occupiers: again they would surely be regarded as joint tenants, no matter what the agreement stated.

There is one case at least, where it is doubtful whether a licence would be overriden by sub-s. (1). This is where there was in fact no separate dwelling within s. 28 (1) and thus no security of tenure within Chapter II at all. There is no separate dwelling where there is no letting of a living unit e.g. the unit is incapable of being regarded as separate from the remainder of a larger entity, not let to the individual separately: *Neale* v. *Del Soto* [1945] 1 All E.R. 191, C.A.; *Curl* v. *Angelo* [1948] 2 All E.R. 189, C.A. There is likewise no separate dwelling if there is a significant degree of sharing: *Goodrich* v. *Paisner* [1957] A.C. 65; [1956] 2 All E.R. 176, H.L.

A final remark: it is still possible of course for the licences of the type nullified in relation to the public sector to be granted at law under the present Rent Act rules; so why did this Act not likewise nullify these licences in that area? The question may only be asked; an amendment to achieve *inter alia* in the private sector exactly the same result as s. 48 achieves in the public sector was voted down by the government in Committee: H.C. Committee, Cols 2318–2327. Nevertheless, should the political complexion of the government alter after the next election, legislation to close the licence and holiday let loopholes may be expected: *ibid.*, Col 2328.

LICENCE
As to licences generally and the differences between tenancies and licences, see 23 Halsbury's Laws (3rd Edn.), pp. 427 *et seq.*

THIS PART OF THIS ACT
I.e., Part I (ss. 1, 50) of this Act.

JURISDICTION OF COUNTY COURT
See the note to s. 1, *ante.*

DEFINITIONS
For "secure tenancy", see ss. 28, *ante*, and 49 (2), *post*; for "dwelling-house", see s. 50 (2), *post.*

Housing associations

49. Exclusion of certain housing associations from Chapter II

(1) In this section—

"registered association" means a housing association which falls within paragraph (*a*) of section 15 (3) of the 1977 Act (associations registered with the Housing Corporation); and

"registered society" means a housing association which falls within paragraph (*d*) of section 15 (3) (certain associations registered under the Industrial and Provident Societies Act 1965).

(2) A tenancy is not a secure tenancy at any time when the interest of the landlord belongs to a housing association which is both a registered association and a registered society.

(3) Sections 35 to 46 of this Act do not apply to a tenancy at any time when the interest of the landlord belongs to a housing association which is a registered society.

(4) If a housing association which is a registered society has been a registered association but at any time after the commencement of this Chapter has ceased to be such an association it shall notify those of its tenants who thereby become secure tenants that they have become secure tenants.

(5) Notice under subsection (4) above shall be given in writing to each tenant concerned, within the period of 21 days beginning with the date on which the association ceased to be a registered association. **[378]**

COMMENCEMENT
See the note to s. 28, *ante.*

HOUSING ASSOCIATION
Cf. the note to s. 1, *ante.*

COMMENCEMENT OF THIS CHAPTER
See the note "Commencement" to s. 28, *ante.*

WRITING
See the note "Written; writing" to s. 5, *ante.*

21 DAYS BEGINNING WITH, ETC.
    See the note "Three months beginning with, etc." to s. 12, *ante*.

DEFINITIONS
    For "secure tenancy" and "secure tenant", see s. 28, *ante* and s, 150, *post*. Note as to "registered association" and "registered society", sub-s(1) above.

1977 ACT
    I.e., the Rent Act 1977; see s. 150, *post*. For s. 15 (3) (*a*) and (*d*) of that Act, see A.L.S. Vol. 255.

Supplementary

50. Interpretation of Chapter II

(1) In this Chapter—

"development corporation" means a development corporation established by an order made, or having effect as if made, under the New Towns Act 1965;

"housing co-operative" has the meaning given by paragraph 1 of Schedule 20 to this Act;

"housing co-operative agreement" means an agreement to which Schedule 20 applies;

"housing trust" has the same meaning as in section 15 of the 1977 Act;

"improvement" has the meaning given by section 81;

"landlord authority" has the meaning given by section 42 (1);

"local authority" means the council of a district, the Greater London Council, the council of a London borough, the Common Council of the City of London or the Council of the Isles of Scilly;

"rental period" means a period in respect of which a payment of rent falls to be made;

"successor" has the meaning given by section 31; and

"term", in relation to a secure tenancy, includes a condition of the tenancy.

(2) For the purposes of this Chapter—

(*a*) a dwelling-house may be a house or part of a house;

(*b*) land let together with a dwelling-house shall be treated as part of the dwelling-house unless the land is agricultural land exceeding two acres;

and in this subsection "agricultural land" has the meaning set out in section 26 (3) (*a*) of the General Rate Act 1967.

(3) A person is a member of another's family within the meaning of this Chapter if he is his spouse, parent, grandparent, child, grandchild, brother, sister, uncle, aunt, nephew or niece; treating—

(*a*) any relationship by marriage as a relationship by blood, any relationship of the half blood as a relationship of the whole blood and the stepchild of any person as his child; and

(*b*) an illegitimate person as the legitimate child of his mother and reputed father;

or if they live together as husband and wife. **[379]**

COMMENCEMENT
    See the note to s. 28, *ante*.

THIS CHAPTER
    I.e., Chapter II (ss. 28–50) of Part I of this Act.

COUNCIL OF A DISTRICT
See the note "Council of any district" to s. 43, *ante.*

GREATER LONDON COUNCIL
This council is constituted by the Local Government Act 1972, s. 8, Sch. 2, Vol. 42, pp. 860, 1115.

COUNCIL OF A LONDON BOROUGH
See the note "London borough" to s. 43, *ante.*

COMMON COUNCIL OF THE CITY OF LONDON
I.e., the mayor, aldermen and commons of the City of London in common council assembled; see the City of London (Various Powers) Act 1958, s. 5, Vol. 20, p. 398.

COUNCIL OF THE ISLES OF SCILLY
The Council of the Isles of Scilly is continued in being by the Local Government Act 1972, s. 265 (1), Vol. 42, p. 1094, and is now constituted by the Isles of Scilly Order 1978, S.I. 1978 No. 1844, art. 4 (made under s. 265 (2) of that Act, Vol. 42, p. 1094).

SECURE TENANCY
For meaning, see ss. 28 and 49 (2), *ante.*

FOR THE PURPOSES OF THIS CHAPTER, ETC.
Sub-s. (2) above is modelled on provisions contained in the Rent Act 1977, ss. 1, 26, Vol. 47, pp. 393, 427.

DWELLING-HOUSE
See the note to s. 3, *ante.*

LAND LET TOGETHER WITH A DWELLING-HOUSE, ETC.
It is supposed that the dwelling-house must be the dominant feature of the letting, so that a letting primarily for business purposes with a dwelling as a subsidiary adjunct only would be outside Part I; cf. the position under the Rent Act 1977, A.L.S. Vol. 255, ss. 6 and 26 and *Whiteley* v. *Wilson* [1952] 2 All E.R. 940, C.A. The question is primarily one of fact; cf. *Wimbush* v. *Cibulia* [1949] 2 K.B. 564; [1949] 2 All E.R. 432, C.A. If s. 49 (2) applies, then what is covered by it is, so to speak, a composite entity composed of the dwelling-house and the land: *Langford Property Co Ltd.* v. *Batten* [1950] 2 All E.R. 1079, H.L.
Thus, s. 50 (2) would mean that Part I would apply to land let as an adjunct to the dwelling-house, such as a garage or garden. "Together with" is not thought to mean that the land and the dwelling be let in the same document: *Mann* v. *Merrill* [1945] 1 All E.R. 708, C.A., and the two need not even adjoin physically, but some reasonably close connection would presumably be required: *Feyereisel* v. *Parry* [1952] 1 All E.R. 728, C.A.

NEW TOWNS ACT 1965
For the establishment of development corporations, see s. 2 of that Act, Vol. 36, p. 377.

1977 ACT
I.e., the Rent Act 1977; see s. 150, *post.* For the definition of "housing trust" in s. 15, see s. 15 (5) of that Act as substituted by s. 74 (2), *post.*

GENERAL RATE ACT 1967, s. 26 (3) (*a*)
See Vol. 27. p. 106. The definition contained in the General Rate Act 1967, s. 26 (3) (*a*), has been extended by the Rating Act 1971, Part I, Vol. 41, pp. 1169 *et seq.*

PART II

PRIVATE SECTOR TENANTS

PUBLICATION OF INFORMATION
As to the publication by local authorities of information for the assistance of landlords and tenants and others as to their rights and duties under this Part of this Act and s. 136, *post*, and as to the procedure for enforcing those rights and securing the performance of those duties, see the Rent Act 1977, s. 149, Vol. 47, p. 550, as amended by s. 152 (1) and Sch. 25, para. 53, post.

Protected shorthold tenancies

51. Preliminary

Sections 53 to 55 below modify the operation of the 1977 Act in relation to protected shorthold tenancies as defined in section 52 below. **[380]**

Government. See s. 153 (4), *post*, and the note "Orders under this section" thereto.

1977 Act. *I.e.*, the Rent Act 1977, A.L.S. Vol. 255; see s. 150 *post*.

52. Protected shorthold tenancies

(1) A protected shorthold tenancy is a protected tenancy granted after the commencement of this section which is granted for a term certain of not less than one year nor more than five years and satisfies the following conditions, that is to say,—

(a) it cannot be brought to an end by the landlord before the expiry of the term, except in pursuance of a provision for re-entry or forfeiture for non-payment of rent or breach of any other obligation of the tenancy; and

(b) before the grant the landlord has given the tenant a valid notice stating that the tenancy is to be a protected shorthold tenancy; and

(c) either a rent for the dwelling-house is registered at the time the tenancy is granted or—

(i) a certificate of fair rent has, before the grant, been issued under section 69 of the 1977 Act in respect of the dwelling-house and the rent payable under the tenancy, for any period before a rent is registered for the dwelling-house, does not exceed the rent specified in the certificate; and

(ii) an application for the registration of a rent for the dwelling-house is made not later than 28 days after the beginning of the term and is not withdrawn.

(2) A tenancy of a dwelling-house is not a protected shorthold tenancy if it is granted to a person who, immediately before it was granted, was a protected or statutory tenant of that dwelling-house.

(3) A notice is not valid for the purposes of subsection (1) (b) above unless it complies with the requirements of regulations made by the Secretary of State.

(4) The Secretary of State may by order direct that subsection (1) above shall have effect, either generally or in relation to any registration area specified in the order, as if paragraph (c) were omitted.

(5) If a protected tenancy is granted after the commencement of this section—

(a) for such a term certain as is mentioned in subsection (1) above, to be followed, at the option of the tenant, by a further term; or

(b) for such a term certain and thereafter from year to year or some other period;

and satisfies the conditions stated in that subsection, the tenancy is a protected shorthold tenancy until the end of the term certain. **[381]**

COMMENCEMENT
 See s. 153 (4), *post*, and the note "Orders under this section" thereto.

SUB-S. (I): PROTECTED SHORTHOLD TENANCY
 This means that the Rent Act 1977, A.L.S. Vol. 255, will apply for the duration of the fixed term and also for any term derived from it under sub-s. (5) of this section. By s. 1 of the 1977 Act, to be protected, there must be a tenancy under which a dwelling-house (which may be a house or part of a house) is let as a separate dwelling.
 As to this, see s. 28 and the notes thereto, which apply here.

Tenancy not licence

It is a question of intention whether a licence or a tenancy is created: *Addiscombe Garden Estates Ltd.* v. *Crabbe* [1958] 1 Q.B. 513; [1957] 3 All E.R. 563, C.A.; *Somma* v. *Hazlehurst* [1978] 2 All E.R. 1011, C.A. As to the principles of construction where a "sham" agreement is suspected, see *Walsh* v. *Griffiths-Jones* [1978] 2 All E.R. 1002; *Somma* v. *Hazlehurst, supra; O'Malley* v. *Seymour* (1979) 250 E.G. 1083, C.A.; *Demuren & Adefope* v. *Seal Estates* (1979) 250 E.G. 440, C.A.: the court asks whether the document does not truly represent or reproduce the real transaction.

An informal agreement under which household bills are paid by an occupier may confer only a licence on the latter: *Barnes* v. *Barratt* [1970] 2 Q.B. 657; [1970] 2 All E.R. 483, C.A. There may be a licence not a lease where it is shown that there is no intention to create legal relations: *Booker* v. *Palmer* [1942] 2 All E.R. 674, C.A.; *Heslop* v. *Burns* [1974] 3 All E.R. 406, C.A.

In a proper case, exclusive possession may lead the court to conclude that a tenancy has been created: *Cobb* v. *Lane* [1952] 1 All E.R. 1199, C.A.; *Facchini* v. *Bryson* [1952] 1 T.L.R. 1386, C.A. In this, it is thought that merely to reserve oneself a right of access may not prevent there from being held to be a lease: *Walsh* v. *Griffiths-Jones, supra*. A term which enables the owner to introduce another occupier with the "licensee" denies exclusive possession to them both: *Somma* v. *Hazlehurst, supra*. Temporary occupation may be a ground for holding there only to be a licence: *Marchant* v. *Charters* [1977] 3 All E.R. 918, C.A. A sharing of essential living facilities such as a dining room may well negate, of itself, the intention to create a tenancy: *R.* v. *South Middlesex Rent Tribunal, ex p. Beswick* (1976) 32 P. & C.R. 67.

For an exhaustive analysis of this problem, see an article in [1980] Conv. 27 (P. Robson and P. Watchman).

GRANTED

It is presumed that express rather than implied grant is what is required, cf. *City Permanent Building Society* v. *Miller*, [1952] 2 All E.R. 621, C.A. If it is desired to pass the legal estate and thus create a "term of years absolute" within the Law of Property Act 1925, s. 205 (1) (xxvii), then the neessary formalities must be complied with: by *ibid.*, s. 52 (1) there must be a deed where the term exceeds three years (s. 54 (2)). If the term is under this period, then the legal estate passes provided that the lease takes effect in possession i.e. it confers a right to immediate as opposed to future possession: *Foster* v. *Reeves* [1892] 2 Q.B. 255.

a term in equity, which is governed in principle by the same rules as apply to a term at law: *Walsh* v. *Lonsdale* (1882) 21 Ch.D. 9, C.A. Covenants in an equitable term would now appear to be enforceable as though a legal estate had been created: see *Industrial Properties (Barton Hill) Ltd.* v. *Associated Electrical Industries Ltd.* [1977] Q.B. 580; [1977] 2 All E.R. 293, C.A.

TERM CERTAIN

The contrast is with a periodic tenancy, which cannot be a protected shorthold tenancy, even though the duration of a periodic tenancy may, for want of service of a notice to quit, run for well over one year, or because there is a fetter on the landlord's power to serve a notice to quit which has the result of granting a tenancy for a very considerable time: cf. *Re Midland Railway Co's Agreement* [1971] Ch. 725; [1971] 1 All E.R. 1007, C.A., and *Centaploy Ltd.* v. *Matlodge Ltd.* [1974] Ch. 1; [1973] 2 All E.R. 720.

The date of commencement and of termination of the term certain must be stated in the habendum of the lease: *Lace* v. *Chantler* [1944] K.B. 368; [1944] 1 All E.R. 305, C.A. If not, then only a periodic tenancy may arise by implication from the payment and acceptance of rent: *Re Midland Railway Co's Agreement, supra*.

There being no limitation on the persons who may grant a protected shorthold tenancy, a lessee might (in the absence of covenant with his lessor) grant a protected shorthold tenancy provided that his reversion is sufficient to support it: if not, then there is an assignment of the residue of the term: *Milmo* v. *Carreras* [1946] K.B. 306; [1946] 1 All E.R. 288, C.A.

RENT ... REGISTERED (SUB-S. (1) (*c*))

A protected shorthold tenancy differs from other regulated tenancies in that, subject to the court's dispensation power in s. 55 (2), it is one of the conditions precedent to there being a shortlet that a fair rent must be registered, certified or applied for. In the case of any other kind of regulated tenancy, registration requires the initiative of the landlord, tenant or local authority: see the Rent Act 1977, ss. 67 and 68. It may be of interest, *passim*, to note that it was stated that in 1978 only 4·8 per cent of applications for registration of a fair rent were by tenants: H.L. Committee, 2nd July 1980, Col. 459.

As to the application for registration of a fair rent, see the Rent Act 1977, s. 67 (as amended from the commencement of Part II of this Act by ss. 60 and 61 (5)). Failure to specify a rent is fatal to an application; *Chapman* v. *Earl* [1968] 2 All E.R. 1214, unless the rent is capable of calculation with certainty: *R.* v. *London Rent Assessment Panel, ex parte Braq Investments Ltd.* [1969] 2 All E.R. 1012.

SECTION 69 OF THE 1977 ACT
This section enables a landlord intending to let a dwelling-house where no rent is registered to apply to the rent officer for a certificate of fair rent: this specifies the rent which, in the opinion of the rent officer, would be the fair rent. See also Sch. 12 to the 1977 Act.

SUB-S (2)
Owing to Sch. 25, para. 58, the offer of a shorthold tenancy in another dwelling-house of the landlord to a sitting protected or statutory tenant is not to be deemed suitable alternative accommodation in proceedings for possession by the landlord. This would not prevent, of itself, surrender by the tenant of his existing tenancy in return for a shortlet of another dwelling-house, and a variation in accommodation, following surrender, would not be caught: cf. *Gluchowska* v. *Tottenham B.C.*, [1954] 1 All E.R. 408.

SUB-S. (5)
Even if a tenant's renewal option (para. (*a*)) or a periodic tenancy following the fixed term certain (para. (*b*)) are included in the *original* grant of the shortlet, Case 19 will still be available at the end of the renewed term or the ending of the periodic tenancy as the case may be. Where no provision as to tenant's renewal, etc., is made in the grant of the term certain, then: (i) on its expiry, in the event of the sitting tenant (protected or statutory) remaining in possession, even if the landlord accepts rent for any period from this person, Case 19 remains available to the landlord even where he failed to serve an "appropriate notice" on the tenant in the last 3 months of the protected shorthold tenancy: see s. 55 (1) (*a*); but (ii) the landlord must beware of re-grant of a periodic (or any other) tenancy to a person not the sitting (protected or statutory) tenant: if there is such an one in possession, then he should not accept rent from him, though even if the landlord did this, the court would, in the event of his promptly asking for possession, be reluctant to infer an implied grant of a protected tenancy: *Marcroft Wagons Ltd.* v. *Smith* [1951] 2 K.B. 496; [1951] 2 All E.R. 271, C.A. In this, the parties may agree or the circumstances may justify an implied re-grant: *Murray Bull & Co Ltd* v. *Murray* [1953] 1 Q.B. 211; [1952] 2 All E.R. 1079.

DWELLING-HOUSE
Cf. the note to s. 3, *ante*.

NOT LATER THAN 28 DAYS AFTER, ETC.
See the note "Not later than three months after, etc." to s. 11, *ante*.

SUB-S. (3): SECRETARY OF STATE
See the note to s. 2, *ante*.

SUB-S. (4): REGISTRATION AREA
As to these, see the Rent Act 1977, s. 62, A.L.S. Vol. 255.

DEFINITIONS
By virtue of s. 150, *post*, for "protected tenant", see the Rent Act 1977, s. 1, and for "statutory tenant", see s. 2 of that Act.

1977 ACT
I.e., the Rent Act 1977; see s. 150, *post*. For s. 69 of that Act, see Vol. 47, p. 475.

REGULATIONS UNDER THIS SECTION
At the time of going to press no regulations had been made under sub-s. (3) above.
As to regulations generally, see s. 151, *post*.

ORDERS UNDER THIS SECTION
At the time of going to press no order had been made under sub-s. (4) above.
As to orders generally, see s. 151, *post*; and note, in particular, sub-s. (2) thereof.

53. Right of tenant to terminate protected shorthold tenancy

(1) A protected shorthold tenancy may be brought to an end (by virtue of this section and notwithstanding anything in the terms of the tenancy) before the expiry

of the term certain by notice in writing of the appropriate length given by the tenant to the landlord; and the appropriate length of the notice is—

    (*a*) one month if the term certain is two years or less; and

    (*b*) three months if it is more than two years.

(2) Any agreement relating to a protected shorthold tenancy (whether or not contained in the instrument creating the tenancy) shall be void in so far as it purports to impose any penalty or disability on the tenant in the event of his giving a notice under this section. **[382]**

COMMENCEMENT
    See s. 153 (4), *post*, and the note "Orders under this section" thereto.

PROTECTED SHORTHOLD TENANCY
    The operation of the Rent Act 1977, A.L.S. Vol. 255, is modified by this section and ss. 54 and 55, *post*, as respects protected shorthold tenancies as defined by s. 52, *ante*.

THE TERM CERTAIN
    I.e., the term certain mentioned in s. 52 (1), *ante*.

WRITING
    See the note "Written; writing" to s. 5, *ante*.

MONTH; MONTHS
    "Month" means calendar month; see the Interpretation Act 1978, s. 5, Sch. 1, A.L.S. Vol. 258.

VOID
    It is an open question whether this means exactly what it says, because of public policy requiring a strict construction (see *R.* v. *Hipswell* (1828), 8 B & C. 467) or voidable at the option of the tenant: cf. *Re London Celluloid Co.* (1888) 39 Ch.D. 190, C.A.

PENALTY OR DISABILITY
    A penalty is a sum of money stipulated *in terrorem* of the offending party, but contrast liquidated damages, which are not within the vice of this subsection, and which are essentially a genuine pre-estimate of damages: *Dunlop Pneumatic Tyre Co. Ltd.* v. *New Garage & Motor Co Ltd.* [1915] A.C. 79, H.L. A sum which is extravagant in amount compared with the greatest loss which could possibly be proved is a penalty: *Re Newman* (1876) 4 Ch.D. 724, C.A. Accordingly, if in a lease there was a term stating that damage must be made good on a fixed financial basis, this would not be a penalty if the sums payable represented a genuine pre-estimate of the loss or damage: *Lord Elphinstone* v. *Monkland Iron Co.* (1886) 11 App. Cas. 332, H.L.; *Willson* v. *Love* [1896] 1 Q.B. 626, C.A. The terminology is not decisive; what is described as a "penalty" may be liquidated damages and *vice versa*: *Willson* v. *Love, supra*. Also, a sum of £40 payable on quitting towards redecoration is not a penalty but an agreed sum towards dilapidations, and may therefore be inserted without falling foul of sub-s. (2) of this section: see *Boyer* v. *Warbey* [1953] 1 Q.B. 234; [1952] 2 All E.R. 976, C.A. But a clause in the lease requiring the payment of the landlord's costs in any event was held to infringe the Landlord and Tenant Act 1954, s. 38, as a penalty: *Stevenson & Rush (Holdings) Ltd.* v. *Langdon* (1978) 122 Sol. Jo. 827, C.A.

54. Subletting or assignment

(1) Where the whole or part of a dwelling-house let under a protected shorthold tenancy has been sublet at any time during the continuous period specified in subsection (3) below, and, during that period, the landlord becomes entitled, as against the tenant, to possession of the dwelling-house, he shall also be entitled to possession against the sub-tenant and section 137 of the 1977 Act shall not apply.

(2) A protected shorthold tenancy of a dwelling-house and any protected tenancy of the same dwelling-house granted during the continuous period specified in subsection (3) below shall not be capable of being assigned, except in pursuance of an order under section 24 of the Matrimonial Causes Act 1973.

(3) The continuous period mentioned in subsections (1) and (2) above is the period beginning with the grant of the protected shorthold tenancy and continuing until either—

(a) no person is in possession of the dwelling-house as a protected or statutory tenant; or

(b) a protected tenancy of the dwelling-house is granted to a person who is not, immediately before the grant, in possession of the dwelling-house as a protected or statutory tenant. **[383]**

COMMENCEMENT
See s. 153 (4), *post*, and the note "Orders under this section" thereto.

DWELLING-HOUSE
Cf. the note to s. 3, *ante*.

PROTECTED SHORTHOLD TENANCY
The operation of the Rent Act 1977, A.L.S. Vol. 255, is modified by this section and s. 53, *ante*, and s. 55, *post*, as respects protected shorthold tenancies as defined by s. 52, *ante*.

LANDLORD BECOMES ENTITLED ... TO POSSESSION OF THE DWELLING-HOUSE
For the grounds for possession of dwelling-houses let on a protected tenancy, see the Rent Act 1977, s. 98, Sch. 15, as amended, in the case of Sch. 15, by s. 55, *post*.

PROTECTED TENANCY
As to these tenancies, see the Rent Act 1977, s. 1, and the notes thereto.

DEFINITIONS
For "protected shorthold tenancy", see s. 52, *ante*; by virtue of s. 150, *post*, for "protected tenant", see the Rent Act 1977, s. 1, and for "statutory tenant", see s. 2 of that Act.

1977 ACT
I.e., the Rent Act 1977; see s. 150, *post*.

MATRIMONIAL CAUSES ACT 1973, S. 24
See A.L.S. Vol. 217.

55. Orders for possession

(1) The following Case shall be added to the Cases in Part II of Schedule 15 to the 1977 Act (mandatory orders for possession):

"Case 19

Where the dwelling-house was let under a protected short hold tenancy (or is treated under section 55 of the Housing Act 1980 as having been so let) and—

(a) there either has been no grant of a further tenancy of the dwelling-house since the end of the protected shorthold tenancy or, if there was such a grant, it was to a person who immediately before the grant was in possession of the dwelling-house as a protected or statutory tenant; and

(b) the proceedings for possession were commenced after appropriate notice by the landlord to the tenant and not later than 3 months after the expiry of the notice.

A notice is appropriate for this Case if—

(i) it is in writing and states that proceedings for possession under this Case may be brought after its expiry; and

(ii) it expires not earlier than 3 months after it is served nor, if, when it is served, the tenancy is a periodic tenancy, before that periodic tenancy could be brought to an end by a notice to quit served by the landlord on the same day;

   (iii) it is served—

       (*a*) in the period of 3 months immediately preceding the date on which the protected shorthold tenancy comes to an end; or

       (*b*) if that date has passed, in the period of 3 months immediately preceding any anniversary of that date; and

   (iv) in a case where a previous notice has been served by the landlord on the tenant in respect of the dwelling-house, and that notice was an appropriate notice, it is served not earlier than 3 months after the expiry of the previous notice."

(2) If, in proceedings for possession under Case 19 set out above, the court is of opinion that, notwithstanding that the condition of paragraph (*b*) or (*c*) of section 52 (1) above is not satisfied, it is just and equitable to make an order for possession, it may treat the tenancy under which the dwelling-house was let as a protected shorthold tenancy. **[384]**

COMMENCEMENT
    See s. 153 (4), *post*, and the note "Orders under this section" thereto.

GENERAL NOTE
    The following deals with the relationship between an "appropriate notice" under this section and a notice to quit a periodic protected tenancy following the term certain under s. 52 (5).
    When a protected shorthold tenancy is followed by a protected periodic tenancy as a result of express grant contemplated by s. 52 (5), the term certain will, of course, expire on its last day automatically. To be able to rely on Case 19 to obtain vacant possession, the landlord must, as a matter of procedure, serve an "appropriate notice" on the tenant. If he wishes to obtain possession as soon as he is able on expiry of the term certain, he must take very great care, where s. 52 (5) (*b*) applies, to serve a suitable and correct notice to quit in addition, so as to end the protected periodic tenancy following the protected shorthold tenancy at law. Suppose L grants T a one -year PST in July 1981 to expire on 30th June 1982, to be followed by a monthly tenancy. The earliest date, it seems on which the term may expire at law is, thanks to s. 52 (5), 31st July 1982. If, therefore, L wishes to rely on Case 19 to obtain possession as soon as may be after that date: (i) he must serve a notice to quit on T to end the periodic protected tenancy at law on 31st July 1982; (ii) he must also serve an "appropriate notice" which expires not earlier than 3 months after it is served nor before 31st July, 1982, this being the earliest date on which the periodic tenancy may be brought to an end: s. 55 (1) (ii). Also, both notices must be served in the period of 3 months immediately preceding the date of expiry of the shortlet (30th June 1982 in the example): s. 55 (1) (iii).
    If, in this, and dealing only with the case of monthly or shorter periodic protected tenancies following the PST under s. 52 (5), the notice to quit is bad, e.g. because it states that wrong date of termination, or is served out of time, then, unless L can put matters right in time, two unpleasant consequences appear to follow: (i) If the notice to quit is ineffective, then the periodic protected tenancy following the PST is not ended thereby; if no suitable notice to quit is served before the expiry of the PST, possession cannot be obtained promptly because the landlord's "appropriate notice" is merely procedural and depends, in this instance, on the periodic protected tenancy having been effectually determined: see s. 55 (1) (ii). (ii) If the above is correct, then L would, where his notice to quit was bad, or not served, have to wait for at least 9 further months from the expiry of the PST before being able to serve a fresh notice to quit plus an apppropriate notice: see s. 55 (1) (iii) (*b*). Meantime, the tenant (protected or statutory) will enjoy full Rent Act protection.
    It was assumed in the above that the landlord stated a date of termination. In that the courts do not necessarily require a notice to quit in the case of a yearly or presumably other periodic tenancy, expressly to state a date of termination provided that sense may be made of the notice, it would be much safer for a landlord to omit all specific reference

to a date of termination unless he is quite sure of it. See e.g. *Addis* v. *Burrows* [1948] 1 All E.R. 177, C.A.; *Davis* v. *Huntley* [1947] 1 All E.R. 246, C.A.

But it was also assumed in the above discussion that if the landlord gets the date of termination wrong where he states one in the notice, this is fatal to its validity. This was held to be so in relation to notices to determine an option to determine: *Hankey* v. *Clavering* [1942] 2 K.B. 326; [1942] 2 All E.R. 311, C.A. But latterly, some doubt as to this has arisen: it has been held that if the mistake is so absurd (e.g. stating a date of termination which was manifestly absurd becccause it had already passed) that a reasonable tenant could make sense of the notice, then it will be upheld: *Carradine Properties Ltd.* v. *Aslam* [1976] 1 All E.R. 373, approved in *Germax Securities Ltd.* v. *Spiegal* (1979) 250 E.G. 449, C.A. (See further some criticisms of these cases in 251 E.G. 653.) It is also self-evident that a trivial error in the landlord's notice to quit will not render it bad of itself, e.g. stating an incorrect date of service: *Germax Securities Ltd.* v. *Spiegal*, *supra*; or stating the incorrect name: *Frankland* v. *Capstick* [1959] 1 All E.R. 209, C.A., *Safeway Food Stores Ltd.* v. *Morris* (1980) 254 F.G. 1091. Finally, if the landlord tries to have the best of all worlds and leaves too much to the tenant to resolve, the notice may for this reason be held bad: *Phipps & Co.* v. *Rogers* [1925] 1 K.B. 14, C.A.

One final remark: if the landlord in the example had granted the tenant a one-year PST on 1st July 1981 to be followed by a yearly tenancy (protected: s. 52 (5)) than L could not obtain possession in principle until after 30th June 1983 under s. 55 at any rate and, L will have to serve the notice to quit on or before 1st January 1983 to expire on the last day of the yearly tenancy or the anniversary thereof: *Sidebotham* v. *Holland* [1895] 1 Q.B. 378, C.A., and then follow it up with an appropriate notice on or after 1st April 1983 but no later than 1st July of that year: cf. *Dodds* v. *Walker* (1980) 255 E.G. 53, C.A.

FOLLOWING CASE SHALL BE ADDED TO THE CASES IN PART II OF SCH. 15, ETC.
It is provided by the Rent Act 1977, s. 98 (2) A.L.S. Vol. 255 that if, apart from s. 98 (1) of that Act, *ibid.*, the landlord would be entitled to recover possession of a dwelling-house let on or subject to a regulated tenancy (as defined by s. 18 of that Act, as partly repealed by s. 152 (3) and Sch. 26, *post*), the Court shall make an order for possession if the circumstances are as specified in any of the Cases in Part II of Sch. 15 to that Act. See also the provisions of the Act of 1977 metnioned in the note "Case 11" to Part II of Sch. 15 to the Act of 1977.

DWELLING-HOUSE
See the note to the Rent Act 1977, s. 1.

PROTECTED SHORTHOLD TENANCY
The operation of the Rent Act 1977, is modified by this section and ss. 53 and 54, *ante*, as respects protected shorthold tenancies as defined by s. 52, *ante*.

NOT LATER (EARLIER) THAN 3 MONTHS AFTER, ETC.
See the note "Not later than three months after, etc." to s. 11, *ante*.

WRITING
See the note "Written; writing" to s. 5, *ante*.

PERIODIC TENANCY
As to periodic tenancies, see 23 Halsburys Laws (3rd Edn.), pp. 529 *et seq.*

ON THE SAME DAY
I.e., the day on which the appropriate notice is served.

MONTHS
I.e., calendar months; see the Interpretation Act 1978, s. 5, Sch. 1, A.L.S. Vol. 258.

THE COURT
Cf. the note "A court" to the Rent Act 1977, s. 98.

DEFINITIONS
For "protected shorthold tenancy", see s. 52, *ante*; for "protected tenant", see the Rent Act 1977; for "statutory tenant", see s. 2 of that Act; for "landlord", "let", "tenancy" and "tenant", see s. 152 (1) of that Act.

1977 ACT
I.e., the Rent Act 1977; see s. 150, *post*.

Assured tenancies

56. Assured tenancies

(1) A tenancy under which a dwelling-house is let as a separate dwelling is an assured tenancy and not a housing association tenancy (within the meaning of section 86 of the 1977 Act) or a protected tenancy if—

    (*a*) it would, when created, have been a protected tenancy or, as the case may be, housing association tenancy but for this section; and

    (*b*) the conditions described in subsection (3) below are satisfied.

(2) In this Part of this Act "assured tenant" means the tenant under an assured tenancy.

(3) The conditions are that—

    (*a*) the interest of the landlord has, since the creation of the tenancy, belonged to an approved body;

    (*b*) the dwelling-house is, or forms part of a building which was erected (and on which construction work first began) after the passing of this Act; and

    (*c*) before the tenant first occupied the dwelling-house under the tenancy, no part of it had been occupied by any person as his residence except under an assured tenancy.

(4) In this Part of this Act "approved body" means a body, or one of a description of bodies, for the time being specified for the purposes of this Part of this Act in an order made by the Secretary of State.

(5) After section 16 of the 1977 Act there is inserted the following section—

"16A. Assured tenancies

A tenancy shall not be a protected tenancy at any time when it is an assured tenancy within the meaning of section 56 of the Housing Act 1980.".

(6) The preceding provisions of this section do not apply to a tenancy if, before the grant of the tenancy, the landlord has given the tenant a valid notice stating that the tenancy is to be a protected tenancy or, as the case may be, a housing association tenancy and not an assured tenancy.

(7) A notice is not valid for the purposes of subsection (6) above unless it complies with the requirements of regulations made by the Secretary of State. **[385]**

COMMENCEMENT
    See s. 153 (4), *post*, and the note "Orders under this section" thereto.

SUB-S. (1): GENERALLY
    As to the conditions which have to be satisfied for there to be a protected tenancy, see the Rent Act 1977 s. 1: some aspects of this are considered in the note to s. 28. As to housing association tenancies, see *ibid.*, s. 86.

DWELLING-HOUSE
    Cf. the note to s. 3, *ante*.

LET AS A SEPARATE DWELLING
    Cf. the decisions on the meaning of the words "let as a separate dwelling" in the Rent Act 1977, s. 1, and its predecessors, which are discussed in the notes to that section, A.L.S. Vol. 255.

ASSURED TENANCY
    For other provisions as to assured tenancies, see s. 57, *post* (effect of interest of landlord ceasing to belong to approved body), and s. 58 and Sch. 5, *post* (application of Landlord and Tenant Act 1954). Note also that by virtue of the Housing Finance Act 1972, s. 19 (5) (*d*), as substituted by s. 118 and Sch. 15, para. 3, *post*, a person is a private tenant

for the purposes of the provisions of Part II of that Act, (as amended by s. 118 and Sch. 15, *post*), relating to rent allowances if he occupies a dwelling let under an assured tenancy within the meaning of the present section.

PROTECTED TENANCY
As to those tenancies, see the Rent Act 1977, s. 1, and the notes thereto.

SUB-S. (2): THIS PART OF THIS ACT
I.e., Part II (ss. 51–79) of this Act.

SUB-S. (3): BUILDING
A structure or erection must form part of the realty to be a "building" and thus change the physical character of the land: *Cheshire County Council* v. *Woodward* [1962] 2 Q.B. 126 [1962] 1 All E.R. 517. Cf. the definition in the Leasehold Reform Act 1967, A.L.S. Vol. 162, s. 2 (1) (*b*), which envisages that only flats are "buildings"; but also in a development of terraces, it is thought that, contrary to the decision in *Parsons* v. *Viscount Gage* [1974] 1 All E.R. 1162, H.L., each terraced house could be a building on its own or the whole series a building taken as a whole, as a matter of fact and degree. See also *Bardrick* v. *Haycock* (1976) 31 P. & C.R. 421, C.A.; *Bell* v. *Edinburgh Workers' Dwelling-House Improvement Co. Ltd.* 1957 S.L.T. 10 (Sh. Ct.).

PASSING OF THIS ACT
This Act was passed, *i.e.*, received the Royal Assent, on 8th August 1980.

AS HIS RESIDENCE
The occupation by the person previous to the tenant "as his residence" resembles the requirement in the Rent Act 1977, s. 2 (1) (*a*) as to statutory tenancies; and so it is thought that to satisfy the condition in sub-s. (3) (*c*), substantial rather than merely nominal occupation is required: *Remon* v. *City of London* Real Property Co. [1921] 1 K.B. 49; *Hutchinson* v. *Jauncey* [1950] 1 K.B. 574; [1950] 1 All E.R. 165. The person's occupation must have a domestic quality about it: *Reidy* v. *Walker* [1933] 2 K.B. 266. If the person assigns the whole premises (*Crowhurst* v. *Maidment* [1952] 2 All E.R. 808, C.A.) or sub-lets the whole of them (*Haskins* v. *Lewis* [1931] 2 K.B. 1; *Skinner* v. *Geary* [1931] 2 K.B. 546, C.A.) then there is no occupation as his residence and the condition in sub-s. (3) (*c*) is not complied with. This is also the case where the tenant is not personally in occupation as where he allows other persons, such as his relatives, into occupation: see *Cove* v. *Flick* [1954] 2 Q.B. 326, n.; [1954] 2 All E.R. 441, C.A.
  In this connection, it is not thought that "person" is apt to include "company": this is because, in relation to the Rent Acts, it has been held that no trading company may claim security of tenure: *Hiller* v. *United Dairies (London) Ltd.* [1934] 1 K.B. 57, C.A., and this, irrespective of whether there is a term in the lease allowing for occupation by the company or by its agent or employee: see *S. L. Dando Ltd.* v. *Hitchcock and Another* [1954] 2 Q.B. 317; 1954 2 All E.R. 335, C.A.; *Firstcross Ltd.* v. *East West (Export/Import) Ltd. and Another* (1980) 255 E.G. 355, C.A.

SUB-S. (4): SECRETARY OF STATE
See the note to s. 2, *ante*.

DEFINITIONS
In the section substituted by sub-s. (5) above for "protected tenancy", see the Rent Act 1977, s. 1, and for "tenancy", see s. 152 (1) of that Act. Note as to "approved body", sub-s. (4) above.

1977 ACT
I.e., the Rent Act 1977; see s. 150, *post*. S. 86 is amended by s. 77 and Sch. 10, para. 1, *post*, and is partly repealed by s. 152(3) and Sch. 26, *post*.

ORDERS UNDER THIS SECTION
See The Assured Tenancies (Approved Body) (No. 1) Order 1980, S.I. 1980 No. 1694.
  As to orders generally, see s. 151, *post*.

REGULATIONS UNDER THIS SECTION
At the time of going to press no regulations had been made under sub-s. (7) above.
  As to regulations generally, see s. 151, *post*.

57. Effect of interest of landlord ceasing to belong to approved body

(1) If the landlord under an assured tenancy ceases to be an approved body by reason only of a variation in the bodies or descriptions of bodies for the time specified in an order under section 56 (4) of this Act, then in relation to—

    (*a*) that tenancy; and

    (*b*) any further tenancy granted by the landlord to the person who immediately before the grant was in possession of the dwelling-house as an assured tenant;

the landlord shall be treated, for the purposes of the condition in section 56 (3) (*a*) above, as if it had remained an approved body.

(2) If, for any period—

    (*a*) the interest of the landlord under an assured tenancy has ceased to belong to an approved body, for any reason other than that mentioned in subsection (1) above; and

    (*b*) but for this subsection the tenancy would thereby have become a housing association tenancy (within the meaning of section 86 of the 1977 Act) or a protected tenancy;

then so much of that period as does not exceed 3 months shall be disregarded in determining whether the condition in section 56 (3) (*a*) above is satisfied in relation to that tenancy. **[386]**

COMMENCEMENT
    See s. 153 (4), *post*, and the note "Orders under this section" thereto.

GRANTED
    See s. 51 and the note thereto.

IN POSSESSION
    For a detailed discussion of this term, see Farrand, "Contract and Conveyance", 3rd Edn. (1979) p. 218. In leasehold conveyancing, the contrast is between a term taking effect in possession at once and a term whose commencement is postponed until a future date: see *Foster* v. *Reeves* [1892] 2 Q.B. 255, at p. 257; *District Bank Ltd.* v. *Webb* [1958] 1 All E.R. 126.

ASSURED TENANCY
    As to assured tenancies, see s. 56, *ante*, and the other provisions mentioned in the note "Assured tenancy" thereto.

DWELLING-HOUSE
    Cf. the note to s. 3, *ante*.

PROTECTED TENANCY
    As to these tenancies, see the Rent Act 1977, s. 1, A.L.S. Vol. 255, and the notes thereto.

MONTHS
    I.e., calendar months; see the Interpretation Act 1978, s. 5, Sch. 1, A.L.S. Vol. 258.

DEFINITIONS
    For "assured tenant", see s. 56 (2), *ante*; for "approved body", see s. 56 (4), *ante*.

1977 ACT
    I.e., the Rent Act 1977; see s. 150, *post*. Section 86 is amended by s. 77 and Sch. 10, para. 1, *post*, and is partly repealed by s. 152 (3) and Sch. 26, *post*.

58. Application of Landlord and Tenant Act 1954

(1) Part II of the Landlord and Tenant Act 1954 (renewal and continuation of tenancies) applies to assured tenancies as it applies to certain business and other

tenancies by virtue of section 23 of that Act, but subject to the exceptions and modifications mentioned in Schedule 5 to this Act.

(2) Part IV of that Act (miscellaneous and supplementary provisions) applies to assured tenancies subject to the exceptions and modifications mentioned in Schedule 5. **[387]**

COMMENCEMENT
   See s. 153 (4), *post*, and the note "Orders under this section" thereto.

ASSURED TENANCIES
   As to assured tenancies, see s. 56, *ante*, and the other provisions mentioned in the note "Assured tenancy" thereto.

LANDLORD AND TENANT ACT 1954, PARTS II, IV, S. 23
   See A.L.S. Vols. 87, 155.

Rents

59. Rent officers and applications for registration of rent

(1) In section 63 (2) of the 1977 Act (provisions to be made by rent officer schemes) there is inserted, at the end of paragraph (*d*) "; and

  (*e*) may require the proper officer—
    (i) to designate one of the rent officers as chief rent officer; and
    (ii) to delegate to him such of the duties imposed on the proper officer by virtue of paragraph (*d*) above as may be specified in the scheme."

(2) In section 67 of the 1977 Act (application for registration of rent) for subsection (2) there is substituted the following subsection—

  "(2) Any such application must be in the prescribed form and must—
    (*a*) specify the rent which it is sought to register;
    (*b*) where the rent includes any sum payable by the tenant to the landlord for services and the application is made by the landlord, specify that sum and be accompanied by details of the expenditure incurred by the landlord in providing those services; and
    (*c*) contain such other particulars as may be prescribed."

(3) Schedule 6 to this Act has effect, in relation to applications made after the commencement of this subsection, for the purpose of amending the procedure provided for by the 1977 Act in relation to applications for the registration of rent.

[388]

COMMENCEMENT
   See s. 153 (4), *post*, and the note "Orders under this section" thereto.

PROPER OFFICER
   As to the meaning of this expression, cf. the Local Government Act, s. 270 (3), A.L.S. Vol. 209.

PRESCRIBED FORM; SUCH OTHER PARTICULARS AS MAY BE PRESCRIBED
   I.e., prescribed by regulations under the Rent Act 1977, s. 74, A.L.S. Vol. 255; see s. 75 (1) of that Act, *ibid*, (under which a form substantially to the same effect as the prescribed form may also be used). At the time of going to press no regulations had been made for the purposes of the Rent Act 1977, s. 67 (2), as substituted by sub-s. (2) above, but it is thought that, if they are still in force at the commencement of this section, the Rent Regulation (Forms etc.) Regulations 1978, S.I. 1978 No 495, regs. 7, 8, Sch. 4, Forms Nos. 5–7, will have effect for the purposes of that subsection, and the Rent (Agriculture) (Rent Registration) Regulations 1978, S.I. 1978 No. 494, will have effect for the purposes of that subsection as applied by the Rent (Agriculture) Act 1976, s. 13, A.L.S. Vol. 250.

MUST ... SPECIFY THE RENT WHICH IT IS SOUGHT TO REGISTER
Failure by an applicant to specify in his application the rent which it is sought to register is a fatal defect having the consequence that the application and subsequent proceedings on it are a nullity and that certiorari has to quash the determination of the fair rent (*Chapman* v. *Earl*, [1968] 2 All E.R. 1213). It is, however, sufficient if words are used from which the rent can be calculated with certainty (*R* v. *London Rent Assessment Panel, Ex Parte Braq Investments, Ltd.*, [1969] 2 All E.R. 1012).

SERVICES
See the note to the Rent Act 1977, s. 30.

DEFINITIONS
For "prescribed", see the Rent Act 1977, s. 78 (1); for "landlord" and "tenant", see s. 152 (1) of that Act.

1977 ACT
I.e., the Rent Act 1977: see s. 150, *post*.

60. Applications for new registered rents and phasing of increases

(1) In section 67 of the 1977 Act (which, among other things, prevents an application for a new registered rent from being made within 3 years of the date of an existing registration and which is applied by section 13 (2) of the Rent (Agriculture) Act 1976 to rents registered under that Act) in subsections (3) and (4) for the words "3 years" there are substituted, in each case, the words "2 years".

(2) Subsection (1) above does not apply in any case where, on the determination or confirmation of a rent by the rent officer, the rent determined by him is registered, or his confirmation is noted in the register, before the commencement of this section.

(3) In Schedule 6 to the 1976 Act and in Schedule 8 to the 1977 Act (phasing of increases in registered rents) there is substituted, in each case for paragraph 3, the following paragraph—

"3.—(1) Subject to sub-paragraph (2) below, the permitted increase for a period falling within the period of delay is an increase to an amount calculated by applying the formula—

$$\tfrac{1}{2}(P+S+R)$$

where—

P is the previous rent limit,
S is the service element, and
R is the registered rent.

(2) The maximum permitted increase by virtue of this Schedule is an increase to the registered rent".

(4) Sections 56 and 114 of, and Schedule 9 to, the 1977 Act (special phasing rules in cases where controlled tenancies have been converted into regulated tenancies and where certain improvements have been made to dwelling-houses) are hereby repealed); and the general rules relating to the phasing of rent increases contained in section 55 of, and Schedule 8 to, that Act shall apply in those cases.

(5) The Secretary of State may by order make provision—

(a) reducing or increasing the period for the time being mentioned in section 67 (3) and (4) of the 1977 Act; or

(b) reducing or increasing the period of delay for the time being imposed by the Schedules mentioned in subsection (3) above; or

(c) repealing section 55 of the 1977 Act and section 15 of the 1976 Act (phasing of rent increases).

(6) An order under subsection (5) (*a*) above may make a corresponding reduction or increase in any of the periods for the time being mentioned in section 13 of the 1976 Act (application for registration of rent) and sections 73 (1) (*a*) and (1A) (*a*) (cancellation of registration of rent under Part IV), 80 (2) (reconsideration of rent under restricted contract) and 81A (cancellation of registration of rent under Part V) of the 1977 Act.

(7) An order under subsection (5) above may make such supplemental, incidental and consequential provision as the Secretary of State considers necessary or expedient, including provision amending any enactment (including this Act). **[389]**

COMMENCEMENT
See s. 153, *post*, and the note "Orders under this section" thereto; and note sub-s. (2) above.

SUB-S. (2): DETERMINATION OR CONFIRMATION . . . BY THE RENT OFFICER
I.e., under the Rent Act 1977, Sch. 11, para. 5, A.L.S. Vol. 255; and cf. paras. 3 (1) and 10 (2) of that Schedule. As to the appointment of rent officers, see s. 63 of that Act Vol. 255 (as amended by s. 59 (1), *ante*).

THE REGISTER
I.e., the register kept under the Rent Act 1977, s. 66.

SUB-S. (5): SECRETARY OF STATE
See the note to s. 2, *ante*.

DEFINITIONS
In the provisions substituted by sub-s. (3) above for "period of delay", "permitted increase", "previous rent limit" and "service", see the Rent (Agriculture) Act 1976, Sch. 6,, para. 1 (1). A.L.S. Vol. 250, or the Rent Act 1977, Sch. 8, para. 1 (1), as amended in each case by s. 61 (6), *post* and for "registered", see s. 19 of the Act of 1976, or Sch. 8, para. 1 (1), to the Act of 1977, Vol. 47, p. 576.

1977 ACT
I.e., the Rent Act 1977; see s. 150, *post*. For ss. 55, 56, 67 (3), (4), 73 (1), (*a*), 80 (2) and 114 of, and Schs. 8 and 9 to, that Act, see A.L.S. Vol. 255; s. 73 (1A) is inserted by s. 62 (1), (2), *post*, and s. 81A is inserted by s. 71 (1), *post*. For the meaning of "period of delay" in Sch. 8 to that Act, see para. 1 (1) thereof, as amended by s. 61 (6), *post*. S. 55 of that Act is amended by s. 152 (1) and Sch. 25, para. 39, *post*; ss. 56 and 114 of, and Sch. 9 to, that Act are also repealed by s. 152 (3) and Sch. 26, *post*; and Sch. 8 is also amended and partly repealed by ss. 61 (6) and 152 (3) and Sch. 26, *post*.

RENT (AGRICULTURE) ACT 1976, S. 13 (2)
See A.L.S. Vol. 250.

1976 ACT
This expression is not defined by this Act but it clearly means the Rent (Agriculture) Act 1976; see sub-s. (1) above. For ss. 13 and 15 of, and Sch. 6, para. 3, to that Act, see A.L.S. Vol. 250: and for the meaning of "period delay" in Sch. 6 to that Act, see para. 1 (1) thereof, as amended by s. 61 (6), *post*.

ORDERS UNDER THIS SECTION
At the time of going to press no order had been made under sub-s (5) above.
As to orders generally, see s. 151, *post*; and note, in particular, sub-s. (2) thereof.

TRANSITIONAL PROVISION
See s. 152 (2) and Sch. 25, para. 63, *post*.

61. Effect of registration of rent etc.

(1) For section 72 of the 1977 Act (effect of registration of rent) there is substituted the following section—

"72. Effect of registration of rent

(1) The registration of a rent for a dwelling-house takes effect—

(*a*) if the rent is determined by the rent officer, from the date when it is registered, and

(*b*) if the rent is determined by a rent assessment committee, from the date when the committee make their decision.

(2) If the rent for the time being registered is confirmed, the confirmation takes effect—

(*a*) if it is made by the rent officer, from the date when it is noted in the register, and

(*b*) if it is made by a rent assessment committee, from the date when the committee make their decision.

(3) If (by virtue of section 67 (4) of this Act) an application for registration of a rent is made before the expiry of the period mentioned in section 67 (3) and the resulting registration of a rent for the dwelling-house, or confirmation of the rent for the time being registered, would, but for this subsection, take effect before the expiry of that period it shall take effect on the expiry of that period.

(4) The date from which the registration or confirmation of a rent takes effect shall be entered in the register.

(5) As from the date on which the registration of a rent takes effect any previous registration of a rent for the dwelling-house ceases to have effect.

(6) Where a valid notice of increase under any provision of Part III of this Act has been served on a tenant and, in consequence of the registration of a rent, part but not the whole of the increase specified in the notice becomes irrecoverable from the tenant, the registration shall not invalidate the notice, but the notice shall, as from the date from which the registration takes effect, have effect as if it specified such part only of the increase as has not become irrecoverable.".

(2) For subsections (4) to (6) of section 13 of the Rent (Agriculture) Act 1976 (effect of registration of rent) there are substituted the following subsections—

"(4) The registration of a rent in the said part of the register takes effect—

(*a*) if the rent is determined by the rent officer, from the date when it is registered, and

(*b*) if the rent is determined by a rent assessment committee, from the date when the committee make their decision.

(5) If the rent for the time being registered in the said part of the register is confirmed, the confirmation takes effect—

(*a*) if it is made by the rent officer, from the date when it is noted in the register, and

(*b*) if it is made by a rent assessment committee, from the date when the committee make their decision.

(6) If (by virtue of section 67 (4) of the Rent Act 1977, as applied by subsection (2) above) an application for registration of a rent is made before the expiry of the period mentioned in section 67 (3) and the resulting registration of a rent for the dwelling-house, or confirmation of the rent for the time being registered, would, but for this subsection, take effect before the expiry of that period it shall take effect on the expiry of that period.

(6A) The date from which the registration or confirmation of a rent takes effect shall be entered in the said part of the register.

(6B) As from the date on which the registration of a rent takes effect any previous registration of a rent for the dwelling-house ceases to have effect."

(3) In Part VI of the 1977 Act (rent limit for dwellings let by housing associations, housing trusts and the Housing Corporation)

(a) in section 87 (registration of rent), in subsection (2) (a) for the words "and 70" there are substituted the words "70 and 72" and subsections (3) to (5) are hereby repealed; and

(b) subsections (1) and (2) of section 96 (effect of determination by rent assessment committee) are hereby repealed."

(4) In section 45 of the 1977 Act (limit of rent during statutory periods) in subsection (3) for the words "on which the rent was registered" there are substituted the words "from which the registration of the rent took effect".

(5) In section 67 of the 1977 Act, for subsection (5) (meaning of "relevant date" in relation to applications for registration of rent) there is substituted the following subsection—

"(5) In this section and sections 68 and 69 of this Act "relevant date", in relation to a rent which has been registered under this Part of this Act, means the date from which the registration took effect or, in the case of a registered rent which has been confirmed, the date from which the confirmation (or, where there have been two or more successive confirmations, the last of them) took effect.".

(6) In Schedule 6 to the Rent (Agriculture) Act 1976 and in Schedule 8 to the 1977 Act (phasing of rent increases)—

(a) in paragraph 1 (1)—

(i) in the definition of "period of delay" for the words from "means" to the end there are substituted the words "means—

(a) if the registered rent has been confirmed by a rent assessment committee, a period beginning with the date from which the registration of the rent took effect and ending one year after the date on which the committee took their decision; and

(b) in any other case, a period of one year beginning with the date from which the registration took effect.".

(ii) in the definition of "previous rent limit" for the words "at the date of registration" there are substituted the words "immediately before the relevant date"; and

(iii) before the definition of "service element" there is inserted the following definition—

"relevant date" means, in relation to a registered rent—

(a) if the rent was determined by the rent officer (and whether or not it was confirmed by a rent assessment committee), the date on which the rent was registered by the rent officer; and

(b) if the rent was determined by a rent assessment committee, the date on which the rent officer registered the rent determined by him or, as the case may be, noted in the register his confirmation of the rent for the time being registered;

(b) for paragraph 4 there is substituted the following paragraph—
"4. Where the registration of a rent takes effect in a period of delay which began by reference to an earlier registration, then—

(a) from the date on which the later registration takes effect the limitation under that period of delay shall cease to apply; and

(b) a fresh period of delay shall begin by reference to the later registration"; and

(c) paragraphs 7 (in Schedule 6) and 8 (in Schedule 8) are hereby repealed.

(7) In Schedule 11 to the 1977 Act (procedure on application for registration of rent), in paragraph 9 (2) for the word "accordingly" there are substituted the words "of their decision and of the date on which it was made".

(8) Subsections (1) to (5) above do not apply in any case where, on the determination or confirmation of a rent by the rent officer, the rent determined by him is registered, or his confirmation is noted in the register, before the commencement of this section. **[390]**

COMMENCEMENT
See s. 153 (4), *post*, and the note "Orders under this section" thereto; and note sub-s (8) above.

SUB-S. (1): S. 72 (1): DWELLING-HOUSE
See the note to the Rent Act 1977, s. 1, A.L.S. Vol. 255.

RENT IS DETERMINED BY THE RENT OFFICER
I.e., under the Rent Act 1977, Sch. 11, para. 3A, as substituted by s. 59 (3), *ante*, and Sch. 6, para. 2, *post*, or under Sch. 11, para. 5, to the Act of 1977; and cf. para. 2 (1) of that Schedule as substituted by s. 59 (3), *ante*, and Sch. 6, para. 2, *post*, and para. 10 (2) of Sch. 11 to the Act of 1977.

RENT IS DETERMINED BY A RENT ASSESSMENT COMMITTEE
I.e., under the Rent Act 1977, Sch. 11, para. 9 (1); and cf. para. 12 (2) of that Schedule. As to rent assessment committees, see s. 65 of, and Sch. 10 to, the Act of 1977.

S. 72 (2): IF IT IS MADE BY THE RENT OFFICER
As to confirmation by the rent officer of a rent for the time being registered, see the Rent Act 1977, Sch. 11, para. 3A, as substituted by s. 59 (3), *ante*, and Sch. 6, para. 2, *post*, or Sch. 11, para. 5, to that Act.

IF IT IS MADE BY A RENT ASSESSMENT COMMITTEE
As to confirmation by a rent assessment committee of a rent for the time being registered, see the Rent Act 1977, Sch. 11, para. 9 (1).

S. 72 (4): THE REGISTER
I.e., the register kept under the Rent Act 1977, s. 66.

S. 72 (6): VALID NOTICE OF INCREASE UNDER . . . PART III
I.e., a notice of increase under the Rent Act 1977, s. 45 (2) or 46 (2). See also, as to notices of increase generally, s. 49 of that Act.

IN CONSEQUENCE OF THE REGISTRATION . . . POST . . . OF THE INCREASE . . . BECOMES IRRECOVERABLE
This restriction on the increase might be imposed because of the provisions of the Rent Act 1977, s. 44 (1), (2) or 45 (2) (a).

SUB-S. (2): S. 13 (4): SAID PART OF THE REGISTER
I.e., the part created by the Rent (Agriculture) Act 1976, s. 13 (1), *A.L.S.* Vol. 250.

RENT IS DETERMINED BY THE RENT OFFICER
I.e., under the Rent Act 1977, Sch. 11, para. 3A, as substituted by s. 59 (3), *ante*, and Sch. 6, para. 2, *post*, or under Sch. 11, para. 5, to the Act of 1977; and cf. para. 2 (1) of that Schedule as substituted by s. 59 (3), *ante*, and Sch. 6. para. 2, *post*. Those provisions are applied by the Rent (Agriculture) Act 1976, s. 13 (2).

RENT IS DETERMINED BY A RENT ASSESSMENT COMMITTEE
I.e., under the Rent Act 1977, Sch. 11, para. 9 (1), as applied by the Rent (Agriculture) Act 1976, s. 13 (2).

S. 13 (5): IF IT IS MADE BY THE RENT OFFICER
As to confirmation by the rent officer of a rent for the time being registered, see the Rent Act 1977, Sch. 11, para. 3A, as substituted by s. 59 (3), *ante*, and Sch. 6, para. 2, *post*,

or Sch. 11, para. 5, to that Act. Those provisions are applied by the Rent (Agriculture) Act 1976, s. 13 (2).

IF IT IS MADE BY THE RENT ASSESSMENT COMMITTEE
As to confirmation by a rent assessment committee of a rent for the time being registered, see the Rent Act 1977, Sch. 11, para. 9 (1), as applied by the Rent (Agriculture) Act 1976, s. 13 (2).

SUB-S. (4): REGISTRATION OF THE RENT TOOK EFFECT
I.e., in accordance with the Rent Act 1977, s. 72 (1)–(3), as substituted by sub-s, (1) above.

SUB-S. (5): THIS PART OF THIS ACT
I.e., the Rent Act 1977, Part IV.

SUB-S. (6): DATE FOR WHICH THE REGISTRATION OF THE RENT TOOK EFFECT
I.e., in accordance with the Rent (Agriculture) Act 1976, s. 13 (4)–(6), as substituted by sub-s. (2) above, or the Rent Act 1977, s. 72 (1)–(3), as substituted by sub-s. (1) above.

ONE YEAR AFTER, ETC.
See the note "Not later than three months after, etc." to s. 11, *ante*.

ONE YEAR BEGINNING WITH, ETC.
See the note "Three months beginning with, etc," to s. 12, *ante*.

DEFINITIONS
For "the rent officer", see the Rent Act 1977, s. 63 (4); for "tenant", see s. 152 (1) of that Act; for "period of delay", see the Rent (Agriculture) Act 1976, Sch. 6, para. 1 (1), or the Rent Act 1977, Sch. 8, para. 1 (1), as amended, in each case, by sub-s (6) (*a*) above; for "registered" see s. 19 of the Act of 1976, or Sch. 8, para. 1 (1), to the Act of 1977.

1977 ACT
I.e., the Rent Act 1977; see s. 150, *post*. S. 67 (3) and (4) of that Act are amended by s. 60 (1), (2), *ante* (see also s. 60 (5) (*a*), (7), *ante*); and ss. 87 (3) (5) and 96 (1), (2) and Sch. 8, para. 8, are also repealed by s. 152 (3) and Sch. 26, *post*.

RENT (AGRICULTURE) ACT 1976, S. 13 (4)–(6), SCH. 6, PARAS. 1 (1), 4, 7
See A.L.S. Vol. 250. Sch. 6, para. 7, to that Act is also repealed by s. 152 (3) and Sch. 26, *post*.

RENT ACT 1977, S. 67 (3), (4)
See A.L.S. Vol. 255. These subsections are amended by s. 60 (1), (2), *ante*; see also s. 60 (5) (*a*), (7), *ante*.

TRANSITIONAL PROVISION
In connection with the provisions substituted by sub-s, (1) above, see the Rent Act 1977, Sch. 24, para. 16, as amended by s. 152 (1) and Sch. 25, para. 60, *post*.

62. Cancellation of registration of rent

(1) Section 73 of the 1977 Act is amended as follows.

(2) After subsection (1) there is inserted the following subsection:—

"(1A) Such an application may also be made where—

(*a*) not less than two years have elapsed since the relevant date (as defined in section 67 (5) of this Act); and

(*b*) the dwelling-house is not for the time being subject to a regulated tenancy; and

(*c*) the application is made by the person who would be the landlord if the dwelling-house were let on such a tenancy."

(3) For subsection (3) there is substituted the following subsection—

"(3) An application under this section must—

(*a*) be in the form prescribed for the application concerned and contain the prescribed particulars; and

(*b*) be accompanied, in the case of an application under subsection (1) above, by a copy of the rent agreement."

(4) In subsection (4)—

(*a*) after the word "If" there are inserted the words "the application is made under subsection (1) above and"; and

(*b*) at the end there are inserted the words "and he shall also cancel the registration if the application is made under subsection (1A) above".

(5) In subsection (5) after the word "Where" there are inserted the words "the application is made under subsection (1) above and".

(6) In subsection (6) for the words "The cancellation" there are substituted the words "A cancellation made in pursuance of an application under subsection (1) above". **[391]**

COMMENCEMENT
See s. 153 (4), *post*, and the note "Orders under this section" thereto.

SUB-S. (2): SUCH AN APPLICATION
I.e., an application for the cancellation of the registration of a rent.

NOT LESS THAN TWO YEARS
This period may be reduced or increased by order made in accordance with s. 60 (5) (*a*), (6), (7), *ante*.

DWELLING-HOUSE
See the note to the Rent Act 1977, s. 1. A.L.S. Vol. 255.

SUB-S. (3): FORM PRESCRIBED; PRESCRIBED PARTICULARS
I.e., prescribed by regulations under the Rent Act 1977, s. 74: see s. 75 (1) of that Act, *ibid.* (under which a form substantially to the same effect as the prescribed form may also be used). At the time of going to press no regulations had been made for the purposes of s. 73 (3) of the Act of 1977 as substituted by sub-s. (3) above.

DEFINITIONS
For "regulated tenancy", see the Rent Act 1977, s. 18 (1), as partly repealed by s. 152 (3) and Sch. 26, *post*; for "rent agreement", see s. 73 (9) of that Act: for "prescribed", see s. 75 (1) of that Act; for "landlord", see s. 152 (1) of that Act.

1977 ACT
I.e., the Rent Act 1977; see s. 150, *post*. S. 67 (5) of that Act is substituted by s. 61 (5), *ante*.

63. Repeal of sections 48 and 50 of Rent Act 1977

Section 48 of the 1977 Act (increase, on account of improvements, of recoverable rent for statutory periods before registration) and section 50 of that Act (private street works to count as improvements) are hereby repealed. **[392]**

COMMENCEMENT
See s. 153 (4), *post*, and the note "Orders under this section" thereto.

1977 ACT
I.e., the Rent Act 1977; see s. 150, *post*. For ss. 48 and 50 of that Act, see A.L.S. Vol. 255. Those sections are also repealed by s. 152 (3) and Sch. 26, *post*.

TRANSITIONAL PROVISION
See s. 152 (2) and Sch. 25, para, 64, *post*.

Conversion of controlled tenancies

64. Conversion of controlled tenancies into regulated tenancies

(1) At the commencement of this section every controlled tenancy shall cease to be a controlled tenancy and become a regulated tenancy, except in the case mentioned in subsection (2) below.

(2) If the controlled tenancy is one to which Part II of the Landlord and Tenant Act 1954 would apply, apart from section 24 (2) of the 1977 Act, or would so apply if it were a tenancy within the meaning of the Act of 1954, it shall, when it ceases to be a controlled tenancy, be treated as a tenancy continuing by virtue of section 24 of the Act of 1954 after the expiry of a term of years certain. **[393]**

COMMENCEMENT
   See s. 153 (4), *post*, and the note "Orders under this section" thereto.

GENERAL NOTE
   When this section is brought into force all controlled tenancies as defined by the Rent Act 1977, s. 17, A.L.S. Vol. 255, will cease to be such tenancies and will become regulated tenancies as defined by s. 18 (1) of that Act (as partly repealed by s. 152 (3) and Sch. 26, *post*), except in the case mentioned in sub-s. (2) above under which controlled tenancies with a partial business use are to be treated, on ceasing to be controlled, as tenancies continued under the Landlord and Tenant Act 1954, Part II. See further the note to sub-s. (2), *infra*. When the general conversion of controlled tenancies into regulated tenancies takes effect the rents of the tenancies affected will cease to be governed by Part II of the Act of 1977 (rents under controlled tenancies) and will become subject to Parts III and IV of that Act (rents under regulated tenancies and registration of rents under regulated tenancies), as amended by the present Act, and the provisions for phasing of rent increases contained in s. 55 of, and Sch. 8 to, that Act, as so amended, will accordingly apply unless those provisions are repealed by order under s. 60 (5), *ante*. Under s. 52 of the Act of 1977 as substituted by s. 68 (2), *post*, an agreement which purports to increase the rent payable under a tenancy converted into a regulated tenancy by this section is in general void if entered into at a time when no rent is registered under Part IV of the Act of 1977. Another effect of the conversion under this section will be that the court will be required to make an order for possession in the circumstances set out in Part II of Sch. 15 to the Act of 1977, as amended by ss. 66 and 67, *post* (see s. 98 (2) of that Act) (as well as being able to make an order for possession where the provisions of s. 98 (1) of, and Sch. 15, Part I, to, that Act are satisfied).
   For a power to release dwelling-houses from rent regulation, see the Rent Act 1977, s. 143.

SUB-S. (2) GENERALLY
   By the Rent Act 1977, s. 24 (2), Part II of the Landlord and Tenant Act 1954 is not to apply where there is a controlled tenancy of a dwelling-house but with user of part of the premises as a shop or office for business, trade or professional purposes. In such cases (*semble*, mainly small shops) then sub-s. (2) overrides s. 24 (2) of the 1977 Act where there is automatic decontrol by sub-s. (2), in much the same was as was done by the Housing Finance Act 1972, A.L.S. Vol. 202, s. 27 (3).
   If the tenant is only a statutory controlled tenant at the date of automatic decontrol, then Part II of the 1954 Act will not apply in any event, it is thought: in *Piper* v. *Muggleton* [1956] 2 Q.B. 569; [1956] 2 All E.R. 269, C.A., it was held that, where a tenant's contractual (controlled) tenancy of premises with partial business user was determined, he was not a "landlord" vis-à-vis a subtenant within s. 44 of the 1954 Act because he was, as statutory tenant, not the owner of an interest in the property.
   The highly artificial fiction adopted for continuation under s. 24 of the 1954 Act—a non-existent term of years which is deemed to have come to an end and then to continue under s. 24—would not, presumably, mean that the terms of the decontrolled contractual tenancy will not be continued: for instance it was held in *Poster* v. *Slough Estates Ltd.* [1969] 1 Ch. 495; [1968] 3 All E.R. 257, that the tenant's contractual right to the use of buildings free from removal by the landlord was continued by Part II.

CONTROLLED TENANCY
   I.e., a controlled tenancy as defined by the Rent Act 1977, s. 17, (prospectively repealed by s. 152 (3) and Sch. 26, *post*).

REGULATED TENANCY
This expression is defined by the Rent Act 1977, s. 18 (prospectively repealed in part by s. 152 (3) and Sch. 26, *post*).

MODIFICATIONS OF RENT ACT 1977
For modifications of the Rent Act 1977, in relation to a tenancy converted from a controlled tenancy into a regulated tenancy by, *inter alia*, this section, see s. 18A of that Act as inserted by s. 152 (1) and Sch. 25, para. 35, *post*, and Sch. 17 to that Act, as amended by s. 152 (1) and Sch. 25, para. 59, *post*.

RENTS OF SUBSIDISED PRIVATE HOUSES
As to the rent limit under a tenancy of a subsidised private house which is converted into a regulated tenancy by, *inter alia*, this section, see the Rent Act 1977, s. 145, as amended by s. 152 (1) and Sch. 25, para. 52, *post*, and in particular sub-s. (3) (*b*) thereof as so amended.

CONSEQUENTIAL REPEALS
Consequent upon this section certain enactments are prospectively repealed by s. 152 (3) and Sch. 26, *post*; these include the Rent Act 1977, s. 17, Sch. 3 (definition of "controlled tenancy"). Part II (ss. 27–43) of, and Schs. 4 and 6 to, that Act (rents under controlled tenancies), and ss. 108–113 of, and Sch. 11, Part III, to that Act (conversion from controlled tenancy into regulated tenancy where local authority certifies that the dwelling-house has all the standard amenities and is in good repair, etc.).

LANDLORD AND TENANT ACT 1954
For the tenancies to which Part II of that Act applies, see s. 23 thereof and for the meaning of "tenancy" in that Act, see s. 69 (1) thereof.

TRANSITIONAL PROVISION
See s. 152 (2) and Sch. 25, para, 75, *post*.

Regulated tenancies

65. Resident landlords

(1) In section 12 (1) of the 1977 Act (certain tenancies granted by resident landlords not to be protected tenancies) for paragraphs (*a*) to (*c*) there are substituted the following paragraphs—

"(*a*) the dwelling-house forms part only of a building and, except in'a case where the dwelling-house also forms part of a flat, the building is not a purpose-built block of flats; and

(*b*) the tenancy was granted by a person who, at the time when he granted it, occupied as his residence another dwelling-house which—
   (i) in the case mentioned in paragraph (*a*) above, also forms part of the flat; or
   (ii) in any other case, also forms part of the building; and

(*c*) subject to paragraph 1 of Schedule 2 to this Act, at all times since the tenancy was granted the interest of the landlord under the tenancy has belonged to a person who, at the time he owned that interest, occupied as his residence another dwelling-house which—
   (i) in the case mentioned in paragraph (*a*) above, also formed part of the flat; or
   (ii) in any other case, also formed part of the building."

(2) Schedule 2 to the 1977 Act (provisions for determining application of section 12) is amended as follows.

(3) In paragraph 1—

(*a*) in sub-paragraph (*a*) for the words "14 days" there are substituted the words "28 days" and after the word "building" there are inserted the words "or, as the case may be, flat";

175

(b) in sub-paragraph (b) for the words "such dwelling-house as is referred to in that paragraph" there are substituted the words "dwelling-house in the building or, as the case may be, flat concerned"; and

(c) in sub-paragraph (c) for the words "12 months" there are substituted the words "2 years" and paragraph (i) is hereby repealed.

(4) In paragraph 2 (b) after the word "building" there are inserted the words "or, as the case may be, flat".

(5) After paragraph 2 there is inserted the following paragraph—

"2A.—(1) The tenancy referred to in section 12 (1) falls within this paragraph if the interest of the landlord under the tenancy becomes vested in the personal representatives of a deceased person acting in that capacity.

(2) If the tenancy falls within this paragraph, the condition in section 12 (1) (c) shall be deemed to be fulfilled for any period, beginning with the date on which the interest becomes vested in the personal representatives and not exceeding two years, during which the interest of the landlord remains so vested."

(6) Subject to subsection (7) below, this section, except subsection (1), applies to tenancies granted before as well as those granted after the commencement of this section.

(7) In any case where the interest of the landlord under a tenancy vested in the personal representatives (acting in that capacity) of a person who died before the commencement of this section, Schedule 2 to the 1977 Act applies as if paragraph 2A had not been inserted and paragraph 1 (c) (i) had not been repealed. **[394]**

COMMENCEMENT

See s. 153 (4), *post*, and the note "Orders under this section" thereto; and note sub-s. (6) above.

GENERAL NOTE

The new words in sub-s. (1) (a) "except in a case where the dwelling-house also forms part of a flat" and the consequential amendments on this inserted into the rest of the new s. 12 (1) of the 1977 Act, will enable a landlord who shares a flat with a tenant to be a resident landlord; equally, should the landlord live merely in another flat not in the same building, he will continue not to be within s. 12.

The new s. 12 continues the previous s. 12's references to a building, and the difficult question as to the meaning of this will persist. In relation to any structure, the question whether one is resident in another part of the same building as the tenant is one of fact: *Bardrick* v. *Haycock* (1976) 31 P. & C.R. 420, C.A. It was there held by the county court judge, whose decision was not disturbed, that an extension to a house (the latter having been converted into flats) was, being essentially a separate living unit, not part of the same building as the flats and so the owner was outside s. 12. Presumably, by analogy with *Humpherey* v. *Young* [1903] 1 K.B. 44, the fact that there is a continuous roof common to several units will not of itself mean that the whole area covered by the roof is to be treated as one single building. The mischief test was applied in *Bardrick* v. *Haycock, supra*, the issue being therefore whether, in relation to s. 12, one has separate living units within a given larger structure.

Sub-ss. (3) and (5) generally

To the government, a one-year "wait and see" period to allow for the administration of a deceased resident landlord's estate is too short: H.C. Committee, Col. 2210. This is retrospectively altered to two years as part of a wider relaxation; the period available for a new owner-occupier to move in (where there is no prior notice) is likewise doubled to 28 days by s. 65 (3).

The question of the effect on the tenant's status of the two suspensory periods, which does not apply (sub-s. (5)) to vesting in personal representatives was considered at length in *Landau* v. *Sloane* [1980] 2 All E.R. 539, C.A. It was held that, during and after the relevant periods of disregard, the tenant was a protected or statutory tenant against anyone except a resident landlord who could show a continuous period of resident landlords broken only by a disregard period. This meant that a notice to quit served during either period of disregard by a non-resident purchaser or, at that time, by non-resident personal representatives, which expired before the end of the disregard period (without the moving in of a new resident landlord during the disregard period at any rate) only converted the protected tenancy into a statutory tenancy. If, by the end of the disregard periods, there was again a resident landlord, then the tenancy ceases to be protected or statutory; but if not, it remained protected or statutory. In *Beebe* v. *Mason* (1980) 254 E.G. 987, C.A., the deceased resident landlord's personal representative, as sole beneficiary, moved in during the relevant disregard period (without having assented to the vesting of the landlord's interest in himself) but was held nevertheless entitled to rely on a notice to quit served by him after moving in: the tenant was no longer a protected tenant.

SUB-S. (1): DWELLING-HOUSE
See the note to the Rent Act 1977, s. 1, A.L.S. Vol. 255.

BUILDING
See the note to s. 3, *ante*.

RESIDENCE
See the note "Resident" to Sch. 3, para. 6, *post*.

SUB-S. (5): PERIOD, BEGINNING WITH, ETC.
See the note "Three months beginning with, etc." to s. 12, *ante*.

DEFINITIONS
For "landlord" and "tenancy", see the Rent Act 1977, s. 152 (1); for "purpose-built block of flats", see Sch. 2, para. 4, to that Act: as to "occupying a dwelling-house as his residence", see Sch. 2, para. 5, to that Act.

1977 ACT
I.e., the Rent Act 1977; see s. 150, *post*. S. 12 of that Act is also amended by s. 69 (4), *post*; and para. 1 (*c*) (i) of Sch. 2 is also repealed by s. 152 (3) and Sch. 26, *post*.

66. Amendment of Cases 11 and 12 of Schedule 15 to Rent Act 1977

(1) In Case 11 in Schedule 15 to the 1977 Act (dwelling-house required by a person who was owner-occupier at time of letting) for paragraph (*c*) there is substituted the following paragraph—

"(*c*) the court is of the opinion that of the conditions set out in Part V of this Schedule one of those in paragraphs (*a*) and (*c*) to (*f*) is satisfied."

(2) In Case 12 in Schedule 15 (dwelling-house required for use by owner on his retirement) for paragraph (*c*) there is substituted the following paragraph—

"(*c*) the court is of the opinion that of the conditions set out in Part V of this Schedule one of those in paragraphs (*b*) to (*e*) is satisfied.".

(3) There are inserted in Schedule 15, as a new Part V, the provisions set out in Schedule 7 to this Act; and in section 98 of the 1977 Act (which, among other things, introduces Schedule 15) there is added, at the end, the following subsection—

"(5) Part V of Schedule 15 shall have effect for the purpose of setting out conditions which are relevant to Cases 11 and 12 of that Schedule.".

(4) In Case 12 for the words from the beginning to "employment let" there are substituted the words "Where the landlord (in this Case referred to as "the owner") intends to occupy the dwelling-house as his residence at such time as he might retire from regular employment and has let."

(5) Subject to subsection (6) below, Cases 11 and 12, as amended by this section, apply to tenancies granted before, as well as those granted after, the commencement of this section; and nothing in this section invalidates a notice that possession might be recovered under Case 11 or Case 12 which was duly given to a tenant before then.

(6) Paragraphs (c) and (d) of Part V of Schedule 15 do not apply to Case 11 if the tenancy was granted, and the owner died, before the commencement of this section; and paragraph (d) does not apply to Case 12 in any such case. **[395]**

COMMENCEMENT
> See s. 153 (4), *post*, and the note "Orders under this section" thereto; and note sub-ss. (5) and (6) above.

SUB-S. (1): THE COURT
> Cf. the note "A court" to the Rent Act 1977, s. 98, A.L.S. Vol. 255.

SUB-S. (4): DWELLING-HOUSE
> See the note to the Rent Act 1977, s. 1.

RESIDENCE
> See the note "Resident" to Sch. 3, para. 6, *post*.

SUB-S. (5): NOTICE THAT POSSESSION MIGHT BE RECOVERED UNDER CASE 11 OR CASE 12
> *I.e.*, a notice given under the Rent Act 1977, Sch. 15, Part II, Case 11 (*a*) or Case 12 (*a*).

DEFINITIONS
> For "landlord", "let" and "tenancy", see the Rent Act 1977, s. 152 (1); for "owner", in relation to Case 11, see para. 1 of Part V of Sch. 15 to that Act as inserted by sub-s. (3) above and Sch. 7, *post*; for "owner" in relation to Case 12, see that Case, as amended by sub-s. (4) above.

1977 ACT
> *I.e.*, the Rent Act 1977; see s. 150, *post*. The reference in sub-s. (6) above to paras. (*c*) and (*d*) of Part V of Sch. 15 is clearly intended as a reference to para. 2 (*c*) and (*d*) of that Part as inserted by sub-s. (3) above and Sch. 7, *post*.

67. Lettings by servicemen

The following Case shall be added to the Cases in Part II of Schedule 15 to the 1977 Act (mandatory orders for possession) after the Case inserted in Part II by section 55 of this Act—

"Case 20

Where the dwelling-house was let by a person (in this Case referred to as "the owner") at any time after the commencement of section 67 of the Housing Act 1980 and–

(*a*) at the time when the owner acquired the dwelling-house he was a member of the regular armed forces of the Crown;

(*b*) at the relevant date the owner was a member of the regular armed forces of the Crown;

(*c*) not later than the relevant date the owner gave notice in writing to the tenant that possession might be recovered under this Case;

(*d*) the dwelling-house has not, since the commmencement of section 67 of the Act of 1980 been let by the owner on a protected tenancy with respect to which the condition mentioned in paragraph (*c*) above was not satisfied; and

(*e*) the court is of the opinion that—
    (i) the dwelling-house is required as a residence for the owner; or
    (ii) of the conditions set out in Part V of this Schedule one of those in paragraphs (*c*) to (*f*) is satisfied.

If the court is of the opinion that, notwithstanding that the condition in paragraph (*c*) or (*d*) above is not complied with, it is just and equitable to make an order for possession of the dwelling-house, the court may dispense with the requirements of either or both of these paragraphs, as the case may require.

For the purposes of this Case "regular armed forces of the Crown" has the same meaning as in section 1 of the House of Commons Disqualification Act 1975." **[396]**

COMMENCEMENT
See s. 153 (4), *post*, and the note "Orders under this section" thereto.

FOLLOWING CASE SHALL BE ADDED TO THE CASES IN PART II OF SCH. 15, ETC.
See the note to s. 55, *ante*.

DWELLING-HOUSE
See the note to the Rent Act 1977, s. 1, A.L.S. Vol. 255.

WRITING
For meaning, see the note "Written: writing" to s. 5, *ante*.

THE COURT
Cf. the note "A court" to the Rent Act 1977, s. 98.

RESIDENCE
See the note "Resident" to Sch, 3, para. 6, *post*.

DEFINITIONS
For "protected tenancy", see the Rent Act 1977, s. 1; for "let" and "tenant", see s. 152 (1) of that Act; for "the relevant date", see Sch. 15, Part III, para. 2, to that Act, or Sch. 8, para. 3, *post*.

1977 ACT
I.e., the Rent Act 1977; see s. 150, *post*. Part V of Sch. 15 is inserted by s. 66 (3), *ante*, and Sch. 7, *post*.

HOUSE OF COMMONS DISQUALIFICATION ACT 1975, S. 1
See 45, Halsbury's Statutes (3rd edn.), p. 1505.

Rent agreements

68. Rent agreements with tenants having security of tenure

(1) In section 51 (4) of the 1977 Act (requirements to be observed in rent agreements with tenants having security of tenure), in paragraph (*b*) the following sub-paragraph is inserted after sub-paragraph (i)—

"(ia) that if the agreement were not made but instead a rent were registered under Part IV of this Act, then part only of any increase over the rent previously recoverable by the landlord would be payable by the tenant during the first year; and".

(2) For section 52 of the 1977 Act (which makes special provision, in the case of converted tenancies, in relation to rent agreements with tenants having security of tenure) there is substituted the following section—

"52. Protection: special provisions following conversion

(1) This section applies to an agreement with a tenant having security of tenure which is entered into after the commencement of section 68 (2) of the Housing Act 1980 if the tenancy has become or, as the case may be, the previous tenancy became a regulated tenancy by conversion.

(2) Any such agreement which purports to increase the rent payable under a protected tenancy shall, if entered into at a time when no rent is registered for the dwelling-house under Part IV of this Act, be void.

179

(3) If any such agreement constitutes a grant of a regulated tenancy and is made at a time when no rent is so registered, any excess of the rent payable under the tenancy so granted (for any contractual or statutory period of the tenancy) over the rent limit applicable to the previous tenancy, shall be irrecoverable from the tenant; but this subsection ceases to apply if a rent is subsequently so registered.

(4) For the purposes of this section a tenancy is a regulated tenancy by conversion if it has become a regulated tenancy by virtue of—

(a) Part VIII of this Act, section 43 of the Housing Act 1969 or Part III or IV of the Housing Finance Act 1972 (conversion of controlled tenancies into regulated tenancies); or

(b) section 18 (3) of this Act or paragraph 5 of Schedule 2 to the Rent Act 1968 (conversion on death of first successor); or

(c) section 64 of the Housing Act 1980 (conversion of all remaining controlled tenancies).

(5) This section does not apply to any agreement where the tenant is neither the person who, at the time of the conversion, was the tenant nor a person who might succeed the tenant at that time as a statutory tenant.

(6) Where a rent is registered for the dwelling-house and the registration is subsequently cancelled, this section shall not apply to the agreement submitted to the rent officer in connection with the cancellation nor to any agreement made so as to take effect after the cancellation."

(3) In section 57 of the 1977 Act (recovery from landlord of sums paid in excess of recoverable rent, etc.) for subsection (3) there is substituted the following subsection—

"(3) No amount which a tenant is entitled to recover under subsection (1) above shall be recoverable at any time after the expiry of—

(a) one year, in the case of an amount which is irrecoverable by virtue of section 54 of this Act; or

(b) two years, in any other case." **[397]**

COMMENCEMENT
See s. 153 (4), *post*, and the note "Orders under this section" thereto.

SUB-S. (2): S. 52 (2): DWELLING-HOUSE
See the note to the Rent Act 1977, s. 1, A.L.S. Vol. 255.

S. 52 (3): EXCESS ... SHALL BE IRRECOVERABLE
As to the recovery by the tenant of overpaid rent, see the Rent Act 1977, s. 57, as amended by sub-s. (3) above.

S. 52 (5): PERSON WHO MIGHT SUCCEED THE TENANT .... AS A STATUTORY TENANT
For the provisions which have effect for determining who is to be statutory tenant by succession, see the Rent Act 1977, s. 2 (1) (b), Sch. 1, Part I, as amended in the case of Sch. 1, Part I, by s. 76 (1), (2), *post*, and partly repealed by s. 152 (3) and Sch. 26, *post*.

S. 52 (6): REGULATION IS SUBSEQUENTLY CANCELLED
I.e., under the Rent Act 1977, s. 73, as amended by s. 62, *ante*.

AGREEMENT SUBMITTED ... IN CONNECTION WITH THE CANCELLATION
This refers to the agreement which must be sent with the application for cancellation under the Rent Act 1977, s. 73 (3) (b), as substituted by s. 62 (1), (3), *ante*.

SUB-S. (3): AFTER THE EXPIRY OF ... ONE YEAR (TWO YEARS)
Presumably this means after the expiry of one year (or two years) from the date of payment of the amount in question; see the Rent Act 1977, s. 57 (3), as originally enacted.

DEFINITIONS
For "protected tenancy", see the Rent Act 1977, s. 1; for "statutory tenant", see s. 2 of that Act; for "regulated tenancy", see s. 18 of that Act (as partly repealed by s. 152 (3) and Sch. 26, *post*); for "agreement with a tenant having security of tenure", cf. s. 51 (1) of that Act; for "contractual period" and "statutory period", see s. 61 (1) of that Act; for "rent officer", cf. s. 63 (4) of that Act; for "landlord" and "tenant", see s. 152 (1) of that Act. Note as to "regulated tenancy by conversion", s. 52 (4) of the Act of 1977 as substituted by sub-s. (2) above.

1977 ACT
I.e., the Rent Act 1977; see s. 150, *post*. Part IV (ss. 62–75 and Schs. 10–12) is amended by ss. 59, 60 (1), (2), 61 (1), (5), (7) and 62, *ante*, and ss. 71 (2), 152 (1), (3), Sch. 6, Sch. 25, paras. 40, 41, 56, and Sch. 26, *post*; and s. 18 (3) and the provisions of Part VIII providing for conversion of controlled tenancies into regulated tenancies (*i.e.*, ss. 108–113) are repealed by s. 152 (3) and Sch, 26, *post*.

HOUSING ACT 1969, S. 43
That section was repealed by the Housing Finance Act 1972, s. 108 (4), Sch. 11, Part VI.

HOUSING FINANCE ACT 1972, PARTS III, IV
See A.L.S. Vol. 202. Part III of that Act was repealed by the Rent Act 1977, s. 155 (5), Sch. 25; and the provisions of Part IV providing for conversion of controlled tenancies into regulated tenancies (*i.e.*, ss. 35 and 36) were repealed by the Housing Rents and Subsidies Act 1975, s. 17 (5), Sch. 6, Part III.

RENT ACT 1968, SCH. 2, PARA. 5
See A.L.S. Vol. 179. That Act was repealed by the Rent Act 1977, s. 155 (5), Sch. 25.

TRANSITIONAL PROVISIONS
See s. 152 (2) and Sch. 25, paras. 65, 66, *post*.

Restricted contracts

69. Restricted contracts: security of tenure

(1) In section 3 of the Protection from Eviction Act 1977 (prohibition of eviction without due process of law), after subsection (2) there is inserted the following subsection—

"(2A) Subsections (1) and (2) above apply in relation to any restricted contract (within the meaning of the Rent Act 1977) which—

(*a*) creates a licence; and
(*b*) is entered into after the commencement of section 69 of the Housing Act 1980;

as they apply in relation to a restricted contract which creates a tenancy.".

(2) After section 106 of the 1977 Act there is inserted the following section:—

"106A. Discretion of court in certain proceedings for possession

(1) This section applies to any dwelling-house which is the subject of a restricted contract entered into after the commencement of section 69 of the Housing Act 1980.

(2) On the making of an order for possession of such a dwelling-house, or at any time before the execution of such an order, the court may—

(*a*) stay or suspend execution of the order, or
(*b*) postpone the date of possession,

for such period or periods as, subject to subsection (3) below, the court thinks fit.

(3) Where a court makes an order for possession of such a dwelling-house, the giving up of possession shall not be postponed (whether by the order or any

variation, suspension or stay of execution) to a date later than 3 months after the making of the order.

(4) On any such stay, suspension or postponement as is referred to in subsection (2) above, the court shall, unless it considers that to do so would cause exceptional hardship to the lessee or would otherwise be unreasonable, impose conditions with regard to payment by the lessee of arrears of rent (if any) and rent or payments in respect of occupation after termination of the tenancy (mesne profits) and may impose such other conditions as it thinks fit.

(5) Subsection (6) below applies in any case where—

    (*a*) proceedings are brought for possession of such a dwelling-house;

    (*b*) the lessee's spouse or former spouse, having rights of occupation under the Matrimonial Homes Act 1967, is then in occupation of the dwelling-house; and

    (*c*) the restricted contract is terminated as a result of those proceedings.

(6) In any case to which this subsection applies, the spouse or former spouse shall, so long as he or she remains in occupation, have the same rights in relation to, or in connection with, any such stay, suspension or postponement as is referred to in subsection (2) above, as he or she would have if those rights of occupation were not affected by the termination of the restricted contract.".

(3) Sections 103 to 106 of the 1977 Act (security of tenure in respect of restricted contracts) shall not apply to restricted contracts entered into after the commencement of this section; and accordingly after section 102 of that Act there is inserted the following section—

"102A. Restricted application of sections 103 to 106

Sections 103 to 106 of this Act apply only to restricted contracts entered into before the commencement of section 69 of the Housing Act 1980.".

(4) In section 12 of the 1977 Act, for subsections (2) and (3) (cases where tenancies granted by resident landlords are not exempted by section 12 from being protected tenancies), there is substituted the following subsection—

"(2) This section does not apply to a tenancy of a dwelling-house which forms part of a building if the tenancy is granted to a person who, immediately before it was granted, was a protected or statutory tenant of that dwelling-house or of any other dwelling-house in that building." **[398]**

COMMENCEMENT
    See 153 (4), *post*, and the note "Orders under this section" thereto.

SUB-S. (1): GENERALLY
    A restricted contract is defined in the Rent Act 1977, s. 19 (2), as a contract under which one person grants to another person, in consideration of a rent which includes payment for the use of furniture or services, the right to occupy a dwelling as a residence. Now, the extension of the Protection from Eviction Act 1977, s. 3, by the new s. 3 (2A) seems to be aimed at residential licences such as prevail in hotels or boarding houses: see *e.g. Luganda* v. *Service Hotels Ltd.* [1969] 2 Ch. 209; [1969] 2 All E.R. 692, C.A.; *Marchant* v. *Charters* [1977] 3 All E.R. 918, C.A. But it is thought that s. 3 would have applied to them in any case (see below).
    If there is a licence which, being drafted to avoid the Rent Acts, denies the licensees exclusive possession of *any part* of the premises, services and furniture or not, then there is no restricted contract. (For examples of such licences, see *Somma* v. *Hazlehurst* [1978] 2 All E.R. 1011, C.A., and *Aldrington Garages Ltd.* v. *Fielder* (1979) 37 P. & C.R. 461, C.A.) This is owing to s. 19 (6) of the Rent Act 1977: "... a contract falling within subsection (2) ... and relating to a dwelling which consists of only part of a house is a restricted contract whether or not the lessee is entitled, *in addition to exclusive occupation* of that part, to the use in common with any other person of other rooms ..." (italics supplied). That being so, the new s. 3 (2A) of the Protection from Eviction Act 1977 will not apply to such licences.

It therefore applies where the section as unamended would have applied and does not to a case it perhaps might have been extended to cover.

At any rate, the new s. 3 (2A) means that, where it applies, s. 3 (1) of the Protection from Eviction Act 1977 will apply, and so the only way in which the "owner" (this includes, be it noted, "mortgagee": *Bolton Building Society* v. *Cobb* [1965] 3 All E.R. 814) may obtain possession if the "occupier" has not quit voluntarily is by means of an action for possession in the county court: see *Borzak* v. *Ahmed* [1965] 2 Q.B. 320; [1965] 1 All E.R. 808. However, in that the amendment only deals with licences, no notice to quit is additionally required on the part of the "owner"; the writ for possession indicating an intention to determine the licence: *Martinali* v. *Ramuz* [1953] 2 All E.R. 892, C.A.; *Crane* v. *Morris* [1965] 3 All E.R. 77, C.A. In this, just to mention one more difficulty, suppose there is a counterclaim that the licence was wrongfully revoked? Revocation depends in the case of contractual licences on the terms of the contract (*Winter Garden Theatre (London) Ltd.* v. *Millenium Productions Ltd.* [1948] A.C. 173; [1947] 2 All E.R. 331, H.L.) and so, if the licence is wrongfully revoked, there may be an injunction to enforce the statutory duty in s. 3 (as in *Warder* v. *Cooper* [1970] Ch. 495; [1970] 1 All E.R. 1102) or even, if it is desired to reverse the wrongful revocation, specific performance of the licence: see *Verrall* v. *Great Yarmouth B.C.* [1980] 1 All E.R. 839, C.A.

It does not much matter whether the amendment of the 1977 Act was really required (it is not stated to be merely declaratory) but in *Warder* v. *Cooper*, *supra*, it was held that a service occupier—*i.e.* a licensee—was within what is now s. 3. But though the new s. 3 (2A) applies to post-commencement restricted contracts which create a licence, s. 5 of the 1977 Act (minimum period of notice to quit) is not expressly applied: and as was said above, no notice to quit is required at law to determine a licence. Contravention of any part of s. 3 by the occupier is an offence: see s. 1.

SUB-S. (2): GENERALLY
This inserts a new s. 106A into the Rent Act 1977 and the references below are to the subsections in s. 106A.

Exceptional hardship (sub-s. (4))
This is a far narrower term than "greater hardship" in the Rent Act 1977, A.L.S. Vol. 255, Sch. 15, Part III, para. 1. The burden of proof of exceptional hardship will be on the tenant, as is the case with greater hardship: *Sims* v. *Wilson* [1946] 2 All E.R. 261, C.A.

Unreasonable (sub-s. (4))
Again, it is thought that the onus of proof of unreasonableness will be on the tenant— *not*, as is the case with "reasonable" in s. 33 of this Act, on the landlord: cf. *Sims* v. *Wilson*, *supra*. In judging unreasonableness, presumably the county court could take into account all relevant circumstances existing at the date of the hearing: *Cumming* v. *Danson* [1942] 2 All E.R. 653.

Rights of occupation under the Matrimonial Homes Act 1967 (sub-s. (5))
Under s. 1 (1) of the 1967 Act, a spouse entitled to occupy or to re-enter and occupy a dwelling-house is so entitled against the other spouse. The right ends with the termination of the marriage (*ibid.*, s. 2 (2) (*a*)). A wife may be within the 1967 Act because of the mere fact of being a wife or owing to occupation under say the Rent Act 1977. The effect of sub-s. (5) (*b*) and sub-s. (6) is that the wife is given the same limited rights to a stay, etc., as the husband.

See also the note to s. 87.

THE COURT
Cf. the note "A court" to the Rent Act 1977, s. 98, A.L.S. Vol. 255.

S. 106A (3): NOT .... LATER THAN 3 MONTHS AFTER, ETC.
See the note to s. 11, *ante*.

SUB-S. (4): BUILDING
See the note to s. 3, *ante*.

CONSEQUENTIAL AMENDMENT
Consequent upon sub-s. (2) above the Reserve and Auxiliary Forces (Protection of Civil Interests) Act 1951, s. 15, is amended by s. 152 (1) and Sch. 25, para. 1, *post*.

DEFINITIONS
For "restricted contract", see the Rent Act 1977, s. 19, as amended by ss. 73 (2), 152 (1), (3), Sch. 25, para. 36, and Sch. 26, *post*; for "protected tenant", see s. 1 of that Act; for "statutory tenant", see s. 2 of that Act; for "lessee", see s. 107 (1) of that Act; for "tenancy",

see s. 152 (1) of that Act, or, in relation to sub-s. (1) above, the Protection from Eviction Act 1977, s. 8 (2).

PROTECTION FROM EVICTION ACT 1977, S. 3 (2)
    See 47, Halsbury's Statutes (3rd edn.), p. 665.

RENT ACT 1977
    For the meaing of "restricted contract", see s. 19 of that Act, as amended by ss. 73 (2), 152 (1), (3), Sch. 25, para. 36, and Sch. 26, *post*.

1977 ACT
    I.e., the Rent Act 1977; see s. 150, *post*. S. 12 of that Act is also amended by s. 65 (1), *ante*; see also s. 65 (2)–(7), *ante*.

MATRIMONIAL HOMES ACT 1967
    See A.L.S. Vol. 164. That Act is amended by s. 152 (1) and Sch. 25, paras. 14–17, *post*.

TRANSITIONAL PROVISION
    See s. 152 (2) and Sch. 25, para. 67, *post*.

70. Reconsideration of registered rents under Part V of Rent Act 1977

(1) In section 80 (2) of the 1977 Act (which in certain circumstances prevents an application for a new registered rent for a dwelling-house which is the subject of a restricted contract from being made within 3 years of the date of an existing registration), for the words "3 years" there are substituted the words "2 years".

(2) This section does not apply in any case where the date from which the period during which no application for registration can be made is to be calculated falls before the commencement of this section. **[399]**

COMMENCEMENT
    See s. 153 (4), *post*, and the note "Orders under this section" thereto; and note sub-s. (2) above.

1977 ACT
    I.e., the Rent Act 1977; see s. 150, *post*.

71. Cancellation of rents registered under Part V of Rent Act 1977

(1) After section 81 of the 1977 Act (effect of registration of rent under section 79) there is inserted the following section—

> ### "81A. Cancellation of registration of rent
>
> (1) Where the rent payable for any dwelling is entered in the register under section 79 of this Act, the rent tribunal shall cancel the entry, on an application made under this section, if—
>
> (a) not less than two years have elapsed since the date of entry;
> (b) the dwelling is not for the time being subject to a restricted contract; and
> (c) the application is made by the person who would be the lessor if the dwelling were subject to a restricted contract.
>
> (2) An application under this section must be in the prescribed form, and contain the prescribed particulars.
>
> (3) Cancellation of the registration shall be without prejudice to a further registration of a rent at any time after the cancellation.
>
> (4) The rent tribunal shall notify the applicant of their decision to grant, or to refuse, any application under this section."

(2) In Schedule 10 to the 1977 Act (rent assessment committees), in paragraph 5 for the words "paragraph 6" there are substituted the words "paragraphs 6 and 6A" and after paragraph 6 there is inserted the following paragraph—

"6A. When dealing with an application under section 81A of this Act a rent assessment committee carrying out the functions of a rent tribunal shall consist of the chairman of the committee sitting alone." **[400]**

COMMENCEMENT
See s. 153 (4), *post*, and the note "Orders under this section" thereto.

RENT TRIBUNAL
Rent tribunals were constituted by the Rent Act 1977, s. 76, Sch. 13, A.L.S. Vol. 255, but they are abolished and these provisions were repealed by ss. 72 (1), 152 (3) and Sch. 26, *post*, as from a day to be appointed under s. 153 (4), *post*. On the abolition of the tribunals their functions are to be transferred to rent assessment committees constituted under s. 65 of, and Sch. 10 to, the Act of 1977 (as amended, in the case, of Sch. 10, by sub-s. (2) above and s. 152 (1), (3), Sch. 25, para. 56, and Sch. 26, *post*) (s. 72 (2), *post*) and rent assessment committees are, when constituted to carry out those functions, to be known as rent tribunals (s. 72 (3), *post*).

NOT LESS THAN TWO YEARS
This period may be reduced or increased by order made in accordance with s. 60 (5) (*a*), (6), (7), *ante*.

PRESCRIBED FORM; PRESCRIBED PARTICULARS
I.e., prescribed by regulations under the Rent Act 1977, s. 84. At the time of going to press no regulations had been made for the purposes of s. 81A (2) of that Act as inserted by sub-s. (1) above.

RENT ASSESSMENT COMMITTEE CARRYING OUT THE FUNCTIONS OF A RENT TRIBUNAL
I.e., by virtue of s. 72 (2), *post*.

DEFINITIONS
For "restricted contract", see the Rent Act 1977, s. 19, as amended by ss. 73 (2), 152 (1), (3), Sch. 25, para. 36, and Sch. 26, *post*; for "dwelling", "lessor", "register" and "rent tribunal", see s. 85 (1) of that Act, as amended by s. 152 (1) and Sch. 25, para. 45, *post*; as to "rent", see s. 85 (3) of that Act.

1977 ACT
I.e., the Rent Act 1977; see s. 150, *post*. S. 79 of that Act is amended by s. 152 (1), (3), Sch. 25, paras. 43, 44, and Sch. 26, *post*.

72. Functions of rent tribunals

(1) Rent tribunals, as constituted for the purposes of the 1977 Act, are hereby abolished and section 76 of the 1977 Act (constitution etc. of rent tribunals) is hereby repealed.

(2) As from the commencement of this section the functions which, under the 1977 Act, are conferred on rent tribunals shall be carried out by rent assessment committees.

(3) A rent assessment committee shall, when constituted to carry out functions so conferred, be known as a rent tribunal. **[401]**

COMMENCEMENT
See s. 153 (4), *post*, and the note "Orders under this section" thereto.

RENT TRIBUNALS
Those tribunals were constituted by the Rent Act 1977, s. 76, Sch. 13, A.L.S. Vol. 255 (repealed by sub-s. (1) above and s. 152 (3) and Sch. 26, *post*).

RENT ASSESSMENT COMMITTEES
These committees are constituted under the Rent Act 1977, s. 65, Sch. 10, as amended, in the case of Sch. 10, by s. 71 (2), *ante*, and s. 152 (1), (3), Sch. 25, para. 56, and Sch. 26, *post*.

1977 ACT
I.e., the Rent Act 1977; see s. 150, *post*. Section 76, together with Sch. 13 to that Act, is also repealed by s. 152 (3) and Sch. 26, *post*.

Miscellaneous

73. Dwellings forming part of Crown Estate or belonging to Duchies

(1) The following section is substituted for section 13 of the 1977 Act:

"**13.**—(1) Except as provided by subsection (2) below—

(a) a tenancy shall not be a protected tenancy at any time when the interest of the landlord under the tenancy belongs to Her Majesty in right of the Crown or to a government department or is held in trust for Her Majesty for the purposes of a government department; and

(b) a person shall not at any time be a statutory tenant of a dwelling-house if the interest of his immediate landlord would at that time belong or be held as mentioned in paragraph (a) above.

(2) An interest belonging to Her Majesty in right of the Crown shall not prevent a tenancy from being a protected tenancy or a person from being a statutory tenant if the interest is under the management of the Crown Estate Commissioners.".

(2) In subsection (5) of section 19 of the 1977 Act the words (in paragraph (b)) "or of the Duchy of Lancaster or to the Duchy of Cornwall" are omitted and at the end of the subsection there are inserted the words "except that an interest belonging to Her Majesty in right of the Crown does not prevent a contract from being a restricted contract if the interest is under the management of the Crown Estate Commissioners".

(3) In section 5 of the Rent (Agriculture) Act 1976 the following is substituted for subsection (1):

"(1) A person shall not at any time be a statutory tenant of a dwelling-house if the interest of his immediate landlord would, at that time—

(a) belong to Her Majesty in right of the Crown or to a government department, or

(b) be held in trust for Her Majesty for the purposes of a government department;

except that an interest belonging to Her Majesty in right of the Crown shall not prevent a person from being a statutory tenant if the interest is under the management of the Crown Estate Commissioners.".

(4) In the Landlord and Tenant Act 1954—

(a) the following is inserted at the end of section 56:

"(7) Part I of this Act shall apply where—

(a) there is an interest belonging to Her Majesty in right of the Crown and that interest is under the management of the Crown Estate Commissioners; or

(b) there is an interest belonging to Her Majesty in right of the Duchy of Lancaster or belonging to the Duchy of Cornwall;

as if it were an interest not so belonging.";

(b) in section 21 (6) the following is substituted for the definition of "interest not bound by this Part of this Act":

"In this subsection 'interest not bound by this Part of this Act" means an interest which belongs to Her Majesty in right of the Crown and is not under the management of the Crown Estate Commissioners or an interest belonging to a government department or held on behalf of Her Majesty for the purposes of a government department.".

(5) Schedule 8 to this Act has effect for making certain provisions consequential on this section. **[402]**

COMMENCEMENT
See s. 153 (4), *post*, and the note "Orders under this section" thereto.

GENERAL NOTE
This section extends the protection afforded by the Rent Act 1977, A.L.S. Vol. 255, the Rent (Agriculture) Act 1976, A.L.S. Vol. 250, and the Landlord and Tenant Act 1954, Part I, to interests in land under the management of the Crown Estate Commissioners and in land held by the Duchy of Lancaster or the Duchy of Cornwall. Other property belonging to the Crown and property belonging to a government department continue to be outside the protection afforded by that legislation but this Crown exemption does not extend to sub-tenants or assignees from the Crown; see the General Note to s. 154 of the Act of 1977, and to s. 36 of the Act of 1976.

DWELLING-HOUSE
See the note to the Rent Act 1977, s. 1.

CROWN ESTATE COMMISSIONERS
I.e., the Commissioners referred to in the Crown Estate Act 1961, s. 1; see the Interpretation Act 1978, s. 5. Sch. 1, A.L.S. Vol. 258.

DEFINITIONS
In the provisions substituted by sub-s. (1) above for "protected tenancy"; see the Rent Act 1977, s. 1; for "statutory tenant", see s. 2 of that Act, and for "landlord" and "tenancy", see s. 152 (1) of that Act. In the provisions substituted by sub-s. (3) above for "statutory tenant" see the Rent (Agriculture) Act 1976, s. 4, for "landlord", see s. 34 (1) of that Act, and as to "dwelling-house", see s. 34 (3) of that Act, *ibid*.

1977 ACT
I.e., the Rent Act 1977; see s. 150, *post*. S. 19 (5) of that Act is also amended by s. 152 (1) and Sch. 25, para. 36, *post*, and the words to be omitted from that subsection are also repealed by s. 152 (3) and Sch. 26, *post*.

RENT (AGRICULTURE) ACT 1976, S. 5 (1)
See A.L.S. Vol. 250.

LANDLORD AND TENANT ACT 1954, PART I, SS. 21 (6), 56
See A.L.S. Vols. 87, 155.

74. Housing association and housing trust tenancies under Rent Act 1977

(1) In section 15 of the 1977 Act (tenancies not protected when landlord's interest belongs to housing association or housing trust etc.) subsection (4), and in subsection (1) the words "in respect of which any of the conditions specified in subsection (4) below is fulfilled", are hereby repealed.

(2) For subsection (5) of section 15 there is substituted the following subsection—

"(5) In subsection (2) above 'housing trust' means a corporation or body of persons which—

(a) is required by the terms of its constituent instrument to use the whole of its funds, including any surplus which may arise from its operations, for the purpose of providing housing accommodation; or

187

(b) is required by the terms of its constituent instrument to devote the whole, or substantially the whole, of its funds to charitable purposes and in fact uses the whole, or substantially the whole, of its funds for the purpose of providing housing accommodation.''.

(3) Schedule 9 to this Act has effect for the purpose of supplementing this section.

[403]

COMMENCEMENT
See s. 153 (4), *post*, and the note "Orders under this section" thereto.

HOUSING TRUST
By virtue of the Housing Finance Act 1972, s. 19 (5) (c), as substituted by s. 118 and Sch. 15, para. 3, *post*, a person is a private tenant for the purposes of the provisions of Part II of that Act, A.L.S. Vol. 202 (as amended by s. 118 and Sch. 15, *post*), relating to rent allowances if he occupies a dwelling let to him by a housing trust within the meaning of the Rent Act 1977, s. 15, A.L.S. Vol. 255, as amended by this section, a his tenancy would be a protected tenancy for the purposes of that Act but for the said s. 15.
    Note also that no provisional notice or improvement notice may be served under the Housing Act 1974, Part VIII, A.L.S. Vol. 223, if the person having control of the dwelling in question is a housing trust as defined by s. 15 of the Act of 1977 which is also a charity within the meaning of the Charities Act 1960, A.L.S. Vol. 132; see s. 99 (2) of the Act of 1974.

CORPORATION
As to the nature of corporations, see 9 Halsbury's Laws (4th Edn.), paras. 120 *et seq.*

CHARITABLE PURPOSES
As to charitable purposes and non-charitable purposes generally, see 5 Halsbury's Laws (4th Edn.), paras. 501 *et seq.*

1977 ACT
I.e., the Rent Act 1977; see s. 150, *post*. That section is also partly repealed by s. 152 (3) and Sch. 26, *post*.

TRANSITIONAL PROVISION
See s. 152 (2) and Sch. 25, para. 68, *post*.

75. Proceedings for possession of certain dwelling-houses

(1) Section 100 of the 1977 Act (which gives the court an extended discretion in actions for possession of certain dwelling-houses) is amended as follows.

(2) For subsection (3) there is substituted the following subsection—

"(3) On any such adjournment as is referred to in subsection (1) above or any such stay, suspension or postponement as is referred to in subsection (2) above, the court shall, unless it considers that to do so would cause exceptional hardship to the tenant or would otherwise be unreasonable, impose conditions with regard to payment by the tenant of arrears of rent (if any) and rent or payments in respect of occupation after termination of the tenancy (mesne profits) and may impose such other conditions as it thinks fit."

(3) After subsection (4) there are inserted the following subsections—

"(4A) Subsection (4B) below applies in any case where—
(a) proceedings are brought for possession of a dwelling-house which is let on a protected tenancy or subject to a statutory tenancy;
(b) the tenant's spouse or former spouse, having rights of occupation under the Matrimonial Homes Act 1967, is then in occupation of the dwelling-house; and
(c) the tenancy is terminated as a result of those proceedings.

(4B) In any case to which this subsection applies, the spouse or former spouse shall, so long as he or she remains in occupation, have the same rights in relation to, or in connection with, any such adjournment as is referred to in subsection (1) above or any such stay, suspension or postponement as is referred to in subsection (2) above, as he or she would have if those rights of occupation were not affected by the termination of the tenancy.''.

(4) Section 7 of the Rent (Agriculture) Act 1976 (which corresponds to section 100 of the 1977 Act) is amended as follows.

(5) After subsection (2) there is inserted the following subsection—

"(2A) In those cases the court may adjourn for such period or periods as it thinks fit".

(6) For subsection (4) there is substituted the following subsection—

"(4) On any such adjournment as is referred to in subsection (2A) above or any such stay, suspension or postponement as is referred to in subsection (3) above, the court shall, unless it considers that to do so would cause exceptional hardship to the tenant or would otherwise be unreasonable, impose conditions with regard to payment by the tenant or arrears of rent (if any) and rent or payments in respect of occupation after termination of the tenancy (mesne profits) and may impose such other conditions as it thinks fit.''.

(7) After subsection (5) there are inserted the following subsections—

"(5A) Subsection (5B) below applies in any case where—

　(a) proceedings are brought for possession of a dwelling-house which is subject to a protected occupancy or statutory tenancy;
　(b) the tenant's spouse or former spouse, having rights of occupation under the Matrimonial Homes Act 1967, is then in occupation of the dwelling-house; and
　(c) the tenancy is terminated as a result of those proceedings.

(5B) In any case to which this subsection applies, the spouse or former spouse shall, so long as he or she remains in occupation, have the same rights in relation to or in connection with any such adjournment as is referred to in subsection (2A) above or any such stay, suspension of postponement as is referred to in subsection (3) above as he or she would have if those rights of occupation were not affected by the termination of the tenancy." **[404]**

COMMENCEMENT
　See s. 153 (4), *post*, and the note "Orders under this section" thereto.

SUB-S. (2): THE COURT
　Cf. the note "A court" to the Rent Act 1977, s. 98, A.L.S. Vol. 255.

SUB-S. (3): DWELLING-HOUSE
　See the note to the Rent Act 1977, s. 1.

SUB-S. (5): THE COURT
　See the note "A court" to the Rent (Agriculture) Act 1976, s. 6, A.L.S. Vol. 250.

DEFINITIONS
　In the provisions substituted or inserted by sub-ss. (1)–(3) above for "protected tenancy", see the Rent Act 1977, s. 1, for "statutory tenancy", see s. 2 of that Act, and for "let", "tenant" and "tenancy", see s. 152 (1) of that Act. In the provisions substituted or inserted by sub-ss. (4)–(7) above for "dwelling-house subject to a protected occupancy" see the Rent (Agriculture) Act 1976, s. 3 (6); for "dwelling-house subject to a statutory tenancy", see s. 4 (6) of that Act; for "tenancy" and "tenant", see s. 34 (1) of that Act; as to "dwelling-house", see s. 34 (3) of that Act.

1977 ACT
  I.e., the Rent Act 1977; see s. 150, *post.*

MATRIMONIAL HOMES ACT 1967
  See A.L.S. Vol. 164. That Act is amended by s. 152 (1) and Sch. 25, paras. 14–17, *post.*

RENT (AGRICULTURE) ACT 1976, S. 7
  See A.L.S. Vol. 250.

76. Statutory tenancies by succession

(1) In Schedule 1 to the 1977 Act, for paragraph 2 (under which on the death of the original tenant under a protected or statutory tenancy his widow if residing with him at his death becomes a statutory tenant by succession) there is substituted the following paragraph—

> "2. The surviving spouse (if any) of the original tenant, if residing in the dwelling-house immediately before the death of the original tenant, shall after the death be the statutory tenant if and so long as he or she occupies the dwelling-house as his or her residence.".

(2) For paragraph 6 of that Schedule (similar provision in relation to death of first successor) there is substituted the following paragraph—

> "6. The surviving spouse (if any) of the first successor, if residing in the dwelling-house immediately before the death of the first successor, shall after the death be the statutory tenant if and so long as he or she occupies the dwelling-house as his or her residence.".

(3) In section 3 (2) and (3) (*a*) and 4 (3) and (4) (*a*) of the Rent (Agriculture) Act 1976 (which correspond to provisions in Schedule 1 to the 1977 Act) for the words "with him at his death" there shall be substituted in each case, the words "in the dwelling-house immediately before his death".

(4) The amendments made by this section have effect only in relation to deaths occurring after the commencement of the subsection concerned. **[405]**

COMMENCEMENT
  See s. 153 (4), *post*, and the note "Orders under this section" thereto; and note sub-s. (4) above.

GENERAL NOTE
  This section amends the provisions of the Rent Act 1977, Sch. 1, A.L.S. Vol. 255, under which a widow may succeed as statutory tenant on the death of the original tenant or of a statutory tenant by succession so that they apply equally to a surviving widower where he himself was not previously the tenant (sub-ss. (1) 1 (2)). Those provisions are also amended so that the right of succession arises where the surviving spouse was "residing in the dwelling-house immediately before the death" instead of where she was "residing with him at his death" (sub-ss. (1), (2)).
  This section also amends the corresponding provisions of the Rent (Agriculture) Act 1976, ss. 3, 4, A.L.S. Vol. 250, so that right of succession arises where the surviving spouse was "residing in the dwelling-house immediately before the death" instead of where she (or he) was "residing with him (or her) at the death" (sub-s. (3)). That Act already conferred rights of succession on the surviving widower as well as the surviving widow and the Act of 1977 is brought into line in this respect as mentioned above.

RESIDING
  See the note "Resident" to Sch. 3, para. 6, *post.*

SURVIVING SPOUSE
  This term is a replacement of "widow" in the relevant provisions of the Rent Act 1977 (Sch. 1, paras. 2 and 6). The previous term was blindly repeated from the Increase of Rent and Mortgage Interest (Restrictions) Act 1920, s. 12 (1) (*g*). It is said in Megarry "The Rent Acts", p. 212, that "widow" bore its ordinary meaning and would not therefore

include a divorced wife, citing *MacAlister* v. *Black* 1956 S.L.T. (Sh. Ct.) 74; and see also *Cheshire and North Wales Property Co.* v. *Bull* [1952] C.L.Y. 3007, C.A. It is also thought that "surviving spouse" would not include either a divorced widow or a divorced widower, unless the courts extend the meaning of the term in similar manner to the inclusion of some mistresses in the term "family" in paras 3 and 7 of Sch. 1 to the 1977 Act: see *Dyson Holdings Ltd.* v. *Fox* [1976] Q.B. 503; [1975] 3 All E.R. 1030, C.A.; also *Watson* v. *Lucas*, [1980] 3 All E.R. 647, C.A. It is clear of course that the term "surviving spouse" includes male successors, in keeping with modern notions of reverse sex equality.

IF RESIDING IN THE DWELLING-HOUSE
This replaces, in the case of Sch. 1, paras 2 and 6, to the Rent Act 1977, the following: "residing with him ..." If it be correct to regard the main change as being from the new word "in" rather than "with", while there may not be much real difference most of the time, it may be that there is a shift from personal residence to impersonal occupation in the premises: it may be that even where the personal element of even minimal cohabitation is lacking, the survivor may succeed if physically residing: cf. *Collier* v. *Stoneman* [1957] 3 All E.R. 20, C.A.; *Morgan* v. *Murch* [1970] 2 All E.R. 100, C.A. "Residing" means, as before, that there should be some degree of permanence: see Megarry, *op cit.*, p. 213; but, in this, it appears to be the case that a spouse in an asylum or hospital, even for quite a long time, may still, as a matter of fact and degree, be "residing": see *Greenway* v. *Rawlings* (1952) 102 L.J. News 360; *Alston* v. *Andrews* (1965) 105 L.J. News 188.

Also, there is, for the first time it seems, an express requirement in the new paragraphs that the residence should in fact be in the dwelling-house. Oddly enough, also, the "family" succession provisions in the Rent Act 1977, Sch. 1, paras 3 and 7, remain unaffected and so all the learning on "with him" and the like, will continue to apply to those rules.

IF AND SO LONG AS HE OR SHE OCCUPIES THE DWELLING-HOUSE AS HIS OR HER RESIDENCE
This phrase is to be construed in accordance with the Rent Act 1977, s. 2 (3); and see also the note "After the termination of a protected tenancy ..." to s. 2 of that Act.

DEFINITIONS
For "the original tenant", see the Rent Act 1977, Sch. 1, paras. 1, 10 (1); for "the first successor", see Sch. 1, paras. 4, 10 (1) to that Act; as to "dwelling-house", see the Rent (Agriculture) Act 1976, s. 34 (3).

1977 ACT
I.e., the Rent Act 1977; see s. 150, *post.*

RENT (AGRICULTURE) ACT 1976, SS. 3, 4.
See A.L.S. Vol. 250.

77. Amendment of Part VI of Rent Act 1977

Part VI of the 1977 Act (rent limit for dwellings let by housing associations, housing trusts and the Housing Corporation) is amended in accordance with the provisions of Schedule 10 to this Act. **[406]**

COMMENCEMENT
See s. 153 (4), *post*, and the note "Orders under this section" thereto.

1977 ACT
I.e., the Rent Act 1977; see s. 150, *post.*

78. Allowable premiums in relation to certain long tenancies

(1) Section 127 of the 1977 Act shall have effect and be deemed always to have had effect as if for paragraph (c) of subsection (2) there were substituted the paragraph set out in subsection (2) below and at the end of subsection (5) there were added the words set out in subsection (3) below.

(2) The substituted paragraph is—

"(c) that the terms of the tenancy do not inhibit both the assignment and the underletting of the whole of the premises comprised in the tenancy.".

(3) The added words are "and for the purposes of subsections (2) (c) and (3B) (d) above the terms of a tenancy inhibit an assignment or underletting if they—

(a) preclude it; or

(b) permit it subject to a consent but exclude section 144 of the Law of Property Act 1925 (no payment in nature of fine); or

(c) permit it subject to a consent but require in connection with a request for consent the making of an offer to surrender the tenancy.".

(4) After subsection (3) of section 127 there are inserted the following subsections—

"(3A) If the conditions in subsection (3B) below are satisfied in respect of a tenancy, this Part of this Act shall not apply to that tenancy and, together with Part VII of the Rent Act 1968 and the enactments replaced by Part VII, shall be deemed never to have applied to it.

(3B) The conditions are that—

(a) the tenancy was granted before 16th July 1980;

(b) a premium was lawfully required and paid on the grant of the tenancy;

(c) the tenancy was, at the time when it was granted, a tenancy at a low rent; and

(d) the terms of the tenancy do not inhibit both the assignment and the underletting of the whole of the premises comprised in the tenancy.

(3C) If the conditions in subsection (3D) below are satisfied in respect of a tenancy, this section shall have effect, in relation to that tenancy, as if for the words "20 years" and "21 years", in subsections (2) (b) and (3) above there were substituted, respectively, the words "6 years" and "7 years".

(3D) The conditions are that—

(a) the tenancy is granted after 15th July 1980;

(b) at the time when it is granted it is a tenancy at a low rent; and

(c) the terms of the tenancy ensure that any variation of the sums payable by the tenant otherwise than in respect of rates, services, repairs or maintenance, cannot lead to those sums exceeding an annual rate of two-thirds of the rateable value of the dwelling-house at the date when the variation is made.

For the purposes of this subsection the rateable value of a dwelling-house shall be ascertained in accordance with section 25 of this Act (disregarding subsection (4)) by reference to the value shown in the valuation list at the date when the variation is made.". **[407]**

COMMENCEMENT

See s. 153 (4), *post*, and the note "Orders under this section" thereto. Note, however, that the amendments made by this section are expressed to have retrospective effect.

GENERAL NOTE

This section clarifies the circumstances in which a premium may be charged for the grant or assignment of a tenancy which is both a long tenancy as defined by the Landlord and Tenant Act 1954, s. 2 (4) and a protected tenancy as defined by the Rent Act 1977. By s. 127 (1) (a) of the Rent Act 1977, a long tenancy which is a protected tenancy, which satisfies the conditions set out in s. 127 (2) and (3) lies outside the prohibition on "premiums" in Part IX of the Act, so that the value of the lease may be fully realised by the lessee. But should any of the conditions *not* be satisfied, then by s. 127 (1) (b), Part II of Sch. 18 will apply for allowing a limited amount only of the "premium". If therefore the lease contains an "Adler" clause, the effect will, from the commencement of s. 78 of this Act, be to attract Part II of Sch. 18, owing to the amendments made by sub-ss. (2) and (3) to s. 127 (2) and (3) of the 1977 Act. The new para. (c) of s. 127 (2) speaks of "inhibit" in relation to assignments or sub-lettings of the whole premises rather than the previous terminology and the new words added by sub-s. (3) to s. 127 (3) obviously catch clauses which require the lessee to offer the lease for surrender to the lessor as a condition precedent to consent, upheld in *Adler* v. *Upper Grosvenor Street Investments Ltd.* [1957] 1 All E.R. 229 and confirmed, despite doubts expressed *obiter* in *Greene* v. *Church Commissioners* [1974] 3 All E.R. 609, C.A., in *Bocardo S.A.* v. *S. & M. Hotels* [1979] 3 All E.R. 737, C.A. (and see further Prof. J. E. Adams, 252 E.G. 897). These clauses will still not infringe the Landlord and Tenant Act 1927, s. 19 (2), at common law.

SERVICES
See the note to the Rent Act 1977, s. 30, A.L.S. Vol. 255.

REPAIRS
Cf. the note to the Rent Act 1977, Sch. 6, para. 1, and the note "Does not include . . . decoration or repair" to s. 43 of that Act.

DWELLING-HOUSE
See the note to the Rent Act 1977, s. 1.

DEFINITIONS
For "tenancy at a low rent", see the Rent Act 1977, s. 5; for "grant", see s. 127 (5) of that Act; for "rates", "tenancy" and "tenant", see s. 152 (1) of that Act. Note as to "terms of a tenancy inhibit an assignment or underletting", s. 127 (5) of that Act, as amended by sub-s. (3) above.

1977 ACT
I.e., the Rent Act 1977; see s. 150, *post.*

LAW OF PROPERTY ACT 1925, S. 144
See 27, Halsbury's Statute (3rd edn.), p. 562.

RENT ACT 1968, PART VII
That Act was repealed by the Rent Act 1977, s. 155 (5), Sch. 25.

79. Meaning of "premium" in Part IX of Rent Act 1977

In section 128 of the 1977 Act (interpretation of Part IX, which prohibits premiums etc.) for the definition of "premium", in subsection (1), there is substituted the following definition—

"'premium' includes—

    (*a*) any fine or other like sum;

    (*b*) any other pecuniary consideration in addition to rent; and

    (*c*) any sum paid by way of a deposit, other than one which does not exceed one-sixth of the annual rent and is reasonable in relation to the potential liability in respect of which it is paid." **[408]**

COMMENCEMENT
See s. 153 (4), *post,* and the note "Orders under this section" thereto.

GENERAL NOTE
The question of what is a premium is one of substance: *Elmdene Estates Ltd.* v. *White* [1960] A.C. 528; [1960] 1 All E.R. 306, H.L. A sale at less than market value is a premium within the Rent Act 1977, s. 128 (1); *ibid.* If a landlord required a contribution in money from a tenant for repairs for which the tenant was not responsible, this might be a premium: see *R.* v. *Fulham, Hammersmith and Kensington Rent Tribunal, ex parte Phillipe* [1950] 2 All E.R. 211.

Payments of rent in advance may be caught, quite apart from para. (*c*) of the substituted s. 128 (1) of the 1977 Act, by s. 126 of that Act, which does not apply to restricted contracts, unlike the definition in s. 128 (1), which does apply to them.

To come within the exception to para. (*c*), the sum must be "reasonable in relation to the potential liability": accordingly, a penalty stipulated *in terrorem* would be within para. (*c*) even if within the one-sixth limit in a proper case. As to what is a penalty, see *Re Newman* (1876) 4 Ch. D. 724, C.A.

Apart from the exception in para. (*c*) for sums not exceeding one sixth of the annual rent, para. (*c*) is apt to catch a deposit paid in advance against dilapidations and outgoings, reversing *R.* v. *Ewing* (1977) 65 Cr. App. Rep. 4, C.A. However, a sum payable on quitting is arguably not a "sum paid by way of a deposit" and if this is so, then no matter what its size, it would fall outside para. (*c*): an example would be a sum payable on quitting towards redecoration: *Boyer* v. *Warbey* [1953] 1 Q.B. 234; [1952] 2 All E.R. 976, C.A.

PREMIUM
See the note to the Rent Act 1977, s. 128, A.L.S. Vol. 255.

1977 ACT
I.e., the Rent Act 1977; see s. 150, *post*.

PART III

TENANT'S REPAIRS AND IMPROVEMENTS

Provision of information. As to the publication by landlords under secure tenancies of information explaining, *inter alia*, the provisions of this Part of this Act and the supply to tenants of a copy of such information, see s. 41, *ante*.

80. Repairing obligations in short leases

(1) Section 32 of the Housing Act 1961 (covenant by landlord to repair to be implied in short leases) does not apply to any lease granted after the commencement of this section—

(*a*) to a specified educational institution or other specified body;

(*b*) to a housing association falling within section 15 (3) of the 1977 Act;

(*c*) to a body of a kind mentioned in section 14 of the 1977 Act (local authorities etc);

(*d*) to Her Majesty in right of the Crown unless the lease is under the management of the Crown Estate Commissioners; or

(*e*) to a government department, or to any person holding in trust for Her Majesty for the purposes of a government department.

(2) In subsection (1) above "specified" means specified, or of a class specified, by regulations made by the Secretary of State under section 8 of the 1977 Act.

(3) In section 33 (1) of the Housing Act 1961 (leases to which section 32 applies) after the words "this section" there are inserted the words "and section 80 of the Housing Act 1980". **[409]**

COMMENCEMENT
See s. 153 (4) *post*, and the note "Orders under this section" thereto. Note that by sub-s. (1) above the restriction of the Housing Act 1961, s. 32, A.L.S. Vol. 131, applies only to leases granted after the commencement of this section. It follows that s. 85 (2), *post*, which provides that this Part of this Act applies to tenancies granted before as well as after the commencement of this Part, can have no application to the present section.

HOUSING ASSOCIATION FALLING WITHIN S. 15 (3) OF THE 1977 ACT
It is provided by s. 84, *post*, however, that this Part of this Act does not apply in relation to a housing association which falls within the Rent Act 1977, s. 15 (3) (*d*). A.L.S. Vol. 255 (which relates to certain societies registered under the Industrial and Provident Societies Act 1965).

CROWN ESTATE COMMISSIONERS
See the note to s. 73, *ante*.

PERSON
See the note to s. 24, *ante*.

HOUSING ACT 1961, SS. 32, 33 (1)
    See A.L.S. Vol. 131.

1977 ACT
    I.e., the Rent Act 1977; see s. 150, *post.*

81. Tenant's improvements

(1) The following provisions of this section have effect with respect to secure tenancies, protected tenancies and statutory tenancies in place of section 19 (2) of the Landlord and Tenant Act 1927.

(2) It is by virtue of this section a term of every such tenancy that the tenant will not make any improvement without the written consent of the landlord.

(3) The consent required by virtue of subsection (2) above is not to be unreasonably withheld and, if unreasonably withheld, shall be treated as given.

(4) Subsections (1) to (3) above do not apply in any case where the tenant has been given a notice—

    (*a*) of a kind mentioned in one of Cases 11 to 18 and 20 in Schedule 15 to the 1977 Act (notice that possession might be recovered under that Case); or

    (*b*) under section 52 (1) (*b*) of this Act (notice that a tenancy is to be a protected shorthold tenancy);

unless the tenant proves that, at the time when the landlord gave the notice, it was unreasonable for the landlord to expect to be able in due course to recover possession of the dwelling-house under that Case or, as the case may be, Case 19 of Schedule 15 (added by section 55 of this Act).

(5) In Part I, and in this Part, of this Act "improvement" means any alteration in, or addition to, a dwelling-house and includes—

    (*a*) any addition to, or alteration in, landlord's fixtures and fittings and any addition or alteration connected with the provision of any services to a dwelling-house;

    (*b*) the erection of any wireless or television aerial; and

    (*c*) the carrying out of external decoration;

but paragraph (*c*) above does not apply in relation to a protected or statutory tenancy if the landlord is under an obligation to carry out external decoration or to keep the exterior of the dwelling-house in repair. **[410]**

COMMENCEMENT
    See s. 153 (4), *post,* and the note "Orders under this section" thereto; and see also s. 85 (2), *post.*

SUB-S. (2): WILL NOT MAKE ANY IMPROVEMENT WITHOUT THE WRITTEN CONSENT OF THE LANDLORD
    For further provisions to such consents, see sub-s. (3) above and s. 82, *post* (and see also s. 83, *post*). Note that the term of a secure tenancy implied by virtue of this section may not be varied; see s. 40 (2), *ante.* See also the note "Written; writing" to s. 5, *ante.*

SUB-S. (3): CONSENT . . . IS NOT TO BE UNREASONABLY WITHHELD
    As to the determination of the question whether the withholding of consent was unreasonable, see s. 82 (1), *post,* and as to the giving of consent subject to an unreasonable condition, see s. 82 (3) (*b*), (4), *post.*
    The question whether or not the withholding of consent is in the particular circumstances reasonable or unreasonable must always depend on the facts of the particular case (*Re Gibbs and Houlder Brothers & Co. Ltd's Lease, Houlder Brothers & Co. Ltd.* v. *Gibbs,*

[1925] Ch. 575, C.A., at p. 584; *Lee* v. *K. Carter, Ltd.*, [1949] 1 K.B. 85; [1948] 2 All E.R. 690, C.A., at p. 92 and p. 693, respectively). Consent must be asked for and the landlord given reasonable time to consider the matter (*Wilson v Fynn*, [1948] 2 All E.R. 40).

The tenant may sue for a declaration (*Mills* v. *Cannon Brewery Co.*, [1920] 2 Ch. 38; *Lambert* v. *F. W. Woolworth & Co. Ltd.* (*No. 2*), [1938] Ch. 883; [1938] 2 All E.R. 664; and see s. 86 (2), *post*). or he can ignore the refusal and proceed (*Balls Brothers, Ltd.* v. *Sinclair*, [1931] 2 Ch. 325; [1931] All E.R. Rep. 803. See also *Treloar* v. *Bigge* (1874), L.R. 9 Exch. 151; and see the note to s. 36 (1), *supra*.

SUB-S. (5): PART I
I.e., ss. 1–50, *ante*.

THIS PART
I.e., Part III (see 80–85) of this Act.

IMPROVEMENT
See for a statutory definition, sub-s. (5). It is thought that, while from the tenant's point of view there may be an improvement which does not raise the value of the landlord's reversion, a landlord might be able reasonably to withhold his consent (or only give it and make it subject to, say, a re-instatement condition: see s. 82 (2)) in such a case. It may be noted that under the Landlord and Tenant Act 1927, s. 19 (2), it is what is an improvement from the tenant's point of view that is to be considered: *F. W. Woolworth & Co. Ltd.* v. *Lambert* [1937] Ch. 37; [1936] 2 All E.R. 1523, C.A.; and *Lambert* v. *F. W. Woolworth & Co. Ltd.* (*No. 2*) [1938] Ch. 883; [1938] 2 All E.R. 664, C.A. As to fixtures, see sub-s. (5) and also *Boswell* v. *Crucible Steel Co.* [1925] 1 K.B. 119, C.A.

EXTERNAL DECORATION
On the meaning of "external", it was held in *Brown* v. *Liverpool Cpn.* [1969] 3 All E.R. 1345, C.A., that "exterior" in relation to the Housing Act 1961, A.L.S. Vol. 131, s. 32 (1) includes the front steps of a dwelling-house and access paths, but not necessarily those at the back where not used for access: *Hopwood* v. *Cannock Chase D.C.* [1975] 1 All E.R. 796, C.A.

If the landlord is under a statutory obligation to carry out external repairs, then none of s. 81 will apply: examples would be under the Housing Act 1957, ss. 4 & 6, and the Housing Act 1961, s. 32.

FIXTURES AND FITTINGS
"A fixture is an article which by its annexation to the land has lost its chattel nature and has become, in the eyes of the law, part and parcel of the realty" (*Hulme* v. *Brigham*, [1943] 1 All E.R. 204, at p. 207). "Fittings" on the other hand, seems to cover everything fitted to the premises which is not a fixture. See, further, 23 Halsbury's Laws (3rd Edn.), pp. 489 *et seq.*

SERVICES
Cf. the note to the Rent Act 1977, s. 30, A.L.S. Vol. 255.

EXCLUSION OF CERTAIN HOUSING ASSOCIATIONS
See s. 84, *post*.

JURISDICTION OF COUNTY COURT
By s. 86 (1), *post*, a county court has jurisdiction to determine any question arising under this Part of this Act and to entertain any proceedings brought thereunder, and by s. 86 (2), *post*, this jurisdiction includes jurisdiction to entertain proceedings on any question whether any consent required by this section was withheld or unreasonably withheld. See also s. 86 (3), *post*, as to non-recovery of costs of proceedings in the High Court, and s. 86 (4)–(6), *post*, as to procedure, etc., in the county court.

DEFINITIONS
By virtue of s. 85 (1), *post*, for "secure tenancy", see ss. 28 and 49 (2), *ante*, for "protected tenancy", see the Rent Act 1977, s. 1, for "statutory tenancy", see s. 2 of that Act, for "dwelling-house", see s. 50 (2), *ante*, or s. 1 of the Act of 1977, and for "landlord" and "tenant", see s. 152 (1) of the Act of 1977. Note as to "improvement", sub-s. (5) above.

LANDLORD AND TENANT ACT 1927, S. 19 (2)
18, Halsbury's Statutes (3rd edn.), p. 464.

1977 ACT
I.e., the Rent Act 1977; see s. 150, *post.* Cases 11 and 12 are amended by s. 66, *ante*, and Case 20 is added to Sch. 15 by s. 67, *ante*.

82. Provisions as to consents required by section 81

(1) If any question arises whether the withholding of a consent required by virtue of section 81 above was unreasonable it is for the landlord to show that it was not; and in determining that question the court shall, in particular, have regard to the extent to which the improvement would be likely—

    (*a*) to make the dwelling-house, or any other premises, less safe for occupiers;

    (*b*) to cause the landlord to incur expenditure which it would be unlikely to incur if the improvement were not made; or

    (*c*) to reduce the price which the dwelling-house would fetch if sold on the open market or the rent which the landlord would be able to charge on letting the dwelling-house.

(2) A consent required by virtue of section 81 may be validly given notwithstanding that it follows, instead of preceding, the action requiring it and may be given subject to a condition.

(3) Where the tenant has applied in writing for a consent which is required by virtue of section 81 then—

    (*a*) if the landlord refuses to give the consent it shall give to the tenant a written statement of the reasons why the consent was refused; and

    (*b*) if the landlord neither gives nor refuses to give the consent within a reasonable time, the consent shall be taken to have been withheld, and if the landlord gives the consent but subject to an unreasonable condition, the consent shall be taken to have been unreasonably withheld.

(4) If any question arises whether a condition attached to a consent was reasonable, it is for the landlord to show that it was. **[411]**

COMMENCEMENT
    See s. 153 (4), *post*, and the note "Orders under this section" thereto; and see also s. 85 (2), *post*.

IT IS FOR THE LANDLORD TO SHOW
    In the case of matters covered by the Landlord and Tenant Act 1927, s. 19 (2), the burden of proof of unreasonableness is on the tenant: *Lambert* v. *F. W. Woolworth & Co. Ltd.* [1938] Ch. 883; [1938] 2 All E.R. 664, C.A. This is reversed where s. 81 applies and the tenant will benefit from the deeming provision in s. 81 (3).

THE COURT
    See the note "Jurisdiction of county court" to s. 81, *ante*.

LIKELY
    What is "likely" is probably essentially a question of fact: cf. the use of this term in the Administration of Justice Act 1970, A.L.S. Vol. 194, s. 36 (1) and *Royal Trust Co. of Canada* v. *Markham* [1975] 3 All E.R. 433, C.A.
    In general, it is thought that to be "likely" what has to be shown is a tendency or real possibility; accordingly, one may succeed in showing a thing to be likely without it being essential to show a reasonable chance of the event in fact materialising. Thus, in relation to the Trade Marks Act 1938, s. 11, "likely to succeed" was held not to mean in all cases proof of potential success in any action: *Berlei (U.K.) Ltd.* v. *Bali Brassiere Co. Inc.* [1969] 2 All E.R. 812, H.L. In relation to the Factories Act 1937, s. 47 (1), "likely to be injurious" was a term which was required to be interpreted by reference to the employee's state of knowledge: *Carmichael* v. *Cockburn & Co. Ltd.* 1955 S.C. 487.
    Since "likely" is a hypothetical postulate, it must involve the court in some cases in looking into the future: cf. *General Electric Co.* v. *The General Electric Co. Ltd.* [1972] 2 All E.R. 507. This may be a wider consideration than would be involved by providing

(say) "to cause the landlord": cf. *Doble* v. *David Grieg Ltd.* [1972] 2 All E.R. 195; *Dunning* v. *United Liverpool Hospitals' Board of Governors* [1973] 2 All E.R. 454, C.A. A mere hope or suspicion is not a likelihood.

PREMISES (SUB-S. (I) (*a*))

This is thought to have a wide meaning, so that it may include land and buildings. The popular sense of the term is presumably applicable: *Metropolitan Water Board* v. *Paine* [1907] 1 K.B. 285. Accordingly, land surrounding buildings are part of the premises: *Whitley* v. *Stumbles* [1930] A.C. 544, H.L.: in that case it was held that, in the context of the Landlord and Tenant Act 1927, s. 5, "premises" could even include an incorporeal hereditament. While in the context of a taxing statute "premises" may be taken to mean premises as a whole, not all its separate constituent parts (*Cadbury Bros. Ltd.* v. *Sinclair* [1934] 2 K.B. 389) it is thought that in this context each part may have to be looked at separately: cf. *Kingston-upon-Hull Corporation* v. *North Eastern Railway* [1916] 1 Ch. 31, C.A.

LESS SAFE FOR OCCUPIERS (SUB-S. (I) (*a*))

If this were so, then the landlord might face a possible liability under the Defective Premises Act 1972, s. 4. The occupiers to whom this duty is owed covers licencees as well as protected tenants.

   If the landlord feared that the improvement might involve a liability to third parties, then he would have to base his refusal on sub-s. (I) (*b*): for instance, the term "visitor" is not used in sub-s. (I) (*a*) and a liability in respect of such an one would be outside it.

EXPENDITURE (SUB-S. (I) (*b*))

It is possible that, if as a result of an improvement, the risk of a liability to a lawful visitor were increased significantly, the landlord could rely on this as a ground for withholding consent. It is, *passim*, difficult for him to contract out of a "business" liability to visitors owing to the Unfair Contract Terms Act 1977, A.L.S. Vol. 251.

SOLD IN THE OPEN MARKET

See the note to s. 6, *ante*.

RENT

At common law the position—reversed by sub-s. (I) (*c*)—is that even if the letting value of the premises is reduced, it is not reasonable to refuse consent on that ground alone: *F. W. Woolworth & Co Ltd.* v. *Lambert* [1937] Ch. 37; [1936] 2 All E.R. 1523, C.A.

CONSENT

This means that the landlord may give his consent *ex post facto* and may impose conditions as to re-instatement at the end of the term even where in the action, his refusal of consent was held to be unreasonable and he failed to require compensation beforehand. This again reverses the position at common law, where it was held that if the landlord failed to ask for compensation and unreasonably withheld his consent, he was too late to ask for it once the refusal was held unreasonable: see the *Woolworth* litigation, *supra*.

MAY BE GIVEN SUBJECT TO A CONDITION

As to the effect of failure by a tenant to satisfy a reasonable condition imposed by virtue of sub-s. (2) above, see s. 83, *post*.

WRITING; WRITTEN

See the corresponding note to s. 5, *ante*.

WITHIN A REASONABLE TIME

In this context it must be that what is a reasonable time is a question of fact: see also the discussion of this in s. 31 and note thereto.

TAKEN TO HAVE BEEN WITHHELD

Accordingly, in the case of a secure, protected or statutory tenancy, the tenant may carry out the improvement without going to court for a declaration where the consent is deemed under sub-s. (3) to have been withheld. He may alternatively apply to court on the basis that it is unreasonably withheld or that a condition imposed by the landlord is unreasonable: the court will be, by s. 82, the county court. See further *Balls Bros. Ltd.* v. *Sinclair* [1931] 2 Ch. 325; *Lilley* and *Skinner Ltd.* v. *Crump* (1929) 73 Sol. Jo. 366: it was there held that if the alteration or addition would in fact effect an improvement (and see now s. 81 (5)) then the landlord could not reasonably on that ground refuse his consent to it.

DEFINITIONS
  For "improvement", see s. 81 (5), *ante*; by virtue of s. 85 (1), *post*, for "dwelling-house",
  see s. 50 (2), *ante*, or the Rent Act 1977, s. 1, A.L.S. Vol. 255, and for "landlord" and
  "tenant", see s. 152 (1) of the Act of 1977.

83. Conditional consent to tenant's improvements

Any failure by a secure tenant, a protected tenant or a statutory tenant to satisfy any reasonable condition imposed by his landlord in giving consent to an improvement which the tenant proposes to make, or has made, shall be treated for the purposes of Chapter II of Part I of this Act or, as the case may be, for the purposes of the 1977 Act as a breach by the tenant of an obligation of his tenancy or, as the case may be, of an obligation of the previous protected tenancy which is applicable to the statutory tenancy. **[412]**

COMMENCEMENT
  See s. 153 (4), *post*, and the note "Orders under this section" thereto, and see also s. 85
  (2), *post*.

REASONABLE CONDITION IMPOSED ... IN GIVING CONSENT TO AN IMPROVEMENT
  Such a condition may be imposed under s. 82 (2), *ante*. See also s. 82 (4), *ante*.

CHAPTER II OF PART I
  I.e., ss. 28–50, *ante*; and as to orders for possession where an obligation of the tenancy
  has been broken, see s. 34, *ante*, and Sch. 4, Part I, ground 1, *post*.

DEFINITIONS
  For "improvement", see s. 81 (5), *ante*; for "secure tenant", see s. 150, *post*; by virtue of
  s. 85 (1), *post*, for "protected tenancy" and "protected tenant", see the Rent Act 1977,
  s. 1, A.L.S. Vol. 255, for "statutory tenancy" and "statutory tenant", see s. 2 of that Act,
  and for "landlord", see s. 152 (1) of that Act.

1977 ACT
  I.e., the Rent Act 1977; see s. 150, *post*. As to orders for possession where an obligation
  of the tenancy has been broken, see s. 98 (1) of, and Sch. 15, Part I, Case 1, to that Act.

84. Exclusion of certain housing associations from Part III

This Part of this Act does not apply in relation to a housing association which falls within paragraph (*d*) of section 15 (3) of the 1977 Act (certain societies registered under the Industrial and Provident Societies Act 1965). **[413]**

COMMENCEMENT
  See s. 153 (4), *post*, and the note "Orders under this section" thereto; and see also s. 85
  (2), *post*.

THIS PART OF THIS ACT
  I.e., Part III (ss. 80–85) of this Act.

1977 ACT
  I.e., the Rent Act 1977; see s. 150, *post*.

INDUSTRIAL AND PROVIDENT SOCIETIES ACT 1965
  See 17, Halsbury's Statutes (3rd edn.), p. 333.

85. Interpretation and application of Part III

(1) In this Part of this Act any expression used in Chapter II of Part I of this Act or in the 1977 Act has the same meaning as in that Chapter or, as the case may be, that Act.

(2) This Part of this Act applies to tenancies granted before as well as tenancies granted after the commencement of this Part of this Act. **[414]**

COMMENCEMENT; COMMENCEMENT OF THIS PART
See s. 153 (4), *post*, and the note "Orders under this section" thereto; and note sub-s. (2) above.

THIS PART OF THIS ACT
I.e., Part III (ss. 80–85) of this Act.

CHAPTER II OF PART I
I.e., ss. 28–50, *ante*.

1977 ACT
I.e., the Rent Act 1977, A.L.S. Vol. 255, see s. 150, *post*.

PART IV

JURISDICTION AND PROCEDURE

86. Jurisdiction of county court and rules of procedure

(1) Subject to section 11 of this Act, a county court has jurisdiction to determine any question arising under Part I or III of this Act and to entertain any proceedings brought thereunder and any claim (for whatever amount) in connection with a secure tenancy.

(2) The jurisdiction conferred by this section includes jurisdiction to entertain proceedings on any question arising under Chapter I of Part I and any question—

    (a) whether any consent required by section 35 or section 81 was withheld or unreasonably withheld; or

    (b) whether a statement supplied in pursuance of section 41 (3) (b) is accurate;

notwithstanding that no other relief is sought than a declaration.

(3) If a person takes proceedings in the High Court which, by virtue of this section, he could have taken in the county court he is not entitled to recover any costs.

(4) The Lord Chancellor may make such rules and give such directions as he thinks fit for the purpose of giving effect to this Part of this Act.

(5) The rules and directions may provide—

    (a) for the exercise by any registrar of a county court of any jurisdiction exercisable under this section; and

    (b) for the conduct of any proceedings in private.

(6) The power to make rules under this section is exercisable by statutory instrument and any such instrument is subject to annulment in pursuance of a resolution of either House of Parliament. **[415]**

COMMENCEMENT
Sde s. 153 (4), *post*, and the note "Orders under this section" thereto.

GENERAL NOTE
This section may be compared with the provisions relating to the jurisdiction of the county court and rules of procedure contained in the Rent Act 1977, ss. 141, 142, A.L.S. Vol. 255, and some assistance in determining the effect of sub-ss. (1)–(3) above may be derived from the notes on the effect of s. 141 (3)–(5) of the Act of 1977.

COUNTY COURT
See the note to s. 12, *ante*.

87. Extended discretion of court in certain proceedings for possession

(1) Where proceedings are brought for possession of a dwelling-house let under a secure tenancy on any of grounds 1 to 6 or 10 to 13 in Part I of Schedule 4 to this Act, the court may adjourn the proceedings for such period or periods as it thinks fit.

(2) On the making of an order for possession of such a dwelling-house on any of those grounds, or at any time before the execution of the order, the court may—

(a) stay or suspend execution of the order, or
(b) postpone the date of possession,

for such period or periods as the court thinks fit.

(3) On any such adjournment as is referred to in subsection (1) above or any such stay, suspension or postponement as is referred to in subsection (2) above, the court shall, unless it considers that to do so would cause exceptional hardship to the tenant or would otherwise be unreasonable, impose conditions with regard to payment by the tenant of arrears of rent (if any) and rent or payments in respect of occupation after termination of the tenancy (mesne profits) and may impose such other conditions as it thinks fit.

(4) If such conditions as are referred to in subsection (3) above are complied with, the court may, if it thinks fit, discharge or rescind the order concerned.

(5) Subsection (6) below applies in any case where—

(a) proceedings are brought for possession of a dwelling-house which is let under a secure tenancy;
(b) the tenant's spouse or former spouse, having rights of occupation under the Matrimonial Homes Act 1967, is then in occupation of the dwelling-house; and
(c) the tenancy is terminated as a result of those proceedings.

(6) In any case to which this subsection applies, the spouse or former spouse shall, so long as he or she remains in occupation, have the same rights in relation to,

or in connection with, any such adjournment as is referred to in subsection (1) above or any such stay, suspension or postponement as is referred to in subsection (2) above, as he or she would have if those rights of occupation were not affected by the termination of the tenancy. **[416]**

COMMENCEMENT
See s. 153 (4), *post*, and the note "Orders under this section" thereto.

GENERAL NOTE
As with the Rent Act 1977, s. 100 (2), the court's power is discretionary not obligatory: *Taylor* v. *Faires* (1920) 90 L.J.K.B. 391. *Semble*, however, that once an absolute order for possession against a secure tenant is made, this excludes the discretionary powers in sub-s. (2): *American Economic Laundry Ltd.* v. *Little* [1950] 2 All E.R. 1186, C.A. The court may convert an absolute order into a conditional order—whereupon the powers in sub-s. (2) will apply—by making a subsequent conditional order: *Payne* v. *Cooper* [1957] 3 All E.R. 335, C.A. This order may be compendious in form: it is not necessary to obtain first a conditional order followed by a further order discharging the original order: *Sherrin* v. *Brand* [1956] 1 All E.R. 196, C.A.

SUB-S. (1): PROCEEDINGS . . . FOR POSSESSION OF A DWELLING-HOUSE LET UNDER A SECURE TENANCY
For the main provisions concerning recovery of possession of dwelling-houses let under secure tenancies, see ss. 32–34, *ante*, and Sch. 4, *post*. As to the meaning of "dwelling-house", cf. s. 50 (2), *ante* (and see the note to s. 3, *ante*); and for the meaning of "secure tenancy", see ss. 28 and 49 (2), *ante*.

THE COURT
See the note to s. 32, *ante*.

SUB-S. (2): FOR SUCH PERIOD OR PERIODS AS THE COURT THINKS FIT
Note, however, that by s. 89, *post*, the discretion of the court in relation to the postponement of giving up possession is restricted except where under s. 34 (2) (*a*), (*c*), (3) (*a*), *ante*, the court had power to make the order for possession only if it considered it reasonable.

SUB-S. (3): MESNE PROFITS
Mesne profits may only be claimed against a trespasser and are damages for trespass between landlord and tenant: *Bramwell* v. *Bramwell* [1942] 1 All E.R. 137, at p. 138, C.A. It will be rare, therefore, for a claim to mesne profits to arise in the case of actions for possession of secure tenancies.
     Mesne profits are assessable from the date of the service of the writ in the action: *Canas Property Co. Ltd.* v. *K.L. Television Services Ltd.* [1970] 2 Q.B. 433; [1970] 2 All E.R. 795, C.A. Under R.S.C. Ord. 29, r. 18 (reversing *Moore* v. *Assignment Courier Ltd.* [1977] 2 All E.R. 842, C.A.) the court has power to award interim mesne profits, but not where the defendant has a bona fide claim against the landlord for an amount which exceeds that of the claim for mesne profits: *Old Grovebury Manor Farm Ltd.* v. *W. Seymour Plant Sales and Hire* [1979] 1 All E.R. 573.

MATRIMONIAL HOMES ACT 1967
The occupation of a spouse or former spouse under s. 1 (5) of the Matrimonial Homes Act 1967 means that such occupation is treated as that of the other spouse, and to incorporate secure tenancies into this, s. 1 (5) of the 1967 Act is amended by Sch. 25, para.14, to this Act.

SUB-S. (6) GENERALLY
The reason for this extension of the rights of a spouse or former spouse in relation only to secure tenancies may be found in the fact that, while in a case where a statutory tenancy under the Rent Acts is sought to be determined by the landlord, and he asks for possession against both husband (H) and wife (W), to obtain an order, he must make out grounds for possession against both H and W: *Middleton* v. *Baldock* [1950] 1 K.B. 657; [1950] 1 All E.R. 708, C.A.; *Grange Lane South Flats Ltd.* v. *Cook* (1980) 254 E.G. 499, C.A., it may be otherwise if the order is sought and obtained against H alone. Suppose that H leaves W and the landlord ends H's statutory tenancy by an order for possession. W's possession through him is treated as ended with the termination of H's statutory tenancy: *Penn* v. *Dunn* [1970] 2 Q.B. 686; [1970] 2 All E.R. 858, C.A. In case this should happen, sub-s. (6) gives W the *locus standi* to apply for an adjournment, postponement, etc., under sub-ss. (1) and (2) which she is still not always able to obtain under the Rent Acts.

88. Discretion of court in certain proceedings for possession

(1) Where, under the terms of a rental purchase agreement, a person has been let into possession of a dwelling-house and, on the termination of the agreement or of his right to possession under it, proceedings are brought for the possession of the dwelling-house, the court may—

(a) adjourn the proceedings; or ·

(b) on making an order for the possession of the dwelling-house, stay or suspend execution of the order or postpone the date of possession;

for such period or periods as the court thinks fit.

(2) On any such adjournment, stay, suspension or postponement the court may impose such conditions with regard to payments by the person in possession in respect of his continued occupation of the dwelling-house and such other conditions as the court thinks fit.

(3) The court may revoke or from time to time vary any condition imposed by virtue of this section.

(4) In this section "rental purchase agreement" means an agreement for the purchase of a dwelling-house (whether freehold or leasehold property) under which the whole or part of the purchase price is to be paid in three or more instalments and the completion of the purchase is deferred until the whole or a specified part of the purchase price has been paid.

(5) This section extends to proceedings for the possession of a dwelling-house which were begun before the commencement of this section unless an order for the possession of the dwelling-house was made in the proceedings and executed before the commencement of this section. **[417]**

COMMENCEMENT
    See s. 153 (4), *post*, and the note "Orders under this section" thereto; and note sub-s. (5) above.

GENERAL NOTE
    It is thought that the discussion in the note to s. 111 (6) and (7) applies to this section. The powers in s. 87 are based on the Administration of Justice Act 1970, A.L.S. Vol. 194, s. 36. In the House of Lords, where the section was introduced, it was stated that rental purchase was used by persons who failed to meet the lending criteria of institutional sources of funds (H.L. Committee, 3rd July 1980, cols. 593–594). Until s. 88 was enacted, Parliament gave these people no protection whatsoever, because, on the one hand, they were not mortgagees and so outside s. 36 of the 1970 Act (*supra*) and, on the other hand, they were not tenants and so no part of the Rent Acts applied to them either. It will be noted (for what is is worth) that there is, in this section, no requirement that the court be satisfied that, by the end of the period of suspension, etc., the person is likely to be able to pay his instalments in future under the contract. There is such a futuristic requirement where the Administration of Justice Act 1973, A.L.S. Vol. 216, s. 8 (1) is applied by a court to a default clause in a mortgage under s. 8 (2) of that Act.

DWELLING-HOUSE
    See the note to s. 3, *ante*.

FOR SUCH PERIOD OR PERIODS AS THE COURT THINKS FIT
    Note that by virtue of s. 89 (2), (e), *post*, the discretion of the court to postpone the date of possession under sub-s. (1) above is not restricted by s. 89.

APPLICATION OF PROTECTION FROM EVICTION ACT 1977
    As to the application of the Protection from Eviction Act 1977, Vol. 47, p. 661, where a person has been let into possession of a dwelling-house under a rental purchase agreement within the meaning of this section, see s. 152 (1) and Sch. 25, para. 61, *post*.

89. Restriction on discretion of court in making orders for possession of land

(1) Where a court makes an order for the possession of any land in a case not falling within the exceptions mentioned in subsection (2) below, the giving up of possession shall not be postponed (whether by the order or any variation, suspension or stay of execution) to a date later than fourteen days after the making of the order, unless it appears to the court that exceptional hardship would be caused by requiring possession to be given up by that date; and shall not in any event be postponed to a date later than six weeks after the making of the order.

(2) The restrictions in subsection (1) above do not apply if—

   (a) the order is made in an action by a mortgagee for possession; or

   (b) the order is made in an action for forfeiture of a lease; or

   (c) the court had power to make the order only if it considered it reasonable to make it; or

   (d) the order relates to a dwelling-house which is the subject of a restricted contract (within the meaning of section 19 of the 1977 Act); or

   (e) the order is made in proceedings brought as mentioned in section 88 (1) above. **[418]**

COMMENCEMENT
>See s. 153 (4), *post*, and the note "Orders under this section" thereto.

LAND
>For meaning, see the Interpretation Act 1978, s. 5, Sch. 1, A.L.S. Vol. 258.

GIVING UP OF POSSESSION SHALL NOT BE POSTPONED, ETC.
>This section restricts the discretion of the court under s. 87 (2), *ante*, the Rent Act 1977, s. 100 (2), A.L.S. Vol. 255, and the Rent (Agriculture) Act 1976, s. 7 (3), A.L.S. Vol. 250, but it does not restrict that discretion under s. 88 (1), *ante* (sub-s. (2) (*e*)) or under s. 106A (2) of the Act of 1977 as inserted by s. 69 (2), *ante* (sub-s. (2) (*d*); but see s. 106A (3) of that Act as so inserted). Note also sub-s. (2) (*a*)–(*c*) above.

NOT .... LATER THAN FOURTEEN DAYS (SIX WEEKS) AFTER, ETC.
>See the note "Not later than three months after, etc." to s. 11, *ante*.

COURT HAD POWER TO MAKE THE ORDER ONLY IF IT CONSIDERED IT REASONABLE
>See, in particular, s. 34 (2) (*a*), (*c*), (3) (*a*), *ante* (secure tenancies), the Rent Act 1977, s. 98 (1) (protected tenancies and statutory tenancies), and the Rent (Agriculture) Act 1976, s. 7 (2) (protected occupancies and statutory tenancies).

1977 ACT
>*I.e.*, the Rent Act 1977; see s. 150, *ante*. That section is amended by s. 73 (2), *ante*, and s. 152 (1), (3), Sch. 25, para. 36, and Sch. 26, *post*.

PART V

AMENDMENT OF PART V OF HOUSING ACT 1957

90. Review of housing conditions by local authorities

In section 91 of the 1957 Act (duty of every local authority to consider housing conditions and as often as occasion arises to submit proposals to the Minister for the provision of new houses) the words from "and as often" to the end are hereby repealed. **[419]**

COMMENCEMENT
>This Part (ss. 90–95) of this Act came into operation on the passing of this Act on 8th August 1980, see s. 153 (3), *post*.

1957 ACT
I.e., the Housing Act 1957; see s. 150, *post.* The words which are repealed are also repealed by s. 152 (3) and Sch. 26, *post.*

91. Power of local authorities to dispose of land held for purposes of Part V of Housing Act 1957

(1) For section 104 of the 1957 Act (power to dispose of property acquired or appropriated for purposes of Part V) there is substituted the following section—

"104 Power to dispose of land held for purposes of Part V

(1) Without prejudice to the provisions of Chapter I of Part I of the Housing Act 1980 (right to buy public sector houses), a local authority shall have power by this section, but not otherwise, to dispose of any land which they have acquired or appropriated for the purposes of this Part of this Act.

(2) A disposal under this section may be effected in any manner but is not to be made without the consent of the Minister, except in a case falling within subsection (3) below.

(3) No consent is required for the letting of any land under a secure tenancy (within the meaning of section 28 of the Act of 1980) or under what would be a secure tenancy but for any of paragraphs 2 to 13 of Schedule 3 to that Act (certain lettings which do not create secure tenancies).

(4) On the disposal of any house under this section by way of sale or by the grant or assignment of a lease at a premium the local authority may, if they think fit, agree to the price or premium, or any part thereof, and any expenses incurred by the purchaser being secured by a mortgage of the premises.

(5) Subject to section 104A of this Act, on any disposal under this section the local authority may impose such covenants and conditions as they think fit, but a condition of any of the kinds mentioned in subsection (6) below may only be imposed with the consent of the Minister.

(6) The conditions are—

(a) one limiting the price or premium which may be obtained on a further disposal of the house;

(b) in the case of a sale, one precluding the purchaser (including any successor in title of his and any person deriving title under him or any such successor) from selling or leasing the land unless—

(i) he first notifies the authority of the proposed sale or lease and offers to sell or lease the house to them; and

(ii) the authority refuse the offer or fail to accept it within one month after it is made; and

(c) in the case of a lease, one precluding the lessee (including any successor in title of his and any person deriving title under him or any such successor) from assigning the lease, or granting any sub-lease.

(7) Section 26 (1) of the Town and Country Planning Act 1959 (power of local authorities etc. to dispose of land without consent of Minister) does not apply to any disposal under this section.

(8) Sections 128 to 132 of the Lands Clauses Consolidation Act 1845 (which relate to the sale of superfluous land) do not apply to the sale by a local authority, under this section, of any land acquired by the authority for the purposes of this Part of this Act.

(9) For the purposes of this section the grant of an option to purchase the freehold of, or any other interest in, any land is a disposal and any consent given to such a disposal extends to any disposal made in pursuance of the option.".

(2) Sections 105 (1), (2) and (5) (power to deal with land in addition to that given by section 104), and 106 (power of Minister to impose conditions on sale of houses and land), of the 1957 Act are hereby repealed.

(3) Section 39 of the Town and Country Planning Act 1968 (cases where section 26 (1) of the Town and Country Planning Act 1959 does not apply) is hereby repealed.

(4) In section 104 and in the sections inserted in the 1957 Act by sections 92 and 95 below "the Minister" means the Secretary of State. **[420]**

COMMENCEMENT
> See the note to s. 90, *ante.*

SUB-S. (1): S. 104 (1): LOCAL AUTHORITY
> For meaning, see the Housing Act 1957, s. 1 and the note thereto, A.L.S. Vol. 131.

DISPOSE OF ANY LAND, ETC.
> As to the application of the proceeds of sale or any other capital moneys received by a local authority in respect of any transaction under the Housing Act 1957, s. 104, see s. 142 of that Act.

ACQUIRED OR APPROPRIATED FOR THE PURPOSES OF THIS PART OF THIS ACT
> *I.e.,* for the purposes of the Housing Act 1957, Part V. As to the acquisition or appropriation of land, see ss. 96, 97 and 99 of that Act; see also s. 93 (*a*), *post,* and s. 110A of the Act of 1957 as inserted by s. 95, *post.*

S. 104 (2): CONSENT OF THE MINISTER
> For provisions to such consents, see the Housing Act 1957, s. 104A, as inserted by s. 92, *post;* and for provisions which apply where a discount has been given to the purchaser in accordance with a consent given under s. 102 (2) of that Act, see s. 104B thereof as so inserted.

S. 104 (4): THINK FIT
> See the note "Appear" to s. 2, *ante.*

S. 104 (5). SUCH COVENANTS AND CONDITIONS AS THEY THINK FIT
> As to covenants limiting freedom to dispose of houses in National Parks, areas of outstanding natural beauty, etc, see the Housing Act 1957, s. 104C, as inserted by s. 92, *post;* and as to the enforcement of covenants against the owner for the time being, see s. 151 of that Act.

S. 104 (6): WITHIN ONE MONTH AFTER, ETC.
> See the note "Within six months of, etc." to s. 3, *ante.*

SUB-S. (4): SECRETARY OF STATE
> See note to s. 2, *ante.*

FURTHER PROVISIONS
> See s. 94, *post* (options granted before commencement of this section; s. 112, *post* (provisions as to vesting of mortgaged property in local authorities where property sold under Housing Act 1957, s. 104 (1), before commencement of sub-s. (1) above); and s. 137, *post* (avoidance of unauthorised disposals).

CONSEQUENTIAL REPEALS
> Consequent upon sub-s. (1) above the Housing (Amendment) Act 1973, s. 2, and the amendment of the Housing Act 1957, s. 104, in the Local Land Charges Act 1957, Sch. 1, are repealed by s. 152 (3) and Sch. 26, *post;* and consequent upon sub-s. (2) above s. 96 (*c*) of the Act of 1957, is repealed by s. 152 (1), (3), Sch. 25, para. 5, and Sch. 26, *post.*

DEFINITIONS
   For "house" and "land", see the Housing Act 1957, s. 189 (1). Note as to "disposal",
   s. 104 (9) of the Act of 1957 as substituted by sub-s. (1) above, and as to "the Minister",
   sub-s. (4) above.

1957 ACT
   I.e., the Housing Act 1957; see s. 150, *post.* Section 124A is inserted by s. 92, *post.* Ss.
   105 (1), (2), (5) and 106 of the Act of 1957 are also repealed by s. 152 (3) and Sch. 26,
   post.

TOWN AND COUNTRY PLANNING ACT 1959, S. 26 (1)
   See A.L.S. Vol. 116.

LANDS CLAUSES CONSOLIDATION ACT 1845, SS. 128–132
   See 6, Halsbury's Statutes (3rd edn.) pp. 56–57.

TOWN AND COUNTRY PLANNING ACT 1968, S. 39
   See A.L.S. Vol. 176. That section is also repealed by s. 152 (3) and Sch. 26, *post.*

TRANSITIONAL PROVISION
   See s. 152 (2) and Sch. 25, para. 69, *post.*

92. Consent to disposals and recovery of discount

After section 104 of the 1957 Act there are inserted the following sections—

"104A. Consents under section 104

(1) Any consent of the Minister required under section 104 (2) or (5) of this Act may be given either generally to all local authorities or to any particular local authority or description of authority and either in relation to any particular land or description of land.

(2) Any such consent may be given subject to such conditions as the Minister sees fit to impose.

(3) Without prejudice to the generality of subsection (2) above, any such consent may be given subject to conditions as to the price, premium or rent to be obtained on a disposal under section 104, including conditions as to the amount by which, on the disposal of a house by way of sale or by the grant or assignment of a lease at a premium, the price or premium is to be, or may be, discounted by the local authority.

104B. Repayment of discount on early disposal of freehold or lease

(1) This section applies where, on a disposal under section 104 of this Act (the "first disposal"), a discount has been given to the purchaser by the local authority in accordance with a consent given by the Minister under subsection (2) of that section; but this section does not apply in any such case if the consent so provides.

(2) On the first disposal, the conveyance, grant or assignment shall contain a covenant binding on the purchaser and his successors in title to pay to the local authority on demand the amount specified in subsection (3) below if, within a period of five years, there is a disposal falling within subsection (4) below, (the "further disposal"); but if there is more than one further disposal, then only on the first of them.

(3) The amount payable under the covenant is an amount equal to the discount given to the purchaser, but reduced by 20 per cent. of that discount for each complete year which elapses after the first disposal and before the further disposal.

207

(4) A disposal falls within this subsection if it is—

(*a*) a conveyance of the freehold or an assignment of the lease; or

(*b*) the grant of a lease or sub-lease for a term of more than twenty-one years otherwise than at a rack rent;

whether the disposal is of the whole or part of the house; but a disposal in pursuance of an order under section 24 of the Matrimonial Causes Act 1973 or under section 2 of the Inheritance (Provision for Family and Dependants) Act 1975 or a vesting in a person taking under a will or on an intestacy is not a disposal falling within this subsection.

(5) The liability that may arise under the covenant required by subsection (2) above shall be a charge on the house—

(*a*) taking effect as if it had been created by deed expressed to be by way of legal mortgage; and

(*b*) having priority immediately after any legal charge securing any amount left outstanding by the purchaser or advanced to him by a body specified in subsection (6) below for the purpose of enabling him to acquire the interest disposed of on the first disposal or further advanced to him by that body.

(6) The bodies referred to in subsection (5) (*b*) above are any building society and any of the bodies specified in paragraph 6, 7 or 8 of the Schedule to the Home Purchase Assistance and Housing Corporation Guarantee Act 1978.

(7) A charge taking effect by virtue of subsection (5) above shall, notwithstanding subsection (5) of section 59 of the Land Registration Act 1925, be a land charge for the purposes of that section, and subsection (2) of that section shall apply accordingly with respect to its protection and realisation.

(8) The reference in subsection (4) above to a lease or sub-lease does not include a mortgage term.

(9) In this section "building society" means a building society within the meaning of the Building Societies Act 1962 or the Building Societies Act (Northern Ireland) 1967 and "purchaser" means the person acquiring the interest disposed of by the first disposal; and for the purposes of this section the grant of an option enabling a person to call for a disposal falling within subsection (4) above shall be treated as such a disposal.

104C. Houses in National Parks and areas of outstanding natural beauty, etc.

(1) Where a conveyance, grant or assignment executed under section 104 of this Act (the "first disposal") is of a house situated in a National Park, or an area designated under section 87 of the National Parks and Access to the Countryside Act 1949 as an area of outstanding natural beauty, or an area designated by order of the Secretary of State as a rural area, the conveyance, grant or assignment may (unless it contains a condition of a kind mentioned in section 104 (6) (*b*) or (*c*) above) contain a covenant limiting the freedom of the purchaser and his successors in title to dispose of the house in the manner specified in subsection (2) below.

(2) The limitation is that, until such time (if any) as may be notified in writing by the local authority to the purchaser or his successors in title there will be no disposal falling within subsection (4) below (the "further disposal")

without the written consent of the local authority; but that consent shall not be withheld if the further disposal is to a person satisfying the condition stated in subsection (3) below.

(3) The condition is that the person to whom the further disposal is made (or, if it is made to more than one person, at least one of them) has, throughout the period of three years immediately preceding the application for consent, either—

(a) had his place of work in a designated region which or part of which is comprised in the National Park or area; or

(b) had his only or principal home in such a region;

or has had the one in part or parts of that period and the other in the remainder; but the region need not have been the same throughout the whole of the period.

(4) A disposal falls within this subsection if it is—

(a) a conveyance of the freehold or an assignment of the lease; or

(b) the grant of a lease or sub-lease for a term of more than 21 years otherwise than at a rack rent;

whether the disposal is of the whole or part of the house; but a disposal in pursuance of an order under section 24 of the Matrimonial Causes Act 1973 or under section 2 of the Inheritance (Provision for Family and Dependants) Act 1975 or a vesting in a person taking under a will or on an intestacy is not a disposal falling within this subsection.

(5) If the further disposal is in breach of the covenant mentioned in subsection (1) above, it shall be void.

(6) The limitation imposed by such a covenant shall be a local land charge and, if the land is registered under the Land Registration Act 1925, the Chief Land Registrar shall enter the appropriate restriction on the register of title as if application therefor had been made under section 58 of that Act.

(7) The reference in subsection (4) above to a lease or sub-lease does not include a mortgage term.

(8) In this section "purchaser" means the person acquiring the interest disposed of by the first disposal.

(9) In this section "designated region" means an area designated for the purposes of this section by order of the Secretary of State.

(10) For the purposes of this section the grant to any person of an option enabling him to call for a disposal falling within subsection (4) above shall be treated as such a disposal made to that person and a consent to such a grant as a consent to a disposal made in pursuance of the option.". **[421]**

COMMENCEMENT
See the note to s. 90, *ante.*

S. 104A (1): LOCAL AUTHORITIES
For meaning, see the Housing Act 1957, s. 1, and the notes thereto, A.L.S. Vol. 109.

S. 104A (2): SEES FIT
See the note "Appear" to s. 2, *ante.*

S. 104B (2): WITHIN ... FIVE YEARS
See the note "Within six months of, etc." to s. 3, *ante.*

S. 164B (4): RACK RENT
Cf. the note to s. 8, *ante.*

S. 104B (5): CHARGE ... TAKING EFFECT AS IF IT HAD BEEN CREATED BY ... LEGAL
MORTGAGE
See the note to s. 8, *ante.*

S. 104C (1): NATIONAL PARK
See the note to s. 19, *ante.*

SECRETARY OF STATE
See the note to s. 2, *ante.*

S. 104C (2): NOTIFIED
As to the authentication and service of notices, see the Housing Act 1957, ss. 166 (2), 169.

WRITING
See the note "Written; writing" to s. 5, *ante.*

S. 104C (4): RACK RENT
See the note to s. 8, *ante.*

S. 104C (6): LIMITATION ... SHALL BE A LOCAL LAND CHARGE
As to the registration of local land charges, see the Local Land Charges Act 1975, s. 1,
A.L.S. Vol. 238.

CHIEF LAND REGISTRAR: REGISTER OF TITLE
See notes to s. 19, *ante.*

APPLICATION TO DISPOSALS BY HOUSING ASSOCIATIONS
As to the application of the Housing Act 1957, ss. 104B (2), (9), 104C, as inserted by this
section, to certain disposals of land by registered housing associations, see s. 122 (4)–(6),
post.

DEFINITIONS
For "the Minister", see s. 91 (4), *ante;* for "house" and "land", see the Housing Act 1957,
s. 189 (1). Note as to "first disposal", s. 104B (1) or 104C (1) of the Act of 1957 as inserted
by this section; as to "further disposal", s. 104B (2) or 104C (2) of that Act as so inserted;
as to "disposal falling within subsection (4)",, s. 104B (4) and (9) or 104C (4) and (10) of
that Act; as to "lease" and "sub-lease", s. 104B (8) or 104C (7) of that Act; as to "building
society", s. 104B (9) of that Act; as to "purchaser", s. 104B (9) or 104C (8) of that Act;
and as to "designated region", s. 104C (9) of that Act.

1957 ACT
I.e., the Housing Act 1957; see s. 150, *post.* S. 104 of that Act is substituted by s. 91 (1),
ante.

MATRIMONIAL CAUSES ACT 1973, S. 24
See A.L.S. Vol. 217.

INHERITANCE (PROVISION FOR FAMILY AND DEPENDANTS) ACT 1975, S. 2
See A.L.S. Vol. 236.

HOME PURCHASE ASSISTANCE AND HOUSING CORPORATION GUARANTEE ACT 1978,
SCHEDULE, PARAS. 6–8
See A.L.S. Vol. 258.

LAND REGISTRATION ACT 1925
See 27, Halsbury's Statutes (3rd edn.), p. 778.

BUILDING SOCIETIES ACT 1962
For the meaning of "building society", see s. 1 of that Act.

BUILDING SOCIETIES ACT (NORTHERN IRELAND) 1967
1967 c. 31 (N.I.).

NATIONAL PARKS AND ACCESS TO THE COUNTRYSIDE ACT 1949, S. 87
See A.L.S. Vol. 65.

ORDERS
At the time of going to press no order under the Housing Act 1957, s. 104C (1) or (9) as inserted by this section, had been published in the S.I. series. As to the publication of orders made by the Secretary of State under the Act of 1957, see s. 180 (1) thereof.

93. Acquisition of land for purpose of its subsequent disposal

It is hereby declared that—

(a) the power of a local authority to acquire land under section 96 of the 1957 Act (power of local authority to acquire land for provision of housing accommodation) includes power to do so for the purpose of disposing of houses erected, or to be erected, on the land or of disposing of the land to a person who intends to provide housing accommodation on it; and

(b) the things that a local authority may do under section 92 of that Act (mode of provision of accommodation) may equally be done in relation to land acquired for either of those purposes. **[422]**

COMMENCEMENT
See the note to s. 90, *ante.*

LOCAL AUTHORITY
For meaning, see the Housing Act 1957, s. 1, and the note thereto, A.L.S. Vol. 109.

LAND; HOUSES
These expressions are defined by the Housing Act 1957, s. 189 (1).

DISPOSING OF HOUSES ERECTED, ETC.
As to the disposal of land acquired for the purposes of the Housing Act 1957, Part V, see s. 104 of that Act as substituted by s. 91 (1), *ante*, together with ss. 104A, 104C of that Act as inserted by s. 92, *ante.*

PERSON
See the note to s. 24, *ante.*

1957 ACT
I.e., the Housing Act 1957; see s. 150, *post.*

94. Options granted before commencement of section 91

The limitations on a local authority's statutory power to dispose of houses acquired or appropriated for the purposes of Part V of the 1957 Act shall not be taken to have prevented a local authority, at any time before the commencement of section 91 of this Act, from granting to the tenant of a house an option to purchase the freehold of, or any other interest in, the house. **[423]**

COMMENCEMENT
See note to s. 90, *ante.*

LIMITATIONS ON ... POWER TO DISPOSE OF HOUSES, ETC.
The disposal of such houses as are mentioned in this section was governed by the Housing Act 1957, s. 104, as originally enacted, A.L.S. Vol. 109.

LOCAL AUTHORITY
For meaning, see the Housing Act 1957, s. 1, and the note thereto.

HOUSES
The expression "house" is defined by the Housing Act 1957 189 (1).

ACQUIRED OR APPROPRIATED FOR THE PURPOSES OF PART V OF THE 1957 ACT
As to the acquisition or appropriation of land for those purposes, see the Housing Act 1957, ss. 96, 97, 99; see also s. 93 (*a*), *ante.*

1957 ACT
I.e., the Housing Act 1957; see s. 150, *post*.

95. Appropriation of land

After section 110 of the 1957 Act there is inserted the following section—

"110A. Appropriation of Part V land for other purposes

(1) Where a local authority have acquired or appropriated any land for the purposes of this Part of this Act they shall not, without the consent of the Minister, appropriate any part of that land which consists of a house or part of a house for any other purpose.

(2) Any consent under this section may be given either generally to all local authorities or to any particular local authority or description of authority and either in relation to any particular land or description of land.

(3) Any such consent may be given subject to such conditions as the Minister sees fit to impose.". **[424]**

COMMENCEMENT
See the note to s. 90, *ante*.

LOCAL AUTHORITY
For meaning. see the Housing Act 1957, s. 1, and the note thereto, A.L.S. Vol. 109.

ACQUIRED OR APPROPRIATED ... FOR THE PURPOSES OF THIS PART OF THIS ACT
See the note to s. 91, *ante*.

SEES FIT
See the note "Appear" to s. 2, *ante*.

DEFINITIONS
For "the Minister", s. 91 (4), *ante*; for "house" and "land", see the Housing Act 1957, s. 189 (1).

1957 ACT
I.e., the Housing Act 1957, see s. 150, *post*.

PART VI

HOUSING SUBSIDIES

96. New housing subsidy to replace certain existing subsidies and contributions

(1) For the year 1981–82 and subsequent years—

    (a) a subsidy, to be known as housing subsidy, shall be payable to local authorities, new town corporations and the Development Board for Rural Wales in accordance with this Part of this Act;

    (b) no payment shall be made under any of the enactments listed in Part I of Schedule 11 to this Act; and

    (c) no payment shall be made under any of the enactments listed in Part II of Schedule 11 to this Act in respect of dwellings within a local authority's Housing Revenue Account or a new town corporation's housing account.

(2) No grant shall be made after 31st March 1981 under section 14 of the Housing (Financial Provisions) Act 1958 (grants for building experiments). **[425]**

COMMENCEMENT
By s. 153 (3), *post*, this Part (ss. 96–195) of this Act came into operation on the passing of this Act on 8th August 1980. However, by sub-s. (1) above the new subsidy introduced by this Part is payable, and payments under the enactments listed in Sch. 11, *post*, are not to be made, for the year 1981-82 (beginning 1st April 1981) and subsequent years. and sub-s. (2) above also takes effect from 1st April 1981.

HOUSING SUBSIDY
Housing subsidy is payable to local authorities in accordance with ss. 97–100, *post*, and to new town corporations and the Development Board for Rural Wales in accordance with those sections as modified by s. 101, *post*. As to recoupment of subsidy, see s. 102, *post*, and as to administration, see s. 103, *post*.

DEVELOPMENT BOARD FOR RURAL WALES
See the note to s. 19, *ante*.

THIS PART OF THIS ACT
I.e., Part VI (ss. 96–105) of this Act.

HOUSING REVENUE ACCOUNT
This account is to be kept in accordance with the Housing Finance Act 1972, s. 12, Sch. 1, A.L.S. Vol. 202; see also s. 134, *post*. For the dwellings within the account, see s. 12 (1), (2) of that Act.

DEFINITIONS
For "local authority", new town corporation" and "year", see s. 105, *post*.

HOUSING (FINANCIAL PROVISIONS) ACT 1958, S. 14
See A.L.S. Vol. 109. That section is repealed by s. 152 (3) and Sch. 26, *post*.

Local authorities

97. Housing subsidy for local authorities

(1) The amount of the housing subsidy payable to a local authority for any year (the year of account) shall be calculated from the amounts which are the authority's—

    (*a*) base amounts (BA);
    (*b*) housing costs differential (HCD); and
    (*c*) local contribution differential (LCD);

for that year and shall be so calculated by using the formula $BA + HCD - LCD$.

(2) If the amount so calculated is nil or a negative amount, no housing subsidy is payable to the authority for the year of account. **[426]**

COMMENCEMENT
See the note to s. 96, *ante*.

HOUSING SUBSIDY
See s. 96 (1) (*a*), *ante*, and the note to that section.

BASE AMOUNT; HOUSING COSTS DIFFERENTIAL; LOCAL CONTRIBUTION DIFFEREN-
TIAL
As to these, see ss. 98, 99 and 100, *post*, respectively.

APPLICATION TO NEW TOWN CORPORATIONS AND DEVELOOMENT BOARD FOR RURAL WALES
See s. 101, *post*.

DEFINITIONS
For "local authority" and "year", see s. 105, *post*. Note as to "year of account", sub-s. (1) above.

98. The base amount

(1) A local authority's base amount is, subject to any adjustment under this section,—

(a) for the year 1982–83 or any subsequent year, the amount calculated for the preceding year under section 97, that is to say, the amount of subsidy payable to the authority for the year (or, if none was payable, nil or a negative amount, as the case may be);

(b) for the year 1981–82, the aggregate of the following amounts payable to the authority for the year 1980–81, that is to say—

    (i) the amount of housing subsidy under section 2 of the 1975 Act;

    (ii) the amount (if any) of expanding towns subsidy under section 4 of the 1975 Act; and

    (iii) the amount of any contribution under the enactments listed in Part II of Schedule 11 which is payable in respect of any dwelling within the authority's Housing Revenue Account.

(2) If the Secretary of State is of opinion that particular circumstances require it, he may adjust the base amount for any year by increasing or decreasing it, either generally or in relation to any description of authority or any particular authority; and, without prejudice to the generality of this provision, he may adjust the base amount for the year 1981–82 by excluding from the amount taken into account as housing subsidy under section 2 of the 1975 Act so much of the new capital costs element and the high costs element as was in his opinion attributable to capital costs directly charged to revenue. **[427]**

COMMENCEMENT
See the note to s. 96, *ante.*

BASE AMOUNT
This is one of the elements from which the amount of housing subsidy is to be calculated; see s. 97 (1), *ante.*

HOUSING REVENUE ACCOUNT
See the note to s. 96, *ante.*

SECRETARY OF STATE
See the note to s. 2, *ante.*

OPINION
See the note "Appear" to s. 2, *ante.*

NEW CAPITAL COSTS ELEMENT; HIGH COSTS ELEMENT
As to these see the Housing Rents and Subsidies Act 1975, s. 2 (2), Sch. 1, paras. 2, 4, 7, 8, A.L.S. Vol. 230 (repealed by s. 152 (3) and Sch. 26, *post*).

APPLICATION TO NEW TOWN CORPORATIONS AND DEVELOPMENT BOARD FOR RURAL WALES
See s. 101, *post.*

DEFINITIONS
For "local authority" and "year", see s. 105, *post.*

1975 ACT
I.e., the Housing Rents and Subsidies Act 1975; see s. 150, *post.* Sections 2, 4 of that Act are repealed by s. 152 (3) and Sch. 26, *post*, consequent upon s. 96 (1) (*b*), *ante*, and Sch. 11, Part I, *post.*

99. The housing costs differential

(1) A local authority's housing costs differential for any year of account is the amount by which its reckonable expenditure for that year exceeds its reckonable

expenditure for the preceding year (and accordingly is nil or, as the case may be, a negative amount if its reckonable expenditure for the year of account is the same or less).

(2) A local authority's reckonable expenditure for any year is the aggregate of—

(*a*) so much of the expenditure incurred by the authority in that year and falling to be debited to its Housing Revenue Account as the Secretary of State may determine; and

(*b*) so much of any other expenditure incurred by the local authority in that year or treated, in accordance with any determination made by the Secretary of State, as so incurred, as the Secretary of State may determine to take into account for the purposes of housing subsidy.

(3) A determination under this section may be made for all local authorities or different determinations may be made for authorities of different descriptions or for authorities in England and authorities in Wales or in different parts of England or Wales or for individual authorities; and any such determination may be varied or revoked in relation to all or any of the authorities for which it was made.

(4) Before making a determination for all local authorities the Secretary of State shall consult with organisations appearing to him to be representative of local authorities. **[428]**

COMMENCEMENT
See the note to s. 96, *ante*.

HOUSING COSTS DIFFERENTIAL
This is one of the elements from which the amount of housing subsidy is to be calculated; see s. 97 (1), *ante*.

HOUSING REVENUE ACCOUNT
See the note to s. 96, *ante*.

SECRETARY OF STATE; APPEAR
See the notes to s. 2, *ante*.

HOUSING SUBSIDY
See s. 96 (1) (*a*), *ante*, and the note to that section.

ENGLAND; WALES
For meanings, see the Interpretation Act 1978, s. 5, Sch. 1, A.L.S. Vol. 258.

CONSULT
See the note to s. 26, *ante*.

APPLICATION TO NEW TOWN CORPORATIONS AND DEVELOPMENT BOARD FOR RURAL WALES
See s. 101, *post*.

AGREEMENTS WITH HOUSING CO-OPERATIVES
Where a local authority, a new town corporation or the Development Board for Rural Wales, has made an agreement with a housing co-operative and the agreement is one to which Sch. 20, *post*, applies, neither the agreement nor any letting of land under it is to be taken into account in determining that body's reckonable expenditure or reckonable income under this Part of this Act or as a ground for recovering, withholding or reducing any sum under s. 102, *post*; see s. 139 and Sch. 20, para. 2 (1), *post* (but see also Sch. 20, para. 2 (2), (3), *post*.

DEFINITIONS
For "local authority", "year" and "year of account", see s. 105, *post*. Note as to "reckonable expenditure", sub-s. (2) above.

100. The local contribution differential

(1) A local authority's local contribution differential for any year of account is the amount by which its reckonable income for that year exceeds its reckonable income for the preceding year (and accordingly is nil or, as the case may be, a negative amount if its reckonable income for the year of account is the same or less).

(2) A local authority's reckonable income for any year is the amount which, in accordance with any determination made by the Secretary of State, the local authority is assumed to receive for that year as income which it is required to carry to its Housing Revenue Account, but—

(a) excluding, subject to paragraph (b) below, any income derived from any subsidy, grant or contribution; and

(b) including any contribution made by the authority out of its general rate fund as well as any modified rent rebate subsidy payable under section 3 of the 1975 Act.

(3) A determination under this section shall state the assumptions on which it is based and the method of calculation used in it, and in making it the Secretary of State shall have regard, among other things, to past and expected movements in incomes, costs and prices.

(4) A determination under this section may be made for all local authorities or different determinations may be made for authorities of different descriptions or for authorities in England and authorities in Wales or in different parts of England or Wales or for individual authorities, and every determination shall be made known in the year preceding the year of account to the local authorities for which it is made.

(5) Before making a determination for all local authorities the Secretary of State shall consult with organisations appearing to him to be representative of local authorities. **[429]**

COMMENCEMENT
See the note to s. 96, *ante.*

LOCAL CONTRIBUTION DIFFERENTIAL
This is one of the elements from which the amount of housing subsidy is to be calculated; see s. 97 (1), *ante.*

SECRETARY OF STATE; APPEARING
See the corresponding notes to s. 2, *ante.*

HOUSING REVENUE ACCOUNT
See the note to s. 96, *ante.*

GENERAL RATE FUND
This fund is to be kept under the Local Government Act 1972, s. 148 (1), A.L.S. Vol. 209.

ENGLAND; WALES
See note to s. 99, *ante.*

APPLICATION TO NEW TOWN CORPORATIONS AND DEVELOPMENT BOARD FOR RURAL WALES
See s. 101, *post.*

AGREEMENTS WITH HOUSING CO-OPERATIVES
See the note to s. 99, *ante.*

DEFINITIONS
For "local authority", "year" and "year of account" see s. 105, *post.* Note as to "reckonable income", sub-s. (2) above.

1975 ACT
   I.e., the Housing Rents and Subsidies Act 1975; see s. 150, *post*. For s. 3 of that Act, see A.L.S. Vol. 230.

Other housing authorities

101. Housing subsidy for other bodies

(1) Sections 97 to 100 above apply in relation to new town corporations and the Development Board for Rural Wales as they apply in relation to local authorities, but subject to the following provisions of this section.

(2) In relation to a new town corporation—

(*a*) section 98 has effect as if the aggregate mentioned in subsection (1) (*b*) included so much of the grant made to the corporation for the year 1980–81 under section 42 (2) or 42 (3A) of the New Towns Act 1965 as was to be credited to the corporation's housing account; and

(*b*) sections 98, 99 and 100 have effect as if for references to the Housing Revenue Account there were substituted references to the housing account and for the reference to the general rate fund a reference to the general revenue account.

(3) In relation to the Board,—

(*a*) section 98 has effect as if for the references to section 2 of the 1975 Act there were substituted references to section 18 of the Development of Rural Wales Act 1976 and the aggregate mentioned in subsection (1) (*b*) included so much of the grants made to the Board for the year 1980–81 under section 11 of the Act of 1976 as was to be credited to its housing account; and

(*b*) sections 99 and 100 have effect as if for references to the Housing Revenue Account there were substituted references to the housing account, and the contribution and rent rebate subsidy referred to in section 100 (2) (*b*) were respectively any contribution made by the Board out of revenue and the subsidy payable under section 19 of the Act of 1976.

(4) The consultations required by section 99 (4) or 100 (5) shall be with organisations appearing to the Secretary of State to be representative of new town corporations or, as the case may be, with the Development Board for Rural Wales.

(5) The Commission for the New Towns is to be treated as a separate body in respect of each of its new towns. **[430]**

COMMENCEMENT
   See the note to s. 96, *ante.*

DEVELOPMENT BOARD FOR RURAL WALES
   See the note to s. 19, *ante.*

APPEARING; SECRETARY OF STATE
   See the corresponding notes to s. 2, *ante.*

COMMISSION FOR THE NEW TOWNS
   See the note to s. 28, *ante.*

FURTHER PROVISIONS
   See s. 96, *ante*, and Sch. 11, *post* (introduction of new housing subsidy and replacement of certain existing subsidies, etc.); s. 102, *post* (recoupment of subsidy); and s. 103, *post* (administration of subsidy).

DEFINITIONS
   For "local authority", "new town corporation" and "year", see s. 105, *post.*

NEW TOWNS ACT 1965, S. 42 (2), (3A)
    For s. 42 (2) of that Act, see 36, Halsbury's Statutes (3rd edn.), p. 408; s. 42 (3A) was
    inserted by the Housing Finance Act 1972, s. 14 (1), A.L.S. Vol. 202.

1975 ACT
    I.e., the Housing Rents and Subsidies Act 1975; see s. 150, *post.* That section is repealed
    by s. 152 (3) and Sch. 26, *post*, consequent upon s. 96 (1) (*b*), *ante*, and Sch. 11, Part I,
    post.

DEVELOPMENT OF RURAL WALES ACT 1976, SS. 11, 18, 19
    See 46, Halsbury's Statutes (3rd edn.), pp. 1875, 1880, 1881. S. 18 of that Act is repealed
    by s. 152 (3) and Sch. 26, *post*, consequent upon s. 96 (1) (*b*), *ante*, and Sch. 11, Part I, *post*;
    and s. 19 of that Act is amended by s. 117 (4), (5), *post.*

Recoupment

102. Recoupment of subsidy

(1) Where any subsidy has been paid to any local authority or other body under this
Part of this Act, and it appears to the Secretary of State that—

    (*a*) the purpose for which it was paid has not been fulfilled or not completely
      or adequately or not without unreasonable delay; and

    (*b*) that the case falls within rules published by him;

he may recover from the authority or other body the whole or such part of the
payment as he may determine in accordance with the rules, with interest from such
time and at such rates as he may so determine.

(2) A sum recoverable under this section may be recovered either as a simple
contract debt or by withholding or reducing housing subsidy payable in any year or
in successive years.

(3) The withholding or reduction under this section of housing subsidy payable
to a local authority or other body for any year shall not affect the authority's or other
body's base amount for the following year. **[431]**

COMMENCEMENT
    See the note to s. 96, *ante.*

OTHER BODY
    I.e., a body falling within s. 101 (1), *ante.*

THIS PART OF THIS ACT
    I.e., Part VI (ss. 96–105) of this Act.

APPEARS; SECRETARY OF STATE
    See the corresponding notes to s. 2, *ante.*

HOUSING SUBSIDY
    See s. 96 (1) (*a*), *ante*, and the note to that section.

BASE AMOUNT
    This is one of the elements from which the amount of housing subsidy is to be calculated;
    see s. 97, *ante*, or that section as applied by s. 101, *ante.*

AGREEMENTS WITH HOUSING CO-OPERATIVES
    See the note to s. 99, *ante.*

PAYMENT OF RECEIPTS
    See s. 154 (2), *post.*

DEFINITIONS
    For "local authority" and "year", see s. 105, *post.*

Administration

103. Administration of housing subsidy

(1) Housing subsidy shall be paid out of moneys provided by Parliament and shall be credited—

   (a) if paid to a local authority, to the authority's Housing Revenue Account; and
   (b) if paid to another body, to that body's housing account or appropriate housing account.

(2) Housing subsidy shall be paid by the Secretary of State at such times, in such manner and subject to such conditions as to records, certificates, audit or otherwise as he may, with the agreement of the Treasury, determine.

(3) Payment of subsidy shall be subject to the making of a claim for it in such form, and containing such particulars, as the Secretary of State may from time to time determine. **[432]**

COMMENCEMENT
   See the note to s. 96, *ante*.

HOUSING SUBSIDY
   See s. 96 (1) (a), *ante*, and the note to that section.

LOCAL AUTHORITY
   For meaning, see s. 105, *post*.

HOUSING REVENUE ACCOUNT
   See the note to s. 96, *ante*.

ANOTHER BODY
   I.e., a body falling within s. 101 (1), *ante*.

SECRETARY OF STATE
   See the note to s. 2, *ante*.

TREASURY
   See note to s. 46, *ante*.

Transitional town development subsidy

104. Power to commute transitional town development subsidy and payments to receiving authority

(1) Where, under section 5 of the 1975 Act, transitional town development subsidy is payable to a sending authority for years later than the year 1979–80 the Secretary of State may, with the agreement of the sending authority and of the receiving authority, determine—

   (a) to commute further payments of transitional development subsidy into a single payment of an amount determined by him or calculated in a manner determined by him; and
   (b) to commute the corresponding payments by the sending authority to the receiving authority under subsection (6) of that section into a single payment of an amount four times that payable under paragraph (a) above.

(2) In making a determination under this section the Secretary of State shall make such allowance (if any) as appears to him appropriate for circumstances in which, if there were no commutation, his power under section 5 of the 1975 Act to reduce or discontinue the sending authority's transitional town development subsidy might be exercised. **[433]**

COMMENCEMENT
This section came into operation on the passing of this Act on 8th August 1980; see s. 153 (3), *post*.

SENDING AUTHORITY
By virtue of the Housing Rents and Subsidies Act 1975, s. 5 (1), A.L.S. Vol. 230, this means a sending authority as defined by the Housing Finance Act 1972, s. 10 (1), A.L.S. Vol. 202 (repealed by s. 17 (5) of, and Sch. 6, Part II, to, the Act of 1975).

YEARS
For the meaning of "year", see s. 105, *post*, or the Housing Rents and Subsidies Act 1975, s. 16 (1).

SECRETARY OF STATE; APPEARS
See the corresponding notes to s. 2, *ante*.

RECEIVING AUTHORITY
The expression is defined by the Housing Rents and Subsidies Act 1975, s. 16 (1).

1975 ACT
I.e., the Housing Rents and Subsidies Act 1975; see s. 150, *post*.

Interpretation

105. Interpretation of Part VI

In this Part of this Act—

"local authority" means the council of a district or London borough, the Greater London Council, the Common Council of the City of London or the Council of the Isles of Scilly;

"new town corporation" means a development corporation (within the meaning of the New Towns Act 1965) or the Commission for the New Towns;

"year" means any period of 12 months beginning on a 1st April;

"year of account" means the year for which any housing subsidy is or may be payable under this Part of this Act. **[434]**

COMMENCEMENT
This section came into operation on the passing of this Act on 8th August 1980; see s. 153 (3), *post*.

THIS PART OF THIS ACT
I.e., Part VI (ss. 96–105) of this Act.

COUNCIL OF A DISTRICT OR LONDON BOROUGH
See the corresponding notes to s. 43, *ante*.

GREATER LONDON COUNCIL; COMMON COUNCIL OF THE CITY OF LONDON; COUNCIL
OF THE ISLES OF SCILLY
See the note to s. 50, *ante*.

COMMISSION FOR THE NEW TOWNS
See the note to s. 28, *ante*.

HOUSING SUBSIDY
See s. 96 (1) (*a*), *ante*, and the note to that section.

NEW TOWNS ACT 1965
For the meaning of "development corporation", see s. 2 (9) of that Act.

PART VII

HOUSING: FINANCIAL AND RELATED PROVISIONS

Repairs and improvements

106. Grants for tenants under Part VII of Housing Act 1974

(1) A local authority may entertain an application for a grant under Part VII of the 1974 Act from a person who has, in relation to his dwelling—

    (*a*) a protected tenancy or a statutory tenancy;

    (*b*) a secure tenancy;

    (*c*) a tenancy to which section 1 of the Landlord and Tenant Act 1954 applies and of which less than 5 years remain unexpired at the date of the application;

    (*d*) a protected occupancy or statutory tenancy within the meaning of the Rent (Agriculture) Act 1976; or

    (*e*) a tenancy which satisfies such conditions as may be prescribed,

but not where the application is for an improvement grant in respect of works required for the provision of a dwelling.

(2) A local authority may refuse to entertain the application unless it is accompanied by a certificate given by a qualified person and stating his intention that, throughout the period of 5 years beginning with the certified date—

    (*a*) the dwelling will be let or available for letting as a residence, and not for a holiday, to a person other than a member of the family of the person giving the certificate; or

    (*b*) the dwelling will be occupied or available for occupation by a member of the agricultural population in pursuance of a contract of service and otherwise than as a tenant,

(disregarding any part of that period in which neither of the above paragraphs applies but the dwelling is occupied by a protected occupier under the Rent (Agriculture) Act 1976).

(3) A person is qualified to give a certificate for the purposes of subsection (2) if the local authority could (apart from this section) have entertained an application from him.

(4) Unless the application is accompanied by that certificate, the authority shall not impose any of the grant conditions specified in section 74 (2) of the 1974 Act (future letting of a dwelling).

(5) Expressions defined for the purposes of Part VII of the 1974 Act have the same meanings in this section as they have in that Part. **[435]**

COMMENCEMENT
    See s. 153 (4), *post*, and the note "Orders under this section" thereto.

SUB-S. (1): GRANT
    I.e., a grant of one of the descriptions mentioned in the Housing Act 1974, s. 56 (2), A.L.S. Vol. 223.

FROM A PERSON WHO HAS, ETC.
    Applications from tenants of the kinds mentioned in sub-s. (1) above for grants under the Housing Act 1974, Part VII, were formerly prohibited by s. 57 (3) of that Act, which is consequentially amended by s. 107 and Sch. 12, para. 28, *post*. As to the case where the applicant ceases to have such an interest as is referred to in sub-s. (1) above as s. 57 (3) of the Act of 1974, see s. 81 (2) of that Act, as amended by s. 107 and Sch. 12, para. 32, *post*.

PROTECTED TENANCY; STATUTORY TENANCY

These expressions are not defined in this Act or in the Housing Act 1974, but it is thought that "protected tenancy" has the meaning assigned by the Rent Act 1977, s. 1, A.L.S. Vol. 255, and "statutory tenancy" has the meaning assigned by s. 2 of that Act; cf. the definitions of "protected tenant" and "statutory tenant" applied by s. 150, *post.*

SUCH CONDITIONS AS MAY BE PRESCRIBED

I.e., prescribed by order made by the Secretary of State; see, by virtue of sub-s. (5) above, the Housing Act 1974, s. 84, and as to orders generally, see s. 128 of that Act. At the time of going to press no order had been made for the purposes of sub-s. (1) (*e*) above.

NOT WHERE THE APPLICATION IS FOR AN IMPROVEMENT GRANT . . . FOR THE PROVISION OF A DWELLING

It follows that a tenant within sub-s. (1) above may apply for an improvement grant in respect of works within the Housing Act 1974, s. 56 (2) (*a*), other than those required for the provision of a dwelling, or for a grant falling within s. 56 (2) (*b*)–(*d*) of that Act.

SUB-S. (2): UNLESS IT IS ACCOMPANIED BY A CERTIFICATE, ETC.

The certificate mentioned in sub-s. (2) takes the place of that required from other applicants under the Housing Act 1974, s. 60, as amended by s. 107 and Sch. 12, paras. 5, 29, *post.* As to the making of conditions as to future occupation conditions of the grant under Part VII of the Act of 1974, see s. 73 of that Act, as amended by s. 107 and Sch. 12, paras 21, 30, *post.*

5 YEARS BEGINNING WITH, ETC.

See the note "Three months beginning with, etc." to s. *12, ante.*

CONTRACT OF SERVICE

As to the distinction between a contract of service (or employment) and a contract for service, see 16 Halsbury's Laws (4th Edn.), para. 501.

SUB-S. (3): COULD (APART FROM THIS SECTION) HAVE ENTERTAINED AN APPLICATION FROM HIM

It follows that a person may give a certificate if he could have made an application under the Housing Act 1974, s. 57 (3) or 83.

DEFINITIONS

For "secure tenancy", see ss. 28 and 49 (2), *ante*; by virtue of sub-s. (5) above for "improvement grant", see the Housing Act 1974, s. 56 (2) (*a*), for "agricultural population", "grant", "let", "local authority" and "prescribed", see s. 84 of that Act, for "dwelling", see s. 129 (1) of that Act, and as to "member of the family", see s. 129 (3), (4) of that Act. Note as to "qualified person", sub-s. (3) above.

1974 ACT

I.e., the Housing Act 1974; see s. 150, *post.* Part VII is extensively amended by s. 107 and Sch. 12, *post.*

LANDLORD AND TENANT ACT 1954, S. 1

See A.L.S. Vol. 155.

RENT (AGRICULTURE) ACT 1976

For the meanings of "protected occupancy" and "protected occupier", see ss. 2 and 3 of that Act, A.L.S. Vol. 250, and for the meaning of "statutory tenancy", see ss. 4 and 5 of that Act.

107. Miscellaneous changes in Part VII of Housing Act 1974

The provisions of Part VII of the 1974 Act relating to local authority improvement, repairs and other grants are amended in accordance with Schedule 12 to this Act (amendments to alter certain conditions of grants, relax other conditions, and make other minor and consequential changes). **[436]**

COMMENCEMENT
See s. 153 (4), *post*, and the note "Orders under this section" thereto.

1974 ACT
I.e., the Housing Act 1974; see s. 150, *post*. For Part VII of that Act, see A.L.S. Vol. 223. That Part is extended by s. 106, *ante*, to allow the payment of grants to tenants of the descriptions mentioned in sub-s. (1) of that section.

108. Disposal of houses after repair, improvement or conversion

(1) The Secretary of State may, with the consent of the Treasury, make schemes for making contributions out of moneys provided by Parliament to the net cost (as determined under the schemes) to local authorities of disposing of dwellings in cases of the kind mentioned in subsection (2) below.

(2) Those cases are where an authority—

(a) disposes of a house as one dwelling;
(b) divides a house into two or more separate dwellings and disposes of them; or
(c) combines two houses to form one dwelling and disposes of it,

after carrying out works of repair, improvement or conversion.

(3) The cost towards which contributions may be made under such a scheme shall not exceed £5,000 for any one dwelling, but the Secretary of State may, by order made with the consent of the Treasury, substitute another amount for £5,000.

(4) In this section—

"house" includes a flat;
"local authority" means the council of a district or London borough, the Greater London Council, the Common Council of the City of London or the Council of the Isles of Scilly.

(5) Section 79 of the 1974 Act (payment of improvement contributions to housing authorities) is hereby repealed. **[437]**

COMMENCEMENT
This section came into operation on the passing of this Act on 8th August 1980; see s. 153 (3), *post*.

SECRETARY OF STATE
See the note to s. 2, *ante*.

TREASURY
See the note to s. 46, *ante*.

SCHEMES
Schemes made under this section are not statutory instruments (cf. s. 151, *post*) but particulars of them may be obtained from the Department of the Environment.

COUNCIL OF A DISTRICT OF LONDON BOROUGH
See the corresponding notes to s. 43, *ante*.

GREATER LONDON COUNCIL: COMMON COUNCIL OF THE CITY OF LONDON; COUNCIL OF THE ISLES OF SCILLY
See the notes to s. 50, *ante*.

1974 ACT
I.e., the Housing Act 1974; see s. 150, *post*. For s. 79 of that Act, see A.L.S. Vol. 223. That section is also repealed by s. 152 (3) and Sch. 26, *post*.

ORDERS UNDER THIS SECTION
At the time of going to press no order had been made under sub-s. (3) above.
As to orders generally, see s. 151, *post*.

109. General improvement areas, housing action areas and priority neighbourhoods

(1) The enactments relating to general improvement areas and housing action areas are amended in accordance with Schedule 13 to this Act.

(2) Part VI of the 1974 Act (priority neighbourhoods) shall cease to have effect but without prejudice to the status of any land as part of a priority neighbourhood declared before the commencement of this section.

(3) Section 29B of the 1969 Act (incorporation of priority neighbourhood into general improvement area) shall cease to have effect; but—

    (a) any land comprised in a priority neighbourhood declared before the commencement of this section shall cease to be such land on the area comprising the land becoming a general improvement area; and

    (b) this subsection does not affect the operation of section 29B in any case where a preliminary resolution under that section was passed before the commencement of this section. **[438]**

COMMENCEMENT
    See s. 153 (4), *post*, and the note "Orders under this section" thereto.

LAND
    For meaning, see the Interpretation Act 1978, s. 5, Sch. 1, A.L.S. Vol. 258.

PRIORITY NEIGHBOURHOOD DECLARED
    I.e., under the Housing Act 1974, s. 52, A.L.S. Vol. 223 (repealed by sub-s. (2) above and s. 152 (3) at Sch. 26, *post*.

AREA ... BECOMING A GENERAL IMPROVEMENT AREA
    I.e., by virtue of a declaration made under the Housing Act 1969, s. 28, A.L.S. Vol. 183, as restored by sub-s. (1) above and Sch. 13, para. 1, *post*.

1974 ACT
    I.e., the Housing Act 1974; see s. 150, *post*. Part VI (ss. 52–55) is also repealed by s. 152 (3) and Sch. 26, *post*.

1969 ACT
    I.e., the Housing Act 1969; see s. 150, *post*. S. 29B of that Act was inserted by the Housing Act 1974, s. 51, Sch. 5, Part II, para. 1, and it is also repealed by s. 152 (3) and Sch. 26, *post*.

Mortgages and home ownership

110. Local authority mortgage interest rates

(1) Where, after the commencement of this subsection, a local authority—

    (a) advances money for any of the purposes mentioned in subsection (2) below; or

    (b) on the disposal of any dwelling-house, allows or has to allow any sum to be left outstanding on the security of the dwelling-house; or

    (c) takes a transfer of a mortgage in pursuance of section 111 of this Act;

the provision to be made by it with respect to interest on the sum advanced or remaining outstanding shall comply with the following provisions of this section, unless the advance, disposal or transfer is made in pursuance of a binding contract entered into before the commencement of this subsection or entered into by the acceptance of an offer made by the local authority which was capable of being accepted before the commencement of this subsection.

(2) The purposes mentioned in subsection (1) (a) above are—

    (*a*) acquiring a house;

    (*b*) constructing a house;

    (*c*) converting another building into a house or houses or acquiring another building and converting it into a house or houses;

    (*d*) altering, enlarging, repairing or improving a house; and

    (*e*) facilitating the repayment of an amount outstanding on a previous loan made for any of the purposes specified in paragraphs (*a*) to (*d*) above;

and "house" in this subsection has the same meaning as in the Housing (Financial Provisions) Act 1958.

    (3) The rate of interest shall be whichever is for the time being the higher of the following, namely—

    (*a*) the standard national rate (as defined in subsection (4) below); and

    (*b*) the applicable local average rate (as defined in subsection (5) below);

and shall be capable of being varied by the local authority whenever a change in either or both of those rates requires it; and the amount of the periodic payments shall be capable of being varied correspondingly.

    (4) The standard national rate is the rate for the time being declared as such by the Secretary of State after taking into account interest rates charged by building societies in the United Kingdom and any movement in those rates.

    (5) The applicable local average rate is whichever of the two rates for the time being declared by the local authority in accordance with subsection (6) below is applicable.

    (6) A local authority shall for such period not exceeding six months and beginning at the commencement of subsection (1) above as it may determine and for every subsequent period of six months declare, on a date falling within the month immediately preceding that period, a rate applicable to the advances and transfers mentioned in subsection (1) (*a*) and (*c*) above and a rate applicable to the sums left outstanding as mentioned in subsection (1) (*b*) above; and—

    (*a*) the rate applicable to those advances and transfers shall be a rate exceeding by $\frac{1}{4}$ per cent. that which the authority estimates it has to charge in order to service the loan charges on money borrowed or to be borrowed by the authority for the purpose of such advances and transfers; and

    (*b*) the rate applicable to the sums left outstanding shall be a rate exceeding by $\frac{1}{4}$ per cent. the average, on the date the rate is declared, of the rates at which all loan charges debited to the authority's appropriate account are serviced.

    (7) The appropriate account for the purposes of paragraph (*b*) of subsection (6) above is—

    (*a*) for sums left outstanding on the disposal of dwelling-houses held by a local authority under Part V of the 1957 Act, the authority's Housing Revenue Account; and

    (*b*) for any other sums left outstanding, the general fund if the authority is the Greater London Council or the Council of the Isles of Scilly, the county fund if it is the council of a county, the general rate if it is the Common Council of the City of London and the general rate fund in any other case;

and in that subsection "loan charges" has the meaning given by section 104 (3) (*b*) of the 1972 Act (or, in relation to the council of a county, the meaning that would be so given if the council were a housing authority within the meaning of that Act).

    (8) Where, on any such change as is mentioned in subsection (3) above, a rate of interest is capable of being varied, the local authority shall vary it and shall serve on

the person liable to pay the interest notice in writing of the variation not later than two months after the change; and the variation shall take effect with the first payment of interest due after a date specified in the notice, which—

(a) if the variation is a reduction, shall be not later than one month after the change; and

(b) if the variation is an increase, shall be not earlier than one month nor later than three months after the service of the notice.

(9) On a variation, in accordance with subsection (8) above, of a rate of interest the local authority may make a corresponding variation of the periodic payments, which shall be notified and take effect together with the variation of the rate of interest; and it shall do so if otherwise the period over which the repayment of principal is to be made would be reduced below the period fixed when the mortgage was effected.

(10) The Secretary of State may by notice in writing to a local authority direct it to treat a rate specified in the notice as being the higher of the rates mentioned in subsection (3) above, either during a period specified in the notice or until further notice, and may by a further notice in writing vary or withdraw any direction so given; and where such a direction is given the preceding provisions of this section shall have effect accordingly.

(11) This section shall not prevent a local authority, if the conditions stated in subsection (12) below are satisfied, from giving assistance to a person acquiring a house in need of repair or improvement by making provision for waiving or reducing, for a period ending not later than five years after the date of the advance mentioned in subsection (1) (a) above or the disposal mentioned in subsection (1) (b) above, the interest payable on the sum advanced or remaining outstanding and for dispensing during that period with any repayment of principal.

(12) The conditions mentioned in subsection (11) above are that—

(a) the assistance is given in accordance with a scheme which either has been approved by the Secretary of State or conforms with such requirements as may be specified in an order made by the Secretary of State with the consent of the Treasury; and

(b) the person acquiring the house has entered into an agreement with the local authority to carry out, within a period specified in the agreement, such works of repair or improvement as are so specified.

(13) This section shall not prevent a local authority from giving assistance in the manner provided by section 1 (4) (b) of the Home Purchase Assistance and Housing Corporation Guarantee Act 1978 (part of certain loans to be free of interest for up to five years).

(14) This section does not apply to loans made by local authorities to housing associations under section 119 of the 1957 Act.

(15) In this section "local authority" means the council of a county, the council of a district or London borough, the Greater London Council, the Common Council of the City of London or the Council of the Isles of Scilly. **[439]**

COMMENCEMENT
  See s. 153 (4), *post*, and the note "Orders under this section" thereto.

SUB-S. (1): ADVANCES MONEY FOR ANY OF THE PURPOSES, ETC.
  Such advances may be made under the Housing (Financial Provisions) Act 1958, s. 43, A.L.S. Vol. 109 (as partly repealed by s. 152 (1), (3), Sch, 25, para 9 and Sch. 26, *post*), or under the Small Dwellings Acquisition Acts 1899 to 1923. See also, as respects the Greater London Council, the London County Council (General Powers) Act 1957, s. 78.

ALLOWS ... AND SUM ... ON THE SECURITY OF THE DWELLING-HOUSE
This may be done, in particular, where a secure tenant exercises his right to buy and also exercises his right to a mortgage; see s. 1 (1) (*c*), (2), *ante*.

DWELLING-HOUSE
See the note to s. 3, *ante*.

SUB-S. (2): BUILDING
See the note to s. 3, *ante*.

SUB-S. (4): SECRETARY OF STATE
See the note to s. 2, *ante*.

BUILDING SOCIETIES
The expression "building society" is not defined for the purposes of this section, but cf. s. 8 (8), *ante*, and s. 111 (7), *post*.

UNITED KINGDOM
I.e., Great Britain (as to which, see the note to s. 131, *post*) and Northern Ireland; see the Interpretation Act 1978, s. 5, Sch. 1, A.L.S. Vol. 258.

SUB-S. (6): SIX MONTHS ... BEGINNING AT, ETC.
Cf. the note "Three months beginning with, etc." to s. 12, *ante*.

SUB-S. (7): HOUSING REVENUE ACCOUNT
See the note to s. 96. *ante*.

GENERAL FUND; COUNTY FUND
The general fund is kept by the Greater London Council under the Local Government Act 1972, s. 148 (2), A.L.S. Vol. 209, and the county fund is kept by each county council under the same provision.

GREATER LONDON COUNCIL; COUNCIL OF THE ISLES OF SCILLY; COMMON COUNCIL OF THE CITY OF LONDON
See the notes to s. 50, *ante*.

COUNCIL OF A COUNTY
See the note "County Council" to s. 19, *ante*.

GENERAL RATE FUND
This fund is kept by district councils and London borough councils under the Local Government Act 1972, s. 148 (1).

SUB-S. (8): SERVE ... NOTICE
As to the service and authentication of notices by local authorities, see the Local Government Act 1972, ss. 233, 234.

WRITING
See note "Written; writing" to s. 5, *ante*.

NOT LATER THAN TWO MONTHS (ONE MONTH) (THREE MONTHS) AFTER, ETC.
See the note "Not later than three months after, etc." to s. 11, *ante*.

SUB-S. (10): NOTICE ... TO A LOCAL AUTHORITY
As to the service of notices on local authorities, see the Local Government Act 1972, s. 231.

SUB-S. (11): NOT LATER THAN FIVE YEARS AFTER, ETC.
See the note "Not later than three months after, etc." to s. 11, *ante*.

SUB-S. (12): SCHEME
Schemes made under sub-s. (12) (*a*) above are not statutory instruments (cf. s. 151, *post*), but particulars of them may be obtained from the Department of the Environment.

TREASURY
See the note to s. 46, *ante*.

SUB-S. (15): COUNCIL OF A DISTRICT OR LONDON BOROUGH
See the corresponding notes to s. 43, *ante.*

HOUSING (FINANCIAL PROVISIONS) ACT 1958
For the meaning of "house", see s. 58 (1) of that Act, A.L.S. Vol. 109.

1957 ACT
I.e., the Housing Act 1957; see s. 150, *post.* Part V of that Act is amended by ss. 90–95,

1972 ACT
I.e., the Housing Finance Act 1972; see s. 150, *post.*

HOME PURCHASE ASSISTANCE AND HOUSING CORPORATION GUARANTEE ACT 1978,
S. 1 (4) (*b*)
See A.L.S. Vol. 258.

ORDERS UNDER THIS SECTION
At the time of going to press no order had been made under sub-s. (12) (*a*) above.
As to orders generally, see s. 151, *post.*

111. Local authority and Housing Corporation indemnities for building societies

(1) Local authorities and the Housing Corporation may, with the approval of the Secretary of State, enter into agreements with building societies lending on the security of house property whereby, in the event of default by the mortgagor, and in circumstances and subject to conditions specified in the agreements, an authority or the Corporation binds itself to indemnify the building society in respect of—

(*a*) the whole or part of the mortgagor's outstanding indebtedness; and
(*b*) any loss or expense falling on the building society in consequence of the mortgagor's default.

(2) In subsection (1) above "house property" means any property which is a house for the purposes of the Housing (Financial Provisions) Act 1958.

(3) The agreement may also, where the mortgagor is made party to it, enable or require the authority or the Corporation in specified circumstances to take a transfer of the mortgage and assume rights and liabilities under it, the building society being then discharged in respect of them.

(4) The transfer may be made to take effect—

(*a*) on any terms provided for by the agreement (including terms involving substitution of a new mortgage agreement or modification of the existing one); and
(*b*) so that the authority or the Corporation are treated as acquiring (for and in relation to the purposes of the mortgage) the benefit and burden of all preceding acts, omissions and events.

(5) The Secretary of State may under subsection (1) approve particular agreements or give notice that particular forms of agreement have his approval; and

(*a*) he may in either case make the approval subject to conditions;
(*b*) he shall, before giving notice that a particular form has his approval, consult the Chief Registrar of Friendly Societies and such organisations representative of building societies and local authorities as he thinks expedient.

(6) In this section "local authority" means a county or district council, the Greater London Council, a London borough council, the Common Council of the City of London or the Council of the Isles of Scilly.

(7) In this section "building society" means a society within the Building Societies Act 1962 or the Building Societies Act (Northern Ireland) 1967.

(8) Section 16 (3) and (5) of the Restrictive Trade Practices Act 1976 (recommendations by services supply association to members) shall not apply to recommendations made to building societies about the making of agreements under this section, provided that the recommendations are made with the approval of the Secretary of State, which may be withdrawn at any time on one month's notice.

[440]

COMMENCEMENT
See s. 153 (4), *post*, and the note "Orders under this section" thereto.

SUB-S. (1): HOUSING CORPORATION
See the note to s. 1, *ante*.

SECRETARY OF STATE
See the note to s. 2, *ante*.

SUB-S. (3): TAKE A TRANSFER OF THE MORTGAGE
For provisions as to mortgage interest rates where such a transfer is taken, see s. 110, *ante*.

SUB-S. (5): CONSULT
See the note to s. 26, *ante*.

CHIEF REGISTRAR OF FRIENDLY SOCIETIES
As to this officer, see the Friendly Societies Act 1974, ss. 1, 2, A.L.S. Vol. 234.

SUB-S. (6): COUNTY OR DISTRICT COUNCIL
See the note "County council" to s. 19, *ante*, and the note "Council of any district" to s. 43, *ante*.

GREATER LONDON COUNCIL; COMMON COUNCIL OF THE CITY OF LONDON; COUNCIL OF THE ISLES OF SCILLY
See notes to s. 50, *ante*.

LONDON BOROUGH COUNCIL
See the note "London borough" to s. 43, *ante*.

SUB-S. (8): MONTHS
I.e., one calendar month; see the Interpretation Act, 1978, s. 5, Sch. 1, A.L.S. Vol. 258.

ADDITIONAL SECURITY FOR BUILDING SOCIETY ADVANCES
A guarantee or agreement under this section is a permitted class of additional security for the purposes of the Building Societies Act 1962, s. 26; see s. 26 (1) of, and Sch. 3, para. 3, to, that Act (as amended, in the case of Sch. 3, para. 3, by s. 152 (1) and Sch. 25, para. 11, *post*), and para. 14 of that Schedule as inserted by s. 152 (1) and Sch. 25, para. 12, *post*. See also the Building Societies Act (Northern Ireland) 1967, Sch. 3, para. 3, as amended by s. 152 (1) and Sch. 25, para. 18, *post*, and para. 14 of that Schedule as inserted by s. 152 (1) and Sch. 25, para. 19, *post*.

HOUSING (FINANCIAL PROVISIONS) ACT 1958
For the meaning of "house", see s. 58 (1) of that Act, A.L.S. Vol. 109.

BUILDING SOCIETIES ACT 1962
For the meaning of "building society", see s. 1. of that Act.

BUILDING SOCIETIES ACT (NORTHERN IRELAND) 1967
1967 c. 31 (N.I.).

RESTRICTIVE TRADE PRACTICES 1976, S. 16 (3), (5)
See A.L.S. Vol. 246.

112. Vesting of mortgaged property by local authorities

(1) The following provisions of this section apply where, before the commencement of section 91 (1) above, a local authority has sold any property under the powers of section 104 (1) of the 1957 Act and—

(a) part of the price was secured by a mortgage on the property; and

(b) such a condition was imposed on the sale as is mentioned in section 104 (3) (c) of that Act (right of pre-emption); and

(c) the period during which the authority has the right to re-acquire the property under that condition has not expired.

(2) If the authority as mortgagee has become entitled to exercise the power of sale conferred by section 101 of the Law of Property Act 1925 or by the mortgage deed, it may, if the county court gives it leave to do so, by deed vest the property in itself—

(a) for such estate and interest in the property as is the subject of the mortgage or as it would be authorised to sell or convey under that Act on exercising its power of sale; and

(b) freed from all estates, interests and rights to which the mortgage has priority,

but subject to all estates, interests and rights which have priority to the mortgage.

(3) Accordingly, on the vesting of the property the authority's mortgage term or charge by way of legal mortgage, and any subsequent mortgage term or charge, shall merge or be extinguished as respects the property vested.

(4) Where the title to the property is registered under the Land Registration Acts 1925 to 1971 the Chief Land Registrar shall, on application being made to him by the local authority, register the authority as proprietor of the property, free from all estates, interests and rights to which its mortgage had priority, and he shall not be concerned to inquire whether any of the requirements of this and the following section were complied with.

(5) Where a local authority conveys the property, or part of it, to any person—

(a) he shall not be concerned to inquire whether any of the provisions of this or the following section were complied with; and

(b) his title shall not be impeachable on the ground that the property was not properly vested in the authority or that those provisions were not complied with.

(6) Where application for leave under this section is made to the county court, the county court may adjourn the proceedings or postpone the date for the execution of the local authority's deed for such period or periods as the court thinks reasonable.

(7) Any such adjournment or postponement may be made subject to such conditions with regard to payment by the mortgagor of any sum secured by the mortgage or the remedy of any default as the court thinks fit; and the court may from time to time vary or revoke any such condition.

(8) Property vested under this section shall be treated as acquired under Part V of the 1957 Act. **[441]**

COMMENCEMENT
This section came into force on the passing of this Act on 8th August 1980; see s. 153 (3), *post.*

SUB-S. (1): LOCAL AUTHORITY
For meaning in this context, see the Housing Act 1957, s. 1, and the note thereto, A.L.S. Vol. 109.

SUB-S. (2). POWER OF SALE
In the case of an instalment mortgage, the statutory power of sale arises as soon as default in repayment is made: *Payne* v. *Cardiff R.D.C.* [1932] 1 K.B. 241, but is only exercisable if the Law of Property Act 1925, s. 103, is satisfied. It is thought that, in the event of the mortgagor tendering the principal and interest with costs prior to vesting under this section, then vesting could not take place because the power of sale would be no longer exercisable: *Lord Waring* v. *London and Manchester Assurance Co. Ltd.* [1935] Ch. 310; [1934] All E.R. Rep. 642.

VEST THE PROPERTY IN ITSELF
Where s. 112 applies, *Williams* v. *Wellingborough* B.C. [1975] 3 All E.R. 462, C.A., is reversed. But s. 112 has a limited application: sub-s. (1); and where the sale is after the commencement of s. 91 (1) of this Act, there will be no vesting power. It cannot be implied because a mere re-taking of property is not a sale: *Williams* v. *Wellingborough B.C.*, *supra*, p. 463.

COUNTY COURT
See the note to s. 12, *ante*.

SUB-S. (4): CHIEF LAND REGISTRAR
See the note to s. 19, *ante*.

SUB-S. (5) GENERALLY
The policy of the Law of Property Act 1925, s. 104 (2) is thus adopted. But what sub-s. (5) of this section does not do is to settle the question of a purchaser becoming aware, before completion, of an irregularity or impropriety in the exercise by the mortgagee of the vesting power: sub-s. (5) (*b*) refers to a title (after completion). In relation to the 1925 Act, s. 104 (2), it has been held that a purchaser with notice of such matters before completion is not protected by the statute: *Selwyn* v. *Garfit* (1888) 38 Ch. D. 273, C.A.; *Bailey* v. *Barnes* [1894] 1 Ch. 25, C.A.; *Lord Waring's* case, *supra*.

PERSON
See the note to s. 24, *ante*.

SUB-SS. (6) AND (7): GENERALLY
Though these powers are obviously taken from the Administration of Justice Act 1970, s. 36, it is curious that the powers do not in terms depend on its being shown that, in the event of the exercise of the court's powers, the mortgagor is likely to be able within a reasonable period to pay any sums due under the mortgage, etc. No doubt in view of the terms of sub-s. (7) this likelihood would have to be shown.
    Before any question under either subsection can arise, the power of sale of the mortgagee must have become exercisable: sub-s. (2) above, and so in this, sub-ss. (6) and (7) differ from the Administration of Justice Act 1970, s. 36, because the right of a mortgagee to take possession is independent of whether his statutory power of sale is exercisable: *Western Bank Ltd.* v. *Schindler* [1976] 2 All E.R. 393, C.A.
    By analogy with s. 36 of the 1970 Act, it is thought that the period of the adjournment, etc., cannot be indefinite but must be for a defined or ascertainable period: *Royal Trust Co of Canada* v. *Markham* [1975] 3 All E.R. 433, C.A. *Quaere* whether, under these subsections, a court could not in a proper case specify a definite period of postponement which was to last at all events for the remainder of the pre-emption period, with liberty in the mortgagee to apply; see *Western Bank Ltd.* v. *Schindler* [1976] 2 All E.R. 393, at p. 400 (Buckley, L.J.), C.A.
    The question of the exercise of the discretion is presumably one of fact: *Royal Trust Co of Canada* v. *Markham, supra*. The effect at law and also in equity of the stipulations in the mortgage will be taken into account: *Centrax Trustees Ltd.* v. *Ross* [1979] 2 All E.R. 952.
    As to the conditions which may be imposed, again it is a question of fact, but no doubt in the case of an instalment mortgage, repayment of each instalment might be a condition of a suspension order, though of course the Administration of Justice Act 1973, s. 8, is inapplicable here. See, however, the form of the order in *Centrax Trustees Ltd.* v. *Ross, supra*.

COMPENSATION AND ACCOUNTING
See s. 113, *post*.

1957 ACT
I.e., the Housing Act 1957; see s. 150, *post*. For Part V of that Act and for s. 104 prior

to its substitution by s. 91 (1), *ante*, see A.L.S. Vol. 109.   Part V of that Act is also amended by ss. 90, 91 (2) and 922–95, *ante*.

LAW OF PROPERTY ACT 1925, S. 101
See 27, Halsbury's Statutes (3rd Edn.), p. 504.

113. Compensation and accounting under s. 112

(1) Where, under section 112 above, a local authority has vested any property in itself it shall appropriate a fund equal to the aggregate of—

    (*a*) the price at which the authority could have re-acquired the property by virtue of the condition mentioned in section 112 (1) (*b*) above; and

    (*b*) interest on that price for the period beginning with the vesting and ending with the appropriation at the rate or rates prescribed for that period under section 32 of the Land Compensation Act 1961.

(2) The fund shall be applied—

    (*a*) first, in discharging, or paying sums into court for meeting, any prior incumbrances to which the vesting is not made subject;

    (*b*) secondly, in recovering costs, charges and expenses properly incurred by the authority as incidental to the vesting of the property; and

    (*c*) thirdly, in recovering the mortgage money, interest, costs, and other money (if any) due under the mortgage;

and any residue then remaining in the fund shall be paid to the person entitled to the mortgaged property, or who would have been entitled to give receipts for the proceeds of sale of the property if it had been sold in exercise of the power of sale.

(3) Section 107 (1) of the Law of Property Act 1925 (mortgagee's written receipt sufficient discharge for money arising under power of sale) applies to money payable under this section as it applies to money arising under the power of sale conferred by that Act. **[442]**

COMMENCEMENT
This section came into force on the passing of this Act on 8th August 1980; see s. 153 (3), *post*.

LOCAL AUTHORITY
See the note to s. 112, *ante*.

PRIOR INCUMBRANCES TO WHICH THE VESTING IS NOT MADE SUBJECT
In this connection, cf. s. 112 (2), *ante*.

PERSON
See the note to s. 24, *ante*.

POWER OF SALE
I.e., the power of sale mentioned in s. 112 (2), *ante*.

SECTION 113

LAND COMPENSATION ACT 1961, S. 32 (SUB-S. (1))
This enables the Treasury to prescribe a rate of interest on the notional price from time to time. The latest regulation at the time of going to press is the Acquisition of Land (Rate of Interest after Entry) Regulations S.I. 1979 No 1743: and the rate is 17 per cent. per annum.

SUB-S. (2) GENERALLY
Cf. the Law of Property Act 1925, s. 105 (application of proceeds of sale by a selling mortgagee). It is thought that similar principles would apply here as regards|costs. Accordingly, costs arising out of the wrongful act of a third party may only be allowed if paid to protect title: *Re Smith's Mortgage, Harrison* v. *Edwards* [1931] 2 Ch. 168. A subsequent in-

cumbrancer would appear to be within the benefit of s. 113: cf. *Thorne* v. *Heard and Marsh* [1895] A.C. 495, H.L.

One difference between the present subsection and s. 105 of the 1925 Act is that no trusteeship is imposed in sub-s. (2); presumably, however, this would not preclude the local authority from being under a duty of care to pay the surplus to the person or persons entitled: cf. *West London Commercial Bank* v. *Reliance Permanent Building Society* (1884) 27 Ch. D. 187; *Re Thomson's Mortgage Trusts* [1920] 1 Ch. 508. *Quaere* whether a payment under a mistake of fact would avoid liability. In *Re Allsop* [1914] 1 Ch. 1, C.A., it did, but the case turned on what is now the Trustee Act 1925, s. 61. Overpayments may be recovered by the local authority if *Weld-Blundell* v. *Synott* [1940] 2 K.B. 107; [1940] 2 All E.R. 580, applies here, in the absence of course of negligence, which would estop any such claim: *ibid.*

In cases where the right of redemption of the mortgagor and persons claiming under him is extinguished under the Limitation Act 1939, s. 12, by reason of the mortgagee's possession for the requisite period of time, then any subsequent mortgagee also loses his rights: *Young* v. *Clarey* [1948] 1 All E.R. 197.

LAW OF PROPERTY ACT 1925, S. 107 (1) (SUB-S. (3))

This provides as follows: "The receipt in writing of a mortgagee shall be a sufficient discharge for any money arising under the power of sale conferred by this Act, or for any money or securities comprised in his mortgage, or arising thereunder; and a person paying or transferring the same to the mortgagee shall not be concerned to inquire whether any money remains due under the mortgage."

It is assumed that the vesting order will destroy the mortgagor's equity of redemption: *Lord Waring* v. *London and Manchester Assurance Co Ltd.* [1935] Ch. 310; [1934] All E.R. Rep. 642; *Property and Bloodstock Ltd.* v. *Emerton* [1968] Ch. 94; [1967] 3 All E.R. 321, C.A. Also it is thought that even if the mortgagor had entered into a contract for sale of the property, a local authority whose statutory power of sale was exerciseable would not thereby be disentitled from vesting the property in itself: cf. *Duke* v. *Robson* [1973] 1 All E.R. 481.

114. Subsidised home loans—amendments as to options

(1) If an option notice under Part II of the Housing Subsidies Act 1967 (subsidised loans for house purchase and improvement) is given—

    (a) with the qualifying lender's agreement and in such circumstances or in such cases or descriptions of case as may be specified in directions given by the Secretary of State; or

    (b) not earlier than twelve months after the date of the repayment contract;

it shall have effect notwithstanding that the conditions specified in section 24 (3) (a) and (b) of the Act are not satisfied.

(2) An option notice given under subsection (1) above takes effect from the first day of April falling not less than three months after the notice is given; but if it is given under sub-section (1) (a) above and it is so agreed between the borrower and the qualifying lender, it takes effect on the first day of such month beginning not less than three months after it is given as is so agreed.

(3) An option notice may be cancelled as from any end of March falling not less than twelve months after the date of the repayment contract by a notice given by the borrower to the lender not less than three months before the cancellation.

(4) Unless authorised by order under subsection (5) below—

    (a) an option notice given by virtue of subsection (1) (b) above cannot be cancelled by a notice under subsection (3) above; and

    (b) where an option notice has been cancelled under subsection (3) above no further option notice can be given under subsection (1) (b) above in respect of the same repayment contract.

(5) If it appears to the Secretary of State appropriate to do so having regard to any material change in taxation or other conditions likely to affect a borrower's

decision whether or not to take a subsidised loan, he may by order authorise the giving or cancellation of option notices in accordance with subsections (1) to (3) above in such circumstances or descriptions of case as may be specified in the order.

(6) An order under subsection (5) above shall not authorise the giving of any option notice or of a notice cancelling an option notice later than twelve months after the end of the year in which the order is made.

(7) A notice under subsection (3) above must be in writing and in such form as the Secretary of State may direct; and the reference in that subsection to the borrower includes persons in whom the rights and obligations under the repayment contract are for the time being vested.

(8) Before making an order under subsection (5) above the Secretary of State shall have such consultations with qualifying lenders or organisations representative of them as he thinks appropriate having regard to the purposes of the proposed order.

(9) This section shall be construed, and Part II of the Act of 1967 shall have effect, as if this section were contained in that Part. **[443]**

COMMENCEMENT
    See s. 153 (4), *post*, and the note "Orders under this section" thereto.

SUB-S. (1): QUALIFYING LENDER
    Qualifying lenders are, by virtue of sub-s. (9) above, the bodies specified in, or by order under, the Housing Subsidies Act 1967, s. 27, A.L.S. Vol. 164, as amended by s. 116 (1) and Sch. 14, para. 6 (1), (2), *post*.

SECRETARY OF STATE
    See the note to s. 2, *ante*.

NOT EARLIER THAN TWELVE MONTHS AFTER, ETC.
    See the note "Not later than three months after, etc." to s. 11, *ante*.

SUB-S. (2): NOT LESS THAN THREE MONTHS
    The words "not less than" indicate that three clear months must intervene between the day on which the notice is given and the first day of the month on which it is to take effect; see *R. v. Turner*, [1910] 1 K.B. 346, and *Re Hector Whaling, Ltd.*, [1936] Ch. 208; [1935] All E.R. Rep. 302. "Months" means calendar months by virtue of the Interpretation Act 1978, s. 5, Sch. 1, Vol. 48, pp. 1299, 1319.

SUB-S. (3): NOT LESS THAN TWELVE (THREE) MONTHS
    Cf. the note "Not less than three months" above.

SUB-S. (5): APPEARS
    See the note "Appear" to s. 2, *ante*.

SUBSIDISED LOAN
    I.e., a loan subsidised in accordance with the Housing Subsidies Act 1967, Part II (as amended or affected by this section, and ss. 115, 116 (1) and 152 (3) and Schs 14 and 26, *post*).

SUB-S. (6): NOT .... LATER THAN TWELVE MONTHS AFTER, ETC.
    See the note "Not later than three months after, etc." to s. 11, *ante*.

SUB-S. (7): WRITING
    See the note "Written; writing" to s. 5, *ante*.

SUB-S. (8): CONSULTATIONS
    See the note "Consult" to s. 26, *ante*.

DEFINITIONS
    By virtue of sub-s. (9) above for "repayment contract"; see the Housing Subsidies Act 1967, s. 24 (1) (c); for "option notice", see s. 24 (2) of that Act. Note as to "the borrower", sub-s. (7) above.

HOUSING SUBSIDIES ACT 1967, PART II, S. 24 (3) (*a*), (*b*)
See A.L.S. Vol. 164. That part is also affected by s. 115, *post*, and is amended and partly repealed by ss. 116 (1) and 152 (3) and Sch. 14 and 26, *post*.

ORDERS UNDER THIS SECTION
At the time of going to press no order had been made under sub-s. (5) above.
As to orders generally, see s. 151, *post*.

TRANSITIONAL PROVISION
See s. 152 (2) and Sch. 25, para. 70, *post*.

115. Subsidised loans—further application of Part II of 1967 Act

(1) In relation to a loan which satisfies the two conditions stated in subsections (2) and (3) below Part II of the Housing Subsidies Act 1967 shall have effect as if the loan were for or in connection with one or more of the purposes specified in section 24 (1) (*b*) of that Act.

(2) The first condition is that the loan—

    (*a*) is made as part of a scheme under which not less than nine-tenths of the proceeds of the loan are applied to the purchase by the person or persons to whom it is made of an annuity—

        (i) ending, if the loan is made to one person, with his life or with the life of the survivor of two or more persons who include that person, and

        (ii) ending, if the loan is made to more than one person, with the life of the survivor of two or more persons who include the persons to whom the loan is made; or

    (*b*) was made under such a scheme before the commencement of this section.

(3) The second condition is that each of the persons mentioned in subsection (2) above has attained the age of sixty-five years at the time the loan is made (or, if the loan was made before the commencement of this section, had attained that age at the time the loan was made). **[444]**

COMMENCEMENT
See s. 153 (4), *post*, and the note "Orders under this section" thereto.

ATTAINED THE AGE, ETC.
A person attains a particular age at the commencement of the relevant anniversary of the date of his birth; see the Family Law Reform Act 1969, s. 9, A.L.S. Vol. 189.

HOUSING SUBSIDIES ACT 1967, PART II, S. 24 (1) (*b*)
See A.L.S. Vol. 164. That Part is also affected by s. 114, *ante*, and is amended and partly repealed by ss. 116 (1) and 152 (3) and Schs. 14 and 26, *post*.

116. Other amendments relating to subsidised loans

(1) Part II of the Housing Subsidies Act 1967 is amended as shown in Schedule 14 (amendments to make new or altered provision about the conditions on which subsidised loans are to be available, the duration of subsidy and the bodies who are to be qualifying lenders).

(2) Where a guarantee in respect of an advance by a building society to a borrower in Northern Ireland is given by an insurance company in pursuance of arrangements made under Article 14 of the Housing (Northern Ireland) Order 1978 (guarantee of advances in excess of normal amount)—

    (*a*) the guarantee is to be regarded as an appropriate policy for the purposes of section 33 (1) of the Building Societies Act 1962 (advances for the payment of certain premiums); and (*b*) section 26 (3) of that Act (which limits the amount of an advance where certain guarantees are given) does not apply to the guarantee. **[445]**

COMMENCEMENT
See s. 153 (4), *post*, and the note "Orders under this section" thereto.

HOUSING SUBSIDIES ACT 1967, PART II
See A.L.S. Vol. 164. That Part is also affected by ss. 114 amd 115, *ante*.

HOUSING (NORTHERN IRELAND) ORDER 1978
S.I. 1978 No. 457.

BUILDING SOCIEITIES ACT 1962, SS. 26 (3), 33 (1)
See 3, Halsbury's Statutes (3rd Edn.), pp. 337, 341.

Other provisions about local authority housing finance

117. Rent allowance and rent rebate subsidy

(1) The amount of rent allowance subsidy payable to a local authority (for the credit of the general rate fund) shall be 90 per cent. of the authority's standard amount of rent allowances for the year, as defined by section 20 (8) of the 1972 Act.

(2) In section 3 of the 1975 Act (modified rent rebate subsidy)—

(*a*) in subsection (3) (rate of subsidy) "90 per cent." is substituted for "75 per cent."; and

(*b*) in subsection (4) (*a*) (rate fund contribution) "10 per cent." is substituted for "25 per cent.".

(3) A local authority's rate fund contribution under section 3 (4) of the 1975 Act, so far as payable under paragraph (*a*) of that subsection (percentage of standard amount of rent rebates), is not to count as relevant expenditure for the purposes of section 1 of the Local Government Act 1974 (rate support grant).

(4) In section 19 (2) of the Development of Rural Wales Act 1976 (rate of rent rebate subsidy payable to the Development Board for Rural Wales), "90 per cent." is substituted for "75 per cent.".

(5) This section applies in respect of subsidies payable for 1981–82 and subsequent years. **[446]**

COMMENCEMENT
See s. 153 (4), *post*, and the note "Orders under this section" thereto; and note sub-s. (5) above.

SUB-S. (1): RENT ALLOWANCE SUBSIDY
This subsidy is payable under the Housing Finance Act 1972, s. 1 (1), (2), A.L.S. Vol. 202. Up to the years 1980–81 it was payable in the circumstances set out in s. 8 of that Act, Vol. 42, p. 574, which is repealed by s. 152 (3) and Sch. 26, *post*, consequent upon sub-s. (1) above.

LOCAL AUTHORITY
I.e., a local authority as defined by the Housing Finance Act 1972, s. 104 (1).

GENERAL RATE FUND
See the note to s. 110, *ante*, and the definition in the Housing Finance Act 1972, s. 104 (1).

YEAR
I.e., a financial year; see the Housing Finance Act 1972, s. 104 (1). "Financial year" means the twelve months ending 31st March by virtue of the Interpretation Act 1978, s. 5, Sch. 1, A.L.S. Vol. 258.

    I.e., a local authority as defined by the Housing Rents and Subsidies Act 1975, s. 16 (1),
    A.L.S. Vol. 230.

RATE FUND CONTRIBUTION
    I.e., as defined by the Housing Rents and Subsidies Act 1975, s. 16 (1).

SUB-S. (5): 1981–82 AND SUBSEQUENT YEARS
    The reference is to financial years; see the note to sub-s. (1) above together with the Housing
    Rents and Subsidies Act 1975, s. 16 (1), and the Development of Rural Wales Act 1976,
    s. 19 (2).

1972 ACT
    I.e., the Housing Finance Act 1972; see s. 150, *post*.

1975 ACT
    I.e., the Housing Rents and Subsidies Act 1975; see s. 150, *post*.

LOCAL GOVERNMENT ACT 1974, S. 1
    See A.L.S. Vol. 218.

118. Rent rebates and allowances

Part II of the 1972 Act (rent rebates and allowances) shall have effect, in relation to
the operation of rebate and allowance schemes after such date as the Secretary of
State may by order appoint, subject to the amendments set out in Schedule 15 to this
Act. **[447]**

COMMENCEMENT
    See s. 153 (4), *post*, and the note "Orders under this section" thereto; and note that by
    the present section the amendments made by Sch. 15, *post*, apply in relation to the operation
    of rebate and allowance schemes after such date as may be appointed.   At the time of going
    to press no such date had been appointed.

SECRETARY OF STATE
    See the note to s. 2, *ante*.

1972 ACT
    I.e., the Housing Finance Act 1972; see s. 150, *post*.   For Part II of that Act, see A.L.S.
    Vol. 202, *et seq*.   That Part is also amended and otherwise affected by s. 119, *post*.

ORDER UNDER THIS SECTION
    At the time of going to press no order had been made under this section.
        As to orders generally, see s. 151, *post*.

119. Rent rebates etc. and supplementary benefits

(1) Except in accordance with directions of the Secretary of State, no rebate or
allowance shall be paid by an authority under or by virtue of Part II of the 1972 Act
to any person if, to the authority's knowledge—

    (*a*) he is receiving supplementary benefit; or

    (*b*) his income or resources fall to be aggregated under the 1972 Act or the
        Supplementary Benefits Act 1976 with those of another person who is
        receiving that benefit.

(2) The Secretary of State may also give directions modifying the application of
Part II of the 1972 Act (including Schedules 3 and 4) in circumstances where a
person's entitlement to rebate or allowance is or may be affected by subsection (1) or
directions under it.

(3) Authorities shall supply the Secretary of State with such information in their
possession as may be required to give effect to the Supplementary Benefits Act 1976;

and the Secretary of State shall supply authorities with such information concerning claims for and payments of supplementary benefits as authorities may require to give effect to their rebate and allowance schemes.

(4) Part II of Schedule 3 to the 1972 Act and Part II of Schedule 4 to that Act (provisions superseded by this section regarding relationship between supplementary benefits and rent rebates and allowances) are hereby repealed.

(5) In this section "authority" means any of those bodies which under Part II of the 1972 Act operate rent rebate or rent allowance schemes; and "supplementary benefit" means the same as in that Part of that Act.

(6) In section 22 of the 1972 Act (permitted totals of rent rebates and allowances) after subsection (1) there are inserted the following subsections—

"(1A) The Secretary of State may, on application by an authority, direct that the authority's permitted total of rebates or allowances for such period as may be specified in the direction shall be such proportion of their standard amount of rent rebates or, as the case may be, standard amount of rent allowances, greater than 110 per cent., as may be specified in the direction.

(1B) Any direction given under subsection (1A) above may be made conditional upon compliance by the authority concerned with such conditions as may be specified in the direction." **[448]**

COMMENCEMENT
See s. 153 (4), *post*, and the note "Orders under this section" thereto.

SECRETARY OF STATE
See the note to s. 2, *ante*. It is thought, however, that in sub-s (3) above the Secretary of State referred to is the Secretary of State for Social Services.

REBATE OR ALLOWANCE; REBATE AND ALLOWANCE SCHEMES
I.e., a rebate scheme under the Housing Finance Act 1972, s. 18, as substituted by s. 118, *ante*, and Sch. 15, para. 2, *post*, or a rebate thereunder, or an allowance scheme under s. 19 of that Act, as substituted by s. 118, *ante*, and Sch. 15, para. 3, *post*, or an allowance thereunder.

BODIES WHICH ... OPERATE RENT REBATE OR RENT ALLOWANCE SCHEMES
In the case of rebate schemes the bodies concerned are local authorities as defined by the Housing Finance Act 1972. s. 104 (1), A.L.S. Vol. 202, new town corporations as defined by s. 106 of that Act and the Development Board for Rural Wales and in the case of allowance schemes the bodies concerned are local authorities as defined by s. 104 (1) of the Act of 1972.

DEFINITIONS
In the provisions inserted by sub-s. (6) above for "standard amount of rent rebates" and "standard amount of rent allowances", see the Housing Finance Act 1972, s. 20 (8), and for "authority", see the definition substituted in s. 26 (1) of that Act by the Development of Rural Wales Act 1976, s. 20 (3), Sch. 5, para. 12. Note also as to "authority" and "supplementary benefit", sub-s. (5) above.

1972 ACT
I.e., the Housing Finance Act 1972; see p. 150, *post*.

SUPPLEMENTARY BENEFITS ACT 1976
That Act is extensively amended by the Social Security Act 1980, s. 6 (1), Sch. 2, Part I.

Part VIII

Housing Associations and the Housing Corporation

120. Borrowing powers of Housing Corporation

(1) In section 7 (5) of the 1974 Act (which limits the aggregate amount outstanding in respect of certain advances and loans to the Housing Corporation and its subsidiaries to £400 million but enables the limit to be raised to £750 million) for "£400 million" and "£750 million" there are substituted respectively "£2,000 million" and "£3,000 million".

(2) In ascertaining the limit imposed by that section any interest payable under section 7 (6) of that Act on a loan made by the Secretary of State to the Housing Corporation which, with the approval of the Treasury, is deferred and treated as part of the loan, shall, so far as outstanding, be treated as outstanding by way of principal, whether the loan was made before or is made after the commencement of this section.

[449]

COMMENCEMENT
> This section came into operation on the passing of this Act on 8th August 1980; see s. 153 (3), *post.*

SECRETARY OF STATE
> See the note to s. 2, *ante.*

HOUSING CORPORATION
> See the note to s. 1, *ante.*

TREASURY
> See the note to s. 46, *ante.*

1974 ACT
> *I.e.*, the Housing Act 1974; see s. 150, *post.* For s. 7 of that Act see A.L.S. Vol. 223.

121. Grants to and by Housing Corporation

(1) The Secretary of State may, with the consent of the Treasury, make out of moneys provided by Parliament such grants to the Housing Corporation as appear to him required to enable the Corporation to meet the expenses incurred by it in the exercise of its functions, and any such grant may be made subject to such conditions as he may with the consent of the Treasury determine.

(2) In exercising its functions under section 1 (2) (*a*) and (*b*) of the 1974 Act the Housing Corporation may, with the consent of the Secretary of State and of the Treasury, make grants—

    (*a*) to registered housing association towards the expenses incurred by them in carrying out the objects mentioned in section 13 (3) (*c*) and (*d*) of that Act (advice on formation or running of other housing associations and provision of services for them); and

    (*b*) to other voluntary organisations towards the expenses incurred by them in carrying out the like objects;

and any such grant may be made subject to such conditions as the Corporation may, with the consent of the Secretary of State and of the Treasury, determine.

(3) In this section "voluntary organisation" means a body the activities of which are carried on otherwise than for profit. **[450]**

COMMENCEMENT
See s. 153 (4), *post*, and the note "Orders under this section" thereto.

SECRETARY OF STATE; APPEAR
See the notes to s. 2, *ante*.

TREASURY
See the note to s. 46, *ante*.

HOUSING CORPORATION
See the note to s. 1, *ante*.

BODY ... CARRIED ON OTHERWISE THAN FOR PROFIT
The expression "body" covers a body of persons corporate or unincorporate, cf. the Interpretation Act 1978, s. 5, Sch. 1, A.L.S. Vol. 258.

It seems clear that a body may be "carried on otherwise than for profit" although it makes profits; see, in particular, *National Deposit Friendly Society Trustees* v. *Skegness Urban District Council* [1959] A.C. 293; [1958] 2 All E.R. 601, H.L. In fact there is authority for saying that the making of profits is irrelevant if it is only a subsidiary object, *i.e.*, only a means whereby the main object of the body in question can be furthered or achieved; see, in particular, *National Deposit Friendly Society Trustees* v. *Skegness Urban District Council, supra*, at pp. 319, 320 and p. 612, *per* Lord Denning.

DEFINITIONS
For "registered housing association", see s. 133 (1), *post*. Note as to "voluntary organisation". sub-s. (3) above.

1974 ACT
I.e., the Housing Act 1974; see s. 150, *post*. For ss. 1 (2) and 13 (3) of that Act, see A.L.S. Vol. 223.

122. Disposal of land by registered housing associations

(1) Without prejudice to the provisions of Chapter I of Part I of this Act, every registered housing association shall, subject to section 2 of the 1974 Act (control by Housing Corporation of dispositions by housing associations), have power by virtue of this section, but not otherwise, to dispose in such manner as it thinks fit of any land held by it.

(2) If, in a case where a registered housing association disposes of any land, section 39 of the Settled Land Act 1925 (disposal of land by trustees) would apply but for this subsection, that section shall not apply in relation to the disposal; and accordingly the disposal need not be for the best consideration in money that can reasonably be obtained.

(3) Nothing in subsection (2) above shall be taken to authorise any action on the part of a charity that would conflict with the trusts of the charity.

(4) Subsections (2) to (9) of section 104B of the 1957 Act (repayment of discount on early disposal of freehold or lease), which is inserted in that Act by section 92 of this Act, apply (with the modification specified in subsection (5) below) in relation to a disposal by a registered housing association made under this section with the consent of the Housing Corporation, as they apply to a disposal by the local authority made under section 104 of that Act with the consent of the Secretary of State; and accordingly do not apply in any such case if the consent so provides.

(5) The modification referred to in subsection (4) above is that the Housing Corporation is added to the bodies specified in subsection (6) of section 104B.

(6) Section 104C of the 1957 Act (power to impose covenant limiting freedom to dispose of houses in National Parks and areas of outstanding beauty, etc.), which is also inserted in that Act by section 92 of this Act, shall apply in relation to a

conveyance, grant or assignment executed under this section by a registered housing association as it applies to a conveyance, grant or assignment executed under section 104 of that Act by a local authority. **[451]**

COMMENCEMENT
This section and ss. 123–127, *post*, came into operation on the passing of this Act on 8th August 1980; see s. 153 (3), *post*.

SUB-S. (1): CHAPTER I OF PART I
I.e., ss. 1–27, *ante*.

REGISTERED HOUSING ASSOCIATION
For meaning, see ss. 133 (1), *post*.

LAND
For meaning, see the Interpretation Act 1978, s. 5, Sch. 1, A.L.S. Vol. 258.

SUB-S. (3): CHARITY
As to the meaning of "charity", see 5 Halsbury's Laws (4th Edn.), paras. 501 *et seq*.

SUB-S. (4): CONSENT OF THE HOUSING CORPORATION
This is required by the Housing Act 1974, s. 2, A.L.S. Vol. 223, as amended by s. 123, *post*. See also the note "Housing Corporation" to s. 1, *ante*.

SECRETARY OF STATE
See the note to s. 2, *ante*.

HOUSING ACT 1974, S. 2 (SUB-S. (1))
Registered housing associations are subject to special controls by s. 2 of the 1974 Act, as amended by s. 117 of this Act. By s. 2 (1), the consent of the Housing Corporation is required for a sale, lease, mortgage, charge or other disposal of land by a registered housing association. In the cases set out in s. 2 (2) of the 1974 Act (as substituted by s. 117 (3) of this Act) such consent is not required to dispositions by a charitable unregistered housing association.

SETTLED LAND ACT 1925, S. 39 (SUB-S. (2))
Though the reasons for sub-s. (2) appear obscure and unlikely to arise in many cases, the Settled Land Act 1925 might accidentally apply to land held by a registered housing association (so that presumably it would have to sell as the "statutory owner," *vide* s. 23 of the 1925 Act) because of the extreme width of the definition section in the Settled Land Act (s. 1). An example might be land affected by subsisting family charges (see *ibid.*, s. 1 (1) (v)); for an illustration of the difficulties that this causes, see *Re Ogle's Settled Estates* [1927] 1 Ch. 229. It is much to be hoped than no registered housing association is ever forced to rely on the protection of sub-s. (2). While s. 39 of the 1925 Act is excluded, and therefore the best consideration in money on the sale need not necessarily be obtained, in a case where the 1925 Act applied, the trustees as statutory owners would still have to comply with other parts of the 1925 Act, e.g. s. 72; and so there might be a trap where there was a formal defect in the conveyance: see *Re Cayley and Evans' Contract* [1930] 2 Ch. 143. If a purchaser from the registered housing association fails to comply with for instance s. 18 (1) (b) of the 1925 Act, it is not clear whether he obtains a good title. If the land is only found to be settled land after the conveyance to a purchaser from the registered housing association, then it seems that the purchaser will obtain a good title: s. 110 (2) of the 1925 Act.

1957 ACT
I.e., the Housing Act 1957; see s. 150, *post*. S. 104 of that Act is substituted by s. 91 (1), *ante*.

123. Consent of Housing Corporation to disposals of land by housing associations and housing trusts

(1) Section 2 of the 1974 Act (control by Housing Corporation of dispositions of land by housing associations) is amended as follows.

(2) After subsection (1) there are inserted the following subsections—

"(1A) Any consent of the Corporation may be given either generally to all housing associations or to any particular association or description of association and either in relation to any particular land or description of land.

(1B) Any such consent may be given subject to such conditions as the Corporation sees fit to impose.".

(3) For subsection (2) there is substituted the following subsection—

"(2) Subsection (1) above shall not apply to a disposition by an unregistered housing association which is a charity if the disposition is one which, by virtue of subsection (1) or (2) of section 29 of the Charities Act 1960 (certain disposals not to take place without an order of the court or of the Charity Commissioners), cannot be made without such an order as is mentioned in that section.".

(4) After subsection (3) there is inserted the following subsection—

"(3A) Subsection (1) above shall not apply to the letting, by a registered housing association or by an unregistered housing association which is a housing trust, of any land under a secure tenancy or under what would be a secure tenancy but for any of paragraphs 2 to 13 of Schedule 3 to the Housing Act 1980 or, as the case may be, but for any of paragraphs 2 to 7 of Schedule 1 to the Tenants' Rights, Etc. (Scotland) Act 1980.".

(5) In subsection (4), after the word "grant" there are inserted the words "by an unregistered housing association which does not satisfy the landlord condition in section 28 of the Housing Act 1980 (bodies which are capable of granting secure tenancies)".

(6) After subsection (5) there is inserted the following subsection—

"(5A) Where a housing association has, at any time, made a disposition requiring the consent of the Corporation under this section, then—

(a) in favour of any person claiming under the association, the disposition shall not be invalid by reason that any consent of the Corporation which is required has not been given; and

(b) a person dealing with the association or a person claiming under the association shall not be concerned to see or inquire whether any such consent has been given.".

(7) After subsection (6) there is inserted the following subsection—

"(6A) In this section—

'housing trust' has the same meaning as in section 15 of the Rent Act 1977; and

'secure tenancy' has the same meaning as in section 28 of the Housing Act 1980 or section 10 of the Tenants' Rights, Etc. (Scotland) Act 1980.". **[452]**

COMMENCEMENT
See the note to s. 122, *ante.*

SUB-S. (2): SEES FIT
See the note "Appear" to s. 2, *ante.*

SUB-S. (3): CHARITY
See the note to s. 122, *ante.*

SUB-S. (6): PERSON
See the note to s. 24, *ante.*

FURTHER PROVISIONS
See s. 122, *ante* (disposals of land by registered housing associations) and s. 137, *post*

(avoidance of unauthorised disposal) and note that the Housing Act 1974, s. 2 (5A), as inserted by sub-s. (6) above, is excluded by s. 137 (1), *post*.

DEFINITIONS
As to "consent", see the Housing Act 1974, s. 2 (6), A.L.S. Vol. 223; for "land", see s. 12 of that Act; for "the Corporation", "housing association", "registered and unregistered", see s. 129 (1) of that Act. Note as to "housing trust" and "secure tenancy", s. 2 (6A) of the Act of 1974 as added by sub-s. (7) above.

1974 ACT
I.e., the Housing Act 1974; see s. 150, *post*.

CHARITIES ACT 1960, S. 29
See A.L.S. Vol. 132.

TENANTS' RIGHTS, ETC. (SCOTLAND) ACT 1980
1980 c. 52.

RENT ACT 1977, S. 15
For the meaning of "housing trust" in that section, see sub-s. (5) thereof as substituted by s. 74 (2), *ante*.

TRANSITIONAL PROVISION
See s. 152 (2) and Sch. 25, para. 71, *post*.

124. Accounts and audit

(1) The Secretary of State may by order lay down accounting requirements for registered housing associations with a view to ensuring that the accounts of every registered housing association are prepared in the requisite form and give a true and fair view of the state of affairs of the association, so far as its housing activities are concerned, and of the disposition of funds and assets which are, or at any time have been, in its hands in connection with those activities.

(2) The accounts of every registered housing association must comply with those requirements; and the auditor's report shall state (in addition to any other matters which it is required to state) whether in the auditor's opinion they do so comply.

(3) Every registered housing association shall furnish to the Housing Corporation a copy of its accounts, and auditor's report within 6 months of the end of the period to which they relate.

(4) A registered housing association which is a society registered under the Industrial and Provident Societies Act 1965 shall be subject to section 4 (1) of the Friendly and Industrial and Provident Societies Act 1968 (obligation to appoint auditors), without regard to the volume of its receipts and payments, the number of its members or the value of its assets; and such an association is in no case to be treated as an exempt society under that section.

(5) A registered housing association which is a registered charity but not a society registered under the Act of 1965 shall, in respect of its housing activities (and separately from its other activities, if any) be subject to Part I of Schedule 16 to this Act (provisions corresponding to those of the Act of 1968); but this does not affect any obligation falling on the charity in consequence of section 8 of the Charities Act 1960 (statement of accounts to be transmitted to Charity Commissioners).

(6) The method by which an association shall distinguish in its accounts between its housing activities and other activities shall be as laid down by orders under subsection (1) above.

(7) Subsections (2) to (6) above apply with respect to any period beginning on or after the day on which the first order under subsection (1) comes into force; and the

requirements contained in any order under that subsection shall not apply in relation to any period beginning before the day on which the order comes into force. **[453]**

COMMENCEMENT
See the note to s. 122, *ante*; and note sub-s. (7) above.

SUB-S. (1): SECRETARY OF STATE
See the note to s. 2, *ante*.

SUB-S. (3): HOUSING CORPORATION
See the note to s. 1, *ante*.

WITHIN 6 MONTHS OF, ETC.
See the note to s. 3, *ante*.

ENFORCEMENT
See s. 125, *post*.

DEFINITIONS
For "registered charity" and "registered housing association", see s. 133 (1), *post*; as to "housing activities", see s. 133 (2), *post*.

INDUSTRIAL AND PROVIDENT SOCIETIES ACT 1965
See 17, Halsbury's Statutes (3rd edn.), p. 333.

FRIENDLY AND INDUSTRIAL AND PROVIDENT SOCIETIES ACT 1968, S. 4
See A.L.S. Vol. 180.

CHARITIES ACT 1960, S. 8
See A.L.S. Vol. 132.

ORDERS UNDER THIS SECTION
At the time of going to press no order had been made under sub-s. (1) above.
As to orders generally, see s. 151, *post*; and for further provisions which are to be made by an order under sub-s. (1) above, see s. 131 (2), *post*.

125. Enforcement of s. 124

(1) All persons who are directly concerned with the conduct and management of the affairs of a registered housing association and are in that capacity responsible for the preparation and audit of accounts shall have the duty to ensure that section 124 and (where applicable) Part I of Schedule 16 are complied with by the association.

(2) If—

(a) the accounts of a registered housing association, as furnished to the Housing Corporation under section 124 (3), do not comply with the accounting requirements laid down under section 124 (1); or

(b) section 124 (3) is not complied with in respect of the accounts and auditor's report; or

(c) Part I of Schedule 16 is not complied with by an association which is a registered charity but not a society registered under the Act of 1965,

the association as well as each of the persons on whom the above duty is imposed shall be liable on summary conviction to a fine not exceeding £200.

(3) It is a defence—

(a) for a person charged under subsection (2) above to prove that he did everything that could reasonably have been expected of him by way of discharging the duty imposed by subsection (1) above; and

(b) for an association charged under subsection (2) above to prove that the persons mentioned in subsection (1) above did everything that could reasonably have been expected of them by way of discharging the duty imposed by subsection (1) above in relation to the association.

(4) No proceedings for an offence under this section shall be instituted in England or Wales except by or with the consent of the Director of Public Prosecutions or the Housing Corporation. **[454]**

COMMENCEMENT
See the note to s. 122, *ante*; and note also s. 124 (7) *ante*.

PERSONS
See the note "Person" to s. 24, *ante*.

DIRECTLY CONCERNED WITH
There is little authority as to this; a degree of participation is required and it need not be total: a director in control of an essential part of a business was held to be "concerned" with the management of the business for income tax purposes in *Glanvill, Enthoven & Co* v. *I.R.C.* (1925) 41 T.L.R. 258, H.L.

HOUSING CORPORATION
See the note to s. 1, *ante*.

SUMMARY CONVICTION
Summary jurisdiction and procedure are mainly governed by the Magistrates' Courts Act 1962, the Magistrates' Courts Act 1957, and certain provisions of the Criminal Justice Act 1967, and of the Criminal Law Act 1977. Those provisions are repealed and replaced by the Magistrates' Courts Act 1980, as from a day to be appointed under s. 115 (7) of that Act.

IT IS A DEFENCE, ETC.
The burden of proof resting on the accused is not so onerous as that which is, in general, laid on the prosecutor as regards proving an offence and may be discharged by satisfying the court of the probability or rather the preponderance of probability, of what the accused is called on to prove; see *R.* v. *Carr-Briant*, [1943] K.B. 607; [1943] 2 All E.R. 156; *R.* v. *Dunbar*, [1958] 1 Q.B. 1; [1957] 2 All E.R. 737, and *R.* v. *Hudson*, [1966] 1 Q.B. 448; [1965] 1 All E.R. 721, *R.* v. *Edwards* [1974] 2 All E.R. 1085, C.A.

ENGLAND; WALES
For meanings, see the Interpretation Act 1978, s. 5, Sch. 1, A.L.S. Vol. 258.

DIRECTOR OF PUBLIC PROSECUTIONS
Provision for the appointment of the Director of Public Prosecutions and Assistant Directors is made by the Prosecution of Offences Act 1979, s. 1; by sub-s. (4) of that section an Assistant Director may do any act or thing which the Director is required or authorised to do. See also, in particular, s. 6 of that Act, as to remand, etc., where the consent of the Director has not been granted, and s. 7 thereof, as to evidence of such consent.

DEFINITIONS
For "registered charity" and "registered housing association", see s. 133 (1), *post*.

ACT OF 1965
I.e., the Industrial and Provident Societies Act 1965, 17, Halsbury's Statutes (3rd edn.), p. 333; see s. 124 (4), *ante*.

126. Payments to certain committee members and others

For subsections (3) to (6) of section 26 and for section 27 of the 1974 Act (payments to members etc. of registered 1965 Act associations and contracts with committee members) there shall be substituted the provisions set out in Part II of Schedule 16 to this Act. **[455]**

COMMENCEMENT
See the note to s. 122, *ante*.

1974 ACT
I.e., the Housing Act 1974; see s. 150, *post*. For ss. 26 (3)–(6) and 27 of that Act, see A.L.S. Vol. 223.

127. Registration of housing associations

(1) A housing association which is a society registered under the Industrial and Provident Societies Act 1965 may have among its objects those of—

　　(*a*) acquiring houses to be disposed of on sale or on lease, or building houses to be disposed of on leases falling within subsection (2) below;

　　(*b*) repairing and improving houses, or creating them by conversion of house or other property, with a view to such disposal,

without preventing the association from being or, as the case may be, remaining registered by the Housing Corporation under section 13 of the 1974 Act.

　(2) A lease of a house falls within this subsection if—

　　(*a*) it is granted on payment of a premium which is calculated by reference to a percentage of the value of the house or of the cost of providing it; or

　　(*b*) the tenant (or his personal representatives) will or may be entitled to a sum calculated by reference directly or indirectly to the value of the house.

　(3) In this section "house" includes a flat.

　(4) Section 14 of the 1974 Act (the Housing Associations Registration Advisory Committee) is hereby repealed. **[456]**

COMMENCEMENT
See the note to s. 122, *ante*.

HOUSING CORPORATION
See the note to s. 1, *ante*.

INDUSTRIAL AND PROVIDENT SOCIETIES ACT 1965
See 17, Halsbury's Statutes (3rd edn.), p. 333.

1974 ACT
I.e., the Housing Act 1974; see s. 150, *post*. For ss. 13 and 14 of that Act, see A.L.S. Vol. 223. S. 14 of that Act is also repealed by s. 152 (3) and Sch. 26, *post*.

128. Removal of certain housing associations from register

(1) In section 15 of the 1974 Act—

　　(*a*) after subsection (2) there is inserted the subsection set out below; and

　　(*b*) in subsection (6) for the words "this section" there are substituted the words "subsection (2) above".

　(2) The subsection inserted after subsection (2) is—

　　　"(2A) Where a body which is registered—

　　　　(*a*) has not at any time received a grant under section 29 or section 32 below or any such payment or loan as is specified in paragraph 2 or paragraph 3 of Schedule 2 to this Act; and

　　　　(*b*) requests the Corporation to remove it from the register;

　　the Corporation may, if they think fit, remove it from the register." **[457]**

COMMENCEMENT
See s. 153 (4), *post*, and the note "Orders under this section" thereto.

REGISTER
> *I.e.*, the register of housing associations maintained under the Housing Act 1974, s. 13, A.L.S. Vol. 223.

DEFINITIONS
> For "the Corporation" and "registered", see the Housing Act 1974, s. 129 (1).

1974 ACT
> *I.e.*, the Housing Act 1974; see s. 150, *post*. S. 29 of that Act is amended and otherwise affected by s. 130 and Sch. 18, paras. 1, 2, *post*, and s. 32 is amended by s. 130 (4) and Sch. 18, para. 9, *post*.

129. Inquiries into affairs of registered housing association and power to act for its protection

Sections 19 and 20 of the 1974 Act are amended and extended in accordance with Schedule 17 to this Act. **[458]**

COMMENCEMENT
> See s. 153 (4), *post*, and the note "Orders under this section" thereto.

1974 ACT
> *I.e.*, the Housing Act 1974; see s. 150, *post*. For ss. 19 and 20 of that Act, see A.L.S. Vol. 223.

130. Housing association grant

(1) The Secretary of State may pay housing association grant under section 29 of the 1974 Act to a registered housing association in cases where the association—

    (*a*) disposes of a house as one dwelling;

    (*b*) divides a house into two or more separate dwellings and disposes of them; or

    (*c*) combines two houses to form one dwelling and disposes of it;

after carrying out works of repair, improvement or conversion.

(2) The maximum grant which may be paid in a case of the kind mentioned in subsection (1) above is £5,000 for any one dwelling, but the Secretary of State may, by order made with the consent of the Treasury, substitute another amount for £5,000.

(3) In this section "house" includes a flat.

(4) The provisions of Part III of the 1974 Act relating to housing association grant are amended in accordance with Schedule 18 to this Act. **[459]**

COMMENCEMENT
> This section came into operation on the passing of this Act on 8th August 1980; see s. 153 (3), *post* (but see Sch. 18, para. 1 (2), post).

SECRETARY OF STATE
> See the note to s. 2, *ante*.

TREASURY
> See the note to s. 46, *ante*.

PROVISIONS ... RELATING TO HOUSING ASSOCIATION GRANT ARE AMENDED, ETC.
> The amendments made by Sch. 18, *post*, are not confined to the provisions of the Housing Act 1974, Part III, A.L.S. Vol. 223, relating to housing association grant (as defined by s. 29 (1) of that Act, but extend to the provisions relating to management grants, revenue deficit grant and hostel deficit grant.

DEFINITIONS
For "registered housing association", see s. 133 (1), *post*. Note as to "house", sub-s. (3) above.

1974 ACT
I.e., the Housing Act 1974; see s. 150, *post*. S. 29 of that Act is amended by sub-s. (4) above and Sch. 18, paras. 1, 2, *post*, and Part III is also affected by s. 139 and Sch. 20, para. 6, *post*.

ORDERS UNDER THIS SECTION
At the time of going to press no order had been made under sub-s. (2) above.
As to orders generally, see s. 151, *post*.

131. Recoupment of surplus rental income

(1) Every registered housing association which has at any time received a grant under section 29 of the 1974 Act shall show separately in its accounts for any period the surpluses arising from increased rental income during that period from housing projects in connection with which the grant was made.

(2) The surpluses are to be shown by each association in a fund to be known as the Grant Redemption Fund; and the method of constituting the Fund and of showing it in the association's accounts is to be as required by order of the Secretary of State under section 124 (1) above.

(3) The surpluses in respect of any period are to be calculated in a manner determined by the Secretary of State for housing associations generally, and in determining it the Secretary of State may take account of the rental income received or capable of being received by an association and the management and maintenance costs and loan charges incurred or likely to be incurred by it.

(4) The manner of calculating surpluses shall be determined after consultation with organisations appearing to the Secretary of State to be representative of registered housing associations, and shall be made known to the associations from time to time; and surpluses may be calculated differently for housing associations of different kinds or dwellings in different parts of Great Britain.

(5) The Secretary of State may from time to time give notice to a registered housing association requiring it to pay to him, with interest, if demanded, or to apply or appropriate for purposes he specifies, any sums standing in its Grant Redemption Fund at the end of a period of account.

(6) Any interest demanded under subsection (5) above—

(a) shall be at the rate or rates previously determined by the Secretary of State with the consent of the Treasury for housing associations generally and published by him or, if no such determination has been made, at the rate or rates specified with the consent of the Treasury in the notice; and

(b) shall be payable either from the date of the notice or from such earlier date, but not earlier than the end of the period of account, as the notice may specify.

(7) Subsections (1) and (2) above apply to an association's accounts for any period beginning on or after the date on which the first order under section 124 (1) above comes into force. **[460]**

COMMENCEMENT
This section came into operation on the passing of this Act on 8th August 1980; see s. 153 (3), *post* (but note sub-s. (7) above).

SUB-S. (1): REGISTERED HOUSING ASSOCIATION
For meaning, see s. 133 (1), *post*.

SUB-S. (I): HOUSING PROJECTS
The expression "housing project" is defined by the Housing Act 1974, s. 29 (2), A.L.S. Vol. 223.

SUB-S. (2): SECRETARY OF STATE
See the note to s. 2, *ante*.

SUB-S. (4); CONSULTATIONS
See the note "Consult" to s. 26, *ante*.

APPEARING
See the note "Appear" to s. 2, *ante*.

GREAT BRITAIN
I.e., England, Scotland and Wales; see the Union with Scotland Act 1706, preamble Art. I, as read with the Interpretation Act 1978, s. 22 (I), Sch. 2, para. 5 (*a*), A.L.S. Vol. 258.

SUB-S. (5): PAY TO HIM
Any sums received by the Secretary of State under this section are to be paid into the Consolidated Fund, see s. 154 (2), *post*.

SUB-S. (6): TREASURY
See the note to s. 46, *ante*.

1974 ACT
I.e., the Housing Act 1974; see s. 150, *post*. Section 29 is amended and otherwise effected by s. 130, *ante*, and Sch. 18, paras. I, 2, *post*.

132. Amendment of rules of registered housing association

In section 24 of the 1974 Act the following subsection is inserted after subsection (5)—

"(5A) In relation to a registered 1965 Act association section 10 of the 1965 Act shall have effect as if—

(*a*) in subsection (1) after the words "shall not be valid" there were inserted the words "without the consent of the Housing Corporation given by order under the seal of the Corporation nor" and after paragraph (*b*) there were inserted the words "and there shall also be sent with the copies of the amendment a copy of the Corporation's consent"; and

(*b*) in subsection (2) at the end of the words preceding the paragraphs there were inserted the words "notice of any such change shall be sent to the Housing Corporation and"." **[461]**

COMMENCEMENT
See s. 153 (4), *post*, and the note "Orders under this section" thereto.

REGISTERED 1965 ACT ASSOCIATION
For meaning, see the Housing Act 1974, s. 28, A.L.S. Vol. 223.

HOUSING CORPORATION
See the note to s. I, *ante*.

1974 ACT
I.e., Housing Act 1974; see s. 150, *post*.

1965 ACT
I.e., the Industrial and Provident Societies Act 1965; see the Housing Act 1974, s. 13 (1) (*b*).

133. Interpretation of Part VIII

(1) In this Part of this Act—

> "registered charity" means a charity registered under section 4 of the Charities
> Act 1960, and "exempt charity" has the same meaning as in that Act;
> "registered housing association" means an association registered under section
> 13 of the 1974 Act.

(2) For the purposes of this Part of this Act, the housing activities of a registered
housing association are all those activities by reference to which it is to be regarded
as a housing association (within the meaning given to that expression by section 189
(1) of the 1957 Act or, as the case may be, section 208 (1) of the Housing (Scotland)
Act 1966) and as registrable under Part II of the 1974 Act. **[462]**

COMMENCEMENT
>   This section and ss. 134 and 135, *post*, came into operation on the passing of this Act on
>   8th August 1980; see s. 153 (3), *post*.

THIS PART OF THIS ACT
>   *I.e.*, Part VIII (ss. 120–133) of this Act.

CHARITIES ACT 1960
>   For that Act, see A.L.S. Vol. 132.

1974 ACT
>   *I.e.*, the Housing Act 1974; see s. 150, *post*.

1957 ACT
>   *I.e.*, the Housing Act 1957; see s. 150 *post*. For s. 189 (1) of that Act, see A.L.S. Vol.
>   109.

HOUSING (SCOTLAND) ACT 1966
>   1966 c. 49.

PART IX

GENERAL

Housing Revenue Account and Housing Repairs Account

134. Working balance in Housing Revenue Account

(1) Section 1 (3) of the 1975 Act (restriction on working balances in Housing
Revenue Account) shall cease to have effect.

(2) Any authority which keeps a Housing Revenue Account may from time to
time carry to the credit of its general rate fund (or, as the case may be, the general
fund or the general rate) the whole or part of any balance in its Housing Revenue
Account. **[463]**

COMMENCEMENT
>   See the note to s. 133, *ante*.

AUTHORITY WHICH KEEPS A HOUSING REVENUE ACCOUNT
>   *I.e.*, any local authority as defined by the Housing Finance Act 1972, s. 104 (1), A.L.S.
>   Vol. 202. See also the note "Housing Revenue Account" to s. 96, *ante*.

GENERAL RATE FUND
>   See the note to s. 110, *ante*.

GENERAL FUND
>   The general fund is kept by the Greater London Council under the Local Government Act
>   1972, s. 148 (2), A.L.S. Vol. 209.

GENERAL RATE
   I.e., the general rate of the City of London.

1975 ACT
   I.e., the Housing Rents and Subsidies Act 1975; see s. 150, *post*.

135. Housing Repairs Account

(1) Any local authority may, for the year 1981–82 and for subsequent years, keep an account (to be known as the Housing Repairs Account) in accordance with this section.

(2) Every authority which keeps a Housing Repairs Account shall credit to the account—

   (a) contributions from its Housing Revenue Account;
   (b) income arising from the investment or other use of money credited to the account; and
   (c) sums received by the authority in connection with the repair or maintenance of any of its housing stock, either from its tenants or from the sale of scrapped or salvaged materials.

(3) Every such authority shall debit to its Housing Repairs Account—

   (a) all expenditure incurred by it in connection with the repair or maintenance of any of its housing stock;
   (b) any amount which is carried to the credit of its Housing Revenue Account in accordance with subsection (5) below; and
   (c) such expenditure incurred by it in connection with the improvement or replacement of any of its housing stock as may from time to time be determined by the Secretary of State.

(4) Every such authority shall ensure that sufficient credits are carried to its Housing Repairs Account to secure that the account never shows a debit balance.

(5) If an authority considers that any credit balance in its Housing Repairs Account at the end of a year will not be required for the purposes of that account, it may carry some or all of the balance to the credit of its Housing Revenue Account.

(6) If an authority which has opened a Housing Repairs Account ceases to maintain the account, any balance shall be carried to its Housing Revenue Account.

(7) In paragraph 3 (1) of Schedule 1 to the 1972 Act (items to be debited to Housing Revenue Account)—

   (a) at the end of sub-paragraph (c) there are added the words "(except where that expenditure is properly debited to the Housing Repairs Account)"; and
   (b) after that sub-paragraph there is inserted the following sub-paragraph—

   "(d) contributions from the account to the Housing Repairs Account."

(8) In paragraph 5 (1) of Schedule 1 to the 1972 Act (Secretary of State's directions as to amounts to be credited or debited to Housing Revenue Account), after the words "Revenue Account" there are inserted the words "or, as the case may be, a Housing Repairs Account".

(9) Any determination by the Secretary of State under subsection (3) (c) above may be made to apply to local authorities generally or to a particular authority or group of authorities and may make different provision in respect of different cases or descriptions of case.

(10) In this section—

"expenditure" includes loan charges;

"housing stock" means any house or other property within a local authority's Housing Revenue Account;

"local authority" means the council of a district or London borough, the Greater London Council, the Common Council of the City of London or the Council of the Isles of Scilly. **[464]**

COMMENCEMENT
See the note to s. 133, *ante*.

SUB-S. (1): YEAR 1981–82 AND SUBSEQUENT YEARS
The expression "year" is not defined but it is thought that it means a financial year. By the Interpretation Act 1978, s. 5, Sch. 1, A.L.S. Vol. 258, "financial year" means a period of twelve months ending with 31st March.

HOUSING REPAIRS ACCOUNT
A Housing Repairs Account was formerly required to be kept by every local authority required to keep a Housing Revenue Account by the Housing (Financial Provisions) Act 1968, s. 51, but it was discontinued by the Housing Finance Act 1972, s. 108 (3), Sch. 10, para. 3, A.L.S. Vol. 202, as respects the year 1972–73 and later years, and s. 52 of the Act of 1958 was consequently repealed by s. 108 (4) of, and Sch. 11, Part I to, the Act of 1972.

SUB-S. (2): HOUSING REVENUE ACCOUNT
See the note to s. 96, *ante*.

SUB-S. (3): SECRETARY OF STATE
See the note to s. 2, *ante*.

SUB-S. (10): COUNCIL OF A DISTRICT OR LONDON BOROUGH
See the corresponding note to s. 43, *ante*.

GREATER LONDON COUNCIL; COMMON COUNCIL OF THE CITY OF LONDON; COUNCIL OF THE ISLES OF SCILLY
See the notes to s. 50, *ante*.

1972 ACT
I.e., the Housing Finance Act 1972; see s. 150, *post*.

Service charges

136. Service charges.

(1) Schedule 19 to this Act shall have effect, in place of sections 90 to 91A of the 1972 Act, in relation to periods ending after the commencement of this section, but subject to subsection (2) below.

(2) In relation to works begun earlier than six months after the commencement of this section—

(*a*) paragraphs 2 to 6 of Schedule 19 shall not apply; and

(*b*) sections 90 to 91A shall continue to apply. **[465]**

COMMENCEMENT
See s. 153 (4), *post*; and the note "Orders under this section" thereto; and note sub-s. (2) above.

EARLIER THAN SIX MONTHS AFTER, ETC.
See the note "Not later than three months after, etc." to s. 11, *ante*.

PUBLICATION OF INFORMATION
See the note to Part II of this Act, *ante*.

1972 ACT
I.e., the Housing Finance Act 1972; see s. 150, *post.*

Miscellaneous

137. Avoidance of certain unauthorised disposals

(1) If—

- (*a*) at any time after 18th July 1980 a local authority or a housing association has disposed of a house; and
- (*b*) the disposal was one which, under section 104 of the 1957 Act or section 2 of the 1974 Act, required the consent of the Secretary of State or of the Housing Corporation (or would have required it had the relevant provisions been in force) but was made without that consent;

then, unless the disposal was to an individual (or to two or more individuals) and did not extend to any other house, it shall be void (and, if made before the passing of this Act, be deemed always to have been void) and section 128 (2) of the Local Government Act 1972 or, as the case may be, subsection (5A) (inserted by section 123 (6) of this Act) of section 2 of the 1974 Act (protection of purchasers) shall not apply.

(2) In this section "house" includes a flat and "the relevant provisions" means Part I and sections 91 and 123 of this Act. **[466]**

COMMENCEMENT
    This section an ss. 138–140, *post*, came into operation on the passing of this Act on 8th August 1980; see s. 153 (3), *post.*

LOCAL AUTHORITY
    This must mean a local authority as defined by the Housing Act 1957, s. 1, A.L.S. Vol. 109.

HOUSING ASSOCIATION
    This must mean a housing association of one of the kinds mentioned in the Housing Act 1974, s. 2 (1), A.L.S. Vol. 223.

SECRETARY OF STATE
    See the note to s. 2, *ante.*

HOUSING CORPORATION
    See the note to s. 1, *ante.*

INDIVIDUAL
    See the note to s. 28, *ante.*

PASSING ON THIS ACT
    This Act was passed, *i.e.*, received the Royal Assent, on 8th August 1980.

PART I . . . OF THIS ACT
    I.e., ss. 1–50, *ante.*

1957 ACT
    I.e., the Housing Act 1974; see s. 150, *post.* Section 2 of that Act is amended by s. 123, *ante.*

1974 ACT
    I.e., the Housing Act 1974; see s. 150, *post.* Section 2 of that Act is amended by s. 123, *ante.*

LOCAL GOVERNMENT ACT 1972, S. 128 (2)
    See A.L.S. Vol. 209.

138. Displacement of residential occupiers by housing authority 1973 c. 26

In section 42 (1) of the Land Compensation Act 1973 (which requires an authority acquiring or redeveloping land to indemnify another authority against the cost of rehousing a person displaced by the acquisition or redevelopment but only if the displacing authority is not an authority having functions under Part V of the 1957 Act) after the words "Housing Act 1957" (in paragraph (*b*)) there are inserted the words "or (if they are such an authority) the land is acquired or redeveloped by them otherwise than in the discharge of those functions". **[467]**

COMMENCEMENT
    See the note to s. 137, *ante.*

LAND COMPENSATION ACT 1973, S. 42 (1)
    See A.L.S. Vol. 215.

1957 ACT
    I.e., the Housing Act 1957; see s. 150, *post.* For Part V of that Act, see A.L.S. Vol. 109.
    That Part is amended by ss. 90–95, *ante.*

139. Housing co-operatives

Schedule 20 has effect for making in relation to housing co-operatives provisions corresponding to paragraph 9 of Schedule 1 to the 1975 Act and certain other provisions. **[468]**

COMMENCEMENT
    See the note to s. 137, *ante.*

1975 ACT
    I.e., the Housing Rents and Subsidies Act 1975; see s. 150, *post.* For Sch. 1, para. 9 to
    that Act, see A.L.S. Vol. 230. That paragraph is repealed by s. 152 (3) and Sch. 26, *post,*
    consequent upon s. 96 (1) (*b*), *ante*, and Sch. 11, Part I, *post.*

140. Exclusion of shared ownership tenancies from Leasehold Reform Act 1967

(1) Where, after the commencement of this section, a tenancy of a house is created by the grant of a lease at a premium and either—

    (*a*) the lease is granted by a body mentioned in subsection (2) below and complies with the condition set out in subsection (3) below; or

    (*b*) the lease is granted by a registered housing association and complies with the conditions set out in subsection (4) below;

the tenancy shall not be treated for the purposes of Part I of the Leasehold Reform Act 1967 (enfranchisement and extension of long leaseholds) as being a long tenancy at a low rent at any time when the interest of the landlord belongs to such a body or, as the case may be, to a registered association.

(2) The bodies referred to in subsection (1) (*a*) above are—

    (*a*) the council of a district, the Greater London Council, the council of a London borough, the Common Council of the City of London or the Council of the Isles of Scilly;

    (*b*) a development corporation established by an order made, or having effect as if made, under the New Towns Act 1965;

    (*c*) the Commission for the New Towns;

    (*d*) the Development Board for Rural Wales.

(3) The conditions mentioned in subsection (1) (*a*) above are—

    (*a*) that the lease provides for the tenant to acquire the freehold, whether under an option to purchase or otherwise, for a consideration which is to be calculated in accordance with the terms of the lease and which is reasonable, having regard to the premium or premiums paid by the tenant under the lease; and

    (*b*) that it states the landlord's opinion that by virtue of this section the tenancy will not be a long tenancy at a low rent for the purposes of the Leasehold Reform Act 1967 at any time when the interest of the landlord belongs to a body mentioned in subsection (2) above.

    (4) The conditions mentioned in subsection (1) (*b*) above are—

    (*a*) that the lease is granted at a premium which is calculated by reference to a percentage of the value of the house or of the cost of providing it;

    (*b*) that at the time when it is granted it complies with the requirements of regulations made by the Secretary of State for the purposes of this section; and

    (*c*) that it states the landlord's opinion that by virtue of this section the tenancy will not be a long tenancy at a low rent for the purpose of the Leasehold Reform Act 1967 at any time when the interest of the landlord belongs to a registered housing association.

    (5) If, in any proceedings in which it falls to be determined whether a lease complies with the condition in subsection (3) (*a*) above, the question arises whether the consideration payable by the tenant on acquiring the freehold is reasonable, it is for the landlord to show that it is.

    (6) In this section "registered housing association" means an association registered under section 13 of the 1974 Act. **[469]**

COMMENCEMENT
    See the note to s. 137, *ante.*

SUB-S. (2): COUNCIL OF A DISTRICT; COUNCIL OF A LONDON BOROUGH
    See the corresponding notes to s. 43, *ante.*

GREATER LONDON COUNCIL; COMMON COUNCIL OF THE CITY OF LONDON; COUNCIL OF THE ISLES OF SCILLY
    See the notes to s. 50, *ante.*

COMMISSION FOR THE NEW TOWNS
    See the note to s. 28, *ante.*

DEVELOPMENT BOARD FOR RURAL WALES
    See the note to s. 19, *ante.*

SUB-S. (4): SECRETARY OF STATE
    See the note to s. 2, *ante.*

LEASEHOLD REFORM ACT 1967, PART I
    See A.L.S. Vol. 162. For the meanings of "long tenancy" and "low rent" in that Part, see ss. 3 and 4, respectively, of the Act of 1967, as amended, in the case of s. 3, by s. 141 and Sch. 21, para. 3, *post.* Part I of the Act of 1967 is also amended or affected by ss. 141 and 142 and Sch. 21, *post.*

NEW TOWNS ACT 1965
    As to orders establishing development corporations, see s. 2 of that Act.

1974 ACT
    I.e., the Housing Act 1974; see s. 150, *post.* For s. 13 of that Act, see A.L.S. Vol. 223 (and see also s. 127 (1)–(3), *ante*).

REGULATIONS UNDER THIS SECTION
      At the time of going to press no regulations had been made under sub-s. (4) (*b*) above.
      As to regulations generally, see s. 151, *post.*

141. Amendments of Leasehold Reform Act 1967 etc.

Sections 1, 3, 9, 16, 23 and 29 of, and Schedules 1 and 3 to, the Leasehold Reform Act 1967 and Schedule 8 to the 1974 Act are amended as shown in Schedule 21 to this Act. **[470]**

COMMENCEMENT
      See s. 153 (4), *post*, and the note "Orders under this section" thereto.

LEASEHOLD REFORM ACT 1967, SS. 1, 3, 9, 16, 23, 29, SCHS. 1, 3.
      See A.L.S. Vol. 162. Part I of that Act (in which these provisions are included) is also affected by s. 140, *ante*, and s. 142, *post.*

1974 ACT
      I.e., the Housing Act 1974; see s. 150, *post.* For Sch 8, to that Act, see A.L.S. Vol. 223.

142. Leasehold valuation tribunals

(1) Any matter which under section 21 (1), (2) or (3) of the Leasehold Reform Act 1967 is to be determined by the Lands Tribunal shall instead be determined by a rent assessment committee constituted under Schedule 10 to the 1977 Act.

(2) A rent assessment committee shall, when constituted to make any such determination, be known as a leasehold valuation tribunal.

(3) Part I of Schedule 22 to this Act has effect with respect to leasehold valuation tribunals, and the 1967 Act is amended in accordance with Part II of that Schedule. **[471]**

COMMENCEMENT
      See s. 153 (4), *post*, and the note "Orders under this section" thereto.

LEASEHOLD REFORM ACT 1967
      See A.L.S. Vol. 162. That Act is also amended or affected by ss. 140 and 141, *ante*, and Sch. 21, *post*; and s. 21 is amended by sub-s. (3) above and Sch. 22, para, 8, *post.*

1977 ACT
      I.e., the Rent Act 1977; see s. 150, *post.* For Sch. 10 to that Act, see A.L.S. Vol. 255. That Schedule is amended by s. 71 (2), *ante*, and s. 152 (1), (3), Sch. 25, para. 56, and Sch. 26, *post.*

143. Apportionment of rents

(1) Section 20 (1) of the Landlord and Tenant Act 1927 (apportionment of certain rents and other payments) has effect as respects applications for apportionment made under that section after the passing of this Act with the substitution in the proviso of "£5" for "two pounds".

(2) The Secretary of State may by order vary the amount there mentioned.

(3) After section 20 (1) of the said Act there is inserted the following subsection—

"(1A) An order of apportionment under sections 10 to 14 of the said Act of 1854 may provide for the amount apportioned to any part of the land in respect of which the rent or payment is payable to be nil.". **[472]**

COMMENCEMENT
      Sees.153(4),*post*,andthenote"Ordersunderunder this section" thereto. Note, however, that the amendment made by sub-s. (1) above has effect as respects applications for appor-

tionment made on or after 8th August 1980 (the date on which this Act received the Royal Asssent).

PASSING OF THIS ACT
This Act was passed, *i.e.*, received the Royal Assent, on 8th August 1980.

SECRETARY OF STATE
See the note to s. 2, *ante*.

LANDLORD AND TENANT ACT 1927, S. 20 (1)
See 18, Halsbury's Statutes (3rd edn.), p. 467.

SAID ACT OF 1854
I.e., the Inclosure Act 1854; see the Landlord and Tenant Act 1927, s. 20 (1).

ORDERS UNDER THIS SECTION
At the time of going to press no order had been made under sub-s (2) above.
As to orders generally, see s. 151, *post*.

144. Landlord's failure to disclose identity or give notice of assignment: increased penalties

In relation to offences committed after the commencement of this section section 121 (1) and (5) and section 122 (5) of the 1974 Act shall have effect as if for "£200" there were substituted "£500". **[473]**

COMMENCEMENT
See s. 153 (4), *post*, and the note "Orders under this section" thereto.

1974 ACT
I.e., the Housing Act 1974, see s. 150, *post*. For ss. 121 and 122 (5) of that Act, see A.L.S. Vol. 223.

145. Houses in multiple occupation: revised penalties for certain offences

Schedule 23 to this Act shall have effect, in relation to offences committed after the commencement of this section, for the purpose of altering penalties for certain offences relating to houses in multiple occupations. **[474]**

COMMENCEMENT
See s. 153 (4), *post*, and the note "Orders under this section" thereto.

146. Houses in multiple occupation: overcrowding

(1) For section 90 of the 1957 Act (overcrowding in houses let in lodgings) there is substituted the following section—

"90. Overcrowding in houses let in lodgings

(1) If it appears to a local authority, in the case of a house within their district which is occupied by persons who do not form a single household, that an excessive number of persons is being or is likely to be accommodated on the premises having regard to the rooms available, the local authority may serve on the occupier of the premises or on any person having the control and management thereof, or on both, a notice under this subsection (an "overcrowding notice") complying with subsections (2) and (3) below and including either—

(*a*) the requirement set out in subsection (4); or
(*b*) that set out in subsection (5).

257

(2) An overcrowding notice shall state, in relation to every room on the premises, what is in the authority's opinion the maximum number of persons by whom it is suitable to be occupied as sleeping accommodation at any one time or, as the case may be, that it is in their opinion unsuitable to be occupied as sleeping accommodation.

(3) An overcrowding notice may, in relation to any room, prescribe special maxima applicable in any case where some or all of the persons occupying the room are under such age as may be specified in the notice.

(4) The requirement referred to in subsection (1) (*a*) is that the person on whom the overcrowding notice is served must refrain from—

(*a*) knowingly permitting any room to be occupied as sleeping accommodation otherwise than in accordance with the overcrowding notice; or

(*b*) knowingly permitting such number of persons to occupy the premises as sleeping accommodation that it is not possible, without—

   (i) one or more rooms to which the overcrowding notice relates being occupied as sleeping accommodation otherwise than in accordance with that notice; or

   (ii) any part of the premises which is not a room being occupied as sleeping accommodation;

to avoid persons of opposite sexes and over the age of 12 years (other than persons living together as husband and wife) occupying sleeping accommodation in the same room.

(5) The requirement referred to in subsection (1) (*b*) is that the person on whom the overcrowding notice is served must refrain from—

(*a*) knowingly permitting any room to be occupied by a new resident as sleeping accommodation otherwise than in accordance with the overcrowding notice; or

(*b*) knowingly permitting a new resident to occupy any part of the premises as sleeping accommodation if it is not possible, without—

   (i) one or more rooms to which the overcrowding notice relates being occupied as sleeping accommodation otherwise than in accordance with that notice; or

   (ii) any part of the premises which is not a room being occupied as sleeping accommodation;

both to permit the new resident to so occupy any part of the premises and avoid persons of opposite sexes and over the age of 12 years (other than persons living together as husband and wife) occupying sleeping accommodation in the same room.

(6) In subsection (5) above "new resident" means a person who was not, immediately before the date on which the overcrowding notice was served, living in the house.

(7) Where a local authority have served an overcrowding notice on any person and that notice includes the requirement referred to in subsection (5) above, the local authority may, at any time, withdraw that overcrowding notice and serve on that person, in its place, an overcrowding notice which includes the requirement referred to in subsection (4) above.

(8) Not less than seven days before serving an overcrowding notice, the local authority shall—

(a) in writing inform the occupier of the premises and any person appearing to them to have the control and management thereof of their intention to serve the notice, and

(b) ensure, so far as is reasonably possible, that every person living in the house is informed of that intention;

and shall afford to any such person an opportunity of making representations regarding their proposal to serve the notice.

(9) The local authority may from time to time serve on the occupier of premises in respect of which an overcrowding notice is in force, a notice requiring him to furnish them within 7 days with a statement in writing giving all or any of the following particulars, that is to say—

(a) the number of individuals who are, on a date specified in the notice, occupying any part of the premises as sleeping accommodation;

(b) the number of families or households to which those individuals belong;

(c) the names of those individuals and of the heads of each of those families or households; and

(d) the rooms used by those individuals and families or households respectively.

(10) Any person aggrieved by an overcrowding notice may, within twenty-one days after the date of service of the notice, appeal to the county court and—

(a) on any such appeal the court may make such order confirming, quashing or varying the notice as it thinks fit; and

(b) sections 37 and 38 of this Act shall apply in relation to an appeal under this section as they apply in relation to an appeal to the county court under Part II of this Act.

(11) A local authority may at any time, on the application of any person having an estate or interest in the house, revoke an overcrowding notice or vary it so as to allow more people to be accommodated in the house.

(12) If a local authority refuse an application under subsection (11) above, or do not within 35 days from the making of such an application, or within such further period as the applicant may in writing allow, notify the applicant of their decision on the application, the applicant may appeal to the county court, and on the appeal the court shall have power to revoke the notice or vary it in any manner in which it might have been varied by the local authority.

(13) Any person who contravenes an overcrowding notice shall be guilty of an offence and liable on summary conviction to a fine not exceeding £500.

(14) Any person who knowingly fails to comply with the requirements of a notice under subsection (9) above, or furnishes a statement which he knows is false in a material particular, shall be guilty of an offence and liable on summary conviction to a fine not exceeding £50."

(2) Nothing in this section shall affect the operation of the 1957 Act, as it had effect immediately before the commencement of this section, in relation to any notice served under section 90 before that date. **[475]**

COMMENCEMENT

See s. 153 (4), *post*, and the note "Orders under this section" thereto; and note sub-s (2) above.

HOUSE
Under the old. s. 90 of the 1957 Act, it was held that "house" meant a structure adapted, fitted and used for the purposes of human habitation, albeit not used all the year round: *Reed* v. *Hastings Corporation* (1964) 62 L.G.R. 588, C.A. In relation to the Housing Act 1961, s. 15 (1), it has been held that the term "house" used therein makes no distinction between multiple occupation in undivided parts of a building and such occupation in divided parts thereof: *Okereke* v. *Brent LBC* [1967] 1 Q.B. 42; [1966] 1 All E.R. 150, C.A.

SUB-S. (1): S. 90 (1): LOCAL AUTHORITY
For meaning, see the Housing Act 1957, s. 1, and the note thereto, A.L.S. Vol. 109.

SINGLE HOUSEHOLD
This replaces the words in the original s. 90 (1) "let in lodgings or occupied by members of more than one family". In relation to these latter words, it was held in *Wolkind* v. *Ali* [1975] 1 All E.R. 193, that where the owner allowed his house to be occupied by his large family, and it thereupon ceased to be used as a lodging-house, no offence was committed. Section 90 of the 1957 Act was amended by the Housing Act 1969, s. 58 and Sch. 8, into the form of words now used, *i.e.* "single household"; *quaere*, whether the amendment makes any difference to the result in the case; it was not thought to by Bridge, J., *ibid.*, p. 197.

LIKELY
See the note to s. 43, *ante.*

SERVE
As to the mode of service of notices, see the Housing Act 1957, s. 169 (1).

NOTICE
The prescribed form of notice under the Housing Act 1957, s. 90 (1), as originally enacted, was Form No. 4 in the Housing (Prescribed Forms) Regulations 1972, S.I. 1972 No. 228 (made under s. 178 of the Act of 1957). As to the authentication of notices, see s. 166 (2) of the Act of 1957.

S. 90 (4); KNOWINGLY PERMITTING
As to the penalty, see sub-s. (13). Knowledge on the part of the alleged offender is thought to be an essential ingredient of the offence: *Gaumont British Distributors Ltd.* v. *Henry* [1939] 2 All E.R. 808. But an offence may be committed under these subsections "knowingly" where D. has a state of mind which consists of deliberately refraining from making inquiries: shutting his eyes may be equivalent to actual knowledge. A state of mind which is merely neglecting to make such inquiries as a reasonable person would make, being constructive knowledge, has (generally) no place in the criminal law: see *Taylor's Central Garages (Exeter) Ltd.* v. *Roper* (1951) 115 J.P. 445, pp. 449–450 (Devlin, J.); also *London Computator Ltd.* v. *Seymour* [1944] 2 All E.R. 11.

OVER THE AGE, ETC.
A person attains a particular age at the commencement of the relevant anniversary of the date of his birth; see the Family Law Reform Act 1969, s. 9, A.L.S. Vol. 189.

LIVING TOGETHER AS HUSBAND AND WIFE
Note that the Act says "living together as husband and wife" and not "being husband and wife".

S. 90 (8): NOT LESS THAN SEVEN DAYS, ETC.
See the note "Not less than six months before, etc" to Sch. 19, para. 21, *ante.*

WRITING
See the note "Written; writing" to s. 5, *ante.*

S. 90 (9): WITHIN 7 DAYS
See the note "Within six months of etc" to s. 3, *ante.*

S. 90 (10): PERSON AGGRIEVED
The meaning of a "person aggrieved" may vary substantially according to the context and where, as in this instance, the statute does not define the classes of persons falling into the category of persons aggrieved the court will have to consider the purpose for which the right of appeal has been granted. There have been decisions on the meaning of "person

aggrieved" in a number of statutes and the effect of these is summarised in 1 Halsbury's Laws (4th Edn.), para. 49; see also 4 Words and Phrases (2nd Edn.), pp. 114–116. See also the note "Person" to s. 24, *ante*.

WITHIN TWENTY-ONE DAYS AFTER, ETC.
See the note "Within six months of, etc." to s. 3, *ante*.

COUNTY COURT
See the note to s. 12, *ante*.

S. 90 (12): WITHIN 35 DAYS FROM, ETC.
See the note "Within six months of, etc" to s. 3, *ante*.

S. 90 (13): CONTRAVENES AN OVERCROWDING NOTICE
The offence of contravening an overcrowding notice can only be committed so long as the premises continue to be premises of a kind to which the Housing Act 1957, s. 90 (1), as substituted by sub-s (1) above apply, *i.e.*, a house occupied by persons who do not form a single household; cf. *Wolkind* v. *Ali*, [1975] 1 All E.R. 193.

SUMMARY CONVICTION
See the note to s. 125, *ante*.

S. 90 (14): STATEMENT WHICH HE KNOWS TO BE FALSE IN A MATERIAL PARTICULAR (SUB-S. (14))
A statement may be false because of what it omits, conceals or implies, even though what is said may, taken in isolation, be true, because the statement is so partial that it is made false on account of what is withheld: *R.* v. *Lord Kylsant* [1932] 1 K.B. 442; *R.* v. *Bishirgian* [1936] 1 All E.R. 586. An ambiguous statement intended to mislead, or an expression of opinion which is not genuine, may both amount to a false statement: *R.* v. *Schlesinger* (1847) 10 Q.B.D. 670. To be made "knowingly", the statement must be either known to be false *simpliciter* or because the maker is wilfully blind to its falsity: *Taylor's Central Garages (Exeter) Ltd.* v. *Roper, supra*.

FALSE
A statement may be false on account of what it omits even though it is literally true; see *R.* v. *Lord Kylsant*, [1932] 1 K.B. 442; [1931] All E.R. Rep. 179, and *R.* v. *Bishirgian*, [1936] 1 All E.R. 586; and cf. *Curtis* v. *Chemical Cleaning and Dyeing Co., Ltd.*, [1951] 1 K.B. 805; [1951] 1 All E.R. 631, C.A., at pp. 808, 809 and p. 634 respectively, *per* Denning L.J. Whether or not any advantage accrues from the false statement is immaterial; see *Jones* v. *Meatyard*, [1939] 1 All E.R. 140, and *Stevens and Steeds, Ltd. and Evans* v. *King*, [1943] 1 All E.R. 314.

MATERIAL PARTICULAR
A particular may be material on the ground that it renders more credible another statement; see *R.* v. *Tyson* (1867), L.R. 1 C.C.R. 107.

CONSEQUENTIAL REPEAL
Consequent on this section the Housing Act 1961, s. 20, A.L.S. Vol. 131, which imposed penalties for offences under the Housing Act 1957, s. 90, A.L.S. Vol. 109, is repealed by s. 152 (3) and Sch. 26, *post*.

DEFINITIONS
For "house", see the Housing Act 1957, s. 189 (1). Note as to "overcrowding notice" and "new resident", s. 90 (1) and (6), respectively, of the Act of 1957 as substituted by sub-s. (1) above.

1957 ACT
I.e., the Housing Act 1957, see s. 150 *ante*.

147. Houses in multiple occupation: means of escape from fire

(1) Schedule 24 shall have effect in place of section 16 of the Housing Act 1961 and section 60 of the 1969 Act except in relation to notices served, undertakings accepted or orders made before the commencement of this section.

(2) In relation to a breach after the commencement of this section of an undertaking accepted under section 60 of the 1969 Act subsection (3) of that section (fine on summary conviction) shall have effect as if for "£20" there were substituted "£50".

(3) The amendments and repeals made by this Act (except subsection (2) above) shall not affect the operation of an enactment in relation to any notice served, undertaking given or order made under the provisions replaced by this section.

[476]

COMMENCEMENT
    See s. 153 (4), *post*, and the note "Orders under this section" thereto.

HOUSING ACT 1961, S. 16
    See A.L.S. Vol. 131. That section is repealed by s. 152 (3) and Sch. 26, *post*.

1969 ACT
    I.e., the Housing Act 1969; see s. 150, *post*. For s. 60 of that Act, see A.L.S. Vol. 183. That section is repealed by s. 152 (3) and Sch. 26, *post*.

148. Rent assessment panels: pensions for presidents and vice-presidents

In Schedule 10 to the 1977 Act (rent assessment committees) the following paragraph is inserted after paragraph 7—

> "7A. The Secretary of State may, with the consent of the Minister for the Civil Service, provide for the payment of pensions, allowances or gratuities to or in respect of any person nominated to act as president or vice-president of a panel.". **[477]**

COMMENCEMENT
    See s. 153 (4), *post*, and the note "Orders under this section" thereto.

SECRETARY OF STATE
    See the note to s. 2, *ante*.

PERSONS NOMINATED TO ACT AS PRESIDENT, ETC.
    I.e., under the Rent Act 1977, Sch. 10, para. 3, A.L.S. Vol. 255.

1977 ACT
    I.e., the Rent Act 1977; see s. 150, *ante*.

149. Power of local authority to require repair of houses

In section 9 of the 1957 Act (power of local authority to require repair of unfit house) after subsection (1A) there are inserted the following subsections—

> "(1B) Where a local authority, on a representation made by an occupying tenant, are satisfied that a house is in such a state of disrepair that, although it is not unfit for human habitation, the condition of the house is such as to interfere materially with the personal comfort of the occupying tenant, they may serve upon the person having control of the house such a notice as is mentioned in subsection (1A) above.
>
> (1C) In subsection (1B) above, 'occupying tenant' has the same meaning, in relation to a dwelling which consists, or forms part, of the house concerned as it has in section 104 of the Housing Act 1974". **[478]**

COMMENCEMENT
    See s. 153 (4), *post*, and the note "Orders under this section" thereto.

GENERAL NOTE
Where a house falls into disrepair, there are two separate but parallel systems to enable a local authority to compel the owner to rectify matters. They may on the one hand seek an order from the magistrates under the Public Health Act 1936: s. 92 (1) enables them to make a nuisance order where satisfied that the state of the house is prejudicial to health or a nuisance. Alternatively, the Housing Act 1957, s. 9 (1), compels a local authority itself, where satisfied that a house is unfit for human habitation, to serve a repairs notice on the person having control of the house (see *ibid*, s. 39 (2)) to execute such works as are specified in the notice and which will render the house fit for human habitation, as to which see s. 4 of the 1957 Act. Section 9 (1A) of the 1957 Act empowers a local authority to serve a repairs notice in cases of substantial disrepair but where the house is not rendered unfit thereby for human habitation. Section 9 (1B), added by s. 149 of this Act, extends the procedure further to cases of disrepair causing material interference with the personal comfort of the occupying tenant (see the Housing Act 1974, s. 104, applied by the new s. 9 (1c): s. 149 of this Act). The new s. 9 (1B) would appear apt to cover minor defects such as leaking gutters, broken windows, etc., and perhaps also more serious ones such as leaks in the roof: the overlap with the unfitness provision (s. 9 (1)) is noticeable: thus in *Summers* v. *Salford Corporation* [1943] A.C. 283; [1943] 1 All E.R. 68, H.L., a broken sash-cord has been held to render a house unfit for human habitation. However, the new s. 9 (1B) is not available where the owner is in personal occupation of the whole house.
Before the enactment of s. 149 of this Act there had been some difficulty in deciding on the interaction of the two systems. The 1936 Act procedure was limited by dicta in *Salford City Council* v. *McNally* [1975] 2 All E.R. 860, H.L., to the effect that in the nuisance procedure it was undesirable to consider the question in terms of unfitness for human habitation: health was contrasted somewhat artificially with personal comfort. After this, the Divisional Court in *National Coal Board* v. *Neath B.C.* [1976] 2 All E.R. 478, ruled that the meaning of nuisance in s. 92 (1) of the 1936 Act must be confined to its common-law sense, *i.e.* the 1936 Act procedure did not apply to defects affecting only persons in occupation of the house, but only those defects which interfered for a substantial period with neighbouring property or affecting a class of the public; not, therefore, defective running-boards or windows. Parliament has not overturned these decisions and has accepted by implication their narrowing effect on the 1936 Act procedure; it has replied by extending the 1957 Act repairs notice provisions, and so the two systems remain, as was said in *R.* v. *Kerrier D.C. ex parte Guppys* (1976) 32 P. & C.R. 411, C.A., both separate and parallel.
Notice that the procedure in s. 9 (1B) depends on the initiative in the first place of the occupying tenant. It is not conceived to be mandatory on the local authority: it "may" serve a repairs notice. By contrast, it "shall" do so where s. 9 (1) applies and as a result the s. 9 (1) procedure has been held to be mandatory on the local authority: *R.* v. *Kerrier D.C. ex parte Guppys, supra,* where, however, much was made of the contrast between "shall" in s. 9 (1) and "may" in other parts of the 1957 Act.
The new s. 9 (1B) refers back to s. 9 (1A) and so: (i) a reasonable time, not being less than 21 days, must be allowed to the person having control of the house to carry out the works; and (ii) the works must not be of internal decorative repair. In that s. 9 (1B) is not in terms dependent on its being shown that the house is unfit for human habitation, s. 39 (1) of the 1957 Act does not apply and so the local authority need not have regard to the estimated costs of the works. Also, because s. 9 (1B) applies where there is an occupying tenant, it may be that the financial position of the owner will be regarded as a factor of marginal significance in any appeal by him against a notice: cf. *Hillbank Properties Ltd.* v. *London Borough of Hackney* [1978] 3 All E.R. 343, C.A. The powers to demolish (s. 17) or close (ss. 27 to 28) the house in the event of non-repair by the owner do not apply to s. 9 (1B) as they depend on unfitness for human habitation being shown.

LOCAL AUTHORITY
For meaning, see the Housing Act 1957, s. 1, and the note thereto, A.L.S. Vol. 109.

UNFIT FOR HUMAN HABITATION
For the standard of fitness, see the Housing Act 1957, s. 4.

SERVE ... NOTICE
As to the mode of service and authentication of notices, see the Housing Act 1957, ss. 166 (2), 169 (1).

PERSON HAVING CONTROL
I.e., the person who receives the rack rent whether on his own account or as agent or trustee for any person. or would do so if the house was let at a rack rent, *i.e.*, a rent of not less than two-thirds of the full net annual value of the house: Housing Act 1957 s. 39 (2).

DEFINITIONS
   As to "person having control of the house", see the Housing Act 1957, s. 39 (2); for "house",
   see ss. 9 (3) and 189 (1) of that Act.   Note as to "occupying tenant", s. 9 (1C) of the Act
   of 1957 as inserted by this section.

1957 ACT
   I.e., the Housing Act 1957; see s. 150, *post.*

HOUSING ACT 1974, S. 104
   A.L.S. Vol. 223.

Supplemental

150. Interpretation

In this Act—

> "protected tenant" and "statutory tenant" have the same meanings as in the
> 1977 Act;

> "secure tenant" means the tenant under a secure tenancy and "secure tenancy"
> has the meaning given by section 28;

> "the 1957 Act" means the Housing Act 1957;

> "the 1969 Act" means the Housing Act 1969;

> "the 1972 Act" means the Housing Finance Act 1972;

> "the 1974 Act" means the Housing Act 1974;

> "the 1975 Act" means the Housing Rents and Subsidies Act 1975;

> "the 1977 Act" means the Rent Act 1977. **[479]**

COMMENCEMENT
   This section came into operation on the passing of this Act on 8th August 1980; see s. 153
   (3), *post.*

HOUSING ACT 1957
   See A.L.S. Vol. 109.

HOUSING ACT 1969
   See A.L.S. Vol. 109.

HOUSING FINANCE ACT 1972
   See A.L.S. Vol. 202.

HOUSING ACT 1974
   See A.L.S. Vol. 223.

HOUSING RENTS AND SUBSIDIES ACT 1975
   See A.L.S. Vol. 230.

RENT ACT 1977
   See A.L.S. Vol. 255, and for further meanings of "protected tenant" and "statutory tenant",
   see ss. 1 and 2, respectively, of that Act.

151. Regulations and orders

(1) Any power of the Secretary of State to make an order or regulations under this
Act shall be exercisable by statutory instrument subject, except in the case of
regulations under section 22 (1), 33 (2), 52 (3), 56 (7) or paragraph 11 of Schedule 3
or an order under section 52 (4), 60 or 153 to annulment in pursuance of a resolution
of either House of Parliament.

(2) No order under section 52 (4) or 60 shall be made unless a draft of it has been laid before Parliament and approved by a resolution of each House of Parliament.

(3) Any order or regulation under this Act may make different provision with respect to different cases or descriptions of case, including different provision for different areas.

(4) This section does not apply to the power of the Secretary of State to make vesting orders under section 24. **[480]**

COMMENCEMENT
This section came into operation on the passing of this Act on 8th August 1980; see s. 153 (3), *post*.

SECRETARY OF STATE
See the note to s. 2, *ante*.

STATUTORY INSTRUMENT SUBJECT ... TO ANNULMENT
For provisions as to statutory instruments generally, see the Statutory Instruments Act 1946, A.L.S. Vol. 36, and for provisions as to annulment in pursuance of a resolution of either House of Parliament (or the House of Commons only), see ss. 5 (1) and 7 (1), (2) of that Act, Vol. 32, pp. 672, 673.

LAID BEFORE PARLIAMENT
For meaning, see the Laying of Documents before Parliament (Interpretation) Act 1948, s. 1 (1), A.L.S. Vol. 56.

152. Amendments, savings, transitional provisions and repeals

(1) The enactments mentioned in Part I of Schedule 25 to this Act shall have effect subject to the amendments specified in that Schedule.

(2) The savings and transitional provisions in Part II of that Schedule shall have effect.

(3) The enactments specified in the first column of Schedule 26 to this Act are hereby repealed to the extent specified in column 3 of that Schedule. **[481]**

COMMENCEMENT
As to sub-ss. (1) and (3) above, see s. 153 (4), *post*, and the note "Orders under this section" thereto. Sub-s. (2) above came into operation on the passing of this Act on 8th August 1980, see s. 153 (3), *post*.

153. Commencement

(1) Chapter I of Part I of this Act shall come into operation on the expiry of the period of eight weeks beginning with the day on which this Act is passed.

(2) Chapter II of Part I shall come into operation on such day as the Secretary of State may by order appoint or, if no such order has been made, on the expiry of the period of eight weeks mentioned in subsection (1) above.

(3) Sections 90 to 105, 108, 112, 113, 120, 122 to 127, 130, 131, 133 to 135, 137 to 140, 150, 151, 152 (2) and 153 to 155 shall come into operation on the passing of this Act.

(4) The remaining provisions of this Act shall come into operation on such day as the Secretary of State may by order appoint; and—

    (*a*) different days may be appointed for different provisions; and
    (*b*) any provision may be brought into force on different days for England, Wales and Scotland. **[482]**

CHAPTER I OF PART I
I.e., ss. 1–27, *ante.*

EIGHT WEEKS BEGINNING WITH THE DAY ON WHICH THIS ACT IS PASSED
In calculating this period the day on which this Act was passed (*i.e.* received the Royal Assent) is to be reckoned; see *Hare* v. *Gocher*, [1962] 2 Q.B. 641; [1962] 2 All E.R. 763 and *Trow* v. *Ind Coope* (*West Midlands*), *Ltd.*, [1967] 2 Q.B. 899, at p. 909; [1967] 2 All E.R. 900, C.A. This Act was passed on 8th August 1980 and ChapterI of Part I accordingly came into force on 3rd October 1980.

CHAPTER II OF PART I
I.e., ss. 28–50, *ante.*

SECRETARY OF STATE
See the note to s. 2, *ante.*

EIGHT WEEKS MENTIONED IN SUB-S. (1) ABOVE
Since no order was appointed under sub-s. (2) above Chapter II of Part I came into force on 3rd October 1980.

PASSING OF THIS ACT
This Act was passed (*i.e.*, received the Royal Assent) on 8th August 1980.

ENGLAND; WALES
For meaning, see the Interpretation Act 1958, s. 5, Sch. 1, A.L.S. Vol. 258.

ORDERS UNDER THIS SECTION
No order was made under sub-s. (2) above (and Chapter II of Part I accordingly came into force on 3rd October 1980). The Housing Act 1980 (Commencement No. 1) Order 1980, S.I. 1980 No. 1406 (made under sub-s. (4) above), brought s. 121 into operation on 1st October 1980 and the following provisions into operation on 3rd October 1980; Parts III (ss. 80–85) and Part IV (ss. 86–89); ss. 110, 111, 114; s. 116 (1) in as far as it relates to Sch. 14, para. 6 (1) (2), and s. 116 (2); s. 128, 129, 132, 136; s. 141 except in relation to Sch. 21, para. 7; ss. 143–146, 148; s. 152 (1) in so far as it relates to Sch. 25, paras. 4, 6, 8–16, 18–20, 24–29, 31, 34, 36, 61; and s. 152 (3) in so far as it relates to the repeals in Sch. 26 of or in the Housing Act 1957, ss. 5, 43 (4), 113 (5), 119 (3), the Housing (Financial Provisions) Act 1958, ss. 43 (1), 45, the Housing Act 1961, s. 20, the Housing Act 1964, ss. 65 (1A), 66, the Housing Subsidies Act 1967, s. 24 (5), 26A, the Leasehold Reform Act 1967, Sch. 1, para. 7 (1) (*b*), the Housing Act 1969, s. 61 (6), the Housing Finance Act 1972, ss. 90–91A, the Local Government Act 1972, Sch. 22, para. 2, the Housing Act 1974, ss. 5 (3), 13 (4), (5) (*a*), 14, 19 (1), 30 (5), 31, 32 (1), (4), (8), 33 (6), 104, 114 (1), (6), (7), and the Criminal Law Act 1977, Schs. 6, 12.
The Housing Act 1980 (Commencement No. 2) Order 1980, S.I. 1980 No. 1466 (made under sub-s. (4) above), brought ss. 56–58 into operation on 6th October 1980.
The Housing Act (Commencement No. 3) Order 1980, S.I. 1980 No. 1557 (made under sub-s. (4) above), brought ss. 78, 79 and 118 into operation on 20th October 1980, and s. 107 (except in relation to Sch. 12, paras. 4, 12, 28–32), s. 147, s. 152 (1) (so far as it relates to Sch. 25, paras 21, 30) and s. 152 (3) (for some purposes) on 27th October 1980.
The Housing Act (Commencement No. 4) Order 1980, S.I. 1980 No. 1693 (made under sub-s. (4) above) brought s. 115 into operation on 11th November 1980.
The Housing Act (Commencement No. 5) Order 1980, S.I. 1980 No. 1706 (made under sub-s. (4) above) brought Part II of the Act (so far as not already in operation, and with the exception of s. 59 (3)), ss. 149, 152 (1) (in relation to Sch. 25, paras. 1–3, 17, 32, 33, 35 and 37–60) and s. 152 (3) (in relation to the repeals of 1927 c. 36, s. 16; 1951 c. 65, s. 16 (2) (*c*); 1954 c. 56, s. 43 (1) (*c*); 1964 c. 56, Sch. 4, para. 2; 1971 c. 62, ss. 7 (3), 13 (1), Sch. 1, para. 28 (*a*); 1976 c. 80, Sch. 4, Case X, Sch. 6 paras. 1, 7; 1977 c. 42 (all repeals except that of Sch. 12, paras. 4 (1), (2), 9 (1) (*b*)) into operation on 28th November 1980.
The Housing Act 1980 Commencement No. 6) Order 1980. S.I. 1980 No. 1781 (made under sub-s. (4) above) brought ss. 106, 107 (in relation to those paras. of Sch. 12 not already in operation), 109, 152 (1) (in relation to those paras. of Sch. 25, Part I not already in operation) and s. 152 (3) (in relation to the repeals of 1957 c. 56; s. 96 (*e*); 1958 c. 42, ss. 14, 15; 1969 c. 33, ss. 28A, 29B, 30, 35, 38, 86 (5); 1970 c. 44, s. 3 (1); 1972 c. 5, Sch. 3; 1973 c. 5, ss. 1 (1), 2; 1974 c. 44, ss. 38 (2) (*a*), 42, 50, 52–55, 56 (2) (*d*), 71 (3) (*a*), Sch. 5, Part I and Part II, para. 4; 1975 c. 6, Sch. 1 paras. 1–11, 12 (4) (*a*), Sch. 5, paras. 8 (3), 18; 1975 c. 57, s. 5; 1975 c. 76, Sch. 1) into operation on 15th December 1980.

At the time of going to press no order had been made under sub-s. (4) bringing into operation the other provisions of this Act falling within that subsection.
As to orders generally, see s. 151, *ante*.

154. Expenses and receipts

(1) There shall be paid out of moneys provided by Parliament the administrative expenses of the Secretary of State under this Act and any increase attributable to this Act in the sums so payable under any other enactment.

(2) Any sums received by the Secretary of State under section 102 or 131 shall be paid into the Consolidated Fund. **[483]**

COMMENCEMENT
This section came into operation on the passing of this Act on 8th August 1980; see s. 153 (3), *ante*.

SECRETARY OF STATE
See the note to s. 2, *ante*.

CONSOLIDATED FUND
The Consolidated Fund of the United Kingdom was established by the Consolidated Fund Act 1816, s. 1, see 22, Halsbury's Statutes (3rd edn.), p. 846.

155. Short title and extent

(1) This Act may be cited as the Housing Act 1980.

(2) (*Applies to Scotland.*)

(3) Sections 152 (1), 153, this section and paragraphs 11, 12, 18 and 19 of Part I of Schedule 25 extend to Northern Ireland; but this Act does not otherwise so extend.

[484]

COMMENCEMENT
This section came into operation on the passing of this Act on 8th August 1980; see s. 153 (3), *ante*.

SCHEDULES

SCHEDULE 1

Section 2

EXCEPTIONS TO RIGHT TO BUY

PART I

CIRCUMSTANCES IN WHICH RIGHT DOES NOT ARISE

1. The landlord is a local authority and the dwelling-house is held by it otherwise than under Part V of the 1957 Act.

2. The landlord is a development corporation, the Commission for the New Towns or the Development Board for Rural Wales and—

    (*a*) the dwelling-house is held by it for purposes not corresponding to those for which dwelling-houses are held by local authorities under Part V of the 1957 Act; and

    (*b*) the landlord, or on appeal the Secretary of State, is of opinion that the right to buy ought not to be capable of being exercised with respect to the dwelling-house.

3. The dwelling-house has features which are substantially different from those of ordinary dwelling-houses and which are designed to make it suitable for occupation by physically disabled persons.

4. The dwelling-house is one of a group of dwelling-houses which it is the practice of the landlord to let for occupation by persons of pensionable age and a social service or special

facilities are provided in close proximity to the group of dwelling-houses for the only or main purpose of assisting those persons.

5. The landlord has, within six weeks of the service on it of a notice claiming to exercise the right to buy the dwelling-house, applied to the Secretary of State for a determination under this paragraph, and the Secretary of State has determined that the right to buy is not to be capable of being exercised with respect to the dwelling-house; and he shall so determine if satisfied—

> (a) that the dwelling-house is designed or specially adapted for occupation by persons of pensionable age; and
>
> (b) that it is the practice of the landlord to let it only for occupation by such persons.

[485]

COMMENCEMENT
See the note to s. 1, *ante*.

PARA. 1
Part V of the Housing Act 1957 relates to the provision of housing accommodation by a local authority, which is under a duty to, carry out a periodical review of housing conditions under s. 91 of that Act and is enabled to provide accommodation as mentioned in s. 92. There are the necessary powers to acquire land: s. 96
As to the housing held otherwise than under Part V of the 1957 Act: e.g. sub-standard housing acquired under Part II of the 1957 Act (s. 12) or housing acquired by a local authority which has made a clearance order (see *ibid.*, s. 42 *et seq.*).

PARA. 2: COMMISSION FOR THE NEW TOWNS
See the note to s. 28, *ante*.

PARA. 2 (b)
As to the meaning of "of opinion" see s. 23 (1) and the note thereto.
It is not thought that there could be no judicial review of the decision (on appeal) of the Secretary of State though no appeal on point of law is provided for.

DEVELOPMENT BOARD FOR RURAL WALES
See the note to s. 19, *ante*.

SECRETARY OF STATE
See the note to s. 2, *ante*.

PARA. 4: PENSIONABLE AGE
This expression is not defined for the purposes of this Act but cf. the definition in the Social Security Act 1975, Sch. 20.

PARA. 5; WITHIN SIX WEEKS OF, ETC.
See the note "Within six months of, etc." to s. 3, *ante*.

NOTICE CLAIMING TO EXERCISE THE RIGHT TO BUY
I.e., a notice served by the tenant under s. 5, *ante*.

JURISDICTION OF COUNTY COURT
See the note to s. 1, *ante*.

DEFINITIONS
For "the right to buy", see s. 1 (2), *ante*, for "dwelling-house", see s. 3 (1), (4), *ante*, and s. 50 (2) as applied by s. 27 (1), *ante*; for "landlord", see s. 27 (2), *ante*; for "development corporation" and "local authority", see s. 50 (1) as applied by s. 27 (1), *ante*.

1957 ACT
I.e., the Housing Act 1957; see s. 150, *ante*. For Part V (ss. 91–134) of that Act, see A.L.S. Vol. 109. That Part is amended by ss. 35 (4), 90–95 and 182 (1), *ante*, and Sch. 25, paras. 5–7, *post*, and is partly repealed by s. 153 (3), *ante*, and Sch. 26, *post*.

PART II
CIRCUMSTANCES IN WHICH RIGHT CANNOT BE EXERCISED

1. The tenant is obliged to give up possession of the dwelling-house in pursuance of an order of the court, or will be so obliged at a date specified in such an order.

2. A bankruptcy petition is pending or a receiving order is in force against the person or one of the persons to whom the right to buy belongs or he is an undischarged bankrupt or has made a composition or arrangement with his creditors the terms of which remain to be fulfilled. **[486]**

COMMENCEMENT
See the note to s. 1, *ante*.

TENANT IS OBLIGED TO GIVE UP POSSESSION, ETC
As to proceedings for possession of dwelling-houses let under secure tenancies, see ss. 32–34, 87 and 89, *ante*, and Sch. 4, *post*.

THE COURT
See the note to s. 32, *ante*.

BANKRUPTCY PETITION
As to bankruptcy generally, see the Bankruptcy Act 1914 as amended by the Insolvency Act 1976, s. 1 and Sch. 1, Part I; no bankruptcy petition may, by s. 4 (1) of the 1914 Act, be presented unless the debt or debts owing to the creditor or creditors amount in aggregate to £200 or more.
As to adjudications in bankruptcy, see *ibid.*, s. 18 (1) and for the alternative of a composition scheme, s. 16. As to the discharge in bankruptcy, whereupon para. 2 will not apply to prevent the right to buy being exercised by the person in question, see s. 26 (1). The court has a discretion in the matter: *Re Barker, ex p. Constable* (1890) 25 Q.B.D. 285, C.A.

RECEIVING ORDER
As to such orders, see the Bankruptcy Act 1914, s. 3.

UNDISCHARGED BANKRUPT
For provisions as to the discharge of bankrupts, see in particular, the Bankruptcy Act 1914, s. 26, and the Insolvency Act 1976, ss. 7, 8.

COMPOSITION OR ARRANGEMENT WITH HIS CREDITORS
Arrangements between insolvent debtors and their creditors are described in 3 Halsbury's Laws (4th Edn.), at paras. 999 *et seq.*

DEFINITIONS
For "the right to buy", see s. 1 (2), *ante*; for "dwelling-house", see s. 3 (1), (4), *ante*, and s. 50 (2) as applied by s. 27 (1), *ante*.

SCHEDULE 2

Section 17

CONVEYANCE OF FREEHOLD AND GRANT OF LEASE

PART I

COMMON PROVISIONS

Rights to be conveyed or granted—general

1. The conveyance or grant shall not exclude or restrict the general words implied under section 62 of the Law of Property Act 1925, unless the tenant consents or the exclusion or restriction is made for the purpose of preserving or recognising any existing interest of the landlord in tenant's incumbrances or any existing right or interest of any other person.

[487]

Rights of support, passage of water, etc.

2.—(1) The conveyance or grant shall, by virtue of this Schedule, have the effect stated in sub-paragraph (2) below as regards—

(a) rights of support for any building or part of a building;
(b) rights to the access of light and air to any building or part of a building;

(c) rights to the passage of water or of gas or other piped fuel, or to the drainage or disposal of water, sewage, smoke or fumes, or to the use or maintenance of pipes or other installations for such passage, drainage or disposal;

(d) rights to the use or maintenance of cables or other installations for the supply of electricity, for the telephone or for the receipt directly or by landline of visual or other wireless transmissions.

(2) The effect is—

(a) to grant with the dwelling-house all such easements and rights over other propery, so far as the landlord is capable of granting them, as are necessary to secure to the tenant as nearly as may be the same rights as at the relevant time were available to him under or by virtue of the secure tenancy or any agreement collateral to it, or under or by virtue of any grant, reservation or agreement made on the severance of the dwelling-house from other property then comprised in the same tenancy; and

(b) to make the dwelling-house subject to all such easements and rights for the benefit of other property as are capable of existing in law and are necessary to secure to the person interested in the other property as nearly as may be the same rights as at the relevant time were available against the tenant under or by virtue of the secure tenancy or any agreement collateral to it, or under or by virtue of any grant, reservation or agreement made as mentioned in paragraph (a) above.

(3) This paragraph—

(a) does not restrict any wider operation which the conveyance or grant may have apart from this paragraph; but

(b) is subject to any provision to the contrary that may be included in the conveyance or grant with the consent of the tenant. **[488]**

Rights of way

3. The conveyance or grant shall include—

(a) such provisions (if any) as the tenant may require for the purpose of securing to him rights of way over land not comprised in the dwelling-house, so far as the landlord is capable of granting them, being rights of way that are necessary for the reasonable enjoyment of the dwelling-house; and

(b) such provisions (if any) as the landlord may require for the purpose of making the dwelling-house subject to rights of way necessary for the reasonable enjoyment of other property, being property in which at the relevant time the landlord has an interest, or to rights of way granted or agreed to be granted before the relevant time by the landlord or by the person then entitled to the reversion on the tenancy.
[489]

Covenants and conditions

4. The conveyance or grant shall include such provisions (if any) as the landlord may require to secure that the tenant is bound by, or to indemnify the landlord against breaches of, restrictive covenants (that is to say covenants or agreements restrictive of the use of any land or premises) which affect the dwelling-house otherwise than by virtue of the secure tenancy or any agreement collateral to it and are enforceable for the benefit of other property.

5. Subject to Parts II and III below, the conveyance or grant may include such covenants and conditions as are reasonable in the circumstances. **[490]**

Meaning of "incumbrances", "tenant's incumbrances" and "relevant time"

6. In this Schedule—

(a) "incumbrances" includes personal liabilities attaching in respect of the ownership of land or of an interest in land though not charged on the land or interest;

(b) "tenant's incumbrance" means any incumbrance on the secure tenancy which is also an incumbrance on the reversion, and any interest derived directly or indirectly out of the secure tenancy; and

(c) "the relevant time" means, in all cases, the date on which the tenant's notice claiming to exercise the right to buy is served. **[491]**

See the note to s. 1, *ante.*

PARA. 1

The application to this Schedule of s. 62 of the 1925 Act will mean that a tenant may be able to obtain under implied grant certain additional rights beyond those set out as required to be contained in the conveyance or grant in paras 2, 3 and 5. Section 62 cannot bite on a conveyance unless, first, there is a sufficient diversity of occupation prior to the conveyance: *Long* v. *Gowlett* [1923] 2 Ch. 177. Secondly, the right claimed as passing under s. 62 must be known to the law: *Phipps* v. *Pears* [1965] 1 Q.B. 76; 1964 2 All E.R. 35, C.A.; *vide infra.*

Accordingly, an implied right to any easements required to keep a tenement adjoining the dominant tenement in repair would be capable of passing under para 1 where s. 62 of the 1925 Act was not excluded: see generally *Jones* v. *Pritchard* [1908] 1 Ch. 630. The precise nature of the implied easements is uncertain, but one incident is a right in the dominant owner to enter the servient tenement to effect the repairs: *Sack* v. *Jones* [1925] 1 Ch. 235.

Other advantages which might pass on suitable facts being shown would include: a right to use the grantor's coal-shed if such right were used prior to the conveyance: *Wright* v. *Macadam* [1949] 2 K.B. 744; [1949] 2 All E.R. 565, C.A.; also a right to maintain drains on adjoining land of the grantor, subject to the same condition: *Ward* v. *Kirkland* [1967] Ch. 194; [1966] 1 All E.R. 609.

In the case of landlord and tenant, difficult questions arise under s. 62 where a right of way is enjoyed by the tenant over his landlord's adjacent land, precariously, under a first lease; where a new lease of the same premises is granted, the permissive user is altered into a user as of right by s. 62 where no mention thereof is made at the time of the second grant: *International Tea Stores Co.* v. *Hobbs* [1903] 2 Ch. 165. It may be noted that para. 3 of this Schedule, dealing with the express grant under this Act of a right of way, requires the grant only of "rights of way that are necessary for the reasonable enjoyment of the dwelling-house". There might be a case in which a right of way of an unusual kind might pass under s. 62 because of para. 1, but which was not within para. 3, e.g. possibly a means of alternative or additional access.

As to what para. 1 will not cover, because there are limits on the scope of s. 62 of the 1925 Act, first, if the right claimed to pass is in fact not appurtenant to the tenant's property, then it will not pass under the general words: *Le Strange* v. *Pettefar* (1939) 161 L.T. 300. Secondly, the general words will not pass a right not known to the law, such as a right to weather-protection: *Phipps* v. *Pears, supra.* The right claimed must have some degree of permanence: *Green* v. *Ashco Horticulturalist* [1966] 2 All E.R. 232.

PERSON

See the note to s. 24, *ante.*

PARA. 2(1)

Rights of Support

As to this, see *Dalton* v. *Angus* (1881) 6 App. Cas. 740, H.L. If the servient owner permits his property to deteriorate and imperil the support, the dominant owner may resort to self-help and carry out the repairs necessary to ensure his support: *Bond* v. *Nottingham Corporation* [1940] Ch. 429; [1940] 2 All E.R. 12; also *Jones* v. *Pritchard* [1908] 1 Ch. 630; *Sack* v. *Jones* [1925] Ch. 235.

As to rights of support of party-walls (defined in *Watson* v. *Grey* (1889) 14 Ch. D. 192) see generally the Law of Property Act 1925, s. 38 and Sch. 1, Part V, paras. 1 and 3. These rights may include a right to use the defendant's part of the wall to block recesses: *Upjohn* v. *Seymour Estates Ltd.* [1938] 1 All E.R. 614, *sed quaere:* the decision may not survive *Phipps* v. *Pears* [1965] 1 Q.B. 76; [1964] 2 All E.R. 35, C.A.

Right to Light

A right to light is restricted to particular windows as opposed to doorways: *Levet* v. *Gas Light and Coke Co* [1919] 1 Ch. 24. It is a right in the nature of a negative easement: *Colls* v. *Home and Colonial Stores Ltd.* [1904] A.C. 179, H.L. The amount of light protected by it is a question of fact, though judicial notice is taken of the fact that a higher standard of lighting obtains at the present time: *Ough* v. *King* [1967] 3 All E.R. 859; [1967] 1 W.L.R. 1547, C.A.; *Allen* v. *Greenwood* [1979] 1 All E.R. 819, C.A.

Right to Access of Air

This is the creature of the Act in that at common law there appears to be no right to a free flow of air in general: *Bryant* v. *Lefever* (1879) 4 C.P.D. 172 (no right to a flow of air through chimneys); *Harris* v. *De Pinna* (1886) 33 Ch. D. 238 (no right to flow of air over timber).

Sub-para (c) Generally
Cf. the Leasehold Reform Act 1967, A.L.S. Vol 162, s. 10(2). At common law, rights such as those to a supply of hot water or central heating could not pass under the Law of Property Act 1925, s. 62 (1), because in general, positive easements do not lie in grant: *Regis Property Co. Ltd.* v. *Redman* [1956] 2 Q.B. 612; [1956] 2 All E.R. 335, C.A.

It is thought that, on the other hand, a right to maintain drains and also a right to eaves-drop may exist in law as easements: see Jackson, *The Law of Easements and Profits* (1977) p. 187, citing *inter alia Ward* v. *Kirkland* [1967] Ch. 194; [1966] 1 All E.R. 609, and *Harvey* v. *Walters* (1873) L.R. 8 C.P. 162. But the right of free passage for gas etc., cannot exist at law and is not within s. 62 (1) of the 1925 Act: *Sovmots Investments Ltd.* v. *Secretary of State* [1979] A.C. 144; [1977] 2 All E.R. 385, H.L.

Sub-para (d)
As to the right to run telephone cables over neighbouring land, see *Lancashire Telephone Co.* v. *Manchester Overseers* (1884) 14 Q.B.D. 267.

PARA. 2 (2)

Sub-para (a)
The easements and rights which will pass include not just easements which will lie in grant, but also those passing under the Law of Property Act 1925, s. 62, which may have been precarious in origin: see the discussion under para. 1 above.

Capable of Existing in Law (Sub-para. (b))
This does not mean that the easements and rights must be legal as opposed to equitable, but rather that they were capable before 1926 of existing as legal easements: *E.R. Ives (Investment) Ltd.* v. *High* [1967] 2 Q.B. 379; [1967] 2 All E.R. 504; *Poster* v. *Slough Estates* [1968] 3 All E.R. 257; also 53 L.Q.R. 259 (Davidge) and (1969) 33 Conv. N.S. 135 (P. Jackson). Accordingly, the following cannot form the subject-matter of a grant and cannot burden the tenement referred to in sub-para. (b):
(1) Merely personal rights, e.g., rights to put out pleasure-boats: *Hill* v. *Tupper* (1863) 2 H. & C. 121;
(2) Rights which involve the expenditure of money by the servient owner are less likely to be recognised as capable of lying in grant than merely negative rights. So, there can be no right to require the servient owner to weather-proof: *Phipps* v. *Pears* [1965] 1 Q.B. 76; [1964] 2 All E.R. 35, C.A.;
(3) "Rights" exercisable only with the leave of the servient owner do not lie in grant: *Green* v. *Ashco Horticulturalist* [1966] 2 All E.R. 232; [1966] 1 W.L.R. 889;
(4) Rights whose exercise would depend on having exclusive or joint possession with the servient owner could not pass: e.g. "rights" to dump waste (*Copeland* v. *Greenhalf* [1952] Ch. 488; [1952] 1 All E.R. 809) or to use a cellar (*Grigsby* v. *Melville* [1973] 3 All E.R. 455; [1974] 1 W.L.R. 80); but a right to use a W.C. on another floor is an easement nevertheless: *Miller* v. *Emcer Products Ltd* [1956] Ch. 304; [1956] 1 All E.R. 237, C.A.

PARA. 2 (3) (b)
Section 62 of the Law of Property Act 1925 is not excluded merely by granting one right that would pass thereunder: *Hansford* v. *Jago* [1921] 1 Ch. 322; *Gregg* v. *Richards* [1926] Ch. 521.

BUILDING
See the note to s. 3, *ante*.

EASEMENTS
As to easements generally, see 14 Halsbury's Laws (4th Edn.), paras. 1 *et seq*.

PARA. 3
Necessary (sub-para. (a))
It is thought that this covers far more than mere ways of necessity within the rule of implied grant, which suffer from the defect that they may only be used for the purpose for which the way was used at the time they arose: *London Corporation* v. *Riggs* (1880) 13 Ch. D. 798; *Milner's Safe Co. Ltd.* v. *Great Northern and City Railway Co.* [1907] 1 Ch. 208.
Sub-para. (a) Generally
A grant of a right of way in general terms will permit an increased degree of use at a later stage by the grantee: *South Eastern Railway Co.* v. *Cooper* [1924] 1 Ch. 211, C.A.; *Kain* v. *Norfolk* [1949] Ch. 163; [1949] 1 All E.R. 176; *Jelbert* v. *Davis* [1968] 1 All E.R. 1182; [1968] 1 W.L.R. 589, C.A.

If the user of the grantee's premises alters, this would appear not to affect his right of way: *White* v. *Grand Hotel Eastbourne Ltd* [1913] 1 Ch. 113, C.A.

In dealing with claims to excessive user and the like, the court will take into account the surrounding circumstances, presumably, in this case, those existing at the date of the grant: *St Edmundsbury and Ipswich Diocesan Board of Finance* v. *Clark (No. 2)* [1975] 1 All E.R. 772, C.A.; also *Todrick* v. *Western National Omnibus Co. Ltd.* [1934] Ch. 561; [1934] All E.R. Rep. 25, C.A.

Notice that the grant of a right of way to Plot A cannot, as a rule, confer a right of way to Plot B beyond it: *Harris* v. *Flower* (1904) 74 L.J. Ch. 127, C.A., unless at the time of the grant, Plot A formed an actual means of access to Plot B or was intended for such use: *Nickerson* v. *Barraclough* [1979] 3 All E.R. 312.

Sub-para. (b) Generally

In making an express reservation, no re-grant is required: Law of Property Act 1925, s. 65 (1); also *Johnstone* v. *Holdway* [1963] 1 Q.B. 601; [1963] 1 All E.R. 432, C.A.

LAND

For meaning, see the Interpretation Act 1978, s. 5, Sch. 1, A.L.S. Vol. 258.

PARA. 4

If the land is so burdened, then the landlord as the original covenantor will be liable throughout, and this is the reason for para 4. If the ex-tenant should later convey or assign the property, then he himself ought to take a covenant of indemnity from the grantee or assign to protect himself against a possible liability in damages. All the actions may be heard by bringing in the indemnifiers as third parties: R.S.C. Ord. 16.

INCUMBRANCES (PARA. 6)

As to these, see further para. 1 of this Schedule.

But the difficulties in deciding what is meant by "incumbrances" in this context are not eased. In conveyances it is commonly recited that the vendor is seised "free from incumbrances": see 70 Sol. Jo. 355. In a contract of sale, such freedom is assumed; *Hughes* v. *Parker* (1841), 8 M. & W. 244; *Re Ossemsley* [1937] 3 All E.R. 774; *Re Brine and Davies' Contract* [1935] Ch. 388; *Re Stone and Savilles' Contract* [1963] 1 W.L.R. 163; [1963] 1 All E.R. 353.

It is clear from the wording of para. 1 of this Schedule that any exclusion or restriction to take account of incumbrances must be express and if it is not, a decree of specific performance will not lie for a contract, at the suit of the vendor, which contains undisclosed or unreserved incumbrances: Emmet on Title 17th Edn. pp. 132–133, citing in particular *Nottingham Patent Brick and Tile Co.* v. *Butler* (1886), 16 Q.B.D. 778.

Cf. the definition of "incumbrance" in the Law of Property Act 1925, s. 205 (1) (vii): it includes a legal or equitable mortgage and a trust for securing money, and a lien. An incumbrancer includes, no doubt, a person having authority to demand and receive the principal sum *e.g.*, the Housing Corporation or a local authority mortgagee (cf. *Banham* v. *Maycock* (1928) 138 L.T. 736). It is thought that in para. 6 matters are taken beyond those mentioned in *District Bank Ltd.* v. *Webb* [1958] 1 All E.R. 126; [1958] 1 W.L.R. 148, viz., something in the nature of a mortgage. So, a lease or sub-lease might be an incumbrance, as presumably would the right of a landlord under s. 8 of this Act to repayment of discount under the clawback therein provided in the event of early disposal. Because of para. 6 (a), it is possible that the rights of a solicitor or estate agent to unpaid fees might amount to an incumbrance: cf. *Georgiades* v. *Edward Wolfe & Co. Ltd.* [1965] Ch. 487; [1964] 3 All E.R. 433, C.A. *Quaere*, whether the rights of an individual or company under a personal agreement to remove materials or fixtures from land would be an "incumbrance" within para. 6: see *Thomas* v. *Rose* [1968] 3 All E.R. 765; [1968] 1 W.L.R. 1797, and *Poster* v. *Slough Estates Ltd.* [1969] 1 Ch. 495; [1968] 3 All E.R. 257.

Tenant s notice claiming to exercise the right to buy, i.e., a notice served by the tenant under s. 5, *ante*.

DEFINITIONS

For "the right to buy", see s. 1 (2), *ante*; for "dwelling-house", see s. 3 (1), (4), *ante*, and s. 50 (2) as applied by s. 27 (1), *ante*; for "landlord", see s. 27 (2), *ante*; for "secure tenancy", see ss. 27 (3), 28 and 49 (2), *ante*. Note as to "incumbrances", "tenants' incumbrance" and "relevant time", para. 6 above.

LAW OF PROPERTY ACT 1925, S. 62

See 27, Halsbury's Statutes (3rd edn.), p. 438.

PART II

CONVEYANCE OF FREEHOLD

General

7. The conveyance shall not exclude or restrict the all estate clause implied under section 63 of the Law of Property Act 1925, unless the tenant consents or the exclusion or restriction is made for the purpose of preserving or recognising any existing interest of the landlord in tenant's incumbrances or any existing right or interest of any other person.

8. The conveyance shall be of an estate in fee simple absolute subject to—

(*a*) tenant's incumbrances; and
(*b*) the burdens specified in paragraph 9 below;

but otherwise free of incumbrances.

9. The burdens referred to in paragraph 8 above are burdens in respect of the upkeep or regulation for the benefit of any locality of any land, building, structure, works, ways or watercourse. **[492]**

Covenants

10. The conveyance shall be expressed to be made by the landlord as beneficial owner (thereby implying the covenant set out in Part I of Schedule 2 to the Law of Property Act 1925). **[493]**

COMMENCEMENT
See the note to s. 1, *ante.*

PARA. 7: THE ALL ESTATE CLAUSE
For an excellent analysis of this see Farrand, *Contract and Conveyance* (1979), pp. 293 ff.
The Law of Property Act 1925, s. 63 (1), provides that: "Every conveyance is effectual to pass all the estate, right, title, interest, claim and demand which the conveying parties respectively have in, to or on the property conveyed, or expressed or intended so to be, or which they respectively have power to convey in, to or on the same."
The section is, as a rule, subject to a contrary intention not being expressed (*ibid.*, s. 63 (2)) but, as is the case with the incorporation into this Schedule of s. 62 of the 1925 Act, there can, unless the tenant consents to it, be no exclusion of the section, unless for the purpose of preserving the incumbrances mentioned in para. 7 (see para. 6 and the note thereto) or any existing right or interest of any other person.
The all estate clause is effective whatever the capacity of the vendor: *Taylor* v. *London and County Banking Co.* [1901] 2 Ch. 231. As to the construction of the clause, see *Re Stirrup's Contract* [1961] 1 All E.R. 805. A conveyance of land does not under s. 63 pass a beneficial interest in the proceeds of sale: *Cedar Holdings Ltd.* v. *Green* [1979] 3 All E.R. 117, C.A.; but see now *Williams & Glyn's Bank Ltd.* v. *Boland* [1980] 2 All E.R. 408, H.L. p. 415.

PARA. 9
This was required because, save under the doctrine of mutual benefit and burden (*Halsall* v. *Brizell* [1957] Ch. 169; [1957] 1 All E.R. 371) or where there are chains of indemnity covenant, the burden of positive covenants will not run with freehold land: *Austerberry* v. *Oldham Corporation* (1885) 29 Ch. D. 750, C.A.

PARA. 10
Farrand in *op. cit., supra*, p. 252, has spoken of the "obscure length" of Sch. 2 to the Law of Property Act 1925. The result of the provision is: (i) the beneficial owner covenants that he has full power to convey the subject-matter of the conveyance; (ii) that he will permit the purchaser quiet enjoyment of the property conveyed, without lawful interruption; (iii) free from all incumbrances (note, in this, however, para. 8 above of this Schedule) or indemnified against them; (iv) that the vendor will on request do what is necessary to perfect the title of the purchaser.
It has been held that a vendor is bound to take only reasonable care to get in incumbrances: *David* v. *Sabin* [1893] 1 Ch. 523, C.A. If a defect of title appears on the face of the conveyance or otherwise comes to the notice of the purchaser, these facts will not of themselves avoid liability under the above covenant: *Page* v. *Midland Railway Co.* [1894] 1 Ch. 11; *May* v. *Platt* [1900] 1 Ch. 616.

FULL POWER
  Should a squatter obtain a title to the land in question, then the vendor does not have "full power" and is in breach: *Eastwood* v. *Ashton* [1915] A.C. 900, H.L.

INCUMBRANCES
  But not within the covenant would be an incumbrance, such as a liability for chancel repairs, which was not the result of an act or omission for which the vendor was responsible: *Chivers & Sons Ltd.* v. *Air Ministry* [1955] Ch. 585; [1955] 2 All E.R. 607. A charge which ought to have been paid by the vendor but was not, e.g., for private street works, falls within the covenant: *Stock* v. *Meakin* [1900] 1 Ch. 683.

FURTHER ASSURANCE
  An example would be that of a formal assent by personal representatives: *Re King's WT* [1964] Ch. 543; [1964] 1 All E.R. 833. As to outstanding estates and interests, see *Re Repington* [1904] 1 Ch. 811.

PERSON
  See the note to s. 24, *ante*.

FEE SIMPLE ABSOLUTE
  As to this estate generally, see the Law of Property Act 1927, s. 1.

LAND
  For meaning, see the Interpretation Act 1978, s. 5, Sch. 1, A.L.S. Vol. 258.

BUILDING; STRUCTURE
  See the notes to s. 3, *ante*.

DEFINITIONS
  For "landlord", see s. 27 (2), *ante*; for "incumbrances" and "tenant's incumbrance", see para. 6, *ante*.

LAW OF PROPERTY ACT 1925, S. 63, SCH. 2, PART I
  See 27, Halsbury's Statutes (3rd edn.), pp. 441, 664.

PART III

LEASES

General

11.—(1) The lease shall be for a term of not less than 125 years at a rent not exceeding £10 per annum, and the following provisions shall have effect with respect to the other terms of the lease but subject to sub-paragraph (2) below.

(2) If a building contains two or more dwelling-houses and the landlord has, since the passing of this Act, granted a lease of one of them for a term of not less than 125 years, any lease granted in pursuance of this Chapter of the other or one of the others may be for a term expiring at the end of that term and, if it is for such a term, the assumption stated in section 6 (4) (*a*) shall be modified accordingly. **[494]**

Common use of premises and facilities

12. Where the tenant enjoyed, during the secure tenancy, the use, in common with others, of any premises, facilities or services, the lease shall include rights to the like enjoyment, so far as the landlord is capable of granting them, unless otherwise agreed between the landlord and the tenant. **[495]**

Covenants by landlord

13.—(1) There shall be implied, by virtue of this Schedule, covenants by the landlord—

   (*a*) to keep in repair the structure and exterior of the dwelling-house and of the building in which it is situated (including drains, gutters and external pipes) and to make good any defect affecting that structure;

(b) to keep in repair any other property over or in respect of which the tenant has any rights by virtue of this Schedule;

(c) to ensure, so far as practicable, that any services which are to be provided by the landlord and to which the tenant is entitled (whether by himself or in common with others) are maintained at a reasonable level and to keep in repair any installation connected with the provision of those services.

(2) The covenant to keep in repair implied by virtue of sub-paragraph (1) (a) above includes a requirement that the landlord shall rebuild or re-instate the dwelling-house and the building in which it is situated in the case of destruction or damage by fire, tempest, flood or any other cause against the risk of which it is normal practice to insure.

(3) The county court may, by order made with the consent of the parties, authorise the inclusion in the lease or in any agreement collateral to it, of provisions excluding or modifying the obligations of the landlord under the covenants implied by this paragraph, if it appears to the court that it is reasonable to do so. **[496]**

Covenant by tenant

14. Unless otherwise agreed between the landlord and the tenant there shall be implied, by virtue of this Schedule, a covenant by the tenant to keep the interior of the dwelling-house in good repair (including decorative repair). **[497]**

Avoidance of certain agreements

15. Any provision of the lease or of any agreement collateral to it shall be void in so far as it purports.

(a) to prohibit or restrict the assignment of the lease or the subletting, wholly or in part, of the dwelling-house; or

(b) to enable the landlord to recover from the tenant any part of the costs incurred by the landlord in discharging or insuring against his obligations under paragraph 13 (1) (a) or 13 (1) (b) above, or

(c) to authorise any forfeiture or impose on the tenant any penalty or disability in the event of his enforcing or relying on the preceding provisions of this Schedule;

but subject to section 19 of this Act and paragraph 16 below.

16. A provision is not void by virtue of paragraph 15 above in so far as it requires the tenant to bear a reasonable part of the costs of carrying out repairs not amounting to the making good of structural defects or of the costs of making good any structural defects falling within paragraph 17 below or of insuring against risks involving such repairs or the making good of such defects.

17. A structural defect falls within this paragraph if—

(a) the landlord has notified the tenant of its existence before the lease was granted; or

(b) the landlord does not become aware of it earlier than 10 years after the lease is granted. **[498]**

COMMENCEMENT
See the note to s. 1, *ante.*

PARA. II: BUILDING
See the note to s. 3, *ante.*

PASSING OF THIS ACT
This Act was passed, *i.e.*, received the Royal Assent, on 8th August 1980.

THIS CHAPTER
I.e., Chapter I (ss. 1–27 and Schs. 1 and 2) of Part I of this Act.

PARA. 12
There would pass, *e.g.*, the use of common toilet facilities (*Miller* v. *Emcer Products Ltd.* [1956] Ch. 304; [1956] 1 All E.R. 237, C.A.) or of stairways, lifts, rubbish chutes and the like (*Liverpool City Council* v. *Irwin* [1977] A.C. 239; [1976] 2 All E.R. 39, H.L.).

PARA. 13; SUB-PARA. (1) (a) GENERALLY

As to the standard of repair, in view of the length of the term, it is thought that the rule in *Calthorpe* v. *McOscar* [1924] 1 K.B. 716, C.A., would apply. This means that repair should be such as to maintain the premises to the standard of repair as obtained at the commencement of the term. It is true that the standard of repair required under the Housing Act 1961, A.L.S. Vol. 131, s. 32, has been held to be only that under the rule in *Proudfoot* v. *Hart* (1890) 25 Q.B.D. 42, C.A. (which requires only consideration of the requirements of a reasonably minded incoming tenant): see *Jaquin* v. *Holland* [1960] 1 All E.R. 402, C.A., but the provision there only deals with leases not exceeding seven years.

MEANING OF "REPAIR"

Little turns on the precise formula used to describe what is required of the lessee: *Calthorpe* v. *McOscar, supra*, at p. 722; also *Lister* v. *Lane and Nesham* [1893] 2 Q.B. 212, at p. 216. It is not easy to give guidance as to what is repair as opposed to renewal, because it has recently twice been held that it is a question of fact and degree: *Brew Bros Ltd.* v. *Snax (Ross) Ltd.* [1970] 1 Q.B. 612; [1970] 1 All E.R. 587, C.A.; *Ravenseft Properties Ltd.* v. *Davstone (Holdings) Ltd.* [1979] 1 All E.R. 929. What matters apparently is the proportion of the cost of the remedial work in relation to the cost of the whole building: *ibid.* Repair may thus involve quite extensive subordinate renewal: *Lurcott* v. *Wakely and Wheeler* [1911] 1 K.B. 905, C.A.; *Brew Bros Ltd.* v. *Snax (Ross) Ltd., supra*, and it is certainly no defence that the reason for the work was that the structure was defective originally: *Ravenseft Properties Ltd.* v. *Davstone (Holdings) Ltd., supra*. This appears to be made clear by the concluding words of para. 13 (1) (a).

Nor is it any defence to argue that there is no liability because the whole may collapse in time: *Parkes Drugs Stores* v. *Edwards* (1923) (unrep.), cited in West, *The Law of Dilapidations*, 8th Edn. (1979), p. 112. No covenant to repair covers the total reconstruction or rebuilding of the entire premises, because a landlord is never bound to give a new and different thing from what was demised: *Lister* v. *Lane and Nesham, supra*; *Wright* v. *Lawson* (1903) 19 T.L.R. 510, C.A.; *Pembery* v. *Lamdin* [1940] 2 All E.R. 434, C.A.; *Sotheby* v. *Grundy* [1947] 2 All E.R. 761. See further [1979] Conv. 429 (P.F. Smith). If the total collapse related to insurable risks, then para. 13 (2) would fix the landlord with liability in any event.

STRUCTURE AND EXTERIOR

It is difficult to decide whether windows form part of the structure or not. In *Holliday Fellowship Ltd.* v. *Viscount Hereford* [1959] 1 All E.R. 433; [1959] 1 W.L.R. 211, C.A., it was held that ordinary windows in bays were not part of the "structure" but in *Boswell* v. *Crucible Steel Co.* [1925] 1 K.B. 119, C.A., large plate-glass windows were held to form part of the structure (see also *Bell* v. *Plummer* (1879) "The Times", 17th June 1879: they may be structural if part of the "skin of the house").

Such parts of the building as the roof, main walls and foundations form part of the structure: *Blundell* v. *Obsdale* (1958) 171 E.G. 491; *Granada Theatres Ltd.* v. *Freehold Investment (Leytonstone) Ltd.* [1959] 2 All E.R. 176; [1959] 1 W.L.R. 570, C.A.; *Samuels* v. *Abbints Investments* (1963) 188 E.G. 689 (outside plumbing part of the structure).

To some extent the term "exterior" overlaps with "structure" but in relation to the Housing Act 1961, A.L.S. Vol. 131, s. 32 (1) it has been held that "exterior" includes the access steps and paths to a dwelling: *Brown* v. *Liverpool Corporation* [1969] 3 All E.R. 1345, C.A. Not, however, steps and flagstones at the back of the house not used for access: *Hopwood* v. *Cannock Chase D.C.* [1975] 1 All E.R. 796, C.A.

AND OF THE BUILDING ...

In relation to the matters mentioned in para. 13, the effect of the very narrow interpretation of "dwelling-house" for the purposes of the Housing Act 1961, A.L.S. Vol. 131, s. 32 (1) in *Campden Hill Towers Ltd.* v. *Gardner* [1977] Q.B. 823; [1977] 1 All E.R. 739, C.A., is reversed. It was there held that "dwelling-house" did not mean the whole of the building but only each flat taken separately.

NOTICE

A requirement of notice from the tenant to the landlord of the want of repair is applicable to the obligations to repair in the Housing Act 1957, A.L.S. Vol. 109, ss. 4 and 6, and also to those in the Housing Act 1961, A.L.S. Vol. 131, s. 32; *Morgan* v. *Liverpool Corporation* [1927] 2 K.B. 131, C.A.; *McCarrick* v. *Liverpool Corporation* [1947] A.C. 219; [1946] 2 All E.R. 646, H.L.; *O'Brien* v. *Robinson* [1973] A.C. 912; [1973] 1 All E.R. 583, H.L. It is thought that these principles apply here, whether the defects were patent or latent: *O'Brien* v. *Robinson, supra*.

RE-ENTRY

It is possible that the power of the county court under para. 13 (3) to include terms in the lease might extend to a right of re-entry in the landlord and his agent to inspect for disrepair and execute works, though this would be straining the language. In any event, such a term ought to be inserted in the lease because, if it is not, the common law will only imply a licence to enter and carry out repairs: *Saner* v. *Bilton* (1878) 7 Ch. D. 815. Not a licence to enter to inspect: *Stocker* v. *Planet Building Society* (1879) W.R. 877, C.A.

PARA. 13 (1) (*b*) GENERALLY

As to the repairing issues in this case, see the discussion under para. 13 (1) (*a*) above.

PARA. 13 (1) (*c*) GENERALLY

Services would include presumably a supply of hot water which imports a corresponding obligation on the landlord to ensure that the means of supply function: see *Liverpool City Council* v. *Irwin* [1977] A.C. 239; [1976] 2 All E.R. 39, H.L.; also *Sheldon* v. *West Bromwich Corporation* (1973) 25 P. & C.R. 360.

As to "installation", it was held in *Campden Hill Towers Ltd.* v. *Gardner* [1977] Q.B. 823; [1977] 1 All E.R. 739, C.A., that installations, in the context of the Housing Act 1961, A.L.S. Vol. 131, s. 32, meant those within the dwelling-house narrowly contrued therein— so that a boiler in the basement would not be an installation. While in terms this is not reversed by para. 13 (1) (*c*), it would be odd if it were not: after all, para. 13 involves a wider meaning than in that case to "dwelling-house". Again, while it has been held that the term "fixture" does not include a central refrigeration plant in the building (*Penn* v. *Gatenex Co. Ltd.* [1958] 1 All E.R. 712, C.A.) it is not thought that this applies here: presumably it would be an "installation connected with the provision of those services" within the last words of para. 13 (1) (*c*).

PARA. 13 (2) GENERALLY

As to partial recovery of landlord's costs, see paras. 16 and 17.

Notice that if for some reason there is no money recoverable under the insurance policy, *e.g.*, where the risk is excepted thereunder, there is under para. 13 (2) no liability to re-build: but cf. *Enlayde* v. *Roberts* [1917] 2 Ch. 414, holding the contrary.

As to the application of the insurance monies see the Fires Prevention (Metropolis) Act 1774, s. 83, and further *Sun Insurance Office* v. *Galinsky* (1914) 83 L.J.K.B. 633, C.A.

A covenant to insure is broken by the landlord if the premises are uninsured even for a very short time and no risk covered by the insurance materialises: *Doe d. Muston* v. *Gladwin* (1845) 6 Q.B. 953.

The landlord's covenant to insure only relates to what is mentioned in para. 13 (1) (*a*) and thus does not cover household articles. The insurance ought to be effected so as to cover—account being taken of inflation—the full cost of re-instatement: see *Glenifer Finance Corporation Ltd.* v. *Bamar Wood & Products Ltd.* [1978] 2 Lloyd's Rep. 49.

PARA. 14

As to the meaning of "repair" see the discussion under para. 13 (1) (*a*) above. It is thought that because of the length of the term, the standard of repair is that laid down in *Calthorpe* v. *McOscar* [1924] 1 K.B. 716, C.A. Thus, a deterioration in the locality would not afford of itself a defence to the lessee. If, contrary to this, it should be held that a lower standard applies, then it is relevant to consider the age, character and locality of the house: *Proudfoot* v. *Hart* (1890) 25 Q.B.D. 42, C.A.

As to decorative repairs, if the landlord has served a notice under the Law of Property Act 1925, s. 146 (1), claiming forfeiture, then the lessee may apply for relief under *ibid.*, s. 147 (1), and the court may wholly or partly relieve him from liability for the repairs.

PARA. 15

Sub-para. (*a*).

No doubt a total prohibition on assignment would fall within the vice of this sub-para.; also presumably a qualified covenant not to assign, etc., without the lessor's prior written consent (as to which, see the Landlord and Tenant Act 1927, s. 19 (1), and esp. *Re Gibbs and Houlder Bros' Lease* [1925] Ch. 575, C.A.). If this is right, then it would not matter that the proposed assign was a person to whom the landlord might reasonably object, but for sub-para. (*a*), such as a person with intent to use his nuisance value (see *Pimms* v. *Tallow Chandlers in the City of London* [1964] 2 Q.B. 547; [1964] 2 All E.R. 145, C.A.).

But there is one device which might avoid para. (*a*), because not in the form of a prohibition, though this is its result: a clause in the lease that the lessee, before assigning, etc., should first offer the landlord a surrender of the lease: see *Adler* v. *Upper Grosvenor Street Investment Ltd.* [1957] 1 All E.R. 229, approved in *Bocardo SA* v. *S & M Hotels Ltd.* [1979]

3 All E.R. 737, C.A. It is thought that such a clause would nevertheless fall foul of this paragraph; its result is to prohibit assignment completely: cf. the analysis in *Re Smith's Lease* [1951] 1 All E.R. 346, which the legislature appears to have adopted in preference to that in the *Bocardo* case, *supra.* Cf. Prof J. E. Adams (1979) 252 E.G. 897.

PART IV
CHARGES ON FREEHOLD

18. Where there is a charge (however created or arising) on the freehold which is not a tenant's incumbrance, then—

    (a) if it is not a rentcharge, the conveyance of the freehold in pursuance of the right to buy shall be effective to release the freehold from the charge, but the release shall not affect the personal liability of the landlord or any other person in respect of any obligation which the charge was created to secure; and

    (b) whether or not it is a rentcharge, the charge shall not affect a lease granted in pursuance of the right to buy.

19.—(1) Where the freehold is subject to a rentcharge which does not affect other land the conveyance shall be made subject to the rentcharge.

(2) Where the freehold is subject to a rentcharge which also affects other land the conveyance shall be made subject to the rentcharge but shall contain a covenant by the landlord to indemnify the tenant and his successors in title in respect of any liability arising under the rentcharge.

(3) In a case falling within sub-paragraph (2) above the landlord shall, immediately after the conveyance and if the rentcharge is of a kind which may be redeemed under the Rentcharges Act 1977, take such steps as are necessary to redeem the rentcharge, so far as it affects land owned by the landlord (including land treated by sub-paragraph (4) below as so owned).

(4) For the purposes of the Rentcharges Act 1977 and of sub-paragraph (3) above any land which has been conveyed by the landlord in pursuance of the right to buy, but subject to the rentcharge, shall be treated as if it had not been so conveyed but had continued to be owned by the landlord.

20. In this Part of this Schedule "rentcharge" has the same meaning as in the Rentcharges Act 1977; and for the purposes of paragraph 19 above land is owned by a person if he is the owner of the land within the meaning of section 13 (1) of that Act. **[499]**

COMMENCEMENT
    See the note to s. 1, *ante.*

PERSON
    See the note to s. 24, *ante.*

LAND
    For meaning, see the Interpretation Act 1978, s. 5, Sch. 1, A.L.S. Vol. 258.

DEFINITIONS
    For "the right to buy", see s. 1 (2), *ante*; for "landlord", see s. 27 (2), *ante*; for "incumbrances" and "tenant's incumbrance", see para. 6, *ante.* Note as to "rentcharge" and "land owned", para. 20 above.

RENTCHARGES ACT 1977
    As to redemption of rentcharges, see ss. 8–10 of that Act, 47, Halsbury's Statutes (3rd edn.), pp. 1195–1198; and for the meaning of "rentcharge", see s. 1 of that Act.

SCHEDULE 3

Section 28

TENANCIES WHICH ARE NOT SECURE TENANCIES

Long leases

1.—(1) A tenancy is not a secure tenancy if it is a long tenancy.

(2) For the purposes of this paragraph a long tenancy is a tenancy granted for a term certain exceeding 21 years, whether or not it is (or may become) terminable before the end of that term by notice given by the tenant or by re-entry or forfeiture, and

(a) includes a tenancy for a term fixed by law under a grant with a covenant or obligation for perpetual renewal, unless it is a tenancy by sub-demise from one which is not a long tenancy; but

(b) does not include a tenancy granted so as to become terminable by notice after a death, unless it is a shared ownership tenancy.

(3) For the purposes of this paragraph a tenancy is a "shared ownership tenancy" if—

(a) it is granted by a housing association which, at the time of the grant, is registered under section 13 of the 1974 Act;

(b) it is granted at a premium which is calculated by reference to a percentage of the value of the dwelling-house or of the cost of providing it; and

(c) at the time it is granted it complies with the requirements of the regulations then in force under section 140 (4) (b) of this Act or, in the case of a tenancy granted before any such regulations have been brought into force, it complies with the first such regulations to be in force. **[500]**

Premises occupied under contract of employment

2.—(1) A tenancy is not a secure tenancy if the tenant is an employee of the landlord or, if not such an employee, is an employee of—

(a) a local authority;

(b) a development corporation;

(c) the Commission for the New Towns;

(d) a county council; or

(e) the Development Board for Rural Wales;

and his contract of employment requires him to occupy the dwelling-house for the better performance of his duties.

(2) In this paragraph "contract of employment" means a contract of service or of apprenticeship, whether express or implied and (if express) whether oral or in writing. **[501]**

Social service and educational premises

3. A tenancy is not a secure tenancy if the tenant is an employee of the landlord and—

(a) the terms of the tenancy provide for the tenancy to terminate on the tenant ceasing to be employed by the landlord;

(b) the dwelling-house is held by the landlord for the purpose of any of its functions under the Education Act 1944 or under any of the enactments specified in Schedule 1 to the Local Authority Social Services Act 1970; and

(c) the dwelling-house forms part of a building held for those purposes or is within the curtilage of such a building. **[502]**

Land acquired for development

4. A tenancy is not a secure tenancy if the dwelling-house is on land which has been acquired for development (within the meaning of section 22 of the Town and Country Planning Act 1971) and the dwelling-house is used by the landlord, pending development of the land, as temporary housing accommodation. **[503]**

Accommodation for homeless persons

5. A tenancy granted in pursuance of section 3 (4), 4 (3) or 5 (6) of the Housing (Homeless Persons) Act 1977 is not a secure tenancy before the expiry of a period of twelve months

beginning with the date on which the tenant has received the notification required by section 8 (1) of that Act or, if he received a notification under section 8 (5) of that Act, that notification, unless he has before the expiry of that period been notified by the landlord that the tenancy is to be regarded as a secure tenancy. **[504]**

Temporary accommodation for persons seeking employment

6. A tenancy of a dwelling-house within any district or London borough which was granted to a person who was not immediately before the grant resident in the district or London borough is not a secure tenancy before the expiry of one year from the grant if—

(a) it was granted to that person for the purpose—

(i) of meeting his need for temporary accommodation within the district or London borough in order to work there; and

(ii) of enabling him to find permanent accommodation there; and

(b) before the grant of the tenancy—

(i) the tenant obtained employment, or an offer of employment, within the district or London borough; and

(ii) the landlord notified the tenant in writing of the circumstances in which this exception applies and that in its opinion the proposed tenancy would fall within this exception;

unless the tenant has before the expiry of that year been notified by the landlord that the tenancy is to be regarded as a secure tenancy. **[505]**

Short-term arrangements

7. A tenancy is not a secure tenancy if—

(a) the dwelling-house has been leased to the landlord with vacant possession for use as temporary housing accommodation;

(b) the terms on which it has been leased include provision for the lessor to obtain vacant possession from the landlord on the expiry of a specified period or when required by the lessor;

(c) the lessor is not a body which is capable of granting secure tenancies; and

(d) the landlord has no interest in the dwelling-house other than under the lease in question or as mortgagee. **[506]**

Temporary accommodation during works

8. A tenancy is not a secure tenancy if—

(a) the dwelling-house has been made available for occupation by the tenant or his predecessor in title while works are carried out on the dwelling-house which he previously occupied as his home; and

(b) the tenant (or his predecessor in title) was not a secure tenant of that other dwelling-house at the time when he ceased to occupy it as his home. **[507]**

Agricultural holdings

9. A tenancy is not a secure tenancy if the dwelling-house is comprised in an agricultural holding (within the meaning of the Agricultural Holdings Act 1948) and is occupied by the person responsible for the control (whether as tenant or as servant or agent of the tenant) of the farming of the holding. **[508]**

Licensed premises

10. A tenancy is not a secure tenancy if the dwelling-house consists of or comprises premises licensed for the sale of intoxicating liquor for consumption on the premises. **[509]**

Student lettings

11. A tenancy of a dwelling-house is not a secure tenancy before the expiry of the period of exemption if—

(a) it was granted for the purpose of enabling the tenant to attend a designated course at an educational establishment; and (*b*) before the grant of the tenancy the landlord notified him in writing of the circumstances in which this exception applies and that in its opinion the proposed tenancy would fall within this exception;

unless the tenant has before the expiry of that period been notified by the landlord that the tenancy is to be regarded as a secure tenancy.

A landlord's notice under sub-paragraph (*b*) above shall specify the educational establishment which the person concerned proposes to attend.

In this paragraph—

"designated course" means any course of a kind designated in regulations made by the Secretary of State for the purposes of this paragraph;
"educational establishment" means a university or establishment of further education; and
"the period of exemption" means, in a case where the tenant attends a designated course at the educational establishment specified in the landlord's notice, the period ending six months after the tenant ceases to attend that (or any other) designated course at that educational establishment and, in any other case, the period ending six months after the grant of the tenancy. **[510]**

1954 Act tenancies

12. A tenancy is not a secure tenancy if it is one to which Part II of the Landlord and Tenant Act 1954 applies. **[511]**

Almshouses

13. A licence to occupy a dwelling-house is not a secure tenancy if—

(*a*) the licence was granted by an almshouse charity; and
(*b*) any sum payable by the licensee under the licence does not exceed the maximum contribution that the Charity Commissioners have from time to time authorised or approved for the almshouse charity as a contribution towards the cost of maintaining its almshouses and essential services in them.

In this paragraph "almshouse charity" means a corporation or body of persons which is a charity within the meaning of the Charities Act 1960 and which is prevented by its rules or constituent instrument from granting a tenancy of the dwelling-house. **[512]**

LONG LEASES (PARA. 1)

If the tenant has an option to determine a term certain exceeding 21 years within the first 21 years, its existence will not attract security of tenure and the right to buy; nor its exercise. The same result follows from a right of re-entry or forfeiture in the landlord.

If a landlord has an option to determine enabling him to terminate the tenancy by notice within the first 21 years then it seems that the mere existence of the option (even if it is not in fact exercised) will prevent the tenancy from being a long tenancy within para. 1. This would mean that the tenant would enjoy, *ab initio*, full security and, if applicable, the right to buy.

PARA. 1 (*a*)

A lease with a covenant or obligation for perpetual renewal takes effect, by the Law of Property Act 1922, Sch. 15, para. 5, as a term for 2,000 years from its date of commencement; there is a parallel provision catching contracts for such terms in para. 7 (1), *ibid.*

In view of the penal consequences of these provisions, it has been held that the covenant to renew must plainly state an intention that it should itself be reproduced in the renewed lease: *Green* v. *Palmer* [1944] Ch. 328; [1944] 1 All E.R. 670; *Parkus* v. *Greenwood* [1950] Ch. 644; [1950] 1 All E.R. 436, C.A.; but in *Re Hopkin's Lease, Caerphilly Concrete Products Ltd.* v. *Owen* [1972] 1 All E.R. 248, C.A., there was just such a reproduction, with disastrous consequences for the landlord. See further *Marjorie Burnett, Ltd.* v. *Barclay* (1980), Times, 18th December.

PARA. 1 (*b*)

By the Law of Property Act 1925, s. 149 (6), a lease or underlease for life or for a term determinable with life (which is excluded from the definition of "term of years absolute" in *ibid.*, s. 205 (1) (xxvii)) takes effect as a lease or underlease for a term of ninety years terminable on the death of the original lessee (or the survivor if there was a joint tenancy) by at least one month's notice on the relevant quarter-day, as provided in the Act. This also applies to contracts for a term for life.

The above also applies to terms determinable on the marriage of the lessee.

PARA. 2: PREMISES OCCUPIED UNDER CONTRACT OF EMPLOYMENT
Since even a licence is capable of being a secure tenancy (see s. 48) it was necessary to have a separate exception for service occupancy. The occupation must be related to the services, not for some other reason: see *Smith* v. *Seghill Overseers* (1875) L.R. 10 Q.B. 347. As to instances of occupancy within para 2: see *Tennant* v. *Smith* [1892] A.C. 150, H.L. (bank employees); *Machon* v. *McLoughlin* (1926) 11 T.C. 83 (servant of lunatic asylum); *National Steam Car Co. Ltd.* v. *Barham* (1919) 122 L.T. 315 (chauffeur or resident caretaker); *Langley* v. *Appelby* [1976] 3 All E.R. 391 (policeman). The servant's occupation is deemed to be that of the landlord: *Mayhew* v. *Suttle* (1854) 4 E. & B. 347.

LAND REQUIRED FOR DEVELOPMENT (PARA. 4)
By the Town and Country Planning Act 1971, A.L.S. Vol. 212, s. 22 (1), "development" means the carrying out of building, engineering, mining or other operations in, or over land, or the making of any material change in the use of any buildings or other land.

By s. 22 (2), certain uses are not development, notably, in this context:
   (a) The carrying out of works for the maintenance, improvement, or other alteration of any building affecting only the interior of the building;
   (b) The carrying out by a local authority or statutory undertakers of any works for the purpose of inspecting, repairing or renewing any sewers, mains, pipes, cables or other apparatus.

ACCOMMODATION FOR HOMELESS PERSONS (PARA. 5)
By the Housing (Homeless Persons) Act 1977, s. 3 (4), if a local authority have reason to believe that an applicant may be homeless (as to which, see s. 1) and have a priority need (see s. 2) they must secure that accommodation is made available for his occupation pending any decision which they may make as a result of their inquiries. It is thought that they must actually believe: *Re Banks* [1916] 2 K.B. 621; *Nakkuda Ali* v. *M.F. de S. Jayaratne* [1951] A.C. 66, P.C. A civil action in damages will lie against a housing authority for loss or damage suffered by the applicant as a result of a breach of duty by the authority: *Thornton* v. *Kirklees Metropolitan Borough Council* [1979] Q.B. 626; [1979] 2 All E.R. 349, C.A. A declaration injunction may be: *De Falco* v. *Crawley B.C.*, [1980] 1 All E.R. 913, C.A.

Where a person is homeless or threatened with homelessness, then by s. 4 (3), a housing authority must secure that accommodation is available for his occupation for such period as they consider will give him a reasonable opportunity of himself securing accommodation.

AGRICULTURAL HOLDINGS (PARA. 9)
For the definition of "agricultural holding" see the Agricultural Holdings Act 1948, s. 1 (1): it is the aggregate of the agricultural land comprised in a contract of tenancy, but not a contract under which the land is let to the tenant during his continuance in any office, appointment or employment held under the landlord. (In such cases see, however, the Rent (Agriculture) Act 1976, A.L.S. Vol. 250, and the Rent (Agriculture) Amendment Act 1977.)

"Agricultural land" means, by the Agricultural Holdings Act 1948, s. 1 (2), land used for agriculture for the purposes of a trade or business, and also land designated by the Minister of Agriculture under the Agriculture Act 1947, A.L.S. Vol. 46, s. 109 (1). "Contract of tenancy" is defined in the 1948 Act, s. 2: it includes land let on a tenancy for less than from year to year (e.g. 364 days: overruling *Land Settlement Association Ltd.* v. *Carr* [1944] K.B. 657; 1944 2 All E.R. 126, C.A.). The test is whether the land used as a whole is substantially used for agricultural purposes: *Hawkins* v. *Jardine* [1951] 1 K.B. 614; [1951] 1 All E.R. 320, C.A. A dwelling-house used as part of the agricultural land may be agricultural land, but this is a question of fact: cf. *Harrison-Broadley* v. *Smith* [1964] 1 All E.R. 867, C.A.

LICENSED PREMISES (PARA. 10)
Whereas an off-licence tenancy would fall within the Landlord and Tenant Act 1954, Part II, A.L.S. Vol. 87, s. 23 (1) as a "business", an on-licence tenancy is excluded from that Act by *ibid.*, s. 43 (1) (d).

STUDENT LETTINGS (PARA. 11)
Unlike the exemption from the Rent Act 1977, A.L.S. Vol. 255, s. 8, the present exception is not limited to landlords who are specified educational or other institutions (as to which see the Protected Tenancies (Exceptions) Regulations 1974, S.I. No. 1366 and the Restricted Tenancies (Further Exceptions) Regulations 1976, S.I. No. 905).

Regulations under this para. See The Secure Tenancies (Designated Courses) Regulations 1980, S.I. 1980 No. 1407 (providing that tenancies granted to enable tenant to attend designated courses at university or in further education are not secure).

BUSINESS PREMISES (PARA. 12)
By the Landlord and Tenant Act 1954, Part II, A.L.S. Vol. 87, s. 23 (1), the 1954 Act applies to any tenancy where the property comprised in the tenancy is or includes premises which are occupied by the tenant for the purposes of a business carried on by him or for those and other purposes.

Premises
The term is to be understood in a wide, popular sense: *Metropolitan Water Board* v. *Paine* [1907] 1 K.B. 285; *Whitley* v. *Stumbles* [1930] A.C. 544, H.L. "Premises" include the whole property in one occupation or ownership: *Cadbury Bros. Ltd.* v. *Sinclair* [1934] 2 K.B. 389.

Business
(i) *In general*
"Business" is an imprecise term but it is wider that mere trade. In general, there ought to be an undertaking carried on for gain or reward, though a profit need neither result nor even be aimed at: *South-West Suburban Water Co.* v. *St Marylebone Union* [1904] 2 K.B. 174. It is thought that there must be a continuous process (*Smith* v. *Anderson* (1880) 15 Ch. D. 247, C.A.) but within a general area of a businessman's activities, even isolated speculations outside his usual area of operations are still business or trading activities: cf. *Martin* v. *Lowry* [1927] A.C. 312, H.L. (venture into linen sales); *Rutledge* v. *I.R.C.* (1929) 14 T.C. 490; *I.R.C.* v. *Livingston* (1926) 11 T.C. 538.

(ii) *Scope of Landlord and Tenant Act 1954, s. 23 (1)*
    (a) *"Occupied"*
The fact that the tenant is forced out of occupation by, *e.g.*, a fire will not prevent his being in occupation for the purposes of the Act if he has an *animus revertendi*: *I & H Caplan* v. *Caplan (No. 2)* [1963] 2 All E.R. 930; *Morrison Holdings Ltd.* v. *Manders Property Ltd.* [1976] 2 All E.R. 205, C.A. A seaside seasonal business is within the 1954 Act Part II: *Teasdale* v. *Walker* [1958] 3 All E.R. 207, C.A., but not an incorporeal right: *Land Reclamation Co Ltd.* v. *Basildon D.C.* [1979] 2 All E.R. 993, C.A.

    (b) *"Business"*
See above for a general discussion of the term. Under the 1954 Act, Part II, it has been held that a board of hospital governors may run a business: *Hills (Patents) Ltd.* v. *University College Hospital Board of Governors* [1956] 1 Q.B. 90; [1955] 3 All E.R. 365, C.A.; as may a tennis club (*Addiscombe Garden Estates Ltd.* v. *Crabbe* [1958] 1 Q.B. 513; [1957] 3 All E.R. 563, C.A.).
    A tenant who sub-lets flats but who is resident on the premises running them may have a business tenancy: *Lee-Verhulst (Investments) Ltd.* v. *Harwood Trust* [1972] 3 All E.R. 619, C.A.; but see however *Bagettes Ltd.* v. *G.P. Estates Co. Ltd.* [1956] Ch. 290; [1956] 1 All E.R. 729, C.A.
    If the user of the premises is primarily residential, then the fact that there is a small, incidental or insignificant business user will not of itself bring the matter within s. 23 (1) of the 1954 Act: *Cheryl Investments Ltd.* v. *Saldanha* [1979] 1 All E.R. 5, C.A. (some trading carried on from a residential flat); *Lewis* v. *Weldcrest Ltd.* [1978] 3 All E.R. 1226, C.A. (taking in of lodgers). Part-time activity (*e.g.* a Sunday School) may not be a business: *Abernethie* v. *Kleiman* [1970] 1 Q.B. 10; [1969] 2 All E.R. 790, C.A.

    (c) *Mixed business and residential user*
Plainly, if the lease states the purpose of the tenancy, then this should be conclusive. If it does not, then the purpose may be inferred from the nature of the premises and the circumstances: *Wolfe* v. *Hogan* [1949] 2 K.B. 194; [1949] 1 All E.R. 70, C.A. Residential *de facto* occupation of business premises will not convert them into a dwelling: cf. *Williams* v. *Perry* [1924] 1 K.B. 436. As to the purpose of the letting, it is a question of fact for the county court judge to decide: *Whiteley* v. *Wilson* [1953] 1 Q.B. 77; [1952] 2 All E.R. 940, C.A. Equally, a residential tenancy cannot be converted into a business tenancy by some business user: *Vickery* v. *Martin* [1944] K.B. 679; [1944] 2 All E.R. 167, C.A.

SCHEDULE 4

GROUNDS FOR POSSESSION OF DWELLING-HOUSE LET UNDER SECURE TENANCIES

PART I

GROUNDS ON WHICH COURT MAY ORDER POSSESSION

Ground 1

Any rent lawfully due from the tenant has not been paid or any obligation of the tenancy has been broken or not performed. **[513]**

Ground 2

The tenant or any person residing in the dwelling-house has been guilty of conduct which is a nuisance or annoyance to neighbours, or has been convicted of using the dwelling-house or allowing it to be used for immoral or illegal purposes. **[514]**

Ground 3

The condition of the dwelling-house or of any of the common parts has deteriorated owing to acts of waste by, or the neglect or default of, the tenant or any person residing in the dwelling-house and, in the case of any act of waste by, or the neglect or default of, a person lodging with the tenant or a sub-tenant of his, the tenant has not taken such steps as he ought reasonably to have taken for the removal of the lodger or sub-tenant.

In this paragraph "the common parts" means any part of a building comprising the dwelling-house, and any other premises which the tenant is entitled under the terms of the tenancy to use in common with the occupiers of other dwelling-houses let by the landlord.

[515]

Ground 4

The condition of any relevant furniture has deteriorated owing to ill-treatment by the tenant or any person residing in the dwelling-house and, in the case of any ill-treatment by a person lodging with the tenant or a sub-tenant of his, the tenant has not taken such steps as he ought reasonably to have taken for the removal of the lodger or sub-tenant.

In this paragraph "relevant furniture" means any furniture provided by the landlord for use under the tenancy or for use in any of the common parts (within the meaning given in ground 3). **[516]**

Ground 5

The tenant is the person, or one of the person, to whom the tenancy was granted and the landlord was induced to grant the tenancy by a false statement made knowingly or recklessly by the tenant. **[517]**

Ground 6

The dwelling-house was made available for occupation by the tenant or his predecessor in title while works were carried out on the dwelling-house which he previously occupied as his only or principal home and—

(a) he (or his predecessor in title) was a secure tenant of that other dwelling-house at the time when he ceased to occupy it as his home;

(b) he (or his predecessor in title) accepted the tenancy of the dwelling-house of which possession is sought on the understanding that he would give up occupation when, on completion of the works, the other dwelling-house was again available for occupation by him under a secure tenancy; and

(c) the works have been completed and the other dwelling-house is so available. **[518]**

Ground 7

The dwelling-house is overcrowded, within the meaning of the 1957 Act, in such circumstances as to render the occupier guilty of an offence. **[519]**

Ground 8

The landlord intends, within a reasonable time of obtaining possession of the dwelling-house—

- (a) to demolish or reconstruct the building or part of the building comprising the dwelling-house; or
- (b) to carry out work on that building or on land let together with, and thus treated as part of, the dwelling-house;

and cannot reasonably do so without obtaining possession of the dwelling-house. **[520]**

Ground 9

The landlord is a charity within the meaning of the Charities Act 1960 and the tenant's continued occupation of the dwelling-house would conflict with the objects of the charity.

[521]

Ground 10

The dwelling-house has features which are substantially different from those of ordinary dwelling-houses and which are designed to make it suitable for occupation by a physically disabled person who requires accommodation of a kind provided by the dwelling-house and—

- (a) there is no longer such a person residing in the dwelling-house; and
- (b) the landlord requires it for occupation (whether alone or with other members of his family) by such a person. **[522]**

Ground 11

The landlord is a housing association or housing trust which lets dwelling-houses only for occupation (alone or with others) by persons whose circumstances (other than merely financial circumstances) make it especially difficult for them to satisfy their need for housing; and—

- (a) either there is no longer such a person residing in the dwelling-house or the tenant has received from a local authority an offer of accommodation in premises which are to be let as a separate dwelling under a secure tenancy; and
- (b) the landlord requires the dwelling-house for occupation (whether alone or with other members of his family) by such a person. **[523]**

Ground 12

The dwelling-house is one of a group of dwelling-houses which it is the practice of the landlord to let for occupation by persons with special needs and—

- (a) a social service or special facility is provided in close proximity to the group of dwelling-houses in order to assist persons with those special needs;
- (b) there is no longer a person with those special needs residing in the dwelling-house; and
- (c) the landlord requires the dwelling-house for occupation (whether alone or with other members of his family) by a person who has those special needs. **[524]**

Ground 13

The accommodation afforded by the dwelling-house is more extensive than is reasonably required by the tenant and—

- (a) the tenancy vested in the tenant, by virtue of section 30 of this Act, on the death of the previous tenant;
- (b) the tenant was qualified to succeed by virtue of subsection (2) (b) of that section; and
- (c) notice of the proceedings for possession was served under section 33 of this Act more than six months, but less than twelve months, after the date of the previous tenant's death. **[525]**

PART I

GROUNDS ON WHICH COURT MAY ORDER POSSESSION

GENERAL NOTE

By s. 34 (3) (*a*), the court may not make an order for possession unless it considers it reasonable to do so. By analogy with identical words in the Rent Act 1977, A.L.S. Vol. 255, s. 98 (1), a further obstacle is thus imposed on a landlord's right to possession on the termination of the lease at common law: see *Kennealy* v. *Dunne* [1977] 2 All E.R. 16, p. 22. As to the burden of proof of reasonableness, see further s. 34 (3) and the note thereto: it is conceived that it will be on the landlord. As to the rules for the exercise of the county court judge's discretion, see also s. 34 (3) and the note thereto.

GROUND I: RENT LAWFULLY DUE

Cf. this term in the Rent Act 1977, A.L.S. Vol. 255, Sch. 15, Part I, para. 1. Rent is not lawfully due in relation to this provision, if it is tendered, albeit late, by the tenant before the institution of proceedings: *Bird* v. *Hildage* [1948] 1 K.B. 91; 1947 2 All E.R. 7, C.A. If the rent arrears are only paid before judgment is given, however, it is lawfully due, but *prima facie* such a payment would make it unreasonable to make the order for possession, unless for instance the tenant was shown to have a bad record: *Dallenty* v. *Pellow* [1951] 2 K.B. 858; [1951] 2 All E.R. 716, C.A.; also *Hayman* v. *Rowlands* [1957] 1 All E.R. 321, C.A. It is thought that these principles will apply to Ground I *mutatis mutandis*.

ANY OBLIGATION OF THE TENANCY

Cf. the same words used in the Rent Act 1977, A.L.S. Vol. 255, Sch. 15, Part I, para. 1. It is thought accordingly that, as under the Rent Acts, personal covenants will not come within this Ground for possession: cf. *R.M.R. Housing Society* v. *Combs* [1951] 1 K.B. 486; [1951] 1 All E.R. 16, C.A. Taking in lodgers amounts to breach of a covenant against business user: *Tender* v. *Sproule* [1947] 1 All E.R. 193, C.A.

As to waiver, an unqualified acceptance of rent for a period after the breach has taken place will waive the breach, as will a demand for such rent, though waiver does not operate forwards so that in the case of continuing breaches, *e.g.* the covenant to repair, a fresh cause of action accrues after the period of waiver lapses. The landlord, his agent or servant must have actual, imputed or presumed knowledge, as the case may be, of the basic facts which in law constitute a breach, but actions are judged objectively and one cannot both demand rent for a future period and elect for forfeiture. See generally: *Central Estates (Belgravia) Ltd.* v. *Woolgar (No. 2)* [1972] 3 All E.R. 610, C.A.; *David Blackstone Ltd.* v. *Burnetts (West End) Ltd.* [1973] 3 All E.R. 782; *Metropolitan Properties Co Ltd.* v. *Cordery* (1979) 251 E.G. 567, C.A.

As a rule, a demand for rent "without prejudice" to the right to forfeit is regarded as self-contradictory and operates nevertheless as waiver: *Segal Securities Ltd.* v. *Thoseby* [1963] 1 Q.B. 887; 1963 1 All E.R. 500; also *Richards* v. *De Freitas* (1975) 29 P. & C.R. 1. If, however, the same attitude is adopted as prevails under the Rent Acts, then it may be that a qualified acceptance of rent in the case of a non-continuing breach will not necessarily be waiver, the matter being a question of fact: *Oak Property Co Ltd.* v. *Chapman* [1947] K.B. 886; [1947] 2 All E.R. 1, C.A.

A demand for rent arrears due before the breach is not waiver: *Price* v. *Worwood* (1859) 4 H. & N. 512. A landlord's mere silence cannot of itself amount to waiver: *West Country Cleaners (Falmouth) Ltd.* v. *Saly* [1966] 3 All E.R. 210, C.A.

GROUND 2: NUISANCE OR ANNOYANCE

If the same interpretation of this term obtains as is the case with the Rent Act 1977, A.L.S. Vol. 255, Sch. 15, Part I, Case 2, "annoyance" widens the ambit of the case beyond the common-law understanding of "nuisance": it is any conduct likely to trouble an occupier: *Tod-Heatley* v. *Benham* (1889) 40 Ch. D. 80, C.A.; *Frederick Platts & Co Ltd.* v. *Grigor* [1950] 1 All E.R. 941, C.A. So even if noise created was insufficient to amount to a nuisance, it could be an annoyance: *Chapman* v. *Hughes* (1923) T.L.R. 260.

Of itself, it may be presumed by analogy with the Rent Acts, the occupation of the premises by the mistress of the tenant would not necessarily be an annoyance: *Frederick Platts & Co Ltd.* v. *Grigor, supra*, but should the tenant be convicted of using the premises for immoral purposes, *aliter*. Again, the use of premises for an illegal purpose such as storing stolen goods or drugs is "allowing" the premises to be used for an illegal purpose though the user of the premises might not form an essential constituent element in the crime: *S Schneiders & Sons Ltd.* v. *Abrahams* [1925] 1 K.B. 301, C.A. Nor is it necessary, in this, that the user for an illegal purpose be continuous or frequent. A completely incidental user of the premises for the crime does not fall within Ground 2: cf. *Waller & Son Ltd.* v. *Thomas* [1921] 1 K.B. 541 (illegal user of television); *Abrahams* v. *Wilson* [1971] 2 All E.R. 1114, C.A. (unknowing possession of drugs).

GROUND 3

The present Ground is wider than that in the Rent Act 1977, A.L.S. Vol. 255, Sch. 15, Part I, Case 3, in that it includes the common user parts, such as lifts and staircases, which do not form part of the "dwelling-house" let to the tenant if he has a flat: see *Liverpool City Council* v. *Irwin* [1977] A.C. 239; [1976] 2 All E.R. 39, H.L., and *Campden Hill Towers Ltd.* v. *Gardner* [1977] Q.B. 823; [1977] 1 All E.R. 739, C.A. Accordingly, deliberate damage to commonly used toilets might be covered: see *Miller* v. *Emcer Products Ltd.* [1956] Ch. 304; [1956] 1 All E.R. 237, C.A.

WASTE

Waste is tortious and independent of covenant. There are two kinds of waste which are relevant here. Voluntary waste is the first category: it is damage caused by an injurious act on the land such as demolition of a house: *Buckland* v. *Butterfield* (1820) 2 Brod. and Bing. 54; *Cole* v. *Green* (1672) 1 Lev. 390. It does not matter that what is replaced is an improvement: cf. *Doherty* v. *Allman* (1878) 3 App. Cas. 709, H.L.; *Meux* v. *Cobley* [1892] 2 Ch. 253. *Quaere*, whether it would be reasonable to order possession in such a case.

The second type of waste is permissive waste, i.e. wrongfully allowing by neglect the premises to fall into a dilapidated or ruinous condition. Thus it is permissive waste to allow the rafters or spars of a house to rot because the house is uncovered: see Coke, Co. Litt. 53a and 53b; also *Cheetham* v. *Hampson* (1791) 4 T.R. 318; *Anon* (1702) 11 Mod. Rep. 7 (non-repair of rooves and fences); *Hutton* v. *Warren* (1836) 1 M. & W. 466 (leaving land uncultivated is not waste at common law); *Robertson* v. *Wilson* 1922 S.L.T. (Sh. Ct.) 21 (damp caused by absence of tenant for winter is waste).

A reasonable user of the premises for the purposes for which they were let is not waste, *e.g.* destruction of the floor by its use as a warehouse-floor: *Manchester Bonded Warehouse Co* v. *Carr* (1880) 5 C.P.D. 507; also *Saner* v. *Bilton* (1878) 7 Ch. D. 815.

GROUND 5: FALSE STATEMENT MADE KNOWINGLY OR RECKLESSLY

A statement may be false because of what it omits, conceals or implies, even though what is said may, taken in isolation, be true, because the statement is so partial that it is made false on account of what is withheld: *R.* v. *Lord Kylsant* [1932] 1 K.B. 442; *R.* v. *Bishirgian* [1936] 1 All E.R. 586. An ambiguous statement intended to mislead, or an expression of opinion which is not genuine, may both amount to a false statement: *R.* v. *Schlesinger* (1847) 10 Q.B.D. 670. To be made "knowingly", the statement must either be known to be false *simpliciter* or false because the tenant is wilfully blind to its falsity: *Roper* v. *Taylor's Central Garages (Exeter) Ltd.* (1951) 2 T.L.R. 284; *R.* v. *Parker* [1977] 2 All E.R. 37.

As to "recklessly", on a subjective view, this would involve making a false statement not caring whether it were true or false: *R.* v. *Mackinnon* [1959] 1 Q.B. 150; [1958] 3 All E.R. 657; *R.* v. *Staines* (1974) 60 Cr. App. Rep. 160.

It is not possible to predict whether the subjective test above as to "recklessly" will be adopted in relation to Ground 5 by the courts, or whether they will opt for an objective view, under which what is required to be shown is a high degree of negligence on the part of the maker of the statement, irrespective of his honest belief in the truth of what was said: see *R.* v. *Russell* [1953] 1 W.L.R. 77; [1952] 2 All E.R. 842, C.A.; *R.* v. *Grunwald* [1963] 1 Q.B. 935; [1960] 3 All E.R. 380. A subjective test was adopted in relation to the Criminal Damage Act 1971, A.L.S. Vol. 199, s. 1 (1), *viz.* that a man is reckless when he knows of the risk but continues in his action: *R.* v. *Briggs* [1977] 1 All E.R. 475.

GROUND 7: OVERCROWDING

Under the Housing Act 1957, A.L.S. Vol. 109, s. 77 (1), a dwelling-house is deemed to be overcrowded at any time when the number of persons sleeping in the house either

     (*a*) is such that any two of those persons, being persons ten years old or more of opposite sexes and not being persons living together as husband and wife, must sleep in the same room; or

     (*b*) is, in relation to the number and floor-area of the rooms of which the house consists, in excess of the permitted number of persons, as to which see *ibid.*, Sch. 6.

By s. 77 (2), in determining the number of persons sleeping in a house, no account is to be taken of a child under one year old; a child between one and ten years counts as a one-half unit.

Section 78 of the 1957 Act provides for offences. By s. 78 (1) (as amended by the Criminal Law Act 1977, A.L.S. Vol. 249, s. 31 (6) and (9)) if the occupier of a dwelling-house causes or permits it to be overcrowded, he is guilty of an offence with a penalty of a fine on summary conviction not exceeding £25 plus a further £25 for each subsequent day of continuance of the offence after conviction.

"Cause", presumably, in this context, means to bring about the overcrowding: *Stiles* v. *Galinski* [1904] 1 K.B. 615. But to "permit" is far wider: in *Korton* v. *West Sussex*

288

County Council (1903) 72 L.J.K.B. 514, dealing with "causes or permits" in the Fertilizers and Feeding Stuffs Act 1893, it was said that "causes" *prima facie* referred to a person taking part in an act; but "permits" was a wider word, as where a state of affairs came about by leave of the persons permitting it. A degree of control and direction is required both to cause and to permit: cf. *Shave* v. *Rosner* [1954] 2 Q.B. 113; [1954] 2 All E.R. 280. In relation to the Dangerous Drugs Act 1965, s. 5 (a), an occupier only "permits" the use of cannabis if he has reason to suspect the user: *Sweet* v. *Parsley* [1970] A.C. 132; [1969] 1 All E.R. 347, H.L.

GROUND 8: LANDLORD INTENDS

In relation to the use of the same terms in the Landlord and Tenant Act 1954, s. 30 (1) (f) (as a ground for obtaining possession, that the landlord may show an intention to demolish, etc., the premises) it has been held, in reasoning which it is presumed would be applicable here also, that the burden of proof is on the landlord to show a firm intention or decision. This is contrasted with a mere hope: *Cunliffe* v. *Goodman* [1950] 2 K.B. 237; [1950] 1 All E.R. 720, C.A. The relevant time for proof of the requisite intention is that of the hearing: *Betty's Café Ltd.* v. *Phillips Furnishing Stores Ltd.* [1957] Ch. 67; [1957] 1 All E.R. 1, C.A. *Quaere* though, what would happen if the landlord did not in fact then put his intentions into action: it is thought that, by analogy with the 1954 Act, he would not thereby be unable to retain possession: see *Reohorn* v. *Barry Corporation* [1956] 2 All E.R. 742, C.A.

REASONABLE TIME

As to this, it is thought, again by analogy with the 1954 Act, that it ought to be understood as meaning a reasonably short time, *i.e.* a few months at the very most, probably only a few weeks: cf. *Livestock Underwriting Agency* v. *Corbett and Newson* (1955) 165 E.G. 469.

POSSESSION

It is thought that, as was the case with the 1954 Act until the passing of the Law of Property Act 1969, A.L.S. Vol. 187, s. 7 (see now s. 31A of the Landlord and Tenant Act 1954) it will not matter under this Ground for possession that the landlord only requires possession for a short time: *Little Park Service Station Ltd.* v. *Regent Oil Co Ltd.* [1967] 2 Q.B. 655; [1967] 2 All E.R. 257. Also, a landlord who can show a need only for part of the dwelling-house might succeed in obtaining possession of the whole nevertheless: cf. *Fernandez* v. *Walding* [1968] 2 Q.B. 606; [1968] 1 All E.R. 994, C.A.

PART II

SUITABILITY OF ACCOMMODATION

1.—(1) For the purposes of this Part of this Act, accommodation is suitable if it consists of premises—

(a) which are to be let as a separate dwelling under a secure tenancy, or

(b) which are to be let as a separate dwelling under a protected tenancy (other than one of a kind mentioned in sub-paragraph (2) below) within the meaning of the 1977 Act,

and, in the opinion of the court, the accommodation is reasonably suitable to the needs of the tenant and his family.

(2) The kind of protected tenancy referred to in sub-paragraph (1) above is one under which the landlord might recover possession of the dwelling-house under one of the Cases in Part II of Schedule 15 to the 1977 Act (cases where court must order possession).

2. In determining whether it is reasonably suitable to those needs regard shall be had to—

(a) the nature of the accommodation which it is the practice of the landlord to allocate to persons with similar needs;

(b) the distance of the accommodation available from the place of work or education of the tenant and of any members of his family;

(c) its distance from the home of any member of the tenant's family if proximity to it is essential to that member's or the tenant's well-being;

(d) the needs (as regards extent of accommodation) and means of the tenant and his family;

(e) the terms on which the accommodation is available and the terms of the secure tenancy;

(*f*) if any furniture was provided by the landlord for use under the secure tenancy, whether furniture is to be provided for use in the other accommodation, and, if it is, the nature of that furniture;

but where possession is sought on ground 7, accommodation otherwise reasonably suitable to the needs of the tenant and his family shall not be deemed not to be so by reason only that the permitted number of persons, computed under Schedule 6 to the 1957 Act in relation to the number and floor area of the rooms in it, is less than the number of persons living in the dwelling-house of which possession is sought.

3. Where the landlord is not a local authority for the purposes of Part V of the 1957 Act, a certificate of such an authority certifying that the authority will provide suitable accommodation for the tenant by a date specified in the certificate shall be conclusive evidence that suitable accommodation will be available for him by that date, if the dwelling-house of which possession is sought is situated in the district for supplying the needs of which the authority has power under that Part of that Act. **[526]**

PART II
SUITABILITY OF ACCOMMODATION
OTHER THAN OF A KIND MENTIONED IN SUB-PARA. (2) (SUB-PARA (1) (*b*))
In particular, the Rent Act 1977, Sch. 15, Part II, sets out a number of Cases in which, once the landlord has proved the matters set out therein, there is no discretion in the court to refuse to make the order for possession. Of these, in relation to Case 11 (owner-occupiers who can satisfy the "relevant date" requirement) it has been held that it is not necessary for the landlord to prove that his requirement of possession is "reasonable": all that is required is proof of *bona fide* want and genuine intent: *Kennealy* v. *Dunne* [1977] Q.B. 837; [1977] 2 All E.R. 16, C.A., criticised 128 N.L.J. 729. Also, the "greater hardship" provision (this is contained in the Rent Act 1977, A.L.S. Vol. 255, Sch. 15, Part III, para. 1) does not apply to Case 11: but in the case of a landlord who is a joint tenant then both must require the premises for use as their residence: *Tilling* v. *Whiteman* [1978] 3 All E.R. 1103, C.A.

FAMILY (PARA. 2)
See s. 50 (3).

EXTENT OF ACCOMMODATION (PARA. 2 (*d*))
In deciding these question, if the analogy of the Rent Act applies, a court is entitled to take into account not only the physical character of the accommodation, but also environmental matters, *e.g.* whether what is proposed is suitate in a busy thoroughfare as opposed to the tenant's present residence in a quiet locality: *Redspring Ltd.* v. *Francis* [1973] 1 All E.R. 640, C.A. But only in so far as such matters relate to the character of the property itself: *Siddiqui* v. *Rashid*, [1980] 3 All E.R. 184, C.A. In that "extent" is mentioned by Parliament, it is thought that, as with the Rent Acts, the needs of the tenant and his family as regards furniture might be taken into account: cf. *Mykolyshin* v. *Noah* [1971] 1 All E.R. 48, C.A.

PARA. 2 (*e*)
It is thought that shared accommodation intended to replace non-shared accommodation might not be suitable alternative accommodation: cf. *Selwyn* v. *Hamill* [1948] 2 All E.R. 70, C.A.; *Bernard* v. *Towers* [1953] 1 W.L.R. 1203. C.A.

It is not thought that the offer of replacing a term of years with a periodic tenancy is suitable: *Scrace* v. *Windust* [1955] 2 All E.R. 104, C.A.

SCHEDULE 5

Section 58

APPLICATION OF LANDLORD AND TENANT ACT 1954 TO ASSURED TENANCIES

1. The exceptions and modifications referred to in section 58 (1) and (2) of this Act are as follows.

2. Sections 23, 43 and 56 to 60B do not apply.

3. In relation to an assured tenancy the expression "the holding" (which is defined for the purposes of Part II in section 23 (3)) means the property comprised in the tenancy.

4.—(1) Section 30 applies as if—

(a) for paragraph (d) in subsection (1) there were substituted the following paragraph—
"(d) that the landlord has offered and is willing to provide or secure the provision of suitable alternative accommodation for the tenant,";

(b) in subsection (2) for the words from "a tenancy" to the end there were substituted the words "an assured tenancy or successive assured tenancies"; and

(c) at the end there were added the subsections set out in sub-paragraph (2) below.

(2) The following are the subsections added to section 30 in its application to assured tenancies—

"(4) Accommodation shall be deemed to be suitable if it consists of either—

(a) premises which are to be let as a separate dwelling such that they will then be let on an assured tenancy or on a protected or secure tenancy, or

(b) premises to be let as a separate dwelling on terms which will, in the opinion of the court, afford to the tenant security of tenure reasonably equivalent to that afforded by this Part of this Act in the case of an assured tenancy,

and, in the opinion of the court, the accommodation fulfils the conditions mentioned below.

(5) The conditions are that the accommodation is reasonably suitable to—

(a) the needs of the tenant and his family as regards proximity to place of work;

(b) the means of the tenant; and

(c) the needs of the tenant and his family as regards extent and character; and

that if any furniture was provided for use under the assured tenancy in question, furniture is provided for use in the accommodation which is either similar to that so provided or is reasonably suitable to the needs of the tenant and his family.

(6) Accommodation shall not be deemed to be suitable to the needs of the tenant and his family if the result of their occupation of the accommodation would be that it would be an overcrowded dwelling-house for the purposes of the Housing Act 1957.

(7) In this section—

"assured tenancy" has the same meaning as in section 56 of the Housing Act 1980;

"protected tenancy" means a protected tenancy within the meaning of the Rent Act 1977, other than one under which the landlord might recover possession of the dwelling-house under one of the Cases in Part II of Schedule 15 to that Act (cases where the court must order possession); and

"secure tenancy" has the same meaning as in section 28 of the Act of 1980.".

5. Section 31A applies as if in subsection (1) (a) for the words "for the purposes of the business carried on by the tenant" there were substituted "as a residence for the tenant and his family".

6. Section 34 applies as if in subsection (2) (b) for the words from "tenancies" to the end there were substituted the words "assured tenancies (within the meaning of section 56 of the Housing Act 1980); and".

7. Section 37 applies as if for subsections (2) and (3) there were substituted the following subsection—

"(2) The said amount shall be the rateable value of the holding.".

8. Section 38 applies as if in subsection (2) the words from the beginning to the end of paragraph (b), and subsection (3), were omitted.

9. Section 63 (7) (a) applies as if reference to section 23 (3) of the Act of 1954 were a reference to paragraph 3 of this Schedule. **[527]**

PARA. 2
Sections 23, 43, and 56–60B of the 1954 Act are excluded. Section 23 defines "business" and also the "holding", which latter term has a special definition in the case of assured tenancies

in para. 3. Section 43 of the 1954 Act contains specific exclusions from the 1954 Act; in that s. 56 is excluded, there can never be an assured tenancy from the Crown. The other excluded sections deal with cases where the interest of the landlord is held by a government department, etc.

PARA. 3
This gives a definition of holding for the purpose of assured tenancies. Because of the residence requirement in s. 56 (3) (c) of this Act, it is thought that the tenant will in principle occupy the whole of the holding as his residence.

PARA. 4
Section 30 of the 1954 Act is to apply in an altered manner because assured tenancies are residential. Hence the altered para. (d) of s. 30 to apply in the case of assured tenenacies. If the ground is made out, however, then it is thought that the court has no overriding discretion to refuse to make the order for possession: *Lyon* v. *Commercial Properties* [1958] 2 All E.R. 767, C.A.

There is a statutory definition of what is to be suitable alternative accommodation in para. 4 (2)–(7). As to the new s. 30 (4) and (5), see the discussion in Schedule 4 Part II to this Act.

Paragraph 4 does not otherwise modify s. 30 of the 1954 Act; a brief summary of relevant principles as they might apply to assured tenancies may be helpful.

In relation to paras. (a) to (c) of s. 30 (1) (breaches of covenants), a discretion exists in the court to consider all relevant circumstances and the court is not confined to those breaches specified in a landlord's s. 30 notice: *Eichner* v. *Midland Bank Executor & Trustee Co. Ltd.* [1970] 2 All E.R. 597, C.A. The discretion is not even necessarily confined strictly to those matters set out in paras. (a) to (c): *Turner & Bell* v. *Searles* (1977) 33 P. & C.R. 208, C.A.

As to s. 30 (1) (f) (landlord's intention to demolish, etc): "intention" has been taken to connote a firm decision and this is not so if the person said to "intend" has not moved from the zone of contemplation to the valley of decision: *Cunliffe* v. *Goodman* [1950] 2. K.B. 237; [1950] 1 All E.R. 720, C.A. This was so where the landlord lacked the present means or ability to carry out the work: *Reohorn* v. *Barry Corporation* [1956] 2 All E.R. 742, C.A. The evidence of the landlord's intention, in the case of, for instance, a body corporate, is not to be confined to a formal resolution but could be ascertained from minutes or evidence from its officers: see *Poppett's (Caterers) Ltd.* v. *Maidenhead Corporation* [1970] 3 All E.R. 289, C.A. The relevant date for determining whether the landlord has the requisite intention is that of the hearing and not that of service of the landlord's notice of opposition: *Betty's Cafés Ltd.* v. *Phillips Furnishing Stores Ltd.* [1957] Ch. 67; [1957] 1 All E.R. 1, C.A.

But it is vital to note the ill-effects from the landlord's point of view of his having a right of re-entry to do repairs in the lease. If he is to get within the terms of para. (f) of s. 30 (1), the landlord must show a requirement of "possession" but, unfortunately, to the extent that the lease entitles him to re-enter and carry out works of repair or reconstruction, para. (f) will not avail him. This is because it has been held to apply only where the lease does not enable the landlord to re-enter to carry out the works in question: *Heath* v. *Drown* [1973] A.C. 498; [1972] 2 All E.R. 561, H.L.; *Price* v. *Esso Petroleum Co. Ltd.* (1980) 255 E.G. 243, C.A.

In relation to s. 30 (1) (g) (landlord's intention to occupy the holding for the purposes, or partly for the purposes, of his business, or as a residence) it is thought that a resolution by the landlord, if a company, plus counsel's undertaking that on obtaining possession, there would be occupation, establishes a sufficiently fixed intention within para. (g): *Espresso Coffee Machine Co. Ltd.* v. *Guardian Assurance Co. Ltd.* [1959] 1 All E.R. 458, C.A. The occupation by a company controlled by the landlord is not occupation by the landlord: *Tunstall* v. *Stiegmann* [1962] 2 Q.B. 593; [1962] 2 All E.R. 517, C.A.; but that of the landlord personally in partnership with another person suffices: *Re Crowhurst Park* [1974] 1 All E.R. 991.

To "intend" within para. (g), the landlord, as with para. (f), has to establish a reasonable prospect of being able to bring about occupation by means of his own volition: thus, where planning permission is required, the test is whether there is a reasonable prospect of success in the application therefor: *Gregson* v. *Cyril Lord Ltd.* [1962] 3 All E.R. 907, C.A. But it is not always necessary to show an intention to make actual physical use of the whole premises: *Method Developments Ltd.* v. *Jones* [1971] 1 All E.R. 1027, C.A.

PARA. 5
Section 31A (which restricts the ability of the landlord to obtain possession under s. 30 (1) (f)) is modifed so as to include, in the case of assured tenancies, residential user

of the holding for the tenant and his family. If then, under s. 31A (1) (*a*), the tenant agrees to give the landlord, in a new tenancy, rights of access which would reasonably enable the landlord to carry out the work without obtaining possession of the holding and without interfering to a substantial extent or for a substantial time with the residential user of the holding by the tenant or his family, the landlord will fail to obtain possession under para. (*f*).

Section 31A (1) (*a*) is, for all the above, not an easy provision to comprehend: *Price* v. *Esso Petroleum Co. Ltd.* (1980) 255 E.G. 243, p. 245. It appears to cover work which cannot be done by the landlord under any right of re-entry under the contractual term: *Heath* v. *Drown* [1973] A.C. 498; [1972] 2 All E.R. 561, H.L. In dealing with a tenant's defence based on s. 31A (1) (*a*) as applied by para. 5, *semble*, the court will look at the physical effects of the work, not its consequence from a residential point of view: this because, as the amendment in para. 5 does not touch the words "with the holding ..." in s. 31A (1) (*a*) which refer one back to s. 24 of the 1954 Act, the reasoning in *Redfern* v. *Reeves* (1978) 37 P. & C.R. 364, C.A., applies.

PARA. 6
Section 34 of the 1954 Act is modified by para. 6 in such a way that the benefit of s. 34 (1) (*c*) in particular is to apply. Therefore, the effect of any improvement carried out by the tenant or certain of his predecessors in title and completed not more than 21 years before the application for the new tenancy was made will, subject to s. 34 (2), be disregarded in assessing the rent.

This will be beneficial to the tenant under an assured tenancy; but the following may be mentioned as useful to the landlord:

(*a*) The jurisdiction to award an interim rent during interim continuation of the tenancy under s. 24: s. 24A. This applies s. 34 to the court's determination, but regard must be had to the current rent. The court therefore determines a rent for a hypothetical yearly tenancy: *English Exporters (London) Ltd.* v. *Eldonwall Ltd.* [1973] 1 All E.R. 726.

(*b*) If the contractual term contains a rent review clause, then the reviewed rent will reflect the effect on the holding of improvements carried out by the tenant at his own expense, as well as any other improvements: *Ponsford* v. *H.M.S. Aerosols Ltd.* [1978] 2 All E.R. 837, H.L.

PARA. 8
Section 38 of the 1954 Act is modified by para. 8 in such a way as to enable compensation restriction agreements to be made where during the five years immediately preceding that on which the tenant quits, there was a change in the occupier. In any other case, however, the accrued right to compensation conferred by s. 38 (2) on occupiers for five years immediately preceding the date for quitting cannot be excluded or modified by agreement. If the period is less than five years then such agreements are not avoided.

PARA. 9
The jurisdiction of the county court (s. 63) is modified in relation to assured tenancies, so that the special definition of the "holding" in para. 3 is applied to s. 63.

SCHEDULE 6

Section 59

NOTE: Section 59 (3) and Sch. 6 will not be brought into force. In their place, for amendments to the Rent Act 1977, Schs. 11, 12, see the Regulated Tenancies (Procedure) Regulations 1980, S.I. 1980 No. 1696, which became effective on 28th November 1980.

APPLICATIONS FOR REGISTRATION OF RENT

1. Schedule 11 to the 1977 Act (applications for registration of rent) is amended as follows.

2. For paragraphs 2 and 3 there are inserted the following paragraphs—

"2.—(1) Where the application is made jointly by the landlord and the tenant and it appears to the rent officer, after making such inquiry, if any, as he thinks fit and considering any information supplied to him in pursuance of paragraph 1 above, that the rent specified in the application is a fair rent, he may register that rent without further proceedings.

(2) Where the rent officer registers a rent under this paragraph he shall notify the landlord and tenant accordingly.

3.—(1) In the case of an application which does not fall within paragraph 2 above, the officer shall serve on the landlord and on the tenant a notice—

    (*a*) stating the rent specified in the application;

    (*b*) stating any sum specified in the application in accordance with section 67 (2) (*b*) of this Act; and

    (*c*) inviting the person on whom the notice is served to state, within a period of not less than seven days after the service of the notice, whether he wishes the rent officer to consider, in consultation with the landlord and the tenant, what rent ought to be registered for the dwelling-house.

(2) Where, in pursuance of section 67 (2) (*b*), the application was accompanied by details of the landlord's expenditure in connection with the provision of services, a notice under this paragraph shall be accompanied by a copy of those details.

3A. If, after service of a notice by the rent officer under paragraph 3 above, no request is made within the period specified in the notice for the rent to be considered as mentioned in paragraph 3 (1) (*c*) above, the rent officer after considering what rent ought to be registered or, as the case may be, whether a different rent ought to be registered, may—

    (*a*) determine a fair rent and register it as the rent for the dwelling-house; or

    (*b*) confirm the rent for the time being registered and note the confirmation in the register; or

    (*c*) serve a notice under paragraph 4 (2) below."

    3. For sub-paragraph (1) of paragraph 4 there is substituted the following sub-paragraph—

"(1) Where, in response to a notice served by the rent officer under paragraph 3 above, the landlord or the tenant asks for the rent to be considered as mentioned in paragraph 3 (1) (*c*), the rent officer shall serve a notice under this paragraph.".

    4. In sub-paragraph (2) of paragraph 4, for the word "notice" there are inserted the words "notice, or 14 days in a case falling within paragraph 3 (1) (*b*) above".

    5. After sub-paragraph (3) of paragraph 4 there is inserted the following sub-paragraph—

"(4) The rent officer may, where he considers it appropriate, arrange for consultations in respect of one dwelling-house to be held together with consultations in respect of one or more other dwelling-houses."

    6. In paragraph 5, for the words "and shall", immediately after sub-paragraph (*b*), there is substituted—

"5A. Where a rent has been registered or confirmed by the rent officer under paragraph 3A or 5 above, he shall".

    7. In paragraph 6 (1) for "5" there is substituted "5A". **[528]**

GENERAL NOTE

It is thought that one of the aims of the amendments to the Rent Act 1977, Sch. 11, affected by this Schedule is that of reducing the number of consultations between a rent officer and landlord and tenant. Thus, where, say, a landlord applies alone for registration of a fair rent, so that the new para. 3 (1) of Sch. 11 (inserted by para. 2 of this Schedule) applies, the rent officer's notice served on landlord and tenant must invite the person on whom it is served to himself initiate the consultation procedure (new para. 3 (1) (*c*)). If neither party requests consultation, then, by the new para. 3A of Sch. 11 (inserted by para. 2 of this Schedule) the rent officer may determine/confirm a fair rent; equally, at his discretion, he may by notice under Sch. 11, para. 4 (as amended by paras. 3 to 5 of this Schedule) set the consultation procedure in motion.

PARA. 2

In the case of joint applications for registration of a fair rent, where the requirements of the new para. 2 (1) of Sch. 11 to the 1977 Act are satisfied, a rent may be registered by the rent officer without consultation. If these requirements are not satisfied, then the new para. 3 of Sch. 11 will apply: if neither party requests consultation, it is at the rent officer's discretion (new para. 3A (*c*)) whether to require it or not. Under the rules replaced from the commencement of this Schedule, in the case of joint applications, if the rent officer was not satisfied as above, then he had to consult.

The new para. 3 (1) (*b*) of Sch. 11 (inserted by para. 2) requires the rent officer's notice to state any sum payable by the tenant to the landlord for services, which sum must be specified and accompanied by details of the expenditure incurred by the landlord in providing them. This is to enable tenants to challenge such sums, but not where there was a joint application and the rent officer registers a rent without consultation.

PARA. 3

The alteration to para. 4 of Sch. 11 to the 1977 Act is consequential on the changes in the consultation procedure made by para. 2 above.

PARA. 4

In a case where service charges are made by the landlord and challenged by a tenant and either party has then asked for consultation (new para. 4 (1)) the rent officer must serve a para. 4 (2) notice, as is the case where consultation is required for any other reason, but the minimum time for consultation, in the case of service charges challenges, is to be, thanks to para. 4 of this Schedule, 14 days after service of the rent officer's notice.

DEFINITIONS

For "rent officer" see the Rent Act 1977, s. 63 (4), A.L.S. Vol. 255; for "landlord" and "tenant" see s. 152 (1) of that Act.

1977 ACT

I.e., the Rent Act 1977; see s. 150, *ante*. The s. 67 (2) (*b*) referred to is that substituted by s. 59 (2), *ante*.

SCHEDULE 7

Section 66

AMENDMENT OF SCHEDULE 15 TO 1977 ACT

The following new Part is inserted at the end of Schedule 15 to the 1977 Act (grounds for possession of dwelling-houses let on or subject to protected or statutory tenancies)—

"PART V

Provisions applying to Cases 11, 12 and 20

1. In this Part of this Schedule—

'mortgage' includes a charge and 'mortgagee' shall be construed accordingly;
'owner' means, in relation to Case 11, the owner-occupier; and
'successor in title' means any person deriving title from the owner, other than a purchaser for value or a person deriving title from a purchaser for value.

2. The conditions referred to in paragraph (*c*) in each of Cases 11 and 12 and in paragraph (*e*) (ii) of Case 20 are that—

(*a*) the dwelling-house is required as a residence for the owner or any member of his family who resided with the owner when he last occupied the dwelling-house as a residence;

(*b*) the owner has retired from regular employment and requires the dwelling-house as a residence;

(*c*) the owner has died and the dwelling-house is required as a residence for a member of his family who was residing with him at the time of his death;

(*d*) the owner has died and the dwelling-house is required by a successor in title as his residence or for the purpose of disposing of it with vacant possession;

(*e*) the dwelling-house is subject to a mortgage, made by deed and granted before the tenancy, and the mortgagee—

(i) is entitled to exercise a power of sale conferred on him by the mortgage or by section 101 of the Law of Property Act 1925; and

(ii) requires the dwelling-house for the purpose of disposing of it with vacant possession in exercise of that power; and

(*f*) the dwelling-house is not reasonably suitable to the needs of the owner, having regard to his place of work, and he requires it for the purpose of disposing of it with vacant possession and of using the proceeds of that disposal in acquiring, as his residence, a dwelling-house which is more suitable to those needs.". **[529]**

GENERAL NOTE

This Schedule widens the scope of Cases 11 and 12 and also applies to new Case 20 (s. 67), in Sch. 15, Part II, to the Rent Act 1977 (mandatory orders for possession) by stating six requirements which may be fulfilled by an owner-occupier requiring possession, or, in the case of para. 2 (*e*), a mortgagee asking for sale.

PURCHASER FOR VALUE (PARA. 1)

In relation to the Land Registration Act 1925, s. 20 (1) and s. 59 (6), it has been held that a purchaser for valuable consideration does not include a purchaser who has acted in bad faith: *Peffer* v. *Rigg* [1978] 3 All E.R. 745. But, a "purchaser for money or money's worth" within the Land Charges Act 1925, s. 13 (2) (now the Land Charges Act 1972, s. 4 (6)) has been held to include a person who paid a nominal sum: *Midland Bank Trust Co. Ltd.* v. *Green* (1980), Times, 15th December, H.L. If this sort of reasoning were to apply here, then it would mean that such a purchaser could not claim to be a successor in title and within the benefit of the new Part V of Sch. 15 to the Rent Act 1977.

REQUIRED (PARA. 2)

In relation to Case 11, "required" has been held to mean no more than proof by the landlord of a bona fide want and genuine intent of occupation: *Kennealy* v. *Dunne* [1977] 2 All E.R. 16, C.A. No requirement of "reasonably" required will be imported. Both Cases 11 and 12 lack the protection both of the overriding reasonableness discretion (s. 98 (1) of the 1977 Act) and the greater hardship provision (*ibid.*, Sch. 15, Part III, para. 1).

DWELLING-HOUSE

See the note to the Rent Act 1977, s. 1, A.L.S. Vol. 255.

RESIDENCE

See the note "Resident" to Sch. 3, para. 6, *ante*.

MEMBER OF HIS FAMILY

Cf. the note "Member of the original tenant's family" to the Rent Act 1977, Sch. 1, Part I.

RESIDED WITH THE OWNER

See the note "Residing with him" to the Rent Act 1977, Sch. 1, Part I.

PLACE OF WORK

See the note to Sch. 4, Part II, *ante*.

DEFINITIONS

For "tenancy", see the Rent Act 1977, s. 152 (1); for "owner", see Case 12 in Part II of Sch. 15 to that Act, as amended by s. 66 (4), *ante*, or Case 20 in that Part as added by s. 67, *ante* (and note para. 1 of Part V of that Schedule as set out above); for "owner-occupier", see Case 11 in Part II of Sch. 15 to the Act of 1977. Note as to "mortgage", "mortgagee" and "successor in title", para. 1 of Part V of Sch. 15 to the Act of 1977 as set out above.

1977 ACT

I.e., the Rent Act 1977; see s. 150, *ante*.

LAW OF PROPERTY ACT 1925, S. 101

See 27, Halsbury's Statutes (3rd edn.), p. 504.

SCHEDULE 8

CROWN ESTATE AND DUCHIES—

CONSEQUENTIAL PROVISIONS

PART I

Rent Act 1977

1. Where a tenancy granted before the commencement of section 73 of this Act becomes, or would but for its low rent become, a protected tenancy by virtue of that section, section 5 of the 1977 Act applies as if in relation to the dwelling-house the appropriate day were the commencement of that section.

2. In Part I of Schedule 15 to the 1977 Act the following is inserted after paragraph (*b*) of Case 6:

"(*bb*) the commencement of section 73 of the Housing Act 1980, in the case of a tenancy which became a regulated tenancy by virtue of that section."

3. In Part II of Schedule 15 to the 1977 Act any reference to the relevant date shall (notwithstanding paragraph 2 of Part III of that Schedule) be construed, in the case of a tenancy which becomes a regulated tenancy by virtue of section 73 of this Act as meaning the date falling six months after the passing of this Act.

4.—(1) Part II of Schedule 18 to the 1977 Act applies to a tenancy which becomes a regulated tenancy by virtue of section 73 of this Act (unless it is a tenancy falling within sub-paragraph (2) below).

(2) Nothing in Part IX of the 1977 Act applies to the assignment, before the end of the year 1990, of a tenancy which falls within this sub-paragraph; and a tenancy falls within this sub-paragraph if it was granted for a term certain and its terms do not inhibit both the assignment and the underletting of the whole of the premises comprised in the tenancy, and either—

(*a*) it was granted before the commencement of section 73 of this Act and became a regulated tenancy by virtue of that section; or

(*b*) it is a regulated tenancy by virtue of that section and was granted to a person who, at the time of the grant, was the tenant of the premises comprised in it under a regulated tenancy which also fell within this sub-paragraph.

(3) For the purposes of sub-paragraph (2) above the terms of a tenancy inhibit an assignment or underletting if they—

(*a*) preclude it; or

(*b*) permit it subject to a consent but exclude section 144 of the Law of Property Act 1925 (no payment in nature of fine); or

(*c*) permit it subject to a consent but require in connection with a request for consent the making of an offer to surrender the tenancy. **[530]**

COMMENCEMENT
See s. 153 (4), *ante*, and the note "Orders under this section" thereto.

PARA. 1. LOW RENT
This is to be construed in accordance with the Rent Act 1977, s. 5 (1), (4), A.L.S. Vol. 255.

PROTECTED TENANCY
I.e., a protected tenancy as defined by the Rent Act 1977, s. 1.

DWELLING-HOUSE
See the note to the Rent Act 1977, s. 1.

PARA. 3: DATE FALLING SIX MONTHS AFTER THE PASSING OF THIS ACT
"Months" means calendar months by virtue of the Interpretation Act 1978, s. 5, Sch. 1, A.L.S. Vol. 258, and this Act was passed (*i.e.*, received the Royal Assent) on 8th August 1980. It is thought therefore that the date referred to is 8th February 1981.

TERM CERTAIN
    Cf. the note to Sch. 3, para. 1, *ante.*

DEFINITIONS
    For "regulated tenancy", see the Rent Act 1977, s. 18 (as partly repealed by s. 152 (3), *ante,* and Sch. 26, *post*); for "tenancy", see s. 152 (1) of that Act.

1977 ACT
    I.e., the Rent Act 1977; see s. 150, *ante.* Part IX (ss. 119–128) of that Act is amended by ss. 78 and 79, *ante.*; and Sch. 15, Part II, is amended by ss. 55 (1), 66 and 67, *ante.*

LAW OF PROPERTY ACT 1925, S. 144
    See 27, Halsbury's Statutes (3rd edn.), p. 562.

PART II
Rent (Agriculture) Act 1976

5. Whether the question whether a person is a qualifying worker for the purposes of the Rent (Agriculture) Act 1976 arises by virtue of section 73 of this Act, Part II of Schedule 3 to that Act applies as if the date of operation for forestry workers were the commencement of that section.

6. Where a protected occupancy or statutory tenancy within the meaning of the Rent (Agriculture) Act 1976 arises at the commencement of section 73 of this Act, Cases VIII and X in Schedule 4 to that Act apply in relation to it as if the operative date were that commencement.

7. For the purpose of determining whether, at the commencement of section 73 of this Act, a person becomes a statutory tenant for the purposes of the Rent (Agriculture) Act 1976 and of applying that Act to him if he does, paragraph 3 of Schedule 9 to that Act applies as if the operative date were that commencement.

8. Paragraphs 6 and 7 above apply in relation to forestry workers as they apply in relation to other persons and paragraph 7 of Schedule 9 to the Rent (Agriculture) Act 1976 does not apply. **[531]**

COMMENCEMENT
    See s. 153 (4), *ante,* and the note "Orders under this section" thereto.

PARA. 5: DATE OF OPERATION FOR FORESTRY WORKERS
    Apart from para. 5 above this expression would have the meaning assigned by the Rent (Agriculture) Act 1976, Sch. 3, para. 8, A.L.S. Vol. 250.

PARAS. 6, 7: OPERATIVE DATE
    Apart from paras. 6 and 7 above this expression would have the meaning assigned by the Rent (Agriculture) Act 1976, s. 1 (6) (see also Sch. 9, para. 7 (2), (3) to that Act, which are excluded by para. 8 above).

PARA. 8: FORESTRY WORKERS
    As to the meaning of "forestry", see the Rent (Agriculture) Act 1976, s. 1 (1) (*b*); and for provisions postponing the operation of that Act in relation to certain forestry workers, see s. 1 (5) (*b*) of, and Sch. 3, Part II, to, that Act (together with para. 5 above).

RENT (AGRICULTURE) ACT 1976
    See A.L.S. Vol. 250; for the meaning of "qualifying worker", see Sch. 3, para. 1, to that Act; for the meaning of "protected occupancy", see ss. 2 and 3 of that Act; and for the meanings of "statutory tenancy" and "statutory tenant", see ss. 4 and 5 of that Act.

PART III
General

9. Where an interest belongs to Her Majesty in right of the Duchy of Lancaster, then, for the purposes of Part I of the Landlord and Tenant Act 1954, the Rent (Agriculture) Act 1976

or the 1977 Act, the Chancellor of the Duchy of Lancaster shall be deemed to be the owner of the interest.

10. Where an interest belongs to the Duchy of Cornwall, then, for the purposes of Part I of the Landlord and Tenant Act 1954, the Rent (Agriculture) Act 1976 or the 1977 Act, the Secretary of the Duchy of Cornwall shall be deemed to be the owner of the interest. **[532]**

COMMENCEMENT
    See s. 153 (4), *ante*, and the note "Orders under this section" thereto.

LANDLORD AND TENANT ACT 1954, PART I
    See A.L.S. Vols. 87, 155.

RENT (AGRICULTURE) ACT 1976
    See A.L.S. Vol. 250.

1977 ACT
    I.e., the Rent Act 1977; see s. 150, *ante*.

SCHEDULE 9

Section 74

PROVISIONS SUPPLEMENTING SECTION 74

1. Paragraphs 2 to 6 below apply to any tenancy which was a protected or statutory tenancy but which, by virtue of the landlord becoming a "housing trust" within the meaning of section 15 of the 1977 Act, has ceased to be such a tenancy.

2. If the tenancy—
    (*a*) was a statutory tenancy; and
    (*b*) would have become a secure tenancy had it previously been a protected tenancy;
it shall be treated for the purposes of Chapter II of Part I of this Act as if it were a secure tenancy for a term certain which, at the time when it ceased to be a statutory tenancy, came to an end by effluxion of time.

3. Registration of a rent, or of a different rent, for the dwelling-house shall be effected in pursuance of section 87 of the 1977 Act; but until such time as a rent is so registered—
    (*a*) the rent recoverable under the tenancy; and
    (*b*) where a rent was registered for the dwelling-house under Part IV of the 1977 Act, the time at which an application for a different registered rent may be made;
shall be determined as if the tenancy had continued to be a regulated tenancy.

4. If the tenant was a successor within the meaning of Schedule 1 to the 1977 Act he shall not be treated as a successor for the purposes of Chapter II of Part I of this Act.

5. Section 33 of this Act does not apply in any case where proceedings for possession were begun before the tenancy ceased to be a protected or statutory tenancy; but in such a case the court shall allow the parties to take such steps in relation to the proceedings as it considers appropriate in consequence of the tenancy becoming a secure tenancy.

6.—(1) This paragraph applies in any case where—
    (*a*) the tenant died before the date on which the tenancy ceased to be a protected or statutory tenancy; and
    (*b*) there was then more than one member of his family entitled to succeed him as statutory tenant but no decision had, by that date, been reached as to which of them was to succeed.

(2) In a case to which this paragraph applies, the person who is to be the secure tenant of the dwelling-house on the tenancy becoming a secure tenancy shall be selected by the landlord from among those mentioned in sub-paragraph (1) (*b*) above notwithstanding that the question may have been referred to the county court in accordance with paragraph 1 (7) of Schedule 1 to the 1977 Act. **[533]**

COMMENCEMENT
See s. 153 (4), *ante*, and the note "Orders under this section" thereto.

PARA. 1: PROTECTED OR STATUTORY TENANCY
I.e., a protected tenancy within the meaning of the Rent Act 1977, s. 1, A.L.S. Vol. 255, or a statutory tenancy within the meaning of s. 2 of that Act.

PARA. 2: SECURE TENANCY
I.e., a secure tenancy as defined by s. 28, *ante*.

IT SHALL BE TREATED FOR THE PURPOSES OF CHAPTER II OF PART I, ETC.
I.e., for the purposes of ss. 28–50, *ante*; and see, in particular, s. 29, *ante*.

PARA. 3: DWELLING-HOUSE
See the note to the Rent Act 1977, s. 1.

TIME AT WHICH AN APPLICATION FOR A DIFFERENT REGISTERED RENT MAY BE MADE
This is governed by the Rent Act 1977, s. 67 (3), (4), as amended by s. 60, *ante*.

REGULATED TENANCY
I.e., a regulated tenancy as defined by the Rent Act 1977, s. 18 (as partly repealed by s. 152 (3), *ante*, and Sch. 26, *post*).

PARA. 4: SHALL NOT BE TREATED AS A SUCCESSOR FOR THE PURPOSES OF CHAPTER II OF PART I
See, in particular, ss. 30 and 31, *ante*.

PARA. 5: THE COURT
Cf. the note "A court" to the Rent Act 1977, s. 98.

PARA. 6: MORE THAN ONE MEMBER OF HIS FAMILY ENTITLED TO SUCCEED HIM AS STATUTORY TENANT
I.e., under the terms of the Rent Act 1977, Sch. 1, para. 3 or 7.

1977 ACT
I.e., the Rent Act 1977; see s. 150, *ante*. For the meaning of "housing trust" in s. 15 of that Act, see sub-s. (5) thereof, as substituted by s. 74 (2), *ante*. There is no para. 1 (7) of Sch. 1 to the Act of 1977, but a reference may be made to the county court under para. 3 or 7 of that Schedule.

SCHEDULE 10

Section 77

AMENDMENT OF PART VI OF RENT ACT 1977

1.—(1) Section 86 of the 1977 Act is amended as follows.

(2) In subsection (2) after the word "tenancy", where it first occurs, there are inserted the words "(other than a co-ownership tenancy)".

(3) In subsection (3), for the words from "is a registered society" to the end there are substituted the words "falls within section 15 (3) (c) of this Act".

(4) After subsection (3) there is inserted the following subsection—

"(3A) For the purposes of this section a tenancy is a 'co-ownership tenancy' if—

(a) it was granted by a housing association which falls within section 15 (3) (d) of this Act; and

(b) the tenant (or his personal representatives) will, under the terms of the tenancy agreement or of the agreement under which he became a member of the association, be entitled, on his ceasing to be a member and subject to any conditions stated in either agreement, to a sum calculated by reference directly or indirectly to the value of the dwelling-house.".

(5) For subsection (4) there is substituted the following subsection—

"(4) In this Part of this Act "housing trust" has the same meaning as in section 15 of this Act.". **[534]**

2.—(1) For section 89 of the 1977 Act (phasing of progression to registered rent) there is substituted the following section—

"89. Phasing of progression to registered rent

(1) This section applies where a rent is registered for a dwelling-house (whether it is the first or any subsequent registration) unless at the date of registration there is no tenant and no person to whom a tenancy has been granted.

(2) The rent for any rental period, or part of a rental period, falling within the period of delay imposed by Schedule 8 to this Act may be increased in accordance with that Schedule.

(3) A notice of increase which purports to increase the rent further than permitted by Schedule 8 shall have effect to increase it to the extent permitted, but no further.

(4) Nothing in this section or in Schedule 8 prevents or limits any increase in rent by virtue of section 71 (4) of this Act as applied by section 87 (2) of this Act.".

(2) In relation to a rent registered before the commencement of sub-paragraph (1) above, that sub-paragraph and Schedule 8 to the 1977 Act as applied by that sub-paragraph are subject to the following modifications.

(3) The period of delay is a period ending one year after the end of the stage (within the meaning of section 89 of the 1977 Act as originally enacted) which last began before the commencement of sub-paragraph (1) above; and—

(a) for any period falling within that stage section 89 applies as originally enacted; and
(b) for any later period falling within the period of delay the permitted increase is whichever of the following is the greater—

(i) the increase that would have been permitted if this Act had not been passed; and
(ii) the increase that would be permitted under Schedule 8 to the 1977 Act if the formula set out in paragraph 3 (as substituted by section 60 (3) of this Act) were $P + \frac{1}{2} (R - P)$. **[535]**

3. Sections 90 (special rent limit where previous rent limit exceeds registered rent) and 91 (procedure on application to Secretary of State under section 90) of the 1977 Act are hereby repealed.

4. In section 92 (conversion of housing association tenancies into regulated tenancies) in subsection (1) the words "in such form as may be prescribed" are hereby repealed.

5.—(1) Section 93 of the 1977 Act (increase of rent without notice to quit) is amended as follows.

(2) In subsection (1), for the words from "given by the landlord" to the end there are substituted the words "specifying the date on which the increase is to take effect and given by the landlord to the tenant not later than four weeks before that date.".

(3) For subsection (2) there is substituted the following subsection—

"(2) Where a notice of increase is given under subsection (1) above and the tenant, before the date specified in the notice of increase, gives a valid notice to quit, the notice of increase does not take effect unless the tenant, with the written agreement of the landlord, withdraws his notice to quit before that date.".

(4) Subsection (3) is hereby repealed.

(5) This paragraph only applies to notices of increase given after the commencement of this paragraph. **[536]**

COMMENCEMENT
See s. 153 (4), *ante*, and the note "Orders under this section" thereto.

PARA. 1: DWELLING-HOUSE
See the note to the Rent Act 1977, s. 1, A.L.S. Vol. 255.

THIS PART OF THIS ACT
I.e., the Rent Act 1977, Part VI.

PARA. 2: THIS SECTION APPLIES, ETC.
As to phasing of rent increases where the Rent Act 1977, s. 89, as substituted by para.
2 above, does not apply see s. 55 of, and Sch. 8 to, that Act, as amended and partly repealed
by ss. 60 (3), 61 (6) and 152 (1), (3), *ante*, and Sch. 25, para. 39, and Sch. 26, *post* (but
note that s. 55 of the Act of 1977 may be repealed by order made under s. 60 (5), *ante*).

PARA. 5: WRITTEN
See the note "Written; writing" to s. 5, *ante*.

DEFINITIONS
For "housing association", see the Rent Act 1977, s. 86 (3), as amended by para. 1 (1)
(3) above; for "tenancy", see ss. 97 (1) and 152 (1) of that Act; for "registered", see s.
97 (2) of that Act; for "the landlord" in s. 93 of that Act, see sub-s. (1) thereof; for "rental
found" and "tenant", see s. 152 (1) of that Act. Note as to "co-ownership tenancy", s.
86 (3A) of the Act of 1977 as inserted by para. 1 (1), (4) above.

1977 ACT
I.e., the Rent Act 1977; see s. 150, *ante*. For the meaning of "housing trust" in s. 15 of
that Act, see sub-s. (5) thereof as substituted by s. 74 (2), *ante*, and for the meaning of
"period of delay" in Sch. 8, see para. 1 (1) thereof, as amended by s. 61 (6) (*a*), *ante*. Ss.
90 and 91 are also repealed and ss. 92 and 93 are partly repealed, by s. 152 (3), *ante*, and
Sch. 26, *post*; and Sch. 8 is amended and partly repealed by ss. 60 (3), 61 (6) and 152 (3),
ante, and Sch. 26, *post*.

TRANSITIONAL PROVISIONS
See s. 152 (2), *ante*, and Sch. 25, para. 77, *post*.

SCHEDULE 11
Section 96
SUPERSEDED ENACTMENTS RELATING TO SUBSIDIES, GRANTS AND
CONTRIBUTIONS TO HOUSING AUTHORITIES

PART I

SUBSIDIES PAYABLE UNTIL 1980–81

The Housing Rents and Subsidies Act 1975 sections 2 and 4.

The Development of Rural Wales Act 1976 section 18. **[537]**

PART II

CONTRIBUTIONS TOWARDS COSTS OF IMPROVEMENT OR
CONVERSION

The Housing Act 1969 sections 17 to 19.

The Housing Act 1971 sections 1 and 2.

The Housing Act 1974 section 79. **[538]**

COMMENCEMENT
See the note to s. 96, *ante*.

HOUSING RENTS AND SUBSIDIES ACT 1975, SS. 2, 4
See A.L.S. Vol. 230. These sections are repealed by s. 152 (3), *ante*, and Sch. 26, *post*.

DEVELOPMENT OF RURAL WALES ACT 1976, S. 18
That section is repealed by s. 152 (3), *ante*, and Sch, 26, *post*.

HOUSING ACT 1969, SS. 17–19
See A.L.S. Vol. 183. Those sections were repealed with a saving by the Housing Act 1974,
s. 130 (3), (4), Sch. 14, para. 5, Sch. 15, A.L.S. Vol. 223.

HOUSING ACT 1971, SS. 1, 2
    See A.L.S. Vol. 199.

HOUSING ACT 1974, S. 79
    See A.L.S. Vol. 223. That section is repealed by s. 152 (3), *ante*, and Sch. 26, *post*.

SCHEDULE 12

Section 107

AMENDMENTS OF HOUSING ACT 1974 (c. 44).

PART VII (LOCAL AUTHORITY GRANTS)

Consideration of application for grant

1. In section 57 (3) (application not to be entertained unless certain conditions are complied with) for "entertain" substitute "approve". **[539]**

Withdrawal of application for grant and submission of new one

2. In section 57 (6), omit the words "Except in so far as this Act otherwise provides"; and after that subsection insert—

"(6A) Subsection (6) does not apply if the relevant works have not been begun and either—

(*a*) more than 2 years have elapsed since the date on which the previous application was approved; or

(*b*) the application is made with a view to taking advantage of orders under section 59 below." **[540]**

Standard amenities

3. After section 58 (2) insert—

"(3) An order under subsection (2) above shall be subject to annulment in pursuance of a resolution of the House of Commons." **[541]**

"Appropriate percentage" for determining amount, or maximum amount, of grant

4. For section 59 substitute—

"59. Appropriate percentage

(1) In this Part of this Act "the appropriate percentage" (which is relevant for determining the amount or the maximum amount of grant) shall be a percentage ascertained from orders made by the Secretary of State with the consent of the Treasury and in force when the application for grant is approved.

(2) Orders under this section shall operate with respect to applications for grant approved after such date as may be specified in the applicable order; but an order shall not be made unless a draft of it has been approved by resolution of the House of Commons, and shall not specify a date earlier than the date of the laying of the draft."
[542]

Certificates of future occupation

5. In section 60, substitute the following for subsections (3) and (4)—

"(3) A "certificate of owner-occupation" is a certificate stating that the applicant for the grant intends that, on or before the first anniversary of the certified date and throughout the period of 4 years beginning on that first anniversary, the dwelling will be the only or main residence of, and will be occupied exclusively by, either—

(*a*) the applicant himself and members of his household (if any); or

(*b*) a person who is a member of the applicant's family, or a grandparent or grandchild of the applicant or his spouse, and members of that person's household (if any).

(4) But in a case where application for grant is made by the personal representatives of a deceased person or by trustees, it is a certificate stating that the applicants are personal representatives or trustees and intend that, on or before the first anniversary of the certified date and throughout the period of 4 years beginning on that first anniversary, the dwelling will be the only or main residence of, and exclusively occupied by, either—

> (a) a beneficiary and members of his household (if any); or
> (b) a person related to a beneficiary by being a member of his family or a grandparent or grandchild of the beneficiary or his spouse, and members of that person's household (if any);

and "beneficiary" means a person who, under the will or intestacy or, as the case may require, under the terms of the trust, is beneficially entitled to an interest in the dwelling or the proceeds of sale of it."

6. In section 60 (5), add at the end—

"(disregarding any part of that period in which neither of the above paragraphs applies but the dwelling is occupied by a person who is a protected occupier under the Rent (Agriculture) Act 1976).". **[543]**

Improvement grants

7. After section 62 (4) insert—

"(5) Subsections (1) and (2) above do not apply to dwellings in housing action areas.

(6) Those subsections do not apply where the application for an improvement grant is made in respect of a dwelling for a disabled occupant and it appears to the local authority that the works are needed to meet a requirement arising from the particular disability from which the disabled occupant suffers."

8. Omit section 64 (7). **[544]**

Intermediate grants

9. For section 66 substitute—

"66. Conditions of approval

A local authority shall not approve an application for an intermediate grant unless—

> (a) they are satisfied that on completion of the relevant works the dwellings or, as the case may be each of the dwellings, to which the application relates will be fit for human habitation (to be determined in accordance with section 4 of the Housing Act 1957); or
> (b) it seems reasonable in all the circumstances to do so even though the dwelling or dwellings will not reach that standard on completion of the relevant works."

10.—(1) In section 67 (2) omit paragraph (b) and the word "and" immediately preceding it.

(2) For section 67 (3) substitute—

"(3) Where the relevant works specified in an application for an intermediate grant include works of repair or replacement which go beyond those needed, in the opinion of the local authority, to put the dwelling into reasonable repair (disregarding the state of internal decorative repair) having regard to its age and character and the locality in which it is situated and the period during which it is likely to be available for use as a dwelling, the local authority may, with the consent of the applicant, treat the application as varied so that the relevant works—

> (a) are confined to works other than works of repair or replacement; or
> (b) include only such works of repair or replacement as (taken with the rest of the relevant works) will, in the opinion of the local authority, put the dwelling into reasonable repair,

and may approve the application as so varied."

(3) (omit section 67 (4).

304

11.—(1) In section 68 (3) (*a*) for "£800 or such other amount as may be prescribed" substitute "the relevant limit".

(2) In section 68, after subsection (3) insert—

"(3A) The relevant limit for the purposes of subsection (3) (*a*) above is—

(*a*) £2,000 or such other amount as may be prescribed in a case where either—

(i) the dwelling will, in the opinion of the local authority, be put on completion of the relevant works into reasonable repair (disregarding the state of internal decorative repair) having regard to its age and character and the locality in which it is situated and the period during which it is likely to be available for use as a dwelling; or

(ii) it appears to the local authority that the applicant could not without undue hardship finance the cost of the works necessary to put the dwelling into reasonable repair;

(*b*) in any other case, the amount obtained by multiplying the number of standard amenities to be provided on completion of the relevant works by £200 or such other amount as may be prescribed, but subject to a maximum of £800 or such amount as may be prescribed.

(3B) An order under subsection (3A) above prescribing an amount shall be subject to annulment in pursuance of a resolution of the House of Commons.". **[545]**

Repairs grant

12.—(1) In section 71, for subsection (2) substitute—

"(2) A local authority shall not in any case approve an application for a repairs grant unless—

(*a*) they are satisfied that the relevant works are of a substantial and structural character; or

(*b*) the relevant works satisfy requirements prescribed (with the consent of the Treasury)."

(2) In section 71 (3), omit paragraph (*a*) and after that subsection insert—

"(3A) But an application for a repairs grant shall not be approved—

(*a*) unless it is in respect of an old dwelling (within any meaning given to that expression by an order made by the Secretary of State); and

(*b*) in the case of a dwelling situated elsewhere than in a housing action area where the application is accompanied by a certificate of owner-occupation, unless the rateable value (at the date of the application) is within limits specified by an order so made.

(3B) Orders under subsection (3A) (*b*) require the consent of the Treasury."

13. After section 71 insert—

"71A. Mandatory repairs grant

In so far as an application for a repairs grant relates to the execution of works required by a notice under section 9 of the Housing Act 1957

(*a*) section 60 above shall not apply; and

(*b*) the authority shall not refuse it if it is duly made and the authority are satisfied that the works are necessary for compliance with the notice."

14.—(1) After section 72 (3), insert—

"(3A) An order under this section prescribing an amount shall be subject to annulment in pursuance of a resolution of the House of Commons."

(2) For section 72 (4) substitute—

"(4) The amount of a repairs grant—

(*a*) so far as the grant is made in pursuance of section 71A above, shall be the appropriate percentage of the eligible expense; and

(b) otherwise shall be such as may be fixed by the local authority when they approve the application for the grant, but shall not exceed the appropriate percentage of the eligible expense.

(4A) With the notification under subsection (1) above the local authority shall send to the applicant a notification of the amount of the grant."

(3) In section 72 (5), for "subsection (4)" substitute "subsection (4A)". **[546]**

Special grants for houses in multiple occupation

15. In section 56 (2) of the Act, for paragraph (c) substitute—

"(c) a "special grant" in respect of works required for the improvement of a house in multiple occupation by the provision of (both or either)—
    (i) standard amenities,
    (ii) means of escape from fire".

16.—(1) In section 69, for subsection (2) substitute—

"(2) An application for a special grant must state by how many households and individuals the house concerned is occupied and (as applicable)—

(a) the standard amenities with which it is already provided;
(b) the means of escape from fire which are already available.

(2A) Subject to section 69A, the application shall not be approved unless the local authority are satisfied that on completion of the relevant works the house will attain the relevant standard of repair.

(2B) If, in the opinion of the authority, the relevant works are more extensive than is necessary for the purpose of securing that the house will attain that standard, the authority may (with the consent of the applicant) treat the application as varied so that the relevant works include only such works as seem to the local authority necessary for that purpose; and they may then approve the application as so varied.

(2C) For the purposes of this section a house shall be taken to attain the relevant standard of repair if it is in reasonable repair (disregarding the state of internal decorative repair) having regard to its age and character and the locality in which it is situated.".

(2) In section 84, at the end of the definition of "the relevant standard" add "and

(d) in relation to a special grant, the relevant standard referred to in section 69 (2C) above."

17. After section 69 insert—

"69A. Mandatory special grants

(1) In so far as an application for a special grant relates to the provision of standard amenities, the authority shall not refuse it if it is duly made and the authority are satisfied that the relevant works are necessary for compliance with so much of a notice under section 15 of the Housing Act 1961 as relates to standard amenities.

(2) In so far as such an application relates to the provision of means of escape from fire, the authority shall not refuse it if it is duly made and the authority are satisfied that the relevant works are necessary for compliance with a notice under Schedule 24 to the Housing Act 1980."

18.—(1) For section 70 substitute—

"70.—(1) Where a local authority approve an application for a special grant they shall determine the amounts of the expenses which they think proper to be incurred respectively for those of the relevant works which—

(a) consist in providing standard amenities;
(b) relate to the provision of means of escape from fire; and
(c) consist of works of repair or replacement;

and the authority shall notify the applicant of the amounts so determined by them.

(2) If the applicant satisfies the local authority that the relevant works cannot be, or could not have been, carried out without additional works and that this could not have been

reasonably foreseen at the time the application was made, the local authority may determine a higher amount under any of paragraphs (*a*) to (*c*) of subsection (1).

(3) The amount of a special grant—

    (*a*) so far as the grant is made in pursuance of section 69A above, shall be the appropriate percentage of the eligible expense ascertained under section 70A below; and

    (*b*) otherwise shall be such as may be fixed by the local authority when they approve the application for the grant but shall not exceed the appropriate percentage of the eligible expense ascertained under section 70A below.

(4) With the notification under subsection (1) above, the local authority shall send to the applicant a notification of the amount of the grant.

(5) If, after the amount of a special grant has been notified, the local authority under subsection (2) determine a higher amount under any of the heads of subsection (1), the eligible expense shall be recalculated under section 70A; and if the amount of it is then greater than when the application for grant was approved, the amount of the grant shall be increased, and the applicant notified, accordingly.".

(2) In section 82 (2) for "70 (3)" substitute "70 (2)".

19. After section 70 insert—

"70A. Eligible for purposes of special grant

(1) Except in a case or description of case in respect of which the Secretary of State approves a higher eligible expense, the eligible expense for the purposes of a special grant shall be the aggregate of the contributory elements specified in the following subsections.

(2) As regards the provisions of standard amenities, the contributory element is so much of the amount determined under section 70 (1) (*a*) as does not exceed the aggregate of the amounts specified in the second column of Part I of Schedule 6 to this Act in relation to each of the standard amenities which are to be provided by the relevant works (so that, where the relevant works make provision for more than one standard amenity of the same description, a separate amount shall be aggregated for each of those amenities).

(3) As regards the provision of means of escape from fire, the contributory element is so much of the amount determined under section 70 (1) (*b*) as does not exceed £6,750 or such other amount as may be prescribed.

(4) As regards works of repair or replacement, the contributory element is so much of the amount determined under section 70 (1) (*c*) as does not exceed £2,000 or such other amount as may be prescribed.

(5) An order under this section prescribing an amount shall be subject to annulment in pursuance of a resolution of the House of Commons." **[547]**

Standard of improvement, repair, etc.

20.—(1) In section 61 (3) (*b*) for "good repair" substitute "reasonable repair".

(2) In section 61 insert after subsection (4)—

"(4A) A local authority may dispense, to the extent they think fit, with any of the conditions specified in paragraphs (*a*) to (*c*) of subsection (3) if they are satisfied that the applicant could not, without undue hardship, finance the cost of the works without the assistance of a grant."

(3) In section 71 (5) for "good repair" substitute "reasonable repair". **[548]**

Grant conditions

21. In section 73 (3)—

    (*a*) for paragraph (*a*) substitute—

        "(*a*) the applicant for the grant and—

            (i) in a case where the application was accompanied by a certificate of owner-occupation with respect to the dwelling, any person who derives title to the dwelling through or under the applicant; or

(ii) in a case where the application was accompanied by a certificate of availability for letting with respect to the dwelling, any person who derives title to the dwelling through or under the applicant otherwise than by a conveyance for value;".

(*b*) after paragraph (*a*), insert—

"(*aa*) a person who is a member of the applicant's family or a grandparent or grandchild of the applicant or his spouse; and"

(*c*) at the end of paragraph (*b*) insert—

"and

(*bb*) a person related to one who qualifies under paragraph (*b*) above, by being a member of his family or a grandparent or grandchild of his or of his spouse".

22. At the end of section 73 (4) insert—

"(disregarding any part of that period in which neither of the above paragraphs applies but the dwelling is occupied by a person who is a protected occupier under the Rent (Agriculture) Act 1976)".

23. In section 74 (1) after "they shall" insert "(subject to subsection (2A) below)" and after section 74 (2) insert—

"(2A) Where, apart from this subsection, a local authority would be required to impose the conditions specified in subsection (2) above with respect to a dwelling in respect of which a certificate of owner-occupation has been given but it appears to the local authority that in the special circumstances of the case it would be reasonable to dispense with the conditions they shall not be required to impose the conditions.".

24.—(1) In section 74 (3), after paragraph (*c*) insert "Or

(*d*) which is occupied by a person who is a protected occupier or statutory tenant under the Rent (Agriculture) Act 1976."

(2) In section 74, after subsection (3), insert—

(3A) There shall be disregarded for the purposes of subsection (3) (*b*) above any letting to the applicant for the grant or a member of his family, or a grandparent or grandchild of the applicant or his spouse." **[549]**

Payment of grant by instalments

25. In section 82, for subsection (4) substitute—

"(4) Where grant is paid in instalments, the aggregate of the instalments paid before the completion of the works shall not at any time exceed—

(*a*) in the case of intermediate grant, the appropriate percentage of the total cost of the works so far executed;

(*b*) in the case of improvement grant, special grant or repairs grant, an amount bearing to that total cost the same proportion as the fixed amount of the grant bears to the eligible expense." **[550]**

Repair and special grants (consequential)

26.—(1) In section 57 (3) for "section 83" substitute "sections 69A, 71A and 83".

(2) At the beginning of section 57 (5) insert "Except under section 69A or 71A". **[551]**

Parliamentary control

27. In section 128 (4) after "46" insert "58" and after "64" insert "68, 70A, 72". **[552]**

Tenants' grants (consequential)

28. In section 57 (3), after "below" insert "and section 106 of the Housing Act 1980".

29. In section 60 insert after subsection (1)—

"(1A) This section does not apply to an application made under section 106 of the Housing Act 1980".

30.—(1) At the end of section 73 (3) insert—

"and where an application for a grant is accompanied by a certificate under section 106 (2) of the Housing Act 1980 this subsection shall apply with the substitution for references to the applicant of references to the person who gave the certificate."

(2) In section 73 (4) after "certificate of availability for letting" insert "or a certificate under the said section 106 (2)".

31. In section 74 (1), after "subsection (3) below" insert "and section 106 (4) of the Housing Act 1980."

32. In section 81 (2), after "section 57 (3) above" insert "or section 106 (1) of the Housing Act 1980". **[553]**

COMMENCEMENT
See s. 153 (4), *ante*, and the note "Orders under this section" thereto.

PARA. 1
Section 57 (3) of the Housing Act 1974 requires the applicant to own an estate in fee simple or a term of years absolute with at least 5 years unexpired at the date of the application for grant-aid, before an application may be entertained. Para. 1 removes the word "entertained" and substitutes "approve" so that, from the commencement of Sch. 12 to this Act, a prospective purchaser of property in need of improvement, etc., may apply for grant-aid to the local authority, which may then go up to formal approval of the application before the purchase goes through. In this way, a prospective purchaser will be able to have some notion of what his prospects of obtaining grant-aid will be if he decides to go ahead with the purchase, before entering into a binding contract of sale.

PARA. 3: SUBJECT TO ANNULMENT, ETC.
For provisions as to statutory instruments which are subject to annulment in pursuance of a resolution of the Commons, see the Statutory Instruments Act 1946, ss. 5 (1), 7 (1), (2), A.L.S. Vol. 36.

PARA. 4: THIS PART OF THIS ACT
I.e., the Housing Act 1974, Part VII, A.L.S. Vol. 223.

SECRETARY OF STATE
See the note to s. 2, *ante*.

TREASURY
See the note to s. 46, *ante*.

PARA. 5: 4 YEARS BEGINNING ON, ETC.
Cf. the note "Three months beginning with, etc." to s. 12, *ante*.

ONLY OR MAIN
Cf. the note "Wholly or mainly" to Sch. 19 *post*.

RESIDENCE
See the note "Resident" to Sch. 3, para. 6, *ante*.

PARA. 7: HOUSING ACTION AREAS
As to these areas, see the Housing Act 1974, Part IV, *et seq*., as amended by s. 109 (1), *ante*, and Sch. 13, paras. 7–10, *post*.

APPEARS
See the note "Appear" to s. 2, *ante*.

PARA. 9: INTERMEDIATE GRANTS
As amended by the Housing Act 1969, A.L.S. Vol. 183, s. 71, the Housing Act 1957, A.L.S. Vol. 109, s. 4, states that in determining whether a dwelling-house is unfit for human habitation, regard shall be had to: (*a*) repair; (*b*) stability; (*c*) freedom from damp; (*d*) internal arrangement; (*e*) natural lighting; (*f*) ventilation; (*g*) water supply; (*h*) drainage and sanitary conveniences; (*i*) facilities for preparation and cooking of food and for the

disposal of waste water. In addition to these requirements, a house will be unfit for human habitation at common law if it is bug-infested (*Smith* v. *Marrable* (1843) 11 M. & W. 5) or had bad drains (*Wilson* v. *Finch Hatton* (1877) 2 Ex. D. 336) or has a defective ceiling (*O'Brien* v. *Robinson* [1973] 1 All E.R. 583, H.L.), defective steps (*McCarrick* v. *Liverpool Corporation* [1946] 2 All E.R. 646, H.L.), leaking gutters (*Horrex* v. *Pidwell* [1958] C.L.Y. 1461) or a defective floor (*Ryall* v. *Kidwell* [1914] 3 K.B. 135).

SATISFIED
See the note "Appear" to s. 2, *ante*.

PARA. 10: OPINION
See the note "Appear" to s. 2, *ante*.

LIKELY
See the note to s. 43, *ante*.

PARA. 10 (2): REASONABLE REPAIR
This is the standard laid down in *Proudfoot* v. *Hart* (1890) 25 Q.B.D. 42, C.A.: a deterioration in the neighbourhood will lower the standard of repair as a result.

PARA. 10 (2): OTHER THAN WORKS OF REPAIR OR REPLACEMENT
I.e., of improvement in the sense discussed in s. 81 and the note thereto. Repair does not include the total reconstruction of the property necessitated by old age: *Lister* v. *Lane and Nesham* [1893] 2 Q.B. 212, C.A.; *Sotheby* v. *Grundy* [1947] 2 All E.R. 761; *Pembery* v. *Lamdin* [1940] 2 All E.R. 434, C.A. This would however fall within the term "replacement" used in para. 11.

The two categories of repair and replacement are not mutually exclusive (the wording might suggest that they were): repair may often include extensive subordinate renewal: *Lurcott* v. *Wakely and Wheeler* [1911] 1 K.B. 905, C.A. Examples would be the rebuilding of a collapsed flank wall (*ibid.*) or the replacement of a defective front window with its modern equivalent (*Wright* v. *Lawson* (1903) 19 T.L.R. 510, C.A.) or replacement of stone external cladding: *Ravenseft Properties Ltd.* v. *Davstone (Holdings) Ltd.* [1979] 1 All E.R. 929.

It is also thought that "replacement" in para 10 is dependent on repair: in other words a replacement which amounted to an improvement would fall outside para. 10.

PARA. 11: SUCH OTHER AMOUNT AS MAY BE PRESCRIBED
I.e., prescribed by order made by the Secretary of State: see the Housing Act 1974, s. 84, and as to orders generally, see s. 128 of that Act, as amended by para. 27, *post* (and note s. 68 (3B) of that Act as inserted by para. 11 (2) above). At the time of going to press no order had been made for the purposes of s. 68 (3A) of the Act of 1974 as inserted by para. 11 (2) above.

PARA. 12: SUBSTANTIAL AND STRUCTURAL CHARACTER
Accordingly, work which was of a minor repairing character would fail to qualify for a repairs grant. Obviously, the replacement of defective fittings or running-boards and any other interior repairs of a decorative or semi-decorative nature would fail to qualify because such would be neither substantial nor structural. So those matters mentioned in *Proudfoot* v. *Hart* (1890) 25 Q.B.D. 42, C.A., as being tenant-like repairs would not qualify: re-papering, re-plastering, etc. It is not thought, because the following would not be structural, that the installing of a new floor (cf. *Wates* v. *Rowland* [1952] 1 All E.R. 470, C.A.) or sanitary facilities (cf. *Strood Estates* v. *Gregory* [1936] 2 K.B. 605; [1936] 2 All E.R. 355, C.A.) would qualify for a repairs grant: these works would be improvements only.

The terms "substantial and structural" being juxtaposed it is thought that the repair must involve the fabric of the house itself: as to this see *Boswell* v. *The Crucible Steel Co. of America* [1925] 1 K.B. 119, C.A.; *Samuels* v. *Abbints Investments* (1963) 188 E.G. 689. Accordingly, "substantial" does not only refer to the extent of the repair, so as to disqualify a small defect extravagantly repaired, but is to be construed *ejusdem* with "structural": see further *Granada Theatres Ltd* v. *Freehold Investment (Leytonstone) Ltd.* [1959] 2 All E.R. 176, C.A.

It is thus thought that the rebuilding of the whole or even part of the external walls or the roof would qualify (see *Lurcott* v. *Wakely and Wheeler* [1911] 1 K.B. 905, C.A.) as would replacing structural windows such as plate-glass windows (see *Boswell* v. *The Crucible Steel Co of America, supra*) or structured windows (*Wright* v. *Lawson* (1903) 19 T.L.R. 510, C.A.). So too would replacing outside stone cladding (*Ravenseft Properties Ltd.* v. *Davstone (Holdings) Ltd.* [1979] 1 All E.R. 929).

What was more extensive than this, and not a repair at all, but rather the complete replacement of the whole or substantially the whole of the property, would not qualify for a repair grant because such work is outside the scope of the term "repair"; see *Lister* v. *Lane and Nesham* [1893] 2 Q.B. 212, C.A.; *Pembery* v. *Lamdin* [1940] 2 All E.R. 434, C.A.; *Brew Bros Ltd.* v. *Snax (Ross) Ltd.* [1970] 1 All E.R. 575, C.A.

REQUIREMENTS PRESCRIBED
I.e., prescribed by order made by the Secretary of State: see the Housing Act 1974, s. 84, and as to orders generally, see s. 128 of that Act. At the time of going to press no order had been made for the purposes of s. 71 (2) (*b*) of that Act as substituted by para. 12 (1) above.

RATEABLE VALUE
As to the ascertainment of rateable value, see the General Rate Act 1967, ss. 19 *et. seq.*, A.L.S. Vol. 166.

PARA. 13: SECTION 9 OF THE HOUSING ACT 1957
By the Housing Act 1957, A.L.S. Vol. 109, s. 9 (1), where a local authority are satisfied that a house is unfit for human habitation they shall, unless they are satisfied that it cannot be made fit at reasonable expense, serve on the person having control of the house (as to which, see s. 39 (2)) a notice requiring him within a reasonable time (not less than 21 days) to execute the works specified in the notice, and stating that, in the opinion of the authority, those works would render the house fit for human habitation.

Where a house is not unfit for human habitation, then by the Housing Act 1957, s. 9 1A (added by the Housing Act 1969, A.L.S. Vol. 183, s. 72) in a case where substantial repairs are required to bring it up to a reasonable standard, having regard to its age, character and locality, they may serve a notice—as above—on the person having control of the house to execute the works specified in the notice, not being works of internal decorative repair.

In determining whether a house can be made fit for human habitation at reasonable expense, the local authority must have regard, by s. 39 (1) of the 1957 Act, to the estimated cost of the works and the value of the house on completion thereof. In *Bacon* v. *Grimsby Corporation* [1949] 2 All E.R. 875, C.A., it was held that the local authority did not have to have detailed items of estimate; and that the "value" was that to the freeholder, whatever the interest of the person having "control" of the house might be. A local authority may not adduce evidence to show a different value from open market value: *Inworth Property* v. *Southwark L.B.C.* (1977) 34 P. & C.R. 186, C.A.; but "value" in s. 39 (1) means value with vacant possession (ignoring any sitting tenant) after the repairs had been carried out: *Hillbank Properties Ltd.* v. *Hackney L.B.C.* [1978] 3 All E.R. 343, C.A. As to the issue of "reasonable cost" and other matters, see Morgan [1979] Conv. 414. Section 9 of the 1957 Act is extended by s. 149 of this Act.

PARA. 16: AGE AND CHARACTER AND LOCALITY
By para. 1, the new s. 69 (2c) adopts, as is done throughout this Schedule, the standard of repair laid down in *Proudfoot* v. *Hart* (1890) 25 Q.B.D. 42, C.A. The crucial passage in that case laid down the standard for "good tenantable repair" and applies equally to "reasonable repair". It was said: "Good tenantable repair is such repair as, having regard to the age, character and locality of the house, would make it reasonably fit for the occupation of a reasonably minded tenant of the class who would be likely to take it. The age of the house must be taken into account, because nobody could reasonably expect that a house 200 years old should be in the same condition of repair as a house lately built ..." (*ibid.*, at p. 52).

In this fashion, Parliament has once again preferred the lower standard of repair in the above to the high standard mentioned in *Calthorpe* v. *McOscar* [1924] 1 K.B. 616, C.A., wherein it was held that in the case of a long lease (95 years in that case) there could be no defence to liability to repair to the standard obtaining at the commencement of the term because the locality had deteriorated meantime. Cf. in this the like adoption of the lower standard of repair by the Housing Act 1961, A.L.S. Vol. 131, s. 32: *Jaquin* v. *Holland* [1960] 1 All E.R. 462, C.A.

PARA. 17: STANDARD AMENITIES
As to this, see the Housing Act 1974, A.L.S. Vol. 223, s. 58 and Sch. 6.
It has been held that "standard amenities" in Part VIII of the Housing Act 1974 mean amenities for the exclusive use of the occupants of the dwelling-house. If there is more than one dwelling-house in a building, then separate standard amenities may be required for each in an improvement notice served under ss. 89 and 91 of the 1974 Act: see *F.F.F. Estates Ltd.* v. *Hackney L.B.C.*, [1980] 3 W.L.R. 909, C.A.

PARA. 17: SECTION 15 OF THE HOUSING ACT 1961
This empowers a local authority to serve a notice to remedy defective conditions on the premises on anyone responsible for managing a house occupied by persons who do not form a single household.

PARA. 18: REPAIR
See the discussion in the notes to paras 10 and 12, *supra.*

PARA. 19: SUCH OTHER AMOUNT AS MAY BE PRESCRIBED
I.e., prescribed by order made by the Secretary of State; see the Housing Act 1974, s. 84, and as to orders generally, see s. 128 of that Act, as amended by para. 27, *post* (and note s. 70A (5) of that Act as inserted by para. 19 above). At the time of going to press no order had been made for the purposes of s. 70A (3) or (4) of the Act of 1974 as inserted by para. 19 above.

PARA. 20: REASONABLE REPAIR
As with much else in this Schedule, it cannot be doubted that Parliament had it in mind to reduce the overall standard of repair which is to govern: see also the note to para. 16 above. It is submitted that the difference between "good" and "reasonable" repair is more apparent than real. It has for instance been held that, in relation to words in a covenant to repair such as "good", "necessary", "sufficient", etc., that the particular form of words used is unimportant: what is required is an obligation to repair: *Calthorpe* v. *McOscar* [1924] 1 K.B. 724, C.A., at pp. 722, 729 and 731.
No doubt the object is to adopt the standard in *Proudfoot* v. *Hart*, (1890) 25 Q.B.D. 42, C.A. (see note to para. 16) but "reasonable" is hardly a conveyancer's term.

THINK FIT
See the note "Appear" to s. 2, *ante.*

PARA. 23: GENERAL NOTE
As a result of the Housing Act 1974, s. 74 (1) and (3), no grant-aid is available for improvement of an owner-occupied house within a housing action area or a general improvement area if that house was let within the previous 12 months. The object of this rule is to stop an owner removing the tenant by whatever means, obtaining grant-aid, and then selling for a better price as a result. The rule is retained but with the relaxation allowed by para. 23 which amends s. 74 so that the local authority will have a discretion to dispense with the rule (and also any other condition mentioned in s. 74 (2)) if it appears to them reasonable to do so in the special circumstances of the case.

DEFINITIONS
For "improvement grant", "intermediate grant", "special grant" and "repairs grant", see the Housing Act 1974, s. 56 (2), as amended by para. 15 above; for "the relevant works", see s. 57 (2) (*b*) of that Act; for "standard amenities", see s. 58 of, and Sch. 6 to, that Act, as amended, in the case of s. 58, by para. 3 above; for "the appropriate percentage", see s. 59 of that Act as substituted by para. 4 above; for "certificate of owner-occupation", see s. 60 (3), (4) of that Act as substituted by para. 5 above; for "certificate of availability for letting", see s. 60 (5) of that Act, as amended by para. 6 above; for "eligible expense", see s. 64 (3) or 72 (3) of that Act, or s. 70A thereof as inserted by para. 19 above; for "grant", "local authority", "prescribed" and the relevant standard, see s. 84 of that Act, as amended by para. 16 (2) above; for "dwelling" and "house in multiple occupation", see s. 129 (1) of that Act; as to "member of family", see s. 129 (3), (4) of that Act.

HOUSING ACT 1974, SS. 56 (2) (*c*), 57, 58 (2), 59–61, 62 (4), 64 (7), 66–74, 81 (2), 82, 84, 128 (4), SCH. 6, PART I
See A.L.S. Vol. 223. The provisions to be omitted are also repealed by s. 152 (3), *ante*, and Sch. 26, *post.*

RENT (AGRICULTURE) ACT 1976
For the meaning of "protected occupier", see ss. 2 and 3 of that Act, A.L.S. Vol. 250, and for the meaning of "statutory tenant", see ss. 4 and 5 of that Act.

HOUSING ACT 1957, SS. 4, 9
See A.L.S. Vol. 109.

HOUSING ACT 1961, S. 15
See A.L.S. Vol. 131.

ORDERS

At the time of going to press no order had been made under the Housing Act 1974, s. 59 (1), as substituted by para. 4 above, or under s. 71 (3A) (*a*) or (*b*), as inserted by para. 12 (2) above. For general provisions as to orders, see s. 128, of that Act, Vol. 44, p. 520, as amended by para. 27 above. Note also s. 59 (2) of the Act of 1974 as substituted by para. 4 above and s. 71 (3B) thereof as inserted by para. 12 (2) above; and see the notes to paras. 11, 12 and 19 above concerning matters to be prescribed by order.

SCHEDULE 13

Section 109

GENERAL IMPROVEMENT AREAS AND HOUSING ACTION AREAS

General improvement areas

1.—(1) In Part II of the 1969 Act section 28 (for which subsection (1) of section 50 of the 1974 Act substituted the two sections set out in Part I of Schedule 5 to that Act) is restored as originally enacted, but with the substitution in subsection (1) of the words "can most appropriately be improved" for the original "ought to be improved".

(2) Sub-paragraph (1) above does not affect the operation of the sections so substituted in any case where a preliminary resolution under the first of those sections was passed before the commencement of this Schedule.

2. Subsections (2) to (4) of subsection 50 of the 1974 Act (termination by Secretary of State of status of general improvement area) shall cease to have affect.

3. In relation to any resolution passed by a local authority after the commencement of this Schedule section 30 of the 1969 Act (changes with respect to general improvement areas) shall have effect with the omission of the words "but such a resolution shall be of no effect unless approved by the Minister".

4. In section 35 of the 1969 Act (disposal and appropriation of land)—

(*a*) subsections (1), (3), (5) and (7) are hereby repealed;
(*b*) in subsection (2) for the words from the beginning to "without his consent" there are substituted the words "Where any land is vested in a local authority for the purposes of this Part of this Act they shall not, without the consent of the Secretary of State";
(*c*) in subsection (4) the words "the consent of the Minister under subsection (2) of this section" are hereby repealed; and

(*d*) in subsection (6) the words from "with the approval" to "particular case" are hereby repealed.

5. For section 37 of the 1969 Act (contributions to local authority expenditure incurred under Part II) there is substituted the following section:—

"37.—(1) The Secretary of State may pay contributions to a local authority towards such expenditure incurred by them under this Part of this Act as he may determine.

(2) A contribution under this section shall be a sum payable annually for a period of 20 years beginning with the financial year in which the expenditure towards which the contribution is made is incurred and that sum shall be equal to one-half of the annual loan charges referable to that expenditure.

(3) The aggregate of the expenditure towards which contributions may be made under this section with respect to any general improvement area shall not exceed the sum arrived at by multiplying £400 by the number of dwellings stated by the local authority under the preceding provisions of this Part of this Act to be in the area; but two adjoining general improvement areas may for the purposes of this subsection be treated as one.

(4) The Secretary of State may, with the consent of the Treasury, by order substitute, in subsection (2) above, another fraction for one-half and, in subsection (3) above, another amount for £400; and he may, with the consent of the Treasury, direct that, in the case of a general improvement area specified in the direction or of a general improvement area of a description so specified, subsections (2) and (3) above shall have

313

effect as if a higher fraction or a greater amount were substituted for the fraction or amount for the time being specified therein.

(5) An order under subsection (4) above shall be made by statutory instrument which shall be subject to annulment in pursuance of a resolution of the House of Commons."

6. In section 38 of the 1969 Act after the word "Where" there are inserted the words "any contribution has been paid under section 37 of this Act towards" and the words from "has been approved" to "this Act" are omitted. **[554]**

COMMENCEMENT
See s. 153 (4), *ante*, and the note "Orders under this section" thereto.

PARA. 3: LOCAL AUTHORITY
I.e., an authority specified in the Housing Act 1969, s. 39, A.L.S. Vol. 183, as amended; see also s. 40 of that Act.

PARA. 4: THIS PART OF THIS ACT
I.e., the Housing Act 1969, Part II.

SECRETARY OF STATE
See the note to s. 2, *ante*.

PARA. 5: FINANCIAL YEAR
I.e., the twelve months ending with 31st March; see the Interpretation Act 1978, s. 5, Sch. 1, A.L.S. Vol. 258.

GENERAL IMPROVEMENT AREA
I.e., an area declared to be a general improvement area under the Housing Act 1969 (as to which, see para. 1 above).

TREASURY
See the note to s. 46, *ante*.

STATUTORY INSTRUMENT ... SUBJECT TO ANNULMENT
See the note to s. 151, *ante*.

DEFINITIONS
For "land", see the Housing Act 1969, s. 86 (1); as to "annual loan charges", see s. 86 (5) of that Act, as partly repealed by s. 152 (3), *ante*, and Sch. 26, *post*.

1969 ACT
I.e., the Housing Act 1969; see s. 150, *ante*. The provisions which are to be omitted or are repealed are also repealed by s. 152 (3), *ante*, and Sch. 26, *post*, and s. 28A of the Act of 1969, is repealed by the same provisions consequent upon para. 1 above.

1974 ACT
I.e., the Housing Act 1974; see s. 150, *ante*. Those provisions are repealed by s. 152 (3), *ante*, and Sch. 26, *post*.

ORDERS
At the time of going to press no order had been made under the Housing Act 1969, s. 37 (4), as substituted by para. 5 above.

Housing action areas

7. In relation to any resolution passed by a local authority after the commencement of this Schedule, section 38 (2) (*a*) of the 1974 Act (incorporation of general improvement area or part thereof into housing action area) shall have effect with the omission of the words "and approved by the Secretary of State".

8. Section 42 of the 1974 Act (duty to inform Secretary of State of action taken) shall cease to have effect.

9.—(1) Section 45 of the 1974 Act is amended as follows.

(2) For subsection (1) there is substituted the following subsection:—

"(1) For the purpose of improving the amenities in a housing action area, the local authority may—

(*a*) carry out on any land belonging to them works other than works to the interior of housing accommodation; and

(*b*) give assistance in accordance with this section towards the carrying out of such works by others;

and works which may be carried out or towards the carrying out of which assistance may be given under this section are in this section referred to as "environmental works".

(3) For subsection (3) there is substituted the following subsection:—

"(3) No assistance may be given under subsection (1) above towards works in respect of which an application for a grant under Part VII of this Act has been approved."

10.—(1) For section 46 of the 1974 Act there is substituted the following section:—

"46.—(1) The Secretary of State may pay contributions to local authorities in respect of such expenditure incurred by them under section 45 (1) above as he may determine.

(2) A contribution under this section shall be a sum payable annually for a period of 20 years beginning with the financial year in which the expenditure towards which the contribution is made is incurred and that sum shall be equal to one-half of the annual loan charges referable to that expenditure.

(3) For the purposes of subsection (2) above, the annual loan charges referable to any expenditure are the annual sum that, in the opinion of the Secretary of State, would fall to be paid by the local authority for the repayment of principal and payment of interest on a loan repayable over 20 years of an amount equal to the expenditure.

(4) The aggregate of the expenditure towards which contributions may be made under this section with respect to any housing action area shall not exceed the sum arrived at by multiplying £400 by the aggregate of the number of dwellings, houses in multiple occupation and hostels stated by the local authority, in accordance with section 36 (4) (*c*) above, to be in the area; but two adjoining housing action areas may for the purposes of this subsection be treated as one.

(5) The Secretary of State may, with the consent of the Treasury, by order substitute, in subsection (2) above, another fraction for one-half and, in subsection (4) above, another amount for £400; and he may, with the consent of the Treasury, direct that, in the case of a housing action area specified in the direction or of a housing action area of a description so specified, subsections (2) and (4) above shall have effect as if a higher fraction or a greater amount were substituted for the fraction or amount for the time being specified therein.

(6) An order under subsection (5) above shall be made by statutory instrument which shall be subject to annulment in pursuance of a resolution of the House of Commons.

(7) Where a contribution has been paid under this section towards any expenditure, neither the expenditure nor the contribution shall be carried to the authority's Housing Revenue Account except with the consent of the Secretary of State." **[555]**

COMMENCEMENT

See s. 153 (4), *ante*, and the note "Orders under this section" thereto.

PARA. 7: LOCAL AUTHORITY

I.e., an authority specified in the Housing Act 1974, s. 49, A.L.S. Vol. 223.

PARA. 9: AMENITIES

See the note to s. 42, *ante*.

HOUSING ACTION AREA

I.e., an area declared to be a housing action area under the Housing Act 1974, s. 36.

LAND
For meaning, see the Interpretation Act 1978, s. 5, Sch. 1, A.L.S. Vol. 258.

PARA. 10: SECRETARY OF STATE
See the note to s. 2, *ante*.

FINANCIAL YEAR
See the note to para. 5, *ante*.

OPINION
See the note "Appear" to s. 2, *ante*.

TREASURY
See the note to s. 46, *ante*.

STATUTORY INSTRUMENT ... SUBJECT TO ANNULMENT
See the note to s. 151, *ante*.

HOUSING REVENUE ACCOUNT
See the note to s. 96, *ante*.

DEFINITIONS
For "housing accommodation", see the Housing Act 1974, s. 36 (6); for "dwelling", "hostel" and "house in multiple occupation", see s. 129 (1) of that Act.

1974 ACT
I.e., the Housing Act 1974; see s. 150, *ante*. The provisions to be omitted or which cease to have effect are also repealed by s. 152 (3), *ante*, and Sch. 26, *post*; and Part VII of that Act is amended by s. 107 and Sch. 12, *ante*, and extended by s. 106, *ante*.

ORDERS
At the time of going to press no order had been made under the Housing Act 1974, s. 46 (5), as substituted by para. 10 above.

SCHEDULE 14

Section 116

AMENDMENTS OF HOUSING SUBSIDIES ACT 1967 (c. 29) Part II

1. In section 24 of the 1967 Act, after subsection (2) insert—

"(2A) Prescribed conditions governing entitlement to subsidy may be imposed by reference to—

    (*a*) a borrower's personal circumstances;

    (*b*) the amount of the loan and the terms of repayment;

    (*c*) the use and occupation foreseen for the property on which the loan is secured; and

    (*d*) the existence and terms of any loans taken by a borrower or his spouse before the option notice;

and such other conditions may be prescribed as the Secretary of State thinks necessary to ensure that loans are subsidised only in proper cases, that subsidy is withdrawn when the conditions cease to be fulfilled, and that the borrower repays to the Secretary of State any sums paid by him under subsection (2) (*a*) (ii).".

2. In section 24 (3) (*c*) of the Act, for the words from "a declaration" to "section 24B of this Act is fulfilled" substitute—

"the prescribed declaration with respect to his personal circumstances and the fulfilment of the subsidy conditions";

and in that subsection omit paragraph (*d*) and all after it.

3. In that section, omit subsections (4), (5) and (5A).

4. For sections 24A and 24B substitute—

"24A. Duration of subsidy

(1) An option notice shall have effect for the period beginning with the date on which it is signed and ending with whichever of the following events first occurs, namely—

    (*a*) the satisfaction of the borrower's debt to the lender;

    (*b*) the realisation of the security on the interest in land in question, whether or not the borrower's debt is fully satisfied thereby;

    (*c*) that interest's ceasing to be security for the loan;

    (*d*) the vesting of the rights and obligations under the repayment contract of the borrower (or, in the case of joint borrowers, of both or all of them) in some other person who has become beneficially entitled to the interest;

    (*e*) subject to subsection (2) below, the vesting of the lender's rights under the repayment contract in some other person;

    (*f*) if the number of the periodical payments referred to in section 24 (1) (*c*) is not fixed by or ascertainable under the repayment contract, the expiration of 30 years from the beginning of the period for which the option notice has effect;

    (*g*) the taking effect of a direction under section 24 (3A) with respect to the loan;

    (*h*) any event which by regulations under section 24 (2A) is made to terminate subsidy entitlement, in consequence of the subsidy conditions having ceased to be fulfilled or otherwise.

(2) If at the expiration of the period of 3 months beginning with the date of the vesting referred to in subsection (1) (*e*) above the other person there referred to is a qualifying lender, the option notice shall not cease to have effect by virtue of that paragraph; and the notice and the provisions of this Part of this Act shall be treated as having continued to have effect during that period as if the other person were a qualifying lender, notwithstanding that at any time during that period he was not so."

5.—(1) In section 26 (1), for "subsections (2) to (6) of the said section 24" substitute "sections 24 (2) to (6) and 24A above."

(2) In section 26 (2) for "subsections (2) to (6) of that section" substitute "sections 24 (2) to (6) and 24A above" and for "the said subsections (2) to (6)" substitute "sections 24 (2) to (6) and 24A above".

6.—(1) In section 27 (1) (*c*) after sub-paragraph (iii) insert—

"and

    (iv) other bodies whose activities and objects appear to him to qualify them for inclusion in this subsection".

(2) At the end of section 27 (1) insert—

"(*g*) trustee savings banks;

  (*h*) the Scottish Special Housing Association;

  (*j*) the Development Board for Rural Wales.".

(3) In section 32 (1) at the end insert—

" "subsidy conditions" means conditions prescribed under section 24 (2A) of this Act". **[556]**

COMMENCEMENT
See s. 153 (4), *ante*, and the note "Orders under this section" thereto.

PARA. I: PRESCRIBED CONDITIONS; SUCH OTHER CONDITIONS MAY BE PRESCRIBED
I.e., prescribed by regulations made by the Secretary of State; see the Housing Subsidies Act 1974, s. 32 (1), as amended by the Housing Act 1974, s. 119 (1), Sch. 11, para. 7, A.L.S. Vol. 223. At the time of going to press nothing had been prescribed for the purposes of the Housing Subsidies Act 1967, s. 24 (2A), as inserted by para. 1 above.

SECRETARY OF STATE
See the note to s. 2, *ante*.

PARA. 2: PRESCRIBED DECLARATION
Cf. the first note to para. 1 above. At the time of going to press no declaration had been

prescribed for the purposes of the Housing Subsidies Act 1967, s. 24 (3) (*c*), as amended by para. 2 above.

PARA. 4: PERSON
See the note to s. 24, *ante*.

3 MONTHS BEGINNING WITH, ETC.
See the note to s. 12, *ante*.

QUALIFYING LENDER
Qualifying lenders are the bodies specified in, or by order under, the Housing Subsidies Act 1967, s. 27, as amended by para. 6 (1), (2) above.

THIS PART OF THIS ACT
I.e., the Housing Subsidies Act 1967, Part II (as amended or affected by ss. 114, 115, 116 (1) and 152 (3), *ante*, and by this Schedule and Sch. 26, *post*).

PARA. 6: APPEAR
See the note to s. 2, *ante*.

SCOTTISH SPECIAL HOUSING ASSOCIATION
This Association was established in 1937; it is not a statutory body but was approved by the Secretary of State under the Housing (Financial Provisions) (Scotland) Act 1938, s. 2.

DEVELOPMENT BOARD FOR RURAL WALES
See the note to s. 19, *ante*.

DEFINITIONS
For "repayment contract", see the Housing Subsidies Act 1967, s. 24 (1) (*c*); for "option notice", see s. 24 (2) of that Act; for "prescribed" and "subsidy conditions", see s. 32 (1) of that Act, as amended by the Housing Act 1974, s. 119 (1), Sch. 11, para. 7, and by para. 6 (3) above.

1967 ACT
I.e., the Housing Subsidies Act 1967; see s. 116 (1), *ante*.

SCHEDULE 15

Section 118

RENT REBATES AND ALLOWANCES

1. Part II of the 1972 Act is amended as follows.

2. For section 18 there is substituted the following section—

"18. Rent Rebates

(1) It shall be the duty of every authority to maintain a scheme for granting, to persons who occupy as their homes dwellings let to them by the authority, rebates from rent calculated in accordance with the provisions of the scheme by reference to their needs and resources.

(2) A scheme under this section is referred to in this Part of this Act as a 'rebate scheme'.

(3) No rebate from the rent for any dwelling shall be granted by virtue of this section to any person—

(*a*) if he occupies the dwelling under a licence which was granted as a temporary expedient to a person who entered it, or any other land, as a trespasser (whether or not before the grant another licence of that or any other dwelling has been granted to him); or

(*b*) if he occupies the dwelling in pursuance of a contract of service with the authority the terms of which require that he shall be provided with a dwelling at a rent specified in the contract; or

(*c*) if Part II of the Landlord and Tenant Act 1954 (security of business tenants) applies to his tenancy.

318

(4) Where a person who is not the tenant of a dwelling has a licence to occupy the dwelling, granted for a consideration, this Part of this Act, so far as it relates to rebate schemes, applies to the licence as it applies to a tenancy and, as so applied, has effect as if expressions appropriate to a licence were substituted for those appropriate to a tenancy.".

3. For section 19 there is substituted the following section—

"19. Rent allowances

19.—(1) It shall be the duty of every local authority to maintain a scheme for granting to private tenants who occupy as their homes dwellings in the authority's area allowances, calculated in accordance with the provisions of the scheme by reference to their needs and resources, towards the rent payable under their tenancies.

(2) A scheme under this section is referred to in this Part of this Act as an 'allowance scheme'.

(3) No allowance towards the rent of a dwelling shall be granted by virtue of this section to any person who occupies a dwelling in pursuance of a contract of service the terms of which require that he shall be provided with a dwelling at a rent specified in the contract.

(4) In this Part of this Act 'private tenant' means a person who is a private tenant by virtue of any of the following provisions of this section.

(5) A person is a private tenant if—

    (a) he is protected or statutory tenant for the purposes of the Rent Act 1977;

    (b) he occupies a dwelling under a contract which is a restricted contract for the purposes of that Act;

    (c) he occupies a dwelling under a contract which would be a restricted contract but for section 19 (5) (c) of the Act of 1977;

    (d) he occupies a dwelling let to him under an assured tenancy within the meaning of section 56 of the Housing Act 1980;

    (e) he occupies a dwelling let to him by—

        (i) a county council;

        (ii) the Housing Corporation;

        (iii) a housing association;

        (iv) a housing trust within the meaning of section 15 of the Act of 1977;

    and his tenancy would be a protected tenancy for the purposes of that Act but for section 14 or 15 of the Act of 1977;

    (f) he occupies a dwelling let to him by a housing co-operative, as defined in paragraph 1 of Schedule 20 to the Housing Act 1980, and his tenancy would be a protected tenancy but for section 16 of the Act of 1977 or, where the housing co-operative is a housing association, but for sections 15 and 16 of the Act of 1977;

    (g) he is a statutory tenant of premises under the Rent (Agriculture) Act 1976 and the rent payable under his tenancy is not less than two-thirds of the rateable value which is or was the rateable value of his dwelling on the appropriate day for the purposes of the Act of 1977; or

    (h) he occupies hostel accommodation or shared accommodation.

(6) In subsection (5) (h) above—

'hostel accommodation' means accommodation in a building in which there is provided, for persons generally or for a class or classes of person, residential accommodation otherwise than in separate and self-contained sets of premises; and

'shared accommodation' means accommodation which a person occupies together with one or more other persons and of which he would be a private tenant by virtue of any of paragraphs (a) to (g) of subsection (5) above if he had the right to exclusive occupation of the accommodation.

319

(7) A person is not a private tenant if he occupies a dwelling let to him by a housing association and he (or his personal representative) will, under the terms of the tenancy agreement or of the agreement under which he became a member of the association, be entitled, on his ceasing to be a member and subject to any conditions stated in either agreement, to a sum calculated by reference directly or indirectly to the value of the dwelling.

(8) Where a person occupies hostel accommodation under a licence, granted for a consideration, this Part of this Act, so far as it relates to allowance schemes, applies to the licence as it applies to a tenancy and, as so applied, has effect as if expressions appropriate to a licence were substituted for those appropriate to a tenancy.

(9) In this section 'local authority' does not include the Greater London Council.".

4. In section 19A (1) for "(4)" there is substituted "(3)".

5.—(1) In section 20 (5)—

(a) for paragraph (a) there is substituted the following paragraph—
  "(a) that the general level of the rents charged by an authority is exceptionally high by comparison with the general level of the rents charged by other authorities.";
(b) for paragraph (c) there is substituted the following paragraph—
  "(c) that the general level of the rents charged by an authority for a class of dwelling, or of the rents paid by private tenants for a class of dwelling in the area of an authority, is exceptionally high by comparison with the general level of the rents charged by other authorities or, as the case may be, with the general level of the rents paid by private tenants elsewhere"; and
(c) paragraph (d) is hereby repealed.

(2) In section 20 (7) the words from "section 19 (8)" to "Schedule 3 to this Act" are hereby repealed.

6.—(1) In section 24 (5) the words "or their allowance scheme, as may be appropriate" and the words from "of Housing Revenue" to "housing account dwellings" are hereby repealed.

(2) For subsection (6) of section 24 there is substituted the following subsection—

"(6) An authority shall also furnish the statutory particulars of their rebate scheme to any person who becomes their tenant, on or before the date on which his tenancy commences.".

(3) In section 24 (9), for the words "tenant of a dwelling" there are substituted the words "private tenant".

7.—(1) In section 25 (2), after paragraph (c) there are inserted the following words—
", and
  (d) exclusive of any part of the rent or residue which is fairly attributable to the provision of board".

(2) In section 25 (5), after the word "services" there are inserted the words "or board".

8.—(1) In section 26 (1), the following are hereby repealed—
(a) in the definition of "allowance" the words from "but also" to the end;
(b) in the definition of "allowance scheme" the words from "and includes" to the end; and
(c) the definition of "housing account dwelling".

(2) In section 26 (1) for the definition of "dwelling" there are substituted the following definitions—

" 'dwelling' means—
  (a) in relation to a rebate scheme, any residential accommodation provided by an authority, whether or not comprising separate and self-contained premises; and
  (b) in relation to an allowance scheme, any premises of which a person is a private tenant for the purposes of this Part of this Act;

'housing association' has the meaning assigned to it for the purposes of the Housing Act 1957 by section 189 (1) of that Act.".

(3) In section 26 (1), for the definition of "tenant" there is substituted the following definition—

" 'tenant' means—

    (a) in relation to a rebate scheme, a person who occupies a dwelling as mentioned in section 18 of this Act, including a successor in title of the person to whom the dwelling was originally let, and

    (b) in relation to an allowance scheme, a private tenant.".

9. In Schedule 4, in paragraph 1 (3) (a) the words from "Housing" to "account" are hereby repealed. **[557]**

COMMENCEMENT
See the note to s. 118, *ante*.

PARA. 2: IT SHALL BE THE DUTY
See the note to s. 43, *ante*.

THIS PART OF THIS ACT
I.e., the Housing Finance Act 1972, Part II, A.L.S. Vol. 202.

LICENCE
As to licences generally and the differences between tenancies and licences, see 23 Halsbury's Laws (3rd Edn.), pp. 427 *et seq*.

CONTRACT OF SERVICE
As to the destination between a contract of service (or employment) and a contract for services, see 16 Halsbury's Laws (4th Edn.), para. 501.

PARA. 3: COUNTY COUNCIL
See the note to s. 19, *ante*.

HOUSING CORPORATION
See the note to s. 2, *ante*.

BUILDING
See the note to s. 3, *ante*.

GREATER LONDON COUNCIL
See the note to s. 50, *ante*.

DEFINITIONS
For "statutory particulars", see the Housing Finance Act 1972, s. 24 (4); for "allowance", "authority", "dwelling", "housing association", "rebate", "tenant" and "tenancy", see s. 26 (1) of that Act, as amended by para. 8 above; for "land" and "local authority", see s. 104 (1) of that Act (and note also as to "local authority", s. 19 (9) of that Act as substituted by para. 3 above). Note as to "rebate scheme", s. 18 (2) of the Act of 1972 as substituted by para. 2 above; as to "allowance scheme", s. 19 (2) of the Act of 1972 as substituted by para. 3 above; as to "private tenant", s. 19 (4), (5), (7) of that Act as so substituted; and as to "hostel accommodation" and "shared accommodation", s. 19 (6) of that Act as so substituted.

1972 ACT
I.e., the Housing Finance Act 1972; see s. 150, *ante*. S. 19A was inserted by the Housing Rents and Subsidies Act 1975, s. 12, A.L.S. Vol. 230; and s. 25 (2) (c) was added by the Rent Act 1974, s. 11 (7), A.L.S. Vol. 224. The provisions which are repealed are also repealed by s. 152 (3), *ante*, and Sch. 26, *post*.

LANDLORD AND TENANT ACT 1954, PART II
See A.L.S. Vols. 87, 155, and for the tenancies to which that Part applies, see s. 23 of that Act and the note thereto, and s. 58 (1), *ante*.

RENT ACT 1977
See A.L.S. Vol. 255.

RENT (AGRICULTURE) ACT 1976
For the meaning of "statutory tenant", see ss. 4 and 5 of that Act, A.L.S. Vol. 250.

HOUSING ACT 1957, S. 189 (1)
See A.L.S. Vol. 109.

SCHEDULE 16

Sections 124 and 126

REGISTERED HOUSING ASSOCIATIONS

PART I

ACCOUNTING REQUIREMENTS FOR CHARITABLE HOUSING ASSOCIATIONS

1.—(1) The charity shall in respect of its housing activities—

   (a) cause to be kept proper books of account showing its transactions and its assets and liabilities; and

   (b) establish and maintain a satisfactory system of control of its books of account, its cash holdings and all its receipts and remittances.

(2) The books of account must be such as to enable a true and fair view to be given of the state of affairs of the society in respect of its housing activities, and to explain its transactions in the course of those activities.

2.—(1) The charity shall for each period of account prepare—

   (a) a revenue account giving a true and fair view of the charity's income and expenditure in the period, so far as arising in connection with its housing activities,

   (b) a balance sheet giving a true and fair view (as at the end of the period) of the state of the charity's affairs.

(2) The revenue account and balance sheet must be signed by at least two trustees of the charity.

3.—(1) The charity shall in each period of account appoint a qualified auditor to audit the accounts prepared to comply with paragraph 2.

(2) A person is qualified for the purposes of this paragraph if he is either a member of one of the following bodies—

   (a) the Institute of Chartered Accountants in England and Wales;

   (b) the Institute of Chartered Accountants of Scotland;

   (c) the Association of Certified Accountants;

   (d) the Institute of Chartered Accountants in Ireland;

   (e) any other body of accountants established in the United Kingdom and recognised by the Secretary of State for the purposes of section 161 (1) (a) of the Companies Act 1948,

or a person who is for the time being authorised by the Secretary of State under section 161 (1) (b) of that Act as being a person with similar qualifications obtained outside the United Kingdom.

(3) But none of the following shall be appointed—

   (a) any trustee, officer or servant of the charity or of an associated body;

   (b) any person who is a partner of or in the employment of, or who employs, a trustee, officer or servant of the charity or of an associated body; or

   (c) a body corporate;

and any body of persons is "associated" for this purpose (whether a corporate or unincorporated body, and whether or not itself a charity) if it is essentially under the same management or control as the charity.

(4) A Scottish firm is qualified for appointment as auditor, notwithstanding sub-paragraph (3) (c) above, if each of the partners in it is qualified for appointment.

4.—(1) The charity's auditor appointed under this Schedule shall make a report to the charity on the accounts examined by him.

(2) The report shall state whether, in the auditor's opinion—

(a) the revenue account gives a true and fair view of the income and expenditure of the charity in respect of its housing activities and of any other matters to which it relates; and

(b) the balance sheet gives a true and fair view of the state of affairs of the charity as at the end of the period of account.

5.—(1) It shall be the duty of the charity's auditor so appointed, in preparing his report, to carry out such investigations as will enable him to form an opinion as to the following matters—

(a) whether the charity has kept, in respect of its housing activities, proper books of account in accordance with the requirements of this Schedule;

(b) whether the charity has maintained a satisfactory system of control over its transactions in accordance with all those requirements; and

(c) whether the accounts are in agreement with the charity's books.

(2) If the auditor is of opinion that the charity has failed in any respect to comply with this Schedule, or if the accounts are not in agreement with the books, the auditor shall state that fact in his report.

(3) The auditor—

(a) shall have a right of access at all times to the books, deeds and accounts of the charity, so far as relating to its housing activities, and to all other documents relating to those activities; and

(b) shall be entitled to require from the trustees or officers of the charity such information and explanations as he thinks necessary for the performance of his duties.

(4) If the auditor fails to obtain all the information and explanations which, to the best of his knowledge and belief, are necessary for the purposes of his audit, he shall state that fact in his report.

6. A period of account for the purposes of this Schedule is 12 months or such other period not less than 6 months and not more than 18 months as the charity may with the consent of the Housing Corporation determine. **[558]**

COMMENCEMENT

This Schedule came into operation on the passing of the Act on 8th August 1980 by virtue of s. 153 (3), *ante*, but by virtue of s. 124 (7), *ante*, this Part of the Schedule only applies with respect to any period beginning on or after the day on which the first order under s. 124 (1), *ante*, comes into force. At the time of going to press no such order had been made.

PARA. 1: THE CHARITY

By s. 124 (5), *ante*, this Part of this Schedule applies to any registered housing association (as defined by s. 133 (1), *ante*) which is a registered charity (as so defined) but not a society registered under the Industrial and Provident Societies Act 1965.

PARA. 3: UNITED KINGDOM

See the note to s. 110, *ante*.

SECRETARY OF STATE

Cf. the note to s. 2, *ante*. The Secretary of State referred to in para. 3 (2) above is the Secretary of State for Trade.

PARA. 6: MONTHS

I.e., calendar months; see the Interpretation Act 1978, s. 5, Sch. 1, A.L.S. Vol. 258.

HOUSING CORPORATION

See the note to s. 1, *ante*.

ENFORCEMENT

See s. 125, *ante*.

323

DEFINITIONS
As to "housing activities", see s. 133 (2), *ante*. Note as to "period of account", para. 6 above.

COMPANIES ACT 1948, S. 161 (1)
See 5, Halsbury's Statutes (3rd edn.), p. 240.

PART II
PAYMENTS TO CERTAIN COMMITTEE MEMBERS AND OTHERS
Provisions substituted for subsections (3) to (6) of section 26 of the 1974 Act

"(3) The Corporation may from time to time specify the maximum amounts which may be paid by a registered 1965 Act association—

    (*a*) by way of fees or other remuneration or by way of expenses to a member of the association who is not a member of its committee or an officer or employee of the association;

    (*b*) by way of expenses to a member of its committee who is not an officer or employee of the association; or

    (*c*) by way of expenses to an officer of the association who does not have a contract of employment with the association.

(4) Different amounts may be specified under subsection (3) above for different purposes.

(5) Where a registered 1965 Act association—

    (*a*) pays any sum or makes any gift in breach of subsection (1) above; or

    (*b*) pays to any person a sum which exceeds any maximum amount specified in relation to that person under sub-section (3) above;

the sum or, as the case may be, the value of the gift or, in a case falling within paragraph (*b*) above, the amount by which the sum exceeds the maximum shall be recoverable by the association; and proceedings for its recovery shall be taken by the association if the Corporation gives the association a direction to that effect.

(6) For the purposes of subsection (3) (*b*) above and section 27 below, a person co-opted by the committee of a registered 1965 Act association to serve on the committee (whether he is a member of the association or not) shall be treated as a member of the committee."

Provision substituted for section 27 of the 1974 Act

"27. Payments and grant of benefits by registered 1965 Act associations

(1) Subject to subsection (5) below, a registered 1965 Act association shall not make any payment or grant any benefit to—

    (*a*) a person who is, or at any time within the relevant period has been, a committee member, officer or employee of the association;

    (*b*) a close relative of such a person; or

    (*c*) a business trading for profit in which a person falling within paragraph (*a*) above has a personal interest.

(2) In subsection (1) (*a*) above, "the relevant period" means the period of 12 months immediately preceding the making of the payment or the grant of the benefit.

(3) For the purposes of subsection (1) (*c*) above, a person has a personal interest in a business if he, or a close relative of his, either is one of the principal proprietors of the business or is directly concerned with its management.

(4) Any sum paid, or the value of any benefit granted, by a registered 1965 Act association in breach of sub-section (1) above shall be recoverable by the association; and proceedings for its recovery shall be taken by the association if the Corporation gives it a direction to that effect.

(5) This section does not apply to—

(a) any payment made or benefit granted by a registered 1965 Act association to an officer or employee under his contract of employment with the association;

(b) any payment of expenses made by such an association to a member of its committee;

(c) any payment to which, by virtue of subsection (2) of section 26 above, subsection (1) of that section does not apply; or

(d) any payment of expenses to which section 26 (3) (c) above applies.

(6) Where a tenancy of a house has been granted to, or to a close relative of, a person who later became a committee member, officer or employee of an association, nothing in this section prevents the grant to that tenant of a new tenancy (whether of that or any other house).

(7) Nothing in this section prevents the grant or renewal of a tenancy by an association whose rules restrict membership to persons who are tenants or prospective tenants of the association and preclude the granting or assignment of tenancies to persons other than members.

(8) No sum shall be recoverable under this section in respect of a payment made or a benefit granted by a registered 1965 Act association in a case where an obligation to make the payment or grant the benefit was incurred by the association before the passing of the Housing Act 1980.". **[559]**

COMMENCEMENT
This Part of this Schedule came into force on the passing of this Act on 8th August 1980 by virtue of s. 153 (3), *ante.*

Note—references in this annotation are to the new Housing Act 1974, s. 27.

SUB-SS. (1) (b) AND (3): CLOSE RELATIVE
This is not defined at all and one is left to infer, first that blood ties are to be included only (*e.g.* not mistresses and the like) and second that it is spouses, fathers, mothers, children and possibly grandparents and grandchildren who are chiefly within the vice of s. 27. *Quaere* whether uncles, nephews etc., are within s. 27?

SUB-SS. (1) (c) AND (3): BUSINESS
For a discussion of this wide term, see the note to Sch. 3, para. 12.

SUB-S. (3): DIRECTLY CONCERNED
An example may be given as to the great width of this section as a whole. Suppose that it were possible for Q Housing Association to pay the rates of the X Co. Ltd. on some premises the latter holds on a lease from Q. Surely this is a "benefit"? It then transpires that one M, the spouse of R, who is an employee of Q Assn., is the sales director of the X Co. Ltd. and "directly concerned" in its business: see *Glanvill, Enthoven & Co.* v. *I.R.C.* (1925) 41 T.L.R. 258, H.L. This gives R a personal interest in the X Co. Ltd. within sub-s. (3) and so the benefit is caught because of R's employment with the Q Assn.

This also contains another quite obvious trap. Suppose that in the above, the benefit was conferred eleven and a half months after R (say a quite junior employee: note the absence of a requirement of direct concern as concerns employees or officers of a housing association) resigned from Q Assn. It is still caught as it is within the "relevant period" in s. 27 (2).

SCHEDULE 17

Section 129

AMENDMENT AND EXTENSION OF SECTIONS 19 AND 20 OF HOUSING ACT 1974 (C. 44)

Appointment of persons to conduct inquiries

1. In section 19, in subsection (1), the words "(who may or may not be a member of the Corporation's staff)" are hereby repealed; and after subsection (1) there is inserted the following subsection—

"(1A) No person who is, or at any time has been, a member of the Corporation's staff shall be appointed to conduct an inquiry under subsection (1) above.". **[560]**

Duty of agents to give information

2. In subsection (2) of section 19 after "officer" there is inserted "agent" and at the end of the section there is added the following:—

"(8) In subsection (2) above "agent" includes banker, solicitor and auditor; but nothing in this section requires the disclosure—

(a) by a solicitor, of any privileged communication made to him in his capacity of a solicitor; or

(b) by a housing association's banker's, of any information as to the affairs of any of their other customers." **[561]**

Suspension of committee members and others

3. In section 20—

(a) after subsection (1) (a) there is inserted—

"(aa) by order suspend such a person for up to 6 months, pending determination whether he should be removed;";

(b) after subsection (1) there is inserted—

"(1A) Where a person is suspended, the Corporation may give directions with respect to the performance of his functions and otherwise as to matters arising from the suspension.";

(c) in subsection (5) after "subsection (2) above" there is inserted "or suspended under subsection (1) (aa) above". **[562]**

Extension to registered charities which are not exempt charities

4. The powers exercisable by the Housing Corporation under sections 19 and 20 may be exercised in relation to any registered housing association—

(a) which is a registered charity and not an exempt charity; and

(b) with respect to which, at the time the powers are exercised (in this Schedule referred to as the relevant time), the condition stated in paragraph 5 below is satisfied;

but subject to the following provisions of this Schedule.

5. The condition mentioned in paragraph 4 above is that the housing association has at any time received a grant or loan under section 119 (3) of the 1957 Act, section 9, 29, 31, 32 or 33 of the 1974 Act or under any enactment mentioned in paragraph 2 or 3 of Schedule 2 to that Act.

6. Sections 19 and 20 shall have effect in their application by virtue of paragraph 4 above as if—

(a) the references in either section to a registered 1965 Act association included such an association as is mentioned in that paragraph;

(b) the references in either section to an officer, agent or member or to a member of the committee included a trustee;

(c) the references in section 19 to the association's business did not include any activities other than the association's housing activities;

(d) the references in section 19 to the association's accounts did not include revenue accounts not relating to the association's housing activities, except in so far as such accounts are necessary for the auditing of revenue accounts which do so relate or of the association's balance sheet; and

(e) the auditor referred to in section 19 (4) were an auditor qualified for the purposes of paragraph 3 of Schedule 16 to this Act.

7. The power under section 19 (1), section 20 (1) (a), section 20 (1) (aa) or section 20 (3) shall not be exercised by virtue of paragraph 4 above except after consultation with the Charity Commissioners; and nothing in this Schedule shall be taken to enable the Housing Corporation

to appoint a trustee in excess of the maximum number permissible under the constitution of the housing association with respect to which the power under section 20 (3) is exercisable.

8. A person appointed under section 20 (3) as a member of the committee or a trustee of a housing association shall be entitled—

    (*a*) to attend, speak and vote at any general meeting of the association and to receive all notices of and other communications relating to any general meeting which a member of the association is entitled to receive; and

    (*b*) to require a general meeting of the association to be convened within 21 days of a request to that effect made in writing to the committee or the trustees of the association. **[563]**

Proceedings for an offence

9. In section 20 (7), after "the consent of" there is inserted "the Director of Public Prosecutions or". **[564]**

COMMENCEMENT
See s. 153 (4), *ante*, and the note "Orders under this section" thereto.

PARA. 2 : PRIVILEGED COMMUNICATION
Communications to a solicitor are exempted from the duty to disclose in the Housing Act 1974, s. 19 (2), if privileged. Curiously, it is not provided that communications *from* such an one are exempt from the duty to disclose.

Subject to this matter, a communication between a client and solicitor is privileged from disclosure though no litigation is contemplated by the client: *Greenough* v. *Gaskell* (1833) 1 My. and K. 98, H.L. The relationship of solicitor and client must at least be contemplated : privilege will not attach simply because the person to whom the communication is addressed is a solicitor: *Minter* v. *Priest* [1930] A.C. 558, H.L. But communications from a legal adviser to a third party to obtain information are not privileged where no litigation is existing or contemplated: *Wheeler* v. *Le Marchant* (1881) 17 Ch. D. 675, C.A. The fact that the adviser is an employee of the client will not exclude the privilege: *Alfred Crompton Amusement Machines Ltd.* v. *Comrs of Customs and Excise (No. 2)* [1972] 2 Q.B. 102; [1972] 2 All E.R. 353, C.A.; on appeal the point was not dealt with by their Lordships: [1974] A.C. 405; [1973] 2 All E.R. 1169. The privilege may be waived by the client: *Wilson* v. *Rastall* (1792) 4 Term Rep. 753, and enures for the benefit of the client's successors in title: *Minet* v. *Morgan* (1873) 8 Ch. App. 361; *Crescent Farm (Sidcup) Sports Ltd.* v. *Sterling Offices Ltd. and Another* [1972] Ch. 553; [1971] 3 All E.R. 1192.

Communications made to a solicitor by his client before the commission of a crime or fraud for the purpose of being guided or helped in the commission of the same are not privileged from disclosure: *R.* v. *Cox and Railton* (1884) 14 Q.B.D. 153; *R.* v. *Smith* (1915) 11 Cr. App. Rep. 229; for an application of this doctrine to civil fraud, see *Williams* v. *Quebrada Railway, Land and Copper Co.* [1895] 2 Ch. 751, but fraud in this context means fraud or dishonesty, not inducement of breach of contract: *Crescent Farm* case *supra*.

As to the bankers mentioned in para. 2, this is not a claim which the common law would recognise: thus there is no privilege in an accountant in relation to documents relating to his client's tax affairs: *Chantrey Martin & Co* v. *Martin* [1953] 2 Q.B. 286; [1953] 2 All E.R. 691. *Aliter* if the documents are the client's property; cf. *Leicestershire County Council* v. *Michael Faraday & Partners Ltd.* [1941] 2 K.B. 205; [1941] 2 All E.R. 483, C.A.

PARA. 3 : MONTHS
I.e., calendar months; see the Interpretation Act 1978, s. 5, Sch. 1, A.L.S. Vol. 258.

PARA 4 : HOUSING CORPORATION
See the note to s. 1, *ante*.

PARA. 7 : CONSULTATION
See the note "Consult" to s. 26, *ante*.

CHARITY COMMISSIONERS
I.e., the Charity Commissioners for England and Wales referred to in the Charities Act 1960, s. 1, A.L.S. Vol. 132; see the Interpretation Act 1978, s. 5, Sch. 1.

PARA. 8 : WITHIN 21 DAYS OF, ETC.
See the note" Within six months of, etc." to s. 3, *ante*.

WRITING
See the note "Written; writing" to s. 5, *ante*.

PARA 9: DIRECTOR OF PUBLIC PROSECUTIONS
See the note to s. 125, *ante*.

DEFINITIONS
For "registered charity", "exempt charity" and "registered housing association", see s. 133 (1), *ante*; as to "housing activities", see s. 133 (2), *ante*; for "the Corporation" and "housing association", see the Housing Act 1974, s. 129 (1), A.L.S. Vol. 223.

HOUSING ACT 1974, SS. 19, 20
The words in s. 19 (1) of that Act which are repealed are also repealed by s. 152 (3), *ante*, and Sch. 26, *post*.

1957 ACT
I.e., the Housing Act 1957; see s. 150, *ante*.

1974 ACT
I.e., the Housing Act 1974; see s. 150 ante. S. 29 of that Act is amended and otherwise affected by s. 130, *ante*, and Sch. 18, paras, 1, 2, *post*; s. 31 is repealed by ss. 130 (4) and 152 (3), *ante*, and Sch. 18, para. 8, and Sch. 26, *post*, except in relation to grants payable in pursuance of applications made before 8th August 1980; and ss. 32 and 33 are amended by s. 130 (4), *ante*, and Sch. 18, paras. 9, 10, *post*.

SCHEDULE 18

Section 130

AMENDMENTS OF HOUSING ACT 1974 (c. 44) PART III

Shared ownership schemes

1.—(1) In section 29 of the 1974 Act (housing association grant) after subsection (2) there is inserted the following subsection:—

"(2A) For the purposes of this section, "letting" includes the grant of a lease or licence to occupy—

(a) on payment of a premium calculated by reference to a percentage of the value of the dwelling or of the cost of providing it; or

(b) under which the tenant (or his personal representatives) will or may be entitled to a sum calculated by reference directly or indirectly to the value of the dwelling." **[565]**

(2) This paragraph shall be deemed always to have had effect.

Cost of housing projects

2. In section 29, after subsection (6) there is inserted the following subsection—

"(6A) In determining the net cost of a housing project under subsection (6) above the Secretary of State may adopt the assessment of the body forwarding the application under sub-section (3) above." **[566]**

Approved development programmes

3. After section 29 there is inserted the following section—

"29A. Approved development programmes

(1) In this section "approved development programme" means any programme for the development of housing by registered housing associations prepared by the Housing Corporation or—

(a) in England and Wales, by a council which has power under section 119 of the Housing Act 1957 to make loans to registered housing associations; or

(b) *(applies to Scotland.)*

and approved for the time being by the Secretary of State for the purposes of this section.

(2) Where a registered housing association undertake a housing project which falls within an approved development programme, housing association grant may be paid under section 29 in respect of that project, notwithstanding that it has not been approved by the Secretary of State under section 29 (1).". **[567]**

Payment of housing association grant

4. In subsection (1) of section 30—

(a) after the words "the project is completed" where they occur in paragraphs (a) and (b) there are inserted the words "or its completion has become impossible"; and

(b) for the words "before the project is completed" there are substituted the words "at an earlier time".

5. After subsection (2) of section 30 there is inserted the following subsection—

"(2A) In any case where, by virtue of section 29A above, a housing project has not required the approval of the Secretary of State under section 29 (1), the Secretary of State may impose such conditions as are mentioned in subsection (2) above before first making payment of housing association grant in respect of that project.".

6. For subsection (3) of section 30 there are substituted the following subsections—

"(3) If, after the making of a housing association grant to a registered housing association—

(a) any land to which the grant relates has been disposed of by the association in any manner;

(b) any condition imposed under subsection (2) above has not been complied with; or

(c) the Secretary of State is satisfied that any land to which the grant relates has ceased to be used, or to be available for use, for the purpose for which, at the time the project concerned was approved, it was intended that it should be used;

the Secretary of State may reduce the amount of, or of any payment in respect of, the grant or suspend or discontinue any instalment of it or, where any payment has been made to the association in respect of the grant, direct the association to pay to him an amount equal to the whole, or such proportion as he may determine, of the amount so paid to the association.

(3A) Any amount which a registered housing association is directed to repay to the Secretary of State under subsection (3) above shall be recoverable as a simple contract debt, or in Scotland as a debt due under a contract, in any court of competent jurisdiction.".

7. Subsection (5) of section 30 is hereby repealed. **[568]**

Management grant

8. No grant shall be made under section 31 (management grants) except in pursuance of an application made before the passing of this Act; and accordingly that section shall cease to have effect except in relation to grants payable in pursuance of such applications. **[569]**

Revenue deficit grant

9. In section 32 (deficit grants)—

(a) in subsection (1), the word "annual" is omitted and for the words "an accounting year of the association" there are substituted the words "any period";

(b) in subsection (2)—

(i) in the words preceding the paragraphs for the words from "in respect of" to "association" there are substituted the words "to a registered housing association in respect of any period";

(ii) in paragraph (a) for the words from "in respect of that year" to "end of that year" there are substituted the words "in respect of that period is made by the association to the Secretary of State not later than 15 months after the end of that period"; and

   (iii) in paragraph (c) for the words "accounting year" there is substituted the word "period";

  (c) for subsection (3) there is substituted the following subsection:—

"(3) For the purposes of this section, a registered housing association shall be treated as incurring a deficit on its revenue account for any period, if—

    (a) its expenditure for that period which, in the opinion of the Secretary of State, is attributable to its housing activities and is reasonable and appropriate, having regard to all the circumstances; exceeds

    (b) the income which, in the opinion of the Secretary of State, it might reasonably be expected to receive for that period in respect of its housing activities, including sums by way of grant or subsidy under any enactment other than this section;

and for this purpose—

    (i) an association's housing activities are any of its activities not relating to hostels or, if the association is a registered charity and not an exempt charity, those of its activities not relating to hostels which fall within section 133 (2) of the Housing Act 1980; and

    (ii) an association's expenditure and income shall be calculated in such manner as the Secretary of State may, with the consent of the Treasury, from time to time determine.";

  (d) subsection (4) shall cease to have effect except in relation to grants made in pursuance of applications made before the passing of this Act;

  (e) in subsection (5) for the words "accounting year" there is substituted the word "period" and for the words "that year" the words "that period";

  (f) in subsection (6) for the words "accounting year", in both places, there is substituted the word "period"; and

  (g) subsection (8) is hereby repealed. **[570]**

Hostel deficit grant

10. In section 33—

  (a) in subsection (1) for the words "an accounting year of the association" there are substituted the words "any period";

  (b) in subsection (2) for the words from "any accounting year" to "end of that year" there are substituted the words "any period unless an application in respect of that period is made by the association to the Secretary of State not later than 15 months after the end of that period";

  (c) in subsection (3)—

    (i) in the words preceding the paragraphs, for the words "an accounting year of the association" there are substituted the words "any period"; and

    (ii) in paragraphs (a) and (b) for the word "year", wherever it occurs, there is substituted the word "period";

  (d) in subsection (4) for the words "accounting year of the association" there is substituted the word "period" and for the words "that year" the words "that period";

  (e) in subsection (5) for the words "accounting year" there is substituted the word "period" and for the words "that year" the words "that period"; and

  (f) in subsection (6) for the words "accounting year", in both places, there is substituted the word "period" and the words "before the expiry of that year" are omitted.

[571]

COMMENCEMENT

This Schedule came into operation on the passing of this Act on 8th August 1980 by virtue of s. 153 (3), *ante* (but note para. 1 (2) above).

330

PARA. 1: LICENCE
As to licences generally and the differences between tenancies and licences, see 23 Halsbury's Laws (3rd Edn.), pp. 427 *et seq.*

PARA. 2: SECRETARY OF STATE
See the note to s. 2, *ante.*

PARA. 3: HOUSING CORPORATION
See the note to s. 1, *ante.*

ENGLAND; WALES
For meanings, see the Interpretation Act 1978, s. 5, Sch. 1, A.L.S. Vol. 258.

PARA. 6: LAND
For meaning, see the Interpretation Act 1978, s. 5, Sch. 1.

SATISFIED
See the note "Appear" to s. 2, *ante.*

PARA. 8: PASSING OF THIS ACT
This Act was passed, *i.e.,* received the Royal Assent, on 8th August 1980.

PARA. 9: NOT LATER THAN 15 MONTHS AFTER, ETC.
See the note "Not later than three months after, etc." to s. 11, *ante.*

OPINION
See the note "Appear" to s. 2, *ante.*

TREASURY
See the note to s. 46, *ante.*

DEFINITIONS
For "housing association grant", see the Housing Act 1974, s. 29 (1); for "housing project", see s. 29 (2) of that Act; for "dwelling", "hostel", "housing association", "registered" and "registered charity", see s. 129 (1) of that Act; as to "exempt charity", cf. s. 133 (1), *ante.* Note as to "approved development programme", s. 29A (1) of the Act of 1974 as inserted by para. 3 above.

1974 ACT
I.e., the Housing Act 1974; see s. 150, *ante.* The provisions which are repealed or omitted or cease to have effect are also repealed by s. 152 (3), *ante,* and Sch. 26, *post.*

HOUSING ACT 1957, S. 119
See A.L.S. Vol. 109. That section is partly repealed by s. 152 (1), (3), *ante,* and Sch. 25, para. 6, and Sch. 26, *post.*

SCHEDULE 19

Section 136

PROVISIONS REPLACING SECTIONS 90 TO 91A OF HOUSING FINANCE ACT 1972

Service charge and relevant costs

1.—(1) For the purposes of this Schedule, a service charge is an amount payable by the tenant of a flat as part of or in addition to the rent—

(*a*) which is payable, directly or indirectly, for services, repairs, maintenance or insurance or the landlord's costs of management; and

(*b*) the whole or part of which varies or may vary according to the relevant costs;

and the relevant costs are the costs or estimated costs (including overheads) incurred or to be incurred in any period (whether the period for which the service charge is payable or an earlier or later period) by or on behalf of the landlord or a superior landlord in connection with the matters for which the service charge is payable.

(2) Other expressions used in this Schedule are to be construed in accordance with paragraphs 16 to 20 below. **[572]**

Limitation of service charge

2. The extent to which relevant costs are taken into account in determining the amount of a service charge payable for any period shall be limited in accordance with the following paragraphs, and the amount payable shall be limited accordingly; and where the service charge is payable before the relevant costs are incurred—

    (*a*) no greater amount shall be so payable than is reasonable; and

    (*b*) after the relevant costs have been incurred any necessary adjustments shall be made by repayment, reduction of subsequent charges or otherwise.

3. Costs are to be taken into account only to the extent that they are reasonably incurred, and costs incurred on the provision of services or the carrying out of works only if the services or works are of a reasonable standard.

4.—(1) Where costs incurred on the carrying out of works on a building exceed the amount prescribed by or under this paragraph the excess is not to be taken into account unless the requirements of paragraph 5 below have been complied with or are dispensed with under paragraph 6 below.

(2) The prescribed amount is £25 multiplied by the number of flats in the building or £500, whichever is the greater, but the Secretary of State may by order substitute a different amount for £25 or £500 or both.

5.—(1) The requirements are as follows.

(2) At least two estimates for the works shall be obtained, one of them from a person wholly unconnected with the landlord.

(3) A notice accompanied by a copy of the estimates shall be given to each of the tenants concerned or shall be displayed in the building so as to be likely to come to the notice of all those tenants and, if there is a recognised tenants' association for the building, the notice and copy of the estimates shall also be given to the secretary of the association.

(4) The notice shall describe the works to be carried out and invite observations on them and on the estimates and shall state the name and the address in the United Kingdom of the person to whom the observations may be sent and the date by which they are to be received.

(5) The date stated in the notice shall not be earlier than one month after the date on which it is given or displayed as required by sub-paragraph (3) above.

(6) The landlord shall have regard to any observations received in pursuance of the notice and, unless the works are urgently required, they shall not be begun earlier than the date specified in the notice.

(7) For the purposes of this paragraph the tenants concerned are all the landlord's tenants of flats in the building by whom a service charge is payable to which the costs of the proposed works are relevant.

6. In any proceedings relating to a service charge the court, if satisfied that the landlord acted reasonably, may dispense with all or any of the requirements. **[573]**

Information as to relevant costs

7.—(1) If a tenant requests the landlord in writing to supply him with a written summary of the costs incurred in the relevant period defined in sub-paragraph (5) below which are relevant to the service charges payable or demanded as payable by the tenant in that or any other period, the landlord shall do so within six months of the end of the period or within one month of the request, whichever is the later.

(2) If there is a recognised tenants' association for the building and the tenant consents, a request under sub-paragraph (1) above may be made by the secretary of the association instead of by the tenant and may then be for the supply of the summary to the secretary.

(3) The summary shall set out those costs in a way showing how they are or will be reflected in demands for service charges and, if there are more than four flats in the building or the relevant costs relate also to another building, it must be certified by a qualified accountant as in his opinion a fair summary complying with this requirement and as being sufficiently supported by accounts, receipts and other documents which have been produced to him.

(4) Where a tenant or the secretary has obtained such a summary as is referred to in sub-paragraph (1) above (whether in pursuance of this paragraph or otherwise) the tenant, or the secretary with the consent of the tenant may, within six months of obtaining it, require the landlord in writing to afford him reasonable facilities for inspecting the accounts, receipts and other documents supporting the summary and for taking copies or extracts from them, and the landlord shall then make such facilities available to the tenant or secretary for a period of two months beginning not later than one month after the request is made.

(5) The relevant period mentioned in sub-paragraph (1) above is—

    (*a*) if the relevant accounts are made up for periods of 12 months, the last such period ending not later than the date of the request; and

    (*b*) if none are made up for such a period, the period of 12 months ending with the request. **[574]**

Information held by superior landlord

8.—(1) If a request under paragraph 7 (1) above relates in whole or in part to relevant costs incurred by or on behalf of a superior landlord, and the landlord to whom the request is made is not in possession of the relevant information—

    (*a*) he shall in turn make a written request for the relevant information to the person who is his landlord (and so on if that person is not himself the superior landlord) and the superior landlord shall then comply with the request within a reasonable time; and

    (*b*) it shall be the duty of the immediate landlord to comply with the tenant's or secretary's request, or that part of it which relates to the relevant costs incurred by or on behalf of the superior landlord, within the time allowed by paragraph 7 or within such further time, if any, as is reasonable in the circumstances.

(2) If a request made under paragraph 7 (4) above relates to a summary of costs incurred by or on behalf of a superior landlord, the landlord to whom the request is made shall forthwith inform the tenant or secretary of that fact and of the name and address of the superior landlord, and sub-paragraph (4) shall then apply as if the superior landlord were the immediate landlord. **[575]**

Service of requests under paragraph 7

9. A request under paragraph 7 above shall be deemed to be duly served on a landlord if it is served on any agent of the landlord named as such in the rent book or similar document, or on the person who receives the rent on behalf of the landlord; and a person on whom a request is so served shall forward it as soon as may be to the landlord. **[576]**

Effect of assignment

10. The assignment of a tenancy shall not affect the validity of a request made under paragraph 7 or 8 above before the assignment, but a person shall not be obliged to provide a summary or make facilities available more than once for the same flat and for the same period. **[577]**

Determination of reasonableness

11. Any agreement made by a tenant of a flat, other than an arbitration agreement within the meaning of section 32 of the Arbitration Act 1950, shall be void in so far as it purports to provide for a determination in a particular manner or on particular evidence of any question whether any amount payable before costs for services, repair, maintenance, insurance or management are incurred is reasonable, whether such costs were reasonably incurred or whether services or works for which costs were incurred are of a reasonable standard.

12. A county court may make a declaration that any such amount is or is not reasonable, that any such costs were or were not reasonably incurred or that any services or works are or are not of a reasonable standard, notwithstanding that no other relief is sought in the proceedings. **[578]**

Offences

13.—(1) If any person without reasonable excuse fails to perform any duty imposed on him by this Schedule he shall be guilty of an offence and liable on summary conviction to a fine not exceeding £500.

(2) Where an offence under this Schedule which has been committed by a body corporate is proved to have been committed with the consent or connivance of, or to be attributable to any neglect on the part of, a director, manager, secretary or other similar officer of the body corporate, or any person who was purporting to act in any such capacity, he, as well as the body corporate, shall be guilty of an offence and be liable to be proceeded against and punished accordingly.

(3) Where the affairs of a body corporate are managed by its members, sub-paragraph (2) above shall apply in relation to the acts and defaults of a member in connection with his functions of management as if he were a director of the body corporate. **[579]**

Exceptions

14.—(1) This Schedule does not apply to service charges payable by a tenant of any of the following bodies, that is to say—

(a) a local authority or development corporation (as defined in section 50 (1) of this Act),
(b) the council of a county,
(c) the Commission for the New Towns,
(d) the Development Board for Rural Wales,

unless the tenancy is a long tenancy for the purposes of paragraph 1 of Schedule 3 to this Act.

(2) Where this Schedule applies to a service charge payable by the tenant of a body mentioned in sub-paragraph (1) above—

(a) paragraph 13 does not apply, and
(b) the persons who are qualified accountants include a member of the Chartered Institute of Public Finance and Accountancy and paragraph 17 (2) (b) below does not apply.

15. This Schedule does not apply to service charges payable by the tenant of a flat the rent of which is registered under Part IV of the 1977 Act, unless the amount registered is, in pursuance of section 71 (4) of that Act, entered as a variable amount. **[580]**

Definition of "flat", "qualified accountant", "landlord",
"tenant" and "recognised tenants' association"

16. A flat is a separate set of premises, whether or not on the same floor, which—

(a) forms part of a building; and
(b) is divided horizontally from some other part of that building; and
(c) is constructed or adapted for use for the purposes of a dwelling and is occupied wholly or mainly as a private dwelling.

17.—(1) A qualified accountant is a person qualified for the purposes of paragraph 3 of Schedule 16, but subject to sub-paragraph (2) below.

(2) None of the following is a qualified accountant—

(a) a body corporate, except a Scottish firm;
(b) an officer or employee of the landlord or, where the landlord is a company, of a company which is the landlord's holding company or subsidiary (within the meaning of section 154 of the Companies Act 1948) or a subsidiary of the landlord's holding company; and
(c) a person who is a partner or employee of any such officer or employee.

18. "Landlord" includes any person who has a right to enforce payment of a service charge and, in relation to a flat occupied by a tenant under a right conferred by an enactment, also includes the person who, apart from that right, would be entitled to possession of the flat.

19. "Tenant" includes a person occupying a flat under a right conferred by an enactment, and, where the whole or any part of the flat is sublet, includes also the sub-tenant.

334

20. A recognised tenants' association is an association of tenants of flats in a building which is recognised for the purposes of this Schedule either—

(*a*) by a notice in writing given by the landlord to the secretary of the association; or

(*b*) by a certificate of one of the persons appointed by the Lord Chancellor under the 1977 Act to the panel of persons to act as members of a rent assessment committee for the registration area in which the building is situated.

21.—(1) A notice given under paragraph 20 (*a*) above may be withdrawn by the landlord by notice in writing given to the secretary of the association not less than six months before the date on which it is to be withdrawn; and a certificate given under paragraph 20 (*b*) above may be cancelled by one of the persons there mentioned.

(2) The Secretary of State may by regulations specify the matters to which regard is to be had in giving or cancelling a certificate under paragraph 20 (*b*) above. **[581]**

COMMENCEMENT

See s. 153 (4), *ante*, and the note "Orders under this section" thereto; but see also s. 136 (2), *ante*.

GENERAL NOTE

A new element in the definition of "service charge" is that, by para. 1 (1), the landlord's costs of management are recoverable as part of a service charge, subject as provided in paras. 2–5.

Another new element is that, by para. 1 (1), costs "to be incurred" are recoverable, as limited by paras. 2–5: see the note to paras. 1 and 2 below. The right to consultation about service charges in certain cases disappears and is replaced by provisions enabling the (individual) tenant or recognised tenants' association (para 20), on their initiative, to obtain information from the landlord: paras. 7–8.

The scope of the provisions in Sch. 19 is restricted in particular by the fact that Sch. 19 has no application where a flat has a fair rent registered in respect of it—unless the amount is entered as a variable amount (para. 15).

Another restriction on the recovery of service charges apart from Sch. 19 is that where the landlord is subject to the obligations to repair the structure and exterior of a flat and the installations in the flat to which the Housing Act 1961, s. 32 (1), applies, then no service charges in respect of these obligations is recoverable. But in *Campden Hill Towers* v. *Gardner* [1977] 1 All E.R. 739, C.A., the word "dwelling-house" in s. 32 (1) was held to mean, in relation to flats, only the particular flat demised to the lessee, not the whole block. Equally, in that decision, "installations" in s. 32 (1) was restricted to installations in the physical confines of the flat and did not cover those situated outside the flat, such as a central heating boiler. So even where s. 32 (1) applies, a landlord may recover service charges subject to Sch. 19 in respect of, *e.g.*, (i) the common parts of a block of flats such as the stairs, rubbish chutes, lavatories outside the flats and passages and (ii) installations outside the physical confines of the flat such as the central heating boiler mentioned above. There are, quite apart from s. 32 (1) and the narrow interpretation put on it in *Campden Hill Towers* v. *Gardner, supra*, installations outside s. 32 (1) such as a central refrigeration plant: the only limitation on service charges would be those in Sch. 19 (unless excluded by paras. 14–15): cf. *Penn* v. *Gatenex Co* [1958] 1 All E.R. 712, C.A.

Lastly, if a service charge is recoverable under Sch. 19, the Landlord and Tenant Act 1927, s. 18 (this limits the recoverable damages for breach of a covenant to repair), will not render the charges irrecoverable: *Moss Empires* v. *Olympia* [1939] A.C. 544; [1939] 3 All E.R. 460, H.L.

PARAS. 1 AND 2: RELEVANT COSTS

If there is claimed as an item in a service charge, costs to be incurred by the landlord in the future, then the claim is a "relevant cost" within para. 1 (1). It may then only be recovered in so far as it is reasonable in amount (para. 2 (*a*)) and so the tenant may challenge the amount or reasonableness in the county court (para. 12). Also, after the costs have been in fact incurred, there must then be a re-adjustment of the service charge under para. 2 (*b*). All the same, subject to the restrictions imposed in paras. 1 and 2, interim or advance payments by a landlord to meet the eventual cost of future expenditure may be recovered as part of a landlord's service charge, and to this extent the decision in *Frobisher (Second Investments) Ltd.* v. *Kiloran Trust Co. Ltd.* [1980] 1 All E.R. 488, is reversed.

Para. 1 (1) (*a*) refers to the landlord's costs of management and these are recoverable subject to the restrictions imposed in the rest of the Schedule. It is not clear from the wording of para. 1 (*a*) whether a landlord could not recover interest on money borrowed by his agents, assuming the tenancy agreement was so drafted as to enable him to claim it. In the *Frobisher* case it was held that no term to enable such recovery would be implied.

SERVICES
As to the meaning of this expression, cf. the note to the Rent Act 1977, s. 30.

PARA. 3: REASONABLE STANDARD
Even at common law, it is not taken to be the intention of the parties to a lease that the landlords should have an unfettered discretion to adopt the highest conceivable standard of maintenance for a block of flats and charge a tenant therewith: a reasonable standard only will be implied (the usual standard of implied obligation to repair): *Finchbourne Ltd.* v. *Rodrigues* [1976] 3 All E.R. 581, C.A., applying *Liverpool City Council* v. *Irwin* [1976] 2 All E.R. 39, H.L.

PARA. 4: BUILDING
See the note to s. 3, *ante*.

SECRETARY OF STATE
See the note to s. 2, *ante*.

PARA. 5: LIKELY
See the note to s. 43, *ante*.

UNITED KINGDOM
See the note to s. 110, *ante*.

NOT EARLIER THAN ONE MONTH AFTER, ETC.
See the note "Not later than three months after, etc." to s. 11, *ante*.

PARA. 7: WRITING; WRITTEN
See the corresponding note to s. 5, *ante*.

WITHIN SIX MONTHS (ONE MONTH) OF, ETC.
See the note "Within six months of, etc." to s. 3, *ante*.

MONTHS
I.e., calendar months; see the Interpretation Act 1978, s. 5, Sch. 1, A.L.S. Vol. 258.

PARA. 8: WITHIN A REASONABLE TIME
See the note to s. 36, *ante*.

FORTHWITH
A provision to the effect that a thing must be done "forthwith" or "immediately" means that it must be done as soon as possible in the circumstances, the nature of the act to be done being taken into account; see *Re Southam, Ex parte Lamb* (1881), 19 Ch. D. 169, C.A.; [1881–5] All E.R. Rep. 391; *Re Muscovitch, Ex parte Muscovitch*, [1939] Ch. 694; [1939] 1 All E.R. 135, C.A.; and *Sameen* v. *Abeyewickrema*, [1963] A.C. 597; [1963] 3 All E.R. 382, P.C. Provided, however, that no harm is done, "forthwith" means "at any reasonable time thereafter", and in the absence of some detriment suffered by the person affected failure to act "forthwith" does not invalidate the action taken; see *London Borough of Hillingdon* v. *Cutler*, [1968] 1 Q.B. 124; [1967] 2 All E.R. 361, C.A. See, further, on the meaning of "forthwith", 37 Halsbury's Laws (3rd Edn.), p. 103 and 2 Words and Phrases (2nd Edn.) 273–275.

PARA. 12: COUNTY COURT
See the note to s. 12, *ante*.

PARA. 13: IF ANY PERSON, ETC.
See the note "Person" to s. 24, *ante*; and note the exclusion of para. 13 above by para. 14 (2) (*a*).

REASONABLE EXCUSE
What is a reasonable excuse is largely a question of fact; cf. *Leck* v. *Epsom Rural District Council*, [1922] 1 K.B. 383; [1922] All E.R. Rep. 784. Yet there is authority for saying that ignorance of the statutory provisions provides no reasonable excuse (cf. *Aldridge* v. *Warwickshire Coal Co., Ltd.* (1925), 133 L.T. 439, C.A.); nor does a mistaken view of the effect of those provisions (*R.* v. *Reid (Philip)*, [1973] 3 All E.R. 1020, C.A.).

Once evidence of a reasonable excuse emerges it is for the prosecution to eliminate the existence of that defence to the court's satisfaction; see *R.* v. *Clarke*, [1969] 2 All E.R. 1008, C.A.

SUMMARY CONVICTION
See the note to s. 125, *ante.*

OFFENCE . . . COMMITTED BY A BODY CORPORATE
Except where the penalty is inappropriate or where, by the nature of the offence, it must be committed by an individual, a corporation may be convicted for the criminal acts of the directors and managers who represent the directing mind and will of the corporation and control what it does; see *Director of Public Prosecutions* v. *Kent and Sussex Contractors, Ltd.*, [1944] K.B. 146; [1944] 1 All E.R. 119; *R.* v. *I.C.R. Haulage Ltd.*, [1944] K.B. 551; [1944] 1 All E.R. 691, C.C.A.; and *Tesco Supermarkets, Ltd.* v. *Nattrass*, [1972] A.C. 153; [1971] 2 All E.R. 127, H.L.

For the general law relating to corporations, see 9 Halsbury's Laws (4th Edn.), paras. 120–1 *et seq.*

CONSENT
"Consent" requires awareness of the thing consented to: *Ex parte Ford* (1876) 1 Ch. D. 521, at p. 528. As to "connivance", knowledge is again required before one can be said to connive, or the means of knowledge which the conniver has made himself wilfully blind in respect of: *Somerset* v. *Hart* (1884) 12 Q.B.D. 360, at p. 364.

As to the duty of a director in general: he does not have to supervise his co-directors, nor to acquaint himself with all the details of the running of the company, but should make inquiry should he have reason to believe that there exists a breach of law by a co-director: *Re City Equitable Fire Insurance Co Ltd.* [1925] Ch. 407; *Huckerby* v. *Elliott* [1970] 1 All E.R. 189.

For the purposes of the offence constituted by para. 13 (2) it is irrelevant whether the director is or is not validly appointed under the company rules: this is the reason for the words "or who was purporting to act in any such capapcity". This reverses the rule where there is no like statutory language—see *Dean* v. *Hiesler* [1942] 2 All E.R. 340.

CONNIVANCE
There are many decisions on the meaning of this word in matrimonial law; see *Godfrey* v. *Godfrey*, [1965], A.C. 444; [1964] 3 All E.R. 154, H.L., especially the speech of Lord Guest, in which earlier decisions are reviewed. It would seem that an element of encouragement is essential. The word has been used in many statutes in the same context as in this section, but there is little authority as to its meaning in this context; see Glanville Williams, *Criminal Law: The General Part*, para. 222, and *Gregory* v. *Walker* (1912), 77 J.P. 55; 29 T.L.R. 51.

NEGLECT
This term, in the words of Simonds, J., in *Re Hughes, Rea* v. *Black*, [1943] Ch. 296; [1943] 2 All E.R. 269, at p. 298 and p. 271, respectively, "in its legal connotation implies failure to perform a duty which the person knows or ought to know". See also *Crickitt* v. *Kursaal Casino, Ltd. (No. 2)*, [1968] 1 All E.R. 139, H.L., at pp. 146, 147, and *Huckerby* v. *Elliott*, [1970] 1 All E.R. 189.

ANY PERSON WHO WAS PURPORTING TO ACT
These words are introduced in view of *Dean* v. *Hiesler*, [1942] 2 All E.R. 340, where a director who had not been duly appointed was held not liable for an offence committed by the company.

PARA. 14: COUNCIL OF A COUNTY
See the note "County council" to s. 19, *ante.*

COMMISSION FOR THE NEW TOWNS
See the note to s. 28, *ante.*

DEVELOPMENT BOARD FOR RURAL WALES
See the note to s. 19, *ante.*

PARA. 16: CONSTRUCTED OR ADAPTED
It is thought that this means originally constructed or subsequently altered so as to make apt; cf. *French* v. *Champkin*, [1920] 1 K.B. 76, and *Hubbard* v. *Messenger*, [1938] 1 K.B.

300, at p. 307; [1937] 4 All E.R. 48, at p. 50; and see also *Taylor* v. *Mead*, [1961] 1 All E.R. 626; *Maddox* v. *Storer*, [1963] 1 Q.B. 451; [1962] 1 All E.R. 831; *Flower Freight Co., Ltd.* v. *Hammond*, [1963] 1 Q.B. 275; [1962] 3 All E.R. 950; and *Popperwell* v. *Cockerton*, [1968] 1 All E.R. 1038.

FLAT
Parliament thus adopts the narrow construction of the term which appealed to the court which decided *Campden Hill Towers Ltd.* v. *Gardner* [1977] 1 All E.R. 739, C.A.

PARA. 16 (*c*)
A small, incidental business user will not prevent the occupation from being residential: *Vickery* v. *Martin* [1944] 2 All E.R. 167, C.A. If the lease is silent then whether the user is primarily business is a question of fact: *Whiteley* v. *Wilson* [1952] 2 All E.R. 940, C.A.

WHOLLY OR MAINLY
The word "mainly" probably means "more than half"; see *Fawcett Properties, Ltd.*, v. *Buckingham County Council*, [1961] A.C. 636, at p. 669; [1960] 3 All E.R. 503, at p. 512, H.L., *per* Lord Morton of Henryton. See also *Re Hatschek's Patents, Ex parte Zerenner*, [1909] 2 Ch. 68: *Miller* v. *Owners of Ottilie*, [1944] 1 K.B. 188; [1944] 1 All E.R. 277; *Franklin* v. *Gramophone Co., Ltd.*, [1948] 1 K.B. 542, at p. 555; [1948] 1 All E.R. 353, C.A., at p. 358, *per* Sommervell, L.J.; and *Berthelemy* v. *Neale*, [1952] 1 All E.R. 437, C.A.

PARA. 17: QUALIFIED ACCOUNTANTS
Para. 17 above should be read subject to para. 14 (2) (*b*).

PARA. 20: REGISTRATION AREA
I.e., a registration area as defined by the Rent Act 1977, s. 62, A.L.S. Vol. 255.

PARA. 21: NOT LESS THAN SIX MONTHS BEFORE, ETC.
The words "not less than" indicate that six clear months must intervene between the day on which notice is given and that on which this notice under para. 20 (*a*) above is withdrawn; see *R.* v. *Turner*, [1910] 1 K.B. 346; *Re Hector Whaling, Ltd.*, [1936] Ch. 208; [1935] All E.R. Rep 302; and the cases cited in 37 Halsbury's Laws (3rd Edn.), p. 98, para. 167.

ARBITRATION ACT 1950, S. 32
See A.L.S. Vol. 71.

1977 ACT
I.e., the Rent Act 1977; see s. 150, *ante*, and as the panels of persons to act as members of rent assessment committees, see Sch. 10, paras. 1–3, to that Act. Part IV (ss. 62–75 and Schs. 10–12) of the Act of 1977 is amended by ss. 59, 60 (1), (2), 61 (1), (5), (7), 62, 71 (2) and 152 (1), (3), *ante*, and Sch. 25, paras. 40, 41, 56, and Sch. 26, *post*.

COMPANIES ACT 1948, S. 154
See 5, Halsbury's Statutes (3rd edn.), p. 234.

ORDERS UNDER PARA. 4
At the time of going to press no order had been made under para. 4 (2) above. As to orders generally, see s. 151, *ante*.

REGULATIONS UNDER PARA. 21
At the time of going to press no regulations had been made under para. 21 (2) above. As to regulations generally, see s. 151, *ante*.

SCHEDULE 20

Section 139

HOUSING CO-OPERATIVES

1. In this Schedule "housing co-operative" means a society, company or body of trustees for the time being approved by the Secretary of State for the purposes of this Schedule.

2.—(1) Where a local authority a new town corporation or the Development Board for Rural Wales has made an agreement with a housing co-operative and the agreement is one which this Schedule applies, neither the agreement nor any letting of land in pursuance of it shall be taken into account in determining the authority's, corporation's or Board's reckonable expenditure or reckonable income under Part VI of this Act or as a ground for recovering, withholding or reducing any sum under section 102; but subject to sub-paragraph (2) below.

(2) Sub-paragraph (1) above does not apply where the letting is a lease constituting shared ownership, except if, and to the extent that, the Secretary of State otherwise determines.

(3) For the purposes of sub-paragraph (2) above a lease constituting shared ownership is a lease of a dwelling—

(*a*) which is granted on payment of a premium calculated by reference to a percentage of the value of the dwelling or of the cost of providing it; or

(*b*) under which the tenant (or his personal representatives) will or may be entitled to a sum calculated by reference directly or indirectly to the value of the dwelling.

3. The agreements to which this Schedule applies are agreements with a local authority made (whether before or after the passing of this Act) with the approval of the Secretary of State—

(*a*) for the exercise by the co-operative, on such terms as may be provided in the agreement, of any of the local authority's powers relating to land in which it has a legal estate and which the authority for the time being holds for the purposes of Part V of the 1957 Act, and the performance by the co-operative of any of the local authority's duties relating to such land; or

(*b*) for the exercise by the co-operative, in connection with any such land as is referred to in paragraph (*a*) above, of any of the local authority's powers under section 94 or 95 of the 1957 Act (powers to provide furniture, board and laundry facilities),

and agreements with a new town corporation or the Development Board for Rural Wales for the exercise by the co-operative, on such terms as may be provided in the agreement, of any of the corporation's or Board's powers under the New Towns Act 1965 or the Development of Rural Wales Act 1976 relating to land in which it has a legal estate.

4. The Secretary of State's approval to the making of any such agreement may be given either generally to local authorities or new town corporations or to any local authority or description of local authority or any new town corporation or description of new town corporation or the Development Board for Rural Wales, or in any particular case, and may be given unconditionally or subject to conditions.

5. Without prejudice to any power to let land conferred on a local authority a new town corporation or the Development Board for Rural Wales by an enactment, the terms of an agreement to which this Schedule applies may include terms providing for the letting of land to the housing co-operative by the local authority, new town corporation or Board.

6. A housing association registered under Part II of the 1974 Act shall not be entitled to a grant under Part III of that Act in respect of land for the time being comprised in an agreement to which this Schedule applies. **[582]**

COMMENCEMENT

This Schedule came into operation on the passing of this Act on 8th August 1980 by virtue of s. 153 (3), *ante*.

PARA. 1: HOUSING CO-OPERATIVE

A tenancy is not a protected tenancy for the purposes of the Rent Act 1977 when the interest of the landlord belongs to a housing co-operative as defined in para. 1 above and the dwelling-house is comprised in an agreement to which this Schedule applies (as to which, see para. 3 above): see s. 16 of the Act of 1977, A.L.S. Vol. 255, as amended by s. 152 (1), *ante*, and Sch. 25, para. 34, *post*.

By virtue of the Housing Finance Act 1972, s. 19 (5) (*f*), as substituted by s. 118 and Sch. 15, para. 3, *ante*, a person is a private tenant for the purposes of the provisions of Part II of that Act, A.L.S. Vol. 202, as amended by s. 118 and Sch. 15, *ante*, relating to rent allowances if he occupies a dwelling let to him by a housing co-operative as defined in para. 1 above and his tenancy would be a protected tenancy but for the Rent Act 1977, s. 16, or, where the housing co-operative is a housing association, but for ss. 15 and 16 of that Act.

SECRETARY OF STATE
See the note to s. 2, *ante*.

PARA. 2: LOCAL AUTHORITY; NEW TOWN CORPORATION
Neither of these expressions is defined for the purposes of this Schedule, but it is thought that they have the meanings assigned by s. 105, *ante*.

DEVELOPMENT BOARD FOR RURAL WALES
See the note to s. 19, *ante*.

AGREEMENT ... TO WHICH THIS SCHEDULE APPLIES
See para. 3 above.

LAND
For meaning, see the Interpretation Act 1978, s. 5, Sch. 1.

RECKONABLE EXPENDITURE; RECKONABLE INCOME
As to these; see ss. 99 (2) and 100 (2), *ante*, or those provisions as applied by s. 10 (1), *ante*.

1957 ACT
I.e., the Housing Act 1957; see s. 150, *ante*.   Part V is amended by ss. 90–95, *ante*.

NEW TOWNS ACT 1965
See 36, Halsbury's Statutes (3rd edn.), p. 1863.

DEVELOPMENT OF RURAL WALES ACT 1976
See 46, Halsbury's Statutes (3rd edn.), p. 1863.

1974 ACT
I.e., the Housing Act 1974; see s. 150, *ante*.   The provisions in Part II of the Act of 1974 relating to registration of housing associations are amended or affected by ss. 127 and 128, *ante*, and the provisions of Part III are amended or affected by s. 130 and Sch. 18, *ante*.

TRANSITIONAL PROVISION
See s. 152 (2), *ante*, and Sch. 25, para. 74, *post*.

SCHEDULE 21

Section 141

AMENDMENTS OF LEASEHOLD REFORM ACT 1967 (c. 88) AND HOUSING ACT 1974 (c. 44), SCHEDULE 8

1.—In section 1 (1) (*b*) of the 1967 Act (period during which tenant must have occupied the premises as his residence) for "five years", in both places, substitute "three years".

(2) In sections 9 (3) (*b*) and 23 (2) (*b*) of the 1967 Act (application for enfranchisement or extension of lease not to be made within five years of previous application) for "five years" substitute, in each case, "three years".

2. For section 1 (4A) of the 1967 Act (reduction of rateable value in consequence of tenants' improvements), substitute—

"(4A) Schedule 8 to the Housing Act 1974 shall have effect to enable a tenant to have the rateable value of the house and premises reduced for purposes of this section in consequence of tenant's improvements.".

3. In section 3 (1) of the 1967 Act (meaning of "long tenancy"), the following words are inserted at the end of the proviso: "if either—

(*a*) it was granted before 18th April 1980 or in pursuance of a contract entered into before that date; or

(*b*) the notice is capable of being given at any time after the death or marriage of the tenant, the length of the notice is not more than three months and the terms of the tenancy preclude both its assignment and the subletting of the whole of the premises comprised in it".

4. In section 16 of the 1967 Act (exclusion of rights which would otherwise accrue under extended tenancies), after subsection (1) insert—

"(1A) The Rent Act 1977 shall not apply to a tenancy extended under section 14 above; but if when this provision comes into force a rent is registered under Part IV of the 1977 Act for a dwelling-house which is the subject of an extended tenancy, the tenant shall not be obliged to pay more than the registered rent under the extended tenancy until the next rental period (within the meaning of the 1977 Act) after the landlord has served on him a notice in writing that the registered rent no longer applies.".

5. In section 29 of the 1967 Act (reservation of future right to develop), after subsection (6A) insert—

"(6B) Where the landlord is a university body, the possible development for which land may be reserved by a covenant entered into to give effect to subsection (1) or (2) above includes development by a related university body (within the meaning of section 28 (6) (*b*) above."

6. In paragraph 7 (1) (*b*) of Schedule 1 to the 1967 Act, at the beginning insert "subject to paragraph 7A", omit "(subject to paragraph 8 below)" and after paragraph 7 insert—

"7A.—(1) The price payable for a minor superior tenancy shall be calculated (except where it has been determined by agreement or otherwise before this paragraph comes into force) by applying the formula set out in sub-paragraph (5) instead of in accordance with section 9.

(2) "A minor superior tenancy" means a superior tenancy having an expectation of possession of not more than one month and in respect of which the profit rent is not more than £5 per year.

(3) "Profit rent" means an amount equal to that of the rent payable under the tenancy on which the minor superior tenancy is in immediate reversion, less that of the rent payable under the minor superior tenancy.

(4) Where the minor superior tenancy or that on which it is in immediate reversion comprises property other than the house and premises, the reference in sub-paragraph (3) to the rent payable under it means so much of that rent as is apportioned to the house and premises.

(5) The formula is—

$$P = £\frac{R}{Y} - \frac{R}{Y(1+Y)^n}$$

where—

  P = the price payable;
  R = the profit rent;
  Y = the yield (expressed as a decimal fraction) from $2\frac{1}{2}$ per cent. Consolidated Stock;
  n = the period, expressed in years (taking any part of a year as a whole year) which the minor superior tenancy would have to run if it were not extinguished by enfranchisement.

(6) In calculating the yield from $2\frac{1}{2}$ per cent. Consolidated Stock, the price of that stock shall be taken to be the middle market price at the close of business on the last trading day in the week before the tenant gives notice in accordance with this Act of his desire to have the freehold".

7. In paragraph 6 (1) (*b*) of Schedule 3 to the 1967 Act (particulars to be included in tenants' notices of desire to have freehold or extended lease), after "show that" insert "(i)", and at the end insert—

"(ii) at the material time the rateable value was within the limits specified for the purposes of section 1;".

8. In Schedule 8 to the 1974 Act (procedure for obtaining reduction of rateable value for purposes of the 1967 Act)—

(*a*) in paragraph 1 (1) (notice to landlord requiring agreement to reduction), for "subsection (1) of section 1 of this Act" substitute "section 1 of the Leasehold Reform Act 1967";

(*b*) in paragraph 2 (2) (determinations by county court), omit from "and any such determination" onwards;

(*c*) in paragraph 3 (2) (*a*) (valuation officer's certificate) for "sub-section (1) of section 1 of this Act" substitute "section 1 of the Leasehold Reform Act 1967";

(*d*) after paragraph 3 insert—
> "4. Where a notice under paragraph 1 of this Schedule is served on or after 21st December 1979, the tenant shall bear the reasonable costs incurred by the landlord in investigating any matter specified in it.".

(*e*) in paragraph 2 of the second Form set out in the Schedule, for the words "Schedule Seven to the Leasehold Reform Act 1967" substitute "Schedule 8 to the Housing Act 1974", and in paragraph 3 of that Form for "Seven" substitute "8". **[583]**

COMMENCEMENT
See s. 153 (4), *ante*, and the note "Orders under this section" thereto.

PARA. 3: MONTHS
I.e., calendar months; see the Interpretation Act 1978, s. 5, Sch. 1, A.L.S. Vol. 258.

PARA. 4: WRITING
See the note "Written; writing" to s. 5, *ante*.

PARA. 5: UNIVERSITY BODY
It is thought that this refers to a University body as defined by the Leasehold Reform Act 1967, s. 28 (5) (*c*), Vol. 18, p. 685.

PARA. 6: BEFORE THIS PARAGRAPH COMES INTO FORCE
See s. 153 (4), *ante*, and the note "Orders under this section" thereto.

NOTICE ... OF HIS DESIRE TO HAVE THE FREEHOLD
Such a notice may be given under the Leasehold Reform Act 1967, s. 8 (1), A.L.S. Vol. 162.

DEFINITIONS
For "house and premises", see the Leasehold Reform Act 1967, s. 2; as to "tenant" and "landlord", see s. 5 (1) of that Act; for "tenancy", see s. 37 (1) of that Act. Note as to "minor superior tenancy" and "profit rent", para. 7A (2) and (3) of Sch. 1 to the Act of 1967 as inserted by para. 6 above.

1967 ACT
I.e., the Leasehold Reform Act 1967, see s. 141, *ante*. The words to be omitted from Sch. 1, para. 7 (1) (*b*), to the Act of 1967 are also repealed by s. 152 (3), *ante*, and Sch. 26, *post*.

HOUSING ACT 1974, S. 8
See A.L.S. Vol. 223. That Schedule is amended by para. 8 above.

RENT ACT 1977
See A.L.S. Vol. 255. Part IV (ss. 62–75 and Schs. 10–12) of that Act is amended by ss. 59, 60 (1), (2), 61 (1), (5), (7), 62, 71 (2) and 152 (1), (3), *ante*, and Sch. 25, paras. 40, 41, 56, and Sch. 26, *post*.

1974 ACT
I.e., the Housing Act 1974; see s. 150, *ante*. The words to be omitted from para. 2 (2) of that Schedule are also repealed by s. 152 (3), *ante*, and Sch. 26, *post*.

LEASEHOLD REFORM ACT 1967, S. 1
See A.L.S. Vol. 162. That section is amended by paras 1 (1) and 2 above.

SCHEDULE 22

LEASEHOLD VALUATION TRIBUNALS

PART I

SUPPLEMENTARY PROVISIONS

Constitution of tribunals

1. The president of a panel drawn up under Schedule 10 to the 1977 Act shall, when constituting a leasehold valuation tribunal, ensure that at least one of its members is a person who has experience in the valuation of land. **[584]**

Appeals

2. No appeal shall lie from a decision of a leasehold valuation tribunal to the High Court by virtue of section 13 (1) of the Tribunals and Inquiries Act 1971 and no case may be stated for the opinion of the High Court in respect of such a decision, but any person who—

(*a*) appeared before a tribunal in proceedings to which he was a party; and
(*b*) is dissatisfied with its decision,

may, within such time as rules under section 3 (6) of the Lands Tribunal Act 1949 may specify, appeal to the Lands Tribunal.

3. A leasehold valuation tribunal shall not be treated as a person aggrieved for the purposes of section 3 (4) of the Lands Tribunal Act 1949 (which enables a person aggrieved by a decision of the Tribunal on a point of law to require the Tribunal to state a case for decision of the Court of Appeal).

4. For the purposes of Part I of the Leasehold Reform Act 1967 a matter is to be treated as determined by a leasehold valuation tribunal—

(*a*) if the tribunal's decision is not appealed against, on the expiration of the time for bringing an appeal; or
(*b*) if the decision is appealed against, and not set aside in consequence of the appeal, at the time when the appeal and any further appeal is disposed of by the determination of it and the expiration of the time for bringing a further appeal if any) or by its being abandoned or otherwise ceasing to have effect. **[585]**

Costs

5. The costs which a person may be required to bear under section 9 (4) or 14 (2) of the 1967 Act (matters the costs of which are to be borne by person giving notice of his desire to have the freehold or an extended lease) do not include costs incurred by a landlord in connection with a reference to a leasehold valuation tribunal.

6. Where the county court gives any such certificate as is authorised by section 20 (4) of or paragraph 8 (1) of Schedule 2 to the 1967 Act (certificate of unreasonable delay or default by landlord or tenant) the Lands Tribunal may make the like order as to costs of proceedings on an appeal before the Tribunal in relation to the matter in question as the county court is authorised to make by section 20 (4) or paragraph 8 (1). **[586]**

Provision of information

7.—(1) Where a matter is referred to a leasehold valuation tribunal for determination, the tribunal may by notice in writing served on the tenant or landlord or on a superior landlord require him to give to the tribunal, within such period but not less than 14 days from the service of the notice as may be specified in the notice, such information as the tribunal may reasonably require.

(2) If any person fails without reasonable cause to comply with any notice served on him under this paragraph he shall be liable, on summary conviction, to a fine not exceeding £200.

[587]

COMMENCEMENT
See s. 153 (4), *ante*, and the note "Orders under this section" thereto.

PARA. 1: LEASEHOLD VALUATION TRIBUNAL
I.e., a rent assessment committee when constituted to make any determination under the Leasehold Reform Act 1967, s. 21 (1), (3), A.L.S. Vol. 162; see s. 142 (2), *ante*.

PARA. 2: PERSON
See the note to s. 24, *ante*.

LANDS TRIBUNAL
The Lands Tribunal was established by the Lands Tribunal Act 1949, s. 1, Vol. 6, p. 191.

PARA. 4: TIME FOR BRINGING AN APPEAL
I.e., the time specified by rules under the Lands Tribunal Act 1949, s. 3 (6), A.L.S. Vol. 61, cf. the last part of para. 2 above.

PARA. 6: COUNTY COURT
See the note to s. 12, *ante*.

PARA. 7: WRITING
See the note "Written; writing" to s. 5, *ante*.

TENANT; LANDLORD
These expressions should be construed in accordance with the second limit of the Leasehold Reform Act 1967, s. 5 (1).

WITHIN SUCH PERIOD, ETC
See the note "Within six months of, etc." to s. 3, *ante*.

REASONABLE CAUSE
Cf. the note "Reasonable excuse" to Sch. 19, *ante*.

SUMMARY CONVICTION
See the note to s. 125, *ante*.

1977 ACT
I.e., the Rent Act 1977; see s. 150, *ante*.

TRIBUNALS AND INQUIRIES ACT 1971, S. 13 (1)
See A.L.S. Vol. 191.

LANDS TRIBUNAL ACT 1949, S. 3
See A.L.S. Vol. 61.

LEASEHOLD REFORM ACT 1967, PART I, SS. 9 (4), 14 (2), 20 (4), SCH. 2, PARA. 8 (1).
See A.L.S. Vol. 162.

Part II

Amendments of 1967 Act

8.—(1) In section 21 (1) (jurisdiction of Lands Tribunal) for "the Lands Tribunal" substitute "a leasehold valuation tribunal".

(2) After section 21 (1) insert—

"(1A) An application to a leasehold valuation tribunal under subsection (1) above must be in the prescribed form and contain the prescribed particulars.

(1B) No application may be made to a leasehold valuation tribunal under subsection (1) above to determine the price for a house and premises unless either—
(a) the landlord has informed the tenant of the price he is asking; or
(b) two months have elapsed without his doing so since the tenant gave notice of his desire to have the freehold under this Part of this Act.".

(3) In section 21 (2), for "the Lands Tribunal" substitute "a leasehold valuation tribunal" and for "the Tribunal" substitute "a tribunal".

(4) In section 21 (3) for "the Lands Tribunal" (twice) substitute "a leasehold valuation tribunal" and for "the Tribunal" substitute "a tribunal".

(5) For section 21 (4) substitute—

"(4) Without prejudice to the generality of section 102 of the County Courts Act 1959 or section 74 of the Rent Act 1977, the powers thereby conferred to make rules of procedure shall extend to prescribing the procedure consequent on any such transfer.".

(6) After section 21 (4) insert—

"(4A) The Secretary of State may make regulations prescribing—

(a) the form of any application under subsection (1) above; and
(b) the particulars which it must contain;

and any such regulations shall be made by statutory instrument subject to annulment in pursuance of a resolution of either House of Parliament.".

(7) Section 21 (5) (costs of proceedings before Lands Tribunal) is repealed.

9. In section 31 (2) (a) (consent of Church Commissioners required to provisions of conveyance) after "the court" insert "a leasehold valuation tribunal".

10. In paragraph 5 (3) of Schedule 1 (price for intermediate leasehold interests) for "the Lands Tribunal" (twice) substitute "a leasehold valuation tribunal".

11. In paragraph 2 (2) of Schedule 2 (compensation payable to tenant for loss of house and premises) for "the Lands Tribunal" substitute "a leasehold valuation tribunal".

12. Paragraph 8 (2) of Schedule 2 (costs of proceedings before Lands Tribunal) is hereby repealed. **[588]**

COMMENCEMENT
See s. 153 (4), *ante*, and the note "Orders under this section" thereto.

PARA. 8: LEASEHOLD VALUATION TRIBUNAL
See the note to Part I of this Schedule, *ante*.

MONTHS
I.e., calendar months; see the Interpretation Act 1978, s. 5, Sch. 1, A.L.S. Vol. 258.

NOTICE OF HIS DESIRE TO HAVE THE FREEHOLD
Such a notice may be given under the Leasehold Reform Act 1967, s. 8 (1), A.L.S. Vol. 162.

THIS PART OF THIS ACT
I.e., the Leasehold Reform Act 1967, Part I.

SECRETARY OF STATE
See the note to s. 2, *ante*.

STATUTORY INSTRUMENT SUBJECT TO ANNULMENT
See the note to s. 151, *ante*.

DEFINITIONS
For "house and premises", see the Leasehold Reform Act 1967, s. 2; as to "tenant" and "landlord", see s. 5 (1) of that Act.

1967 ACT
I.e., the Leasehold Reform Act 1967; see s. 142 (1), (3), *ante*. S. 21 (5) and Sch. 2, para. 8 (2), are also repealed by s. 152 (3), *ante*, and Sch. 26, *post*.

COUNTY COURTS ACT 1959, S. 102
See 7, Halsbury's Statutes (3rd edn.), p. 366.

RENT ACT 1977, S. 74
See A.L.S. Vol. 255.

REGULATIONS AND RULES
At the time of going to press no regulations had been made under the Leasehold Reform Act 1967, s. 21 (4A), as inserted by para. 8 (6) above.

SCHEDULE 23

Section 145

HOUSES IN MULTIPLE OCCUPATION: REVISED PENALTIES FOR CERTAIN OFFENCES

1. Sections 20 of the Housing Act 1961 and 61 (6) of the 1969 Act are hereby repealed.

2. In section 13 (4) of the Housing Act 1961 (contravention of, or failure to comply with, regulations prescribing management code) for paragraphs (a) and (b) there are substituted the words "to a fine not exceeding £200".

3. In section 19 of the Act of 1961 (directions to prevent or reduce overcrowding in houses in multiple occupation)—

   (a) in subsection (9) (penalty for making false statement) for the words "twenty pounds" there is substituted "£50"; and
   (b) for subsection (11) (penalty for failing to comply with requirements of subsection (10)) there is substituted the following subsection—

      "(11) A person committing an offence under sub-section (10) above shall be liable, on summary conviction, to a fine not exceeding £500.".

4. In section 22 (4) of the Act of 1961 (penalty for failing to provide information to local authority) for the words "ten pounds" there is substituted "£50".

5.—(1) In Part II of the Act of 1961, after section 26, there is inserted the following section—

   26A. Execution of works under Part II
   If any person, after receiving notice of the intended action—

   (a) being the occupier of any premises, prevents the owner thereof or his officers, agents, servants or workmen, from carrying into effect with respect to those premises any of the provisions of this Part of this Act; or
   (b) being the owner or occupier of any premises, prevents any officer, agent, servant or workman of the local authority, from so doing;

   a magistrates' court may order him to permit to be done on the premises all things requisite for carrying into effect those provisions and if he fails to comply with the order he shall be liable, on summary conviction, to a fine not exceeding £200 and to a further fine of £20 for every day or part of a day during which the failure continues.".

   (2) Section 66 of the Housing Act 1964 is hereby repealed.

6.—(1) In section 65 (1) of the Housing Act 1964 (penalty for failure to execute works in respect of houses in multiple occupation) for paragraphs (a) and (b) there are substituted the words "to a fine not exceeding £500".

   (2) In Schedule 6 to the Criminal Law Act 1977 the entry relating to section 65 (1) of the Act of 1964 is hereby repealed.

7. In section 75 (6) of the Act of 1964 (penalty for failure to comply with magistrates' court order) for the words from "in respect of each day" to the end there are substituted the words "be liable, on summary conviction, to a fine not exceeding £200 and to a further fine of £20 for every day or part of a day during which the failure continues".

8.—(1) In section 61 of the Housing Act 1969 (offences and penalties) for "£100" there is substituted "£500".

   (2) In Schedule 6 to the Criminal Law Act 1977 the entry relating to section 61 of the 1969 Act is hereby repealed.

9. In section 64 (7) of the 1969 Act (offence to contravene or fail to comply with scheme for registering houses in multiple occupation) for paragraphs (a) to (c) there are substituted the following paragraphs—

"(*a*) if the offence is a contravention of so much of the control provisions as relate—

  (i) to occupation, to a greater extent than permitted thereunder, of a house not registered in pursuance of those provisions; or

  (ii) to the occupation of a house registered in pursuance of those provisions by more households or persons than the registration permits;

  to a fine not exceeding £500; and

(*b*) in any other case to a fine not exceeding £50.". **[589]**

COMMENCEMENT
See s. 153 (4), *ante*, and the note "Orders under this section" thereto.

PARA. 3: PERSON
See the note to s. 24, *ante*.

SUMMARY CONVICTION
See the note to s. 125, *ante*.

PARA. 5: THIS PART OF THIS ACT
I.e., the Housing Act 1961, Part II, A.L.S. Vol. 131; but see also Sch. 24, para. 12, *post*.

LOCAL AUTHORITY
For meaning see, by virtue of the Housing Act 1961, s. 28 (2), the Housing Act 1957, s. 1, and the note thereto.

EVERY DAY ... DURING WHICH THE FAILURE CONTINUES
The fine must not be calculated by reference to a period of more than six months before the information was laid; see the Magistrates' Courts Act 1952, s. 104, Vol. 21, p. 273 (replaced by the Magistrates' Courts Act 1980, s. 127 (1), as from a day to be appointed under s. 155 (7) of that Act); *R.* v. *Slade, Ex parte Saunders*, [1895] 2 Q.B. 247; *R.* v. *Struve, etc., Glamorganshire Justices* (1895), 59 J.P. 584; and *R.* v. *Chertsey Justices, Ex parte Franks*, [1961] 2 Q.B. 152; [1961] 1 All E.R. 825. However, the period over which the daily penalty accrues does not stop at the date on which the information was laid but continues until the date on which the information is heard or alternatively until a known earlier date when the offence ceased; see *Grice* v. *Needs*, [1979] 3 All E.R. 501.

DEFINITIONS
For "owner" in the provisions inserted by para. 5 (1) above, see, by virtue of the Housing Act 1961, s. 28 (2), the Housing Act 1957, s. 189 (1); for "control provisions" in the provisions substituted by para. 9 above, see the Housing Act 1969, s. 64 (2).

HOUSING ACT 1961, PART II, SS. 13 (4), 19, 20, 22 (4), 26
See A.L.S. Vol. 131. S. 20 of that Act is also repealed by s. 152 (3), *ante*, and Sch. 26, *post*.

1969 ACT
I.e., the Housing Act 1969; see s. 150, *ante*. S. 61 (6) of that Act is also repealed by s. 152 (3), *ante*, and Sch. 26, *post*.

HOUSING ACT 1964, SS. 65 (1), 66, 75 (6)
See A.L.S. Vol. 149. S. 66 of that Act is also repealed by s. 152 (3) *ante*, and Sch. 26, *post*.

CRIMINAL LAW ACT 1977, SCH. 6
See A.L.S. Vol. 249. The entries in that Schedule which are repealed are also repealed by s. 152 (3), *ante*, and Sch. 26, *post*.

HOUSING ACT 1969, S. 61
See A.L.S. Vol. 187. The reference to £100 mentioned in para. 8 (1) above occurs in s. 61 (2) of the Act of 1969.

SCHEDULE 24

Section 147

HOUSES IN MULTIPLE OCCUPATION:
MEANS OF ESCAPE FROM FIRE

Exercise of powers of local authority

1. If it appears to a local authority that a house which is occupied by persons who do not form a single household is not provided with such means of escape from fire as the local authority considers necessary the local authority may exercise such of its powers under this Schedule as appear to it most appropriate; and it shall do so if the house is of such description or occupied in such manner as the Secretary of State may by order specify. **[590]**

Powers available to local authority

2.—(1) The local authority may serve a notice on any person on whom a notice may be served under section 15 of the Housing Act 1961 specifying the works which in the opinion of the local authority are required to provide the necessary means of escape from fire and requiring the person on whom the notice is served to execute those works within such period, not less than twenty-one days from the service of the notice, as may be specified in the notice.

(2) The period specified in the notice may from time to time be extended by the local authority.

(3) Where the local authority serves a notice on any person under this paragraph it shall inform any other person who to its knowledge is an owner, lessee or mortgagee of the house of the fact that the notice has been served.

3. If it appears to the local authority that the means of escape from fire would be adequate if part of the house were not used for human habitation the local authority may secure that that part is not so used.

4. The local authority may secure that part of the house is not used for human habitation and serve a notice under paragraph 2 above specifying such works only as in the opinion of the authority are required to provide the means of escape from fire which will be necessary if that part is not so used.

5. For the purpose of securing that a part of the house is not used for human habitation the local authority may, if after consultation with any owner or mortgagee it thinks fit to do so, accept an undertaking from him that that part will not be used for human habitation without the permission of the local authority.

6. If the local authority does not accept an undertaking under paragraph 5 above with respect to a part of the house, or if, in a case where it has accepted such an undertaking, that part of the house is at any time used in contravention of the undertaking, the local authority may make a closing order with respect to that part of the house. **[591]**

Enforcement

7. Any person who, knowing that an undertaking has been accepted under paragraph 5 above, uses the part of the house to which the undertaking relates in contravention of the undertaking, or permits that part of the house to be so used, shall be guilty of an offence and liable on summary conviction to a fine not exceeding £50 and to a further fine of £5 for every day, or part of a day, on which he so uses it or permits it to be so used after conviction. **[592]**

Consultation with fire authority

8. A local authority shall, before serving a notice, accepting an undertaking or making a closing order under this Schedule, consult with the fire authority concerned. **[593]**

Exclusion of Rent Act protection

9. Nothing in the 1977 Act shall prevent possession being obtained of any part of a house which, in accordance with any undertaking in pursuance of this Schedule, cannot for the time being be used for human habitation. **[594]**

Interpretation

10. In this Schedule expressions defined in the 1957 Act have the same meanings as in that Act. **[595]**

Application and amendment of enactments

11. Part II of the 1957 Act shall apply to a closing order made under this Schedule as it applies to a closing order under section 18 (1) of that Act, but the ground on which, under section 27 (2) of that Act, the local authority is required to determine the order shall be that it is satisfied that the means of escape from fire with which the house is provided is adequate (owing to a change of circumstances) and will remain adequate if the part of the house with respect to which the order was made is again used for human habitation.

12. Any reference in the provisions relating to houses in multiple occupation (that is to say Part II of the Housing Act 1961, Part IV of the Housing Act 1964 and Part IV of the 1969 Act) to section 16 or Part II of the Housing Act 1961 shall be construed as including a reference to this Schedule; but the functions of a local authority under this Schedule shall not be among those referred to in section 70 of the 1969 Act (review of housing conditions by local authorities).

13. In section 29 (7) of the Land Compensation Act 1973 for the words "section 60 of the Housing Act 1969" there are substituted the words "Schedule 24 to the Housing Act 1980" and for the words "section 60 (2) of the said Act of 1969" the words "paragraph 5 of the said Schedule 24.". **[596]**

COMMENCEMENT
> See s. 153 (4), *ante*, and the note "Orders under this section" thereto.

PARA. 1: LOCAL AUTHORITY
> For meaning, see, by virtue of para. 10 above, the Housing Act 1957, s. 1, and the note thereto, Vol. 16, p. 115.

MEANS OF ESCAPE
> This may include a smoke screen; see *Horgan* v. *Birmingham Corpn.* (1964), 63 L.G.R. 33, C.A.

SECRETARY OF STATE
> See the note to s. 2, *ante*.

PARA. 2: NOTICE

> The persons on whom a notice under the Housing Act 1961, s. 15, may be served are either, by s. 15 (1): (a) the person having "control" of the house (as to this, see the Housing Act 1957, s. 39 (2)), or (b) any person to whom the house is let at a rack rent, or any person who, as the agent or trustee of a person to whom the house is let at a rack rent, receives rents or other payments from tenants of parts of the house or lodgers in the house. In this connection, it would appear that "rack rent" connotes a rent which represents the full annual value of the holding: *Re The Solicitors' Remuneration Act 1881, ex parte Sheridan and Russell* [1900] 1 I.R. 1, p. 6; also *Re C. R. Sawyer and Withall* [1919] 2 Ch. 333. Where the Rent Acts apply it would seem that "rack rent" involves the full amount a landlord could reasonably be expected to get from a tenant: *Rawlence* v. *Croydon Corporation* [1952] 2 Q.B. 803; [1952] 2 All E.R. 335, C.A. "Agent" within s. 15 (1) of the 1961 Act apparently does not include the secretary of the owner not clothed with actual or apparent authority to receive the rent: *Bottomley* v. *Harrison* [1952] 1 All E.R. 368.

PARA. 2 (3): OWNER
> For a definition of "owner", see the Housing Act 1957, s. 189 (1), applied by para. 10 of this Schedule.

PERSON
> See the note to s. 24, *ante*.

WITHIN SUCH PERIOD, ETC.
> See the note "Within six months of, etc." to s. 3, *ante*

PARA. 5: CONSULTATION
> See the note "Consult" to s. 26, *ante*.

PARA. 6: CLOSING ORDER

As to the power to make a closing order, see the Housing Act 1957, ss. 17 and 18, and as to the nature thereof, *ibid.*, s. 27. There is a power to revoke a closing order and substitute a demolition order: s. 28. Para. 11 of this Schedule makes consequential amendments to ss. 18 (1) and 27 (2) of the 1957 Act.

PARA. 7: KNOWING

See the note "Knowingly; knows" to s. 146, *ante*.

SUMMARY CONVICTION

See the note to s. 125, *ante*.

EVERY DAY ... ON WHICH HE SO USES IT, ETC.

See the note "Every day ... during which the failure continues" to Sch. 23, *ante*.

PARA. 8: FIRE AUTHORITY

As to fire authorities, see the Fire Services Act 1947, ss. 4, *et seq.*

SUPPLEMENTAL PROVISIONS

For miscellaneous provisions, supplementing this Schedule, see, by virtue of para. 12 above, the Housing Act 1961, s. 23, A.L.S. Vol. 131.

CONTROL ORDERS

Where a control order under the Housing Act 1964, s. 73, A.L.S. Vol. 149, is in force as respects the house in question or is revoked the provisions of this Schedule should be read together with certain provisions of that Act as construed in accordance with para. 12 above; see, in particular, ss. 74 (4), 77 (1), 79 (2) (*a*), 84 (2), (3), (5), 85 (1) (*a*), 86 (9), 88 (3) (*a*) of the Act of 1964.

SPECIAL GRANTS

In so far as an application for a special grant under the Housing Act 1974, Part VII, as amended by s. 107 and Sch. 12, *ante*, relates to the provision of means of escape from fire, the authority concerned is not to refuse it if it is duly made and its authority are satisfied that the relevant works are necessary for compliance with a notice under this Schedule; see s. 69A (2) of the Act of 1974 as inserted by s. 107 and Sch. 12, para. 17, *ante*.

HOME LOSS PAYMENTS

As to the making of home loss payments to persons displaced from dwellings in consequence of the making of a closing order under para. 6 above or the acceptance of an undertaking under para. 5 above, see the Land Compensation Act 1973, s. 29, A.L.S. Vol. 215, as amended by para. 13 above.

DEFINITIONS

By virtue of para. 10 above for "house" and "owner", see the Housing Act 1957, s. 189 (1), A.L.S. Vol. 109, by virtue of para. 12 above as to "lessee", see the Housing Act 1961, s. 23 (7), A.L.S. Vol. 131.

HOUSING ACT 1961, PART II, SS. 15, 16

S. 16 of that Act is repealed by s. 152 (3), *ante*, and Sch. 26, *post*, consequent upon s. 147 (1), *ante*, and this Schedule. For the persons on whom a notice may be served under s. 15 of the Act of 1961, see sub-s. (1) of that section, and see also in this connection the Housing Act 1964, ss. 102, 103 (2).

1977 ACT

I.e., the Rent Act 1977; see s. 150, *ante*. For limitations on the right to recover possession see, in particular, ss. 98 *et seq.*, of that Act.

1957 ACT

I.e., the Housing Act 1957; see s. 150, *ante*.

HOUSING ACT 1964, PART IV

See A.L.S. Vol. 149.

1969 ACT

I.e., the Housing Act 1969; see s. 150, *ante*.

LAND COMPENSATION ACT 1973, S. 29 (7)
    See A.L.S. Vol. 215.

ORDERS UNDER PARA. I
    At the time of going to press no order had been made under para. I above.   As to orders
    generally, see s. 151, *ante*.

SCHEDULE 25

Section 152

MINOR AND CONSEQUENTIAL AMENDMENTS,
TRANSITIONAL PROVISIONS AND SAVINGS

PART I

MINOR AND CONSEQUENTIAL AMENDMENTS

*Reserve and Auxiliary Forces (Protection of Civil Interests)
Act 1951 (c. 65)*

1. In section 15 of the Reserve and Auxiliary Forces (Protection of Civil Interests) Act
1951 (protection of tenure of furnished, and certain other, rented premises by extension of
provisions of the 1977 Act applying to restricted contracts) there is inserted, after subsection
(1), the following subsection—

"(1A) This section does not apply in relation to any tenancy entered into after the
commencement of section 69 (2) of the Housing Act 1980.".

2. In section 16 of the Act of 1951 (protection of tenure of rented premises not within
section 15, by extension of the Rent Acts) for subsections (4) to (7) there are substituted the
following subsections—

"(4) The rent for any rental period shall be the amount payable for the last rental
period of the tenancy qualifying for protection but subject to adjustment from time to
time in accordance with section 46 or 47 of the Rent Act 1977 (adjustment, with respect
to rates, services and furniture, of recoverable rent for statutory periods before
resignation).

(5) Subsection (4) above has effect subject to any agreement between the parties for
the payment of a lower rent; and where a lower rent is agreed it shall not be increased
in accordance with section 46 or 47 of the Act of 1977 but may, notwithstanding
anything in any other enactment, be increased by agreement in writing between the
parties up to the amount payable under subsection (4) above.".

3. In sections 17 and 18 of the Act of 1951 (which relate respectively to premises which
include accommodation shared otherwise than with the landlord and to premises occupied in
connection with employment under a licence or a rent-free letting) in each case in subsection
(2) for the words "to (7)" there are substituted the words "and (5)". **[597]**

COMMENCEMENT
    See s. 153 (4), *ante*, and the note "Orders under this section" thereto.

TENANCY
    For meaning, see the Reserve and Auxiliary Forces (Protection of Civil Interests) Act 1951,
    s. 23 (1).

WRITING
    See the note "Written, writing" to s. 5, *ante*.

1977 ACT
    I.e., the Rent Act 1977, A.L.S. Vol. 225.

Housing Act 1957 (c. 56)

4. Section 5 of the 1957 Act (prohibition of back-to back houses) is hereby repealed.

5. In section 96 of the 1957 Act, in paragraph (*d*) the words "by them", and paragraph (*e*), are hereby repealed.

6. In section 119 (3) of the 1957 Act (Financial assistance for housing associations) the words from "with the consent" to "the Minister" and the words from "The Minister's power" to the end are hereby repealed.

7. In section 126 of the 1957 Act (power of county councils to provide houses for their employees) there are added, at the end, the words "and any land so acquired or appropriated may be disposed of by the council as if the council were a local authority".

8. In Schedule 3 to the 1957 Act (procedure for authorising compulsory purchases under Part III) for sub-paragraph (4) of paragraph 3 there is substituted the following sub-paragraph—

> "(4) Where any objection not withdrawn has been made on the ground that a building included in the order is not unfit for human habitation, the local authority shall not later than 28 days before the date of the enquiry or hearing—
>
> > (*a*) serve upon the objector a notice in writing stating what facts have emerged as their principal grounds for being satisfied that the building is so unfit; and
> > (*b*) send a copy of the notice to the Secretary of State."

This paragraph does not apply in relation to an order under sections 43 or 51 of the 1957 Act made before the commencement of this paragraph. **[598]**

COMMENCEMENT
    See s. 153 (4), *ante*, and the note "Orders under this section" thereto.

PARA. 4
    The government repealed the prohibition on back-to-back houses because, it stated in Committee, it preferred to have developments for small households dealt with by planning controls and building regulations. Moreover, its spokesman claimed that s. 5 of the 1957 Act was out of date, imprecise and increasingly irrelevant: H.C. Committee, Col. 2591.
    Unfit housing will remain governed by s. 4 of the 1957 Act. It may be noted, *passim*, that the government rejected a proposed committee amendment extending s. 4 to cover the provision of standard amenities (see the Housing Act 1974, Sch. 6) and provision of sufficient artificial lighting. This was pending further consideration of the matter: H.C. Committee, Col. 2586.
    How correct were the government's views on the inadequacy of s. 5 of the 1957 Act is a matter of judgment; but the scope of the repealed prohibition on back-to-back houses was shown to be uncertain in *Chorley B.C.* v. *Barratt Developments (North West) Ltd.* [1979] 3 All E.R. 634. The type of development in that case may have been what the government had it in mind to encourage when repealing s. 5 of the 1957 Act; there, the houses were in blocks of four with two walls of the four external walls back-to-back. The development was held to fall outside s. 5, which was held directed at a case where three of the four walls were back-to-back. Section 5 was also limited by the fact that it only applied to dwellings "intended to be used ... for the working classes", an outdated term considered in *Guinness Trust (London Fund)* v. *Green* [1955] 3 All E.R. 871, C.A. *Quaere*, how far poverty is relevant to this term.

LOCAL AUTHORITY
    For meaning, see the Housing Act 1957, s. 1, and the note thereto, A.L.S. Vol. 109.

UNFIT FOR HUMAN HABITATION
    As to the standard of fitness for human habitation, see the Housing Act 1957.

WRITING
    See the note "Written, writing" to s. 5, *ante*.

PRINCIPAL GROUNDS FOR BEING SATISFIED, ETC.
As to the sufficiency of the grounds for being satisfied that a building is unfit for human habitation, see *R.* v. *Minister of Health, Ex parte Hack*, [1937] 3 All E.R. 176.

SECRETARY OF STATE
See the note to s. 2, *ante*.

1957 ACT
I.e., the Housing Act 1957; see s. 150, *ante*. Ss. 5 and 96 (*e*) of that Act and the words in s. 119 (3) mentioned in para. 6 above are also repealed by s. 152 (3), *ante*, and Sch. 26, *post*.

Housing (Financial Provisions) Act 1958 (c. 42)

9. In section 43 (1) of the Housing (Financial Provisions) Act 1958 (power of local authorities to make advances) the words "subject to such conditions as may be approved by the Minister" are omitted. **[599]**

COMMENCEMENT
See s. 153 (4), *ante*, and the note "Orders under this section" thereto.

HOUSING (FINANCIAL PROVISIONS) ACT 1958, S. 43 (1)
See A.L.S. Vol. 109. The words to be omitted are also repealed by s. 152 (3), *ante*, and Sch. 26, *post*.

County Courts Act 1959 (c. 22)

10. In section 109 (4) (*b*) of the County Courts Act 1959 for the word "document" there is substituted the word "enactment". **[600]**

COMMENCEMENT
See s. 153 (4), *ante*, and the note "Orders under this section" thereto.

COUNTY COURTS ACT 1959, S. 109 (4) (*b*)
That paragraph was substituted by the Rent Act 1977, s. 155 (2), Sch. 23, para. 30, A.L.S. Vol. 255.

Building Societies Act 1962 (c. 37)

11. In Schedule 3 to the Building Societies Act 1962 (permitted classes of additional security) in paragraph 3 (1) for "local authorities" substitute "bodies" and in paragraph 3 (2) (*a*), after "England and Wales" insert "section 111 of the Housing Act 1980" and in paragraph 3 (2) (*c*) after "Northern Ireland" insert "any statutory provision for the time being in force in Northern Ireland and made for purposes corresponding to those of section 111 of the Housing Act 1980".

12. After paragraph 13 of that Schedule insert—

"14. An agreement under section 111 of the Housing Act 1980 (agreement by local authority or Housing Corporation to indemnify building society in respect of mortgagor's default) or under any statutory provision for the time being in force in Northern Ireland and made for purposes corresponding to those of that section.". **[601]**

COMMENCEMENT
See s. 153 (4), *ante*, and the note "Orders under this section" thereto.

BUILDING SOCIETIES ACT 1962, SCH. 3, PARAS. 3, 13
Sch. 3, para. 13, was added by the Building Societies (Additional Security) Order 1974, S.I. 1974, No. 1408.

Housing Act 1964 (c. 56)

13. In Schedule 1 to the Housing Act 1964, for paragraph 4 (1) (authentication of fixing of Corporation's seal by signature of chairman or member) substitute—

"(1) The fixing of the Corporation's seal may be authenticated by the signature of the Chairman or of any other person authorised for that purpose.". **[602]**

COMMENCEMENT
See s. 153 (4), *ante*, and the note "Orders under this section" thereto.

THE CORPORATION
I.e., the Housing Corporation; see the Housing Act 1964, s. 1 (1), A.L.S. Vol. 149.

HOUSING ACT 1964, SCH. 1, PARA. 4 (1)
See A.L.S. Vol. 149.

Matrimonial Homes Act 1967 (c. 75)

14. In section 1 (5) of the Matrimonial Homes Act 1967 after "be treated as possession by the other spouse" insert "and for purposes of Chapter II of Part I of the Housing Act 1980 be treated as occupation by the other spouse".

15. In section 7 (1) of that Act, after paragraph (*b*) insert—

"or
(*c*) a secure tenancy within the meaning of section 28 of the Housing Act 1980";

and for "subsection (2) or (3)" substitute "subsection (2), (3) or (3A)".

16. In section 7 (2) of that Act, after "the Rent Act 1977" insert "or a secure tenancy within the meaning of section 28 of the Housing Act 1980"; and at the end of the subsection add "and where the said spouse is a successor within the meaning of Chapter II of Part I of that Act, his or her former spouse shall be deemed also to be a successor within the meaning of that Chapter".

17. In section 7 (3) of that Act for "widow" substitute "the surviving spouse". **[603]**

COMMENCEMENT
See s. 153 (4), *ante*, and the note "Orders under this section" thereto.

PARA. 14
This means that occupation by virtue of s. 1 of the 1967 Act by a "bare" spouse is treated as that of the other spouse where that other is the secure tenant; accordingly, the "bare" spouse will continue to have security despite the tenant's desertion, etc.

CHAPTER II OF PART I OF THE HOUSING ACT 1980
I.e., ss. 28–50, *ante*. For the meaning of "successor" in that Chapter, see s. 31, *ante*.

MATRIMONIAL HOMES ACT 1967, SS. 1 (5), 7
See A.L.S. Vol. 164. S. 7 (3A) of that Act was inserted by the Rent (Agriculture) Act 1976, s. 40 (2), Sch. 8, para. 16, A.L.S. Vol. 250.

Building Societies Act (Northern Ireland) 1967 (c. 31 N.I.)

18. In Schedule 3 to the Building Societies Act (Northern Ireland) 1967 (permitted classes of additional security) in paragraph 3 (1) after "certain local authorities" insert "or the Housing Corporation" and in paragraph 3 (2) (*b*), after "England and Wales" insert "section 111 of the Housing Act 1980."

19. After paragraph 13 of that Schedule insert—

"14. An agreement under section 111 of the Housing Act 1980 (agreement by local authority or Housing Corporation to indemnify building society in respect of mortgagor's default).". **[604]**

COMMENCEMENT
See s. 153 (4), *ante*, and the note "Orders under this section" thereto.

BUILDING SOCIETIES ACT (NORTHERN IRELAND) 1967
1967 c. 31 (N.I.).

Prices and Incomes Act 1968 (c. 42)

20. In section 12 (1) of the Prices and Incomes Act 1968 (provision for local authorities to increase rents under periodic tenancies without giving notice to quit) after "tenancy", where first occurring, insert "which is not a secure tenancy within the meaning of section 28 of the Housing Act 1980". **[605]**

COMMENCEMENT
See s. 153 (4), *ante*, and the note "Orders under this section" thereto.

PARA. 20
In relation to secure tenancies, the procedure for serving a notice of increase of rent without notice to quit is inapplicable; but s. 12 (1) of the 1968 Act will continue to apply to non-secure tenancies, *e.g.* short-life tenancies under Sch. 3, para. 7.

PRICES AND INCOMES ACT 1968, S. 12 (1)
See A.L.S. Vol. 175.

Housing Act 1969 (c. 33)

21. In section 85 of the 1969 Act (provisions relating to orders and regulations under the Act), after subsection (1) there is inserted the following subsection—

"(1A) Any order or regulation made under this Act may make different provision with respect to different cases or descriptions of case, including different provision for different areas". **[606]**

COMMENCEMENT
See s. 153 (4), *ante*, and the note "Orders under this section" thereto.

1969 ACT
I.e., the Housing Act 1969; see s. 150, *ante*. For s. 85 (1) of that Act, see A.L.S. Vol. 183.

Chronically Sick and Disabled Persons Act 1970 (c. 44)

22. In section 3 (1) of the Chronically Sick and Disabled Persons Act 1970 (duty of housing authorities to have regard to special needs of chronically sick or disabled persons) the words from "and any proposals" to the end are hereby repealed. **[607]**

COMMENCEMENT
See s. 153 (4), *ante*, and the note "Orders under this section" thereto.

CHRONICALLY SICK AND DISABLED PERSONS ACT 1970, S. 3 (1)
See A.L.S. Vol. 192. The words which are repealed are also repealed by s. 152 (3), *ante*, and Sch. 26, *post*.

Local Government Act 1972 (c. 70)

23. In section 131 (2) of the Local Government Act 1972 (enactments which are not affected by Parts VII and VIII of that Act) after paragraph (k) there is inserted the following paragraph—

"(l) the Housing Act 1980". **[608]**

COMMENCEMENT
See s. 153 (4), *ante*, and the note "Orders under this section" thereto.

LOCAL GOVERNMENT ACT 1972, S. 131 (2) (k)
See A.L.S. Vol. 209.

Housing Act 1974 (c. 44)

24. In section 5 of the 1974 Act (disposal of land by Housing Corporation), in subsection (3) omit all after paragraph (*f*), and after that subsection insert—

"(3A) The Corporation may sell or lease individual dwellings to persons for their own occupation; but where the dwelling concerned was acquired by the Corporation by compulsory purchase under section 3 (3), it shall not be disposed of under this subsection without the written consent of the Secretary of State.".

25. In section 26 (2) of the 1974 Act (cases in which payments may be made by registered housing associations to members) in paragraph (*b*) (iii) after "person" insert "either under his tenancy agreement with the association or".

26. After section 103 of the 1974 Act insert—

103A "Full and reduced standard
(1) For the purposes of this Part of this Act, a dwelling shall be taken to attain the full standard if the following conditions are fulfilled with respect to it, namely—

- (*a*) that it is provided with all the standard amenities for the exclusive use of its occupants; and
- (*b*) that it is in reasonable repair (disregarding the state of internal decorative repair) having regard to its age and character and the locality in which it is situated; and
- (*c*) that it conforms with such requirements with respect to thermal insulation as may for the time being be specified by the Secretary of State for the purposes of this section; and
- (*d*) that it is in all other respects fit for human habitation (to be determined in accordance with section 4 of the Housing Act 1957); and
- (*e*) that it is likely to be available for use as a dwelling for a period of 15 years or such other period as may for the time being be specified by the Secretary of State for the purposes of this subsection.

(2) Subject to subsection (3) below, a local authority may, if they consider it reasonable to do so, dispense wholly or in part with any of the conditions in subsection (1), and a dwelling shall be taken to attain the reduced standard if the conditions not dispensed with are fulfilled.

(3) A local authority shall not dispense with the conditions in paragraph (*a*) of subsection (1) in a case where they are satisfied that the dwelling is, or forms part of, a house or building in respect of which they could by notice under section 15 of the Housing Act 1961 (power to require execution of works) require the execution of such works as are referred to in subsection (1) of that section.".

27. In section 104 of the 1974 Act (Interpretation of Part VIII) the definitions of "the full standard" and "the reduced standard" are repealed.

28.—(1) In section 114 (1) of the 1974 Act (rehabilitation orders) paragraph (*c*) and the word "or" immediately preceding it are omitted, and after that subsection there is inserted the following subsection—

"(1A) In the case of a clearance area comprising houses within subsection (1) (*a*) or (*b*) above, this section also applies to houses comprised in the area which have been included in it by virtue of section 49 of the Housing Act 1957.".

(2) Subsections (6) and (7) of section 114 are repealed.

(3) In section 114 (8)—

- (*a*) in the definition of "full standard" for "section 66 (2)" substitute "section 103A (1)";
- (*b*) in paragraph (*b*) of the definition of "Part III land", for "section 43 (2)" substitute "section 43".

29. After section 114 of the 1974 Act there is inserted the following section—

114A(1) "Effects of rehabilitation order
Where in the case of a rehabilitation order a local authority are freed by section 114 (5) above from the duty to demolish or secure the demolition of houses included in a

356

clearance area as being unfit for human habitation, the authority shall take such steps as are necessary—

    (*a*) to restore the houses so as to provide one or more dwellings to the full standard of section 103A above;

    (*b*) where they are not vested in the authority, to ensure that the houses are restored with that object.

(2) A local authority may accept undertakings for the purposes of subsection (1) (*b*) above from the owner of the houses, or any other person who has or will have an interest in them or any of them, concerning works to be carried out to restore the houses as mentioned in that subsection, and the time within which the works are to be carried out."

30. In section 128 of the 1974 Act (provisions relating to orders under the Act), after subsection (1) there is inserted the following sub-section—

"(1A) An order made by the Secretary of State under any provision of this Act may make different provision with respect to different cases or descriptions of case, including different provision for different areas."

31. In Schedule 10 to the 1974 Act (rehabilitation orders), in paragraph 6, there is added after sub-paragraph (*b*) the following sub-paragraph—

"and

(*c*) the notice land, so far as not comprised within sub-paragraph (*a*) or (*b*) above.". **[609]**

COMMENCEMENT
    See s. 153 (4), *ante*, and the note "Orders under this section" thereto.

PARA. 24: WRITTEN
    See the note "Written: writing" to s. 5, *ante*.

SECRETARY OF STATE
    See the note to s. 2, *ante*.

PARA. 26
    In place of the definition of "full standard" in the Housing Act 1974, s. 104, which referred in turn to s. 66 of that Act (a new s. 66 is substituted, it may be recalled, by Sch. 12, para. 9, to this Act, and alters the basis of intermediate grants, leaving out all reference to "full standard") there is a new definition in para. 26. The new s. 103A (1) of the Housing Act 1974 is, as regards paras. (*a*), (*c*), and (*e*) thereof, identical with the provision it replaces. Para. (*d*), however, refers only to the Housing Act 1957, s. 4, in determining fitness for human habitation, rather than, as before, the whole of Part II of that Act. Para. (*b*), refers, instead of to "good repair", as the standard of repair, to "reasonable repair". This is in line with the rest of this Act: see the note to Sch. 12, para. 20.

THIS PART OF THIS ACT
    I.e., the Housing Act 1974, Part VIII (ss. 85, 104), A.L.S. Vol. 223.

LIKELY
    See the note to s. 43, *ante*.

PARA. 29: LOCAL AUTHORITY
    I.e., a local authority as defined by the Housing Act 1974, s. 114 (8), as substituted by the Housing Rents and Subsidies Act 1975, s. 17 (4), Sch. 5, para. 21, A.L.S. Vol. 230.

DEFINITIONS
    In the provisions inserted by para. 24 above for "the Corporation" and "dwelling", see the Housing Act 1974, s. 129 (1). In the provisions inserted by para. 26 above by virtue of s. 104 (1) of the Act of 1974, for "local authority", see s. 84 thereof; and for "standard amenities", see s. 58 of, and Sch. 6 to, that Act (as amended, in the case of s. 58, by s. 107 and Sch. 12, para. 3, *ante*). In the provisions inserted by para. 29 above for "rehabilitation order", cf. s. 114 (2) of the Act of 1974 as substituted by the Housing Rents and Subsidies Act 1975, s. 17 (4), Sch. 5, para. 21. In the provisions added by para. 31 above for "notice and", see Sch. 10, para. 1 (1), to the Act of 1974 as substituted by s. 17 (4) of, and Sch. 5, para. 25, to the Act of 1975.

1974 ACT
    I.e., the Housing Act 1974; see s. 150, *ante.* The provisions which are omitted or repealed
    are also repealed by s. 152 (3), *ante*, and Sch. 26, *post.*

HOUSING ACT 1957, SS. 4, 49
    See A.L.S. Vol. 109.

HOUSING ACT 1961, S. 15
    See A.L.S. Vol. 131.

Rent (Agriculture) Act 1976 (c. 80)

32. In section 7 of the Rent (Agriculture) Act 1976, at the end of subsection (6) (definition
of "tenant"), there are added the words "and 'tenancy' shall be construed accordingly".

33. In section 13 of the Act of 1976 (application for registration of rent)—

    (a) for the words "three years" in subsection (7) there are substituted the words "two
        years"; and
    (b) in subsection (3) for the words "Schedule 7" there are substituted the words "Schedule
        12". **[610]**

COMMENCEMENT
    See s. 153 (4), *ante*, and the note "Orders under this section" thereto.

RENT (AGRICULTURE) ACT 1976, SS. 7 (6), 13
    See A.L.S. Vol. 250.

Rent Act 1977 (c. 42)

34. In section 16 of the 1977 Act (landlord's interest belonging to housing co-operative) for
the words "paragraph 9 of Schedule 1 to the Housing Rents and Subsidies Act 1975" there are
substituted the words "paragraph 1 of Schedule 20 to the Housing Act 1980".

35. Sections 18 (4) and 115 of the 1977 Act (modification of Act in cases where controlled
tenancies converted into regulated tenancies) are hereby repealed; and in that Act, after
section 18, there is inserted the following section—

    18A. "Modification of Act for controlled tenancies converted into regulated tenancies
    Schedule 17 to this Act applies for the purpose of modifying the provisions of this Act
    in relation to a tenancy which, by virtue of any of the following enactments, was
    converted from a controlled tenancy into a regulated tenancy, that is to say—

        (a) section 18 (3) of this Act;
        (b) paragraph 5 of Schedule 2 to the Rent Act 1968 (which was superseded by
            section 18 (3));
        (c) Part VIII of this Act;
        (d) Part III of the Housing Finance Act 1972 (which was superseded by Part
            VIII);
        (e) Part IV of the Act of 1972 (conversion by reference to rateable values);
        (f) section 64 of the Housing Act 1980 (conversion of remaining controlled
            tenancies into regulated tenancies)."

36. In section 19 (5) of the 1977 Act (furnished lettings etc. which are not restricted
contracts) after paragraph (a) insert—

    "(aa) under the contract the interest of the lessor belongs to a body mentioned in section
        14 of this Act;".

37. In section 45 (4) of the 1977 Act, for the words "to 48" there are substituted the words
"and 47".

38. In section 49 of the 1977 Act, for the words "46 (2) or 48 (3)" there substituted the
words "or 46".

39. In section 55 of the 1977 Act (general provisions for phasing of rent increases), in
subsection (3), for paragraph (b) there is substituted the following paragraph—

    "(b) the provisions of section 89 of this Act do not apply to it; and".

40. In sections 68 (4), 69 (1) (*b*) (ii) and (4), 73 (1) (*a*), and 88 (4) (*b*) of the 1977 Act for the words "three years" and "3 years," wherever occurring, there are substituted the words "2 years".

This paragraph does not apply in any case where, on the determination or confirmation of a rent by the rent officer, the rent determined by him is registered, or his confirmation is noted in the register, before the commencement of this paragraph.

41. In section 70 (3) of the 1977 Act (matters to be disregarded in determining fair rent) paragraphs (*c*) and (*d*) are hereby repealed.

42. In section 78 (5) of the 1977 Act, for the words "subsection (1)" there are substituted the words "subsection (2)".

43. In section 79 of the 1977 Act—

    (*a*) in subsection (1) for the words "local authority" there are substituted the words "president of every rent assessment panel";

    (*b*) in subsection (2) for the words "local authority" there are substituted the words "rent assessment panel";

    (*c*) subsection (4) is hereby repealed; and

    (*d*) in subsection (5) for the words "local authority" there are substituted the words "president of the rent assessment panel concerned".

44. In section 79 of the 1977 Act there is inserted, at the end, the following subsection—

"(6A) Every local authority shall, before the expiry of the period of three months beginning with the commencement of paragraph 44 of Schedule 25 to the Housing Act 1980, send to the president of the appropriate rent assessment panel the register previously kept by the authority under this section."

45. In section 85 of the 1977 Act—

    (*a*) in the definition of "register" for the words "local authority" there are substituted the words "president of the rent assessment panel concerned"; and

    (*b*) in the definition of "rent tribunal" for the words from "has" onwards there are substituted the words "shall be construed in accordance with section 72 of the Housing Act 1980".

46. In section 88 (2) of the 1977 Act (rent limits for housing association tenancies) for the words "sections 89 and 90" there are substituted the words "section 89".

47.—(1) Section 116 of the 1977 Act (provision where tenant refuses to allow landlord to carry out works) is amended as follows.

(2) For sub-section (1) there is substituted the following subsection—

"(1) This section applies where a dwelling-house is subject to a statutory tenancy and the landlord wishes to carry out works which cannot be carried out without the consent of the tenant."

(3) For subsection (3) there is substituted the following subsection—

"(3) The condition is—

    (*a*) that the works were specified in an application for an improvement, or intermediate, grant under Part VII of the Housing Act 1974 and the application has been approved, or

    (*b*) that the works are specified in a certificate issued by a local authority and stating that if an application were to be made by the landlord for such a grant in respect of the works, the application would be likely to be approved."

(4) In subsection (5) the words "sections 4 (4) or 10 of the Housing Act 1969 or" are hereby repealed.

48. In section 129 (1) of the 1977 Act (mortgages to which Part X applies), for paragraph (*b*) there is substituted the following paragraph—

"(*b*) are regulated mortgages as defined in section 131 of this Act".

49. In section 132 (1) of the 1977 Act (powers of court to mitigate hardship to mortgagors under regulated mortgages), for the words from "relate only" to "such a mortgage" there are substituted the words "become exercisable, in relation to a regulated mortgage,".

50. In section 136 of the 1977 Act (interpretation of Part X), in paragraph (*b*) for the words from "and 'mortgage'" to "include" there is substituted the word "includes".

51. Section 138 (3) of the 1977 Act (effect on furnished sub-tenancy of determination of superior unfurnished tenancy) shall have effect, and be deemed always to have had effect, as if for the words from "meaning" to the end there were substituted the words "same meaning as it has for the purposes of section 137 (2) of this Act".

52. In section 145 of the 1977 Act (which limits the rent recoverable under tenancies of certain subsidised private houses), for subsections (3) and (4) (which apply to conditions limiting the rent under controlled tenancies) and subsection (5) (which applies Schedule 21 to that Act to conditions limiting the rent under other tenancies) there are substituted the following subsections—

> "(3) If any condition to which this section applies limits the rent under a tenancy, the condition shall limit, or have effect as if it limited, the rent—
>> (*a*) if the tenancy is a regulated tenancy which is not a converted tenancy within the meaning of Schedule 17 to this Act, to the rent which would be recoverable if the tenancy had been converted from being a controlled tenancy upon the commencement of section 64 of the Housing Act 1980 and accordingly as if it were a converted tenancy;
>> (*b*) if the tenancy is a converted tenancy, or a housing association tenancy within the meaning of Part VI of this Act, to the rent recoverable under this Act;
>> (*c*) if the tenancy is a protected occupancy or statutory tenancy within the meaning of the Rent (Agriculture) Act 1976, to the rent recoverable in accordance with that Act; and
>> (*d*) in any other case, to such rent as may from time to time be, or have been, agreed between the landlord and the local authority or as may, in default of agreement, be or have been determined by the Secretary of State.
>
> (4) Subject to subsection (5) below, in subsection (3) above 'local authority', in relation to any premises, means the council of the London borough or district in which the premises are situated or, if they are situated in the City of London, the Common Council of the City of London.
>
> (5) In the case of houses the construction of which was promoted by the Greater London Council or in respect of which improvement grants were made by that council under the Housing (Financial Provisions) Act 1958, the reference in subsection (3) above to the local authority shall be construed as a reference to the Greater London Council.".

53. In section 149 of the 1977 Act (powers of local authorities for purposes of giving information), in subsection (1) (*a*), for sub-paragraph (iii) there is substituted the following sub-paragraph—

> "(iii) Part II, and section 136, of the Housing Act 1980;".

54. In section 153 (1) of the 1977 Act (application to Isles of Scilly), for the words "103 to 106" there are substituted the words "102A to 106A".

55. Section 155 (1) of the 1977 Act (which modifies provisions of that Act in relation to certain old controlled tenancies) is hereby repealed.

56. In Schedule 10 to the 1977 Act (rent assessment committees)—

> (*a*) in paragraph 2 the words from "and, if the Secretary of State" to the end; and
> (*b*) paragraph 10;

are hereby repealed.

57. In Schedule 15 to the 1977 Act (grounds for possession of dwelling-houses), in paragraph (i) in Case 9, for the words "controlled tenancy" there are substituted the words "tenancy which was then a controlled tenancy".

Case 9 has effect, as so amended, in relation to any tenancy which was a controlled tenancy on the date mentioned in paragraph (i) notwithstanding that it ceased to be a controlled tenancy before the commencement of this paragraph.

58. In Schedule 15 to the 1977 Act, in paragraph 4 in Part IV, for the words "paragraph 1"

there are substituted the words "paragraph 3", at the end of paragraph (*a*) there are inserted the words "(other than one under which the landlord might recover possession of the dwelling-house under one of the Cases in Part II of this Schedule)", and at the end of paragraph (*b*) there are inserted the words "of a kind mentioned in paragraph (*a*) above".

59. In Schedule 17 to the 1977 Act (modification of Act where controlled tenancy converted into regulated tenancy)—

    (*a*) in the definition of "converted tenancy", for paragraphs (*a*) and (*b*) there are substituted the words "any of the enactments mentioned in section 18A of this Act."; and

    (*b*) paragraphs 3 and 4 are hereby repealed; and

    (*c*) in paragraph 7, for the words from the beginning to "shall not" there are substituted the words "None of the enactments mentioned in section 18A of this Act shall".

60. In Schedule 24 to the 1977 Act (savings and transitional provisions)—

    (*a*) in paragraph 6 (4) for the words "paragraph 1 (1)" there are substituted the words "paragraph 1 (c)"; and

    (*b*) in paragraph 16 for the words "sections 44 (1), (2), 38 and 72 (4)" there are substituted the words "sections 44 (1), 45 (2), 57 and 72 (7)". **[611]**

COMMENCEMENT
    See s. 153 (a), *ante*, and the note "Orders under this section" thereto.

PARA. 36
    Section 14 of the Rent Act 1977 will thus apply to exclude a restricted contract from protection where the interest of the landlord belongs to the local authorities therein mentioned; also where the landlord is the Commission for the New Towns, certain development corporations and the Development Board for Rural Wales. So a local authority, etc., will be able to provide services such as central heating, without there being a restricted contract as a result.

PARA. 37
    The exclusion of the Rent Act 1977, s. 48, in determinations of what is the rent recoverable during a "statutory period" (defined in s. 61 (1) of the 1977 Act) where no rent is registered under Part IV of the 1977 Act means that no increases in the statutory period will be permissible on account of improvements completed after 7th December 1965 and after the time when the rent under the regulated tenancy was agreed, after the commencement of this Schedule. The exclusion of even a step-by-step procedure for increases on account of improvements is in accordance with the general policy of this Act.

PARA. 39
    The exclusion of the Rent Act 1977, s. 89, is in consequence of the alterations to phasing in this Act: see, generally, Sch. 10.

PARA. 40
    The time-bar on fresh applications for a new registered rent is reduced from 3 years to 2 years from the "relevant date" (Rent Act 1977, s. 67 (5) as substituted by s. 61 (5) of this Act) in the following cases: where a local authority has applied for registration of a fair rent (Rent Act 1977, s. 68); where an intending landlord has applied for a certificate of fair rent (*ibid.*, s. 69); where a registration of a fair rent is cancelled (s. 73); and the period of time before a tenancy began when dealing with the recoverable rent limit is reduced to 2 years by para. 40: see Rent Act 1977, s. 88.

PARA. 40: RENT OFFICER
    This expression defined by the Rent Act 1977, s. 63 (4), A.L.S. Vol. 255.

REGISTER
    I.e., the register kept under the Rent Act 1977, s. 66.

PARA. 41
    As a result of the deletion of paras. (*c*) and (*d*) of s. 70 of the Rent Act 1977, there may be taken into account, in determining a fair rent (from the commencement of this Schedule):

    (*a*) the provision in the locality after the "material date" (this is usually the date of registration of rent) of any new amenity or the improvement of certain amenities;

(*b*) the effect of (in effect) deterioration in local amenities.

Notice that nowhere in the Rent Act 1977 is there a definition of "amenity"; but in *Metropolitan Properties Ltd.* v. *Finegold* [1975] 1 All E.R. 389, the nearness of schools, zoos or theatres were mentioned as a possible list of amenities.

PARA. 43: RENT ASSESSMENT PANEL

As to these panels, see the Rent Act 1977, Sch. 10, paras. 1–3, as partly repealed, in the case of para. 2, by para. 56 above.

PARA. 44: LOCAL AUTHORITY

I.e., the local authority as defined by the Rent Act 1977, s. 83 (1).

THREE MONTHS BEGINNING WITH, ETC.

See the note to s. 12, *ante*.

PARA. 47: DWELLING-HOUSE

See the note to the Rent Act 1977, s. 1.

LOCAL AUTHORITY

I.e., a local authority as defined by the Rent Act 1977, s. 118 (1).

PARAS. 48 AND 49

Owing to de-control, the definition of a controlled mortgage in the Rent Act 1977, s. 130, has been repealed; the sole relevant definition will therefore, after the commencement of this Schedule, be that in s. 131 of the 1977 Act. This results from para. 48. Para. 49 therefore makes consequential amendment to s. 132 (1) of the 1977 Act, so as to exclude controlled mortgages from its ambit.

PARA. 50

This excludes controlled mortgages from the ambit of the relevant definition section in the Rent Act 1977 (s. 136).

PARA. 52

Owing to de-control, the rent limit on subsidised private houses in the Rent Act 1977, s. 145 (3) to (5) had to be modified by para. 52, which substitutes new s. 145 (3) to (5).

PARA. 53

To the list of matters on which a local authority may publish information in the Rent Act 1977, s. 149, there is added Part II and the service charges rules in this Act. In that the service charges rules in this Act replace those of the Housing Finance Act 1972, s. 90 *et seq.*, the reference in s. 149 of the 1977 Act to these rules is deleted.

PARAS. 55 AND 57

De-control: Further provisions

The modifications of the Rent Act 1977, when applied to controlled tenancies (s. 155 and Sch. 22) are repealed by para. 55 in consequence of de-control. Para. 57 makes amendments to the Rent Act 1977, Sch. 15, Case 9, so that the Case will apply to a tenancy which was at the "relevant date" (7th November 1956) a controlled tenancy but which has ceased so to be as a result of de-control by the date of the action for possession.

PARA. 58

The alteration to the reference to the Rent Act 1977, Sch. 15, Part IV, "para. 1," in para. 4, to read "para. 3" may have been to correct a misprint.

Para. 58 so alters para. 4 of Sch. 15, Part IV, to that Act that the offer of accommodation such that the landlord would be able, on expiry of the term, to recover possession under one of the mandatory Cases (11 to 20) in Sch. 15, Part II, to the 1977 Act, is not deemed to be suitable alternative accommodation. Thus, for instance, the offer to a sitting protected tenant of a new tenancy in another dwelling-house under a protected shorthold tenancy (to which the new Case 19 applied) would not be of suitable alternative accommodation. *Quaere*, whether this would not have been held to be the case in any event, as reasonably equivalent security of tenure would arguably not be offered in such a case: cf. the note to Sch. 4, Part II, para. 1 (*b*), to this Act.

COUNCIL OF THE LONDON BOROUGH OR DISTRICT

See the corresponding notes to s. 43, *ante*.

COMMON COUNCIL OF THE CITY OF LONDON; GREATER LONDON COUNCIL
    See the notes to s. 50, *ante*.

PARA. 60: 72 (7)
    I.e., the Rent Act 1977, s. 72 (7). There is no sub-s. (7) in s. 72 of that Act as substituted
    by s. 61 (1), *ante* (or in s. 72 as originally enacted) and it is thought that its reference in
    para. 60 (*b*) above to s. 72 (7) of the Act of 1977 should be read as a reference to s. 72
    (6) thereof as substituted by s. 61 (1), *ante*.

DEFINITIONS
    For "statutory tenancy", see the Rent Act 1977, s. 2; for "controlled tenancy", see s. 17
    of that Act; for "regulated tenancy", see s. 18 of that Act (as partly repealed by para.
    35 above and s. 152 (3) *ante*, and Sch. 26, *post*); for "lessor", see s. 19 (8) of that Act; for
    "regulated mortgage", see s. 131 of that Act; for "landlord", "tenant" and "tenancy",
    see s. 152 (a) of that Act.

1977 ACT
    I.e., the Rent Act 1977; see s. 150, *ante*. S. 18 (3) of that Act is repealed by s. 152 (3),
    ante, and Sch. 26, *post*, as from a day to be appointed under s. 153 (4), *ante*, consequent
    upon s. 64 (1), *ante*; s. 89 is substituted by s. 77 and Sch. 10, para. 2, *ante*; s. 102A is inserted
    by s. 69 (3), *ante*, and s. 106A is inserted by s. 69 (2), *ante*. The provisions of the Act of
    1977 which are repealed are also repealed by s. 152 (3), *ante*, and Sch. 26, *post*.

RENT ACT 1968, SCH. 2, PARA. 5
    That Act was repealed by the Rent Act 1977, s. 155 (5), Sch. 25.

HOUSING FINANCE ACT 1972, PARTS III, IV
    See A.L.S. Vol. 202. Part III was repealed by the Rent Act 1977, s. 155 (5), Sch. 25, and
    the provisions in Part IV relating to decontrol by reference to rateable value (*i.e.* ss. 35
    and 36) were repealed by the Housing Rents and Subsidies Act 1975, s. 17 (5), Sch. 6, Part
    III, consequent on the termination of such decontrol by s. 9 of the Act of 1975.

HOUSING ACT 1974, PART VII
    See A.L.S. Vol. 223. That Part is amended by s. 107 and Sch. 12, *ante*, and it is extended
    by s. 106, *ante*.

RENT (AGRICULTURE) ACT 1976
    See A.L.S. Vol. 250; and for the meanings of "protected occupancy" and "statutory
    tenancy", see ss. 2 and 3, and ss. 4 and 5 thereof respectively.

HOUSING (FINANCIAL PROVISIONS) ACT 1958
    See A.L.S. Vol. 109. The provisions of that Act relating to improvement grants (*i.e.* ss.
    30–42) were repealed by the Housing Act 1969, s. 89 (3), Sch. 10.

TRANSITIONAL PROVISION
    See s. 152 (2), *ante*, and para. 78 in Part II of this Schedule, *post*.

Protection from Eviction Act 1977 (c. 43)

    61. The Protection from Eviction Act 1977 shall apply, where a person has been let into
possession of a dwelling-house under the terms of a rental purchase agreement (within the
meaning of section 88 of this Act) as if—
    (*a*) the dwelling-house had been let to him as a dwelling under a tenancy which is not a
        statutorily protected tenancy (within the meaning of section 3 of that Act); and
    (*b*) that tenancy had come to an end on the termination of the agreement or of his right
        to possession under it. **[612]**

COMMENCEMENT
    See s. 153 (4), *ante*, and the note "Orders under this section" thereto.

DWELLING-HOUSE
    See the note to s. 3, *ante*.

PROTECTION FROM EVICTION ACT 1977
    See 47, Halsbury's Statutes (3rd edn.), p. 661.

PART II

TRANSITIONAL PROVISIONS AND SAVINGS

62. For the purposes of section 33 of this Act a notice served at any time after regulations are first made for the purposes of subsection (2) of that section, but before the commencement of that section shall be treated as duly served under that section if it would have been so treated had Chapter II of Part I of this Act then been in force.

63. Where, immediately before the commencement of section 60 of this Act, an increase in rent was subject to the provisions as to phasing of rent increases in Schedule 6 to the Rent (Agriculture) Act 1976 or in Schedule 8 or 9 to the 1977 Act that increase shall continue to be subject to those provisions as if this Act had not been passed.

64. Where the recoverable rent for any statutory period has been increased by a notice under section 48 of the 1977 Act, nothing in section 63 of this Act affects that increase or the operation of subsections (4) and (5) of section 48 in relation to the notice.

65. In a case where, by virtue of subsection (4) of section 52 of the 1977 Act, that section would not have applied to an agreement with a tenant having security of tenure had it not been replaced by the section substituted by section 68 (2) of this Act, the substituted section 52 shall also not apply in relation to that agreement.

66. The repeal by this Act of subsections (4) and (5) of section 54 of the 1977 Act does not affect the operation of those subsections in relation to defaults occuring before the commencement of section 68 of this Act.

67. Where, immediately before the commencement of section 69 (4) of this Act, a tenancy was, by virtue of section 12 (2) (*b*) of the 1977 Act, a protected tenancy and not a restricted contract, the 1977 Act shall continue to apply in relation to that tenancy as if section 69 (4) had not been enacted.

68. The repeals made by section 74 of this Act in section 15 of the 1977 Act shall not affect any tenancy which was, immediately before the commencement of section 74 (1), a protected, or statutory tenancy but which would, were it not for this paragraph, have ceased to be such a tenancy by virtue of the repeal of section 15 (4) (*f*).

69—(1) Any condition which, immediately before the commencement of section 91 of this Act, was a local land charge by virtue of section 104 (5) of the 1957 Act shall continue to be a local land charge notwithstanding the provisions of section 91.

(2) Section 104 (3) of the 1957 Act shall have effect, in the period between the commencement of section 91 and the commencement of Chapter II of Part I of this Act as if Chapter II were in force.

70. Any directions given by the Secretary of State under section 24 (5) of the Housing Subsidies Act 1967 shall, if in force at the commencement of section 114 of this Act, continue in force as if given under subsection (1) (*a*) of section 114 until revoked or varied.

71. Subsection (3A) of section 2 of the 1974 Act (inserted by section 123 (4) of this Act) shall have effect, in the period between the commencement of section 123 (4) and the commencement of Chapter II of Part I of this Act as if Chapter II were in force.

72—(1) This paragraph applies in relation to the exceptions in paragraphs 6 and 11 of Schedule 3 to this Act.

(2) Notice given to a tenant at any time after 31st March 1980 but before the commencement of Schedule 3 shall be treated—

> (*a*) as duly given in accordance with paragraph 6 (*b*) (ii) if it would have been so treated had paragraph 6 then been in force; or
> (*b*) as duly given in accordance with paragraph 11 (*b*) if it would have been so treated had paragraph 11, and the regulations first made under that paragraph designating courses, then been in force.

73. In relation to a tenancy (or licence) granted before 8th May 1980 Schedule 3 to this Act has effect as if the following paragraph were added at the end of it:

"14. A tenancy is not a secure tenancy if—
  (a) the landlord is a charity within the meaning of the Charities Act 1960; and
  (b) before the tenancy was granted the tenant was informed in writing that the landlord intended to carry out works on the building or part of the building comprising the dwelling-house and could not reasonably do so without obtaining possession of the dwelling-house."

74. Any approval given for the purposes of paragraph 9 of Schedule 1 to the 1975 Act shall have effect as an approval given for the purposes of Schedule 20 to this Act.

75. Section 5 of the 1977 Act (tenancies at low rents) shall continue not to apply to any tenancy which, immediately before the repeal by this Act of section 17 of the 1977 Act (categories of controlled tenancies) was a controlled tenancy by virtue of subsection (2) of section 17.

76. The repeals made by this Act in the 1975 Act do not affect the operation of orders made under paragraph 23 of Schedule 1 to that Act (power to apply subsidy provisions to housing associations).

77. Section 90 of the 1977 Act continues to have effect, notwithstanding its repeal by this Act, in relation to any direction given by the Secretary of State under that section.

78. Paragraphs 3 and 4 of Schedule 17 to the 1977 Act continue to have effect, notwithstanding paragraph 59 of this Schedule, in relation to a notice of increase served under paragraph 4 before the commencement of paragraph 59. **[613]**

COMMENCEMENT
This Part of this Schedule came into force on the passing of this Act on 8th August 1980 by virtue of s. 153 (3), *ante*.

PARA. 62: CHAPTER II OF PART I
I.e., ss. 28–50, *ante*.

PARA. 64: STATUTORY PERIOD
I.e., a statutory period as defined by the Rent Act 1977, s. 61 (1), A.L.S. Vol. 255.

PARA. 65: AGREEMENT WITH A TENANT HAVING SECURITY OF TENURE
For meaning, cf. the definition of "rent agreement with a tenant having security of tenure" in the Rent Act 1977, s. 51 (1).

PARA. 67: PROTECTED TENANCY, RESTRICTED CONTRACT
These expressions are defined by the Rent Act 1977, ss. 1, 19, respectively.

PARA. 68: PROTECTED OR STATUTORY TENANCY
For the meanings of "protected tenancy" and "statutory tenancy", see the Rent Act 1977, ss. 1, 2, respectively.

PARA. 69: LOCAL LAND CHARGE
As to local land charges generally, see the Local Land Charges Act 1975, A.L.S. Vol. 238.

COMMENCEMENT OF S. 91: COMMENCEMENT OF CHAPTER II OF PART I
S. 91, *ante*, came into force on the passing of this Act on 8th August 1980 by virtue of s. 153 (3), *ante*, and Chapter II of Part I came into force on 3rd October 1980 by virtue of s. 153 (2), *ante*.

PARA. 70: SECRETARY OF STATE
See the note to s. 2, *ante*.

PARA. 71: COMMENCEMENT OF S. 123 (4): COMMENCEMENT OF CHAPTER II OF PART I
S. 123, *ante*, came into force on the passing of this Act on 8th August 1980 by virtue of s. 153 (3), *ante*, and Chapter II of Part I came into force on 3rd October 1980 by virtue of s. 153 (2), *ante*.

PARA. 73: WRITING
See the note "Written; writing" to s. 5, *ante*.

BUILDING
See the note to s. 3, *ante*.

DWELLING-HOUSE
As to the meaning of this expression, see s. 50 (2), *ante*.

PARA. 77: SECRETARY OF STATE
See the note to s. 2, *ante*.

RENT (AGRICULTURE) ACT 1976, SCH. 6
See A.L.S. Vol. 250.

1977 ACT
I.e., the Rent Act 1977, A.L.S. Vol. 255; see s. 150, *ante*.

1957 ACT
I.e., the Housing Act 1957; see s. 150, *ante*. For s. 104 (3), (5) of that Act, see A.L.S. Vol. 109.

HOUSING SUBSIDIES ACT 1967, S. 24 (5)
See A.L.S. Vol. 164.

1974 ACT
I.e., the Housing Act 1974; see s. 150, *ante*. For s. 2 of that Act, see A.L.S. Vol. 223.

CHARLES ACT 1960
For the meaning of "charity", see s. 45 (1), (2) of that Act, A.L.S. Vol. 132.

1975 ACT
I.e., the Housing Rents and Subsidies Act 1975, A.L.S. Vol. 230; see s. 150, *ante*.

SCHEDULE 26

Section 152

REPEALS

Chapter	Short title	Extent of repeal
1927 c. 36	The Landlord and Tenant Act 1927	In section 16, the words "and shall be so recoverable notwithstanding anything in Part II of the Rent Act 1977".
1951 c. 65	The Reserve Auxiliary Forces (Protection of Civil Interests) Act 1951	In section 16 (2) (c) the words from "and that" to the end. Section 19 (5).
1954 c. 56	The Landlord and tenant Act 1954	Section 43 (1) (c).
1957 c. 56	The Housing Act 1957	Section 5. Section 43 (4). In section 91, the words from "and as often" to the end. Section 96 (e). Sections 105 (1), (2) and (5) and 106. Section 113 (5). In section 119 (3), the words from "with the consent" to "the Minister" and the words from "The Minister's power" to the end.
1958 c. 42	The Housing (Financial Provisions) Act 1958	Sections 14 and 15. In section 43 (1), the words "subject to such conditions as may be approved by the Minister". Section 45.

Chapter	Short title	Extent of repeal
1959 c. 62	The New Towns Act 1959	Section 4 (2) and (5).
1961 c. 65	The Housing Act 1961	Section 16.
		Section 20.
1964 c. 56	The Housing Act 1964	Section 65 (1A).
		Section 66.
		In Schedule 4, paragraph 2.
1967 c. 29	The Housing Subsidies Act 1967	In section 24, in subsection (2), the words "in accordance with subsection (3) of this section"; in subsection (3), the words "Subject to subsections (4) and (5) of this section", and the words from "and" (at the end of paragraph (c)) to the end of the subsection; and subsections (4), (5) and (5A).
		Section 24B.
		In section 26, in subsection (1) (b) (ii), the words from "or the appropriate" to "later"; in subsection (1) (b) (iii), the words "or 1st April 1968, whichever is the later"; in subsection (2), paragraph (a), and the words from "and except" onwards; and subsection (3).
		Section 26A.
		Section 28A.
1967 c. 88	The Leasehold Reform Act 1967	Section 21 (5).
		In Schedule 1, in paragraph 7 (1) (b), the words "(subject to paragraph 8 below)".
		In Schedule 2, paragraph 8 (2).
1968 c. 72	The Town and Country Planning Act 1968	Section 39.
1969 c. 33	The Housing Act 1969	Section 28A.
		Section 29B.
		In section 30 the words "but such a resolution shall be of no effect unless approved by the Minister".
		In section 35, subsections (1) and (3), in subsection (4) the words "the consent of the Minister under subsection (2) of this section", subsection (5), in subsection (6) the words from "with the approval" to "particular case" and subsection (7).
		In section 38, the words from "has been approved" to "this Act".
		Section 60.
		Section 61 (6).
		In section 86 (5), the words "and 37 (7)".

367

Chapter	Short title	Extent of repeal
1970 c. 44	The Chronically Sick and Dis-abled Persons Act 1970	In section 3)1), the words from "and any proposals" to the end.
1971 c. 62	The Tribunals and Inquiries Act 1971	In section 7 (3) the words "28 (*a*)" and the words from "but" onwards. In section 13 (1) the words "(*a*) or". In Schedule 1 paragraph 28 (*a*).
1972 c. 5	The Local Employment Act 1972	In Schedule 3, the entry relating to the Housing Act 1971.
1972 c. 47	The Housing Finance Act 1972	Section 8. In section 20, in subsection (5), paragraph (*d*) and the words "or (*d*) (ii)", and in subsection (7) the words from "section 19 (8)" to "Schedule 3 to this Act". In section 24 (5), the words "or their allowance scheme, as may be appropriate" and the words from "of Housing Revenue" to "housing account dwellings". In section 26 (1), in the definition of "allowance" the words from "but also" to the end, in the definition of "allowance scheme" the words from "and includes" to the end, and the definition of "housing account dwelling". Sections 90 to 91A. In Schedule 3, Part II. In Schedule 4, in paragraph 1 (3) (*a*) the words from "Housing" to "account", in paragraph 14 (1), sub-paragraph (*a*), in sub-para-graph (*b*) the words "or 9" and sub-paragraph (*f*), and para-graphs 16 and 17.
1972 c. 70	The Local Government Act 1972	In Schedule 22, paragraph 2.
1973 c. 5	The Housing (Amendment) Act 1973	Section 1 (1). Section 2.
1974 c. 44	The Housing Act 1974	In section 5 (3), all after paragraph (*f*). In section 13, in subsection (4) the words from "after consultation" to "section 14 below" and the words "after such consultation" and subsection (5) (*a*). Section 14. In section 19 (1) the words from "(who" to "staff)". Section 30 (5). Section 31. In section 32, in subsection (1) the word "annual", and subsections (4) and (8).

Chapter	Short title	Extent of repeal
1974 c. 44— *cont.*	The Housing Act 1974—*cont.*	In section 33 (6), the words "before the expiry of that year". In section 38 (2) (*a*), the words "and approved by the Secretary of State". Section 42. Section 50. Sections 52 to 55. In section 56, in subsection (1) (*d*), the words "by the provision of standard amenities", and in subsection (2) (*d*), the words "in a housing action area or a general improvement area". In section 57 (6), the words "Except in so far as this Act otherwise provides", and paragraph (*b*). In section 62 (3) the words from "and different limits" to the end. Section 64 (7). Section 67 (2) (*b*) and (4). In section 71 (3), paragraph (*a*). Section 79. In section 84, paragraph (*b*) of the definition of "the relevant standard". In section 104, the definitions of "the full standard" and "the reduced standard". In section 114, in subsection (1) paragraph (*c*) and the word "or" immediately preceding it, and subsections (6) and (7). In Schedule 5, Part I, and in Part II, paragraph 4. In Schedule 8, in paragraph 2 (2) the words from "and any such determination" onwards. In Schedule 11, in paragraph 1, in sub-paragraph (2) the words following paragraph (*b*), sub-paragraph (3), and sub-paragraph (5) and (6).
1975 c. 6	The Housing Rents and Subsidies Act 1975	Section 1 (3). Section 2. Section 4. In Schedule 1, paragraphs 1 to 11, and 12 (4) (*a*). In Schedule 5, paragraphs 8 (3) and 18.
1975 c. 57	The Remuneration, Charges and Grants Act 1975	Section 5.
1975 c. 76	The Local Land Charges Act 1975	In Schedule 1, the entry relating to the Housing Act 1957.

Chapter	Short title	Extent of repeal
1976 c. 68	The New Towns (Amendment) Act 1976	Section 9 (4) to (6).
1976 c. 71	The Supplementary Benefits Act 1976	In Schedule 7, paragraph 28.
1976 c. 75	The Development of Rural Wales Act 1976	Section 18. In section 22, the word "18". In Schedule 5, paragraphs 1 to 6 and, in paragraph 7 (3), the words "or any element of a subsidy".
1976 c. 80	The Rent (Agriculture) Act 1976	In Schedule 4, in Case X, the words "Part II", where they first occur. In Schedule 6, in paragraph 1 the definition of "specified sum" and sub-paragraphs (2) and (3) and paragraph 7.
1977 c. 42	The Rent Act 1977	In section 5 (1), the words "subject to section 17 (2) of this Act". In section 15, in subsection (1) the words from "in respect" to "is fulfilled" and subsections (4) and (6). Section 17. In section 18, in subsection (1) the words from "which" to the end and subsections (3) and (4). In section 19 (5) (*b*), the words "or of the Duchy of Lancaster or to the Duchy of Cornwall". In section 24, subsection (1) and (2). Sections 27 to 43. In section 44 (1), the words "schedule 9". In section 45 (2), the words "paragraph 8 (4) of Schedule 9". Sections 48 and 50. In section 51 (3), paragraph (*b*) and the word "and" immediately before it. Section 53. In section 54, in subsection (1) the words "52 (6) or 53", and subsections (4) and (5). Section 56. In section 61 (1), the definition of "improvement". Section 67 (6). Section 68 (6). In section 69 (4) the words "Subject to section 67 (6) of this Act" and paragraph (*b*). In section 70, in subsection (3), paragraphs (*c*) and (*d*) and subsection (5).

Chapter	Short title	Extent of repeal
1977 c. 42—*cont.*	The Rent Act 1977—*cont.*	In section 71 (3) (*a*), the words from "subject to" "this Act". Section 76. In section 77 (1) the words "for the district in question". In section 78 (2) the words "and the local authority". Section 79 (4). Section 84 (*a*) and (*b*). Section 86 (5). In section 87, subsections (3) to (5). Sections 90 and 91. In section 92, in subsection (1), the words "in such form as may be prescribed", in subsection (5) the definition of "prescribed" and the word "and" immediately before it, and subsections (6) and (7). Section 93 (3). Section 96 (1) and (2). Sections 108 to 115. In section 116, in subsection (5) the words "sections 4 (4) or 10 of the Housing Act 1969 or". Section 117. In section 118, in subsection (1) the words from "prescribed" to the end, and subsection (2). Section 130. In section 131 (1), the words "but which is not a controlled mortgage". Sections 133 to 135. In section 141, subsections (1) (*c*), (2) and (5) (*a*) and in subsection (1) (*a*) the words from "or whether a mortgage" to "of this Act". In section 150, the words from "(other" to "31 (9))". In section 152 (1), the definition of "controlled tenancy". Section 155 (1). In Schedule 1, paragraph 8. In Schedule 2, paragraph (1) (*c*) (i). Schedules 3, 4 and 6. In Schedule 7, paragraph 4. In Schedule 8, in paragraph 1 the definition of "specified sum" and sub-paragraphs (5) and (6) and paragraph 8. Schedule 9. In Schedule 10, in paragraph 2 the words from "and, if the

Chapter	Short title	Extent of repeal
1977 c. 42— *cont.*	The Rent Act 1977–*cont.*	Secretary of State" to the end and paragraph 10. In Schedule 11, paragraphs 13, 14 and 15 to 25. In Schedule 12, in paragraph 1 (*c*) the words from "(but" to "Act)", in paragraph 3 the words from "in the case" to "111 (1) of this Act", in paragraph 4, sub-paragraph (1) and in sub-paragraph (2) the words from "in the case" to "section" and in paragraph 9 (1), paragraph (*b*) and the word "or" immediately before. Schedule 13. In Schedule 14, paragraph 6. In Schedule 15, in Case 6 paragraph (*a*), Case 7 and in Case 10 the words "Part II or, as the case may be". In Schedule 17, paragraphs 3, 4, 10 and 11. Schedule 19. In Schedule 20, in paragraph 1 (1) the words "or controlled" and sub-paragraphs (6) and (7), in paragraph 3 (2) (*c*) the words "or, as the case may be, Schedule 9", paragraph 4 and in paragraph 5 the definitions of "dwelling", "notice of increase" and "rent limit". Schedules 21 and 22. In Schedule 23, paragraph 1, in paragraph 4 sub-paragraphs (*g*) to (*i*) and paragraphs 37 38 and 56 (*a*).
1977 c. 45	The Criminal Law Act 1977	In Schedule 3, paragraph 25. In Schedule 6, the entries relating to sections 65 (1) of the Housing Act 1964 and 61 of the Housing Act 1969. In Schedule 12, the entry relating to section 65 of the Housing Act 1964.

COMMENCEMENT
See s. 153 (4), *ante*, and the note "Orders under this section" thereto.

INDEX

Index

DUCHIES, 530

DWELLING HOUSE,
definition, 14, 332
value of, 27

EXTENDED TENANCY,
registered rent, and, 303

FIRE,
escape from,
houses in multiple occupation, 319
special grant, and, 256
means of escape from, 476, 590–596
consultation with fire authority, 593
enforcement, 592
exclusion of Rent Act protection, 594
powers available to local authority, 591

FIXED-TERM TENANCY,
death of tenant, 73 *et seq.*
security of tenure, and, 90

FLAT, 14
definition, 332, 581

FLAT-SHARING, 186

FORFEITURE, 93–95

FREEHOLD,
charges on, 499
right of public sector tenant to acquire, 330

GENERAL IMPROVEMENT AREA, 262
et seq., 438, 554
aim of, 262
removal of Ministerial Controls, 263

GRANTS
calculation of appropriate percentage, 241, 542
certificate of future occupation, 543
conditions, 549
consideration of application for, 539
multiple occupation, and, 547
Parliamentary control, 552
payment by instalments, 550
standard amenities, 541
standard of repair, 548
tenants', 553
withdrawal of application for, 540

HOMELESS PERSONS,
accommodation for,
secure tenancy, and, 504

HOUSE,
definition, 14, 332

HOUSING ACTION AREA, 262 *et seq.*, 438, 555
basis of Central Government Contribution, 272
environmental works, 271
removal of Ministerial Controls, 270

HOUSING ALLOCATION, 118

HOUSING ASSOCIATIONS, 22, 378, 403 413

HOUSING ASSOCIATIONS—*cont.*
accounts, 453
amendment of rules, 461
approved development programmes, 567
audit, 453
cost of housing projects, 566
disposal by,
avoidance of, 466
grant, 459
hostel deficit grant, 571
inquiries into affairs of, 458
management grant, 569
payment of grant, 568
payments to certain committee members, 455
recoupment of surplus rental income, 460
registered
disposal of land by, 451
registration of, 456
removal from register, 457
revenue deficit grant, 570
shared ownership schemes, 565

HOUSING CO-OPERATIVES, 22, 297,
general conditions, 259–260
definition, 582

HOUSING CORPORATION, 22, 286, 287
appointment of persons to conduct inquiries, 560
borrowing powers of, 449
consent to disposals of land by, 452
duty of agents to give information, 561
grants by, 450
grants to, 450
indemnities for building societies, 440
non-exempt charities, and, 563
offences, and, 564
payments to committee members, 559
suspension of committee members, 562

HOUSING MANAGEMENT, 117
definition, 371

HOUSING POLICY, 7

HOUSING REPAIRS ACCOUNT, 464

HOUSING REVENUE ACCOUNT,
working balance, 296, 463

HOUSING REVENUE ACCOUNT
DWELLINGS, 237

HOUSING SUBSIDIES, 225 *et seq.*, 425 *et seq.*
"additional financial assistance", 228
administration of, 432
calculation, 226, 230
expanding towns subsidy, 226
mortgage, and, 278
recoupment, 431
to whom payable, 226–229
transitional town development subsidy, 433

HOUSING SUBSIDIES ACT 1967,
amendments of, 556

References are to paragraph numbers

374

References are to paragraph numbers

References are to paragraph numbers

References are to paragraph numbers

References are to paragraph numbers